Because He Has Spoken to Us

Because He Has Spoken to Us
Structures of Proclamation from Rahner to Ratzinger

Brad Bursa

FOREWORD BY
Frank P. Lane

☙PICKWICK *Publications* · Eugene, Oregon

BECAUSE HE HAS SPOKEN TO US
Structures of Proclamation from Rahner to Ratzinger

Copyright © 2022 Brad Bursa. All rights reserved. Except for brief quotations in critical publications or reviews, no part of this book may be reproduced in any manner without prior written permission from the publisher. Write: Permissions, Wipf and Stock Publishers, 199 W. 8th Ave., Suite 3, Eugene, OR 97401.

Pickwick Publications
An Imprint of Wipf and Stock Publishers
199 W. 8th Ave., Suite 3
Eugene, OR 97401

www.wipfandstock.com

PAPERBACK ISBN: 978-1-6667-3583-3
HARDCOVER ISBN: 978-1-6667-9338-3
EBOOK ISBN: 978-1-6667-9339-0

Cataloguing-in-Publication data:

Names: Bursa, Brad [author]. | Lane, Frank P. [foreword writer].

Title: Because he has spoken to us : structures of proclamation from Rahner to Ratzinger / by Brad Bursa ; foreword by Frank P. Lane.

Description: Eugene, OR: Pickwick Publications, 2022 | Includes bibliographical references.

Identifiers: ISBN 978-1-6667-3583-3 (paperback) | ISBN 978-1-6667-9338-3 (hardcover) | ISBN 978-1-6667-9339-0 (ebook)

Subjects: LCSH: Rahner, Karl, 1904–1984 | Benedict XVI, Pope, 1927– | Catholic Church—Doctrines | Theology—Study and teaching—Catholic Church | Catholic Church | Evangelistic work | Catholic Church—Catechisms

Classification: BX1751.3 B87 2022 (print) | BX1751.3 (ebook)

05/04/22

Scripture quotations are from Revised Standard Version of the Bible—Second Catholic Edition (Ignatius Edition) Copyright © 2006 National Council of the Churches of Christ in the United States of America. Used by permission. All rights reserved worldwide.

For FPL

Contents

Foreword by Frank P. Lane | ix
Abbreviations | xiii

Introduction | 1

Part I: The Rahner Project: Evangelization and Catechesis after Vatican II

1 A Rahnerian Blueprint for Catechetical Renewal | 31
2 Master Builders of a "Vulgarized Rahnerian" Catechesis after Vatican II | 63
3 Recontextualizing Rahner: A Postmodern Project | 93
4 The Gospel according to Postmodernity: Recontextualizing Evangelization | 127

Part II: A Ratzingerian Response to the Crisis

5 The New Pagans, the Council, and the Hermeneutic of Discontinuity | 147
6 Ratzinger Report: An Analysis of Catechetical Renewal Today | 164
7 The Revelation of the *Logos* | 194
8 A Theological Anthropology Revealed by the *Logos* | 233
9 Freedom—Sin—Death | 254
10 Christian Faith as Encounter | 269
11 Evangelization as Participation in the "Yes" of God | 300
12 Communicating the Gospel Today | 340

Conclusion | 385

Bibliography | 395

Foreword

Msgr. Frank P. Lane, PhD

I would like to express my appreciation to Brad Bursa for this remarkable book. It offers serious scholarly consequences for the field of Catholic Theology and some long-awaited resolution to personal questions that have lingered for decades. It has, in fact, brought closure for me concerning unanswered questions that arose during my lengthy journey in the Catholic priesthood.

I did my theological studies at the Leopold-Franzens University in Innsbruck, Austria from 1963–67. It was the time of the Council and the era at the university of the dominant presence of Karl Rahner who moved on to Munich and Münster in 1964 but returned for lectures and various academic events. For years he remained a pervasive influence on the intellectual life of the Theology Faculty of Innsbruck. In addition to Rahner, names like Jungmann, Schlier, Marcel, Fransen, Coreth, others, and, in 1966, a major lecture in a crowded auditorium by Dr. Ratzinger of Tübingen were only some of the academic strengths of the University.

Arriving back in the States in the summer of 1967 after four years' absence, I encountered a Catholic world that I barely recognized. The liturgy was in chaos and the popular journals of Catholic thought contained, at best, only a caricature of what I had experienced in the intellectual world of Innsbruck. The quintessentially speculative Father Rahner had become a sort of catechetical system. People were getting MAs in theology in Rahner's thought with no philosophical requirements. Self-declared Rahner scholars who had visited him in either Munich or Münster, were speaking a theological language that was, at times, rather mystifying. I first presumed my lack of understanding but, eventually, moved back somewhat from that self-doubt.

In my first assignment as a curate in a small Ohio city, I was assigned to teach religion to juniors in the local Catholic High School. I was handed a "new" textbook to teach from. It was its first year to be used as the foundation of the new religious education curriculum. It was, honestly, unintelligible. There was no real content and it glossed over reality with page after page of narrative about the alienation of youth within our society. The students laughed when they read it, especially when I explained what "alienation" meant. I could in no way justify trying to spend an entire year talking about something that wasn't even remotely intelligible in the context of the student's lived experience. I negotiated with them about alternatives. After consulting an older and very accomplished religious sister, I considered the alternative of using contemporary periodicals with some theological content.

There were two publications at the time that seemed worthwhile, Dan Herr's *Critic* and *Commonweal*. I turned to *Commonweal*, which was running a series on "God" in 1967. I negotiated with the students: If they would listen to me teaching from *Commonweal* four days a week, they could have a free period the fifth day—study hall, listen to music, etc. Strangely enough, it worked. I had entered the world of modern American catechetics albeit in a confused and clumsy way. The real challenge persisted throughout the years in classroom and pulpit, trying to provide something of substance for young people to carry with them in life. I suspect I was only minimally successful. The world of catechetics seemed to me to continue to disintegrate. Stick figures replaced the "age-inappropriate art" of the great masters. Doctrinal substance became pre-Vatican II and the exploration of the mystery of the Divine, passé. Religious artifacts were considered out of date and the crucifix, a symbol of the greatest act of human love ever known, dismissed as maudlin and anachronistic.

I have always maintained that those of us who lived through the "revolution" were excellent primary witnesses but would never be able to unravel the mystery of the cultural upheaval of the mid to late Twentieth Century. I thought it would take someone much younger, looking back critically and with great insight to interpret the experience we had. I have found that younger person in Dr. Brad Bursa and have seen the mystery solved in his exceptional work, *Because He Has Spoken to Us*.

Bursa has unraveled the subtle, intricate and bewildering labyrinthine journey from the Baltimore Catechism to the notion of "Alienation" and from alienation to contemporary subjectivity in the theology of "Re-Contextualization." Each of these have been seen, in turn, as foundational theological structures of contemporary belief and proclamation. The world that proclamation envisions might best be viewed through Marcuse's distinction between *Epic* and *Novel*. Marcuse maintains that the Epic is the story of a people, a tracing of their journey through History. The novel, as a fairly recent genre, opens to whole generations new possibilities for the future, leaving those in the present "alienated" from the world in which they live. For Marcuse, the novel sets society on the course of revolution. Alienation became the thematic of many and various activists within the Church who sought revolution and its promised "brave new world" with which we have become all too familiar. Bursa steps beyond that rather primitive insight. He identifies alienation's brave new world and dissolves the intellectual process by which many strove to reach those hallowed shores.

Bursa begins to recover the Epic and place us on a real road to the future by using the great Ratzinger insight. Ratzinger reoriented twentieth-century theology with the fundamental realization that Being Itself, "Das Sein," is not the real quest of the Christian believer. The real object of faith is what Being Itself reveals of itself to us, i.e., the Logos. Logos is Being's fullness of revelation. Logos is reason, mind, and person. Here we encounter all that is knowable about Being itself, about God. We have the experience that without the Word made flesh dwelling among us, we cannot know God. Jesus/Logos becomes the starting point of the quest for knowledge and understanding of the infinite God. The search for understanding begins with Logos as the "Given," the Heideggerian "Es Gibt." Ratzinger brings this insight to life and offers humanity an encounter with a person in whom all knowledge exists, through whom all things are made and without whom nothing is made. According to Bernard of Clairvaux, Logos is both source and destiny, Logos is meaning.

We are all deeply indebted to Bursa's work and his willingness to share it. Perhaps clarity will enable us to recover the epic story of ourselves as a people and move us forward in a way consistent with who we are, with our ancestors in the faith, yet still discovering new horizons that are real and not simply figments of muddled imagination and singular minds. By now we might have learned that, separated from our whole experience, we are always less than we could be and separated from the Person of the Word, from Logos, we wander in an endless desert overcome by an unquenchable thirst for meaning and tormented by mirages of understanding that fade, ultimately, into obscurity.

I am grateful for Bursa's work and have great hope for its power to exert a strong influence on current theological exploration and on contemporary catechetics. He has clearly interpreted the recent past and shown us faithful and creative ways for discovering those new horizons that humanity has always striven for—and sometimes found.

Abbreviations

Works by Joseph Ratzinger/Benedict XVI

CC	*Called to Communion*
Christian Brotherhood	*The Meaning of Christian Brotherhood*
"Christmas Greetings 2005"	"2005 Address to the Roman Curia Offering Them His Christmas Greetings"
"Christmas Greetings 2012"	"2012 Address on the Occasion of Christmas Greetings to the Roman Curia"
DCE	*Deus caritas est*
Dogma	*Dogma and Preaching*
"The Eucharist"	"The Eucharist—Heart of the Church"
GCC	*Gospel, Catechesis, Catechism*
Introduction	*Introduction to Christianity*
Jesus I	*Jesus of Nazareth: From the Baptism in the Jordan to the Transfiguration*
Jesus II	*Jesus of Nazareth: Holy Week*
"Meditation 2012"	"Meditation During the First General Congregation."
Nature and Mission	*The Nature and Mission of Theology*
New Outpourings	*New Outpourings of the Holy Spirit*
"New Pagans"	"The New Pagans and the Church"
New Song	*A New Song for the Lord*
"Notion of Person"	"Concerning the Notion of Person"

"Parish Priests 2013"	"Address on the Occasion of Meeting with the Parish Priests and the Clergy of Rome."
Pierced One	*Behold the Pierced One*
Pilgrim Fellowship	*Pilgrim Fellowship of Faith*
Principles	*Principles of Catholic Theology*
Theology of History	*The Theology of History in Bonaventure*
Transforming Power	*The Transforming Power of Faith*
TT	*Truth and Tolerance*
What It Means	*What It Means to Be a Christian*
On the Way	*On the Way to Jesus Christ*
Yes of Jesus	*The Yes of Jesus Christ*

Works by Gabriel Moran

Catechesis	*Catechesis of Revelation*
Revelation	*Theology of Revelation*

Works by Lieven Boeve

Crossroads	*Theology at the Crossroads of University, Church and Society*
God Interrupts	*God Interrupts History*
Lyotard	*Lyotard and Theology*

Works by Karl Rahner

Foundations	*Foundations of Christian Faith*

Works by Thomas Groome

CRE	*Christian Religious Education*
Sharing	*Sharing Faith*

Ecclesial Documents

CCC *Catechism of the Catholic Church*
GDC *General Directory for Catechesis*

Introduction

The terse imperative read: "The triune God, Father, Son and Holy Spirit—do not presuppose him, but present him!"[1] Such was Hans Urs von Balthasar's critical feedback to Joseph Ratzinger regarding a paper the young theologian had submitted for Balthasar's review.

This correspondence took place early in the postconciliar period, as many theologians and ecclesiastical figures hastened Vatican II's call for renewal. "New issues were appearing on the horizon, and it was becoming necessary to find new methods," Ratzinger recalls. "It seemed self-evident that a theologian who wanted to be up to date and who rightly understood his task should temporarily suspend the old discussions and devote all of his energies to the new questions pressing in from every side."[2] For example, just a year after the close of the Council, seismic shifts in catechetics shook the field, as theorists and practitioners replaced the traditional content of catechesis with human experience. Piet Schoonenberg (1911–99), a Dutch theologian and a key contributor in the creation of the anthropologically-inspired Dutch Catechism, explains that now "experience has become the theme itself of catechesis. Catechesis has become the interpretation of experience. It has to clarify experience, that is, it has to articulate and enlighten the experience

---

1. Benedict XVI, *Western Culture*, 164. See also Ratzinger, *GCC*, 23. Authorial references to Joseph Ratzinger will be made according to his title at the time in which the piece being referred to was written. In other words, the paper will attempt to be consistent in referring to the author as Ratzinger prior to his papal election in April 2005. Any works published following his election will refer to him as Benedict XVI. That said, when speaking about the author and his work in general, the paper will refer to him as Ratzinger in interest of the ease of the reader. As a way of further narrowing the scope of the present study and keeping in mind Benedict XVI's own statement that he did not write any of the documents of the Congregation for the Doctrine of the Faith (see Benedict XVI, *Last Testament*, 172), documents from the Congregation have not been considered part of Ratzinger's corpus within this paper.

2. Ratzinger, *GCC*, 23. See also Ratzinger, *Introduction*, 41.

and existence of those for whom the message is intended."[3] A "horizontalizing" effect was at play, as anthropology became the beginning, and ultimately the end for catechetics. Balthasar sensed the shift and sounded an early alarm to warn against a radical anthropocentrism at work in the Church immediately after Vatican II and of which the Council unwittingly acted as a catalyst. His message to Ratzinger is indicative of this.

At the time, during the latter part of the 1960s, Ratzinger remained cautiously optimistic of catechetical endeavors. In 1968, he acknowledged certain limitations of the Dutch Catechism but issued certain hopes as well. He did not reject the "new" catechism outright, instead seeing it as an opportunity for catechesis to be both enriched and challenged.[4] In the decades that followed, however, a process of "fermentation" took place. The threats Balthasar foresaw from afar had become reality. By 1983, any inkling of optimism Ratzinger had been holding onto regarding catechesis had waned. That year, he opened a lecture by simply taking it as a given that "catechesis is having a difficult time." He called this observation "a platitude that does not need to be demonstrated at great length."[5] The builders of renewal, "with their hasty *aggiornamento*," expedited the creation of new catechisms following the Council, only to abandon the whole idea of a catechism altogether. An anthropocentric attitude saw the constant changes of life outpacing dogmatic teaching, which no longer seemed relevant. With the human being in his ever-changing present context becoming the "given" for catechetics, Ratzinger says, "catechesis had to be constantly written anew."[6] While there had certainly been some advances in catechetical creativity and other bright spots since the Council,[7] Ratzinger ultimately concludes that

---

3. Schoonenberg, "Revelation and Experience," 304. To be sure, Christianity has historically acknowledged the role of experience (one thinks of Augustine or Newman, for example). The novelty of the anthropological shift, however, appears in the reduction of catechetics to experience and in rendering faith implicit in every human experience.

4. Ratzinger, *Dogma*, 74.

5. Ratzinger, *Handing on the Faith*, 13n1.

6. Ratzinger and Schönborn, *Introduction to the Catechism*, 12–13. Kevane comments on this speech and the evacuation of the concept of a catechism in "Toward Research in Fundamental Catechetics," 357–58.

7. See the final report from the 1985 Extraordinary Synod of Bishops, "The Final Report of the 1985 Extraordinary Synod." Another example: Ratzinger acknowledges the achievement of the *New Catechism* produced by the Dutch bishops (hence, it is often referred to as the Dutch Catechism) which was published in 1966. To its credit, this catechism addresses man's humanity that is "moved by a deep, true, and warm religiosity," the reality and seriousness of sin, and the life of Christ (Ratzinger, *Dogma*, 64–65). However, the Dutch Catechism contains limitations as well, which Ratzinger outlines (65–73).

with all its "multifarious experimentation,"[8] modern catechetics, that is, catechesis following the Second Vatican Council, has been an "all too obvious ... catastrophic failure."[9]

Ratzinger was not alone in his criticism. Nearly twenty years after the Council, Johannes Hofinger (1905–84), an Austrian Jesuit and a prominent force in twentieth century renewal efforts, reflected on those efforts by likening them to the construction of a house. He said, "The pioneers did the hard and dirty groundwork; the kerygmatic renewal built a noble construction on that basis, but it still needed a crowning roof."[10] He continued with an assessment of the builders of anthropological renewal, by noting "the promoters of the human approach provided us with a fine roof; but unfortunately, instead of placing the roof upon the walls, they

---

8. Ratzinger, *On the Way*, 142.

9. Ratzinger, *Yes of Jesus*, 34–35. To be sure, not everyone felt this way. Many, in fact, denounced the whole project of developing a new catechism. Avery Dulles' "The Challenge of the Catechism" offers a succinct overview of the project, along with commentary from its detractors, and Ratzinger comments on this in his "Is the *Catechism of the Catholic Church* Up-to-Date?," a reflection ten years after the publication of the *Catechism*, which appears in Ratzinger, *On the Way*, 142–65.

10. Hofinger identifies three key phases within renewal. During Phase 1, pioneers like Heinrich Stieglitz and his "Munich Method" poured the foundation for renewal by incorporating methodological insights from secular education and psychology in child-centered movements of the early twentieth century (Tilmann, "Origin and Development," 86; see also Boys, *Biblical Interpretation*, 79). Stieglitz sought a solution in developments within secular education rooted in psychological developments which provided insight into the cognitive development of children. In the foremost, this meant beginning with "the visual and the concrete" instead of text and explanation (see Posset, *American Catechetics*, 55; Hofinger, *The Art of Teaching*, 3). The second phase emerged in the mid-twentieth century as Josef Jungmann's "Kerygmatic Renewal" grounded the content of catechesis in the person of Jesus Christ as found in the biblical narrative of salvation history, thus erecting the metaphorical walls of Hofinger's house in the years leading up to Vatican II. Catherine Dooley notes that, "kerygmatic renewal called for a cohesive and unified presentation of the Christian faith by an integration of the sources or 'four signs' of revelation: liturgy, scripture, Church teaching, and the witness of Christian living" ("The Religious Education," 157). Luis Erdozain expounds upon these four aspects of the kerygmatic method in "The Evolution of Catechetics," 86–109. Jungmann (1889–1975), the founder of this movement, did not slacken the moral demands of Christianity, but sought to organize them around a kerygmatic core. Hofinger, perhaps Jungmann's greatest student, explains, "the name *kerygma* (a publicly announced message) has come to be more and more generally given to those aspects of revelation which were meant to be explicitly and emphatically proclaimed ... the essential content of the Christian glad tidings" (Hofinger, *The Art of Teaching*, 6). Pauley also addresses the kerygmatic movement in *Liturgical Catechesis*, 42–48, 57–65. The third phase of construction began around the time of Vatican II, and it is rightly called the "anthropological stage." For an in-depth survey of each of these phases, see Brian Pedraza's excellent summaries throughout the whole of Pedraza, "Reform and Renewal in Catechesis," 1–31; Pedraza, *Catechesis for the New Evangelization*, 70–102.

constructed the roof on the grounds beside the edifice; and now it needs a fourth phase for elevating this valuable roof to its proper place on the walls."[11] The proximity of this observation to his death carries with it a certain *gravitas*, like a last testament exposing a depleted inheritance. In a certain sense, Hofinger's metaphorical house illustrates what happened as the "baby" (i.e., dogmatic theology) got thrown out with the "bathwater" (i.e., the Suárezian scholasticism that played a significant role in shaping catechetics prior to the Council and that which the renewal movement reacted against). Dogmatic theology is critical for a successful catechesis, even if it is not the primary, fundamental thing. Catechetics needed to become more personalist and more Trinitarian but not de-ratiocinated. Catechetical movers and shakers after the Council overreacted.

In the end, such a movement frittered away sacred tradition, and left people stranded in their own experiences. Ratzinger likens the phenomenon to the German folk tale of "Clever Hans," a boy inconvenienced by the weight of his lump of gold, who trades it for a horse, a cow, a pig, a goose, and ultimately a whetstone that he tosses into the river to (finally) gain "the precious gift of complete freedom" from his burden.[12] For Ratzinger, jettisoning tradition means throwing away "the precondition for man's humanness." He adds that "whoever destroys tradition destroys man—he is like a traveler in space who destroys the possibility of ground control, of contact with earth."[13] Tracey Rowland describes the scene over fifty years after the Council, claiming that "members of the millennial generation find themselves in a situation where they have rarely experienced a fully functional Catholic culture." She continues, "To find out about Christianity, especially the Catholic version of it, they watch documentaries and movies, they interrogate older Catholics, they google information about the saints, liturgies, and cultural practices. The cultural capital that should follow as a natural endowment upon their baptism has been frittered away, buried, and

---

11. Hofinger, "Looking Backward and Forward," 356. Hofinger was not alone in his self-critique of the catechetical renewal movement. Ten years prior, Alfonso Nebrada issued a host of concerns about the state of catechetics, including an express concern about Gabriel Moran and the whole question of implicit versus explicit faith. See Nebrada, "Some Reflections," 85–98. This is not to say the third phase of catechetical renewal—the human, or anthropological phase—is entirely valueless. Pedraza catalogues the renewal's effect on post-conciliar magisterial teaching in *Catechesis for the New Evangelization*, 108–14, 122–38. Here, he highlights both accolades and words of caution in magisterial texts and measures renewal with the textual guidance provided by Vatican II.

12. Ratzinger, *Introduction*, 31.

13. Ratzinger, *Principles*, 90.

in some cases even deliberately suppressed by previous generations."[14] Keep in mind that Rowland is describing that minority of millennial Catholics who still care enough to google such queries.

While cultural centripetal forces contribute to the bleak ecclesial landscape described by Ratzinger, Hofinger, and Rowland, certain centrifugal forces at work in catechetics are of particular interest here, amid what is described as the postconciliar "anthropological phase" of catechetical renewal. Though the beginnings of such decline predate the Council, this book grapples with how catechesis came to have such a "difficult time" in the anthropological phase from the immediate postconciliar years to the postmodern present, as the rise of an anthropocentric catechesis contributed to the field's demise. Generally, the anthropological phase consists of two "moments," the first of which is a distinctly modern one that relegates the role of the Church's tradition in catechesis and replaces it with human experience. The second one, which is postmodern in nature, risks losing touch with the Church's tradition altogether. In response, I will argue that the anthropological movement ends up revolving around itself, and it can now be displaced by attending to Ratzinger's considerations for evangelization and catechesis. Ratzinger's thought, shaped by Balthasar's imperative, offers an alternate path grounded in the life of the Church, personal renewal in Christ, and a call for a fresh proposal of the faith in every age and every place.[15]

Broadly speaking, this book examines the hermeneutical debates surrounding Vatican II, and specifically focuses on the implications of such disputes for evangelization and catechesis. This book, then, will not propose a concrete methodology, nor will it lay out practical plans or strategies for parishes, dioceses, or schools. It is more fundamental than that. It aims

---

14. Rowland, "*Catechism of the Catholic Church*," 219. The vaporizing of Catholic culture has been well-documented in recent years. See, for example, McCarthy and Vitek, *Going, Going, Gone*; Pew Research Center, "America's Changing Religious Landscape"; Pew Research Center "Decline of Christianity"; Reiss, "Religion Declining in Importance." Clearly the number of millennial Catholics is shrinking and with increasing rapidity. Additionally, the average age of disaffiliation amongst Catholics is surprisingly low. McCarty and Vitek report that "when asked at what age they no longer identified themselves as Catholic, 74 percent of the sample said between the ages of 10 and 20, with the median age being 13 years old" (*Going, Going, Gone*, 6). This further corroborates the findings of the National Study for Youth and Religion, a study largely conducted in the early 2000s with millennials, which found that one's faith trajectory was set by age fourteen, saying, "The vast majority, then, of those youth—85 percent—who have by the age of 18–23 ever committed to lives their lives for God appear to have made their first commitments before age 14. Most first religious commitments thus appear to be made during childhood and the preteen or very early teen years" (Smith, *Souls in Transition*, loc. 5358).

15. Ratzinger, *GCC*, 23–24. See also Balthasar, *Razing the Bastions*, 34.

to contribute on the level of principles by exploring the thread between fundamental theology and structures of proclamation (i.e., preaching and teaching; evangelization and catechesis), insofar as this linkage appears in the trajectories set by the two most prominent theologians after Vatican II: Karl Rahner and Joseph Ratzinger. In other words, this book illustrates how *determinations in fundamental theology shape the theological foundations of, and methodological approaches to evangelization and catechesis*. Therefore, this book will not provide a step-by-step methodology for evangelization or catechesis, but will consider, theologically, their very foundations. It is about developing, or, more accurately, discovering an adequate and legitimate theological foundation for evangelization amid a post-Christian, postmodern world, and one that will not result in a roof on the ground.

Context: Vatican II as a Catechetical Council

Vatican II's stated objective basically ratified the catechetical renewal movement and functioned as a catalyst for its progress. It was as if the Council brought catechetical renewal from functioning as a tributary in ecclesial renewal right into the mainstream. Petroc Willey describes Vatican II as "a *uniquely* catechetical Council of the Church, one whose attention is focused upon the *transmission* of the Gospel of Christ."[16] This claim does provide a concentrated understanding of the Council's objective, which can be gleaned from St. Pope John XXIII's opening address, where he called for "the sacred heritage of Christian truth be safeguarded and expounded with greater efficacy."[17] Though it did discuss doctrine to some degree, ultimately producing two dogmatic constitutions, the Council's primary aim was not doctrinal.[18] Rather, as John XXIII notes:

> What is needed at the present time is a new enthusiasm, a new joy and serenity of mind in the unreserved acceptance by all of the entire Christian faith, without forfeiting that accuracy and precision in its presentation which characterized the proceedings of the Council of Trent and the First Vatican Council. What is needed, and what everyone imbued with a truly Christian, Catholic and apostolic spirit craves today, is that this doctrine shall be *more widely known, more deeply understood, and more penetrating in its effects* on men's moral lives.[19]

16. Willey, "The Catechism Enshrines the Pedagogy of God."
17. John XXIII, "Opening Address," 428.
18. See Paruch, "The Catechism," 189.
19. John XXIII, "Opening Address," 430; emphasis added. Ratzinger says John

For the Church to remain faithful to her mission in the face of modernity, John XXIII challenges the Church's apostolate to impact the men and women more deeply in this day with her teaching, without losing any of the doctrinal purity and clarity brought forth by Trent and Vatican I.

Pope Paul VI, elected following John XXIII's untimely death during the Council, reinforced the original objectives of Vatican II. He argued that these can be "definitively summed up in this single one: to make the Church of the twentieth century ever better fitted for proclaiming the Gospel to the people of the twentieth century."[20] Conciliar documents echo such statements. For example, *Ad gentes* emphasizes that the Church is "missionary by her very nature,"[21] and *Lumen gentium* notes that the Church exists to "reveal to the world, faithfully though darkly, the mystery of its Lord until, in the end, it will be manifested in full light."[22] Echoing this general sentiment, Benedict XVI claims, "At the end of the day, the point of the Church is to turn us toward God and to enable God to enter into the world."[23] Applying this essential point to Vatican II, he argues that the Council should be known as neither "progressive" nor "conservative," but as "missionary."[24] Vatican II sought to situate the Church within the modern world as an entity capable of effectively evangelizing and catechizing. Thus, Vatican II can rightly be called a catechetical council, or, perhaps even more broadly, an evangelizing one.

In addition to its catechetical nature, Vatican II could also be classified according to its emphasis on renewal. For his part, John O'Malley, author of *What Happened at Vatican II*, claims, "Vatican II . . . falls under the rubric of a reform council."[25] The link here, between evangelization and renewal, is rather straightforward. Ratzinger observes that for evangelization to be fruitfully carried out in any age, for the Gospel to be "more widely known, more deeply understood, and more penetrating in its effects," the Church's evangelizing structures, programs, and language must

---

XXIII's purpose for the Council was rather broad in nature, leaving "the Fathers with an almost unlimited freedom to give things concrete shape." For his part, he sees John XXIII's intention as this: "The faith, while remaining the same in its contents, was to be proclaimed to our era in a new way, and, after a period of demarcations and defensive maneuvers, we were now no longer to condemn but to apply the 'medicine of mercy'" (Ratzinger, *Milestones*, 121–22).

20. Paul VI, *Evangelii nuntiandi*, §2.
21. Second Vatican Council, *Ad gentes*, §2.
22. Second Vatican Council, *Lumen gentium*, §8.
23. Benedict XVI, *Light of the World*, 155.
24. Ratzinger and Messori, *The Ratzinger Report*, 13.
25. O'Malley, *What Happened at Vatican II*, 300.

be well-suited for the communication of the Gospel within the cultural contexts. However, while the Church has constant need of such human "vehicles" to transmit the Gospel, she must remain aware of and admit to the obsolescence of such vehicles over time. Ratzinger notes that they can set "themselves up as the essence of the Church," and prevent "us from seeing through to what is truly essential."[26] While they begin as seemingly necessary constructs for mission, these vehicles or structures often and eventually "smack" of ideology, bureaucracy, and so on, greatly diminishing their reach and effectiveness.[27] In short, the Church (and her man-made structures) risks becoming self-referential, instead of the sacrament of salvation pointing to Christ. Ratzinger describes this reality:

> In the Church . . . there are of course also institutions of purely human law for the many purposes of management, organization, and coordination, which may grow in accordance with the demands of the time and may have to grow. Yet we would have to say this: the Church needs such institutions of her own, yet if they become too numerous and too strong, then they threaten the order and the life of her spiritual essence. The Church always has to scrutinize her own institutional structure so that it does not become too heavy—lest it harden into an armor that stifles her actual spiritual life.[28]

The Church stands in need of constant renewal. Therefore, Ratzinger concludes that "in her human structures the Church is always *semper reformanda*, but one must be clear in this question as to how and up to what point."[29]

Lumen gentium also calls for constant renewal: "while Christ . . . knew nothing of sin, but came to expiate only the sins of the people, the Church, embracing in its bosom sinners, at the same time holy and always in need of being purified, *always follows the way of penance and renewal*."[30] The Church needs renewal inasmuch as the human is not always directed to and subordinate to the divine, the visible directed to and subordinate to the invisible,

---

26. Ratzinger, *CC*, 142.

27. Ratzinger, *CC*, 136. Elsewhere, Ratzinger claims, "we have too much bureaucracy. Therefore, it will be necessary to simplify things. Everything should not take place by way of committees; there must even also be the personal encounter. And not everything can be dealt with rationally. However, much Christianity makes a claim on reason and claims to speak to it, there are other dimensions of the perception of reality that we also need" (*Salt of the Earth*, 266). See also Ratzinger, *New Outpourings*, 24–25, 27, 69, 73–74.

28. Ratzinger, *New Outpourings*, 24–25.

29. Ratzinger and Messori, *The Ratzinger Report*, 50.

30. Second Vatican Council, *Lumen gentium*, §8; emphasis added.

action directed to and subordinate to contemplation of the divine mysteries, and the present world directed to that which is to come.[31] Renewal, therefore, exists, as Ratzinger says, so the Church might "speak the Gospel of Christ in a way understandable to contemporary man—i.e., in a contemporary fashion (*aggiornamento* means bringing up to date) . . . the objective is precisely that Christ may become understood."[32] Vatican II, then, confirms the apparent need for renewal that had surfaced within various movements of the late nineteenth and early twentieth centuries—with catechetical renewal attaining a certain pride-of-place given John XXIII's objective—and encourages the advancement of such efforts for the sake of the Church's communication of the Gospel in the modern world. Risking an over-extension of Hofinger's analogy, it is almost as if Vatican II passed a levy for the completion of a half-built catechetical edifice and placed a spotlight on the construction site that all may witness the finishing touches. Unfortunately, the builders depleted the funds and left the project in shambles.

Quarreling Hermeneutics

Given the assessments of Ratzinger, Hofinger, and Rowland, one must ask: Why has the implementation of the Council's vision been so difficult? In his 2005 Christmas Greetings to the Roman Curia, Benedict XVI offers the following answer:

> It all depends on the correct interpretation of the Council or— as we would say today—on its proper hermeneutics, the correct key to its interpretation and application. The problems in its implementation arose from the fact that two contrary hermeneutics came face to face and quarreled with each other. One caused confusion, the other, silently but more and more visibly, bore and is bearing fruit.[33]

On the one hand, Benedict XVI points out a "hermeneutic of discontinuity and rupture," which has "frequently availed itself of the sympathies of

---

31. See Second Vatican Council, *Sacrosanctum concilium*, §2. Here, the Council Fathers teach that the Church is "both human and divine, visible yet invisibly equipped, eager to act and yet intent on contemplation, present in this world and yet not at home in it; and she is all these things in such wise that in her the human is directed and subordinated to the divine, the visible likewise to the invisible, action to contemplation, and this present world to that city yet to come, which we seek."

32. Ratzinger, *Theological Highlights of Vatican II*, ix.

33. Benedict XVI, "Christmas Greetings 2005."

the mass media, and also *one trend of modern theology.*"[34] On the other, he notes a "hermeneutic of reform," or "renewal in the continuity of the one subject-Church which the Lord has given to us. She is a subject which increases in time and develops, yet always remaining the same, the one subject of the journeying People of God."[35] With this assessment and explanation, Benedict XVI cuts to the core of the problem. Underneath the stated objective of the Council, one tied to catechetical renewal, *the question of the Council had to do with the manner in which the Church understood revelation in light of the "Heideggerian problematic,"* that is, the indictment that Western philosophy and theology has been marked by a "forgetfulness of being,"[36] and a challenge to address "the problem of the relationship of history and ontology, of the mediation of history in the realm of ontology."[37] Martin Heidegger (1889–1976), whose thought gained traction beyond the purely academic sphere, questioned Being itself and the manner in which Being appears within time, within history and context. How does Being reveal itself *within* time?

The battlefield, so to speak, for the quarreling hermeneutics, then, appears in the debates regarding fundamental theology—the implications of which spill over into nearly every area of the Church's life and mission, if not all of it. Susan Baumert describes theology of revelation as something of "ground zero" for the debate between those of a neo-scholastic bent and those of differing theological opinions.[38] Rowland emphasizes this point as well, saying:

34. Benedict XVI, "Christmas Greetings 2005"; emphasis added.

35. Benedict XVI, "Christmas Greetings 2005."

36. Sweeney, *Sacramental Presence*, 42.

37. Ratzinger, *Principles*, 158. Tracey Rowland, in "Catholic Theology in the Twentieth Century," 41, notes that the Conciliar debates were shaped by three theological "camps": "Those wedded to pre-Conciliar scholasticism, in particular to a Suárezian-infused Thomism, those fostering a synthesis of Thomist and Kantian thought, often described as Transcendental Thomism, such as Karl Rahner, and those who followed the decidedly anti-Kantian trajectory of the *ressourcement* theologians, above all, Henri de Lubac" (41). See also Rowland, *Catholic Theology*, 55.

38. Baumert, "Instruments of Change," 63–64. For a brief overview of the significant tenants of Neo-scholasticism, see Gleason, *Contending with Modernity*, 114–23; Kerr, *Twentieth-Century Catholic Theologians*, 1–16. Neo-scholasticism was enshrined by Pope Leo XIII as the *optimus modus philosophandi* and the antidote to "the heresy of Modernism" in 1879 (See Boys' brief treatment on this historical development in *Biblical Interpretation*, 70–72). Though difficult to define with precision, Rowland describes Modernism in theology as "a tendency to rely exclusively on historical science so as to determine the theological meaning of biblical and other texts, without acknowledging any role for tradition in the hermeneutical process" (*Ratzinger's Faith*, 2). Broadly speaking, Neo-scholasticism aimed to immunize Catholic theology from Modernist

Unlike in other periods of Church history when there has been some dominant theological issue creating a pastoral crisis, such as the battles in the early Church over Christology, or the battles in the medieval period over the reception of Greek philosophy or the battles in the sixteenth century over ecclesiology and sacramentality, today if we name *any* area in the field of fundamental theology we usually find that it is a battle zone.[39]

Baumert goes on to explain that prior to the Council, many theologians, educators, and biblical scholars were increasingly dissatisfied with the dominant interpretation drawn from the thought of Francisco Suárez (1548–1617) that basically says divine revelation is "the communication of a system of ideas rather than a manifestation and self-giving of a Person [Jesus Christ] who is Truth."[40] It was no different at the Council. Many theo-

---

tendencies by following Aquinas' trajectory of modifying and bringing Aristotelian realism into harmony with Christianity (Gleason, *Contending with Modernity*, 116). Its main proponents, however, are accused of an ahistorical reading of Aquinas based upon what Marie-Dominique Chenu (1895–1990) calls a "Baroque Thomism." That is to say, Neo-scholasticism builds upon commentaries produced by Thomist scholars (e.g., Cajetan [1469–1534] and Suárez [1548–1617] who were responding to Protestant opposition in the late scholastic era. Rowland further explains, "Modernists wanted history without tradition and ... Roman proponents of a Strict Observance Thomism [i.e., Neo-scholasticism] wanted tradition without history" (Rowland, "Catholic Theology in the Twentieth Century," 38). Given its privileged status, Neo-scholasticism played a significant role in shaping theology, seminary training, and catechetics during latter part of the nineteenth century and the first part of the twentieth.

39. Rowland, "Joseph Ratzinger," 236.

40. Baumert, "Instruments of Change," 63. The nineteenth-century followers of Suárez aimed to find common ground between Catholic and non-Catholics by anachronistically and historically reading Aquinas as an interlocutor amid the strains of Cartesian and Kantian rationalism that dominated the intellectual and cultural landscape. Their position has become known as Neo-scholasticism. Alasdair MacIntyre criticizes such Leonine Thomists (Thomists at the time of Pope Leo XIII (1810–1903) who had adopted Suárez's Neo-scholasticism) for "deforming central Christian positions for apologetic purposes" (*Three Rival Versions of Moral Enquiry*, 70, quoted in Rowland, *Ratzinger's Faith*, 19). Rowland criticizes them for "reworking Thomistic themes in Kantian terms" (*Ratzinger's Faith*, 19). Rowland explains, "The idea was that Catholics and non-Catholics could find common ground on the territory of 'pure nature' [and, concomitantly, "pure reason"], while the more socially contentious supernatural beliefs and aspirations of Catholics could be relegated to the privacy of the individual soul" (Rowland, *Ratzinger's Faith*, 20). A "two-tier" theory of nature and grace allowed for such a thing. This theory was originally developed by Cajetan (1469–1534) who, as described by Gerard O'Shea, speculated "that a *Duplex Ordo* theory was taught by St. Thomas Aquinas, with antecedents in Aristotelian philosophy. In explaining this thesis, Cajetan needed to raise the question of whether it was possible for human beings to have a natural desire for God. His answer was no. (Herein lies the root of the Catholic acceptance of arguing only from natural premises when dealing with 'natural' human

logians at the time of Vatican II challenged a Suárez-infused neo-scholastic theological tenor marked by what they perceived as a Kantian emphasis on "pure reason" and "pure nature,"[41] and which Fergus Kerr describes as a theological "straightjacket."[42] A certain "propositionalism" had encroached upon the more personal aspects of the faith.[43]

Reacting against a reduction of faith to the acceptance of propositions, a young Ratzinger admits that "scholasticism has its greatness," but he finds that in it "everything is very impersonal." As a young theologian, Ratzinger held that this school of thought contained an academic fear that

---

beings.)" (O'Shea, "Nature or Grace," 4). O'Shea goes on to point out that Ruard Tapper (1487–1559) and Luis de Molina (1535–1600) advanced Cajetan's thesis by developing the idea of a *finis naturalis*—"a natural end for a natural order." Suárez inherited these positions, and proposed the theory of "pure nature," which O'Shea describes as "a human nature that was completely devoid of any natural orientation to the grace of God, thus taking Cajetan's speculations into the mainstream of theology." Suárezian scholasticism does not see faith as a response to God's act of self-revealing, but as the ratification of revealed truths. Faith now ratifies propositions—it becomes a theoretical matter that may or may not touch the everyday realities of life. Rowland explains that "For Suárez, revelation does not disclose God himself, rather it concerns pieces of information which God has decided to disclose and whereas for St. Thomas, things revealed led to faith, for Suárez faith confirms what is revealed" (*Benedict XVI*, 49). Elsewhere, Rowland adds, "Suárez fostered a propositional account of Revelation by which Revelation does not disclose God himself so much as pieces of information about God" (*Catholic Theology*, 48; see also Rowland, *Ratzinger's Faith*, 48). To be clear, the critique of Neo-scholasticism presented here is not a criticism aimed at Aquinas' thought. Rather, it is a criticism of an anachronistic application of Aquinas' thought without due consideration for the historical context in which Aquinas was writing. See also Montag, "The False Legacy of Suárez," 38–63.

41. See Rowland, *Ratzinger's Faith*, 5. Additionally, Kerr notes the paradox of this revival in Thomistic philosophy following Leo XIII's directive that intended to keep modern philosophy out of Catholicism, "kept to very much the same canons of rationality as we find in the Enlightenment. The Enlightenment ideal was to attain timeless, universal and objective conclusions by exercising a unitary and ahistorical form of reasoning. . . . Neoscholastic theology 'identified truth and life with immutability and rationality; it opposed being to history and ignored concreteness in human life and in the economy of salvation.' For neothomists, as for Enlightenment philosophers, appealing to experience, tradition and historical studies was the wrong way to get to truth" (Kerr, *Twentieth-Century Catholic Theologians*, 2).

42. See Rowland, "Catholic Theology in the Twentieth Century," 55.

43. Even biographical material in the early twentieth century hints at a reduction of faith to proposition. For example, Bede Jarrett explains that "The Christian faith comprises a series of statements or truths revealed by God, and explaining either the inner side of the divine Being as we note It in the mystery of the Trinity or the relationship of man to the Creator by the laws of providence or the destiny and purpose of creation. But these statements were made known to us that precisely by means of our knowledge of them we might more closely hold on to God" (Jarrett, *The Life of Saint Dominic*, 109).

would not confront the "Heideggerian problematic."[44] In response, Ratzinger prefers a Bonaventurian and personalist understanding of revelation, as opposed to a Suárezian propositional one.[45] This is not to say Ratzinger is anti-metaphysical or anti-dogmatic, but simply that he did not declare a pocketbook of dogmas itself to be the very heart of the Christian life—the personal relationship with the Trinity is. The dogmatic teachings buttress this relationship, ensuring that one does not veer off into error, yet if they become the whole thing, the Catholic faith can be reduced to a certain intellectualism or moralism.[46] As will become clear, Ratzinger's position shaped Vatican II as a whole, and *Dei verbum* in particular.[47]

Neo-scholasticism drove fundamental theology prior to the Council, and catechetics as well. The two are inextricably linked. In areas still untouched by catechetical renewal efforts, neo-scholastic conceptions of revelation produced question-and-answer catechisms, religious education models emphasizing rote memorization, and the like. These methods offered content-rich presentations of the faith, but often ones that, according to their critics, failed to connect the doctrines of the faith to life shaped by the machinations of modernity. The Church needed to bridge the ever-widening gap between faith and life, and neo-scholastic forms of catechesis alone would not suffice. Instead, they were accused of causing a certain pedagogical bondage. In language that echoes Kerr's, though it predates Kerr's assessment, American catechist Gerard Sloyan (b. 1919) claims the "exclusive use of the question and answer method," was "a pedagogical straight jacket."[48] Brian Pedraza comments, "Though this emphasis on the memorization of doctrine may have been a valuable asset for the Church in previous eras, such a methodology was, the pioneers of renewal claimed, now significantly less effective in its ability to pass on the faith in all its vitality."[49]

Generally speaking, progressive conciliar reformers sought to exorcise the remaining vestiges of a Suárezian neo-scholastic theology that renewal movements had been confronting for decades. "Vatican II," as Tracey Rowland notes, "had the effect of doing away with the idea that Catholic theology was a monolithic intellectual system."[50] Key players leading up

---

44. Rowland, *Ratzinger's Faith*, 5.

45. See, for example, Ratzinger, *Milestones*, 108–9.

46. Rowland, "Dogmatic and Pastoral Theology," 192. Generally speaking, moralism refers to the reduction of religion to ethics.

47. See Ratzinger, *Milestones*, 124–29.

48. Sloyan, *Speaking of Religious Education*, 16. See also Pauley's brief description of catechesis prior to Vatican II in *Liturgical Catechesis in the 21st Century*, 17.

49. Pedraza, "Reform and Renewal in Catechesis," 6.

50. Rowland, *Catholic Theology*, 91.

to Vatican II, engaged in the Council itself, and in its outworking in the decades that followed, particularly Karl Rahner (1904–84) and Ratzinger, perceived something ossified in the Church's propositional understanding of the deposit of faith. The intellectualizing of revelation had somehow cost it its heart. It had cost the faith something personal. For theologians like Rahner and Ratzinger, recovering the liveliness of faith, overcoming the widening chasm between the world and the Church, and addressing the new paganism that had arisen in the Church combined to form the impetus necessary to work for renewal. Renewing the theology of revelation marked the way forward for the endeavor.

The concept of revelation touches the whole of Christianity; it is foundational in such a way that it cannot be prized apart without affecting virtually everything. This is certainly true for catechetics. On this point, Gabriel Moran (b. 1935), a craftsman of catechetical renewal in the United States following Vatican II, says, "The study of the theology of revelation should be of significance not only to the professional theologian, but to those involved in the pastoral ministry of the Church. The questions raised within this part of theology are so fundamental . . . that they cannot fail to have profound effects upon preaching and catechizing."[51] Again, Moran remarks, "The theology of revelation cannot solve the catechetical problem, but the catechetical problem can become intelligible only through a continuing study of revelation."[52] Avery Dulles echoes, observing that "fundamental theology [does] not try to speak to unbelievers but content[s] itself with analyzing for the sake of believers how God brings human beings to assent to His word."[53] Nevertheless, developments in fundamental theology, which explores the relationship between revelation and faith, directly impact the Church's mediation thereof. A theological grasp of how God reveals and who he reveals himself to be, the role human beings play in the act of God's gratuitous self-manifestation, and what this means for them is the critical foundation upon which one builds structures of proclamation. Evangelization announces the revelation of God and cultivates a process by which one comes to encounter this God. What one understands about the nature of revelation directly relates to how one leads another person to the revealing God (i.e., how one evangelizes). How one understands revelation directly impacts how one communicates it.

Vatican II, as a catechetical renewal council, opened to new questions in fundamental theology, and to new possibilities for catechetics as well. Therefore, one might propose a tentative thesis in response to this

---

51. Moran, *Revelation*, 19.
52. Moran, *Catechesis*, 40.
53. Dulles, "The Rebirth of Apologetics."

study's initial contextual question: how did catechetics reach such a state of crisis after Vatican II? What led to its decline? The answer, in some way, must have to do with certain developments in fundamental theology after Vatican II and a moving away from the "given" of the Church's tradition in this area, which radically impacts catechetics over time. Shifts in fundamental theology ultimately grounded the catechetical roof during the anthropological phase of renewal.

An Architect and His Master Builders

Catechetics, then, rests upon fundamental theology. This is to say, new ventures, debates, or determinations in fundamental theology inevitably impact practical theology.[54] So, who is the theological "architect" behind the metaphorical roof in what Hofinger calls the human, or anthropological phase of catechetical renewal? Avery Dulles answers this question by observing, "the most powerful restatement of the Catholic theology of revelation for the period in which the Church finds itself on the morrow of Vatican Council II is unquestionably to be found in the writings of Karl Rahner."[55] Rahner's influence was neither limited to the field of fundamental theology, nor to the ether of speculative theology, but it functioned as an impetus for further renewal in the areas of evangelization and catechetics. Indeed, Rahner stands, perhaps unintentionally, as the chief architect for the third phase of catechetical renewal—one that ultimately constructs a fine roof but fails to fasten it atop the house. Certain principles drawn from his fundamental theology became the blueprint for the modern catechetical project.

Rahner was born into a middle-class family on March 5, 1904, in Freiburg, Germany. Inspired by Romano Guardini (1885–1968), Karl went on to join his brother Hugo in the Society of Jesus in 1922, where he engaged in the standard neo-scholastic seminary courses from 1924–33.[56] Rahner never intended to become a theologian, and was surprised when he was tasked with teaching philosophy. He began his doctoral work in

---

54. Ratzinger identifies catechetics with practical theology [*praktische Theologie*] in *Handing on the Faith*, 15. Therefore, I will use the expression "practical theology" in the same manner, with regard to the theological study of catechesis as an integral part of evangelization.

55. Dulles, *Revelation Theology*, 158–59.

56. Kerr's claims that Neo-scholasticism and its implementation within seminaries attempted to "inoculate [theologians, seminarians, etc.] them against infection by the idealist, subjectivist and positivist philosophies, which were held to have created 'the modernist crisis'" (Kerr, *Twentieth-Century Catholic Theologians*, 1).

1934 at Freiburg im Breisgau, where he attended lectures given by Heidegger.[57] Heidegger did not supervise Rahner's thesis, however. Instead, Rahner studied under Martin Honecker who failed Rahner's first dissertation, before his second attempt at Innsbruck succeeded. Following a brief stint on the faculty at Innsbruck, the war altered things, and Rahner spent ten years in parish life. Here he discovered "at first hand the problems lay people had with their faith, the context for much of his later writing."[58] In 1948, Rahner returned to Innsbruck where he taught dogmatic theology. Despite criticism from Rome—and even preliminary censorship—Rahner was nominated a *peritus* for Vatican II. In 1964, he began teaching at Munich, only to leave in 1967 when he moved to the University of Münster. He retired in 1971 and continued to engage in various theological and pastoral endeavors until his death on March 30, 1984.[59]

Rahner's theology, taken as a whole, is speculative in nature. It lives and grows in the mid-twentieth century world of ideas. Unconcerned with finding perfectly clear answers to deep theological questions, Rahner's theology is always moving—almost evading a resolution. He simply wants to keep theology flowing in modernity's stream instead of stagnating in pre-modern ways of thinking. Rahner reacted against propositional conceptions of faith and developed a theology on what we might call a transcendental anthropology, a "dynamised and subjectified (or personalised) reflection on the relation between God and humans in a fundamental way, thus opening a place for the human experience of freedom and the sacramental event."[60] At the bottom of it, Rahner's theological enterprise is an exercise in correlation that attempts to show how theology corresponds to the modern context. Lieven Boeve summarizes this mid-twentieth century shift to a correlation approach, saying, "Although this claimed autonomy of the subject was first rejected by the church and theology, afterwards they embraced it." Now, "rationality, human freedom, and social liberation were considered privileged *loci theologici*. . . . Secular culture was no longer considered to be alien from

---

57. For a brief description of Heidegger's influence on Rahner, see Rahner, *Karl Rahner in Dialogue*, 13. Rahner claims he took from Heidegger a style of thinking, a "method or approach by which one does not examine dogmatic truths *merely* as evidence derived from the positive sources, but one seeks to construct a synthesis. One takes the various dogmatic propositions and reduces them to certain fundamental principles. In that way an internal, coherent body of dogmatic truth is established." Rahner was concerned with providing some sort of synthesis made possible by an idea that could organize the immensity of Christian dogma.

58. Kerr, *Twentieth-Century Catholic Theologians*, 88.

59. This brief summary of Rahner's biography is a cursory overview of the one Kerr provides in *Twentieth-Century Theologians*, 87–90.

60. Boeve, "Postmodern Sacramento-Theology," 330.

Christianity, rather it was the place in which God was actively present in the struggle for an authentic subjectivity and social justice."[61] The category of "experience" plays a significant role in building this bridge.[62] By embracing secular culture, modern correlation theology sought to make faith relevant again by establishing a "consensus between culture and faith."[63] Now, Catholic theology endeavors to "dialogue with modernity . . . to identify points at which the Christian narrative could be grafted onto modernity's potential for freedom and liberation."[64] Modern thinking makes theology move again and theology can, in turn, serve modernity's humanistic and liberating mission. Rahner's project is indicative of such motivations.

Rahner's thought belongs to the school of Transcendental Thomism and its adoption of certain Kantian thought-tools.[65] Consequently, Rahner constructs his anthropology along the lines of transcendent experience and freedom, in which he grounds his Christology. He then goes on to argue that the Christ-event renders all human experience always already Christian via his notoriously nebulous concept of the supernatural existential and its practical, soteriological outworking in his thesis known as anonymous Christianity. Thus, Rahner is accused of naturalizing the supernatural.[66] In his attempt "to translate the riches of the Christian faith

---

61. Boeve, *God Interrupts*, 32. For a longer treatment on this shift, see Boeve, *Interrupting Tradition*, 44–49.

62. Boeve provides a long treatment on Schillebeeckx's experiential bridge between Christianity and modernity, along with Antoon Vergote's criticism of this bridge in *God Interrupts History*, 62–70. In many ways, Schillebeeckx's position is sympatico with Rahner's in this regard, where "there can be no revelation without experience," where the subjective element is highlighted, and the objective provides some sort of interpretive direction (63). Boeve clearly does not subscribe to this position in his attempt to recontextualize Christianity. He claims, "As a result of detraditionalization, the overlap between culture and faith has become too narrow. At the cultural level, profound human experiences can no longer be quasi-automatically interpreted within Christian interpretive frameworks. The frequent result of a non-problematized correlation today, therefore, is *de facto* a horizontal and functionalized reduction of Christianity in terms of cultural Christianity, ethics, or aesthetics. . . . [As Vergote points out] there is absolutely no basis for assuming that a profound human experience will be interpreted as a Christian experience" (74). See also Boeve, "Experience according to Edward Schillebeeckx," 199–225.

63. Boeve, *God Interrupts*, 33.

64. Boeve, *God Interrupts*, 4.

65. See, for example, Rausch, *Systematic Theology*, 16; Nichols, *The Shape of Catholic Theology*, 337; Rowland, *Catholic Theology*, 60–65.

66. See Rowland, *Catholic Theology*, 62. See also Cooper, *Naturally Human*, 113, where he claims that "one gets the continual impression that the deifying experience of grace outlined by Rahner takes place in the individual primarily in the form of a heightened consciousness of what is universally already the case."

into contemporary modes of thought," Adam Cooper says, "[Rahner's] theology increasingly came to bear the problematic mark of his concern to 'demythologize' the theological language and concepts of the Bible and the Fathers."[67] Nevertheless, the flow of Rahner's speculative theology manages to move within the banks established by the Church's Magisterium however fluid and difficult to define it remains.

Msgr. Frank Lane, a student at the University of Innsbruck immediately after Rahner's departure for Munich, and while the university situated on the Inn River remained under his theological sway, describes Rahner as a cult-figure after the Council within "popular [American] Catholicism." At the conclusion of his studies and upon his return to the United States, Lane "was shocked to pick up the *National Catholic Reporter* and read what the catechetical minds of American were saying Fr. Rahner had said and was saying."[68] Lane's incredulity lies in the fact that Rahner's deep speculative theology "had fallen into the hands of popularizing journalists and ill-prepared catechists."[69] A form of what Aidan Nichols calls "vulgarized Rahnerianism" swept through the field.[70] This "vulgarised" form could be defined as "an attitude of mind among theological literate, or at least religiously articulate, Catholics which owed much, certainly, to Rahner but on the way had shed too much in the way of nuance and qualification."[71] To this, Rowland adds that Rahner's work is notoriously "ambivalent" and "dense," which "gives a lot of interpretive power to anyone offering a more user-friendly, popularist version."[72] Lane describes the catechetical elite, those vulgarized Rahnerians, as attempting to make of Rahner's fluid, speculative theology something practical by latching onto certain "fixed points" in his thought that proved to be conducive for catechetical experimentation. In other words, to build on Rahner, they had to first stabilize the instability of his thought. They had to somehow do the impossible, by stopping the flow of the speculative stream to grab out building stones for a new catechetics. Rahner had intended to reinvigorate theology such that it might touch the lives of people once again, however the unforeseen impact of such a speculative venture caused catechetics to become speculative and to deteriorate from within. Consequently, Nichols points out that Rahner's

---

67. Cooper, *Naturally Human*, 33.
68. Lane, *Reflections*, 8.
69. Lane, *Reflections*, 8.
70. Nichols, "Rahner and Balthasar," 113.
71. Nichols, "Rahner and Balthasar," 113.
72. Rowland, *Catholic Theology*, 63. Gerard O'Shea also engages this topic in "Vulgarised Rahnerianism," 341–73.

theology "has not simply damaged *theological culture*, the thinking found within the Church," but "*ecclesial practice*, the action which Catholics feel committed to by virtue of their faith."[73]

Therefore, a Rahnerian plan, or "blueprint," guides catechetical construction during catechetical renewal's "anthropological phase." Claiming the blueprint behind the anthropological phase is exclusively Rahnerian would be an exaggeration, but a denial of Rahner's influence would be a gross understatement. Rahner clearly intends for his speculative theology to influence the mission of the Church, though he did not expect elements of his fluid, speculative thought to become fixed theoretical anchors and definitive supports for new, concrete catechetical projects.[74] Some, like Balthasar, for example, had already expressed fear for what would happen to the faithful if aspects of Rahner's speculative thought became concrete in catechetics. His concerns center most poignantly around Rahner's thesis of "anonymous Christianity." In a letter to Rahner, Balthasar admits he is not so much worried about the theory itself, but how it will be understood by ordinary people.[75] For ordinary Catholics, Rahner's theories remain ethereal, inaccessible pieces of speculative theology. However, when catechetical theorists snatch them up and employ them in the renewal efforts of the time, they suddenly gain the force necessary to touch down in and to shape the lives of ordinary people. Many such builders snatched up Rahner's blueprint and begin to construct the next portion of the catechetical edifice in the decades immediately following Vatican II. Of all of them, two stand out as master builders—at least in America: Gabriel Moran and Thomas Groome.

Both Moran and Groome thoroughly embrace the "anthropological turn,"[76] that modernizing trend that shapes what Hofinger describes as the human phase of catechetical renewal. Moran was born in 1935 in Manchester, New Hampshire. He entered the Christian Brothers in 1954, and studied at Catholic University of America, eventually pursuing graduate

---

73. Nichols, "Rahner and Balthasar," 108.

74. See Rahner, *Faith in a Wintry Season*, 166–67. Here, Rahner admits that his theology is closely related to the notions of "anonymous Christian" and "anonymous Christianity," though he is not sure whether he or someone else came up with the concept. Nevertheless, he is indifferent to the word, and "if for religious, pedagogical, or other significant reasons it is found to be dangerous or open to misunderstanding, then simply drop it."

75. As described in Conway, "A Constant Word," 117. For a brief treatment on Balthasar's concern with "Anonymous Christianity," see Balthasar, *The Moment of Christian Witness*, 100–113.

76. Pedraza employs this description as a sure way of describing what happened in the third phase of catechetical renewal. See Pedraza, *Catechesis for the New Evangelization*, 102.

studies under the tutelage of Sloyan. He received his doctorate in Religious Education from Catholic University of America in 1965. In 1985 Moran formally left the Christian Brothers and, in 1986, he married Maria Harris, a former Sister of St. Joseph and a fellow educator. Moran passed away on October 15, 2021. He spent the bulk of his academic career in higher education at New York University and published prodigiously.[77] For his part, Moran latches onto Rahner's transcendental anthropology as his "given," and develops the idea of "ongoing revelation." In his biography on Moran, Robert Parmach quotes Moran's own reflection of the thinkers that shape his thought: "Plato, the Church Fathers, and the like. But . . . Karl Rahner was my salvation as a young man starting out, for he pushed my mind into tight corners and challenged me to open up the pathways of ideas for myself. He also taught me that theology need not be boring if you know where and how to look at it, how it can be both deeply rooted and transformative in one's life."[78]

Moran's fellow catechetical craftsman, Thomas Groome, was born in 1945 in Dublin, Ireland. Eventually the recipient of the equivalent of a Masters of Divinity from St. Patrick's Seminary, Carlow, Groome was ordained to the priesthood 1968. Later, he left the priesthood, married, and studied at Fordham University. He went on to receive a PhD from Union Theological Seminary at Columbia University. Groome is presently a Professor of Theology and Religious Education at Boston College, where he has been since 1977.[79] He has authored a significant number of articles, edited numerous books, and authored seven books from 1980–2019. He has also worked with Sadlier publishing on religious education curriculum since the mid-1980s. Groome essentially concretizes Moran's fundamental insights, along with a host of others, in his method known as *Shared Christian Praxis*. Harold Horell notes the ties between Groome and the thought of Moran and Rahner when he says, "Groome['s] . . . work reflected the insights of developments in post-Vatican II Catholic theology. . . . [He] developed his ideas in dialogue with Catholic religious educators Gabriel Moran and Berard Marthaler, [and] . . . his analysis of education for human freedom resonated with the

---

77. He published twenty-four books between 1963 and 2011, and he has published over two hundred articles. See Paruch, "A Study of the Direct Ramifications," 231–38. In this dissertation, Paruch provides a thorough treatment on the development of Moran's thought throughout his career.

78. Parmach, "Gabriel Moran." See also Pedraza, *Catechesis for the New Evangelization*, 117–18.

79. For further biographical details and a thorough exposition of Groome's catechetical contribution, see Paruch, "A Study of the Direct Ramifications" 313–18. See also O'Shea, *Review of Religious Education*, 99–103; Willey, "The Pedagogue and the Teacher," 46–47.

understanding of freedom that is central to the work of Catholic theologian Karl Rahner."[80] Groome's work would go on to shape American religious education significantly during the 1980s, 1990s, and continues to impact corners of the catechetical landscape today. Moran and Groome, amongst others, brought Rahner's plans to fruition in pastoral practice in a distinctly modern moment of the anthropological phase of catechetical renewal.

Given that Vatican II "updated" the Church just as modernity was in the process of collapsing, the "modern moment" of catechetical renewal was rather brief. The context changed, and the postmodern condition emerged from modernity's sarcophagus. Where there was once an assumed duality for correlation to navigate and synthesize—namely, the "religious" and the "secular"—there is now a multiplicity of positions. Plurality best describes the postmodern condition, with no singular position existing with its own bird's eye view above the diverse panorama of the rest. Here, correlation is simply no longer possible in a one-to-one manner, as there is not a univocal idea of "secular culture" to which theology relates. Thus, Rahner's correlation project must be recontextualized in light of the new, postmodern context if it is to function fruitfully for fundamental and practical theology. Lieven Boeve calls for this recontextualization, and aims to "radicalize modern correlation theory" by allowing for "particularity, contextuality, narrativity, historicity, contingency, and otherness."[81] In short, the straightforward "if you can't beat 'em, join 'em" approach of modern correlation theology is not possible in a plural environment where "em" can stand for an infinite number of positions or entities, and any talk of "winning" reeks of hegemony. Deinstitutionalization, individualization, and detraditionalization are all marks of the postmodern condition—the new context in which theology must be recontextualized if the Rahnerian correlation project is to survive. Boeve and his fellow Leuven colleague, Didier Pollefeyt, are forerunners in the theological movement of recontextualization.

Boeve (b. 1966), a Belgian theologian, received his doctorate in 1995 after writing on postmodernity in relation to theology. He is a professor of Fundamental Theology and the head of the research group Theology in a Postmodern Context at KU Leuven. In 2014, Boeve was appointed as Director-General of the Flemish Office for Catholic Education. He has published over 60 articles and made over seventy contributions to collected volumes. Additionally, he has published six books while co-editing numerous others. His research engages theological epistemology, continental theology and philosophy, neo-Augustinianism in contemporary theology, theological

---

80. Horell, "Thomas Groome."
81. Boeve, *God Interrupts*, 40.

anthropology, and has recently expanded to include questions pertaining to Catholic identity in education.[82] Didier Pollefeyt, also Belgian theologian, was born in 1965. Pollefeyt received his doctorate in theology with a dissertation on ethics after Auschwitz. He is a full professor at KU Leuven where he is a member of the Faculty of Theology and Religious Studies. At KU Leuven, Pollefeyt is also the coordinator of the *Center for Teacher Education*. Like Boeve, Pollefeyt is a prolific researcher and writer, with well over one hundred reviewed articles or books, and over 130 books or articles in other scientific journals.[83] Boeve and Pollefeyt can be considered chief "builders" of recontextualized catechetical renewal today.

Together, Boeve and Pollefeyt's project propels catechetical renewal into something of a "postmodern moment" within the anthropological phase. It is possible to situate this "postmodern moment" within the anthropological phase because the chief motivation (i.e., correlation) and *modus operandi* (i.e., the turn towards anthropology/anthropocentrism) are essentially the same from Rahner to Pollefeyt, even if the context has become radicalized in postmodernity. Modern correlation theology took a modern way of thinking as its "given" and based theological thought on it to make theology relevant again, to get it moving. As a result, modern theology became eerily similar to modern thought and functioned as an advocate for modern project—with catechists serving as its day laborers. The postmodern theological effort follows suit by taking the postmodern condition as "given" and turning Christianity into a herald for the new "gospel" of postmodernity. Here, catechetics becomes something entirely other. The postmodern catechetical project does not put the roof on the house. It is not the fourth phase Hofinger hoped for. Instead, it is a second "moment" within the anthropological phase, and one that basically dismantles the roof, before going on to seemingly deconstruct the whole edifice. The whole movement from Rahner to Pollefeyt in evangelization and catechetics, it seems, manifests precisely what happens when fundamental theology takes some understanding of the human subject as the "given," whether in a modern or postmodern sense, as opposed to taking faith in Jesus Christ as the "given." With the human subject as the "given," a great reversal takes place, and Boeve captures this when he claims, "the best way to convert the world to God is to convert the church to God's

---

82. See Lieven Boeve's biographical webpage at Boeve, "Faculty of Theology and Religious Studies."

83. See Didier Pollefeyt's personal website with complete CV at Pollefeyt, "Biography."

world."[84] Under the sway of this reversal, the Church has little to offer the world, save for serving its dominant modes of thought.

An Architect Who Designs according to the Revelation of the *Logos*

Returning to the question posed above, regarding the difficulty of implementing the Council, Benedict XVI argues that the hermeneutic of rupture "had frequently availed itself of the sympathies of the mass media, and also one trend of modern theology."[85] Though he veils the reference, Benedict XVI seems to tie the hermeneutic to Rahner's theology, which managed to gain a popular foothold. Conversely, the opposing hermeneutic remained silent and has quietly borne fruit over time. Such a hermeneutic, one rooted in a *ressourcement* approach, is his own. Ratzinger, therefore, can easily be considered the architect who proposes an alternate plan for postconciliar catechetical renewal.

In some ways, Ratzinger's life has been marked by a certain significance from the day of his birth, April 16, 1927—Holy Saturday. Born in Marktl am Inn, Germany as the youngest of the three Ratzinger children, Joseph's family lived a modest life and moved about frequently between the Inn and Salzach rivers in Bavaria. Ratzinger entered seminary in 1939, a time that suffered a hiatus as the German armed forces drafted him and other seminarians to serve as members of the anti-aircraft defense of the German army in 1943. Following World War II, Ratzinger's seminary experience resumed at the major seminary of Freising and at the University of Munich, where he studied philosophy and theology, before being ordained to the priesthood on June 29, 1951. In 1953, he obtained his doctorate in theology with his thesis entitled *The People and House of God in Augustine's Doctrine of the Church* and completed his *Habilitationsschrift* on the theology of history in St. Bonaventure in 1957.[86] Following a teaching stint in Freising, Ratzinger taught at the following universities: Bonn (1959–63), Münster (1963–66), Tübingen (1966–69), Regensburg (1969–77). During Vatican II (1962–65), Ratzinger served as a theological expert (*peritus*) for Cardinal Joseph Frings of Cologne.[87] Despite reservations, Ratzinger

---

84. Boeve, "Conversion and Cognitive Dissonance," 254.
85. Benedict XVI, "Christmas Greetings 2005."
86. The *Habilitationsschrift* made him eligible to teach in a German university.
87. It is a well-known fact that Ratzinger participated in the Council as a *peritus* and was instrumental in the development of *Dei verbum*, and the drafting of *Lumen gentium*, *Gaudium et spes*, and *Ad gentes*. For commentaries on Ratzinger's role in the

was appointed by Paul VI as Archbishop of Munich and Freising in 1977, before being appointed by John Paul II as Prefect for the Congregation for the Doctrine of the Faith in 1981. On April 19, 2005, Ratzinger was elected to succeed John Paul II as pope of the universal Church, a position he held until his resignation on February 28, 2013.

As Providence would have it, Vatican II vaulted Ratzinger into the worldwide theological scene. Ratzinger served as the advisor to Cardinal Frings, who assumed a lead role in the Council. The road for the young Ratzinger's ascendency was being paved as he tread upon it. Ratzinger, given his criticism of Neo-scholasticism, was considered a progressive at the time of the Council, and given his general stance on Neo-scholasticism (i.e., if Neo-scholasticism is the measuring stick), this epithet fits. Ratzinger preferred the *ressourcement* movement; his was an historical and Scriptural approach grounded in the Church Fathers. Ratzinger's doctoral work is indicative of this theological position, and this academic work came to bear in several significant theological debates at the Council. In short, at the Council, Ratzinger had arrived.

When it comes to Ratzinger's thought on evangelization and catechesis, one finds that his position proceeds according to the same basic progression from fundamental theology to a theology and consequent methodology of evangelization. By way of illustration, one might consider Benedict XVI's line of questioning from a General Audience on November 28, 2012:

> The important question we ask ourselves today is: how can we talk about God in our time? How can we communicate the Gospel so as to open roads to his saving truth in our contemporaries' hearts—that are all too often closed—and minds—that are at times distracted by the many dazzling lights of society?[88]

That Ratzinger holds the two questions together is itself insightful and educative, though easily overlooked. The first question is not methodological, as it first appears. The question has to do with fundamental theology—how can we say anything at all about God in the first place? This is a clear engagement with the Heideggerian problematic. How has Being (i.e., God) revealed itself such that one can say anything about God at all?

In response to the Heideggerian problematic, Ratzinger argues that the distinctive object of Catholic faith is not Being itself, but what Being has revealed of itself in *logos*. With the incarnation of the *Logos*, Being has

---

Council, see, for example, Gibson, *The Rule of Benedict*, 147–78; Tobin, *Holy Father*, 95–106; Nichols, *The Thought of Pope Benedict XVI*, 53–72; Heim, *Joseph Ratzinger*; Seewald, *Benedict XVI*, 307–463.

88. Benedict XVI, *Transforming Power*, 42.

been revealed precisely by entering into time and space, that is, into the created order in the person of Jesus Christ. Thus, Jesus Christ, the Word, the *Logos*, is the real object of faith for the Christian. Accordingly, Benedict XVI answers his first question—how can we talk about God?—as follows:

> We can talk about God because he has talked to us; so the first condition for speaking of God is listening to all that God himself has said. God has spoken to us! God is therefore not a distant hypothesis concerning the world's origin; he is not a mathematical intelligence far from us. God takes an interest in us, he loves us, he has entered personally into the reality of our history, he has communicated himself, even to the point of taking flesh. Thus God is a reality of our life, he is so great that he has time for us too, he takes an interest in us. In Jesus of Nazareth we encounter the face of God, who came down from his heaven to immerse himself in the human world, in our world, and to teach "the art of living," the road to happiness; to set us free from sin and make us children of God (cf. Eph 1:5; Rom 8:14).[89]

Throughout his theological work, and this is on display again here, Ratzinger clearly takes the revelation of the *Logos* in Jesus Christ as his "given." God is not distant or self-centered thought-thinking-thought, but close and personal. The *logos* reveals itself as *Logos*, Word, as *the* Son, as the second person of the Trinity, and He reveals to humanity the love the Trinity has for man.

The revelation of God in the *Logos* of Jesus Christ, this unveiling—or any unveiling for that matter—requires a receiving subject (i.e., one who receives the gift of the revelation). The human subject is necessary, so to speak, for the revelation of the *Logos* to be revelation, and that act by which man receives the revelation of the *Logos* goes by the name of faith. Faith, according to Ratzinger, is a deeply personal act in response to the personal God who reveals personally. It cannot be otherwise. In Ratzinger's understanding of revelation and faith, then, he moves away from a propositional approach and into a personalist one. Ratzinger bases this move upon the revelation of the *Logos* in the person of Jesus Christ, who reveals the fundamental personhood of the Trinity, and, in doing so, reveals that relationality is at the foundation of all existence.

The encounter with the *Logos* is possible today through the *Logos*' own establishment of the Church and the imparting of the Holy Spirit upon that Church. The Church mediates the Word of God in all times and in all places

---

89. Benedict XVI, *Transforming Power*, 42–43.

where she is present.⁹⁰ Rather than blurring Christ, reordering the tradition, or declaring impossible the revelation of the *Logos* altogether, rather than losing faith in the faith of the Church, which is ultimately to so say, in Christ—as happens in the Rahnerian trajectory—Ratzinger embraces and enters into the faith of the Church and so has access to the revelation of the *Logos* in Jesus Christ who is the same yesterday, today, and forever (cf. Heb 13:8). The Church's growing consciousness, that deepening collective awareness of the *Logos* that comes about precisely through the Church's relationship with Christ, her tradition is, for Ratzinger, the way in which to have access to the *Logos*, who is *the* revelation, the one source of God's revelation. The Church's enduring testimony, located in her Scriptures and her tradition and her teaching office, renders access to the revelation of the *Logos* possible and sure. The Church's act of offering her enduring testimony for the good of mankind, goes by the name of evangelization.

Ratzinger's second question quoted above—how can we communicate the Gospel?—is methodological. If one can say anything at all about God, how ought one say it? One can speak about God today, one can evangelize today, because of the revelation of the *Logos* in Jesus Christ—and faith in that revelation, that Person, in the faith of the Church. However, Benedict XVI proposes that one not only speaks about Being by speaking about the *Logos*, *but* that one speaks according to the *Logos* as well. In other words, the *Logos* is not only the content, but the method as well. The *who* reveals the *how*; person is the method. On this point, Benedict XVI says:

> Speaking of God demands familiarity with Jesus and his Gospel, it implies that we have a real, personal knowledge of God and a strong passion for his plan of salvation without succumbing to the temptation of success, but following God's own method. God's method is that of humility—God makes himself one of us—his method is brought about through the Incarnation in the simple house of Nazareth; through the Grotto of Bethlehem; through the Parable of the Mustard Seed.⁹¹

This "real, personal knowledge of God" is nothing other than faith, as understood in a personalist sense—"the encounter with an event, a person, which gives life a new horizon and a decisive direction."⁹² To speak about God, that is, to evangelize according to faith, according to this radical relationality with God made possible in and through Jesus Christ, means evangelizing according to the *Logos'* own method, which is nothing other

---

90. Cf. Benedict XVI, "Meditation 2012."
91. Benedict XVI, *Transforming Power*, 43.
92. Benedict XVI, *DCE*, §1.

than incarnate humility. Evangelization, then, always begins with God's initiative and proceeds according to God's way. Hofinger had claimed that the "human approach to catechesis has in fact not come to an end," and that the "person-centered approach" of the third phase of catechetical renewal needed to give way to a fourth.[93] Ratzinger offers the corrective to the anthropocentric "given." Ratzinger does not propose an alternate form of a "person-centered" approach, but the establishment of the Person-centered approach in the "given" of the *Logos*. Ratzinger's point is simple: what goes wrong in the catechetical experimentation after Vatican II results from starting with the wrong "given." So renewal must restart, in every age, from the "given" that is Christ.

Thus, one finds in Ratzinger something of a rival architect to Rahner. Both reacted to the same apparent ossification of the faith and both wanted the same thing—for the faith to become personally relevant in the lives of ordinary people. Both had the same awareness of the relationship between fundamental theology and evangelization and catechetics. Ratzinger's questions indicate this: determinations in fundamental theology necessarily impact theological understandings of, and methodological considerations for evangelization. *Who* one believes, *what* one believes, and *how* one believes directly impacts what the *who, what,* and *how* in the Church's preaching and teaching. However, Rahner's and Ratzinger's "design plans" for going about achieving renewal, their concepts of renewal during the postconciliar era, differ significantly. As history now makes clear, the rise of an anthropocentric catechesis according to the Rahnerian plan expeditiously contributes to the vaporizing of a Catholic culture and signals shifts in approaches to fundamental theology that subdue, dismiss, and eventually silence the tradition. Such a project can now be set aside. It can be replaced with Ratzinger's fundamental theology and its emphasis on the *Logos* and principles for a movement in evangelization and catechesis according to the pattern revealed by Christ. Ratzinger's "given," i.e., the revelation of the *Logos* in Jesus Christ, becomes a way forward for evangelization and catechesis—both in terms of content and method. The pages that follow examine the dual aspects of this thesis.

The Book in Outline

The reader will find that Part I of the present study traces the Rahnerian blueprint from Rahner himself to its postmodern reification in Boeve and Pollefeyt. Chapter 1 provides a basic, even cursory, overview of Rahner's

93. Hofinger, "Looking Backward and Forward," 355.

thought—the complexity of which makes such an endeavor rather tentative. Nevertheless, the chapter explores the main points of his thought insofar as they become relevant for catechetics, and how the necessity of Christ begins to become somewhat blurry or subdued in Rahner. Next, chapter 2 engages with the "vulgarized Rahnerian" thought of Moran and Groome. Ultimately, here, Moran and Groome reorder the place of the Church's tradition in catechesis. In the revelational event, tradition is considered secondary—a help for interpreting transcendental experience only when necessary. Chapter 3 explores the Rahnerian project as it manifests itself within the postmodern condition in Boeve's recontextualization project. Following this treatment of Boeve's fundamental theology, and that basic progression from fundamental theology into practical theology, chapter 4 considers a postmodern version of evangelization and catechesis as it appears in the thought of Boeve and Pollefeyt.

Part II presents an alternate path for renewal—a Ratzingerian one. Rather appropriately, chapter 5 explores Ratzinger's role in Vatican II, before examining his criticism of the "hermeneutic of rupture" and its impact on catechesis in chapter 6. Moving from fundamental to practical theology, the remainder of the book attempts to present Ratzinger's own vision for evangelization and catechetics. Chapter 7 examines his understanding of revelation of the *Logos* in Jesus Christ. This revelation "of the incarnate Word [allows] the mystery of man take on light," so chapter 8 presents Ratzinger's theological anthropology, which is properly a Trinitarian and Christocentric anthropology.[94] Chapter 9 addresses the part the receiving subject plays in the revelational act through the act of faith and the implications of faith for one's life, insofar as faith is an encounter that generates conversion and invites one into a path of ongoing healing known as discipleship. Then, moving into practical theology, chapter 10 outlines the basic elements of Ratzinger's understanding of evangelization and catechesis, before chapter 11 theologically engages the question of method.

---

94. Second Vatican Council, *Gaudium et spes*, §22.

Part I

The Rahner Project: Evangelization and Catechesis after Vatican II

CHAPTER ONE

A Rahnerian Blueprint for Catechetical Renewal

Karl Rahner wanted to render mid-twentieth century theology relevant in two ways. First, he sought to make Catholic theology compatible with modern ways of thinking, speaking, and acting. Second, he desired for his systematic theology to impact pastoral ministry in the Church. Regarding the latter, Rahner denounces the thought that theology is an irrelevant and ethereal exercise, instead believing that theology should directly impact the Church's life and mission and "touch down" in the daily lives of believers. Regarding the former, in the years prior to Vatican II, Rahner saw a need reinvigorate Catholic theology. He, along with many others, believed Neo-scholasticism's pre-modern propositional approach ossified theology. The dual motivations are in play when he says, "theology must help the preacher preach the gospel in such a way that it can really be understood and assimilated today; [while also having] a critical function . . . in preventing the Church in its preaching or in its practice from becoming a ghetto or sect within the contemporary world."[1] Hence, Svein Rise concludes, "His writings are characterized by the combination of theory and praxis."[2] Therefore, one could summarize Rahner's mission

---

1. Rahner, *Karl Rahner in Dialogue*, 50.

2. Rise, "Karl Rahner," 225. One must note the historical context in which Rahner's work was generated. Responding to Neo-scholasticism was not his sole task. Rahner was a leading figure in a cast of theologians responding to the horror of the world wars. Centuries before, Luther, Calvin, Zwingli, and other reformers had advanced an alternate understanding of Original Sin that turned Christian anthropology on its head. Msgr. Frank Lane describes the Protestant position on Original Sin as "a damaging" of human nature that actually "destroyed human nature and left us with a fixed and irreversible condition of depravity." The state of human nature after the fall is characterized by Luther's manure pile, with grace being the snow that covers over it. Following the bloodshed of the world wars, it seemed as if Luther and the others may have been right. The Church and her theologians had to respond. The immediate response can

in a rather straightforward manner: Rahner intends to make both theology and pastoral praxis relevant in the face of modernity through correlation by taking postulates drawn from modern thought as his "given."[3]

In Rahner's view, Vatican II gave the Church permission to emerge from the ghetto. The Council gave the Church "the courage to face the modern world." It marked "a real movement away from a more negative, defensive attitude toward a more open and positive one."[4] He sees this openness as "a positive appreciation of modern culture and of modern science and technology," with a deeper "awareness of specifically contemporary problems facing mankind today, of the Church's involvement in these problems, and of her responsibility in helping to find solutions."[5] Following Vatican II, Rahner, and his Transcendental Thomism becomes a catalyst, indeed the single greatest theological force in Catholicism for advancing this positive relationship between the Church and the modern world.[6]

---

be found in the work of the, Karol Wojtyla, Balthasar, and Rahner. Wojtyla turned his attention to Genesis to recover the inherent dignity of the person created in the "image and likeness" of God. Balthasar "gathered the whole of western culture into a synthesis that looked beyond and into the depth." Rahner attempted to theologically reconstruct human nature "as a transcending phenomenon" based upon the work of Aquinas, Kant, and Heidegger. See Lane, *Reflections*, 6–7.

3. See Martin, *Will Many Be Saved?*, 110; Rise, "Karl Rahner," 225.
4. Rahner, *Karl Rahner in Dialogue*, 46.
5. Rahner, *Karl Rahner in Dialogue*, 46.
6. Rausch calls Rahner the "premier example" of this particular branch of Thomism (Rausch, *Systematic Theology*, 18). Transcendental Thomism has its roots in the thought of Maréchal (1878–1944) and Rousselot (1878–1915) and is an "effort to bring theology into dialogue with modern philosophy, particularly Kant, by analyzing the conditions for the transcendental reach of human understanding" (Rausch, *Systematic Theology*, 18). Transcendental Thomism does not begin with metaphysical properties, as is the case in neo-scholastic thought, but with an epistemological principle. It is a "transcendental turn," which begins with the subject and a "theological anthropology or theological view of humanity [which] reveals the human person as spirit-in-the-world, open to the absolute" (Rausch, *Systematic Theology*, 137). Vincelette defines this principle as saying that "what allows for knowledge is that to some degree humans have an a priori *apprehension* of God as Absolute Being (by the light of the agent intellect). The world is intelligent then to Transcendental Thomists because we either seek to, or actually ascend to God (perfectly intelligible being) in every act of knowing" (Vincelette, *Recent Catholic Philosophy*, 82, as quoted in Rowland, *Catholic Theology*, 61). McDermott further explains: "Transcendental Thomism located truth in a judgment or insight, of which the concept is only a part. The mind therefore goes beyond the concept to reach reality; thus are concepts relativized. Moreover truth is realized not in the passive intellect receiving a concept, but in the activity of the judging intellect.... While concepts ground clear distinctions, transcendental judgments transcend them toward a higher unity: God and man, true and good, intellect and will, body and soul, subject and object, natural and supernatural tend to be amalgamated. Not that the value of concepts is denied; without concepts thought is not possible. The best

Rahner's positive stance toward modernity allows him, like Paul Tillich, to correlate theology and the modern context. According to Tillich, in the correlation method, "systematic theology proceeds in the following way: it makes an analysis of the human situation out of which the existential questions arise, and it demonstrates that the symbols used in the Christian message are the answers to these questions."[7] Peter Harrison describes the goal of correlation theology as showing how the Christian message encounters questions implicit in a situation, in a human experience.[8] Rahner takes up correlation as a useful tool for stirring up a stagnant theology, and describes the characteristics of his theological project as being:[9]

- Pluralistic: Rather than a singular, homogenous theology for the whole Church, as there had been for nearly a century with Neo-scholasticism, Rahner calls for a plurality of theologies that express the richness, universality, and diversity of the Church.

- Missionary and Mystagogical: This theology must be missionary in that it serves a faith rooted in personal conviction, and mystagogical in that it brings what the Church believes (*fides quae*) into close unity with the personal act of faith (*fides qua*) so that what the tenets of the faith mean concretely for the individual and society are clear.

- Demythologizing: Transposing and expressing the faith in such a way that it can be assimilated by contemporary people. Rahner adds, "We are and shall always be bound to tradition, of course, but the tradition is the beginning, not the end of theology."

- Transcendental: Theology will highlight the role of the knowing subject.

In sum, Rahner attempts to bring theology to life by injecting it with the thought of modernity, and by attempting to show how theology correlates to modernity.[10] As a result of Rahner's openness to modernity, John Milbank

---

transcendental thinkers tried to preserve concepts and all necessary distinctions but did not absolutise them" (McDermott, "Vatican II," 537). Finally, Rowland notes that, rather than neo-scholastic Thomists and their emphasis on discursive reasoning (*ratio*), "Transcendental Thomists give a higher status to the work of *intellectus* (intuition)" (Rowland, *Catholic Theology*, 62).

7. Tillich, *Systematic Theology*, 62. See also Thorbjørnsen's "Paul Tillich," 107–8.

8. See Harrison "Correlation and Theology," 65–76.

9. See Rahner, *Karl Rahner in Dialogue*, 49.

10. To be sure, Modernism is a rather complex phenomenon and difficult to define. However, Nichols notes that some general characteristics appear within Modern thinking, characteristics that will further define Rahner's thought. Nichols describes these traits as follows: (1) Modernism gives pride-of-place to historical study, wherein

describes the main thrust of Rahner's theology as a movement "toward a universal humanism, a rapprochement with the Enlightenment and an autonomous secular order,"[11] which became, as Rowland notes, the point of departure for many of the liberation theologians of the 1970s and 1980s.[12]

At the bottom of it, Rahner's modern project attempts to seriously engage the "Heideggerian problematic." Connor Sweeney explains that Heidegger accuses metaphysics "of imposing an a priori interpretive grid over top of temporality and historicity, and thereby determining in advance the interpretation of Being in time."[13] "In essence," Sweeney says, "Being is no longer able to reveal itself as Being in any given historical epoch because it's [sic] meaning has already been artificially established in advance."[14] Sweeney points out that Heidegger and his followers accuse onto-theology of a certain numbness to the phenomenon, because in their effort to attain to the essence or "whatness" of entities, to "their timeless self-identity," they end up "suppressing and concealing" the depths of Being.[15] For his part, Rahner contends with Heidegger's challenge that the question of being must be treated phenomenologically "from a perspective of Being via *Dasein* . . . where historicity takes precedence" as opposed to the "timeless, 'bird's eye' view of traditional metaphysics."[16] Heidegger's sharp turn toward temporal-

---

"history becomes everything"; (2) Modernism downplays doctrine, such that it is seen as "a vehicle for the response of a given age to the divine." A doctrine well-suited for one age may not be as accessible or applicable to another, losing its relevance. This results in what may be seen as a "watered down" understanding of the faith, one which has lost sight of the whole for the sake of relevant parts; (3) Modernism claims that, with regard to revelation, the "orientation of the human spirit to transcendence was the entire explanation of the Christian religion. . . . Instead of saying that the immanent orientation of man to God was a necessary complement to the external signs and teachings of divine revelation, interiority becomes everything—not unassisted by Kantian subjectivism and Schleiermacher's sentimentalism" (Nichols, *The Shape of Catholic Theology*, 332–33). Rather simply, Jason Craig describes modernism as "the exaltation of the individual as an autonomous and self-determining being" in his article "Should Men Retire?" This basic attitude becomes more radical in postmodernity.

11. As quoted in Rowland, "Catholic Theology in the Twentieth Century," 45. See Milbank, *Theology and Social Theory*, 207. For more on the question of the secular order, see Rowland, "The World," 109–32.

12. Rowland, "Catholic Theology in the Twentieth Century," 45. See also Ratzinger, *Principles*, 167–68.

13. Sweeney, *Sacramental Presence*, 37.

14. Sweeney, *Sacramental Presence*, 37.

15. Sweeney, *Sacramental Presence*, 37–38. See also Beards, "Addressing Philosophical Currents," 152–53.

16. Sweeney, *Sacramental Presence*, 38. *Dasein*, literally, in German is a compound: *da* = there, *sein* = be; there-be, being-there, existence, presence. For more on this concept, see p. 37 below.

ity concomitantly condemns propositional truth theories that merely *derive* from the primordial encounter with Being and pushes toward recovering the primordial encounter itself.[17] Rahner situates his theological venture right here, in the midst of the turn toward historicity that emerges as a result of the "Heideggerian problematic." In response to Heidegger, as Rise says, Rahner sets "up an encounter between the reality of everyday life and the mystery of faith,"[18] and he does so by grounding his theological endeavor in human experience. It is a turn toward human experience, a prioritizing of human experience that essentially places *ethos* over *logos*.

Following the catechetical Council, catechetical theorists found a willing architect for their renewal plans in Karl Rahner, or Rahner found willing builders in them. Rahner's theology, given its correlation to modernity and pastoral impulse, served as something of a blueprint in fundamental theology for the anthropological phase of catechetical renewal. This is particularly the case in the United States.[19] The problem with this, however, lies in the fact that Rahner's speculative theology is fluid—like a stream—as opposed to a static design drawn up on paper with the hard edges of lines, strokes of finality, and clearly defined dimensions that appear on the modern builder's scroll. Too often, Rahner's concepts remain ambiguous, notoriously difficult to define. This might be allowable in speculative theology. However, when ambiguous concepts become concrete building stones, fixed principles for the foundation of a new catechetical edifice—or part of an edifice, like the support beams of a roof—the structure is tenuous. Those who follow Rahner derive from his theology certain "fixed" specifications from which they built a thoroughly modern catechetical project. Understanding Rahner's theological project, or at least the major elements of what we might call a "Rahnerian blueprint for modern catechetics," then, makes it possible to see more clearly why the anthropological phase remains "grounded."

In what follows, here, I will attempt to highlight several key elements of fundamental theology within the blueprint that shape the more practical outworking of the anthropological phase of renewal. The elements are as follows: (1) Transcendental Anthropology; (2) the Supernatural Existential; (3) Natural and Supernatural Revelation; and (4) "Anonymous Christianity" and the Reconstitution of Evangelization. These Rahnerian

---

17. See Heidegger, *Being and Time*, 268. See also Sweeney, *Sacramental Presence*, 39.

18. Rise, "Karl Rahner," 227.

19. Prior to the Council, Rahner believed the American Church to be more conservative than the German Church, yet in 1970, Rahner claims to find "the willingness and readiness to change in all areas greater in the American Church," a shift that admittedly "brings with it many risks and dangers, but also brings great promise" (Rahner, *Karl Rahner in Dialogue*, 52).

elements provide the basic design for the American catechetical project following Vatican II, of which theorists like Gabriel Moran and Thomas Groome act as master builders.

The Rahnerian Blueprint—Design Element #1: Transcendental Anthropology

The roots of Rahner's transcendental anthropology can be found in the thought of Aquinas, Kant, and Heidegger. The first of these roots appears in Aquinas' *Summa Theologiae* 1.84.7. Here, Aquinas considers whether the human intellect can have some sort of perfect, innate knowledge of things without the assistance of other minds or contact with the world (a position that would later be taken up by Descartes),[20] or whether knowledge comes from "turning without to the sensibly given."[21] Following Aquinas, Rahner claims that "intellectual knowledge is possible only with a simultaneous realization of sense knowledge."[22] As Fergus Kerr puts it, in the human being's present state in life, the intellect is conditioned by "being conjoined with receptive corporeality. There is no purely intellectual intuition.... The world as known is always already the world to which we belong."[23] While he agrees with Aquinas here, Rahner also brings in Kant (the second root), who admits that all knowledge undoubtedly begins with experience, which awakens the agent-intellect. However, just because knowledge begins with experience, "it by no means follows that all arises out of experience." Here, Kant introduces the possibility of *a priori* knowledge, "in contradistinction to empirical knowledge, which has its source *a posteriori*, that is, in experience."[24] Even if human knowledge begins with or comes awake as a result of sense-knowledge, it is not limited to experiential knowledge. Human knowledge has the capacity to transcend sense experience and to become aware of and to access *a priori* knowledge.

Heidegger's thought marks the third root in Rahner's transcendental anthropology. Heidegger sees the positive outcome of Kant's *Critique of Pure Reason* as "the working out of what belongs to any Nature whatsoever, not

---

20. See Descartes, *Discourse on Method*.
21. Kerr, *Twentieth-Century Catholic Theologians*, 90.
22. Rahner, *Spirit in the World*, 236–37.
23. Kerr, *Twentieth-Century Catholic Theologians*, 90.
24. Kant, *Critique of Pure Reason*, xlvii–iii. By *a priori* knowledge, here, Kant refers to as that knowledge which is independent of all experience, which is always *a posteriori* knowledge. He goes on to say that "knowledge *a priori* is either pure or impure. Pure knowledge *a priori* is that with which no empirical element is mixed up" (xlviii).

in a 'theory' of knowledge." Heidegger calls Kant's "transcendental logic . . . an *a priori* logic for the subject-matter of that area of being called 'Nature.'"[25] Heidegger points out that Kant's inquiry acknowledges ontology in its widest sense without considering particular ontologies. In other words, Kant engages in a "primordial" inquiry "over against the ontical inquiry of positive sciences." Rather than researching the "Being of entities," Kant pursues the "meaning of Being in general," and aims at "ascertaining the *a priori* conditions not only for the possibility of the sciences which examine entities . . . but also for the possibility of those ontologies . . . which are prior to the ontological sciences." Therefore, Heidegger concludes, that "basically, all ontology . . . remains blind and perverted from its ownmost aim, if it has not first adequately clarified the meaning of Being."[26] Following Kant, Heidegger concerns himself with what he calls the "fundamental question of metaphysics," namely "why are there beings at all instead of nothing?"[27]

When it comes to questioning Being, Heidegger points out the uniqueness of human beings in this regard, namely that human beings are those unique beings who can question Being. Heidegger calls this type of being *Dasein*.[28] *Dasein* is:

25. Heidegger, *Being and Time*, 31.

26. Heidegger, *Being and Time*, 31.

27. Heidegger, *Introduction to Metaphysics*, 19. Here, Heidegger claims that "'Physics' determines the essence and the history of metaphysics from the inception onward. Even in the doctrine of Being as *actus purus* (Thomas Aquinas), as absolute concept (Hegel), as eternal recurrence of the same will to power (Nietzsche), metaphysics steadfastly remains 'physics.'" Heidegger is concerned that within the purview of metaphysics, shaped as it is by physics, "one can regard the question about Being as such merely as a mechanic repetition of the question about beings as such," which "blocks the way to unfolding [the question about Being as such] in a manner befitting the matter." Here, Heidegger lays out the basic footprint of what will become a critique of "onto-theology." Sweeney notes that Heidegger reads Western philosophy as an attempt to answer the question about the "whatness" of being. This is ontology, the "onto" in onto-theology. Ontology attempts to look for that which all beings share in common. This question about the "whatness" of being is often simultaneously approached "from the perspective of the highest or Supreme Being (the "theo" in onto-theology). Sweeney points out that "metaphysics becomes theology when it attempts to explain 'whatness' via the Supreme Being," and claims that "onto-theology conceives of entities in terms of their essence, their *whatness*, of their timeless self-identity." Onto-theology tends to "'substantialize' our existence" and is laden with a certain "phenomenological numbness" (Sweeney, *Sacramental Presence*, 36–38).

28. Heidegger, *Being and Time*, 32. According to Wheeler, "we might conceive of [*Dasein*] as Heidegger's term for the distinctive kind of *entity* that human beings as such are" (Wheeler, "Martin Heidegger"). Wheeler points out that "entity," in this case, is not in reference to biological make-up, but two *ways* in which human beings engage in life as *Dasein*. First, human beings alone are capable of engaging the question of what it means "to be," by operating with some understanding of Being,however

> [An] entity which does not just occur among other entities . . . [but is] ontically distinguished by the fact that, in its very Being, that Being is an *issue* for it. . . . Dasein, in its Being, has a relationship towards that Being—a relationship which itself is one of Being. . . . It is peculiar to this entity that with and through its Being, this Being is disclosed to it. *Understanding of Being is itself a definite characteristic of Dasein's Being.* Dasein is ontically distinctive in that it *is* ontological. [Yet] "Being-ontological" is not yet tantamount to "developing an ontology" . . . [as] that theoretical inquiry which is explicitly devoted to the meaning of entities . . . [instead] Dasein's "Being-ontological" is to be designated as something "pre-ontological." . . . That kind of Being towards which Dasein can comport itself in one way or another, and always does comport itself somehow, we call "*existence*." . . . Dasein always understands itself in terms of its existence—in terms of a possibility of itself. . . . Only the particular Dasein decides its existence, whether it does so by taking hold or by neglecting. . . . The understanding of oneself which leads *along this way* we call "*existentiell*".²⁹

---

pre-ontological, implicit, or vague, and to reflect back upon it. The second understanding of *Dasein* results from interpreting the *da* of *Da-sein* as "open." In this case, Wheeler defines *Dasein* as "*the having-to-be-open*. In other words, *Dasein* (and so human beings as such) cannot but be open: it is a necessary characteristic of human beings (an a priori structure of our existential constitution, not an exercise of our wills) that we operate with the sense-making capacity to take-other-beings-as." Similarly, Hemming defines *Dasein* as "'the standing open of humans to whatever is, *ek-stasis*,' where historicity takes precedence" (as quoted in Sweeney, *Sacramental Presence*, 38). Wheeler, concludes by noting that the two interpretive paths are not necessarily in conflict as both pertain to "standing out," "standing back," or "standing open." On the one hand, *Dasein* can stand back or outside of itself and reflect back upon itself, and on the other hand, *Dasein* "stands out in an openness to and an opening of Being." Heidegger calls for a "pre-ontological understanding of Being" (Heidegger, *Being and Time*, 35), one that is free of "the errors of the onto-theological tradition," a turn to temporality which "carries with [sic] a transformation of truth as disclosure (*aletheia*) and an attendant condemnation of propositional theories of truth. Truth is most perfectly conceived in terms of a primordial encounter with Being-as-*Dasein* within time" (Sweeney, *Sacramental Presence*, 39). With this, Heidegger lays the groundwork for the dismantling of onto-theology, and with it, the rationalism of the modern project. Sweeney labels this shift the "phenomenological turn," which intimates what will come in a post-onto-theological, post-Enlightenment, postmodern age that "attempts to reconstruct human thought and society according to a non-metaphysical vision" (Sweeney, *Sacramental Presence*, 41).

29. Heidegger, *Being and Time*, 32–34. William Dych, the English translator of Rahner's *Foundations of Christian Faith*, provides this note regarding the two spellings of "existential" and "existentiell": "'Existential' . . . refers to an element in man's ontological constitution precisely as human being, an element which is constitutive of his existence as man prior to his exercise of freedom. It is an aspect of concrete human

Dasein is that peculiar Being which questions Being. It stands open, so to speak, towards Being, in an *a priori,* "pre-ontological" manner that comes *before,* and, in a certain sense, resists, any ontological reductions of its Being to this or that particular anthropology. *Dasein* is fundamentally "pre-ontological," and remains so. It is also "pre-anthropological," so to speak. Hence, Heidegger concludes that to question Being "is nothing other than the radicalization of an essential tendency-of-Being which belongs to *Dasein* itself—the pre-ontological understanding of Being."[30] Heidegger's basic understanding of the human being as *Dasein,* combined with Kant's transcendentalism, provide the modern (and intimate the postmodern) roots that will be fused with basic Thomistic insights (thus tethering it to the tradition) to form Rahner's theological anthropology.[31] Rise argues that all of this can be formulated, with Aquinas, as saying, "the human person is *one who exists* and puts questions vis-à-vis God, but God is *Existence* and the answer to the one who exists."[32] Kerr claims that in sum, Rahner's early works (i.e., *Spirit in the World* [1939] and *Hearer of the Word* [1941]) aim to reconstruct neo-scholastic natural theology by following "the turn to the subject implicit in Aquinas' consideration of the soul," which when combined "with the subject as always already in the world according to his realist-metaphysical emphasis on *conversio ad phantasmata,* yields a theological anthropology in which these finite human beings . . . are by nature open to hearing the Word."[33]

With Aquinas, Kant, and Heidegger as key sources of inspiration, Rahner's blueprint lays out the specifications for profound anthropological turn within theology and ultimately within catechetics as well. Nichols points out that "Rahner was convinced that in a civilization dominated by humanism the only possible starting point for Christian theology is anthropological—one that can show how God is necessary to man."[34] Now, the human subject takes center stage; the spotlight shines on him and his

---

nature precisely as human. 'Existentiell' . . . refers to the free, personal and subjective appropriation and actualization of something which can also be spoken of in abstract theory or objective concepts without such a subjective and personal realization" (see Rahner, *Foundations,* 16n).

30. Heidegger, *Being and Time,* 35.

31. Vandervelde notes that Karl Rahner defines human person along the lines of Heidegger's *dasein.* Vandervelde says that Rahner defines person as "'openness,' even boundless directedness, towards the infinite mystery of fulness, or simply as emptiness" ("The Grammar of Grace," 455).

32. Rise, "Karl Rahner," 231.

33. Kerr, *Twentieth-Century Catholic Theologians,* 91.

34. Nichols, "Rahner and Balthasar," 113.

theological experience. Therefore, as Nichols says, "the only kind of anthropology that will serve theology's turn, however, is a transcendental one—one, that is, which shows God as already somehow implicated in lived humanity, enabling its very possibility."[35] For Rahner, a transcendental anthropology expresses the *"fundamental constitution of the human person*, which is identical with the conditions for being a human person in the world . . . for being spirit in the world. . . . The human person is determined fundamentally as one who exists with particular regard to his *relationship to God.*"[36] In response to Neo-scholasticism, Rahner makes a transcendental anthropology his "given" in an attempt "transform traditional Scholasticism into a theological anthropology that remains . . . oriented toward the mystery of God."[37]

The subject's fundamental openness to being makes a transcendent experience possible. Adam Cooper explains Rahner's concept in simple terms when he says:

> Human life is made up of countless experiences within the finite horizon conditioned by space and time. To these finite experiences Rahner gives the name "categorical experience." Hidden and enclosed within all such categorical experiences, however, lies "transcendental experience," the subtle sense or awareness on the part of the personal subject that she is not simply the product of all these finite experiences, but somehow precedes and transcends them. In this sense of her transcendental subjectivity and origin, the human person possesses an implicit experience of infinite being.[38]

A transcendent *experience* occurs when the ever-open and ever-opening human being engages with categorical experience and becomes implicitly aware of more—of one's subjectivity and relationship with infinite. Rahner describes transcendence as:

> The a priori openness of the subject to being as such, which is present precisely when a person experiences himself as involved

---

35. Nichols, "Rahner and Balthasar," 113. See also Doyle, "The Concept of Inculturation," 7. Here, Doyle notes that Rahner's critics often claim Rahner uses "human experience as a starting point for systematic theological reflection." Others describe his theology, like that of Tillich, as correlational, "allowing human experience to be overly determinative of the questions which revelation would be allowed to answer." For an example of this anthropological starting point, see Crowley, "Mystagogy and Mission," 7–28.

36. Rise, "Karl Rahner," 230–31.

37. Nichols, *The Shape of Catholic Theology*, 337.

38. Cooper, *Naturally Human*, 102.

in the multiplicity of cares and concerns and fears and hopes of his everyday world. Real transcendence is always in the background, so to speak, in those origins of human life and human knowledge over which we have no control. This real transcendence is never captured by metaphysical reflection, and in its purity, that is, as not mediated objectively, it can be approached asymptomatically at most, if at all, in mystical experience. . . . This makes man totally open to this mystery and precisely in this way he becomes conscious of himself as person and subject.[39]

To this, Rahner adds, "Man experiences himself precisely as subject and person insofar as he becomes conscious of himself as the product of what is radically foreign to him."[40] It is precisely man's ability "to see," as Mats Wahlberg puts it, "oneself as conditioned, finite, and reducible," that one discovers he is, properly speaking, "a *subject*, a being with an unlimited horizon of questioning."[41] The human being, precisely in "stepping over" or "stepping through" his or her concrete circumstances or experiences by questioning them, becomes aware of himself or herself as a questioning being, a being capable of, in an "inner moment," stepping "through" and "over" sense experience in time by questioning and becoming aware of himself or herself *as a being that is capable of transcendence.*[42]

The transcendental experience, or the possibility thereof, forms the basis of Rahner's understanding of the person-as-subject. Rahner says, "A person looks inside himself, looks back at his past and looks at the world around him, and he discovers either to his horror or to his relief that he can shift responsibility from himself for all the individual data that make up his reality, and he can place the burden for what he is on what is not him. He discovers that he has come to be through what is other than himself."[43] In other words, man can pay attention to his "I" in action, by questioning and challenging it. He becomes aware that other persons, events, or things, shape his reality. While the human being experiences being as "infinite possibility,"[44] the human being also experiences himself as "dependent and

---

39. Rahner, *Foundations*, 35.
40. Rahner, *Foundations*, 29.
41. Wahlberg, *Revelation as Testimony*, 64.
42. For an example of this type of experience, see Frankl, *Man's Search for Meaning*, 40–41.
43. Rahner, *Foundations*, 27.
44. Rahner, *Foundations*, 32.

conditioned," and incapable of "creating his own unlimited space or infinite horizon."[45] This is clear when he says:

> Man is a transcendent being insofar as all of his knowledge and all of his conscious activity is grounded in pre-apprehension (*Vorgriff*) of "being" as such, in an unthematic but ever-present knowledge of the infinity of reality. . . . But since . . . this pre-apprehension as merely a question is not self-explanatory, it must be understood as due to the working of that to which man is open, namely, being in an absolute sense. . . . He cannot understand himself as subject in the sense of an *absolute* subject, but only in the sense of one who receives being, ultimately only in the sense of grace, . . . the freedom of the ground of being which gives being to man.[46]

Rahner calls transcendence an "a priori openness" and that which is "always in the background," and it becomes known in an exercise known as *Vorgriff*. Nichols notes that *Vorgriff* differs from a concept one entertains (*Begriff*). Instead, *Vorgriff* describes a pre-apprehension, a "pre-grasp" or anticipation of "the wider horizon of being, and ultimately of unconditional or absolute being, in whose perspective I place myself in knowing the object."[47] Adam Cooper claims *Vorgriff* may be better understood as "anticipation" or "dynamic openness," because, he claims it is not limited to epistemology but is situated within ontology. *Vorgriff* "betokens an underlying relatedness, 'a mode of being,' that is inescapably bound up with the human being's simultaneously contingent and transcendent structure, with his being a finite event of God's self-communication." As such, every human experience, when consciously engaged, "presents a transcendent 'horizon'—a real point of contact with and a mute call to enter into the 'silent and uncontrollable' sphere of transcendent and absolute being, which is another name for what the Christian knows as God."[48] *Vorgriff* refers neither to knowledge of being as mediated or handed on propositionally, nor to some sort of predictive understanding of reality, but simply an always already present openness of the human being to Being itself. Transcendent experience, then, is not the result of metaphysical or anthropological study, but the bare, unthematic, ontic experience of Being that is the very foundation of all further reflection on Being. The transcendent experience is possible in and through the person's *a priori* openness to Being, in a way that is difficult to describe in concrete terms, but which happens

---

45. Wahlberg, *Revelation as Testimony*, 64. Cf. Rahner, *Foundations*, 34.
46. Rahner, *Foundations*, 33–34.
47. Nichols, "Rahner and Balthasar," 115.
48. Cooper, *Naturally Human*, 102–3.

mystically, so to speak.[49] Lane corroborates this, saying that Rahner sees the human person as a "self-transcending being . . . with an 'inner moment' of orientation toward the transcendent."[50]

For Rahner, this basic understanding of the human being's subjectivity and transcendent nature is fundamental. It exists prior to any ontologically-based anthropological attempts. Man can become aware of ways in which he can be explained by "empirical anthropologies," even allowing them to "reduce him and dismantle him," yet:

> In the fact that man raises analytical questions about himself and opens himself to the unlimited horizons of such questioning, he has already transcended himself and every conceivable element of such an analysis or of an empirical reconstruction of himself. In doing this he is affirming himself as more than the sum of such analyzable components of his reality. . . . A finite system . . . does not ask questions about itself. It is not a subject.[51]

A system cannot question itself. Only a subject can question systems and itself. In this way, the subject transcends explanations shaped by ontology and reveals itself precisely as person. The limitlessness of man's ability to question reveals something stupendous, which Rahner captures in the following way:

> Man is always present to himself in his entirety. He can place everything in question . . . whatever can come to expression can be at least a question for him. In the fact that he affirms the possibility of a merely *finite* horizon of questioning, this possibility

---

49. Rahner's emphasis on the transcendental experience pushes toward a sort of "mysticism of daily life." He does, however, caution against using the word "mysticism" to describe this experience, which is quite accessible in the very ordinariness of life, because "mysticism" is often associated with some sort of extraordinary phenomenon. For Rahner, "all human experiences tend towards 'an intensification which is directed towards something which one could in fact call mystical experience'" (Rahner, "Reflections on the Problem of the Gradual Ascent to Christian Perfection," 3:23, quoted in Egan, "Karl Rahner," 311). When Rahner says, "in the days ahead, you will either be a mystic (one who has experienced God for real) or nothing at all," he does not have in mind some sort of psychic flight from the present, but a sort of infused contemplation made possible by and in the very "stuff" of ordinary life that is already "engraced" by God, an implicit experience of Him. Therefore, Rahner concludes, "We do have an immediate, pre-conceptual experience of God through the experience of the limitless breadth of our consciousness," therefore, "there is such a thing as a mystical component to Christianity" (*Karl Rahner in Dialogue*, 182).

50. Lane, *Reflections*, 7.

51. Rahner, *Foundations*, 29–30.

is already surpassed, and man shows himself to be a being with an *infinite* horizon . . . as a transcendent being, as spirit."[52]

The subjective consciousness' experience of transcendence is an experience of personal realization, or self-possession—the "I" taking hold of itself, acknowledging itself. The possibility of such an experience always stands in the background for man, amid the regular circumstances of human life, despite any proposed reductions by "particular anthropology[ies]."[53] In other words, the realization of one's person does not come about, first and foremost, by way of traditional or philosophical understandings of humanity, but in the unobjective and unthematic experience of transcendence. In the transcendent experience, man experiences himself as "being *open* to or oriented toward 'the silent and uncontrollable infinity of reality,'"[54] wherein "the infinite horizon of being mak[es] itself manifest" to the subject.[55]

Insofar as the person is a (transcendental) subject, the person is free. Freedom is integral to transcendental anthropology. Transcendental freedom refers to "a person's ultimate responsibility for himself, not only in knowledge, and hence not only as self-consciousness, but also as self-actualization."[56] This means freedom is fundamentally and "in an original sense . . . experienced in the depths of one's own existence."[57] Describing Rahner's theology of freedom, John Galvin notes that it focuses "on personal self-disposal before God, not on the choice of individual objects. Freedom is not only a power to select one thing over another, but, on a deeper level, an ability to make something of oneself. Of its very nature, it seeks permanence, not reversibility, for constant change would be equivalent to indecision."[58] Rahner's treatment on freedom accounts for categorical experience, for the very exercise of freedom is "always actualized in a multiplicity of concrete activities in time and space . . . in history and also in society."[59] One exercises his or her freedom in time. Yet, despite his interaction with time and space, and any restrictions that may be imposed upon his freedom from without, "man's real freedom . . . still continues to be one freedom because it is a transcendental characteristic of the one subject as such."[60]

52. Rahner, *Foundations*, 31–32.
53. Rahner, *Foundations*, 27. Cf. Heidegger, *Being and Time*, 32.
54. Wahlberg, *Revelation as Testimony*, 64–65.
55. Rahner, *Foundations*, 34.
56. Rahner, *Foundations*, 36; see also 94.
57. Rahner, *Foundations*, 37–38.
58. Galvin, "Jesus Christ," 307.
59. Rahner, *Foundations*, 38, 40; Rahner, *Revelation and Tradition*, 17.
60. Rahner, *Foundations*, 38.

In other words, even in a situation wherein one's freedom is significantly restricted, one remains free.[61] In the end, the subject cannot escape freedom and is constantly prompted to accept it, to take responsibility for it, and in taking responsibility in this way, the subject experiences self-actualization. A transcendental anthropology, then, refers to the free human being, the human spirit, who is always already open to and capable of questioning Being, and which becomes aware of itself and accepts itself as a questioning being in the rather intuitive transcendental experience.

The Rahnerian Blueprint—Design Element #2: Supernatural Existential

The second design element culled from Rahner's theological repertoire appears in the concept of the supernatural existential. This supernatural corollary to his transcendental anthropology is, according to Cooper, "an ambiguous and eventually much-controverted term."[62] David Coffey notes that "as with many of his original technical terms, [Rahner] evidently presumed that its meaning would be instantly clear to his readers." It, however, was not.[63]

Rahner developed the concept of the supernatural existential as his response to the nature and grace argument that reached a fever pitch in the mid-twentieth century. Interestingly enough, here, as a response to Neoscholasticism, Rahner's Transcendental Thomism converges, albeit briefly, with the *ressourcement* work of Henri de Lubac (1896–1991). De Lubac's *Surnaturel* (1946) challenged the neo-scholastic view of the relationship between nature and grace that held, as Eamonn Conway puts it, "the most God's revelation in nature could do was to ensure that no contradiction existed between nature and grace. . . . Nature and grace co-existed in two layers, in a *duplex ordo* with grace as a kind of superstructure."[64] De Lubac

---

61. See, for example, Frankl, *Man's Search for Meaning*, 66–67. Here, Frankl, reflecting upon his experience in the Nazi concentration camp famously concluded, "everything can be taken from a man but one thing: the last of the human freedoms—to choose one's attitude in any given set of circumstances, to choose one's own way. . . . It is this spiritual freedom—which cannot be taken away—that makes life meaningful and purposeful."

62. Cooper, *Naturally Human*, 106.

63. Coffey, "The Whole Rahner," 95.

64. Conway, "A Constant Word," 110–11. O'Shea argues that the *duplex ordo* theory arose in the post-Reformation era as a response to Calvinism on the one hand, and Baianism on the other. In an attempt to strike a balance between such positions, theologians in the late sixteenth and early seventeenth centuries developed a thesis that

reacts against the *duplex ordo* theory, by claiming that, in light of human beings' natural desire for God, "God could not create human beings without in some way . . . calling them to union with himself (the beatific vision). Thus, he argued, human beings must have *by nature* a spiritual orientation to the one God."[65] This position was "implicitly condemned" by Pius XII in his 1950 encyclical *Humani Generis*, which warns against positions that destroy "the gratuity of the supernatural order."[66] Rahner's theological work can be viewed, in some ways, as a response to Pius XII. David Coffey notes the convergence of Rahner's thought with de Lubac's, saying:

> That all human beings are oriented to the God of revelation, far from being in dispute, was affirmed by Rahner with a zeal equal to that of de Lubac and his confreres. All parties were united in their opposition to the *duplex ordo* characteristic of [sic] neo-Scholasticism of the day, according to which in human beings the natural and the supernatural orders coexisted as separate "layers" (with the supernatural imposed on the natural). That theology, designed to protect the transcendence of God, had produced the unintended effect of rendering the Christian religion and all that belonged to it, namely: divine revelation, grace, the Church, God, as irrelevant to human beings as they went about their lives in the world.[67]

However, Conway points out that while Rahner was "completely sympathetic to de Lubac's intention," he also thought *Humani Generis* might have a point. Within these circumstances, Rahner introduces the concept of the supernatural existential to thread the theological needle by defending the spiritual orientation of human beings, while protecting the gratuity of grace.[68] In other words, Rahner attempts to avoid the extrinsicism of Neo-

---

there were two ends for humanity—natural and supernatural. O'Shea points out that "According to this view, every human being was created first of all for a natural human happiness to which could later be added a second level of happiness—supernatural beatitude—something totally beyond natural human endowment and accessible only by means of grace." In this case, grace becomes completely extrinsic. O'Shea goes on to argue that in developing this theory, theologians ultimately misread Aquinas. See O'Shea, "Nature or Grace," 3–6.

65. Conway, "A Constant Word," 111.

66. Pius XII, *Humani generis*, §26. De Lubac, however, did not find anything in *Humani generis* that doctrinally affected him or his work. See his *At the Service of the Church*, 37. See also Tracey Rowland's treatment of de Lubac and the *Surnaturel* controversy in "Neo-Scholasticism of the Strict Observance," 29–56.

67. Coffey, "The Whole Rahner," 98.

68. See Rahner, "Eine Antwort," 141–45. This was translated by Cornelius Ernst and published in English as "Concerning the Relationship between Nature and Grace,"

scholasticism and the apparent intrinsicism of de Lubac's collapse of grace into nature that had been condemned by *Humani generis*.[69]

Rahner defines supernatural existential in *Foundations of Christian Faith*, saying, the supernatural existential "is present in all men . . . as an existential [*Existential*] of their concrete existence [*Dasein*]."[70] Coffey explicates this line, saturated as it is in Heideggerian language, as follows:

> The first part of the quoted statement requires no elaboration beyond pointing out that the existential is a consequence of God's universal saving will; the second assertion means that it is an element of the existence rather than of the essence (nature) of human beings. The first part of the statement, Rahner affirms, conflicts in no way with the truth of the second. Because it is not part of human nature, and because it has to do with salvation, the existential must be gratuitous, that is, must pertain in some way to grace. It is clear that the term "existential" is used here as a noun. Rahner goes on to say that as an existential of human beings "it is present prior to their freedom, their self-understanding and their experience." If it were offered to their freedom, that is, after its constitution, it would be something about whose acceptance a decision would need to be made, and would be *existentiell* rather than *existential*. In this sense the term is clearly adjectival. The expression "supernatural existential," while remaining a substantive, combines the two references: it is an element of human existence rather than of the human essence, and its a priori character is asserted and stressed. Since the existential does not of itself bring about justification, "supernatural" cannot at this point indicate sanctifying grace itself, but rather a relationship to this grace, the exact nature of which remains to be clarified.[71]

Therefore, the supernatural existential has its origin in God and not in man, though it "resides," so to speak, in man. That said, it "resides" not in man's essence, but in his existence. Man is not essentially divine; his nature is not supernatural. Instead, God gratuitously establishes human existence (i.e., prior to any exercise of freedom but simply in its very existing) as the point of contact with the divine. Human existence is engraced from the start.

As already indicated, the lexical density of the term leads to an array of possible interpretations. These interpretations can help to illuminate the

---

297–317.

69. Conway, "A Constant Word," 111.

70. Rahner, *Foundations*, 127.

71. Coffey, "The Whole Rahner," 96.

meaning of the complex term, while also illustrating the danger inherent in its ambiguity. A few examples will suffice, here. Eamonn Conway says that the supernatural existential is "the spiritual orientation to God experienced by all human beings" which is "not something owing to them by nature, but by the concrete order of the existence in which all human beings find themselves; an existence which at all times has to do with God, and is addressed by God." Simply by existing, the whole of human existence has to do with God, for it is in existing that God implicitly addresses the human being. Like Coffey, Conway adds that "not by virtue of their nature or essence, but by virtue of their existence, prior to any exercise of their freedom, human beings are graciously and freely addressed by God and invited into fellowship," such that the "acceptance of or refusal of such fellowship takes place in the circumstances of their everyday lives."[72] Similarly, Cooper describes it as "an inner orientation to God that influences human nature but is not actually part of human nature. . . . [The supernatural existential is] the extrinsic divine 'offer' . . . that most intrinsically defines, and, given its gratuitous acceptance, ultimately completes, the human creature."[73] The acceptance, thereof, it seems, would mark that shift from *existential* to *existentiell*. Basically, the extrinsic gift of existence from God makes it intrinsically possible to encounter God implicitly in human experience just by accepting one's existence as a being in time. When one accepts one's humanity, one is accepting the divine always already implicit in one's existence. If the *existential* is a supernatural "element" of human existence, then simply accepting one's existence is to accept the supernatural (*existentiell*). For his part, Aidan Nichols notes that, "since the offer of grace was universal, Rahner deemed it an 'existential,' a constitutive feature of human existence; but . . . Rahner qualified this existential as 'supernatural,' not given in and with humanity as such, but God's free gift to those who stand before his saving mystery."[74] Thomas Groome defines "supernatural existential" as the "ground and horizon of human existence," that opening of the human being toward the other, toward the infinite.[75] Rowland adds that the supernatural existential is "a theological a priori in the very nature of our way of knowing."[76]

Rahner's concept of the "supernatural existential" is basically the supernatural corollary to his transcendental anthropology. It attempts to bring what Heidegger calls the "existential-ecstatic temporality of Being-here" into

72. Conway, "A Constant Word," 111–12.
73. Cooper, *Naturally Human*, 107.
74. Nichols, *The Shape of Catholic Theology*, 337–38.
75. Groome, *Sharing*, 162.
76. Rowland, *Ratzinger's Faith*, 22.

Christian theology. Heidegger claims this "existential-ecstatic temporality" is that "transcendental horizon" towards which "subjective consciousness" tends.[77] It is the "existential level," so to speak, the meeting point between the transcendent human being who stands open toward Being, as a questioning being who is aware of himself as a being capable of an infinite horizon of questioning, and the supernatural grace of existence given by God, from whom and in whom this questioning being has existence.

The supernatural existential is the gratuitous existential "space" in which human existence exists, through which the human being's transcendental experience operates, and of which it eventually becomes aware. The awareness thereof takes place in the transcendental experience. The "transcendental experience in which a person comes into the presence of the absolute mystery which we call 'God,'" is, as Rahner puts it, "an experience which is more primary than reflection."[78] On this point, Balthasar adds that transcendental experience is "the spirit becom[ing] indirectly aware of its own dynamic tendency toward the absolute and of its relation to God, in which God presents himself unobjectively."[79] In other words, the transcendental experience is more than one's experience of oneself as a transcendent being, but of the "supernatural existential," the "transcendental horizon." Precisely in this experience, the person-as-subject discovers God as the "infinite horizon of being," and finds he is, therefore, in this "original experience . . . always present," he is "oriented towards God."[80] The transcendental experience is the conscious experience of this *a priori* existential. Therefore, Rahner adds, "this unthematic and ever-present experience, this knowledge of God which we always have even when we are thinking of and concerned with anything but God, is the permanent ground from out of which that thematic knowledge of God emerges which we have in explicitly religious activity and in philosophical reflection."[81] The supernatural existential is "graspable" not as a result of some sort of thematic, objective study of human nature, but in the very transcendental

77. Heidegger, *Introduction to Metaphysics*, 19–20.
78. Rahner, *Foundations*, 44.
79. Balthasar, *The Moment of Christian Witness*, 83.
80. Rahner, *Foundations*, 53.
81. Rahner, *Foundations*, 53. Dulles describes this as a "supernatural orientation toward the divine." He goes on to quote Rahner, saying this orientation "indelibly affects man's experience in this life, 'the experience of infinite longings, of radical optimism, of unquenchable discontent, of the torment of the insufficiency of everything attainable, of the radical protest against death, the experience of being confronted with an absolute love . . . the experience of a radical guilt and of a still abiding hope, and so forth.'" See Dulles, *Revelation Theology*, 159–60.

experience itself. The supernatural existential is always already present at every moment, whether one is consciously aware of it or not. Transcendence, then, is the fundamental, unthematic, "experience of our orientation towards the ineffable mystery,"[82] and it is proper to the nature of transcendent spirit which participates in the supernatural existential by the nature of its very existence. In light of this relationship between the supernatural existential and transcendental anthropology which meets in transcendental experience, Rahner intimates a conclusion that will be more developed later, that "there is present in this transcendental experience an unthematic an anonymous, as it were, knowledge of God."[83]

The Rahnerian Blueprint—Design Element #3: Reconfiguring Revelation

Rahner bases his theology of revelation on his transcendental anthropology and the corresponding notion of the supernatural existential. In basic terms, Rahner holds that, considering man's transcendent nature and the reality of the supernatural existential, a revelation of the divine occurs in every transcendental experience. He pushes further to note that, in light of the incarnation of Jesus Christ, the supernatural existential is ultimately always already and implicitly a Christian reality—for it has been forever altered by Christ. Revelation becomes a matter of conscious awareness of one's existence in the transcendental experience of the supernatural existential. Therefore, anyone who merely accepts his or her transcendental human existence is already implicitly a Christian.[84]

Rahner, the transcendental experience is a revelatory experience wherein one becomes aware of both Being in time (history) and one's openness to Being. Because God establishes man as a supernatural existential, he establishes the existential ontological condition wherein man can receive the gift of God's self-revelation at any moment in the transcendental experience. And, God's self-communication reaches every man or woman—Christian or non-Christian. Therefore, Rahner claims that "man is the event of God's absolute self-communication."[85] Rahner argues "that man as subject is the

---

82. Rahner, *Foundations*, 53. With regard to questions that may arise pertaining to the supernatural existential and man's freedom, see Rise, "Karl Rahner," 231.

83. Rahner, *Foundations*, 21.

84. This teaching on revelation, then, sets the stage for establishing his theory of "anonymous Christianity." Anonymous Christianity will be discussed starting on p. 56 below.

85. Rahner, *Foundations*, 126.

event of God's self-communication is a statement which refers to absolutely all men, and which expresses an existential of every person." God "gives" the supernatural existential to every man, to everyone "who is a being of unlimited transcendentality as a fulfillment essentially transcending the natural." Therefore, "really and radically *every* person must be understood as the event of a supernatural self-communication of God."[86] The transcendental experience, accepting one's existence, then, is both the experience of and a manifestation of revelation itself. It is the experience and manifestation of God's self-communication in time.

Responding positively to the Heideggerian problematic, Rahner holds that revelation is an event in time and not a clutch purse of propositions outside of it. Rowland once commented that "Transcendental Thomists, especially Rahner, were also highly conscious of the historical embeddedness of concepts."[87] According to Rahner, *Dasein*'s transcendent experience takes place in and through the very "stuff" of life. While it is the case for Rahner that God's self-revelation is "an a priori determination coming from grace and is in itself unreflexive . . . within the realm of consciousness," it is also the case that this "transcendental revelation is itself always mediated categorically in the world, because all of man's transcendentality has a history."[88] This becomes the basis for Rahner's understanding of "natural revelation."

Natural revelation perceives God as one who gives himself "in many and various ways" (Heb 1:1). Ever cognizant of God's universal salvific will (cf. 1 Tim 2:4), Rahner establishes the validity of the religious experience of the *homo religiosus*, and he sees the whole of human history as that which is marked by innumerable transcendent, and, therefore, religious experiences insofar as these experiences tend toward the divine. History is the manifestation of transcendence, on the level of the individual, of communities, and the broad human community, because Spirit (*Geist*) can take on both an individual form and a corporate one (*Gestalten*—a variety of forms). Avery Dulles says this recognition of "interior (or 'transcendental revelation') . . . [makes] due allowance for religious experience and its varied expressions in man's religious history."[89] Rahner calls the experience of transcendence one of "natural revelation" because it "leaves God still

---

86. Rahner, *Foundations*, 127. Rahner encourages a certain inclusivism of all transcendent and religious experience here. Nichols comments on this in "Rahner and Balthasar," when he says, "God *provides in the course of salvation history different forms (Gestalten) of being actively related to that goal, different kinds of human experience of transcendence as ways of appropriating that supernatural transcendentality*" (116–17).

87. Rowland, *Catholic Theology*, 62.

88. Rahner, *Foundations*, 173.

89. Dulles, *Revelation Theology*, 161.

unknown . . . whether God wants to be for us a silent and impenetrable mystery keeping us at a distance in our finiteness, or wants to be the radical closeness of self-communication."[90] At the same time, it is, in a certain sense, most "natural" to the transcendent human being. Here, one can see how Rahner's transcendental anthropology and supernatural existential set the stage for a certain relativizing of revelation and an inclusivist approach to salvation in Jesus Christ wherein all transcendent experiences, all religious experiences and expressions actually subsist in Christ as differing expressions of what is ultimately the same reality.

Rahner continues to develop his thought in light of Heidegger's existential ontology and brings close together (if he does not end up collapsing one into the other) salvation history and the history of man. He says:

> The divine history of salvation . . . always appears in the human history of salvation; revelation always appears in faith. . . . The history of salvation is coexistent with the whole history of the human race (which is not to say identical). . . . Anyone who does not close himself to God in an ultimate act of his life and his freedom through free and personal sin for which he is really and subjectively guilty and for which he cannot shirk responsibility, this person finds salvation.[91]

Here, human history (in general) "coexists" with salvation history (i.e., that work of God in time and space for the sake of man's salvation). These realities coincide in such a way that the person who freely remains open to God "finds salvation." In light of transcendence, Rahner argues that the revelation event has two sides, or aspects: transcendental and historical.[92] The transcendental and historical aspects "are distinct but belong together. Both are necessary so that revelation can exist at all."[93] In other words, the person who accepts his or her personhood as a created being, as one who receives existence and who remains open to Being in and through time, that person finds salvation. This experience of salvation is, in a certain sense, "natural" to man, because it takes place in a revelational experience that is natural to man. Man is a transcendent being always already living within a supernaturally charged existence and who, in freedom, takes up responsibility for his own self-assertion and realization and in this experience "finds" salvation.

90. Rahner, *Foundations*, 170.

91. Rahner, *Foundations*, 142–43. See also Rahner and Ratzinger, *Revelation and Tradition*, 13.

92. Rahner and Ratzinger, *Revelation and Tradition*, 13; Rahner, *Foundations*, 171–75; Wahlberg, *Revelation as Testimony*, 69.

93. Rahner, *Foundations*, 170.

To summarize this element of the Rahnerian blueprint thus far, we must note again that Rahner grounds his theology in transcendent anthropology and the supernatural existential. Now, a "natural" revelation, an experience of the self-communication of God, occurs in any transcendental experience which brings one into contact with, so to speak, the supernatural existential. Here, the human being becomes aware of oneself as a transcendent being existing as, and opening to supernatural existential, which comes from God and is oriented toward God. Yet this revelation is most natural precisely because it takes place in man as he is. The supernatural is naturalized. Becoming aware of and accepting one's transcendent existence as a supernatural gift in the transcendental experience is revelation. Note that up to this point, God has not revealed anything particular about God's very self and nature. This is simply the unthematic, unobjective, religious experience.[94] Clearly, in his attempt to overcome the ahistorical and extrinsic elements of revelation that spring from the neo-scholastic *duplex ordo*, Rahner risks collapsing revelation into man's transcendental experience and salvation history into the history of mankind. He is careful to point out God's prior activity in both cases, but those who fail to acknowledge and promote this nuance, those so-called "vulgarized Rahnerians" do not.

For Rahner, natural revelation is an immanent possibility in one's existence—it is essentially the experience of existing as a transcendent being. Supernatural revelation differs from this conception in that it is a "real revelation of God. . . . [It] is not simply given with the spiritual being of man as transcendence, but rather has the character of event. It is dialogical, and in it God speaks . . . and makes known to him something which cannot be known always and everywhere."[95] As Rahner develops this thought, the real or supernatural revelation of God in history takes place in and becomes unsurpassably manifest in the Incarnation of Jesus Christ. In Christ, Rahner says, "this self-communication [of God] and acceptance [on the part of man] reaches a point in history which is irrevocable and irreversible."[96] In this evolutionary climax of humanity in Jesus Christ, the unity with God that exists as an inherent possibility in every human being is "visible and *realized.*"[97] Balthasar calls this a form of "evolutionistic Christology,"[98] wherein humanity reaches a climax in the Incarnation of

94. Wahlberg ties Rahner's thought, here, to Schleiermacher, in that he "talks about an awareness of God that is not mediated by concepts and that is independent of thought and beliefs" (*Revelation as Testimony*, 64).
95. Rahner, *Foundations*, 171.
96. Rahner, *Foundations*, 193–94.
97. Rise, "Karl Rahner," 231.
98. Balthasar, *The Moment of Christian Witness*, 106.

Jesus Christ, who realizes, as an irrevocable and irreversible high-point in history, what God intended as the intrinsic goal for humanity all along.[99] With the advent of Jesus Christ, Mark Fischer says, "human beings could no longer conceive of God as acting simply upon us from the outside. Jesus is not just God's extrinsic offer of salvation, but also our representative. On our behalf, he accepted God's will as his own."[100] The Christ-event is the realization of the human being's full possession of being—"in whom the search for absolute Being comes to its goal," and, as the high point of Christian revelation, it "simply confirms what any human being tacitly expects or at least hopes for, what he or she anonymously entertains."[101] In other words, natural revelation reaches an unsurpassable high-point in the transcendental experience of Jesus Christ, thus evolving into supernatural revelation. Jesus Christ, in his human nature, takes up this human openness towards God as a totality, "in the expectation that God's gracious self-communication will come to meet this openness."[102]

Jesus Christ, the evolutionary climax of transcendental anthropology, both establishes and reveals the "supernatural existential" as *categorically* christological.[103] The supernatural existential has been penetrated and reconfigured in Christ. In light of Christ, Fischer explains that the supernatural existential is now "a longing and affinity for God's very self that [has reached] its fulfillment in Jesus Christ."[104] The revelation of God in Jesus Christ, rendered in terms of transcendental anthropology, thus alters the transcendental experience in a categorical manner. Gerald McCool describes the tying together of Rahner's supernatural existential and

99. Fischer, "Karl Rahner's Transcendental Christology," 386–87.

100. Fischer, "Karl Rahner's Transcendental Christology," 392. See also Haight, *Jesus Symbol of God*.

101. Nichols, "Rahner and Balthasar," 120.

102. Rise, "Karl Rahner," 231.

103. The Kantian word "categorical" refers to what is "explicit" or "unconditional," or, as Nichols puts it, "the concrete object by whose means in a posteriori fashion we register what the a priori transcendental conditions of possibility of our knowledge enable us to understand" (Nichols, "Rahner and Balthasar," 118). Rahner's christological writings develop over a half-century, with *Foundations* containing the closest approximation to a summary. Galvin notes that Rahner's Christology deals with three theological concerns: (1) "God's universal salvific will"; (2) "Jesus' indispensable role in the mediation of salvation"; and (3) "the completeness of Jesus' humanity." Galvin argues that in addressing these christological issues, Rahner develops his thought as a reflection on the Church's teaching in light of his theological anthropology, which "understands the human being as spirit-in-world, finite openness toward the infinite mystery of God," where "salvation consists fundamentally in participation in divine life . . . [which] is a free gift of God, freely offered to all" (see Galvin, "Jesus Christ," 315–17).

104. Fischer, "Karl Rahner's Transcendental Christology," 386.

Christology, saying, "By his Incarnation the Word has . . . become the ground of man's elevation to the supernatural order and has also become God's historical revelation. . . . Therefore when the human spirit, elevated by the supernatural existential, makes its love surrender to the Horizon of its world, man receives the justifying grace of Christ."[105] Because of Christ, the supernatural existential is always already christological, and, for the person who professes him or herself to be a Christian, the supernatural existential becomes an explicitly Christian "*existentiell*." Furthermore, any transcendental experience is always already an experience of Christianity (as *existential*), whether one knows it or not (i.e., whether one is a professed Christian or an anonymous one). The transcendent experience that is universally accessible to all as an expression of God's salvific will is definitively and indispensably christological. In this way, according to a transcendental anthropology, Rahner maintains the universal salvific necessity of Christ. Hence Rahner can call "Christology . . . the beginning and end of [transcendental] anthropology," and claims that "all theology is therefore, to all eternity, anthropology."[106]

It seems Rahner's evolutionistic Christology, radically tied as it is to a transcendental anthropology, leaves open the question as to whether the Christian event brings something new to humanity or merely perfects and makes explicit what was already imperfectly and implicitly there. Nichols argues this point when he says the categorical nature of the Incarnation mediated historically, remains, "essentially the *interpretation* of that [transcendent] experience."[107] In other words, the transcendent experience remains the primary one, while the historically mediated categorical object (i.e., the Incarnation) perfectly expresses and provides the interpretive key for transcendental experience. Rahner's sensitivity toward Heidegger shines through. Traces of any onto-theological grid that imposes itself upon being's manifestation in time are relegated for the sake of the unthematic and unreflexive transcendental experience. Though Rahner establishes Christ as the categorical object, hence rendering anthropology properly theological and christological, for all intents and purposes, it seems the historical mediation of "supernatural revelation" is secondary. The "unexpressed, unthematic, unobjectified and unspoken" experience of religiosity within man comes to be considered the preeminent experience, even at the expense of liturgical or doctrinal expressions.

105. See McCool's editorial comments in *A Rahner Reader*, 211.

106. As quoted in Balthasar, *The Moment of Christian Witness*, 106. For additional theological opinions, see Colombo, "Rahner and His Critics," 88–89; Kerr, *Twentieth-Century Catholic Theologians*, 92–93; Conway, "A Constant Word," 112, 116.

107. Nichols, "Rahner and Balthasar," 119.

The Rahnerian Blueprint—Design Element #4: Anonymous Christianity and Evangelization

In light of what has been established by Rahner in the categorically christological supernatural existential, the Christian life, then, "can also be lived even by a person who is not a Christian explicitly and does not know in a reflexive way that he is a Christian."[108] This is the essence of the "anonymous Christianity" thesis—the fourth and perhaps most practically significant design element for the roof that lays on the ground in the anthropological phase of catechetical renewal. "Anonymous Christianity" is the name of Rahner's theory regarding the salvation of those persons who have never heard the Gospel, or who have never explicitly professed belief in Jesus Christ. As the name indicates, the "anonymous Christian" is the one who is implicitly and essentially a Christian, while not explicitly professing the faith or calling (i.e., name) him or herself a Christian. Rahner describes anonymous Christianity by saying:

> There is an implicit and anonymous Christianity. . . . There is and has to be an anonymous and yet real relationship between the individual person and the concrete history of salvation, including Jesus Christ, in someone who has not yet had the whole, concrete, historical, explicit and reflexive experience in word and sacrament of this reality of salvation history. Such a person has this real and existentiell relationship merely implicitly in obedience to his orientation in grace towards the God of absolute, historical presence and self-communication. He exercises this obedience by accepting his own existence without reservation.[109]

McCool points out that anonymous Christianity "is an extension of his theology of the supernatural existential."[110] Basically, the anonymous Christian is simply man as he is—man insofar as he accepts himself—precisely because Christ has Christianized the supernatural existential. For, as Rahner says:

> Wherever a person accepts his existence ultimately and unconditionally . . . he is accepting God. . . . The basic and ultimate thrust of Christian life consists not so much in the fact that a Christian is a special instance of mankind in general, but rather in the fact that a Christian is simply man as he is. But

---

108. Rahner, *Foundations*, 430.
109. Rahner, *Theological Foundations*, 306.
110. See McCool's editorial comments in *A Rahner Reader*, 211.

he is a person who accepts without reservations the whole of concrete human life.[111]

Boeve describes this thesis regarding the universal salvation of mankind, or the relationship between Catholic Christianity and non-Catholic Christianity, as an inclusivist strategy, which "argues that while the Christian faith is the true religion, this does not exclude the possibility that elements of truth and salvation may be found in the other religions. As a matter of fact, God's salvific will extends to all people."[112]

Exploring the "anonymous Christianity" thesis a bit further, Nichols notes that the (anonymously) Christian life is manifest through "anonymous opportunities," or "surrogates." While many could be listed, Nichols focuses on what he takes to be Rahner's three chief surrogates: (1) readiness for death; (2) hope for the future; (3) love of neighbor (with this standing as the linchpin for the others).[113] The person, according to Rahner, "discovers his true self in a genuine act of self-realization only if he risks himself radically for another. If he does this, he grasps unthematically or explicitly what we mean by God as the horizon . . . who in his existentiell and historical self-communication made himself the realm within which such love is possible."[114] Love of neighbor implies an experience of God, precisely because "God has made himself the realm within which such love is possible." Again, the ties to the Christological supernatural existential are clear. For Rahner, because salvation history is coextensive with history through the supernatural existential, every human act or good moral action, whether carried out by a Christian or an atheist, "can receive justifying grace and enjoy supernatural sanctification."[115]

At this point, a significant question surfaces: If one has the ability to be Christian anonymously (or implicitly) just by accepting one's humanity in a transcendental experience, why explicitly express Christian belief at all? The question could be rephrased in light of the Church's mission as well: What is the point of the Church and her mission if everyone is, just by embracing and living his or her humanity, already a Christian? Regarding the first question, Rahner argues that implicit faith necessarily moves toward explicit faith. He says, "faith as it exists in the pagan . . . follow[s] its own inherent dynamism in such a way as to develop into that faith which we

---

111. Rahner, *Foundations*, 402.
112. Boeve, *God Interrupts*, 167.
113. Nichols, "Rahner and Balthasar," 121–22.
114. Rahner, *Foundations*, 456.
115. Nichols, "Rahner and Balthasar," 122.

simply call the Christian faith."[116] Implicit faith tends toward explicit faith. At this point, the second question essentially answers itself, for the pagan must be told about the Catholic faith to profess it explicitly. Rahner explains:

> God's gift of himself [revelation] . . . takes place in the historical material of a person's life, but does not for this reason become simply identical with it. If . . . this supernatural determination is to take place in the concrete . . . then God's non-objective and unreflexive self-revelation in grace must always be present as mediated in objective and reflexive knowledge, regardless in the first instance of whether this is an explicitly and thematically religious mediation or not. The attempt is made in every religion, at least on man's part, to mediate the original, unreflexive and non-objective revelation historically, to make it reflexive and to interpret it in propositions.[117]

Rahner links nature to grace through a supernatural existential, and in so doing, he sees something of a continuity between human experience as grace "as belonging to the same ontic plane by stressing the continuity of *ens* [being] and *esse* [existence]."[118] Now, history, social events and movements, and even salvation history simply "make explicit something that was already present in the beginning."[119] However, if God's self-revelation in the Christ-event is to take on the categorical nature proper to it in "objective and reflexive consciousness," it must be made known. In this way, the efforts of evangelization and catechesis are justified.

If God's self-revelation that takes place in Jesus Christ, a perfectly complete and perfectly real, non-objective, unthematic, and unreflexive self-revelation, is to be made known and present, knowledge of it must be mediated. The mediation historically transmits the unsurpassable transcendent experience of mankind in the Incarnation of Jesus Christ, yet in such a way that it does not hinder one's original, ureflexive, unthematic experience. Rahner

---

116. Rahner, *Theological Investigations*, 291, quoted in Nichols, "Rahner and Balthasar," 122.

117. Rahner, *Foundations*, 172–73. Regarding the impact of transcendental anthropology on sacramental theology, Cooper notes that the Sacraments become "the stimulation of a psychological state of awareness, the elicitation of a primarily *gnoseological* orientation. Or, put another way, they have as their aim the making explicit of what hitherto was already present, given, and real at the level of the 'unthematic.' For every categorical, thematic 'yes' or 'no' to God in Christ corresponds to an already-existing transcendental, unthematic 'yes' or 'no' to the absolute" (Cooper, *Naturally Human*, 113–14). For an example of the position identified here by Cooper, see Hughes, *Becoming the Sign*.

118. Rowland, *Ratzinger's Faith*, 22.

119. Rowland, *Ratzinger's Faith*, 22.

notes that in every religion, man attempts to mediate the "original, unreflexive and non-objective revelation [i.e., the transcendental revelation] historically, to make it reflexive [i.e., the object of reflexive, conceptual thought] and to interpret it in propositions."[120] Some of the mediation attempts are successful, and "through these moments God creates for man the possibility of salvation also in the dimension of his objectivity, his concrete historicity."[121] Rahner, therefore, concludes, "In Jesus, God's communication to man in grace and at the same time as categorical self-interpretation in the corporeal, tangible and social dimension . . . have become revelation in an absolute sense. . . . It enables us to distinguish a particular and official history of revelation within the universal history of revelation before Christ."[122]

All of this said, Rahner throws two observations into the mix that eventually horizontalize the catechetical structure. Rahner says, "in the history of man's objectifying self-interpretation of gratuitous revelation, it is only partially successful, it always exists within a still unfinished history, it is intermixed with error, sinful delusions and their objectifications, and these once again co-determine the religious situation of other people."[123] Complicating matters, attempts to disclose God's self-revelation through objective and reflexive knowledge should respect that revelation *is not closed*, as "a point is conceivable at which God's self-communication to the world is indeed not yet concluded."[124] This point will become another anchor for the catechetical theorists who will follow the Rahnerian line and develop the concept of "ongoing revelation" after Vatican II.

Additionally, communicating the Gospel in a pluralist society no longer impregnated with Christianity as a social custom, where men and women are made weary by much communication, and where "even a baptised person is in many respects more 'pagan' than ever anyone has been since Constantine," is difficult at best. Rahner asserts that one must be able to express the essence of Christianity in brief, short formulas of faith.[125] Given the cultural situation, the Church simply does not have time to present secondary things as if they are primary. Instead, she must find some way of briefly and urgently conveying the core of Christianity according to "a clear

---

120. Rahner, *Foundations*, 173. Cf. Wahlberg, *Revelation as Testimony*, 69.

121. Rahner, *Foundations*, 173.

122. Rahner, *Foundations*, 174–75.

123. Rahner, *Foundations*, 172–73.

124. Rahner, *Foundations*, 194.

125. Rahner, "A Short Formula of Christian Faith," 205–11. See also Rahner, *Foundations*, 448–59.

structure in the 'hierarchy of truths.'"[126] Rahner says that without this type of creed, the "Christian faith very quickly becomes amorphous, or a believer very easily places too much value in his religious practice on things which are only secondary."[127] Rahner generates Short Formulas of Faith, or Brief Creedal Statements, in an effort to make the Christian message intelligible today, by separating what is essential from what is secondary so the modern "pagan" can distinguish the essence of Christianity from what might not be inviting in sermons, religious practices, or social relationships.[128] The short formulas of faith are merely to be seen as points of departure. While they may vary in content, the point is to successfully move from this initial creed to "the whole of Christian faith."[129] Therefore, Rahner drives at a message that can "express the essentials *briefly* for busy people today, and to express them again and again. . . . A person will not experience this as an 'ideology' . . . imposed on him from without . . . but . . . as the reality of his very own life as he has experienced it."[130] Again, note the inclusivity. The Christian creed merely names what the person has already "naturally" experienced.

In Summary

Karl Rahner intends for his speculative theology to redesign practical theology and a certain company of catechetical theorists sought to reify his building plans after Vatican II. A Rahnerian blueprint shapes the construction of the roof Hofinger thought would fittingly crown the catechetical edifice following decades of renewal work. Instead, Rahner's roof hugs the ground, too "horizontalized" and anchored to subjective experience. Rahner's design consists of at least four key elements drawn from his fluid theology. First, Rahner makes a turn to the subject, to the being in time, the human being who in its very existence is uniquely open to Being (*Dasein*) with his transcendental anthropology. This transcendental being is capable of a transcendent *experience*, which occurs when the human being engages with categorical experience (the "stuff" of life, of history) and becomes implicitly aware (*Vorgriff*) of its capacity to stand before and to question

---

126. Rahner, *Foundations*, 448. For more on the short formula of faith, see Rahner, *A Rahner Reader*, 205–11. Here, Rahner provides a creed of sorts, with the educated Western man or woman in mind. It serves as something of a summary of the mainlines of his theology.

127. Rahner, *Foundations*, 448.

128. Rahner, *Foundations*, 449.

129. Rahner, *Foundations*, 453.

130. Rahner, *Foundations*, 449.

Being. Next, he establishes the supernatural existential as the supernatural corollary to human transcendence. The "supernatural existential" is a gift of existence from God (hence it is extrinsic and not an inherent part of human existence) which makes it intrinsically possible to encounter God implicitly in human experience. Such an encounter takes place when one accepts one's existence as a being in time. In accepting one's humanity, one embraces the God who establishes human existence and who is always already implicit in one's existence. Because the *existential* (as a noun) is a supernatural "element" of human existence, then simply and freely accepting one's existence is to accept the supernatural (i.e., an *existentiell* decision, with *existentiall* here being used as an adjective describing the type of free acceptance of one's "supernaturalized" existence). The third element flows naturally, as revelation is reconfigured as transcendental experience. Natural revelation is a reality immanent in one's existence—it is essentially the experience of existing as a transcendent being, it essentially occurs in the transcendental experience—and it is accessible to all. Supernatural revelation, the "real" and explicit revelation of God, reaches its high point in the Incarnation of the Word. As an "evolutionary climax," the Incarnation renders the supernatural existential categorically christological. Finally, anonymous Christianity tends to relegate the tradition and reconfigures evangelization. Given that Christ has already rendered the supernatural existential categorically "Christian," one must simply accept his transcendental human existence to implicitly be a Christian. In this way, Christ's redemptive work touches even the non-believer. This sets the stage for relegating evangelization, which of its very nature contains the work of catechesis, along with also limiting the role of Sacred Scripture, Sacred Tradition, and the Church's magisterium. Now, the privileged "place" of encounter is the bare-naked human experience, one unimpeded and unencumbered by tradition. Scripture and tradition become helpful insofar as they may assist with interpreting or thematizing the unthematic experience of the supernatural existential. Evangelization simply helps to make explicit that which was already implicit within transcendent human experience.

Rahner's blueprint brings human experience to the forefront of theology, and, consequently, to the forefront of catechetics, as he tries to make the faith relevant again through a correlation process. Rahner attempted to break away from the metaphysical and propositional trappings of Suárezian scholasticism and a theology far-removed from the ordinary lives of ordinary people. Thus, experience becomes the "jumping off" point for catechetics within "vulgarised Rahnerianism" and it seems to run the risk of assuming tradition (i.e., the thematic and objectified) precludes one's ability to authentically (i.e., transcendentally) encounter or experience an existential-ecstatic relationship with God. Just when it seems Rahner's thought touches down in daily life, his speculation launches again into the theological stratosphere via his Kantian idealism and a Heideggerian existential ontology. Those who take up Rahner's plans and begin to build in the decades following Vatican II—the anthropological phase of catechetical renewal—ultimately end up relativizing revelation and grounding the roof in a type of subjectivism. Rahner's design establishes *ethos* over and against *logos* within catechetics. Those who follow Rahner, those master builders of catechetical renewal following Vatican II, picked up their architect's blueprint and rapidly began to implement it. We now turn to consider their work.

CHAPTER TWO

Master Builders of a "Vulgarized Rahnerian" Catechesis after Vatican II

Following the Council, Rahner exercised significant theological influence, with his work seemingly seeping into every ecclesial crevice. Rahner's theology, for its part, was speculative; it was fluid, something dynamic.[1] In an attempt at correlation, he grounded his theology in human experience. Transcendental anthropology functioned as Rahner's "given," as human experience became the starting point of a new thrust in catechetics. This theological vision appealed to those catechetical theorists who had rejected Neo-scholasticism with its apparent closed-system theology, fixed truths, and air-tight categories. Ironically, in their reaction to theological closed-mindedness they perceived in Neo-scholasticism, renewal architects fixed their own project almost entirely on human experience, emphasizing *ethos* over *logos*. It is worth noting again Schoonenberg's apt description of the shift that was taking place in catechetics: "From a mere approach to the message, experience has become the theme itself of catechesis. Catechesis has become the interpretation of experience. It has to clarify experience, that is, it has to articulate and enlighten the experience and existence of those for whom the message is intended."[2]

For movers and shakers in catechetical renewal after Vatican II, human experience itself becomes the *theologicus locicus* wherein revelation occurs, with doctrine falling out of favor. As Schoonenberg poignantly illustrates, catechetical renewal limited doctrine's role as that which simply names as religious, or interprets as Christian, experiences which have already taken place in ordinary life. Post-conciliar catechesis would make the faith so ordinary and "relatable," it became hardly distinguishable from aspects of the culture at large. Armed with felt banners, secular humanistic "Gospel

1. Moran, *Revelation*, 20.
2. Schoonenberg, "Revelation and Experience," 304.

values," idealistic and self-centered songs, and ranks of de-habited religious sisters (along with former ones) teaching high school religion classes that now featured exegetical work on McLean's "American Pie"—well, at least in one Catholic high school (but probably others)—the revolutionary force charged with tremendous speed after the Council.[3] While this type of transformation was not perfectly universal, it was ubiquitous. Catechesis had been turned on its head. The new paradigm demoted Scripture and tradition, with doctrine now viewed as some sort of onto-theological barrier that prevented the bare-naked transcendental experience from reaching its full potential. "The faith," so to speak, had to be relegated as a secondary value, perhaps helpful in interpreting transcendental experience, or as a tool for somehow correlating the experience to Christianity—thus making one aware of how it was already Christian anyhow. By relegating the role of doctrine in one's encounter with and understanding of God, theological speculation and catechetical renewal in the post-conciliar years revolves more tightly around one axis—the human, transcendent subject.

To be sure, Rahner's speculative theology was not universally embraced. Balthasar was a particularly boisterous critic. He attacked the anonymous Christianity thesis, which, in his mind, synthesized "an interrelated series of errors in Christian thinking" that Aidan Nichols outlines as follows:

> In fundamental theology, as with the belief that a transcendental philosophy can anticipate the distinctive content of Christian revelation; or in soteriology, where the life, death and Resurrection of Christ become exemplary rather than efficacious in force; or in theological ethics where the love of neighbour becomes a surrogate for the love of God and Christological confession no longer necessary for Christian existence; or in the theology of religions which become in fact if not in name ordinary ways of salvation alongside the Christian way; or in ecclesiology where the Church becomes simply the explicit articulation of what is equally present (though only implicitly so) wherever the world opens itself to the Kingdom; or finally in the theology of history where the universal openness of the human spirit to divine transcendence in its supernatural offer of salvation is already deemed to be *Gnadenerfahrung*, "the experience of grace," even without any further intervention of the redeeming God in the special history of revelation.[4]

---

3. The high school shall remain nameless. My inside source was a firsthand recipient of such formation.

4. Nichols, "Rahner and Balthasar," 112. See Balthasar's critique of Rahner's

Balthasar's concern for the impact of Rahner's speculative theology on the faith experience of ordinary, everyday Catholics motivated his broadsweeping indictment of Rahner's speculative work. Balthasar basically believes that without maintaining the incarnate reality of Jesus Christ as the starting point for theological reflection, one which gives priority to Christ crucified,[5] Rahner's approach becomes, as Doyle puts it, "a kind of extreme point on a horizon beyond which one would fall over a cliff."[6] Gerard O'Shea traces the implications of Rahnerian tombstoning by noting the manner in which "Divine Revelation is understood and translated" is the sticking point with regard to Rahner's impact on catechetics.[7] O'Shea claims that in a "vulgarized" form, Rahner's teaching on "the general experience of transcendence—the natural interior impression shared by all human beings of *something more than meets the eye* and a yearning for the infinite—is elevated to a level that can seem at least equivalent in importance to the public revelation of God in Christ."[8] As a result, "some began to interpret these speculations as an endorsement of the principle of *ongoing revelation*, which tended to diminish the unique role of Christ—something that Rahner himself had not done."[9] In light of such developments, Doyle points out that "What was at stake was the transcendent reality of Christian revelation as a gift from God beyond the capacity of any merely human achievement."[10] Things had begun a slide toward subjectivism, and the objectivity of the Catholic faith was at stake—the objectivity of revelation and the place of the traditional "organs of transmission."[11]

Among the many theorists and practitioners who snatched up Rahner's blueprint and assisted with building a Rahnerian "roof" during catechetical renewal following Vatican II, Gabriel Moran and Thomas Groome stand out as prominent figures. This was particularly the case in the United States, where Moran and Groome could be credited as the master builders of the Anthropological Phase of catechetical renewal. Such builders did not

---

Anonymous Christianity in Balthasar, *The Moment of Christian Witness*, 100–113.

5. See Doyle, "The Concept of Inculturation," 7.

6. Doyle, "The Concept of Inculturation," 7.

7. O'Shea, "Vulgarised Rahnerianism," 345. See also Doyle, "The Concept of Inculturation," 6, where Doyle notes that "It is common for critics to distinguish between Rahner's own nuanced positions and those of some of his followers that did not retain such nuance."

8. O'Shea, "Vulgarised Rahnerianism," 347.

9. O'Shea, "Vulgarised Rahnerianism," 347. See also Rise's "Karl Rahner," 230–33, where Rise argues for Rahner's insistence on the unique role of Jesus Christ in salvation.

10. Doyle, "The Concept of Inculturation," 7.

11. Moran, *Revelation*, 18.

only leave the roof on the ground, stuck in a certain subjectivism, but, in following Rahner's plans, they also constructed it on a theological cliff edge. Moran and Groome seem to share in the general sentiment of the twentieth century catechetical reformers, that "more is required of Christian education than the handing on of shopworn formulas, tired customs, and trite devotions."[12] In seeking the "more," Moran develops a theory that locates the possibility of *ongoing* or *continuing revelation* in the transcendental experience—a simple and doctrinally-free experience of being aware of oneself (as a) being aware of itself.[13] The transcendental experience reaches an unsurpassable high-point in human history—an evolutionary breakthrough takes place in Christ who categorically transforms it (see "design elements" 1–3 in the previous chapter) and allows him to move away from the content traditionally associated with catechesis. Because Christ is still alive today (due to the Resurrection and his ongoing presence in the body of believers, the Church), some sort of ongoing, or continuing revelation is possible today in Christ's consciousness, because all transcendental experience is a participation in that most complete transcendental experience

---

12. Marthaler, "The Modern Catechetical Movement," 278. Marthaler summarizes the main thrust of Moran's early work in just two points: as a charge against catechetical language that is (1) "too parochial" and (2) "unduly influenced by theology." Marthaler takes the former to mean that catechesis is often limited in its scope and purview. Designed for children and adolescents, catechetical programs are limited to the mastering the Catechism. The "parochialism" of catechesis limits its purview to "the hierarchical Church [rather] than . . . on the kingdom preached by Jesus." As for the latter, Moran laments that theological ingenuity has little impact on shaping catechetics. Instead, catechesis is deemed effective insofar as it is theologically "orthodox" (see Marthaler, "Introduction," 17). Moran is averse to this.

13. Moran reacts against a view that equates revelation with the contents thereof in the form of the "deposit of faith," to which nothing new can be added after the death of the last apostle. For example, Second Vatican Council, *Dei verbum*, §4 states: "The Christian dispensation, therefore, as the new and definitive covenant, will never pass away and we now await no further new public revelation before the glorious manifestation of our Lord Jesus Christ (see 1 Tim 6:14 and Titus 2:13)." Likewise, Ludwig Ott asserts "With Christ and the Apostles general revelation concluded. Pope Pius X rejected the liberal Protestant and Modernistic doctrine of the evolution of religion through 'New Revelations.' Thus he condemned the proposition that: 'The Revelation, which is the object of Catholic Faith, was not terminated with the Apostles.' The clear teaching of Holy Writ and Tradition is that after Christ, and the Apostles who proclaimed the message of Christ, no further revelation will be made. . . . The full truth of revelation is contained in the doctrine of the Apostles which is preserved unfalsified through the uninterrupted succession of the bishops" (Ott, *Fundamentals of Catholic Dogma*, 7). This does not preclude the development of doctrine or the possibility of "private revelations," which do not improve or complete the deposit of faith but help the faithful to live more faithfully in a given era (cf. *CCC*, §67). For Moran, however, the apparent reduction of revelation to content (i.e., the deposit of faith) precludes the possibility of God's real and onging revelation today.

of Christ. Revelation continues, so to speak, in human experience. Every experience of transcendence is now always already Christian. Experience, as it were, becomes the "seat" of revelation, instead of revelation challenging and shaping experience. Therefore, *the* task of catechesis has to do with cultivating such experiences wherein one can encounter the living God unencumbered by doctrine and the like (see "design element" 4 in the previous chapter). With his transcendental "given," Rahner, perhaps unwittingly, had the stage for what became Moran's the theory of "ongoing revelation." Moran's vision is substantially Rahnerian; it is simply the outworking of Rahner's theological blueprint in the world of catechetical renewal.

Amongst other influences, Groome takes Moran's conception of continuing revelation and the principles Moran lays out for an "evolution" of catechetics, working out what Moran would likely call a "detailed catechetical application."[14] For Groome, this catechetical work crystalizes in his methodology known as *Shared Christian Praxis*. Returning to the roof image from Hofinger, if Rahner provides the blueprint, Moran takes the design and constructs the rafters while also supplying the decking. Groome, then, lays that which is visible, or accessible to all—a tangible method that shapes the landscape—the catechetical shingles.

Moran's Original Inquiry

Moran argues that the Vatican II era's most pressing question deals with a proper understanding of revelation. He believes the Council introduces the question and provides "a framework within which more fruitful discussion may now proceed," but it does not, itself, definitively answer it.[15] Despite the conciliar age's "self-renewal" in the theology of revelation, along with a sense that it is increasingly becoming a service to the pastoral life of the Church, Moran believes an understanding of "the self-disclosure of God in Christ in the present life of the Church has been accomplished only in fragmentary form." He describes the *status quaestionis* as one lacking an understanding of revelation as a "present, personal, conscious, free happening with Christ and our brothers"—a deficiency which must be addressed if the full interrelation between theology and catechetics is to be actualized.[16]

---

14. Moran, *Catechesis*, 17.

15. Moran, *Revelation*, 18; see also 145, where Moran says, "even conciliar definitions are more in the nature of starting points or frameworks within which to live and work than of conclusions."

16. Moran, *Catechesis*, 29. While the debate has been ongoing (see, for example, Moran, *Missed Opportunities*, loc. 2614), Moran believes it is far from over. In fact, it

So, Moran takes up an inquiry addressing the "essence or nature of divine revelation," an area "not yet developed in Catholic circles."[17] He argues that "Catholic doctrine . . . with its insistence upon the closing of revelation, seems committed to the past over the present and exposed to the charge of not taking history seriously."[18] In other words, Moran, along with many others, wants to take the Heideggerian problematic seriously. With this primary motivation, Moran sets out to answer the basic question he believes theologians must ask daily, namely: *What is revelation?*[19] As noted in the Introduction, Moran believes questions raised in the theology of revelation are so fundamental to catechesis, "they cannot fail to have profound effects upon preaching and catechizing . . . despite the fact that the questions raised may seem at first to be abstract and impractical."[20]

Moran criticizes the vision of revelation developed in both Suárezian scholasticism and the Kerygmatic renewal. To him, such theological and catechetical currents were beholden to what Rahner identifies as the Church's traditional view of revelation as an intervention of God "'purely from outside,' speaking to men and conveying to them through the prophets, truths in human statements which they could not attain by themselves."[21] Moran denounces Neo-scholasticism's propositional understanding of revelation, believing it strips revelation of its dynamism by reducing "revelation to doctrinal statements . . . and faith to assent to propositions."[22] Describing these developments from the seventeenth century to the mid-twentieth century, Moran says:

> "Revelation" had come to mean for Catholics the package of truths deposited in the past. . . . It was in the nineteenth century that the phrase "deposit of revelation" came into use as a synonym or replacement for the traditional phrase "deposit of faith." The same century produced the phrase "revelation closed with the death of the last apostle." The vault was sealed; no more deposits were allowed. The "Christian revelation" was secure,

---

is "the intellectual crisis surrounding the very basis of its teaching" (Moran, "A Verb, Not a Noun," 15).

17. Moran, *Revelation*, 18–19.
18. Moran, *Revelation*, 54. Cf. Moran, "What Is Revelation?," 218–19.
19. Moran, *Revelation*, 37.
20. Moran, *Revelation*, 19.
21. Rahner and Ratzinger, *Revelation and Tradition*, 10.
22. See Moran, "What Is Revelation?," 219.

but revelation was equated with a collection of revealed truths instead of divine activity inviting human response.[23]

He also criticizes the "catechetical theorists" of the "kerygmatic" renewal movement who "exalt 'salvation history,'" claiming that the "confident announcements that revelation is history" takes "what is already a wrong conception of history and modif[ies] it according to the peculiar demands of exegetes."[24] For theorists of the Kerygmatic Movement, revelation means "a collection of events in the remote past with interpretations supplied by some extraordinary men of the past," and the "whole scheme of historical events will almost certainly be irrelevant to students if this body of recorded testimony is imposed from the outside as the truths and precepts they must live by."[25] Therefore, Moran argues that "kerygmatic" catechesis, with its insistence on "salvation history," on the past-over-the-present, also fails to adequately address Heidegger's problem with onto-theology, even if it comes from a different place than that of the Neo-scholastics. It remains propositional. The renewal of catechesis, one which will not fall prey to some sort of doctrinal propositionalism or historical extrinsicism, hinges upon a present revelation, the manifestation of Being-in-time.

Both Neo-scholasticism and the "kerygmatic" movement, in Moran's view, fail to address the Heideggerian problematic. Therefore, Moran frames the ensuing dilemma as follows:

> Either revelation is constituted by events in the experience of men in the past and is no longer with us because their experience has ceased; or revelation consists of truths not irrevocably tied to temporal events but communicable through propositions from one generation to another. . . . How can revelation be anything other than truths or objects if it is handed down from one generation to another; or, reversing the question,

---

23. Moran, *Believing in a Revealing God*, 51–52. See also Moran, *Catechesis*, 14–15. In "What is Revelation?," 219, Moran says, "A common Protestant complaint about Catholicism is that of the latter's reduction of revelation to doctrinal statements and the corresponding reduction of faith to assent to propositions."

24. Moran, *Catechesis*, 44; see also 20–29.

25. Moran, *Catechesis*, 44–45. Moran does not believe the "dying catechism" to be the cause of the catechetical crisis apparent in the 1960s, "but the still rising hope that the education of hundreds of millions of people . . . can be carried out with a bit of Scripture and liturgy and much sincerity and good will" (34–35). Moran is dissatisfied with the *status quo* and calls for "patient inquiry, deep understanding, and detailed knowledge" into the heart of revelation.

how can a revelation consisting of personal events in the past ever be a present revelation?[26]

Moran argues that Catholic doctrine, with its insistence upon "the closing of revelation" and a commitment "to the past over the present," is "not taking history seriously," even if it does account for the transcendence of truth, or a deepening in understanding from one generation to the next.[27] Despite various efforts, Catholic theology cannot seem to break free from a propositional and extrinsic understanding of revelation as a collection of "truths, teachings, and historical facts."[28] Moran, however, discovers in non-Catholic theologies an answer to the stated dilemma in the thesis of ongoing or continuing revelation.

Revelation: A Verb, not a Noun

Moran observes that the early Church used two different words, each with the same Greek root, to describe revelation, an unveiling that occurs between God and man: apocalypse (*apocalypsis*) and revelation (*revelatio*).[29] The word "apocalypse" connotes disclosing a secret about the future. The expectation of Jesus' immanent return gave the early Church a certain apocalyptic flair. However, with the delay of the second coming, the early Church leaned on the word "revelation" to describe the unveiling of God that "was given to the prophets and found full expression in Jesus, the Christ."[30] Here, Moran sees the early Church moving decidedly in a direction that understands revelation as *having occurred* rather than one which *will occur*, and taking up a mission of preserving and delivering these revealed truths to the nations instead of anticipating other ones.[31] In short, a split occurs between the concepts of revelation and apocalypse, with one concept which looking to the past and the other into the future. The concept that refers to looking to the past won out.[32] Moran describes

---

26. Moran, *Revelation*, 55–56. See also Moran, *Believing in a Revealing God*, 54; Baumert, "Instruments of Change," 65–67.

27. Moran, *Revelation*, 55.

28. Moran, *Revelation*, 55.

29. In *Believing in a Revealing God*, Moran takes up a longer description of the development of the word "revelation" both in pre-Christian and Christian traditions. See *Believing in a Revealing God*, 40–60. For a longer treatment, see Moran, *Both Sides*, 3–130.

30. Moran, *Believing in a Revealing God*, 46.

31. Moran, *Believing in a Revealing God*, 46.

32. Moran, *Both Sides*, 10–11, 216–18.

this movement as a "domestication," one which reduces revelation to "a message from the past."[33] Over time, this position becomes more and more solidified in Church teaching, until Protestant and Catholic theology would challenge the understanding in the late nineteenth and twentieth centuries.

In his attempt to widen the conversation about revelation and to recover it, Moran does not reduce revelation to mere concepts handled transactionally. "Revelation is not a thing," Moran says, it is an event, "[it] is what happens between persons and exists only as a personal reality."[34] Revelation is a verb, and the "term should be restricted to a verb form."[35] As indicated above, if revelation is not to remain locked in the past, or be understood in a purely propositional manner, it is incumbent upon Moran to establish a more active understanding of revelation. If revelation is not to remain a noun connoting only a "collection of truths from the past,"[36] Moran must recover revelation's verb form as the basis of his theology of revelation.

By emphasizing the verb-form of revelation, Moran establishes revelation as a dialogical exchange between persons. Revelation is, most fundamentally, an unveiling which takes place in an interpersonal encounter; it is an experience of union, in knowledge, between the knowing being and the being known. Moran describes this type of revelation as an unveiling, a removing of the "covering from what could not previously be seen. . . . After a secret is uncovered, revelation ends; a secret revealed is a secret no longer."[37] Unless there is a receiving subject, the veil has not really been lifted and the secret remains undisclosed. Therefore, on the one hand, revelation is an event marked by one's unveiling of what was not previously known. On the other hand, it is the reception by another of that which one was previously ignorant. In other words, the "revelatory experience in the human sphere demands a reciprocal interaction: there is no revelation unless it is received, while to receive is already to give back . . . the impetus to further revelation."[38] As Moran puts it, "all personal knowledge . . . is

33. Moran, *Believing in a Revealing God*, 46.

34. Moran, *Revelation*, 120. Cf. Moran, "What Is Revelation?," 225.

35. Moran, "A Verb, Not a Noun," 15.

36. Moran, "A Verb, Not a Noun," 15. See Moran, *Both Sides*, 10–11.

37. Moran, *Believing in a Revealing God*, 40. See also Moran, *Both Sides*, 5. The word "revelation" comes to us in English from the Latin *revelare*, which literally means "unveil" (from *re-* "opposite of" + *velare* "to cover, veil").

38. Moran, "What Is Revelation?," 223. One ought not overlook the role of freedom, here. One's personal knowledge of the other is completely dependent upon the other's free bestowal and the recipient's free acceptance of this knowledge. Moran says, following Gabriel Marcel, that "for a person to be known in what uniquely distinguishes him, he must choose to be known; if he refuses to reveal his inner self, he cannot be known except by external, nonpersonal description" (Moran, "What Is Revelation?," 221).

truly and accurately called 'revelation,' the reciprocal giving and receiving of knowledge within living experience."[39]

If revelation is the reciprocal act of unveiling what was previously hidden, the act of receptivity is known as faith. Moran denounces a view that sees faith as a complex system of beliefs and practices (a noun, "the faith"), and opts instead for its active verb form: to believe, to believe in.[40] In order to overcome an understanding of faith that is reduced to a series of beliefs, Moran establishes faith in relation to revelation, with the present tense of this verb as primary. Faith, or "believing in," is part of an interpersonal act of revealing-believing. One actively exercises faith in response to the act of revealing, thus receiving that which is revealed. The emphasis on interpersonal relationship in the act of believing in a revelation allows Moran to render secondary the actual "content" of that which is revealed and believed.

For Moran, revelation is an event that takes place "within" human consciousness. It is a conscious event, that, "naturally" speaking, hinges upon an understanding of the human person as a "consciously" transcendent being. This follows closely along Rahner's line. The human being experiences revelation in its consciousness insofar as it is a: (1) knowing being; (2) a spiritual being; (3) an historical being; and (4) a free being.

When describing the human being as a knowing being, Moran refers to the verb "to know" in the biblical sense with its reference on interpersonal union. Moran describes this form of knowing as "the inner presence of being to itself mediated by its relation to the other." In this understanding of biblical knowledge, neither concept nor word are the "content" of knowledge itself, but are part of a process whereby man's intellect comes to a "living knowledge" that is nothing other than "a unity of knower and known."[41] I am aware of myself as myself only in relation to you, the other. This knowledge, then, establishes a union that is a "fundamental pre-predicative comprehension of truth."[42] The truth of the union between knower and being-known, i.e., the truth of the union between the one who

---

39. Moran, "What Is Revelation?," 222.

40. Moran, *Believing in a Revealing God*, 28, 35.

41. Moran, *Revelation*, 84–85. Scholars like Wahlberg debate this point. Wahlberg argues that "if God wants personal communion with us, he must make sure that we know some propositions about him. The 'must' here is the must of logical/conceptual necessity. It is conceptually impossible for something to have a personal relationship to some reality without knowing (or justifiably believing) some proposition about that reality." See Wahlberg, *Revelation as Testimony*, 28.

42. Moran, *Revelation*, 86. Note the Kantian, Heideggerian, and Rahnerian undertones of this line.

believes in and the one who reveals, is not predicated upon some sort of content revealed, but simply upon the interpersonal reality of encountering the other. For this reason, "a question about the 'content' of interpersonal relations would be somewhat peculiar. . . . There is no list of truths that the individuals themselves or an outside examiner could specify as the content of their love."[43] Elsewhere, he explains:

> A knower is simply a being capable of reflecting back upon itself and its relation to others. To know is to be aware of and to possess one's self presence. A being with such perfection and power, one that has to some degree emerged from the conditions of material being dispersed in space and time, we call spiritual. . . . For man, the finite and material being, knowing is always mediated by what is other than himself.[44]

The knower, then, is capable of encountering "what is other than himself," and of transcending it in such a way that he can question what is "other" and its relationship to himself, further knowing, establishing, and possessing oneself. Knowing oneself does not refer to possessing a fact about oneself but is "the taking hold of one's identity in a way which may vary from a simple, global awareness to a detailed, reflexive understanding."[45] Only later is the "content" of this interpersonal, revelatory act "brought to full reflexive consciousness only by progressive conception expression and dialogue."[46]

For Moran, and this is the second point, this knowingly self-conscious being is the very definition of a spiritual being. He says, "To be a spiritual being is to be a conscious being; to be a supernatural being is to be a supernaturally conscious being, with a consciousness that wells up out of life culminating and directing it."[47] According to Moran, man is a spiritual being in that man is capable of an interior movement wherein the "Spirit makes man conscious of what man already is."[48] Third, interior movements, or

---

43. Moran, *Believing in a Revealing God*, 34. In *Belief and Faith*, Josef Pieper claims the dual elements "to believe *something* and to believe *someone*" are not "a structureless parallel, a mere co-ordinate existence of the two elements side by side" (18). This formulation, i.e., to believe *in* someone *that* what he says is true, makes up an integral whole of the act of faith. In Moran's attempt at overcoming the perceived overemphasis on the "content-side" of this formulation belief in both the neo-scholastic and kerygmatic movements, on the *something that is believed*, he emphasizes the other half of the act: *believing in someone* who reveals.

44. Moran, *Revelation*, 67.

45. Moran, *Revelation*, 67.

46. Moran, *Revelation*, 85.

47. Moran, "What Is Revelation?," 224.

48. Moran, "What Is Revelation?," 224.

transcendental experiences, are neither completely idealistic affairs, nor are they cut off from bodily reality or historical events. Instead, objective, historical reality (i.e., the "stuff" of life) makes the transcendental experience possible, for in them one encounters "the other" through whom one becomes aware of oneself precisely as a transcendent being.[49] Finally, the person engaging in the transcendent experience, that act of revelation, engages in it as an act of freedom. Indeed, the revelatory act is the "free bestowal and free acceptance of . . . knowledge."[50]

In marrying the verb form of "revelation" with transcendental anthropology, Moran engages the Heideggerian problematic and establishes the basis for what one could call his "doctrine" of continuing revelation. Continuing revelation maintains God's word as something speaking in the present—a necessary principle for a modernizing of catechetical renewal.

The "Doctrine" of Continuing Revelation Itself

Moran regrets that theologians and theorists reduce his systematic work in *Theology of Revelation* to a slogan: continuing (or ongoing) revelation. This was not his formula of choice, or his sole aim, as if he were merely perpetuating a theory from late nineteenth-century liberal Protestant theology that relegates the Bible and embraces scientific and literary progress as a path of life.[51] Moran argues that the concept of continuing revelation does not immediately deal with content. Because he does not hold revelation as a noun—a reference to a thing revealed—but an act, Moran's thesis does not refer to God's imparting of new, liberalized doctrines or what have you. He is neither concerned with adding objective truths to the deposit of faith, nor does he intend to go beyond Christ. Instead, Moran presents continuing revelation as an answer to how it is that God presently speaks—that God continues to speak, to reveal. For Moran, the question is not *what* continuing revelation says, but *how* it occurs. He concerns himself with form, not content. Moran's continuing revelation thesis, then, is a non-doctrinal doctrine of *praxis*, so to speak, and his inquiry ultimately addresses whether or not this conviction is compatible with Catholic tradition.[52] In short, Moran initiates an understanding of revelation that allows for all Christians (and non-Christians) to participate in "a continuing revelational process" today that is possible or "takes place" within the risen

---

49. Moran, "What Is Revelation?," 224.
50. Moran, "What Is Revelation?," 221.
51. Moran, *Missed Opportunities*, loc. 2673.
52. Moran, *Missed Opportunities*, loc. 2674.

Christ's consciousness—a consciousness which began in the Incarnation and reached its climactic fullness in his Resurrection.[53]

Christ's Consciousness as the "Place" of Ongoing Revelation

Moran, in lockstep with Rahner, grounds his continuing revelation thesis in the consciousness of Christ. Following the Council, he joins in Rahner's attempt to work out a Christology that would account for Christ's consciousness and psychological development in light of Chalcedon's categories.[54] He contends that Christians too often "tend to put the humanity of Christ on God's side rather than man's,"[55] and argues that Jesus Christ's human nature must be taken seriously.[56] For Moran, this means adopting Rahner's evolutionary Christology, and identifying Christ's unique consciousness is the "place" wherein a full and definitive encounter between God and man occurs in what he calls a "redemptive revelation."[57]

The most perfect personal revelation, the most perfect union between God and man, takes place *within* the one person of Christ, in the conscious interaction of his two natures. Moran argues that in the hypostatic union, Christ's human nature is immediately present to the Word (i.e., to the divine nature). If "this union is an act of spiritual being at its highest point," then "the reality of this union cannot be entirely unconscious."[58] As spiritual being at its highest point, Christ's human nature is perfectly, consciously, constantly, and immediately present to the divine and reflecting upon itself in light of this union. As the highest spiritual being (i.e., a knower with perfect self-possession), Jesus Christ, in his human nature's consciousness, would grow in conscious awareness of his union with divinity. This is a real *becoming* aware. Here, Moran asserts:

> Christ was present to God because he was present to himself. The basic self-identity and self-presence that is the *a priori* of objective and conceptual knowledge implies that Christ knew himself in every act of objective knowing. Thus God was attained in the human understanding of Christ as the first reality

---

53. Moran, *Revelation*, 75. See also Moran, *Catechesis*, 37.
54. Moran, *Revelation*, 66.
55. Moran, *Revelation*, 65. See also Moran, *Catechesis*, 59.
56. Moran, *Revelation*, 64.
57. Moran, *Revelation*, 66.
58. Moran, *Revelation*, 68.

known and as always known insofar as a knower knows himself at least implicitly in his knowledge of any other thing.[59]

This statement conjures up Rahner's understanding of the supernatural existential. In being present to himself as a transcendent being, Christ is perfectly oriented towards and receptive of Being. His human, transcendental nature is always perfectly actualized, even as the possibility of conscious awareness grows over time. In being always already present to himself (i.e., in his human nature being always already present to his divine nature) and in reflecting back upon itself (i.e., in his human nature), Christ would have a growing, conscious awareness of God, insofar as the temporal development of his human nature—his human consciousness—would allow for it. In recognizing oneself as a spiritual being, one takes hold of one's identity, and not only in a "simple, global awareness," but in "a detailed, reflexive understanding" (i.e., "reflecting back upon itself and its relation to others").[60]

Tying together the Incarnation and the Cross, Moran argues that revelation reaches its high point in the event of the Paschal Mystery. Moran says, "Revelation reached its fullness . . . only at *the* hour when Christ burst through the gates of death by handing over the Spirit. . . . Revelation as the cognitive expression of redemption was brought to perfection in the consciousness of Christ: he beheld the glory that was his."[61] Moran continues, "The reception of Christ into glory is the never to be surpassed event in the revelational process."[62] Jesus, in his very humanity, perfectly transcends the limits of that humanity and is transformed by the glory of divinity—a perfect revelation that takes place in the human consciousness of Christ. Revelation as an experience of union with the Divine is, therefore, "closed" only in the sense that a high point is reached in the self-consciousness of Christ. However, the revelational process remains open insofar as "the resurrection was not only an event of the past," but is "the beginning of a

---

59. Moran, *Revelation*, 68. Notably, Moran cites Rahner here.

60. Moran, *Revelation*, 67. If this is the case, that is, that Christ's human ability to know "does not exclude a development of knowledge," then it is also possible, according to Moran, that Jesus would have exercised faith (Moran, *Revelation*, 69). If faith is the patient acceptance of God's will, then Jesus "lived in the sheer, naked, unqualified acceptance of what came from the Father" (Moran, *Revelation*, 71). He says, the "man Jesus was the recipient of God's revelation and fulfilled the vocation of the man of faith" (Moran, *Revelation*, 64. See also Moran, *Believing in a Revealing God*, 56). Moran contends that in the understanding of faith-revelation that Vatican II was working towards, "it is impossible for Jesus to be revealer *except* as believer, as the one who perfectly submits to the will of his father" (Moran, *Believing in a Revealing God*, 57).

61. Moran, *Revelation*, 73.

62. Moran, *Revelation*, 74.

new life and the beginning of the total revelation in the risen Christ."[63] In the resurrection, Christ is "constituted as Son of God for us" and begins his "revelatory-redemptive activity in fullness."[64] The perfect and immediate revelation in Christ's consciousness, in his transcendental experience, establishes Christ as the "final standard of human entelechy."[65] If personal revelation is still possible today, Moran argues, the key "lies in the emergence of a human consciousness that is entirely receptive to God revealing and that remains among men to continue that revelation."[66] Jesus Christ's transcendental experience, his consciously-becoming-aware-of-himself, is the unsurpassable foundation of revelation.

For Moran, following Rahner, the resurrection of the incarnate Word, who assumed the whole of the human nature, renders Christological the transcendental experience. Now every transcendent experience even today is always already a participation in Christ's conscious experience, whether one acknowledges it explicitly or not (i.e., anonymous Christianity). Moran follows Rahner in christologizing the supernatural existential. Moran says, "every man is born into a supernatural order and is oriented toward a supernatural end before he becomes consciously and reflexively aware of it."[67] This "supernatural order" is already Christological, such that now, when one does become consciously aware of his or her existence (i.e., of the supernatural existential) one is participating, in greater or lesser degrees, in that which is possible because of the breakthrough of Christ's consciousness in the Paschal Mystery. Therefore, Moran calls Christ the "concrete-universal,"[68] the categorical object who perfectly receives "supernatural" revelation.[69] Christ also makes supernatural revelation accessible for every human being, for "in the psyche of the risen Lord revelation was received (or taken part in receptively) in fullness not only for himself but for all his brothers."[70] Because God assumes a human nature in Jesus Christ, He forever changes humanity's relation to God. Now, the individual's revelatory experience,

63. Moran, *Revelation*, 74.
64. Moran, *Revelation*, 75.
65. Moran, *Revelation*, 76.
66. Moran, *Revelation*, 56.
67. Moran, *Revelation*, 148. See also Moran, "What Is Revelation?," 223–24.
68. Moran, *Revelation*, 76.
69. Moran distinguishes between "natural" and "supernatural" revelation, though he holds the distinction poses a problem and does not resolve their relationship. Moran is concerned about sharply separating the two orders so as to avoid an extrinsicism with regard to revelation that results in a two-story structure of grace building on nature. See Moran, *Catechesis*, 16, 132.
70. Moran, *Revelation*, 75. Cf. Moran, "What Is Revelation?," 228–31.

which is possible through the Spirit "who penetrates human existence at its highest point" (i.e., Christ, the "concrete-universal"), is always already Christological because the Christ-event radically alters "'the *a priori* "mental horizon" which we are conscious of in being conscious of ourselves.'"[71] Thus, Moran grounds an ongoing Christian revelation in the "conscious human experience of Jesus Christ."[72] Hence, Moran, following Rahner, attempts to maintain the unique role of Christ for salvation while avoiding the need for exclusive and explicit faith in Jesus Christ.

Moran's Catechetical Cliff-fall: Relegating the "Organs of Transmission"

Moran's catechetical work essentially brings Rahner's blueprint for the catechetical roof to life. However, following Rahner basically means constructing the roof on the ground and precariously close to the edge of the precipice. The immanent peril of freefall occurs as Moran removes the "guardrails" of Sacred Scripture, tradition, and the magisterium when it comes to the experience of continuing revelation. In promoting some sort of pure, unencumbered transcendental experience as such, Moran relegates any likeness of an onto-theological interpretive grid. Consequently, Moran renders every transcendent experience, even the most secular or seemingly banal, as an implicit experience of revelation capable "of being . . . revelatory instrument[s] of God."[73] Now, unhindered, every experience at least has the implicit capacity of being an instrument of God's revelation, that is, of bringing the transcendent being into contact with the supernatural existential which has been categorically "christologized." In this way, the "doctrine" of continuing revelation sets the stage for a catechetical cliff-fall. By removing constructs purportedly marked by doctrinal extrinsicism, namely Scripture, tradition, and the magisterium, Moran leads individuals to the edge for an unencumbered and subjective leap into the abyss of self-consciousness with the assurance they are actually encountering God. This confuses whether the "revealer" is God, others, or self, and ultimately leaves the transcendental subject as the authority for making such a determination.

In effect, Moran's ongoing revelation, coupled with the relegation of the "organs of transmission," relativizes revelation. Moran argues that revelation as it occurs in transcendental experience is "ecumenical," for "a God who has involved himself in a partnership with all men is revealed wherever

---

71. Moran, *Revelation*, 150. Here, Moran quotes Rahner directly.

72. Moran, *Revelation*, 70.

73. Moran, *Catechesis*, 14; see also 134.

there are such men." Therefore, the church should "give up the language of 'revealed truths' and 'Christian revelation,'" for Christianity exists "within the context of a world history where Christians must search for the truth with everyone else."[74] Pedraza points this out that this is Moran's "proclamation of a catechetical death knell."[75] As Moran's thought progresses, he denounces the "objective norms" of Scripture and doctrine and magisterium, as an imposition on human freedom. Pedraza continues, noting that by 1972, Moran claims that with revelation having as "its core an interpersonal relationship, all truth is therefore *relative*."[76] He then quotes Moran, "Being relative or being related to others becomes the stabilizing and guiding factor for each statement of truth. The whole matrix of interrelationships becomes the starting point for understanding."[77] An imposition of "objective norms" is incompatible with human autonomy, for it manifests an arrangement "whereby someone else is in control and has the answers before the questions are asked."[78] With this, Pedraza concludes:

> Ultimately, then, the scholarship of Gabriel Moran came to give greater weight to present experience over the past, human freedom over absolute truth, and universality over particularity. He thus exploded the boundaries of ecclesial ministry by arguing for its very nonexistence. . . . I believe it is fair to say that the seeds of catechetical discontent were sown in his earlier writings. In them, though Moran had rightly recognized the place of scripture and doctrine in the revelatory process, he nevertheless showed a tendency to prefer the present to the exclusion of the past, embracing an understanding of revelation that, once taken to an extreme, failed to adequately reconcile the particularity of the church with the universality of God's speaking and acting. Catechetically, this likewise opened the door to an inadequate reconciliation of scripture and church teaching—as objective manifestations of revelation—with the subjectivity of human experience.[79]

Rahnerian seeds apparent in *Theology of Revelation* and in *Catechesis of Revelation* come to full flowering as Moran's thought becomes more relativistic

---

74. Moran, *Design for Religion*, 40–41. This is quoted in Pedraza, *Catechesis for the New Evangelization*, 120.
75. Pedraza, *Catechesis for the New Evangelization*, 120.
76. Pedraza, *Catechesis for the New Evangelization*, 121.
77. Moran, *The Present Revelation*, 9.
78. Moran, *The Present Revelation*, 52.
79. Pedraza, *Catechesis for the New Evangelization*, 122.

and more radical, already anticipating that next "moment" (i.e., a postmodern one) of the anthropological phase.[80]

In Moran's attempt to overcome faith-as-belief-in-propositions, catechesis jettisons its previous responsibility of handing on the "contents" of the faith.[81] Catechesis, now "concerned with the understanding of God's revelation now taking place in the student's life,"[82] cultivates present experiences of self-transcendence and aids in their interpretation. Moran claims that starting with "real people" and "real experience" opens up the possibility of wider understanding of revelation, while an imposed set of truths from the outside as a *prior datum* are self-interpretive and restrictive when it comes to one's interaction with his or her personal history. Therefore, Moran fundamentally reconfigures catechesis. Rather than handing on "contents" of faith, it aims at freeing the student from them. Any doctrinal *a priori* is gone. This enables the student to enter unfettered into an unthematic, transcendent, revelatory experience within (or apart from) the community of the Church.

Moran goes so far as to discourage any distinctively Christian "content" as a starting point for catechesis, and instead puts personal history in its place. Indeed, "just as the Jews of old discovered God in their historical experience, the Christian student of today can discover God only through the experience of his own situation of space, time, and community.... God enters the history of each man and ... each man must find God in this present personal history if he is ever to find God."[83] In order for an immediate

---

80. Pedraza notes the tie between Moran and Rahner, here, by citing an article by Guy Mansini. Mansini observes that this sort of relativizing quality appears in the revised edition of Rahner's *Hearers of the Word*, where in approved edits of J. B. Metz, Rahner "had taken the step, seemingly forbidden by the first edition of deducing the content of revelation from the idea of man's supernaturally elevated subjectivity" ("Experiential Expressivism," 134. See Pedraza, *Catechesis for the New Evangelization*, 121n203).

81. See Kevane, *Catechesis in Augustine*, 19–22; Kevane, "Toward Research in Fundamental Catechetics," 357–58.

82. Moran, *Catechesis*, 91. Dulles highlights Moran's antagonism towards a conception of catechesis that, in addition to disregarding the "needs and capacities of the student," while "overburdening him with exegetical and doctrinal materials," demands "a fullness of commitment ... his youth cannot ... sustain" (Dulles, *Revelation Theology*, 168). Moran does not believe a youth is capable of a total commitment, making any sort of catechetical endeavor that takes conversion up as its mission "illusory and dangerous" (Moran, *Catechesis*, 128). Msgr. Eugene Kevane argues against Moran's position. See Kevane, *Catechesis in Augustine*, 19–22, 34–37.

83. Moran, *Catechesis*, 45–46. See Whittle's "Some Theological Reservations," 200–203, which calls for a Rahnerian approach to Christian education according to Rahner's anthropological turn. Reading Moran in light of Whittle makes clear the connection between Rahner's theory and Moran's.

revelation to take place, one must "face his own historical situation and his own community," for one's acceptance of his "own personal history is not only the presupposition of revelation, it is in some way the revelation itself."[84] Attentiveness to history, and personal history in particular, is *the* way to gain immediate access to God's revelation and to live, presently, in salvation history.[85] The human being is active in constructing reality, in shaping time and space, in writing history. With this, Moran's theology of revelation and its corresponding catechetical approach collapses the content of catechesis into the student's own history, and it becomes unclear as to exactly who is being revealed. God? Self?

Only after freeing the concept of revelation from a propositional and extrinsic understanding, and redefining catechesis according to transcendental experience, does Moran consider the role of the Church's preaching, teaching, and interpretation of Scripture. While man stands open to God as a hearer of the Word and God constantly whispers to man in the transcendental experience, it is the case that man may struggle to grasp the meaning of this experience. Moran notes, "If God were to give no further help to man's understanding, revelation might remain on an inchoate and unexplicated level."[86] Therefore, "God completes the revelation process by speaking words of human love, . . . [drawing] forth from the pre-reflexive, entitative, and intentional union a wealth of meaning."[87] The Church's preaching, teaching, and interpretation of Scripture thus manifests its value only after the transcendental experience. It must be relegated to such a position to prevent the transcendental being from being alienated from his or her own transcendental experiences by an onto-theological grid. Dogmatic theology, then, secondarily aids in bringing the unreflexive transcendental experience into reflexive consciousness. It completes the conscious experience of faith, renders explicit what has implicitly taken place, and interprets what is presently unintelligible. Tradition, and specifically Scripture, "bring to conscious and reflexive awareness the meaning of revelation. . . . Scripture . . . becomes the interpretive norm for man's religious experience."[88] Moran's catechetical approach calls for a student to "grasp the mystery 'from the inside out,'" that is, from the interpersonal union of the immediate revelatory act rather than from extrinsic propositions. When this happens, "there are no inherent

---

84. Moran, *Catechesis*, 49.
85. Moran, *Catechesis*, 90.
86. Moran, *Revelation*, 150.
87. Moran, *Revelation*, 150–51.
88. Moran, *Revelation*, 151. See also Moran, *Design for Religion*, 148–51; Baumert, "Instruments of Change," 65.

limits to . . . his doctrinal understanding. . . . No *a priori* and arbitrary limit [should] be imposed upon doctrinal inquiry."[89] This position pushes away from the maintenance of "a system of abstractly defined truths," and instead adopts a position that understands and teaches doctrine insofar as it springs "from human life."[90] Rather than providing an entry into the divine Mystery, the Church's "organs of transmission" are only subsequently necessary when revelation remains consciously inchoate.

Moran's system radically alters the role of the catechists. By 1972, Moran goes so far as to note that insofar as catechists have been recast as religious educators, they are "underminers" who undermine "the faith of their students" and destroy "Catholic tradition." They are to do this "because the educational process itself has that effect upon faith and tradition." He had embraced an educational theory saturated in critical theory that calls into question "whether the words orthodoxy and education are at all compatible."[91] The religious educators (formerly known as catechists) are not to view themselves as dispensers of knowledge, but as both cultivators and "humble interpreters of experience."[92] Moran's position actually cuts through the perceived "inequality" existing between teacher (who has more knowledge, experience, and training) and the student (who has less knowledge, experience, and training) and establishes between them "a more fundamental equality . . . before the bar of human experience."[93] This means the roles are interchangeable. In relation to the "student," the catechist might be "teacher" in one moment, and him or herself the "student" in the next as the one who was "student" becomes "teacher" (i.e., one who might lead the catechist into a religious experience by considering his own personal history and who might help the catechist interpret that experience). This shift challenges the Church's traditional understandings of catechesis and catechist, indeed her entire "traditional" formation structure, and calls on the Church to function as "a community of people dedicated to searching for the divine, reflecting on the implications of the

---

89. Moran, *Catechesis*, 108. Moran admits this sort of "tradition-less" starting point will "undoubtedly lead to problems which are not immediately resolvable," so he encourages teachers to not try to settle all doctrinal and moral questions immediately. He says, "few things could be more detrimental to the appreciation of Christian revelation than facile answers and superficial solutions for every question raised" (109).

90. Moran, *Catechesis*, 114.

91. Moran, *Design for Religion*, 14–15.

92. Moran, *Design for Religion*, 147–48. See also Moran, *Both Sides*, 191; Pedraza, *Catechesis for the New Evangelization*, 119–20.

93. Moran, *Design for Religion*, 147.

quest, and living by the consequences of the reflection."[94] Characteristic of his thrust from noun to verb, Moran emphasizes "showing how" over "knowing how," praxis over content, *ethos* over *logos*.[95] Hence, Moran concludes, "For the catechist, this means recognizing that his is not the divine task of saving children, but rather the human task of freeing men for life in the Spirit by awakening intelligence and freedom."[96]

In his attempt at recovering the dynamism of revelation and reworking catechetics, Moran takes Rahner's transcendental anthropology as his "given," and moves quickly from fundamental theology to catechetical praxis in ongoing revelation and the necessary relegation of the traditional "organs of transmission" for catechesis. The impact on the content and mission of catechesis is immediate.[97] Moran knows this is a significant proposal because religious education is so deeply integrated into every aspect of Church life. Consequently, "changing religious education in the church is equivalent to changing the church."[98] As it turns out, he was right. Moran's work could be likened to that of a magician. He carries out a vanishing act for catechesis. Moran himself describes this as a "disappearance phenomenon," where "as religion is made more 'relevant' it seems to disappear into other fields. What is taught in religion class today may be hardly distinguishable from what transpires in literature or social science class. There is something very peculiar about a field which seems to disappear as it improves."[99] This, of course, assumes that the field was actually improving and not simply making its way over the cliff and into oblivion.

---

94. Moran, *Design for Religion*, 147.

95. See Moran, *Showing How*, 34.

96. Moran, *Catechesis*, 72–73.

97. Moran disputes the use of the word "catechesis," which he sees as an import from Europe that never took root in America. Catechesis remained a "parish-school-CCD project," that universities wanted nothing to do with. Then, in the 1960s, catechetics virtually disappeared with the best theological aspects it contained being absorbed back into theology, and whatever was good educationally was assimilated into general education. The whole of the catechetical movement seems to have collapsed under its own weight (see Moran, "Catechetics in Context," 294–95). In the void, Moran proposes the term "religious education," a "bland and general term [that] could conceivably be saved from its ecclesiocentric bias" (Moran, "Catechetics in Context," 296). Moran argues for religious education to be a genuine field of study, and not simply "a cover for indoctrination" (Moran, "Catechetics in Context," 296).

98. Moran, *Design for Religion*, 145–46.

99. Moran, *Design for Religion*, 15.

Shingles on the Roof: The Practical Outworking of Moran's Thesis in Groome's *Shared Christian Praxis*

Thomas Groome codifies Moran's theories in a methodology known as *Shared Christian Praxis*. The fruit of his life's work, *Shared Christian Praxis* dominated the religious education landscape in the United States during 1980s and 1990s.[100] Its prevalence warrants a far more substantial treatment than what is possible here. Nevertheless, even a cursory glance renders visible the basic contours of Groome's thought.

Groome describes his approach to a Christian religious education as "a participative and dialogical pedagogy in which people reflect critically on their own historical agency in time and place and on their sociocultural reality, have access together to Christian Story/Vision, and personally appropriate it in community with the creative intent of renewed praxis in Christian faith toward God's reign for all creation."[101] In shorthand, Groome refers to this correlation method as one moving "from life to Faith to life,"[102] and describes it as follows:

> In brief, it encourages a teaching-learning community of active participation, conversation and presentation, in which people share their reflections upon their own lives in the world around a generative theme of life or of life in faith, are given persuasive and meaningful access to the truths and spiritual wisdom of

---

100. Groome describes this work briefly in "From Life to Faith to Life," 20.

101. Groome, *Sharing*, 135. Groome prefers to describe his entire enterprise as Christian Religious Education as opposed to "catechesis," though he does not intend to disregard the value of catechesis. Catechesis refers to the "activity of reechoing or retelling the story of Christian faith that has been handed down," and is thus to be situated within the "broader enterprise of CRE" (Groome, *CRE*, 27). This opens the door for other fields (e.g., educational science) to inform religious education. CRE bears several marks for Groome. First, it is "religious" insofar as it is "transcendent." Second, the fact that it is Christian gives it a particularity. And, finally, because it is an education with a social dimension, it is, according to Groome's conception, necessarily political. For more on Groome's understanding of the place and importance of catechesis, see Groome's "The Purposes of Christian Catechesis," 3–27.

102. See Groome, "From Life to Faith to Life," 17. Groome found teaching *about* faith as an ineffective starting point. He opts to begin with the life-experience of people. He describes his influencers in the following way: "[Shared Christian Praxis] proposed a pedagogy and andragogy for CRE that begins with the generative themes of people's own life-situated praxis (Freire), invites participants to reflect critically upon them in communities of conversation and with "communicative competence" (Habermas), to then encounter the liberating and justice-bearing potential of Christian Story and Vision for those themes (Gutiérrez), in order to return to life again with deepened commitment to lived Christian faith" (17). See also Groome, "Religious Education and Practical Theology."

Christian Story and Vision (or of whatever tradition is under study) around the theme, are encouraged to integrate this wisdom into their lives and to make decisions, cognitive, affective or behavioral, in its light.[103]

In Groome's method, people, gathered in community, reflect upon their experience and personally relate the Christian story to that experience. In becoming more aware of God's reign in their lives as individuals, and in the life of their community, they both contribute to and are impelled to take further steps in fostering the reign of God. It basically allows for the becoming aware of and possibility of a Christian interpretation for one's transcendent experiences through a transcendental process. Quezada describes it as a "model of a self-reflection cycle and a methodology that is designed for the preparation of learning experiences or events.... [It] includes a dialectical intersection of narrative and action that is derived from the reflection."[104] One's personal narrative and action are brought into dialogue with aspects of faith, which can alter one's story, one's life.

The name, *Shared Christian Praxis*, expounds the essence of the method. Beginning in reverse word-order, *praxis* refers to "the consciousness and agency that arise from and are expressed in any and every aspect of people's 'being' as agent-subjects-in-relationship, whether realized in actions that are personal, interpersonal, sociopolitical, or cosmic."[105] Groome grounds praxis in an "epistemic ontology" which reflects "an 'ontological turn' to engage all the dimensions and dynamics of human 'being' and... turns participants to the consciousness that arises from their whole 'being' as agent-subjects located and related in place and time."[106] Beaudoin points out that for Groome, "how we *know* is rooted in *who* we are temporally." This "relativity is relative," because of Groome's "transcendental mode of his approach to the historical character of the subject, evident in his emphasis on

---

103. Groome, "From Life to Faith to Life," 19. Interestingly, the *Fundamental Text* of the German Synodal Way adopts such a position when it comes to evangelization and catechesis. The document argues that "the 'outside' of faith, i.e., insights, experiences and developments of time, is not only the context and addressee of the Church's proclamation. It is itself the resonant space of the Gospel and therefore its own irreplaceable and indispensable complex of theologically relevant loci by means of which the Church explores the Gospel: 'Let me study you, your thinking and speaking, your questioning and being, so that by it, I may learn anew the message I have to deliver to you'" (German Synodal Way, *Fundamental Text*, 13).

104. Quezada, "Global Student Teacher Transformation Experiences," 422.

105. Groome, *Sharing*, 136. For a philosophical overview of *praxis*, see Groome, *CRE*, 152–77.

106. Groome, *Sharing*, 85.

'historicity,' the transcendentally derived time-bound condition of being."[107] Additionally, Gerkin points out that a praxis approach takes seriously the story of the person's life. He says, "praxis . . . always involves an essential narrative structure. . . . By means of stories of the self and the world around us we hold together events, persons, and experiences that would otherwise be fragmented. To be a person is therefore to live in a story."[108] Furthermore, Groome claims that "present praxis" has three aspects: active, reflective, and creative. The active aspect involves all mental and volitional activities and exercises through which one realizes that one is an agent-subject in space and time—in the present moment. Next, praxis is reflective in that it encourages reflection on past events, allowing one to see the consequences of the past and opportunities for the future. Finally, the creative aspect permeates the active and reflective aspects, producing and doing, engaging the personal and social imagination, while inspiring ongoing praxis.[109] In other words, a praxis-oriented approach is one that encourages and embraces the transcendental experience as the "place" where revelation occurs, and, in a reflexive act, one takes further possession of oneself and gains insight into how one might act in order to advance the reign of God.

Continuing with the title of Groome's method, *Christian* refers to a "Christian Story and Vision that emerges from the faith of the Christian community in our time and over its history," a Story and Vision that "should not be idealized as monolithic."[110] "Story" includes the Church's Scripture and tradition, but it does not exclude other sources. Groome notes that Christian tradition contains a plurality of stories and a myriad of expressions that make up "the Christian story."[111] "Vision" is ultimately the reign of God for the whole of creation, though more immediately it refers to all the story means and calls for in a person's life.[112]

Finally, *Shared*, as has been intimated, points to "this approach as one of mutual partnership, active participation, and dialogue with oneself, with others, with God, and with Story/Vision of Christian faith."[113] The concept of "shared" refers to two constitutive elements of Groome's transcendental process. First, "shared" refers to the "communal dynamics" present within a "teaching/learning event," dynamics marked by a partnership between teacher/learner, rather than a transactional or one-way model that sees teacher as deliverer and student as receiver. Instead, the teacher is to move

---

107. Beaudoin, "The Theological Anthropology of Thomas Groome," 130.
108. Gerkin, *The Living Human Document*, 52.
109. Groome, *Sharing*, 137–38. See also Clement, "Thomas Groome," 6–7.
110. Groome, *Sharing*, 138.
111. See Groome, *Sharing*, 138–42.
112. Groome, *Sharing*, 139.
113. Groome, *Sharing*, 142.

away from being the "answer person" or "controller of knowledge" and into a position of "'being with participants."[114] These "communal dynamics" also demand active participation, according to the participation style of each individual, and a commitment to dialogue with every dialogical entity involved (self, God, others). Second, "shared" refers to the dialogical or dialectical exchange between one's present praxis and Christian Story/Vision. As one comes to consciously grasp through reflexive activity that which may have previously been unconsciously present in the transcendental experience, of being brought into contact with the supernatural existential, one comes into contact with community's Story/Vision "to encourage appropriation and decision for lived Christian faith."[115] Hence the movement from life to Faith and back to life.

In concrete steps, this approach advances according to five movements.[116] The first movement involves a focusing activity. This aims "to turn people to their present praxis, to some aspect of their lives in the world with shared focus."[117] This largely centers on a symbol that participants "look through . . . to their own situation in life,"[118] with a focus on the "participants' *personal* consciousness of present praxis."[119] The activity turns one's attention to the content and context of his or her own life, the mental horizon from which one "transcends." Mimicking Moran, Groome's *Shared Christian Praxis* begins and ends with the human agent, while relegating the "organs of transmission." Life, in all its dimensions, becomes the primary content of revelation. Through a dialectical process, the participant becomes reflexively aware of his or her "present *praxis*" (i.e., transcendental existence). Second, Groome's method calls for critical reflection on present action, which encourages "participants in critical consciousness and appropriation of present praxis, to promote a dialectic among them and their location in place and time. Critical and historical consciousness emerges as participants un-cover and dis-cover the personal/social sources of and reasons for present praxis and discern its consequences."[120] This is an activity of reflexive consciousness to make thematic the unthematic transcendental experience. Here, human beings, "through reflection on their own present

---

114. Groome, *Sharing*, 143.

115. Groome, *Sharing*, 143.

116. For the purposes of the present study, only Groome's steps in *Sharing* will be considered here, though an earlier form of Shared Christian Praxis appears in Groome, *CRE*, 184–232. *Sharing* is his most systematic and complete treatise on the method that had crystalized over several decades.

117. Groome, *Sharing*, 155–56.

118. Groome, *Sharing*, 156.

119. Groome, *Sharing*, 188.

120. Groome, *Sharing*, 188.

praxis in the world . . . can encounter, recognize, and appropriate God's ongoing self-disclosure."[121] Groome says:

> For existential subjects, God's self-revelation always originates, albeit in an unthematic way, in the depths of human existence, precisely because of our God-gifted "supernatural existential"—it gives us the capacity to encounter and recognize God's self-communication. Thus, every human "experience" can have a transcendental dimension in that it reflects "an unthematic and anonymous, as it were, knowledge of God." At first this might look like a natural knowledge of God, but it is always already more than natural—it is prompted by God's grace, working within.[122]

Groome simply reflects Rahner's argument that all faith "knowing" begins from human "being," with its characteristic "existentials" of self-presence, freedom, and self-transcendence, which permeate what Rahner calls the "supernatural existential" (the "ground and horizon of human existence").[123] Human experience, transcendental experience, unthematic and anonymous as it might be, reveals God.

The third step of *Shared Christian Praxis* makes accessible Christian Story and Vision.[124] This stage brings "to participants a Story/Vision of their faith community as it pertains to the focused theme. . . . As participants have critically interpreted the 'text' and context of their lives, so the educator now brings critical hermeneutics to the texts and contexts of Christian Story/Vision, to make it accessible."[125] The elements of Christian story that pertain to the theme in the focusing activity (Step #1) are presented in an attempt to bring Christian Story/Vision into dialogue with this experience to interpret the transcendental experience. Story/Vision is not necessarily *the* tradition or doctrinal teaching of the Church. Instead, it is that which the leader curates to fit the needs of the group. Christian Story/Vision provides a "thematic" expression of revelation, a "symbolic mediation of God's revelation of Godself,"[126] and one that rejects the same neo-scholastic understanding of revelation highlighted by Moran.[127] Story and Vision are "localized," and not relegated to one mode of expression. They are to be interpreted according to a proper critical hermeneutic as determined and executed by

---

121. Groome, *Sharing*, 162.
122. Groome, *Sharing*, 162.
123. Groome, *Sharing*, 162.
124. Note the omission of the article "the" before "Christian" and the implication that there is not one Christian story, but openness to many Christian stories as developed in various locales.
125. Groome, *Sharing*, 215.
126. Groome, *Sharing*, 218.
127. See Groome, *Sharing*, 219.

the educator and presented to the participants in a way that is accessible. The content and whole of Scripture and tradition (i.e., the analogy of faith), are not considered, but only those parts of Story/Vision that pertain to the present *praxis* as determined by the leader.

From here, participants "make their own" Story/Vision and integrate it into their own experience. Engaging in dialectical hermeneutics, participants appropriate Story/Vision, enabling them "to critically appropriate the faith community's Story/Vision to their own lives and contexts. By 'appropriation' I mean that participants integrate Christian Story/Vision by personal agency into their own identity and understanding."[128] The Story and Vision aim to offer a Christian interpretive voice as a dialogue partner to the critical reflection of Step #2. Clement notes that "Christian Story/Vision has three aspects: it is 'historical and practical'; the 'belonging and ownership' is with the people who share the story; and it is 'engaging and dialogical.'"[129] In short, the one leading the time of sharing and employing the method, as a member of the group, exercises significant influence here. The group exercises its own custody over the Story and Vision, which are to be grounded in the historical-critical method and express a certain pragmatism. They are to cultivate dialogue within the recipient himself or herself, between the recipient and God, and between members of the group. Groome is careful to note that the Story/Vision are to make accessible the "'classic' revelation symbolically mediated through the scriptures and traditions of the Christian community," because Shared Christian Praxis does not limit revelation to the experiential realm in present praxis.[130] However, any "propositional truth claims that are constitutive of [Christianity's] Story/Vision," ought not be taught "as hardened facts from outside to be blindly accepted, but as instances of 'trustworthy guidance' of God's revelation for the present."[131] As with Moran, the continuing revelation of "present praxis" maintains primacy, with doctrine or the Church's tradition relegated to a secondary role of offering "guidance." Beaudoin describes Groome's approach as a theology of teaching that "encourages learning through personal appropriation, where the 'subject' of the teaching is the learner's existential experience, to which the religious tradition speaks in a dialogue involving learners interpreting the tradition, construed very broadly, for their situation, and their situation through the tradition."[132] Who one is, or who one understands himself or herself to be determines, in large part, who one understands, or determines God to be. In this conception, the initiative lies in the life of the person.

128. Groome, *Sharing*, 250.
129. Clement, "Thomas Groome," 7.
130. Groome, *Sharing*, 161.
131. Groome, *Sharing*, 220.
132. Beaudoin, "The Theological Anthropology of Thomas Groome," 127.

Finally, aligned with Groome's emphasis on the "reign of God" and faith intervening "in people's lives as a profoundly political activity,"[133] Shared Christian Praxis aims to produce action; it aims at producing "Christian actors."[134] The last step calls for a decision or response for lived faith. Groome says, "Movement 5 encourages participants to a decision for knowing, desiring, and doing with others what is humanizing and life-giving for all."[135] Here, Christian Story/Vision is applied to life in a practical sense. Therefore, one sees in Shared Christian Praxis the application of Groome's understanding of religious education, namely that it is religious and transcendental,[136] educational, and, according to Groome's understanding of education, one that is essentially political and focused on action.[137]

The Catechist in Groome

Shifting focus slightly to the person of the catechist, Groome's vision mirrors Moran's. Admitting an "identity crisis" in the aftermath of the collapse of neo-scholastic catechesis, Groome attempts to rebuild the catechist's identity, first by universalizing the educational responsibility of members of the Church. In a recent paper, Groome calls for a "total catechetical education." Here, he not only means "total" in the sense that this education should be cognitive, behavioral, and affective, but that virtually everyone and everything can carry out this Christian education.[138] This totalizing, horizontalizing, and open-ended nature of understanding catechesis calls into question what specifically makes a catechist a catechist. What is distinctive about this particular call? Is anyone and everyone a teacher? In *Christian Religious Education*, he says the religious educator is to "represent" Jesus Christ in an "incarnational" ministry of the Word. The task of the teacher is to help people "incarnate the Word in their everyday existence" by staying with the person through the slow process of inculcating a new way of life.[139] Witnesses or representatives, to use Groome's preferred word, "act temporarily for [others] when they cannot act for themselves."[140] In Christianity, this means every Christian represents Christ for the other:

---

133. See Groome, *Sharing*, 13–25; Groome, *CRE*, 63.
134. Groome, *Sharing*, 267.
135. Groome, *Sharing*, 267.
136. Groome, *Sharing*, 11–12. See also Groome, *CRE*, 22.
137. Groome, *Sharing*, 12–24. See also Groome, *CRE*, 25–26.
138. See Groome, "Handing on the Faith," 178–92.
139. Groome, *CRE*, 266.
140. Groome, *CRE*, 267.

The people with whom we work are themselves Christ's representatives to us and Christ's representatives to each other. In this sense, all the participants in an event of Christian religious education participate in an act of ministry. The teacher is distinguished as the leader in creating the context.... But in that context the participants minister to each other, teacher to students, students to teacher, and students to students.[141]

The work of representation for the religious educator means conserving and sharing the Story, proposing the liberating, future-oriented dimension of the ministry as Vision, and to celebrate life by "being with" in present solidarity.[142] The educator leads one into a critical exploration of present praxis by representing Christ in sharing the Story, proposing the Vision, and in being-with the other.

The Removal of the Guardrails

While Moran and Groome do not build a roof for the edifice of catechetical renewal that is exclusively Rahnerian, it is demonstrative of Rahner's fundamental theology on the whole. With the Council's shift from the originally proposed schema on revelation, "The Sources of Divine Revelation," to the promulgated document "On Divine Revelation," Moran believes a shift takes place in the Church's teaching on this subject where the "means of revelation, the organs of transmission, the places where revelation is to be sought ... must be considered secondary."[143] It is easy to overlook this point, which appears towards the beginning of Moran's seminal work, *Theology of Revelation*. This is not simply Moran's description of a postconciliar occurrence; it explains the primary thrust of his catechetical project and its eventual outcome—a creeping separation between revelation and doctrine, along with the slow evaporation of a distinctively Christian revelation.[144]

---

141. Groome, *CRE*, 268. There is a certain resemblance, here, to critical theory. Petroc Willey describes the Frankfurt School's "critical theory" as that which sees "transmission" as "overthrowing a mutuality." Catechesis is problematic in such a view, because "it places the catechist in the position of 'giver' and the learner in the place of a 'receiver,' of one who is taught.... Critical theory interprets 'being taught' as a problem because of an implied superiority of the position of the teacher, the giver. This general concern about a transmission model is intensified in so far as there is also any attempt to take up a position on behalf of an 'authority' which one represents." As a result, critical theorists "play down the importance of any systematic transmission of the faith" (Willey, "Catechetical Thinking," 125–30).

142. Groome, *CRE*, 269–74.

143. Moran, *Revelation*, 18. See also Moran, "What Is Revelation?," 217–18.

144. See Moran, "A Verb, Not a Noun," 15; Moran, *Both Sides*, 222–24.

In what could be called his "doctrine" of continuing revelation, Moran sets to work in building Rahner's design right on the edge of the cliff. Moran's "doctrine" establishes within Christianity the possibility of God's revealing today in light of Rahner's understanding of a "christologized" supernatural existential. Moran and other "vulgarized Rahnerians" (e.g., Groome) take, as O'Shea puts it, Rahner's thesis as an "endorsement of the principle of *ongoing revelation*." In doing so, they seriously risk diminishing "the unique role of Christ." To allow for continuing revelation according to a transcendental anthropology, Moran must remove any sort of doctrinal guardrail which could function as an onto-theological barrier for the bare-naked religious experience. Regarding Rahner on this point, Cooper argues that he "seems to relegate [the sacraments—though by extension, tradition, Scripture, and so forth could be added here] to a secondary role, in favor of a more primordial existential encounter with God," where conversion can be accomplished "by means of the raw materials necessary for daily social existence."[145] If, for Cooper, this *seems* to be the case for Rahner, it simply *becomes* the case for those who follow Rahner's blueprint for catechetical renewal. Those who follow Rahner see the "organs of transmission" as an interpretive and optional "extra," necessary only should one's transcendent experience remain inchoate.

One could, perhaps, go further and say that, if we have followed the main thrust of a thesis drawn from the work of Moran and Groome, the Church's doctrine can even prohibit the revelatory activity of God—or the capacity of the transcendent experience to reach its heights. Here, doctrine acts as a ceiling that prevents the human spirit from soaring to the transcendental heights. This is not to say that God cannot reveal himself outside of the "official" structures of the Church. However, if Moran and Groome's position is correct, if every transcendent experience is implicitly Christian due to the "christologized" supernatural existential, then the need for explicit faith in Jesus Christ fades. Revelation is relativized. The objective role of the Church's mission diminishes. Now the individual decides whether his or her experience is Christian—or if it makes much of a difference at all. Once this happens, evangelization must then be redefined, and approached in terms of common transcendental experiences that are always already Christian. The contents of the faith can only be secondary, and the "organs of transmission" are not viewed as steady guides to ensure that one is encountering God, precisely because they are too Christian. Thus, the project risks dismantling or disfiguring catechetics altogether, and perhaps does so.

---

145. Cooper, *Naturally Human*, 140.

CHAPTER THREE

Recontextualizing Rahner: A Postmodern Project

Following Moran and Groome's distinctly "modern moment" within the Anthropological Phase, Hofinger's allegorical house of catechetical renewal remains roofless. As Hofinger notes, movements in the early-to-mid twentieth century built a new edifice. Following Vatican II, Moran, Groome & Co. took up a blueprint for renewal drawn from Rahner's systematic theology and used it to construct the canopy. They parted ways with Neo-scholasticism in order to correlate modern philosophical and cultural trends with theology, thus breathing new life into old bones. As a result, they "grounded" the catechetical roof in the subject and they do so on a theological cliff edge. When Moran proposes his "doctrine" of continuing revelation and relegates "organs of transmission" within catechetics, he essentially removes the guardrails, relativizing revelation and inviting those in pastoral and educational settings to freefall into the transcendental abyss.

Before his death in 1984, Hofinger broaches the question of how one could affix the horizontalized roof to the house, reattaching it to the tradition. By this point in time, the modern project was in swift decline, with postmodernity filling the vacuum. As will become clear, theologies springing up amid the postmodern condition end up perpetuating the Anthropological Phase of catechetical renewal. Rather than providing a suitable answer to Hofinger's inquiry, the "postmodern moment" within the Anthropological Phase radically deconstructs the roof—and perhaps the house too.

Postmodernity rises from modernity's ashes. According to its stakeholders, it ought not be referred to as an "-ism," for it is not an ideology but a condition. The postmodern condition can best be "understood as radicalized modernity."[1] This describes a continuation of the modernization project that unfolds, now, unimpeded by modern ideological attempts to contain

1. Boeve, *Interrupting Tradition*, 52.

the whole movement under one ideology. Today, it lurches forward in its postmodern form toward the pluralization of the world. For those in Catholic circles concerned with continuing to correlate theology and context, the postmodern condition signals a crisis for modern correlation strategies, while also presenting a new opportunity. Correlation must shift course if it is to be at all effective in relating theology and context. In the postmodern environment, the dialogue is not conducted between two partners—theology and secularism—as conceived by modern correlation theology. Instead, today's plural landscape exhibits a host of detraditionalized and particularized positions, with no single position supposedly standing above the rest. Each position exists equally on the postmodern playing field as "just another position." There is no bird's eye view, no singular way of organizing the whole. Therefore, postmodern theologians like Boeve and Pollefeyt argue for a recontextualization of modern correlation strategies to effectively relate theology to the postmodern context, and vice versa.

The work of Boeve and Pollefeyt offers a critical entry-point into the intersection of postmodern thinking with theology and catechetical renewal. In the space of a few chapters, one cannot attempt to summarize the whole of their thought. Nevertheless, even a cursory glance provides the necessary insight to gain a sense of their approach. Again, we will see that fundamental theology radically alters the shape and meaning of evangelization and catechesis. We will also see Leuven's recontextualization project as one which is Rahnerian at its core. This is not to say Boeve's work adopts Rahnerian theological underpinnings as cleanly as the "vulgarized Rahnerianism" of Moran and Groome. However, Boeve does share in Rahner's basic motivation, the spirit of his theological project, namely, the attempt to correlate Catholicism and context. In recontextualizing theology with postmodernity, Boeve himself dismantles the now passé modern projects of Rahner and the first generation of cliff-jumpers his theology inspires. Boeve replaces Rahner's transcendental given with the theological category of interruption, accounting for postmodern critical consciousness. Eventually, Boeve and Pollefeyt deconstruct the traditional understanding of evangelization altogether, with postmodern theology serving to advance the postmodern project of saving the *differend*—i.e., any position silenced or otherwise threatened by hegemonic metanarratives—and promoting a Christian "open narrative" inspired by Christ, *le différend incarné*.

This chapter proceeds along a rather simple line. First, I will present the main thrust of the recontextualization project flowing out of Leuven. Next, I will explore the basic contours of the postmodern context, the cause of the need for recontextualization. Finally, this chapter will offer a treatment of the theological category of interruption, the means by which Boeve and Pollefeyt make the Christian narrative productive in a postmodern context.

Recontextualization as Postmodern Rahnerianism

Modernity strove to emancipate humanity from the shackles of religion. As Boeve notes, Kant insists that religion is "the principal obstacle to enlightenment." He adds, "Modernity not only forced religion (and religious tradition) onto the defensive at the socio-structural level but also at the level of *fundamental life options*. . . . Master narratives of science saw religion as mere *superstition*; master narratives of emancipation considered it a source of oppression and *alienation*."[2] Modernism stimulates secularization, which Harvey Cox describes as prophesying "the final disappearance of religion, ignorance and superstition."[3] Initially, theology reacted negatively to modernizing trends and maintained a relationship of discontinuity with regard such currents (e.g., Piux X's *Pascendi Dominici gregis*). However, in the decades leading up to Vatican II, and in those immediately following, theologians such as Rahner, Metz, Küng, Schillebeeckx, etc. took up the challenge of relating modernity to theology by, in some way, embracing the modern context.

This modern correlation project built a bridge between culture and faith—a project that required "mutual and critical correlation."[4] Theologians like Rahner considered human experience the link between the two, and they deemed "rationality, human freedom, and social liberation . . . privileged *loci theologici*."[5] While the term "correlation" has come to mean different things, Boeve argues that in "its most general sense, the concept gives expression to the intuition that faith, faith tradition, and reflection

---

2. Boeve, *Interrupting Tradition*, 43. For more on the development of modernity and its use of master narratives in the service of its secularization project, see Boeve, *Interrupting Tradition*, 37–42.

3. Cox, "The Myth of the Twentieth Century," 135, quoted in Boeve, *God Interrupts*, 16. In *Interrupting Tradition*, 39–40, Boeve describes secularization from two perspectives. First, "diverse sub-systems" freed themselves from the "all-embracing religious horizon," only to exclude the religious horizon from its ongoing developments. Now, the religious horizon becomes a sub-system, forced to withdraw from public life and serve only a religious function in society—essentially banished to the private realm. Second, Boeve points out what he calls a "generalization of values," wherein ethical norms are detached from their particular traditions and reconfigured as dictates of moral consensus at the most general level.

4. Boeve, *God Interrupts*, 4.

5. Boeve, *God Interrupts*, 32. For a longer treatment on this shift, see Boeve, *Interrupting Tradition*, 44–49.

on faith do not take place in isolation. On the contrary, they are closely related to life, culture, society, history—the context in which they are embedded."[6] Boeve explains:

> Modern correlation methods work from an essential or factual continuity between Christian faith and the secular context. . . . Correctly understood, Christian faith and modernity are partners on the journey toward a more rational, more human world. Seen as such, the mutually critical correlation functions both as a driving force and a critical instance of a modern Christian faith.[7]

Modern correlation bases itself on the following theoretical presuppositions:[8] (1) that theology is concerned with a dialogue between two partners—Christian tradition and secular culture; (2) the theologies tend to reconstruct Christian tradition in light of the "epistemological standards of the context," meaning the definition of rationality remains profoundly modern and faith simply adds to what human beings know through reason;[9] and (3) correlation assumes a fundamental continuity between modernity and Christianity such that "there should be no discrepancy between being a sincere modern human being and being an authentic Christian."

Boeve sees Rahner's transcendental theology as a significant contributor to the modern theological project. As noted above, Rahner reacted against propositional and "premodern" conceptions of faith, and developed his transcendental theology as a "dynamised and subjectified (or personalised) reflection on the relation between God and humans in a fundamental way, thus opening a place for the human experience of freedom and the sacramental event."[10] For Rahner, God's self-communication, his revelation, is a grace insofar as it is "an inner, constitutive principle of humanity given freely by God."[11] "Wherever people open themselves fully to God," Boeve notes, "the sacramentality of the whole of existence—the self-communication of God to the whole of existence—comes to light."[12]

---

6. Boeve, *God Interrupts*, 31.
7. Boeve, *God Interrupts*, 42–43.
8. For these points, see Boeve, *God Interrupts*, 33–34.
9. Boeve observes that correlation theologians operated according to the epistemological standards of modernity. In this context, as Sweeney points out, faith is "understood as 'adding' to or 'qualifying' a secular standard of rationality" (Sweeney, *Sacramental Presence*, 106). "Adding to" and "qualifying," seem to be apt descriptors for the role of the Christian tradition in the visions of Moran and Groome and betray a system that does not completely evade *duplex ordo* thinking.
10. Boeve, "Postmodern Sacramento-Theology," 330.
11. Boeve, "Postmodern Sacramento-Theology," 331.
12. Boeve, "Postmodern Sacramento-Theology," 331.

In Rahnerian thought, the relationship between God and the human being is described by emphasizing formal causality over efficient causality, a move Sweeney calls an "anthropological shift" that "allows [Rahner] to assert an inner principle of creaturely relation to God within the created order."[13] Despite Rahner's advances, Boeve ultimately describes Rahner's theological attempt as one that aims to "conceptualise the ontological essence of the self-communicating God," and, as such, it is one that "must be understood within the framework of neo-Platonic onto-theology . . . a background which remains primarily classic."[14] In other words, Rahner's theological oeuvre, his attempt to bring Heidegger into dialogue with Kant and Aquinas, remains tinged by elements of the classical thinking that have shaped the West since the time of Plato. Contrary to a neo-scholastic position which could be described as taking a position of discontinuity before modernity, Boeve sums up Rahner's (and all those who stand with him) fundamental assumption as one that claimed, "it was possible to identify *continuity* between modernity and Christian faith as [a] point of departure."[15] This, however, is no longer the case.

The postmodern condition arises amid the gravestones of modern metanarratives. Boeve describes the scene: "The post-modern critique of the modern rationality and emancipation ideologies on the one hand, and in relation to this, the discovery of plurality and heterogeneity on the other have pulled out the rug from under the presuppositions of this modern Christian project."[16] Thus, Boeve notes the following:[17]

1. Plurality has rendered obsolete the notion that Christianity needs to simply dialogue with an "easily identifiable secular culture." Dialogue between two partners is not possible in today's world of dynamic, irreducible, and even conflicting views.

2. The totalizing nature of modern epistemological standards and the resulting "grand narratives" has been criticized by postmodernity and its option for radical plurality, otherness, and difference. Postmodern thinking guards against all totalizing attempts.

3. Postmodernism criticizes "any facile presupposition of consensus, continuity, and harmony."

---

13. Sweeney, *Sacramental Presence*, 120.
14. Boeve, "Postmodern Sacramento-Theology," 331.
15. Boeve, *God Interrupts*, 4.
16. Boeve, "Beyond Correlation Strategies," 246.
17. Boeve, *God Interrupts*, 34–35.

4. The "factual overlap" between Christianity and culture has disappeared. The disappearance of the "factual overlap" means that, in reality, and statistically, many young people have already grown up without belonging to a religion.[18] He says, "In short, Europe has undergone an important transformation at the religious level, moving from a predominantly institutional Christian society to a society in which religiosity and spirituality tend to be a feature of a person's autonomous, subjective establishment of meaning."[19]

The present context is post-Christian and post-secular, and not only chronologically. It is post-Christian and post-secular in the sense that "our relation to the Christian faith and to secularization has changed."[20] Post-Christian means to say that Christianity is no longer the given background that grants meaning. Post-secular describes the reality that the modernization of society did not result in the complete banishment of religion and in the realization of the secular ideal, but in a pluralization of society.[21] In this post-Christian and post-secular context, Boeve notes that the *individual reactions* of detraditionalization, individualization, and pluralization are now the sociocultural processes that change society.[22] The whole thing is radically subjective—there is no "common" from which to work. This means tradition is neither transferred from one generation to another as a "given," nor is one's identity assigned but constructed. It also means that "equal and

---

18. See Boeve, *God Interrupts*, 16–19. This "factual overlap" refers to the nexus of Christianity and human existence, where Christianity provides a sense of meaning even if one is not (actively or a practicing) Christian.

19. Boeve, *God Interrupts*, 19. Boeve explains that for decades "There remained a common cultural horizon, very much influenced by Christian tradition. Up until the beginning of the 1980s, a significant proportion of the population of a large number of Western European countries continued to take their Christian identity for granted as something automatically given at birth" (34). In other words, Christianity was simply taken as a given part of one's identity, whether or not one practiced it. The result is a far higher number of those who called themselves Christians than those who were concretely practicing this religion in the day-to-day. Hence, the "factual overlap." See also Boeve, "Beyond Correlation Strategies," 234–36. See also Boeve, *Interrupting Tradition*, 56–64.

20. Boeve, *Crossroads*, 41.

21. Boeve, *Crossroads*, 41–42.

22. Boeve, *Crossroads*, 44. Boeve prefers the more postmodern -ization suffix over -ism due to the emphasis on the individual reaction and action (-izations) as opposed to the more ideological and totalizing (-isms). Cf. Boeve, *God Interrupts*, 38–39, 41; Boeve, "Religious Education," 145–46.

reciprocal recognition of the philosophical/religious position," or any position, for that matter, must be granted.[23]

In terms of religion, the phenomenon of "believing without belonging" (i.e., being "spiritual but not religious") is a central feature of the postmodern condition.[24] These irreligious believers, often with Christian roots, emphasize autonomy and engage in non-Christian practices and embrace certain non-Christian beliefs. Boeve sums up these developments in Europe as "an important transformation at the religious level, moving from a predominantly institutional Christian society to a society in which religiosity and spirituality tend to be a feature of a person's autonomous, subjective establishment of meaning."[25] He goes on to describe the "spiritual but not religious" person, and the desecularized phenomenon in Europe as distinctly "post-Christian," with "most members of this group . . . only partially initiated . . . [while enjoying] nothing more than a fragmentary involvement with faith and faith communities, . . . [which] becomes manifest . . . in their occasional and declining participation in Christian rites of passage and . . . poor, non-integrated knowledge of the Christian tradition . . . in spite of many years of catechesis and religious education."[26] Modernity's secularization attempt did not succeed in completely stamping out the marks of religion and establishing a homogenous secular society in its place, but it did spark a process of the "deinstitutionalization," "individualization/subjectivization," and "detraditionalization" of religion in Europe and beyond.

Within such heterogenous circumstances, one can no longer correlate a singular secular culture to theology. Boeve's call for a recontextualization, therefore, aims to "radicalize modern correlation theory" by allowing for "particularity, contextuality, narrativity, historicity, contingency, and otherness."[27] Boeve argues that Christianity clings to the cur-

---

23. Boeve, *Crossroads*, 45. See also Boeve, "The Shortest Definition of Religion (Part I)," 8.

24. Boeve describes this position further in *God Interrupts*, 19–21. The use of "religion," as in "spiritual but not religious," can be ambiguous. Boeve notes that "religion" can refer to classical, traditional, or institutional religion, but it can also refer to a general religious attitude. In the past, Christian "believing without belonging" was a real phenomenon. One called himself a Catholic, while distancing himself more and more to the point of a near complete non-practice. However, this type of Christian "believing without belonging" is no longer connoted here. Instead, "believing without belonging" refers to an individual quest for spirituality, "an autonomous answer to questions of ultimate meaning and religious wonder" (20).

25. Boeve, *God Interrupts*, 19.

26. Boeve, *God Interrupts*, 21. For more on this topic, see Boeve, *Crossroads*, 33–53.

27. Boeve, *God Interrupts*, 40.

rent context in any epoch. Deinstitutionalization, individualization, and detraditionalization are all marks of the postmodern condition—the radically subjectivized context in which theology must be recontextualized if the Rahnerian correlation project is to survive. When context or culture shifts, Christian faith must either evolve or risk irrelevance, for "it is theology's task to reflect, in relation to the changing context, on the internal comprehensibility and the external credibility of the Christian faith."[28] Keeping in mind theology's continued engagement with the Heideggerian problematic, Boeve issues something of a mission statement for the fundamental theology from which pastoral implications flow:

> When revelation is primarily understood as God's dialogue with people in concrete histories and contexts; when scripture and tradition are primarily understood as the witness of this meeting inscribed in texts and practices, equally marked by time and context; therefore, when tracing God's Word for today contains an ongoing process of experience and interpretation, and drives at a continuing recontextualization; thus when God's commitment to people leads not away from history and its hermeneutic but directly thereto; in short: when we only can participate in God's dialogue with us, by actively engaging the dialogue ourselves with text and context, community and society, then it is extremely important to get to know the current context.[29]

The continuing revelation thesis is alive and well within the historical, contextual experience of humanity—an experience now distinctly postmodern. If postmodernity describes itself as a radicalized modernity, and the Rahner-Moran continuing revelation thesis is a thoroughly modern attempt at correlating theology and context, then Boeve's recontexualization project within fundamental theology issues forth something of a radicalized "doctrine" of continuing revelation. If Moran successfully relativized revelation, Boeve subjectivizes it in light of postmodernity. There is no such thing as "Revelation," no Christian "supernatural existential" that somehow explains the whole of human existence as an anonymous Christianity. Instead, there are always only lowercase *r* "revelations" brought about in the encounter with the radical otherness of the other. The postmodern condition describes not some sort of universal sameness, but difference, alterity. Recontextualized theology must account for this.

Recontextualization stands as the new watchword for the evolution of Christian faith over time, an evolution that the Church must carry out

---

28. Boeve, *God Interrupts*, 3. See also Boeve, *Lyotard*, 3.
29. Boeve, *Crossroads*, 33.

to ensure a chance at survival from one generation to the next. As Boeve puts it, "the Christian faith can only survive by *recontextualization*, since the credibility thereof is always contextual."[30] However, Boeve aims at more than mere survival. He sees Christianity as a key contributor within the postmodern condition. According to his recontextualization project, Christianity has the capacity to become productive in provoking difference-thinking in the plural field of postmodernity. If Rahner-Moran modernize the Church's mission by encouraging an embrace of one's humanity within the modern context, Boeve postmodernizes it by contributing to and encouraging the embrace of alterity within the postmodern theological context. It is clear, then, that Rahner, Moran, and Boeve all start with what is essentially the same "given," a "given" that is characteristic of an anthropological shift to the subjective, the being-in-time, to history, to context—whether that context is modern or postmodern is the real difference.

Boeve's theological mission, then, can be described as a pursuit to recontextualize theology can in a manner that is both contextually adequate (i.e., acceptable in the eyes of a postmodern critical consciousness) and theologically legitimate (i.e., grounded in the basic premises of Christianity).[31] Understanding his mission, however, can only come about through a clearer understanding of the postmodern context.

Postmodernity: The Next Frontier for Correlation Theology

Boeve's work in the area of postmodern thinking is largely a theological application of the philosophical work of Jean-François Lyotard, a father-figure (along with Jacques Derrida [1930–2004] and Michel Foucault [1926–84]) in "rewriting modernity." Lyotard was born in Versailles in 1924 and studied philosophy at the Sorbonne. His early work dealt with Marx and Freud and a philosophy of desire. Later, he turns toward language pragmatics and aesthetics, while holding various university posts in France and in the United States. Lyotard died in 1998.

Lyotard describes the postmodern state or condition as an "incredulity toward metanarratives" resulting from the "crisis of metaphysical philosophy."[32] By metanarrative, Lyotard means any claim by a so-called

---

30. Boeve, *God Interrupts*, 3. See also Boeve, "The Shortest Definition of Religion (Part I)," 7.

31. See Boeve, *God Interrupts*, 30, 42.

32. Lyotard, *The Postmodern Condition*, xxiv. See also Boeve's brief introduction to the thought of Lyotard and his emphasis on postmodernity as that "point when the

"metasubject" who stands "above" those "people mired in the particular positivity of its traditional knowledge," and explains the whole of reality by a mode of unification.[33] Boeve defines the metanarrative's strategy as unfolding "a discourse that makes all linkings and all strategies for linkings (other discourse-types) hegemonically subordinate to its own finality (for example, the establishment of the classless society, or of the free market, or the restoration of an earlier image of society and of the world, etc.)."[34] The idea or narrative becomes determinative for the whole—for all other ideas or stories. It is all-encompassing either in its rejection or consumption of other ideas or narratives. Metanarratives appear as result of the Enlightment and its many *-isms*: communism, capitalism, conservatism, liberalism, positivism, etc.[35]

---

modern master narratives of knowledge and emancipation . . . lost their legitimacy" and as "radicalized modernity" in *Interrupting Tradition*, 52. See also Boeve, *Lyotard*, 11–12; Boeve, "Postmodern Sacramento-Theology," 334–35. Sweeney notes that Lyotard calls the phenomenon a "condition," rather than a "position" (Sweeney, *Sacramental Presence*, 22). As a celebration of suspension, deferral, and openness, Sweeney describes this condition as "an ongoing process that never achieves a static resting place in certainty and that resists any claim to a totalizing theological discourse . . . theology is not a masternarrative, but must itself be situated by the ever-changing hermeneutical dimension of time" (Sweeney, *Sacramental Presence*, 48; see also O'Shea, "Vulgarised Rahnerianism," 364). Kevin Vanhoozer points out that postmodernism rejects the notion of definition, because definitions can never be "neutral" and always reveal more about the person offering the definition. Postmodernism resists totalizing attempts at explanation and, therefore, it is more accurate to speak of postmodernities, than to speak of postmodernism (Vanhoozer, "Theology and the Condition of Postmodernity," 3).

33. See Lyotard, *The Postmodern Condition*, 34, 37.

34. Boeve, "Critical Consciousness," 461.

35. Vanhoozer, for his part, identifies four principal metanarratives rejected by postmodernity in his "Theology and the Condition of Postmodernity," 10–12. They are as follows: (1) Reason—Postmoderns "do not reject 'reason' but 'Reason.' They deny the notion of universal rationality; reason is rather a contextual and relative affair. What counts as rational is relative to the prevailing narrative in a society or institution." Reason must be viewed not as a universal, but as limited by the context in which it is formed. (2) Truth—Here modernity's metaphysical attempts "of mastering natural reality in a comprehensive conceptual scheme," are criticized. Postmoderns challenge assertions of "that's the way things are," by responding "that's the way things are for you." "Truth on this view is a compelling story told by persons in position of power in order to perpetuate their way of seeing and organizing the natural and social world." (3) History—Postmoderns react against thinkers like Kant, Hegel, and Marx, all moderns who "have attempted to tell the story of humanity, usually in terms of the progress of the race." Rather than accounts that "purport to recount universal history" via continuity, postmoderns favor discontinuity and do not subscribe to "one true story" the describes all of history. (4) Self—"There is no one true way of recounting one's own history and thus no one true way of narrating one's own identity. . . . The postmodern self is not master of but subject to the material and social and linguistic conditions of a historical

Modern metanarratives appear in two main forms: "a speculative narrative [philosophy] or a narrative of emancipation [politics]."[36] In other words, they are metanarratives of knowledge or liberation. The first type of metanarrative, those of knowledge, are narratives of rationality and technology, "which aim at complete transparency and . . . an unlimited mastery and use of reality."[37] Such metanarratives are grounded in a Hegelian idealism that sees knowledge of nature, society, and state as a continued development of *Geist* and a scientific positivism that together attempt to offer a complete and conclusive explanation of the whole with an "efficient course of action."[38] Lyotard categorizes a second group of metanarratives as those centering on emancipation and a utopian vision of human fulfillment. These develop according to a critical understanding of past and present with an optimistic view of the future. They take the form of social ideologies "which reflect what is considered to be the ultimate aim of the human person and society: individual freedom for liberalism, complete solidarity for communism, or general welfare for capitalism."[39]

Postmodern thinking does not legitimate ideals, whether they are related to knowledge or liberation, but performativity. Boeve explains, following Lyotard, "knowledge is . . . characterized by the fact that it works, that it makes things possible."[40] For example, in the field of science, the breaking open of homologous paradigms by the "paralogy of inventors" revolutionizes existing scientific discourse serving as the very key to scientific progress. The reality of scientific progress, then, becomes something of a model for conceptualizing a way out of the hegemony of the metanarrative. For example, in science, "paradigms are to be continually broken open, rules

situation that precedes her." In this way, the self is open-ended and adrift.

36. Lyotard, *The Postmodern Condition*, 37. See also Boeve, "Postmodern Sacramento-Theology," 335. In *Catholic Theology*, 161, Rowland defines metanarrative or "master narrative" in simple terms: "The concept refers to a narrative about narratives of historical meaning, experience or knowledge, which offers a society a legitimation through the anticipated completion of a (as yet unrealised) master idea."

37. Boeve, "Postmodern Sacramento-Theology," 335. See also Boeve, *Interrupting Tradition*, 41.

38. Boeve, "Postmodern Sacramento-Theology," 335.

39. Boeve, "Postmodern Sacramento-Theology," 335. See also Boeve, *Lyotard*, 11–12. Here, Boeve notes that the philosophical-speculative grand narratives of rationality and technology take their form in German Idealism where a speculative metanarrative "legitimizes our knowledge about nature, society and the state by integrating it within the development of the life of the Spirit." The second group of metanarratives concern themselves with politics and the emancipation of humanity. Liberalism and Marxism are examples of such metanarratives.

40. Boeve, *Lyotard*, 12.

of the game to be adjusted, and games changed. The object of science is formed not by what is already known and familiar, but by the unknown and unfamiliar."[41] Lyotard relates such scientific insights to Western society where decisions about the truth determine decisions about goodness and justice. But, if science cannot be described according to one system but is constantly exposed to the breaking-open of its own paradigm, society "and its search for justice," its ethics and politics, cannot be either.

Lyotard's work is, in large part, an application of Ludwig Wittgenstein's "language-games" concept that results in a reality that "can no longer be contained in one grand encompassing narrative."[42] For Wittgenstein, a word is meaningless apart from the rules of the language-game in which it is being used—that which the word stands in relation to, a certain relativity, gives it its meaning. It would seem, then, that there exist an infinite number of language-games in which the same word can be used with a slightly different meaning in each case. In short, "the heterogeneity of language games and their rules . . . and the possibility of dissent, make . . . obligatory striving for consensus dubious. . . . For Lyotard . . . *the question of justice* is no longer able to lean upon such a consensus-oriented model, but should radically start from *dissensus*."[43] In an attempt to provide an alternative to "simplistic consensus thinking," Lyotard's publications of *Le différend* and *Judicieux dans le différend* introduce his language pragmatics as part of the linguistic turn in philosophy that functions as the foundation of his critical analysis of metanarratives. Lyotardian linguistics, then, become essential for understanding the postmodern condition and what a recontextualization of theology will entail.

Language Pragmatics

Lyotard's language pragmatics consist of several basic categories. The first, the most basic, is the *phrase*. Boeve says, "A phrase happens," and "there is an unending multitude of phrases residing simply there as 'given.'"[44] One

---

41. Boeve, *Lyotard*, 12.

42. Boeve, *Lyotard*, 13. Boeve notes that Lyotard's philosophical reflections are primarily in dialogue with Immanuel Kant and Ludwig Wittgenstein. With Wittgenstein, Lyotard takes up the linguistic turn in philosophy and its concerns regarding language and "the heterogeneity of language games" (14). Wittgenstein's language games refer to the different ways in which words or phrases stand in relation to other words or phrases. A word might stand for one thing or serve a specific purpose in one game, and the same word might stand for something completely different in another.

43. Boeve, *Lyotard*, 13.

44. Boeve, *Lyotard*, 15.

might also say a language-game exists, yet it is just one of many possible language-games. The multifarious nature of language-games is the new "given." The new "given" is that there is not one "given." For Lyotard, each phrase is part of a broader *phrase regimen* which determines the rules for the phrase and allows it to be cataloged (e.g., descriptive, interrogative, prescriptive, declarative, exclamatory, etc.). The phrase regimen "consists of a number of rules which determine the forming of suitable phrases" and prevents "a phrase from one regimen [from being] translated as such into another phrase regimen."[45] Now, a phrase that has "happened" is always necessarily followed by another, with silence also counting as a possible following-phrase. While the linking of one phrase to another is necessary, the contents of the phrase are fundamentally contingent. Without "a meta-language or an all-encompassing discourse-type," one cannot adequately fill-in-the-blank, for "no single sentence succeeds in totally expressing the multiplicity of possible linking sentences, or better still, the moment of indeterminacy, of heterogeneity."[46] The movement from one phrase to another, this linking of one to the other, establishes a *discourse genre* or *type*. The *discourse genre* serves a specific goal by forming "a unity of rules that connect heterogenous phrases to each other with the aim of realizing a specific finality." Boeve provides some examples: argumentation, narrative, seduction, rhetoric, pedagogy, and so forth. How a phrase functions in one *discourse genre* could be completely different than how the same phrase would function in another.[47] The multiplicity of realities taking place within a dialogue is known as a *phrase universe*, the contents of which are not prescribed but which appear as instances in "the addressor (the one who utters the phrase); the addressee to whom the phrase is directed; the referent (what is at stake); and the meaning (what is said about that which is at stake)."[48] The meaning of a phrase operating as such within one phrase universe can change when linked to a different discourse genre. Boeve uses the example, here, of the phrase "it is very warm in here." This phrase means one thing in a discourse genre of seduction, while it means something entirely different in a pedagogical discourse.[49] In any one dialogue, multiple phrase universes could "happen," with the same phrase used in multiple ways (hence, given multiple meanings). Finally, in Lyotard's pragmatics, the actual occurrence of a phrase is called an *event*. The phrase happens, its

45. Boeve, *Lyotard*, 15.
46. Boeve, "Postmodern Sacramento-Theology," 339.
47. Boeve, *Lyotard*, 16.
48. Boeve, *Lyotard*, 16.
49. Boeve, *Lyotard*, 16.

utterance happens, though the phrase is neither predetermined, nor is its content, addressor, addressee, or referent imposed. This event of a phrase being issued is then marked by "a kind of 'relative nothingness' between the [event of a phrase] and the phrase to follow. . . . A happened phrase opens an expectation onto an event to come. . . . The only thing which is certain is that a phrase will follow."[50]

The language pragmatics presented above allow Lyotard to introduce the concept of the *differend*. Because the linking of phrases is contingent, with the only necessary thing being a response—*that* a phrase will follow—a conflict will arise. Essentially, this is a conflict at the level of the discourse genre. Only one phrase can follow the preceding one, and the "discourse that wins the conflict ultimately determines the nature of this phrase and closes off the expectation . . . opened up by the preceding phrase. The winning discourse genre defines the phrase which is linked and fills in the 'relative nothingness' in-between the passage from one phrase to the other."[51] Any linking of phrases is the result of an irreducible conflict opened by the preceding phrase, because there is no predetermined rule necessarily imposing, the nature of the phrase that follows. The phrase that follows overcomes the "relative nothingness" between the two phrases—the tense anticipation of the phrase that will determine the discourse genre. Now, Boeve explains that the "conflict between discourse genres over the linking of phrases . . . constitutes a *differend* . . . which is to be distinguished from a litigation."[52] Once a phrase is linked to the event of the preceding one, Lyotard says a litigation occurs. A litigation decides the conflict between competing discourse genres and relaxes the tension of the "relative nothingness" between the phrases. This "relative nothingness," goes by the name *differend*. The *differend* is "the unstable state and instant of language wherein something which must be able to be put into phrases cannot yet be. This state includes silence, which is a negative phrase, but it also calls upon phrases which are in principle possible."[53] The discourse genre that wins out "regulates the linking—in order to achieve its own goal" as if forgetting its own contingency

---

50. Boeve, *Lyotard*, 16.

51. Boeve, *Lyotard*, 17.

52. Boeve, *Lyotard*, 17. See Lyotard, *The Differend*, xi. Here, Lyotard defines a *differend* as "a case of conflict, between (at least) two parties, that cannot be equitably resolved for lack of a rule of judgment applicable to both arguments. One side's legitimacy does not imply the other's lack of legitimacy. However, applying a single rule of judgment to both in order to settle their differend as though it were merely a litigation would wrong (at least) one of them (and both of them if neither side admits this rule). . . . A universal rule of judgment between heterogeneous genres is lacking in general."

53. Lyotard, *The Differend*, 13.

and ending the unstable, uncertain, and open state of the *differend*. A litigation settles the matter. The choice for one phrase "excludes the actualization of the other phrases" and "plurality cannot be radically respected, nor can the legitimate claims of any other phrase (or discourse genre) to realize the linkage."[54] In short, the linking of phrases and the establishing of a discourse genre (i.e., an event of litigation) results in a certain bondage, an injustice, the denial of the opportunity to speak, the condemnation of all other possible phrases to silence. Therefore, *differend* refers to "a wrong or injustice that arises because the prevailing or hegemonic discourse actively precludes the possibility of this wrong being expressed. To put it still another way, it is a wrong or injustice which cannot be proved to have been a wrong or injustice because the means of doing so has (also) been denied the victim."[55] Boeve summarizes, "what is a litigation for the ruling discourse is experienced by the others as a differend, ultimately then as a form of injustice."[56] The *differend* refers to the other, equally contingent phrases which could have been given utterance, but, as victims of a litigation, must remain silent. The *differend* symbolizes and stands for the "relative nothingness," or present absence of that which has not been given utterance.

Lyotard notes that the discourse genre of the narrative is most capable of forgetting the heterogeneity of phrase regimens and discourse genres, because a narrative operates according to a rigid predetermined framework. A narrative has an identifiable beginning and a predetermined end. The narrative affords the *differend* no place, as the "'relative nothingness' between two phrases is immediately qualified through the rule of the story. Each phrase to happen is a suitable phrase, fitting to the realization of the finality of the story."[57] As a result, the narrative forces the *differend* to remain silent, stripped of its "jolting event-character," because of the predetermined litigation.[58] Master narratives, or metanarratives, then, are the most heinous of all narratives, because they offer one all-encompassing narrative of history or reality. They attempt to explain all of history or reality in a predetermined way that does not allow for the possibility of the *differend*. In short, metanarratives forget the *differend*, thus causing some sort of supreme injustice.

Lyotard identifies four characteristics regarding the modern metanarrative, with each of the characteristics regulating an "Idea." First,

---

54. Boeve, *Lyotard*, 18.

55. *Oxford Reference*, s.v. "differend," https://www.oxfordreference.com/view/10.1093/oi/authority.20110803095717700.

56. Boeve, *Lyotard*, 18.

57. Boeve, *Lyotard*, 20.

58. Boeve, *Lyotard*, 20.

metanarratives make a cognitive claim, namely, presenting reality as it is. Second, the metanarrative contains a totalizing power, a closed hegemonic discourse, that regulates "the linking of phrases immediately," and subordinating other discourse genres (i.e., the goal of the linking of two phrases). These initial characteristics are common in all metanarratives. The remaining characteristics render metanarratives distinctly modern. The third characteristic involves being grand narratives of history which legitimate themselves based upon finality (e.g., utopia). The final characteristic reveals the metanarratives of modernity as displaying universal pretensions and claiming to speak on behalf of all of humanity. More simply put, metanarratives appear as "exaggerated *hegemonic discourses of an Idea* that adhere to illegitimate universal and cognitive pretensions," by claiming to (1) pronounce truth in an all-encompassing way, and (2) regulate the linking of phrases by excluding other ones, (3) define the goal of history, and (4) encompass all that happens by universalizing instances.[59] The fundamental point, here, is that "master narratives are hegemonic . . . *discourses regulated by an Idea.*"[60] Metanarratives severely and structurally forget the *differend*. Injustice ensues. As Boeve puts it, "the totalizing way in which a master narrative arranges the linkage of phrases does not allow for otherness to halt—even momentarily—the steady and uninterrupted progression of a narrative."[61]

The Role of Philosophy in the Postmodern Condition

Regarding modern metanarratives, Lyotard inquires about the role of philosophy.[62] Lyotard proposes that philosophy exists to become aware of the *differend* and to bear witness to the *differend*—to not forget the *differend*. It is to exercise a postmodern critical consciousness. Metanarratives are fundamentally closed, and they disregard (either by rejecting or absorbing into its own story) that which is "other." They overstep boundaries and overtake the "other." However, when a narrative operates according to postmodern critical consciousness it engages the "other" at its own boundary (i.e., with a clear awareness of its own boundary or limit) and is open to being challenged by the "other."[63] The awareness of the "other" is the key to postmodern critical consciousness. At the same time, postmodern critical consciousness is keen

---

59. Boeve, *Lyotard*, 25.
60. Boeve, *Lyotard*, 21.
61. Boeve, *Lyotard*, 49.
62. Boeve, *Lyotard*, 25.
63. Boeve, "The Shortest Definition of Religion (Part II)," 5.

on bearing witness to the *differend*, to that which is "other"; it gives voice to the voiceless when totalizing narratives threaten them. When the successive phrase does not bear witness to the relative nothingness, or, more positively put, radical otherness, of the indeterminacy, rule-lessness, or heterogeneity that separates the two phrases, philosophy is to step in and bear witness to the inexpressible heterogeneity that "accompanies every linkage." "No phrase can exhaustively bring into discussion the inexpressible that asks to be put into phrases."[64] Philosophy makes known this certain injustice caused by a litigation and refers to the "inexpressibility of the inexpressible."[65] Therefore, by embracing a postmodern critical consciousness, philosophy at once provokes a *positive* engagement within the context while maintaining a *negative* position of incredulity towards metanarratives. Philosophy functions now, not as disciplined pursuit of truth, but as that which keeps the narrative "open," so to speak, as the supreme witness to the *differend* that is manifest in the "relative nothingness" following a phrase.

In opening to "otherness" and bearing witness to "otherness," philosophy can only pursue this task as a "open narrative," or else it will, itself, become hegemonic.[66] Lyotard ties the concept of an "open narrative" to the *differend* in all its dimensions. Boeve claims there are three dimensions of the *differend*, with the first two referring to the third, more fundamental one. The first dimension of the *differend* is "the experience of conflict—an experience particularly revealed in *not* being able or allowed to speak, to concatenate, to link onto the previous phrase. This occurs when differends are regulated as litigations."[67] In this case, when one discourse genre regulates the discourse and prevents others from linking, the others experience a certain powerlessness and injustice and victimization. The second sense has to do with conflictive or radical plurality. When a phrase "happens," opening the expectation of a second phrase, no supreme rule determines the exact nature of the following phrase. Because, as Boeve says, "a multitude of phrases which are not reducible to one another present themselves to complete the linkage, a situation of radical plurality arises wherein no ultimate,

---

64. Boeve, *Lyotard*, 28.

65. Boeve, *Lyotard*, 28. The German Synodal Way seems to embrace the mission of postmodern philosophy, admitting that "an enlightened and pluralistic society cannot and will not accept . . . [a] structurally rooted abuse of power" as that which appears in the Church. Instead, the Synod works to "expose them, denounce them, punish them and do everything in its power to prevent their continuation" (German Synodal Way, *Fundamental Text*, 9).

66. As Lyotard asks, "Is it [philosophy] narrating the master narrative of the end of master narratives?" (Boeve, *Lyotard*, 27).

67. Boeve, *Lyotard*, 85.

harmonizing or unifying solution is present."[68] Choosing one means denouncing the others and disrespecting plurality. The second dimension is like the first, then, but with the awareness of radical plurality. With this, the third dimension becomes clear. In linking to the preceding phrase and closing the expectation opened by the "happened" phrase, the second phrase does not satisfy the expectation. Boeve says, "the second phrase does not succeed in signifying the indeterminacy, the rule-lessness, or the heterogeneity that separates the first phrase from the second. In fact, we can describe the other side of relative nothingness of this 'moment' in-between phrases as an absolute fullness which can never be grasped or (re)presented in the concatenated phrase."[69] This third dimension refers to a fullness captured in the Idea of heterogeneity. If one is going to bear witness to the *differend*, one would have to bear in mind radical plurality "because no phrase can exhaustively present the inexpressible which asks to be expressed" (the second dimension), because attempting to exhaustively express the inexpressible would disregard the conflictive nature and cause an injustice (the first dimension). Therefore, bearing witness to the *differend* in light of the Idea of heterogeneity, means "linking in such a way that the inexpressibility of the inexpressible is referred to."[70] In other words, the linking must somehow remain in that "moment" of relative nothingness (which is simultaneously a moment of absolute fullness—recognizing the radical heterogeneity of a *differend*, marked as it is by radical plurality, and, thus, preventing a certain injustice caused by litigation). With this, Lyotard reconstitutes what "event" means in his pragmatics. "Event" stands for the occurrence of a phrase (that a phrase "happens" or "happened") and for the closing of a phrase (the linking of a second phrase to that which "happened" first). However, considering the *differend* and its dimensions, a more fundamental "event" precedes the second phrase—it is the "sensing of the impossible phrase, the experience of the relative nothingness and the phrase to happen."[71] This analysis sets the stage for the "open narrative," which situates itself within this third dimension of the *differend* in light of "event."

The "Open Narrative"

The "open narrative," then, is Lyotard's way of accounting for postmodern critical consciousness and dealing with *differends*. Boeve notes that "open

68. Boeve, *Lyotard*, 86.
69. Boeve, *Lyotard*, 87.
70. Boeve, *Lyotard*, 87.
71. Boeve, *Lyotard*, 88. See also Boeve, "Postmodern Sacramento-Theology," 338.

narratives" refuse to put forward claims to absoluteness and universality and are always prepared to recontextualize."[72] An open narrative is essentially a discourse type that is radically aware of "otherness which challenges the narrative from within."[73] This "otherness" provokes an awareness of its own particularity, while bearing witness through the interruptive encounter of the "other" to the Idea of heterogeneity. Thus, the "open narrative" at once acknowledges the radical plurality of the *differend* while avoiding a litigation that causes an injustice to it. In refusing to close the narrative, an "open narrative" remains it that tense state of relative nothingness/absolute fullness that is the event of the *differend*.

In further describing an "open narrative," Boeve notes that it exhibits an *accompanying consciousness* and an *explicit witness*.[74] This *accompanying consciousness* consists of three characteristics. First, it is a consciousness of irreversible plurality, of an inestimable multiplicity, which does not threaten the identity of one's narrative but helps one perceive his or her narrative as one amongst many. The open narrative is marked by "the recognition of the fact that life is made up a multiplicity of narratives" and "no single narrative has a right to claim that it can transcend this multiplicity."[75] Each position on the "field of life options" is situated as "participant" and there is no referee.[76] Boeve says the open narrative is "generated by an *open sensitivity towards otherness*, a specific extraordinary and cultivated sensitivity towards that which interrupts . . . our capacity to be open to strangeness, otherness, and the unexpected."[77] A proclivity to this type of conflict in the encounter with otherness "prevents us from falling back into hegemony ever again, or at least keeps us vigilant against the constant tendency of narratives to do so."[78] Second, accompanying consciousness maintains awareness of the way hegemonic narratives threaten plurality. Boeve is careful to note that there is no such thing as the "open narrative," which would succumb to the level of hegemonic discourse. Instead, the model of "open narrative" offers

---

72. Boeve, "Critical Consciousness," 462.

73. Boeve, *Lyotard*, 95. A *narrative* is a discourse type that offers the reason why it links one phrase to another. A narrative regulates the linking. An *open* narrative renounces a definitive linking.

74. See Boeve, *Lyotard*, 93. What follows here is perhaps a simpler description of the model of the "open narrative" when compared with earlier descriptions in Boeve's work (e.g., Boeve, *Interrupting Tradition*, 90–96).

75. Boeve, *Interrupting Tradition*, 92–93.

76. Boeve, *Interrupting Tradition*, 93. See also Boeve, "The Shortest Definition of Religion (Part I)," 6.

77. Boeve, *Interrupting Tradition*, 95.

78. Boeve, "Postmodern Sacramento-Theology," 337.

characteristics and criteria that allow for the evaluation and criticism of various narratives in light of postmodern critical consciousness.[79] Finally, this accompanying consciousness is aware of conflicts that appear when the linking of phrases occurs. Here, one is conscious that different linkages could have been possible. The sensitivity towards otherness and willingness to witness to the other become "the *critical praxis of an open narrative.*"[80] The praxis appears at the level of decision-making, wherein one is "attentive to the otherness of the other(s)" and will resist "to negate such otherness," or in the resistance to participating in any metanarrative (e.g., marketization).[81] Boeve summarizes these three characteristics of accompanying consciousness as "setting out to keep the narrative open, and fostering the basic open attitude which is both its condition and source."[82]

In addition to this accompanying consciousness, this awareness of the radical particularity or contextuality of one's own narrative, embracing an open narrative calls for an explicit witness. Boeve says, "For Lyotard, philosophy's role, as well as art's, at the present time is *to place such hegemonic narratives*, which want to comprehensively master everything, *under critique*. At the same time, philosophy has its assignment *to bear witness to what escapes such narratives*, to give voice to the other of the narrative, to what differs from the narrative (*le différend*)."[83] Here it becomes clear that apart from its contribution as a negative critique of metanarratives and hegemonic truth claims, postmodern philosophy makes the positive contribution as an open narrative by receiving and giving voice to difference. In other words, "an open narrative . . . strives to offer the language for that which has no language," and, in doing so, "it professes its fundamental choice for non-hegemony."[84] Thus philosophy fosters an "open narrative," while functioning as one. It is at once open to the plurality of narratives and critically conscious of its own

---

79. Boeve, *Interrupting Tradition*, 92; Boeve, *Lyotard*, 94.

80. Boeve, *Interrupting Tradition*, 96. By way of example, the German Synodal Way encourages a culture of conflict. The *Fundamental Text* promotes learning to "live theological diversity in ecclesial unity" in order to "arrive at a new form of conflict of culture in the Church" (6). The "task," the document claims, "is to develop an ecclesial culture of debate and learning from one another in the face of a legitimate diversity of interpretations of how and for what the Church should be good" (15). Such conflict appears as a "work of the Holy Spirit" (15).

81. Boeve, *Interrupting Tradition*, 96.

82. Boeve, *Lyotard*, 93.

83. Boeve, *Crossroads*, 49. See also Boeve, "Postmodern Sacramento-Theology," 339.

84. Boeve, *Lyotard*, 93–94.

contextuality, while simultaneously sensing and bearing witness to heterogeneity and critiquing hegemonic narratives.[85]

The concept of the open narrative shines further light on the postmodern condition. This condition refers to a radical awareness of the *otherness* of being in time, rather than a philosophical position imposed upon being in time. Postmodernity is, simply put, incredulity toward metanarratives, or, as noted by Hanna-Barbara Gerl-Falkovitz, "the admission of heterogeneous subjectivity and cultivation of difference by reflexion."[86] Eugen Rosenstock-Huessy describes the ethos as saying:

> We can drop the methods of the past. The schemes of that era, whatever they might be, were based on either physics or metaphysics. Some were subjective and some were objective; some were idealistic and some were materialistic, and many were a mixture of both. . . . They all set out with abstract generalities on man's mind and on the nature of matter. We renounce their approach to knowledge.[87]

He steps away from the Cartesian *Cogito ergo sum*, as well as Anselm of Canterbury's *Credo ut intelligam*. He says the "*Credo ut intelligam* and the *Cogito ergo sum* worked very well for a time. However, finally the *Credo ut intelligam* led to the Inquisition and the *Cogito ergo sum* into an ammunition factory."[88] Instead, Rosenstock-Huessy calls for adopting another simple formula, *Respondeo etsi mutabor*, "I answer though I have to change."[89] He continues, "We can only try to give a momentary answer, our answer, to the everlasting protean question."[90] Similarly, Sweeney notes that the postmodern condition is "a 'condition' characterized by suspension, deferral, and openness."[91] It is "being-without-confidence," which causes one to defer "reason's aspirations to commensurability with its object."[92] Sweeney quotes James C. Livingston as describing the condition as "'emptiness of self,' 'absence,' 'loss of self,' 'the movement toward silence,' 'the unrepresentable,' 'the crisis of legitimization,'" and notes that "the twilight of certainty means that dimensions once dismissed as irrelevant or unworthy of consideration all suddenly become equally worthy of consideration,

85. See Boeve, "*Christus Postmodernus*," 579.
86. Gerl-Falkovitz, "Recent Developments."
87. Rosenstock-Huessy, *Out of Revolution*, 742.
88. Rosenstock-Huessy, *Out of Revolution*, 753.
89. Rosenstock-Huessy, *Out of Revolution*, 751.
90. Rosenstock-Huessy, *Out of Revolution*, 749.
91. Sweeney, *Sacramental Presence*, 23.
92. Sweeney, *Sacramental Presence*, 23.

given the relativizing of the standards of traditionally privileged modes of discourse."[93] The postmodern condition is the open state of tension amid the "relative nothingness" caused by an incredulity toward metanarratives and the legitimizing of the *differend*.

Recontextualization: Seeking Contextual Adequacy and Theological Legitimacy

What does postmodern thinking make of Christianity? Can it somehow avoid damnation as a metanarrative? For Lyotard, it cannot; the Christian narrative is the preeminent metanarrative.[94] Lyotard holds that the Christian narrative acts as a metanarrative because it perpetuates "the hegemonic discourse of the Idea of love."[95] In *The Differend*, Lyotard establishes the basis of this claim, saying, "The Christian narrative vanquished the other narratives in Rome because by introducing . . . love . . . into narratives and narrations of narratives, it designated what is at stake in the genre itself. . . . As the promise of good news, [it] allows for linking onto whatever happens, including other narratives (and, subsequently, even other genres)."[96] He continues:

> It results from a commandment of universal attraction, *Love one another*. . . . This commandment is authorized by the revelation (itself loving) of a primordial story in which we learn that the god of love was not very well loved by his children and about the misfortunes that ensued. This authorization remains in the circular form common to narratives, but it is extended to all narratives. The obligation to love is decreed by the divine Absolute, it is addressed to all creatures (who are none other than His addressees), and it becomes transitive (in an interested sense, because it is conditional): if you are loved, you ought to love; and you shall be loved only if you love.[97]

Love, God's love, and the love of God, function as elements an all-embracing Christian narrative that goes on to consume all other narratives of love as anticipating that which is fully and finally realized in itself. Additionally, the

---

93. Sweeney, *Sacramental Presence*, 23.

94. In his description of metanarratives in *Le postmoderne expliqué aux enfants*, Lyotard first mentions the Christian narrative, the narrative of the "redemption of original sin through love." See Boeve, *Lyotard*, 49.

95. Boeve, *Lyotard*, 49.

96. Lyotard, *The Differend*, 159.

97. Lyotard, *The Differend*, 159–60.

universal commandment to love appears as the universal condition determining whether or not one is loved by God.

According to Lyotard, Christianity manifests all four determining characteristics of a metanarrative as listed above. First, Christianity legitimates itself according to a universal end: the salvation of all creatures by first grounding the whole of creation in a primordial story. It encompasses beginning and end, legitimating itself in the whole. Second, the Idea of love universalizes instances and overcomes particularity even of local stories by incorporating it into itself. The Idea of love takes over the whole event: Love (God) is the addressor who tells the story of love (referent) and who forces the response on the part of the addressee (as Boeve puts it, "because I, who am love, have loved you, you must love (me)"), thus determining the meaning of whole event as love.[98] Third, the Christian narrative makes a cognitive claim that "love is what reality is about . . . [offering] a reading key to approach and evaluate whatever 'happens.'"[99] Finally, the Christian narrative is implicated as a hegemonic discourse by automatically regulating the linkages between phrases and subordinating other discourse genres. As Lyotard himself puts it, "Christian narration not only tells what has happened, thereby fixing a tradition, but it also prescribes the *caritas* for what can happen, whatever it might be."[100]

In the face of Lyotard's indictment from within the postmodern condition, Boeve raises the question that is at stake in his theological work—the question he believes is at stake for Christian theology in a postmodern context: "Can the Christian narrative reformulate itself as a consciously particular, and contextually embedded way of dealing with plurality and otherness?"[101] From here, Boeve sets out to vindicate the Christian narrative from Lyotard's indictment by recasting the whole of the Christian narrative in a way that is both *contextually* adequate and *theologically* legitimate—as an "open narrative" according to the category of interruption.[102]

---

98. See Boeve, *Lyotard*, 54–55.
99. Boeve, *Lyotard*, 55.
100. Lyotard, *The Differend*, 160.
101. Boeve, *Lyotard*, 95.

102. The recontextualization project ultimately has two criteria: (1) contextual adequacy and (2) theological legitimacy. On the one hand, recontextualization must successfully take the postmodern condition as a "given" and recontextualize theology accordingly. On the other hand, it must show how the recontextualization project is a legitimate exercise in theology—meaning it somehow remains anchored in or correlates to Christian theological tradition. Boeve's criteria for authentic recontextualization appear, for example, in *God Interrupts History*, 30, 42.

The collapse of modern metanarratives leads to the successive collapse of correlation theology. When the singular dialogue partner (i.e., the idea of a perfectly secular society) passes away with the rest of modernity, theology must be recontextualized to account for the "new" plurality of the postmodern condition. Boeve argues that "to the extent that modern correlation theology . . . embraced these modern epistemological presuppositions [i.e., consensus, continuity, and harmony]—whether implicitly or explicitly—it shares in their loss of plausibility. *The presupposition of continuity between tradition and context, legitimated by and expressed in religious experience, no longer works and is often considered as a form of Christian recuperation.*"[103] Boeve goes on to argue that with the dismantling of the singular modern dialogue partner (i.e., secularism), theology must make a choice vis-à-vis the postmodern condition: continuity (i.e., continuing to embrace *the* modern ideal) or discontinuity (i.e., the continuation of various onto-theological projects which have disregarded context, a certain pre-modern approach). Boeve chooses neither, for, though coming at the problem from opposing sides, both result in the same exercise of hegemony. He proposes an alternate path by recontextualizing theology.

If recontextualization is going to radicalize modern correlation theory, due regard must be given not only to continuity (i.e., correlation with the modern context), but also particularity, contextuality, narrativity, historicity, contingency, and otherness (i.e., the distinctly postmodern context). In other words, "the point of departure of such a renewed recontextualization is to be found in the determination to take the radical historicity and contextuality of the Christian faith and theology seriously."[104] Sweeney notes that for Boeve:

> Christians must give up on pretensions to universality . . . [becoming] enabled to more fully embrace the irreducible particularity of their own narrative. . . . Herein lies the paradox of the postmodern condition that Boeve wishes to exploit. Even if we can no longer ontologically ground our discourse, we can nevertheless radically embrace particularity as a valid way of

---

103. Boeve, *God Interrupts*, 75; emphasis added. With regard to modern correlation, Boeve notes that modernity's striving for rationality and the diminishment of the religious horizon, individuals "discovered themselves as subjects both capable of and responsible for their achievement of maturity as subjects." This development was first rejected by the Church, and later embraced. After Vatican II, "rationality, human freedom, and social liberation [are] considered privileged *loci theologici* from which to recontextualize the Christian faith in a God who is salvifically involved with human beings and their histories" (32).

104. Boeve, *God Interrupts*, 40. Boeve's project is best understood as "'post-correlation' in relation to modern correlation theology."

legitimizing the Christian narrative in a postmodern context. . . . Thus, in order to both survive and in order to be truer to its own identity, Christianity must situate itself within the Lyotardian *differend*.[105]

The category of interruption makes this recontextualization possible. Interruption will essentially act as a fulcrum by which Boeve can leverage the Christian narrative as an open narrative (i.e., one that operates within postmodern critical consciousness), thus recontextualizing the Christian narrative in a way that is both contextually adequate and theologically legitimate. Interruption allows Boeve to recontextualize the Christian tradition in postmodern terms, while making that same narrative productive in carrying out postmodernity's mission on behalf of the *differend*. In one fell swoop, Boeve attempts to both vindicate the Christian narrative of Lyotard's charge, and place it at the service of postmodern critical consciousness.[106] Given its centrality in Boeve's work, interruption must be considered in greater detail.

A New Given: Interruption

Johann Baptist Metz's (1928–2019) line "the shortest definition of religion is *interruption*" provides inspiration for the genesis of Boeve's category of interruption.[107] Metz sought to prevent Christianity from becoming a bourgeois religion, comfortably part of mainstream culture, while also not withdrawing from the mainstream. Boeve describes Metz's position:

> After all, Christians are bearers of the subversive, dangerous memory of the suffering, death and resurrection of Jesus Christ. By its very nature, the Christian faith disrupts the histories of conquerer and vanquished, interrupting the ideologies of the powerful and powerlessness of the victims. Metz, therefore, advocates for a theology that is concretely active in history and society—a *political theology*.[108]

---

105. Sweeney, *Sacramental Presence*, 103.

106. See Boeve, *Lyotard*, 94.

107. Boeve, *God Interrupts*, 203; Boeve, *Lyotard*, 125. Here, Boeve is quoting from Metz, *Glaube in Geschichte und Gesellschaft*, 12.

108. Boeve, *Lyotard*, 126.

While Boeve ultimately criticizes Metz's position vis-à-vis postmodernity,[109] he does believe Metz's intuition can inspire a distinctly postmodern conception of interruption.[110]

Interruption encourages tension between continuity and discontinuity. When one's narrative is interrupted, the narrative does not cease to exist—it is not ruptured, annihilated, or discontinued. It is simply interrupted. Eventually, that narrative that was interrupted does continue, but not as before. Now, it speaks with a new awareness—bearing in mind that which interrupted it. Interruption holds continuity and discontinuity together in a tense relationship. Therefore, Boeve defines interruption as "an intrusion that does not destroy the narrative but problematizes the advance thereof. It disturbs the anticipated sequence of sentences following one after the other, and disarms the security devices that protect against disruption."[111] Boeve goes on to explain that interruptions cannot take place without the narrative that is in motion, while they can also not be captured or contained by that same narrative. The "otherness" intrudes and "momentarily but nonetheless intensely halts the narrative sequence"— causing the narrative in motion to "collide with its own borders." This interruption draws "attention to its narrative character and force[s] an opening toward the other within the narrative."[112] Thus, the postmodern condition interrupts modern correlation theology *"from within the context itself."* Now, "rationality and humanity, truth and justice, are no longer univocal terms."[113] In order for a recontextualization to occur, therefore, one which does not result in a rupture or discontinuity from context or an uncritical maintenance of modern continuity, the category of interruption must become productive in a way that is, to use Boeve's criteria, both contextually adequate and theologically legitimate.

Interruption is contextually adequate insofar as it is "the exponent of what can be termed our contemporary *contextual* critical consciousness."[114] Interruption is the concrete realization of the more abstract notion of critical

---

109. See Boeve, *Lyotard*, 128–31. Here, Boeve notes that Metz sees postmodernity as a cultural amnesia and notes his criticism of Lyotard and Derrida for subordinating the human subject to language. Metz ends up taking a discontinuous position with regard to the postmodern context and perhaps commits the same "hermeneutical mistake" that he blames others (e.g., Ratzinger) of committing (i.e., a defensive-traditionalist approach that avoids or stops theory-praxis-dialectics of postmodernity).

110. Boeve, *God Interrupts*, 204.

111. Boeve, *God Interrupts*, 42. See also Boeve, *Lyotard*, 95.

112. Boeve, *God Interrupts*, 42.

113. Boeve, *God Interrupts*, 43.

114. Boeve, *God Interrupts*, 43.

consciousness. In light of the *différend*, contextual critical consciousness refers to the sensitivity one has towards the other in the other's "irreducible otherness and our ultimate witness to that otherness."[115] Boeve claims that interruption is its exponent in two ways. First, the encounter with religious "otherness" calls to mind the particularity of the Christian narrative's truth claim and interrupts "any pretence toward absoluteness." In colliding with and being criticized by the other narrative, the Christian narrative is informed of and becomes aware of its own borders. As Boeve says, it is "thrown back upon its own narrativity and particularity. . . . [It is then] challenged to formulate its truth claims on two fronts: first, with respect to this irreducible narrativity and particularity, and second, as regards the truth claims of others."[116] Now, the Christian narrative cannot claim more than radical particularity will allow while acknowledging the particular truth claims of others. Second, the interruption of the Christian narrative by the "other," a collision that causes the Christian narrative to become aware of its own borders (i.e., particularity), opens the possibility for the Christian narrative to itself become interruptive. The Christian narrative, therefore, can (and dare we say *ought* to) act as a fundamentally "open narrative," becoming productive in the plural arena by engaging "with other narratives that have closed themselves off or harden[ed] themselves in a fundamentalist way."[117] Here, one sees the coinciding of various concepts: open narrative, critical consciousness, and interruption. In the apparent humility that typifies postmodernity, Christianity is to exist "as a small narrative, or better still as an open narrative, as a narrative that offers orientation and integration without thereby being determined to integrate everything in its own narrative in a totalitarian way."[118] Far from Christianity being relegated or serving a functional, to-be-used-only-when-necessary role, as happens in modern correlation theology, in the postmodern context, the Christian narrative, reenergized by interruption and radically aware of its own particularity protests against functionalizing reductions of its own narrative, while challenging today's metanarratives as an agent of postmodern philosophy.[119]

115. Boeve, *Interrupting Tradition*, 91.
116. Boeve, *God Interrupts*, 44.
117. Boeve, *God Interrupts*, 44.
118. Boeve, *Interrupting Tradition*, 175. The implications can be drawn out politico-theologically as well. For example, see Boeve, *God Interrupts*, 48. Sweeney comments on this as well in *Sacramental Presence*, 115, where he says that Christianity is "emboldened to apply this particularity positively to the non-violent embrace of otherness, to victims, and to open dialogue with other 'life options.'"
119. Boeve, *God Interrupts*, 44–45. It is worth noting that Boeve acknowledges that postmodernity can also function, in some cases, as a metanarrative.

According to Boeve, interruption is a contextually adequate way of transforming the Christian narrative into an open narrative that allows theology to play by the rules of postmodernity (if one can say that). However, is it a valid theological position as well? Boeve justifies interruption theologically with four points. Boeve first theologically grounds interruption in apophatic theology according to the maxim: *Deus semper major*. Speech can refer to God, but it cannot "lay hold of God," for even if "language is unmistakably the way to God . . . one has to admit that it does not reach God."[120] He conceives of interruption as reflective of God's relationship with his own creation when parts of that creation attempt to contain Him. As Boeve puts it, "God repeatedly breaks open the narratives of human beings and communities, including narratives about Godself."[121] God's own method of interaction with humanity seems to be shot through with interruption: God is a God who breaks open closed narratives. Boeve says, "The entire metaphorical constitution of the Christian narrative appears to be permeated by the interruption, on God's behalf, of narratives. . . . The Christian narrative is never allowed to close itself. When it does, then the God of love breaks the narrative open. Interruption functions here as a *theological* category."[122]

Second, interruption aligns with an understanding the Incarnation of Jesus Christ as a radical-hermeneutic path. In the interruption of the "other," in the encounter with the "otherness" of the other, the boundaries of one's own narrative are exposed for what they are. God's interruption of human narratives, God's interruption of the faith narrative (in the Old Testament) and the Christian narrative (even today), appears most profoundly in Jesus Christ. Jesus' "otherness" provides a radical hermeneutical path that makes

---

120. Boeve, "Christus Postmodernus," 580. For a more complete treatment of aphophatic theology as the basis of a theological understanding of "open narrative" and interruption, see Boeve, *Interrupting Tradition*, 149–62; Boeve, "Negative Theology and Theological Hermeneutics," 189–207.

121. Boeve, *God Interrupts*, 46. See also 177.

122. Boeve, *God Interrupts*, 46. The German Synodal Way adopts Heidegger's ontological existentialism in its understanding of revelation (see Part 3, pp. 11–15), and, in light of "a handling of complexity that is attentive and sensitive to ambiguity . . . [that is] a basic signature of intellectual contemporaneity—*and also encompasses today's theology*," the *Fundamental Text* holds that while in theology "there is no one central perspective, no one truth of the religious, moral and political world, and no one form of thought that can lay claim to ultimate authority," "in the Church, too, legitimate views and ways of life can compete with each other even in core convictions" (14; emphasis added). Furthermore, the Church's authority does not have "the competence to decide single-handedly on the content of faith and principles of morality; no one has the right to interpret the teachings of faith and morals with the intention of urging others to actions that serve only his interest or correspond to his ideas, but not the convictions of others" (27).

one aware of the Otherness of God. The interrupting God fully reveals this radical hermeneutic in the Incarnation of Jesus Christ.

Boeve theologizes within the Chalcedonian categories,[123] in order to express the manner in which Jesus acts as the "motor of radical hermeneutics."[124] Like Rahner, Boeve carefully maintains the distinctiveness of Christ's two natures, but he does so more radically. Boeve argues that in Christ, the "particular never coincides with God, just as God and humanity are united in a single person, undivided and undiluted. . . . the latter [i.e., humanity] cannot be substituted nor can it be absolutized. [Christ's humanity] speaks of God—and without it there can be no talk about God—but it is not God."[125] He adds:

> In his own person, Jesus Christ signifies what we have called the relation between Word (Logos) and word—the mutually being related of Word (Logos) and word. The Logos incarnated in the word, becomes signified in the word, but does not identify itself with the word. The word "evokes," thereby determining the indeterminable Logos, and precisely in this determining distinguishes itself from the Logos. The word never becomes Logos, but is the way to Logos. To affirm that Jesus Christ is both God and human, means proclaiming that in person, life, speech, and deeds, he was *the definitive hermeneutics of God, but that he—himself being God—can only be approached in a radical-hermeneutical way.* He is the definitive revelation of God, and this precisely in the paradoxical relation of God and humanity established in his person because, as a person, he gives expression to the tension between word and the Word (Logos).[126]

---

123. Boeve, "*Christus Postmodernus*," 584. Boeve notes that Rahner considers the Christological dogma of Chalcedon both the end of the doctrinal development, but also its beginning. Rahner, as Boeve notes, takes Chalcedon as the beginning of further reflection along the lines of transcendental anthropology. Boeve holds that the Chalcedonian Fathers emphasized universality (divinity) as the key to unlocking particularity (humanity). However, within the postmodern context "the universality acknowledged by Christians in Jesus Christ constitutes a problem," therefore, he asks, "How can one think universality starting from particularity?" (588).

124. Boeve, "Negative Theology and Theological Hermeneutics," 205.

125. Boeve, *God Interrupts*, 177.

126. Boeve, "*Christus Postmodernus*," 589. Sweeney summarizes Boeve's position as follows: "Jesus' humanity, as particular, embodies a radical hermeneutical path to God. To say that the Word is made flesh, is to say that in becoming flesh the Word subjects Itself to the hermeneutical condition of the *humanum*. . . . In other words, 'word' (note the lower case), as a phenomenon occurring within the limits of history, is not able to contain the divinity of Logos as such: 'The word never becomes Logos, but is the way to the Logos'" (Sweeney, *Sacramental Presence*, 113).

The "otherness" of Jesus Christ serves, here, as the definitive and radical hermeneutic path in which "otherness" erupts onto the scene and challenges closed (or closing) narratives.[127] In other words, the human word (i.e., Jesus Christ) interrupts and opens one's narrative about the Other (i.e., the unspeakable heterogeneity/relative nothingness/absolute fullness that is God). As Boeve puts it, "christology, does not involve a metaphysics of presence, nor of absence, but of present absence, revealed in the tension between the word and the Word (Logos). In the word, the Word (Logos) is present by its withdrawal."[128] In this conception, the word points the way, as a sign, to Logos, of which there is no onto-theological ground. There is no way for the human intellect to "grasp" Logos. Logos is the ungraspable, and the moment one attempts to lay hold of Logos, Logos itself moves away, breaking free. Jesus Christ, then, as the preeminent "Interrupter" is the "paradigm of the 'open narrative.'"[129] As Sweeney puts it, "It is no longer possible to speak of Incarnation as an ontological event.... Christianity must give up any pretensions of absoluteness and adopt a narrative of interruption."[130]

For Boeve, then, "God's revelation in Jesus Christ forms the hermeneutical key" for understanding the particular and contingent events that become the *loci* of God's self-manifestation. Boeve says:

> Only in the all too concrete, in the all too historical, in the all too contingent—and in an interpretation thereof—does God engage history in an irreducible and definitive way, without, however, coinciding with it. Incarnation never implies the neutralization or cancellation of the historical-particular in terms of the universal, or of the contingent-historical in terms of the absolute.... Only in the all too human is God revealed, not without it—only in the all-too-historical can Christians read God's presence and activity.[131]

If for Rahner, Moran, and Groome, God's revelation in Christ melds with any and every transcendental experience, for Boeve, it seems, revelation (as present absence) takes place every time one encounters the otherness of the other. In the end, it turns out that Jesus was just a forerunner of the postmodern, a prototype of the *differend*, and the Church is that which stands in time and space to give voice to the *differend*—all the while having her own narrative interrupted by it. For Boeve, Jesus Christ "as a human person,

---

127. Boeve, "*Christus Postmodernus*," 591.
128. Boeve, "*Christus Postmodernus*," 592.
129. Boeve, "*Christus Postmodernus*," 590.
130. Sweeney, *Sacramental Presence*, 113.
131. Boeve, *God Interrupts*, 156.

definitively revealed God in history, ... does not mean that God coincides with the concrete and the accidental. Every concrete encounter, no matter how accidental, every particular and contingent event, is the potential locus of God's manifestation."[132] This was basically the case for Rahner, Moran, and Groome as well. The encounter with the concrete, the historical, made the transcendental experience possible—the locus of God's revelation now christologically configured in the supernatural existential. Here, the same basically holds true, but with postmodern sensibilities. The revelation and recognition of God-as-other takes place in and through the interruption of one's own narrative by the "other"—whoever that may be. The "other" basically participates in the "Otherness" of God that reached a high point in Jesus Christ and continues today in the ordinary experience of "otherness." The experience of interruption becomes the "place" or event of revelation when one acknowledges the irreducible heterogeneity of "otherness." Jesus Christ is the revelation of God insofar as he embodies or incarnates the radical hermeneutics of postmodern critical consciousness, always breaking open narratives precisely as other, as the reminder of God's present absence. As one encounters the narrative of the other, the borders of one's own particular Christian narrative become clear. Here, interruption becomes "an adequate means to conceive of God's salvific engagement with history,"[133] and salvation, in this postmodern context, means being saved from the closed narrative—a recontextualized experience of grace.[134] If I am understanding Boeve correctly, it seems that interruption reaches its high point in Christ—something of an evolutionary climax. If so, Boeve appears to be postmodernly reworking Rahner and Moran's Christological supernatural existential. Is every interruption now categorically Christian, because of the always already radical-hermeneutical path established by Christ?

Third, given the previous point, interruption is theologically legitimate in that interreligious dialogue is not merely "a contextual necessity" in a world marked by plurality, but also a theological one.[135] The encounter with the "other" is the postmodern revelational event (as opposed to the encounter with the Christian tradition or an awareness or experience of self in the transcendental experience). Now the "otherness" of the "other" stands in the radically hermeneutical path of Jesus Christ, preventing one's narrative from closing, while raising awareness of the relative nothingness/absolute fullness of the Idea of heterogeneity. This radically impacts

132. Boeve, *God Interrupts*, 176.
133. Boeve, *God Interrupts*, 48.
134. Boeve, *Lyotard*, 73.
135. Boeve, *God Interrupts*, 47.

the notion of tradition, which must now been understood in a non-cumulative, dynamic way. One does not receive tradition as an heir and elucidates or explicates that which was previously only implicitly known, thus building upon a stable foundation. Rather than a "cumulative" and ever-growing, ever expanding approach, Boeve calls for an interruption of tradition that is capable of recontextualization. The outcome of such recontextualization "is . . . *not so much 'more' tradition but rather 'different' tradition.*" Why? He answers:

> We are *not only heirs to the inheritance [i.e., tradition], we are also its testators.* . . . By way of recontextualisation, we are called to experience and reflect upon Christianity's offer of meaning and to pass it on. This certainly does not mean that the tradition simply adapts itself—some will say "surrenders" itself—to time and context. What it does imply is that every time and context challenges us to give shape to the message of God's love revealed in Jesus Christ in a contemporary way. If we do not accept this challenge we run the risk of sliding into inauthenticity.[136]

Following a genealogy of recontextualized traditions over the centuries,[137] Boeve holds that recontextualizing the faith according to context frequently results in a "different" tradition. Context and hermeneutics shape and change the experience of faith tradition to the point where "*The* Christian narrative no longer exists, we only have access to it through its relation to the context. . . . From the perspective of history, the Christian narrative worked its way through a variety of successive contexts, continually recontextualising along the way. As a result it took on a multitude of different forms that were not always reconcilable with those it had left behind."[138] Boeve seems to be describing a detraditionalizing exercise carried out by postmodern critical consciousness. This subjectivizing exercise allows the individual subject to decide whether to accept the tradition, and if so, the individual reconstructs the meaning of a tradition to suit him or herself. To connect the dot back to Moran and modernist correlation, once revelation has been relativized and

---

136. Boeve, *Interrupting Tradition*, 24. See also Rowland, "Catholic Theology in the Twentieth Century," 46.

137. Lieven Boeve, *Interrupting Tradition*, 22–24.

138. Lieven Boeve, *Interrupting Tradition*, 24. Elsewhere, on this point, Boeve cites a current example of such renewal in shifts of language around God who "is no longer interpreted and conceptualized in exclusively patriarchal terms" (Boeve, *God Interrupts*, 53). The encounter with the new context constitutes a language problem, both in terms of how the Christian tradition expresses itself in the postmodern arena (i.e., *ad extra*), and, as a result of this *ad extra* collision with context, the inner perspective, the narrative tradition's self-understanding or self-expression changes *ad intra*.

detached from the Christian tradition, the postmodern position radically subjectivizes it. The movement here goes from "this is what the tradition says, but it does not really matter so much," to "this is what it says or means to me." Under the sway of the detraditionalizing postmodern condition, ultimately the "self," acting as a *testator* now subjectivizes the already relativized tradition and establishes his or her own "different" tradition.

Finally, interruption provides *political-theological* considerations. Closed narratives produce victims by suppressing and excluding other narratives. The Christian position cannot stand for this. Metz's line the "shortest definition of religion is interruption," again, provides the inspiration here.[139] Metz's statement refers to an active Christianity impelled by human suffering, the preferential option for the poor, suffering and oppressed, out of fear that Christianity might devolve into a bourgeois religion.[140] Boeve, however, employs the concept as expressive of postmodern critical consciousness. Now, "where diversity and otherness are being stealthily reduced to the multiplicity of market goods or eradicated in the name of an inviolable hegemonic truth claim, Christians are obliged to interrupt on behalf of God the 'Interrupter.'"[141] Living the Christian identity means contributing to the recontextualization of a narrative tradition by both being open to being interrupted and by taking on the *role of interrupter* of closed narratives. In this way, Christianity becomes productive within postmodernity.

Conclusion

Boeve's project radicalizes Rahner's correlation theology by postmodernly recontextualizing it. Given postmodernity's incredulity toward metanarratives and Lyotard's critique of the Christian metanarrative, Boeve sets out to vindicate Christianity and establish a postmodern theology that is theologically legitimate and contextually adequate. To recontextualize theology, he begins with a non-theological "given" in Lyotardian postmodern critical consciousness and reconstitutes the whole of Christianity in light of its dictates—as an open narrative according to the category of interruption. Having adopted a "radical hermeneutics," Boeve develops a method that "leads irreducibly to particularity, indeed to particular texts and traditions, and to the way these function in a religious context."[142] The emphasis on particularity and alterity interrupts and open traditions, preventing them

---

139. As cited in Boeve, *God Interrupts*, 203.
140. Boeve, *God Interrupts*, 203–4.
141. Boeve, *God Interrupts*, 48.
142. Boeve, "Richard Kearney's Messianism," 15.

from becoming hegemonic. For Christians, Boeve posits, this means starting from "an acceptance of the radical incarnation and inscription of God into a particular history." He goes on to summarize the main thrust of his project in fundamental theology:

> God's revelation is irreducibly historical, bound to the very particularity of a people, of human-being, of communities, and it is only from that level of particularity that it is meaningful, namely, to make a distinction between revelation in general and revelation in particular. Accepting the radicality of incarnation, . . . however, is not the end of hermeneutics, an absolutizing of the historical, but the very start of a radical theological hermeneutics. . . . [Accordingly,] participants in the interreligious conversation . . . venture . . . toward positing religious truth claims, each of which come from their own particular religious narratives and practices. This position . . . develops a critical consciousness precisely *from within* particularity. It is because of the irreducible particularity of religious truth claims that an ongoing hermeneutical process is called for, a process that, in its determination of religious truth today, no longer abandons, but holds fast to precisely this very particularity.[143]

In short, Boeve's project, then, with its postmodern "given," simply perpetuates Rahner and Moran's, but with postmodern sensibilities. In his attempt at theological legitimacy and contextual adequacy, Boeve detraditionalizes the tradition according to the *testator* thesis, reinterprets the Christ-event according to a radical hermeneutics, and ultimately reduces Christianity to an exponent of postmodernity—a plaything of postmodern critical consciousness. Naturally, Boeve's developments for postmodern fundamental theology impact evangelization and catechesis.

---

143. Boeve, "Richard Kearney's Messianism," 16–17.

CHAPTER FOUR

The Gospel according to Postmodernity: Recontextualizing Evangelization

Like Moran's development of ongoing revelation Boeve's theology of interruption, founded on postmodern critical consciousness, profoundly impacts approaches to what are traditionally known as evangelization and catechesis. Moran, followed immediately in Rahner's footsteps, downgrading the importance of evangelization in the mission of the Church and reconfigured catechesis according to transcendent experience. Now, every transcendental experience was a revelation, and one always already implicitly Christian (anonymous Christianity) due to the "christologized" supernatural existential. Moran relativizes revelation and relegates tradition in establishing his doctrine of ongoing revelation. This anthropocentric shift becomes the core of that which theologians like Boeve and Pollefeyt will recontextualize to account for the postmodern condition.

A recontextualization of evangelization basically means postmodernizing it such that evangelization becomes a functional exponent of postmodern critical consciousness. Unlike Moran and Groome, Boeve's conception of "evangelization" allows for and even encourages sharing the Christian narrative, but only insofar as it acts as an open narrative within the plural playing field of fundamental life options. For Boeve, however, the Christian narrative must both be open to being interrupted, and willing to interrupt other narratives that risk becoming hegemonic. In this way, Boeve recontextualizes revelation and the Christian narrative according to the dictates of the postmodern condition, which both limits its narrative capacity and ennobles its functionality as an interruptible-interruptive open narrative. The category of interruption and the reconstitution of the Christian narrative as an open narrative allows Boeve and Pollefeyt to reconfigure the mission of theology, and of the Church, according to Lyotard's conception of the mission of postmodern philosophy of giving voice to the *differend*.

The Question of Salvation and Recontextualizing Evangelization

The relationship between Christianity and other (world) religions has traditionally fallen into one of three categories: exclusivism, inclusivism, and pluralism. Pollefeyt describes exclusivism as the conviction that "believers of other religions or nonbelievers can only be saved when they convert to the only true religion, namely, the religion the exclusivists confess. For Christian exclusivists, this position means . . . people can only be saved when they convert to Christianity and accept . . . Jesus as Christ and Redeemer."[1] Here we confront the age-old motto from St. Cyprian, *extra ecclesiam nulla salus* ("outside of the church, there is no salvation"). This means, as Boeve puts it, "God's universal salvific will is strictly bound to the saving mediation of Jesus Christ and the salvific necessity of the church."[2] Following the Council, the notion of inclusivism became popular. "Inclusivism," Pollefeyt says, "does not deny in advance the value of non-Christian religions . . . salvation outside Christianity is possible, but only thanks to the salvific work of God through Jesus."[3] Boeve explicitly notes Rahner's anonymous Christianity position as illustrative of this position.[4] Pollefeyt believes that Rahner is key in developing this teaching within Catholicism, and that Vatican II's *Lumen gentium* (particularly §16) enshrines it as "the official position of the Catholic Church."[5] If this is the case, than exclusivism is no longer the official position of the Church. Finally, the pluralist paradigm levels the interreligious landscape. Here, one views the vast array of religions as fundamentally equal, "partial expressions of the Ultimate Reality. All religions are relativized as parallel paths to salvation insofar as they are agents working to move human beings away from reliance on ego and orienting them . . . toward the goal of seeking Ultimate Reality."[6] In this case, Jesus Christ is not "unique, irreducible, or complete, because the Christian perspective constitutes only one single part of a more inclusive religious reality." Further illustrating the pluralist point, Boeve likens each religion to facets of the same diamond, "which no one is able to see in its entirety."[7]

---

1. Pollefeyt, "Interreligious Dialogue," 245.
2. Boeve, *God Interrupts*, 167.
3. Pollefeyt, "Interreligious Dialogue," 246.
4. Boeve, *God Interrupts*, 167.
5. Pollefeyt, "Interreligious Dialogue," 246.
6. Pollefeyt, "Interreligious Dialogue," 248.
7. Boeve, *God Interrupts*, 168.

Not surprisingly, all three positions have been sharply criticized according to postmodern critical consciousness. Exclusivism (salvation through *faith in* Christ alone) and inclusivism (salvation through Christ alone) *universalize* the Christian claim and are prone to "'totalitarian features and the denigration of other religious truth claims."[8] Exclusivism sees Christianity as a closed narrative, in that it ultimately does not allow for other narratives. Similarly, critics denounce inclusivism as a position that is "not truly open to the reality of the other," because it restricts "its openness solely to what is compatible in the other with one's own religious identity."[9] Pluralism (many equal pathways to salvation) *particularizes* the Christian claim by making it one truth contained by a higher religious truth that all pathways to God are essentially equal. This strategy weakens the Christian claim the most, limiting or relativizing the claim such that, at most, Jesus represents, but does not incarnate God.[10] Pollefeyt notes that Gavin D'Costa sees agnosticism as the inevitable outcome of pluralism because, in the end, all particularity is ultimately lost in light of the "inclusive religious reality."[11] Similarly, Boeve says it leads to a "relativistic pluralism," wherein "if everything has the same truth value then nothing is ultimately true."[12] Pluralism can even take on the form of exclusivism insofar as it becomes a closed narrative and does not allow for any position other than the pluralist one. Boeve sees pluralism as failing to "maintain the identity and gravity of the Christian truth claim," while "exclusivism and inclusivism find it difficult to ascribe a satisfactory place to other religions and their truth claims."[13] Boeve summarizes the problems, saying, "Exclusivism and inclusivism generalize the confession of Christ, and . . . the religious truth claims of other religions are denied or forced to fit within the Christian truth claim. Pluralism relativizes the confession of Christ by subordinating it to a transcendent, more comprehensive truth, to which other religions also contribute as partial truths or perspectives on truth."[14] Both exclusivism and inclusivism universalize Christianity, though in different ways, while pluralism particularizes it.[15]

8. Sweeney, *Sacramental Presence*, 116. See also Boeve, *God Interrupts*, 166.

9. Pollefeyt, "Interreligious Dialogue," 247.

10. Boeve, *God Interrupts*, 168–69.

11. Pollefeyt, "Interreligious Dialogue," 248. Quote from Boeve, *God Interrupts*, 166.

12. Boeve, *God Interrupts*, 169.

13. Boeve, *God Interrupts*, 170.

14. Boeve, *God Interrupts*, 170–71. For more on exclusivism, inclusivism, and pluralism, see Pollefeyt, "Interreligious Dialogue," 245–59.

15. Boeve, *God Interrupts*, 170. Here, Boeve says that both exclusivism and inclusivism ultimately claim, "the Christian faith is the one and only truth, for all times

Pollefeyt notes that the fundamental problem with the whole understanding of religious dialogue in terms of exclusivism, inclusivism, and pluralism lies in the fact that "Christian scholars created this typology to reflect on Christian questions . . . related to the possibility of salvation for the non-Christian believer. But this soteriological question is a Christian question . . . [hence] an expression of Christian superiority."[16] In other words, none of the positions operate within postmodern critical consciousness, with an understanding of Christianity as an open narrative. One must pursue a position outside the "-isms" if one wishes to recontextualize interreligious dialogue and mission. In place of the three conceptions, then, Boeve attempts to find an alternate, contextually adequate and theologically legitimate path between the universalizing approaches of exclusivism and inclusivism and the particularizing one of pluralism.

In his attempt at a *via media*, Boeve argues for an "alternate form of inclusivism," which opposes the relativizing that happens in pluralism, and distinctly emphasizes particularity and difference.[17] As one comes into contact with other religions, "potential points of mutual kinship emerge side by side with reciprocal difference and an awareness of the uniqueness of the dialogue partners."[18] This approach centers upon plurality and particularity, which do not fit within the traditional typology of exclusivism, inclusivism, and pluralism. In other words, the prior "given" (i.e., salvation—in Christ or in one's religious path) has been recontextualized in terms of alterity. Pollefeyt explains, "the goal of the particularist in interreligious dialogue is no longer to reduce difference to some common denominator or ground outside of difference, but to discover, accept, and respect the differences among partners in dialogue. . . . Each [religion] is a different framework for the expression of a radically different religious experience."[19] Difference is that reality of which all are inclusively a part. An alternate form of inclusion simply means embracing difference as the "given."

All of this, it seems to me, reworks both the inclusivist and pluralist positions according to the dictates of postmodern thinking. Rather than

---

and places and peoples," meaning that other religions are either "completely lacking in truth" (exclusivism) or are "sharing only in a part thereof" (inclusivism). In pluralism, Christian faith "is (only) one perspective on, or part of, a greater truth. It is one specific (particular) truth that is contained in or surpassed by a higher (universal) truth."

16. Pollefeyt, "Interreligious Dialogue," 249.

17. Boeve, *God Interrupts*, 172. He also describes this position as "a different type of inclusivism" (173) and a "sort of 'pluralist' inclusivism" (175).

18. Boeve, *God Interrupts*, 172.

19. Pollefeyt, "Interreligious Dialogue," 249.

inclusivism operating in light of Christian doctrine, it operates within the realm of difference-thinking. Rather than the pluralism theory relativizing Christianity as one path among many, a postmodern reworking simply removes the concept of movement toward some common "salvation." Boeve rejects a "bird's eye perspective on the religious reality" that claims all paths are heading up the same mountain. He says:

> We are all participants. We all follow our own path. We are aware that other paths exist that cross our own from time to time or run parallel with our path. . . . Walking on our own path, however, it is impossible for us to confirm that all these paths actually lead to the same mountaintop. . . . It is thus from our own experiences . . . that we enter into dialogue and that we are able to exchange thoughts and customs, joys and concerns. . . . Aware of the fact that we are participants, and learning about the other inform our contacts with the other, we are capable, to a degree, of changing our perspective, without revoking however the irreducible otherness of the other in the process.[20]

Boeve adds:

> Christians do not have a bird's eye view that allows them to survey religious plurality as detached observers and grant it a place in light of its own truth. Indeed, Christianity's own place in the midst of plurality is part of the picture. The "different inclusivism" to which we refer is conscious of the particularity of the Christian faith and brings it into the dialogue, not in order to relativize its own position but rather to determine it in the plural, interreligious world. In the context of interreligious contacts and communication, Christians will ultimately be confronted with their own specific way of speaking about reality.[21]

Rather than particularizing Christianity as one *part* of some greater whole, Boeve denies the possibility of ever coming to know if there is a greater whole of which everything is a part. In other words, he particularizes everything. One can only know undeniable difference, radical plurality, and boundless multiplicity. Christians cannot approach plurality with a "bird's eye view," a privileged vantage point as appears in exclusivism and inclusivism, but as participants in the radically plural reality of the postmodern condition. Thus, inclusion is recontextualized as way of describing a horizon of difference and an ideal way of approaching the interreligious landscape such

---

20. Boeve, *God Interrupts*, 175.
21. Boeve, *God Interrupts*, 174.

that each position becomes more profoundly aware of its own particularity and contextuality—its own "baggage"—and does not close in on itself as a totalizing grand narrative. This allows for the legitimacy of other paths in a sort of different, or pluralist inclusivism, while leaving as a possibility the "universal salvific will of God," because it leaves open the possibility of "trusting that all humanity is ultimately saved in Christ."[22]

Interreligious Dialogue: The "New" Evangelization

Bereft of any one metanarrative of salvation under which all the others can be organized, Christian evangelization becomes unhinged, a watchword for hegemony. Interreligious dialogue emerges as the only contextually adequate and theologically legitimate way forward for a postmodern Christian religious education. Additionally, Boeve and Pollefeyt argue that an inclusivist approach to interreligious dialogue marked by difference-thinking is a theological necessity. Interreligious dialogue reminds the Christian of the present absence of the "Other" through the "otherness" of the "other" religious position. This revelation of "otherness" prevents one's narrative from overreaching, becoming hegemonic, and closing in upon itself. It reminds one of the ungraspable nature of Being, while allowing time and space for one's own narrative to collide with the narrative boundaries of others. The encounter with the "other" interrupts, particularizing the Christian narrative amid the heterogeneity of the religious landscape and pointing to the present absence of the "Otherness" of God.

Here, one does not, and, in a certain sense, cannot approach interreligious dialogue with evangelization in mind or as a pursuit of *the* truth. This dialogue exists solely for the sake of interrupting and determining one's position "in the plural, interreligious world."[23] Dialogue exists because of difference and for the sake of accounting for and including difference. A different inclusivist interreligious dialogue becomes the new *praxis*, the new "space" for religious education, because now "being a Christian . . . calls one to *a praxis of both being interrupted and interrupting*."[24] Sweeney, summarizing Boeve's position, notes that one who "accepts that the impossibility of a universal point of view means that one cannot assert the primacy of any single religious claim, but that at the same time affirms that Christian particularity is, as particular, irreducibly unique."[25] The Christian narrative can neither

---

22. Boeve, *God Interrupts*, 175.
23. Boeve, *God Interrupts*, 174.
24. Boeve, *Lyotard*, 99.
25. Sweeney, *Sacramental Presence*, 116.

make a totalizing claim on other religions, nor can its uniqueness be denied. It is neither capable of a universal claim, nor is it subject to any universal religious claim. With this, evangelization is recontextualized.

At this point, one must pause and ask how interreligious dialogue possible in an arena where difference *is* the common denominator. Pollefeyt answers this question in two ways. First, because in the realm of religion, particular linguistic systems attempt to describe an "external," namely "God" or a "divine reality" "outside or beyond," each linguistic system itself (i.e., any way a particular religion tries to, in human language, describe "God" or a "divine reality") holds in common the fact that it refers to something outside of the linguistic system itself. Second, "religious linguistic systems are not completely separated from one another historically"; they do not develop in isolation but are mutually influencing each other over time.[26] These two realities provide the basis for the possibility of dialogue that would take place in a manner akin to translation. While all translation risks "losing meaning, changing meaning, perverting meaning," translation does not end with the "loss of meaning." Instead, translation "can discover new meanings."[27] Because experience and language cannot be separated, one's engagement in dialogue will "in some way begin from and remain colored by one's own language. Hence inclusivism, in some way, is always inescapable for religious believers who enter into interreligious dialogue."[28] That a perfect translation is not possible, or that one risks a slight religious inclusivism, is no grounds for a non-engagement in interreligious dialogue. It is precisely in this dialectic between sameness and otherness that prevents one's own narrative from exclusivism or the relativized narrative of pluralism.

All of this indicates, it seems, that the traditional understanding of evangelization clearly betrays Christianity as either an exclusivistic or inclusivistic metannarrative. As such, evangelization is simply unacceptable and inappropriate within a postmodern setting fixated upon difference-thinking and interreligious dialogue. Therefore, evangelization must be recontextualized if it is to survive. Boeve and Pollefeyt recontextualize it in terms of interruption—reconfiguring evangelization as the "saving" engagement of a Christian open narrative within interreligious dialogue. Now, the "good news" offered by a Christian open narrative serves postmodern critical consciousness by breaking open closed narratives, while

---

26. Pollefeyt, "Interreligious Dialogue," 250.
27. Pollefeyt, "Interreligious Dialogue," 251. See also Boeve, *God Interrupts*, 173–74.
28. Pollefeyt, "Interreligious Dialogue," 251.

preserving others from the same fate—saving those it encounters from the most damnable of all sins: hegemony.

Critiquing Current Models

The interruptive value of difference-thinking in interreligious dialogue has serious implications for evangelization, and for postmodernizing catechetics as well. In today's detraditionalized condition, Boeve notes that youth today rarely "consider the Christian story—the Christian tradition that is inherited and can be experienced in life and activity—as a key for interpreting their personal inner life, experience and involvement. . . . Elementary familiarity and acquaintance with the Christian story is lacking."[29] However, youth do welcome experiences of transcendence, which carry them beyond the ordinariness of life, but these experiences rarely connect to the rest of their lives. Boeve believes that such experiences, which he calls religious "kick-experiences" (i.e., experiences of transcendence), have surfaced as a way of dealing with the broken story. The "kick-experience" is a type of transcendent experience wherein one's "boundary" is "transgressed" in a "search for excess," in the escalating need for a greater and more intense "shock."[30] Boeve notes that this pursuit of accumulating kicks may result from two realities. On the one hand, postmodernity seems to eliminate the possibility of experience because real experience takes place within a story, memory, or other platform, and postmodernity has removed such stories and memories. The kick is, therefore, an attempt at forgetting "about the absence of story." On the other hand, the kick can become a way of dealing with the apparent meaninglessness of life without a story. The kick is a way of trying "to hold on to one's identity."[31]

Boeve believes that two current religious movements attempt to present these types of transcendent experiences along with a story that connects to life: "fundamentalist" spirituality and New Age. Boeve sees both movements as presenting religious "kick-experiences" (albeit in different directions) that try to "correct what is missing in the structure and direction of the postmodern."[32] On the one hand, traditional, or "fundamentalist" spirituality groups reject the culture of the "kick," and instead seek

---

29. Boeve, "Religious Bungee Jumping," 54.

30. Boundary transgression refers to the constant shifting or escalation of the boundary and the need for greater or more powerful shocks in order to "transcend" or overcome the newly established boundary. There is a need for constantly new stimuli.

31. Boeve, "Religious Bungee Jumping," 61.

32. Boeve, "Religious Bungee Jumping," 58.

identity outside of the detraditionalized postmodern condition. He says that here, where there "is a strong sense of involvement and an intense spiritual experience that is totally embedded in a life of faith where the specific tradition and life of faith are clear, . . . the experience of transcendence is one of 'feeling comfortable' in their own story."[33] Boeve believes this "feeling comfortable" is the result of maintaining "the letter of tradition," traditional ways of living, and the authority of a leader. Boeve calls this solution to the chaos of postmodernity an *intra-traditional* one that separates "saving faith" from the "perverse culture." The "kick experience," here, is something of an anti-kick, in that it is a rejection of the kick culture and its constantly escalating pursuit of the new. On the other hand, New Age movement embraces the kick culture, as individuals and groups search "for an experience which brings them a certain fulfillment and meaningfulness and which offers them the fullness of human existence."[34] The New Age movement rejects linkage to a single story or religion, instead constructing new religious stories based upon transcendent experiences.[35] In short, New Age "offers the possibility of one structuring a private subjective certainty."[36] Despite their differences, Boeve notes that traditional and New Age groups are structurally similar in that: (1) transcendent experiences are experiences of self-conquest; (2) such experiences are self-affirming; and (3) such experiences attempt to secure an identity through the authority of another or oneself.[37] Boeve finds fault with a Christianity that rejects the culture (e.g., "fundamentalist" groups) and a Christianity entangled with New Age tendencies. The "closed" nature of traditional groups fails to infuse "vital power into its community and its history," while New Age fails as an "integrating and self-directing religious story."[38]

To Boeve's criticism of "kick experiences," Pollefeyt adds his own criticism of correlationist strategies (e.g., Moran and Groome) in religious education. He describes such strategies as "monoreligious" or "mono-correlative," where a direct, albeit implicit connection is assumed between Christian tradition and human experience. Here, as we have seen in Moran and Groome, "the idea behind correlation didactics was that 'tradition' and 'experience' not only refer to one another, but are—on a deeper level—structurally

33. Boeve, "Religious Bungee Jumping," 56.
34. Boeve, "Religious Bungee Jumping," 56–57.
35. See Boeve, "Religious Bungee Jumping," 57. This sounds oddly familiar to themes appearing in chapters 1 and 2.
36. Boeve, "Religious Bungee Jumping," 58.
37. Boeve, "Religious Bungee Jumping," 57–58.
38. Boeve, "Religious Bungee Jumping," 58.

('ontologically') connected."[39] Postmodern critical consciousness does not accept such monocorrelative inclusivism. He explains:

> Teachers of religion who structure their classes by means of monocorrelative didactics are today confronted with the so-called shutter phenomenon. When one addresses the experiences of young peolpe [sic] and children, their response is often enthusiastic. That first instance of enthusiasm, however, is increasingly toned down as the analysis of those experiences is read from the perspective of the Christian tradition. . . . When Christ is mentioned, the teacher witnesses the gradual closing of the pupils' shutters.[40]

According to Pollefeyt, positions like that of Moran and Groome no longer function in the religious education classroom. Students are wary of hidden agendas, a "bait and switch" method of bringing in Christianity and feel their experience "underacknowledged" and even "manipulated." In response to the shutter phenomenon, some teachers simply remain on the level of experience and stay in the realm of behavioral sciences—avoiding religion altogether.[41] Pollefeyt questions how teaching religion can have a future in this environment and considers a recontextualization necessary if any future lies in store.

Religious Education: An Exercise in Alterity

In his attempt at establishing continuity with postmodernity, Boeve calls for a pastoral approach rooted in postmodern critical consciousness. He contends that this will allow for "actual experiences of transcendence" which "are not so much experiences of self-consolidation, self-assurance, immediate experiences of identity (I have arrived!) but, rather, experiences of alterity . . . a breakthrough from the existing safe story."[42] This is the recontextualized transcendental experience, a postmodern experience of alterity, which tears open or interrupts existing stories and provides something of an identity—an identifying with an ever-open identity.[43] It acknowledges a

---

39. Pollefeyt, "The Difference of Alterity," 309.

40. Pollefeyt, "The Difference of Alterity," 310. For more on this position, see Pollefeyt's more recent article "Hermeneutical Learning," 5–6.

41. Pollefeyt, "The Difference of Alterity," 310. Pollefeyt describes this as a type of pluralism in "Hermeneutical Learning," 6.

42. Boeve, "Religious Bungee Jumping," 62.

43. Boeve, "Religious Bungee Jumping," 64. See also Boeve, *Interrupting Tradition*, 88–90.

need for the "other." With this postmodern "given," Boeve recontextualizes religious education, which is allowable insofar as the Christian story "does not allow itself to be closed."⁴⁴ Therefore, Boeve offers three suggestions for recontextualizing pastoral initiatives: (1) the need to bear in mind the "culture of the kick" as the great temptation—an attempt to inoculate oneself against postmodern melancholy; (2) the need to look for models of continuity which are open to the Other (i.e., otherness); and (3) the need to present Christian tradition as something open.⁴⁵

Pollefeyt provides an overview of recontextualized religious education, by identifying six aspects which together mark the shift from a monocorrelative (modernist) pedagogy to a multicorrelative (postmodern) one. They are as follows:⁴⁶

1. From Monocorrelative to Multicorrelative Religious Didactics—Today's students are a heterogenous group of "ideologically diversified individuals" and reading a group in a homogeneous, monoreligious manner would "wrong the singularity of each member." The monocorrelative religious education of the early Moran-Groome project is no longer possible. Alterity *makes* the difference, here. In this context, a multicorrelative methodology employs a threefold hermeneutics which has to account for the individual subject, the present context, and the traditional hermeneutics of text/tradition.⁴⁷ The triple hermeneutical task demands that one becomes aware of the hermeneutics of the tradition (i.e., the way in which the tradition understands itself), the hermeneutics of context (i.e., the radical plurality of the postmodern context), and the hermeneutics of oneself (i.e., how one's own lenses determine and interpret schemas). In the classroom and in life, this means one first becomes aware of philosophical diversity and the radical particularity of one's own position. Following this encounter with plurality, one considers his or her own tradition and what this encounter with "other" means for it, before deepening one's own perspective on his or her position and entering into dialogue with others about it again. This is simply the dynamism

---

44. Boeve, "Religious Bungee Jumping," 65.
45. Boeve, "Religious Bungee Jumping," 66.
46. The list that follows is a summary of Pollefeyt, "The Difference of Alterity," 308–20. Any direct quotes in the descriptions for each aspect appear within these pages in Pollefeyt's article.
47. See also Pollefeyt, "Hermeneutical Learning," 7.

of an "open narrative" at work in the postmodern religious education classroom—a playground of plurality.[48]

2. From a Constitutive to a Representative Christology—Constitutive Christology refers to the way in which Jesus' Paschal Mystery is seen as a series of constitutive acts that bring about redemption. In this case, Jesus' unique death stands at the center and nothing else can bring about mankind's salvation. Representative Christology sees Jesus as a representation of human redemption—he shows what redemption looks like. This allows for the possibility of redemption before and after Christ's coming and does not exclude the possibility of other representations of redemption. Pollefeyt allows for Jesus Christ to remain confessionally constitutive for the Christian, but this does not mean Jesus is exclusively constitutive for all.

3. From Inductive and Deductive Learning to Abductive—Before now, two approaches to religious education typically prevailed: (1) a deductive approach (kerygmatic catechesis) that moves from "faith" to "experience," and (2) an inductive approach (correlative, experience-oriented style) which moves from "experience" to "faith." Today, Pollefeyt calls for an abductive approach which focuses on teaching youth the necessary skills they need "to notice and critically evaluate signs of the tradition in everyday reality." This puts more responsibility on the shoulders of students, as they discover the bridge between Christian tradition and their own experience. Pollefeyt says, "Abductive religious education does not depart from what *is* (cf. induction) or from what *should be* (cf. deduction), but from what *could be*, namely the possible links between knowledge that is already present and eventual new knowledge."[49]

4. From a Closed to an Open Understanding of Tradition—Tradition is not "fixed once and for all," but "believers keep on writing new chapters to its story all of the time." Tradition is a participative event, not a "museum piece." In this conception, the Christian tradition can offer meaning, which is then placed in a context of ideological plurality and which is confronted by the pupil's own ideology and experience (hence

---

48. See Boeve, "Beyond Correlation Strategies," 252; O'Shea, "Vulgarised Rahnerianism," 364–72.

49. In a certain sense, the close ties between Moran and Groome's work and Pollefeyt's become apparent here. Compared to the inductive approach, the abductive approach seems like a sleight of hand. In both cases, one has to wonder how the child is to discover Christianity in situations where the tradition is either relegated or detraditionalized. One does not know what one does not know.

the threefold hermeneutic mentioned earlier). In this case, Christian tradition is not framed in terms of "truth," but in terms of "plausibility" (i.e., a possible approach) and "plurality" (i.e., one of many possible traditions). Here, religious education "is no longer an act of transferring the core elements of the Christian tradition, but rather the 'passing on of life'" to the *testator*.

5. From a Correlative to an Anticorrelative Didactic Structuring—Lessons are to be structured in "non-correlative phases," meaning that throughout the course of a lesson, the teacher does not quickly attempt to correlate experience to tradition. In other words, the teacher functions as one who offers a "continuous questioning" from experience or tradition in order to break open the conversation and to allowing for the "shaping of a deeper persuasion of what the truth may be."

6. From Man as a "Religious Being" to Man as a "Hermeneutical Being"— In a correlative sense, man is a religious being, whose experiences are always already Christian. Christianity fully develops one's religious nature (i.e., the movement from anonymous to explicit Christianity). Multicorrelative didactics allow for a conception of the human being whereby human beings are not necessarily religious beings, but they are hermeneutical ones "capable of ideological deliberation." Here, "the human being is able to question the meaning of existence, and is able to learn new perspectives of meaning, to discover and experience them." In this case, the religious experience (some experience of the divine that comes from without) drops into the "hermeneutical space" of human reality. This calls for religious education to adopt a hermeneutical process of learning marked by the threefold hermeneutics noted above.

The shift from modern "monocorrelative" to postmodern "multicorrelative" education ushers in a new religious education model. For his part, Pollefeyt develops this multicorrelative approach in the form of a "Hermeneutical-Communicative Model," which begins with an "optimistic anthropology" where man is a hermeneutical being seeking meaning and "pessimistic concepts" like sin, evil, and impotence remain secondary.[50] Thus, Pollefeyt recontextualizes religious education according to postmodern sensitivities, while making it useful for postmodernity's mission of giving voice to the *differend*.[51] To this end, the Hermeneuti-

50. Pollefeyt, "The Difference of Alterity," 320.

51. This recasting of religious education has a significant impact on the question of Catholic identity in schools, which, in the Boeve-Pollefeyt model, are to become "dialogue schools." Pollefeyt notes that the "dialogue school" employs a preferential option for the Catholic message, emphasizing its Christian inspiration in a

cal-Communicative Model aims to help people look at reality from different perspectives. The model provides space wherein all "are invited to discover the religious presuppositions that underlie their own opinions and utterances," by confronting the stories of others.[52] This opens to the possibility of students "deconstructing truth" (i.e., their own ideological conceptions) and reconstructing a new view of life. The teacher's role in presenting the Christian synthesis of faith is important in this step, which aims to arouse "hermeneutical intersections," which are the "result of tensions," and "conflicting interpretations."[53] In this sense, the education is truly "hermeneutical-communicative." It does not proceed according to a monocorrelative hermeneutic (that levels diversity by rendering all experiences already Christian), but as an "actual process of communication in which visions of the different participants challenge one another."[54] The whole experience provokes the discomfort of the breaking open of one's prejudicial narrative—including the Christian narrative's hegemonic prejudices—by alterity, by the voice of the *differend* now allowed to speak. At the same time, the Christian open narrative can offer its own interruptive voice amid other hegemonic positions. Boeve and Pollefeyt recast the Church's mission in terms of a Christian "open narrative" that avoids hegemony—while also preventing its relativization—and religious education as "an education towards a more reflexive religious identity, whether that is Christian or not."[55] Thus, Boeve and Pollefeyt recontextualize the Church's fundamental theology and mission in the chaos of heterogenous interruption—calling for the Christian narrative to be interruptible and to

---

hermeneutical-communicative dialogue with the plural society. Pollefeyt favors the "dialogue school" over what the Victoria Scale calls the "monologue school" (which emphasizes Catholic identity and a "closed story"), the "colourless school" (secular and pluralist, with a non-committal attitude towards religion, a watered-down Catholic identity), and the "colourful school" (a school which pays special attention to difference, though with little-to-no regard for the Catholic character of the school). See Pollefeyt and Bouwens, "Framing the Identity of Catholic Schools," 205–7; Pollefeyt and Richards "Catholic Dialogue Schools," 77–113.

52. Pollefeyt, "The Difference of Alterity," 320. There exists, here, an obvious postmodern pedagogical tie for giving voice to the *differend* between Pollefeyt's vision for religious education and, for example, the advancement critical race theory and its antiracial *cri de coeur*. In the United States, Kendi's *How to Be an Antiracist* and DiAngelo's *White Fragility* encourage a similar methodology. For critical commentary on these methods, see Paul, "Against Racialism," 47–50; Reno, "The Woke Script," 61–65; McWhorter "The Dehumanizing Condescension of *White Fragility*."

53. Pollefeyt, "The Difference of Alterity," 321.

54. Pollefeyt, "The Difference of Alterity," 322. See also Sweeney, *Sacramental Presence*, 116.

55. Boeve, "Religious Education," 154.

interrupt. Precisely in this way the Christian "open narrative" can justifiably function within the postmodern condition and advance Lyotard's philosophical vision.

The ~~Catechist~~ Teacher as Witness, Specialist, Moderator

In the Hermeneutical-Communicative Model, the teacher assumes a WSM-function (witness-specialist-moderator). As "moderator," the teacher must be sensitive to youth culture and must join students in their searching, amazement, doubting, and mocking. Pollefeyt says, "this starting point is 'sacred ground' to him or her—there is no place where God comes to pupils than their own world. Being a moderator implies that pupils should be free to make their own choices and . . . that one grant them their 'practice room' for ideological search and reflection."[56] Moderating means one sets the students' search for meaning free and provides space for deconstruction and reconstruction. Additionally, the teacher functions as "witness." In this role, the teacher "does not see him or herself as the one path, truth and life, but as a guide, or rather as the person who shows pupils cliffs and beacons, traps and points of reference in their search for meaning."[57] This understanding of witness aligns with Boeve's call for the *imitatio Christi*, wherein witness refers primarily to an interruptive initiative of the one whose own narrative has been interrupted.[58] Mission and witness are reconstrued in light of interruption. Finally, as a "specialist," the teacher must have a broad knowledge of religions and traditions.

In the Hermeneutical-Communicative Model, teachers choose lessons that vary, and which contain the necessary ingredients to stir up ideological communication and explore hermeneutical intersections. Once these have surfaced, the teacher can then bring in "religious and Christian perspectives" to enrich and deepen the conversation.[59] Here, the method again relegates Christian tradition, but in recontextualized form following the postmodern version of transcendental experience. Religion class basically functions as an exercise of Lyotardian philosophy, assuming postmodern philosophy's role of pointing out and breaking apart metanarratives rather than supposedly perpetuating and encouraging them. Thus, Pollefeyt continues:

---

56. Pollefeyt, "The Difference of Alterity," 323. See also Pollefeyt, "Hermeneutical Learning," 9.
57. Pollefeyt, "The Difference of Alterity," 323.
58. Boeve, *God Interrupts*, 48.
59. Pollefeyt, "The Difference of Alterity," 324.

> The teacher cannot choose the beginning situation and the hermeneutical intersections as they are entirely dependent on the topic and the pupils themselves. What *is* in the teacher's hands are the materials from various sources which can deepen and enrich the materials already present in the pupils' testimonies. Experiences, passages from the Bible, traditions, communities, theologies, magisterium can be brought into the discussion according to the needs of the class. . . . In a communicative learning process aimed at the deconstruction of ill-considered prejudices and the renovation of the already present ideological frame of interpretation by confronting it with source material, an appeal is made to pupils' ideological deliberation.[60]

In sum, religion classes serve the project of postmodernity insofar as they "can be seen as a practice ground of multicorrelational identity construction in dialogue with the Christian tradition" occupying a "position in the middle of ideological absolutism and relativism. . . . All this asks for an open concept of religion, for daring to stand in reality with one's personal faith and be challenged by reality to come to a deeper faith."[61] The Hermeneutical-Communicative model concretizes methodological interruption for the sake of fostering open narratives.

The Rahnerian Trajectory in Sum

Part I of this book has demonstrated the basic movement from Rahner to Pollefeyt as one that first subdues the tradition, then dismisses, and eventually silences it in its successive stages. Rahner, and those who follow his blueprint, or at least his basic motivation for theological renewal, seriously contend with the Heideggerian problematic and aggressively react against the Suárezian position by basically collapsing being into time. As time shifts within the Anthropological Stage of catechetical renewal, catechetics first becomes distinctly modern and then distinctly postmodern. Following a Rahnerian blueprint, Moran and Co. first relativized revelation and horizontalized religious education in a therapeutic, secular humanistic kind of way. Relegating the "organs of transmission" and opening the door for ongoing revelation effectively left the roof detached and on the ground according to Hofinger's read of the matter. Boeve's postmodern "moment" within the

---

60. Pollefeyt, "The Difference of Alterity," 324.

61. Pollefeyt, "The Difference of Alterity," 325. The recontextualization of religious education impacts Catholic school identity in a significant way. See Pollefeyt and Bouwens, "Framing the Identity of Catholic schools," 193–211.

Anthropological Phase basically subjectivizes the whole thing. Ultimately, only the "self" can decide upon anything and only for itself within the shifting sands of the postmodern condition, and even that which is decided upon remains uncertain and highly contingent. As a *testator* of tradition, the "self" determines its meaning, value, and legitimacy. Thus, the Rahnerian response to the hard objectivity of Neo-scholasticism first leads to the relativizing of revelation, before collapsing in postmodern subjectivism. How to properly maintain the tension between the subjective and objective elements of fundamental theology remains to be seen. In the midst of the postmodern moment, the roof for which Hofinger called has been deconstructed, with its parts now strewn on the ground whereupon it had initially been built decades ago. In fact, in this recontextualized postmodern moment, parts of the house now lay strewn across the yard as well—as deconstructed fundamental theology risks dismantling catechetics altogether.

Part II

A Ratzingerian Response to the Catechetical Crisis

CHAPTER FIVE

The New Pagans, the Council, and the Hermeneutic of Discontinuity

Joseph Ratzinger and Karl Rahner were, as Ratzinger puts it, in "agreement in many desires and conclusions." He continues, "He stood for the same things as I did."[1] Ratzinger and Rahner both saw that a creeping separateness had overwhelmed "ordinary Catholicism," with faith and life drifting further apart in the post-WWII years. They both wanted to address the matter, which they saw as a pastoral crisis, a catechetical one, from the perspective of theological renewal. At the Council, however, Ratzinger realized they actually "lived on two different theological planets," and that they might have stood for the same things "but for entirely different reasons." Consequently, their theological differences led to a slow parting of ways that eventually became sharply and "outwardly visible" in the post-conciliar era.[2] In Part I of this book, I attempted to illustrate the progression and results of a Rahnerian blueprint for catechetical renewal as a pathway that ultimately fails to overcome the ever-widening gap, because an anthropological "given"—whether modern or postmodern—only widens the gulf. Part II will trace the basic contours of Ratzinger's response to the Rahnerian trajectory and attempt to trace his own contribution to the renewal of evangelization and catechesis following Vatican II. While Ratzinger's approach maintains some points of convergence with the Rahnerian trajectory, it contains more points of divergence, ultimately ending up on a different planet altogether.

The New Pagans

For his part, Ratzinger's assessment of the Church in the 1950s was something of an indictment that shattered the pristine image of the fortress

1. Ratzinger, *Milestones*, 128.
2. Ratzinger, *Milestones*, 128–29. See also Benedict XVI, *Last Testament*, 134–35.

Church. It marked a young professor's explosive entry onto the theological scene. Following Ratzinger's turbulent yet ultimately successful *habilitation* process, the thirty-one-year-old's *Hochland* article "The New Pagans and the Church," published in 1958, bluntly expressed his disillusionment with the state of Catholicism following the war. The *Hochland* article drew heavily from his pastoral experience in Munich immediately following his 1951 ordination.[3] The contents of the article had been brewing for a while. Peter Seewald points out that Ratzinger anticipated it by remarks offered in sermons at the first Masses of two students. First, on July 4, 1954, Ratzinger describes his naïve and idealistic enthusiasm for proclaiming God's word to the people during his years as a seminarian, hopes that were dashed by a different reality—"people [who] weren't waiting for the sermon but for the end of it. Today God's word is not one of the fashion items people talk about and queue up for. On the contrary: it's fashionable to know better."[4] In another sermon on July 10, 1955, he notes the situation in the cities, where young people "let loose," where all their "common convictions" break down, and where "everyone makes their own rules and just does what they feel is right."[5] Then, in 1958, his "New Pagans" article opens as follows:

> According to religious statistics, old Europe is still a part of the earth that is almost completely Christian. But . . . everyone knows as well . . . the statistic is false: This so-called Christian Europe for almost four hundred years has become the birthplace of a new paganism, which is growing steadily in the heart of the Church, and threatens to undermine her from within. The outward shape of the modern Church is determined essentially by the fact that, in a totally new way, she has become the Church of pagans, and is constantly becoming even more so. She is no longer, as she once was, a Church composed of pagans who have become Christians, but a Church of pagans, who still call themselves Christians, but actually have become pagans.[6]

---

3. Ratzinger, *Milestones*, 101. Here, with regard to his parish catechetical work, Ratzinger notes that it "became evident how far removed the world of life and thinking of many children was from the realities of faith and how little our religious instruction coincided with the actual lives and thinking of our families." He admits that the methods developed between WWI and WWII "would not be able to deal with the changing circumstances of the world we now lived in: we simply had to look for new forms."

4. As quoted in Seewald, *Benedict XVI*, 292.

5. As quoted in Seewald, *Benedict XVI*, 293.

6. Ratzinger, "New Pagans," para. 1.

Peter Seewald calls this an "outrageous statement" and says the article "had the character of a manifesto" in that "it positively called for a revolution."[7] Ratzinger simply "could not remain silent when he saw that things had gone wrong."[8]

Ratzinger's observations and concerns certainly align with Rahner's and with many others who were part of various renewal movements in the mid-twentieth century. For example, Josef Jungmann (1889–1975), a professor at Innsbruck and theorist in the areas of liturgical and catechetical renewal, has this to say about the Church in Europe in the 1950s:

> Christian customs have become a protective armor shielding religious life ... just as the protective bark of a tree develops from the life of a tree. Nor could religious life maintain itself without a sound armor of custom, no more than a tree could flourish without its bark or a plant without its stalk. Of course, it can also happen that, underneath the protective bark of custom, life itself dies out or is restricted to a few pitiful strands of living tissue, while the tree continues to appear outwardly great and mighty.[9]

Jungmann's statement precedes Ratzinger's article by six years. Henri de Lubac (1896–1991), a significant influence on the young Ratzinger,[10] calls for something similar. The foundations of the Church were firm, yet she was in need of renewal. De Lubac argues that, in the face of modernity, the church could not make an idyllic return to ages past in order to overcome the chasm between faith and life but must instead "give [the church] our own style ... a style that meets the needs and questions of our time."[11] The real situation had been found out and the need for catechetical renewal called out.

Additionally, at the heart of the new paganism lay a shifting attitude towards non-Catholics. In the decades, or better, centuries prior to Vatican II, one would have to describe the dominant Catholic position vis-à-vis the salvation of non-Christians with the term "exclusivism." As noted above, the exclusivist position basically says, "the Christian faith alone saves people and that other religions do not lead to salvation."[12] The exclusivist position that "sees in Christ the only real salvation of man," takes up two attitudes toward other religions: (1) it sees a religion as being provisional and

---

7. Seewald, *Benedict XVI*, 296.

8. Seewald, *Benedict XVI*, 297.

9. Jungmann, "An Adult Christian," 6, quoted in Pedraza, "Reform and Renewal in Catechesis," 10–11.

10. Ratzinger, *Milestones*, 98.

11. As quoted in Seewald, *Benedict XVI*, 299.

12. Ratzinger, *TT*, 49.

preparatory for Christianity (i.e., as containing a positive value); or (2) it sees a religion as anti-Christian and antagonistic toward the truth (i.e., containing a negative value) and in need of being rejected.[13] Following the initial age of evangelization in the early Church, the fathers and the great theologians of the Middle Ages operated as if the whole world was Catholic, a view obliterated by the discovery of the New World. With its discovery, the missionaries of the sixteenth century set out for the salvation of the souls they believed would be lost forever without Baptism.

This exclusivist position, however, began to erode with the powerful ascendency of secular humanism in the twentieth century. Ratzinger describes this new *ethos* in "The New Pagans," saying:

> For the modern Christian, it has become unthinkable that Christianity, and in particular the Catholic Church, should be the only way of salvation; therefore, the absoluteness of the Church, and with that, also the strict seriousness of her missionary claim, and, in fact, all of her demands, have become really questionable. . . . We cannot believe that the man next to us, who is an upright, charitable, and good man, will end up going to hell because he is not a practicing Catholic. The idea that all "good" men will be saved today, for the normal Christian, is just as self-evident as formerly was the conviction of the opposite.[14]

Later in his career, Ratzinger readily admits, "probably no one today takes the position of exclusivism in the sense of denying salvation to all non-Christians."[15] Needless to say, the eroding exclusivist position calls the core of the Church's mission into question.

Therefore, by the in the middle of the twentieth century, if catechesis stood in need of renewal, the Church's concept of mission and her relationship with other religions did too. Indeed, the whole of her evangelizing efforts, then, were hanging in the balance during the post-war era. Rather surprisingly, the opportunity to bring the seemingly necessary renewal project to the world's stage arrived in 1959, when John XXIII expressed his intention to convene an ecumenical council in order that the Church might express the faith afresh within modernity.[16]

13. Ratzinger, *TT*, 19–21.

14. Ratzinger, "New Pagans." See also Ratzinger, *What It Means*, 43–46.

15. Ratzinger, *TT*, 80. Regarding the exclusivist position, Boeve says it has "extremely totalitarian features" and that in it, "the step toward Christian fundamentalism is but a short one" (Boeve, *God Interrupts*, 169).

16. Ratzinger recalls John XXIII's motivation for calling for the Council in *Milestones*, saying, "The Pope's view basically amounted to this: The faith, while remaining the same in its contents, was to be proclaimed in our era in a new way, and, after a

Ratzinger's Role at the Council

Pope John XXIII announced the advent of an ecumenical council months after Ratzinger had been offered the chair of fundamental theology at the University of Bonn.[17] As providence would have it, his early years as a professor became intertwined with Vatican II—a foreshadowing of what would dominate the remainder of his theological career and, eventually, his long season as part of the Church's magisterium. The two realities—that is, Ratzinger's young professorial years and Vatican II—collided on February 25, 1961 in Bensberg. Here, Ratzinger spoke on the "Theology of the Council" in front of a large crowd that included Cardinal Josef Frings of Cologne. As soon as the lecture concluded, Frings pulled Ratzinger aside and informed Ratzinger that he had accepted an offer to speak in Genoa on the upcoming Council and its relationship to Vatican I. Uncertain of his ability to complete the task, Frings asked Ratzinger to ghostwrite for him. Ratzinger agreed. Frings delivered the lecture in Genoa on November 20, 1961; it was eventually published in the journal *Geist und Leben*, thus gaining further traction. In fact, the lecture even caught the attention of John XXIII, who, as Seewald points out, grabbed onto Ratzinger's vision for renewal and even his tone, with Ratzinger's text ultimately reflected in John XXIII's opening remarks for the Council.[18] The extent to which divine providence utilized Ratzinger's theological gifts to shape the reform Council has only become clearer in time, as Seewald illustrates in great length in his latest work, *Benedict XVI: A Life* (Vol. 1).[19]

Given John XXIII's warm reception of the Genoa speech, Frings, the president of the German Bishops' Conference and also a member of the

---

period of demarcations and defensive maneuvers, we were now no longer to condemn but to apply the 'medicine of mercy'" (122). See also Benedict XVI, "Reflections Published for the First Time."

17. Interestingly, the decision to take up the post in Bonn meant snubbing his archbishop, Joseph Wendel, who preferred to keep his priests in the diocese rather than serving at State universities. Wendel had wanted him to be a professor at the Pedagogical Institute in Paising, where Ratzinger "would have to teach religion to elementary school teachers, who in turn were called to explain the religion to their little pupils." Ratzinger did not like the idea of going to Paising, because it was not a true university and he "did not consider himself suited for the job that was proposed" (Guerriero, *Benedict XVI*, 121). In *Milestones*, Ratzinger admits he had "scant practical training" (101), a reality that likely contributed to his desire to avoid a pedagogical school.

18. Seewald, *Benedict XVI*, 360–62. Seewald's work in *Benedict XVI: A Life* deepens the observations and insights he previously published on this topic in *Benedict XVI: An Intimate Portrait*, 201–3. See also Guerriero, *Benedict XVI*, 140–45.

19. Seewald offers a succinct list of the reasons why the Council "seemed tailor-made" for Ratzinger in *Benedict XVI*, 387–88.

Council's steering committee, quickly looped Ratzinger into the preparatory work as his chief adviser and eventually as his official conciliar *peritus*. The Council dealt with issues that were tailor-made for Ratzinger, given his experience in fundamental theology and his antagonism towards Suárezian Neo-scholasticism. For Ratzinger, the success of the Council's stated intention—that the Church might announce the Gospel in a more effective way within modernity—hung in a theological balance. The Council would need to reflect a renewal in theology, which had been in the works through the efforts of *nouvelle théologie* with its *ressourcement* methodology, while serving as a catalyst for further renewal. Seewald notes that "Pope John's word *aggiornamento*—'updating'—had mobilized a new energy." It certainly aligned with Ratzinger's progressive, even radical streak.[20] Ratzinger admits, "I was of the opinion that scholastic theology, in the form it had come to have, was no longer an instrument for bringing faith into the contemporary discussion. It had to get out of its armor; it also had to face the situation of the present in a new language, in a new openness. So a greater freedom also had to arise in the Church."[21] Elsewhere in *Salt of the Earth*, Ratzinger describes Scholasticism as having its greatness, "but everything is very impersonal." He prefers Augustine, "the passionate, suffering, questioning man [who] is always right there, and one can identify with him."[22] As Alfred Läpple, Ratzinger's former seminary prefect puts it, for Ratzinger "God is not recognized because He is a *summum bonum* that is able to be grasped and demonstrated with exact formulas, but because He is a You who comes forward and gets Himself recognized . . . [scholasticism] wasn't

20. See Benedict XVI, *Last Testament*, 129. As Gibson points out, "radical" in the sense in which it should be understood with Ratzinger does not have to do with some sort of extreme progressivism, but rather, in the light of the Latin word *radix*, meaning a literal going back to the roots (Gibson, *The Rule of Benedict*, 154). The sense in which Ratzinger was a progressive must also be qualified. Today, progressivism has to do with the implementation of liberal, or post-liberal ideas. In Ratzinger's case, it has to do with a movement away from neo-scholastic ways of thinking and speaking to better engage with the modern world. It does not have to do with leaving the faith of the Church behind, but with leaving behind a certain way of engaging with the faith of the Church.

21. Ratzinger, *Salt of the Earth*, 73. In his 1996 address to the Presidents of the Doctrinal Commissions of the Bishops' Conferences of Latin America, Ratzinger says "I am of the opinion that neo-Scholastic rationalism failed which, with reason totally independent from the faith, tried to reconstruct the with pure rational certainty. The attempts that presume to do the same will have the same result. . . . The historical instrument of the faith can liberate reason as such again so that by introducing it to the path, it can see by itself once again. We must make efforts toward a new dialogue of this kind between faith and philosophy because both need one another reciprocally. Reason will not be saved without the faith, but the faith without reason will not be human" (Ratzinger, "Relativism," 239).

22. Ratzinger, *Salt of the Earth*, 61.

his beer.... He's not interested in defining God by abstract concepts. An abstraction—he once told me—didn't need a mother."[23] During the preparations leading into the Council, Ratzinger looked hesitantly, even skeptically on the Roman Curia, the body largely responsible for developing the preparatory documents. While "everything should become fresher, newer, more vivid," Seewald notes, it was not clear if "the Roman Curia with all its power—and all its guile—would undermine any attempt at reform."[24]

Upon Ratzinger's initial review, the pre-conciliar schemata did not reflect Pope John XXIII's intention—tethered as they were to scholastic language. Ratzinger's slightly anti-Roman outlook, that skepticism present in German theology, certainly colored his assessments of the texts. Nevertheless, Seewald notes that his "expert reports showed circumspection and balance." Ultimately his criticism came from his "attachment to the church, and also from a position less concerned about changing structures than about the faithful's immediate personal experience of Jesus Christ. Ratzinger knew that the truth was not to be voted on and that whoever rushed ahead of God could not be following him."[25]

Though not yet an official conciliar *peritus*, Ratzinger travelled with Frings to Rome for the first session of Vatican II. Even in an "unofficial" capacity, Ratzinger's presence loomed large from the outset. A day after arriving in Rome, Ratzinger addressed the German coalition gathered at Santa Maria dell'Anima, issuing a report on the status of many conciliar schemata, including a harsh assessment of *De fontibus revelationis*, the document on divine revelation.[26] According to Seewald, Ratzinger's report resulted in a pressing question for the Germans, which he captures, saying, "If the schema was so poor and well nigh theologically false, shouldn't it be

---

23. Valente and Azzardo, "Interview with Alfred Läpple," 60. This is quoted in Rowland, *Ratzinger's Faith*, 2–3. Gaál explains, "the epistemology of Augustine seems to [Ratzinger] far more profound, and—more importantly—a closer approximation of human existence. The *ratio naturalis* (natural reason) is always personal and is never *ratio pura* (pure reason)—which does not in fact exist—but rather *ratio purificate* (purified reason)" (Gaál, *The Theology of Pope Benedict XVI*, 65). See also Rowland, *Ratzinger's Faith*, 4–6.

24. Seewald, *Benedict XVI*, 339. See also Benedict XVI, *Last Testament*, 131; Guerriero, *Benedict XVI*, 145–49.

25. Seewald, *Benedict XVI*, 366. Yves Congar corroborates Seewald's sentiment, here, as he said of Ratzinger in *My Journal of the Council*, "[Ratzinger] is reasonable, modest, disinterested, a great help" (as quoted in Guerriero, *Benedict XVI*, 170).

26. Jared Wicks has published the complete text in English in "Six Texts by Prof. Joseph Ratzinger," 269–85. Benedict XVI comments on this meeting in *Last Testament*, 131–32.

blocked or at least altered? And if so, by whom?"[27] Unable to propose an alternate text within the time constraints, the coalition decided it would attempt to postpone the initial vote on the election of the members of the planned commissions via forceful interventions by Cardinal Liénart of Lille, France, and Cardinal Frings. The effort succeeded, effectively shrugging off the possibility of Vatican II becoming a mere formality for the ratification of the efforts of the Roman Curia and opening wide the doors to the possibility of *aggiornamento*.[28]

In the end, Vatican II did effect renewal in various areas, and Ratzinger's fingerprints can certainly be found throughout. Though never part of the official subcommission that produced *Dei verbum*, he worked with Rahner on a counter-draft of a document to replace the originally proposed document on revelation, *De fontibus revelationis*. Theirs would ultimately be rejected, but not before acting as a "transitional document,"[29] one that prepared the way for *Dei verbum*.[30] Ratzinger did contribute to the final texts of *Lumen gentium*, *Ad gentes*, and *Gaudium et Spes*.[31]

Admittedly, Ratzinger knew he had responsibility for urging the German bishops to act,[32] though he did not foresee the "collateral damage" in the realms of politics and the media caused by Liénart and Frings' challenge of the *status quo*. Ratzinger had focused on theological matters and the need for renewal. He approached the Council theologically, and almost myopically so. However, as Ratzinger puts it, "the world at large was interested in quite a different aspect—obstructiveness and rebellion against the Curia. This appealed both to the anti-Roman sentiment and to the basic human desire to kick against the pricks of 'authority.'"[33] Elsewhere he notes that theologically the interventions simply needed to happen, though they "did

---

27. Seewald, *Benedict XVI*, 390–91. In *The Ratzinger Report*, Ratzinger observes that the schemata rejected were "too theoretical, too textbook-like and insufficiently pastoral." These texts did not aim to change doctrine, but to synthesize and define with more precision, hence, to develop it. Nevertheless, "even the rejection of these texts by the Council Fathers was not directed against the doctrine as such, but against the inadequate way of expressing it and certainly also against some definitions that had never existed up to then and are considered unnecessary even today" (41).

28. See Guerriero, *Benedict XVI*, 152–53; Seewald, *Benedict XVI*, 393–95. See also Ratzinger, *Salt of the Earth*, 71–72.

29. Guerriero, *Benedict XVI*, 176. See also Benedict XVI, *Last Testament*, 134.

30. Seewald points out that *Dei verbum* contained "nearly all Ratzinger's desiderata" contained in the report he offered the German bishops before the Council began (*Benedict XVI*, 390).

31. See Guerriero, *Benedict XVI*, 176–77.

32. Seewald, *Benedict XVI*, 388.

33. As quoted in Seewald, *Benedict XVI*, 396.

not correctly assess the political consequences and the actual repercussions. One thought too much of theological matters then, and did not reflect on how these things would come across."³⁴ Damage control would be necessary. As Seewald puts it, "The doors had barely shut on the last session when a Herculean task began for Ratzinger a 50-year battle for the Council's legacy. His watchword was 'To make clear what we really want and what we don't want. This is the task I have undertaken since 1965.'"³⁵

The Tale of Two Hermeneutics

In his 2005 Christmas greetings to the Roman Curia, Pope Benedict XVI opens his remarks on the fortieth anniversary of the closing of Vatican II by likening the Council's results, at least in some way, to St. Basil of Caesarea's description of the fourth century post-Nicaean situation. St. Basil describes that ecclesial landscape was littered with "the raucous shouting of those who through disagreement rise up against one another, the incomprehensible chatter, the confused din of uninterrupted clamoring, [which] has now filled almost the whole of the Church, falsifying through excess or failure the right doctrine of the faith."³⁶ The turbulent post-conciliar era like the present one, raises a question: Why has the implementation of the Council, which has as a primary objective "to determine in a new way the relationship between the Church and the modern era," been so difficult?³⁷ For his part, and I think most would agree with this, Benedict XVI answers that the source of post-conciliar difficulty lies in the interpretation of the Council and the "change" for which it called. It has to do with hermeneutics around the call for renewal.³⁸ As O'Malley summarizes, for the major parties involved, the call for an "updating," here, was not an issue. He says, "[*aggiornamento*] became

---

34. Benedict XVI, *Last Testament*, 142.

35. Seewald, *Benedict XVI*, 463. Gibson argues that as *aggiornamento* sped forward, Ratzinger retreated more deeply into *ressourcement*. He calls Ratzinger a "disillusioned idealist" whose position did not change, but the Church, in effect, did. He says, "the church shifted away from him, leaving him to defend core truths from a stranded center" (*The Rule of Benedict*, 172).

36. Benedict XVI, "Christmas Greetings 2005." Here, he quotes St. Basil directly.

37. Benedict XVI, "Christmas Greetings 2005."

38. To be sure, this has been Ratzinger's position for a number of years. In his 1985 interview published as *The Ratzinger Report* in English, he notes that the last ten years have not been favorable for the Church and that the developments of the Council seem to be in contrast with the expectations of John XXIII and Paul VI. Ten years prior, he had concluded that "It must be clearly stated that a real reform of the Church presupposes an unequivocal turning away from the erroneous paths whose catastrophic consequences are already incontestable" (29–30).

a problem only in terms of its limits (*how far* could it legitimately go?) and its pastoral appropriateness (would it accomplish *what it promised*?)."[39] The point of contention following the Council has to do with precisely how to renew the Church for the sake of the Gospel.

The Conciliar document *Ad gentes* emphasizes that the Church is "missionary by her very nature."[40] In *Lumen gentium*, the Council Fathers added that she exists to "reveal to the world, faithfully though darkly, the mystery of its Lord until, in the end, it will be manifested in full light."[41] Benedict XVI echoes these statements, saying, "At the end of the day, the point of the Church is to turn us toward God and to enable God to enter into the world."[42] The Church exists to evangelize. Yet, in order for evangelization to be fruitful, the Church's evangelizing structures, programs, and language must be well-suited for the communication of the Gospel within the concreteness of the particular context. While the Church is constantly in need of human "vehicles" or "structures" in order to transmit the Gospel, she must remain aware of and admit to the obsolescence of such vehicles over time. It is possible for such vehicles of communication to set "themselves up as the essence of the Church," and prevent "us from seeing through to what is truly essential."[43] What begin as seemingly necessary constructs for mission, these vehicles or structures often and eventually "smack" of institution, ideology, bureaucracy, and everything human, greatly diminishing their reach and effectiveness.[44] In short, the Church (and her man-made structures) risks becoming self-referential, instead of the sacrament of salvation pointing to Another. Therefore, Ratzinger concludes that "in her human structures the Church is always *semper reformanda*, but one must be clear in this question as to how and up to what point."[45] Renewal in the areas of evangelization and catechetics, therefore, exists so the Church might "speak the Gospel of Christ in a way understandable to contemporary man—i.e., in a

---

39. O'Malley, *What Happened at Vatican II*, 300; emphasis added.
40. Second Vatican Council, *Ad gentes*, §2.
41. Second Vatican Council, *Lumen gentium*, §8.
42. Benedict XVI, *Light of the World*, 155.
43. Ratzinger, *CC*, 142.
44. Ratzinger, *CC*, 136. In *Salt of the Earth*, Ratzinger says, "we have too much bureaucracy. Therefore, it will be necessary to simplify things. Everything should not take place by way of committees; there must even also be the personal encounter. And not everything can be dealt with rationally. However, much Christianity makes a claim on reason and claims to speak to it, there are other dimensions of the perception of reality that we also need" (266). See also Ratzinger, *New Outpourings*, 24–25, 27, 69, 73–74.
45. Ratzinger and Messori, *The Ratzinger Report*, 50.

contemporary fashion (*aggiornamento* means bringing up to date) . . . the objective is precisely that Christ may become understood."[46]

Benedict XVI's 2005 address to the Roman Curia contains what is arguably his clearest, most concise analysis of the crisis in renewal efforts that emerged in the Church following Vatican II. He argues that in the post-conciliar confusion, two paths towards renewal emerged based upon two distinct hermeneutics. What one takes as his or her "given" determines the interpretation of the Council and sets the path for renewal attempts. As over fifty years of history have now shown, the paths are not simply alternate routes to the same destination. That is an illusion. Ultimately, the roads end up in different places—perhaps two different planets—altogether. Benedict XVI points out that the two "contrary" post-conciliar hermeneutics came "face to face and quarreled with each other." He identifies one as "a hermeneutic of discontinuity and rupture" which "caused confusion" and "has frequently availed itself of the sympathies of the mass media, and also one trend of modern theology."[47] Here, Benedict XVI draws attention to attempts at correlating theology and context.[48] He describes the problem with this hermeneutic as risking:

> A split between the pre-conciliar Church and the post-conciliar Church. It asserts that the texts of the Council as such do not yet express the true spirit of the Council. It claims that they are the result of compromises in which, to reach unanimity, it was found necessary to keep and reconfirm many old things that are now pointless. However, the true spirit of the Council is not to be found in these compromises but instead in the impulses toward the new that are contained in the texts. These innovations

---

46. Ratzinger, *Theological Highlights of Vatican II*, ix.

47. Benedict XVI, "Christmas Greetings 2005." In *Salt of the Earth*, Ratzinger notes that "it is correct that there are two interpretations of the Council," and that "many people . . . are already saying that the texts are only initial approaches." For those who wish to go "beyond" the texts, detaching themselves from their content once they catch their "spirit," Ratzinger says, "we are no longer speaking of the Council." What the Council Fathers wanted, was "to update the faith . . . in order to present it with its full impact." However, "the impression increasingly gained hold that reform consisted in simply jettisoning ballast, in making it easier for ourselves. Reform thus seemed really to consist, not in a radicalization of the faith, but in any kind of dilution of the faith." This is opposite of the approach Ratzinger proposes, which does not consist of "lightening loads, adapting, and making concessions," but of "simplifying, concentrating on, and deepening the essentials." Ratzinger's path of renewal in continuity, or a hermeneutic of reform, has to do with "renouncing external power and external factors, in order to live all the more by faith," while the hermeneutic of discontinuity encourages "making history more comfortable" (75).

48. Rowland, *Catholic Theology*, 93.

alone were supposed to represent the true spirit of the Council, and starting from and in conformity with them, it would be possible to move ahead. . . . In a word: it would be necessary not to follow the texts of the Council but its spirit.[49]

This position claims the texts of the Council do not express its true spirit. Instead, it is necessary to "go courageously beyond the texts and make room for the newness in which the council's deepest intention would be expressed."[50]

An Enduring Criticism of the Hermeneutic of Discontinuity

Benedict XVI's comments in 2005 build upon prior assessments during the post-conciliar years. For example, ten years after the close of the Council, Ratzinger describes the post-war era of the twentieth century as one pining for meaning, indeed, longing for salvation after the collapse of so many ideals. He identifies two opposing models for redemption which appear and ultimately shape the hermeneutic of rupture. He describes the first as a "the neo-positivistic model, in which the decisive thing is the concept of rational reform, the further development of specialized knowledge."[51] In another document from the same era, he describes this as a psychological attempt wherein "the affluent society seeks out those secular father-confessors whose scientific knowledge of the human soul is supposed to restore order to its shattered, empty existence."[52] Second, a "neo-Marxist model" that is "crypto-theological" emerges, where "politics is deliberately conducted . . . according to Marxist tenets."[53] The neo-Marxist model

---

49. Benedict XVI, "Christmas Greetings 2005." See also Ratzinger and Messori, *The Ratzinger Report*, 28–29, 33–35, 40.

50. Benedict XVI, "Christmas Greetings 2005." Benedict XVI observes that Paul VI, in his closing discourse on the Council, noted that a hermeneutic of discontinuity could become appealing because the Council had to focus on anthropology in its dealings with the relationship between "the Church and her faith on the one hand, and man and the contemporary world on the other" (Benedict XVI, "Christmas Greetings 2005." See also Ratzinger and Messori, *The Ratzinger Report*, 35–36). Benedict XVI concludes that in light of the problem of the the relationship between the Church and modernity, "some kind of discontinuity might emerge" (Benedict XVI, "Christmas Greetings 2005").

51. Ratzinger, *Dogma*, 378.

52. Ratzinger, *Dogma*, 386.

53. Ratzinger, *Dogma*, 379. In *Introduction*, Ratzinger traces the boon of neo-positivism and neo-Marxism in two significant historical turns. First, he identifies Vico's (1668–1744) turn towards history and his claim that "all we can truly know is what we have made ourselves." The second turn marks a movement towards technical thinking.

promises socio-economic redemption by politicizing everything and lighting the charge with a cry for revolution, with the utopian hope of a classless society—whether in the State or in the Church or otherwise. Marxism, as Ratzinger notes, is essentially a "praxis," "which does not presuppose a 'truth' but rather creates one."[54] Praxis is "the domination of things for our needs,"[55] and in such ways of thinking, politics and economics hold sway. In Marxism, man becomes the "eschatological creator," the one who will establish heaven on earth. As Ratzinger puts it, "Eschatology, the expectation of the world to come, is no longer seen within the theology of creation but, rather, replaces creation: the real world worth living in is yet to be created, namely, by man himself... the *pragma* of human work is no longer situated within the *Logos*... but... abolishes the *Logos*."[56] If theology is to offer anything practical, anything really feasible in such an environment, theology needs to be recast politically. Ratzinger goes on to describe Marxism as another sort of positivism, where "praxis" determines the value of something according to the manner in which it is productive.[57] Despite theology's attempts, in the end, God is ultimately not practical, so God is not really necessary. Ratzinger concludes, "If [God] was to be indulged in

---

Here, Marx stands paramount, saying, "So far philosophers have merely interpreted the world in various ways; it is necessary to change it." Knowledge becomes the power to change the world, hence, as Ratzinger concludes, "molding the world" is what matters. It is "a truth centered on future and action" (Ratzinger, *Introduction*, 59–63. The Vico reference appears on p. 59, and Marx on p. 63. See also Ratzinger, *Handing on the Faith*, 14, where he claims, "The fundamental structure of this world is feasibility, and the manner of its certainty is the certainty of what can be calculated"; Benedict XVI, *Western Culture*, 53; Benedict XVI, *Light of the World*, 43–44).

54. Ratzinger, *Introduction*, 14. See also Ratzinger, *Values in a Time of Upheaval*, 16–18.

55. Ratzinger, "Culture and Truth," 268.

56. Ratzinger, *Dogma*, 380.

57. See Ratzinger, "The Church's Teaching," 48. In his 2011 address to the Bundestag, Benedict XVI notes the positivist conception banishes religion and ethics to the realm of the subjective. While the positivist view contains some merit, its exclusivity can result in a dangerous "creaturelessness," a self-made reality that Benedict XVI claims, recognizes "nothing beyond mere functionality [and] resembles a concrete bunker with no windows, in which we ourselves provide lighting and atmospheric conditions, being no longer willing to obtain either from God's wide world. And yet we cannot hide from ourselves the fact that even in this artificial world, we are still covertly drawing upon God's raw materials, which we refashion into our own products. The windows must be flung open again, we must see the wide world, the sky and the earth once more and learn to make proper use of all this" (see Benedict XVI, "The Listening Heart"; see also Ratzinger, *Salt of the Earth*, 163–64).

at all, it would have to be postponed until the most important work had been done," our work.[58] And so, God himself is relegated.

Though distinct, the roots of both redemption attempts (i.e., neo-positivism and neo-Marxism) can be found in the twofold approach to reality that Ratzinger characterizes according to the following slogans: farewell to history and farewell to metaphysics. First, a "farewell to history" means kissing goodbye "the ready-made world," the "establishment," or in church terms, the "ministerial church." Now, one views history as the "oppressor," an impediment to "what is new and the cause of all that is wrong with the present world system."[59] Instead of what once was, the focus shifts to what can be. This operative spirit explains why "the actual statements and intentions of Vatican II could be consigned to oblivion and be replaced at first by the utopia of an impending Vatican III, and, then, by synods that make much of the 'spirit' of Vatican II but ignore the documents. The 'spirit' here means turning to the future as the field of unlimited possibilities."[60] From this vantage point, one somehow stands outside of history and revolts against it, in order to bring it to its proper, and perfectly idealistic, conclusion.

Ratzinger then turns to a second slogan: "Farewell to metaphysics." By metaphysics, here, Ratzinger refers specifically to Being as such, and not any particular school of metaphysical thought. A farewell to metaphysics means ignoring Being, as man shifts his attention to "the pragmatism of what is yet to be created at any moment." The real world to come is that which man can create and will create. This means "the *pragma* of human work is no longer situated within the *Logos* of the creation that has taken place, but, rather, abolishes the *Logos*."[61] Here, *praxis* trumps *logos*, and doing determines being. "*Logos* does not precede [man]," Ratzinger concludes, because "in the beginning is not 'the Word' but 'the deed.'"[62] Now, "man creates his own meaning for himself."[63] Ultimately, as Ratzinger points out, neo-positivism and neo-Marxism cannot answer the human being's deepest questions—why do I exist and where am I going?—but only explain the *how* and offer an illusory vision for its pursuit. Hence, Ratzinger concludes, "they both have nothing to say about anything except power and consumer goods,"[64] and both contribute to shaping a hermeneutic of rupture.

58. Ratzinger, *Introduction*, 14–15.
59. Ratzinger, *Dogma*, 379.
60. Ratzinger, *Dogma*, 379.
61. Ratzinger, *Dogma*, 380.
62. Ratzinger, *Dogma*, 380.
63. Ratzinger, *Dogma*, 388.
64. Ratzinger, *Dogma*, 389. See also Ratzinger, *Handing on the Faith*, 14; Ratzinger,

THE NEW PAGANS, THE COUNCIL, AND THE HERMENEUTIC OF DISCONTINUITY   161

Twenty years after the Council, Ratzinger defends Vatican II "in its official promulgations, in its authentic documents," and holds that the Council "cannot be held responsible for this development which, on the contrary, radically contradicts both the letter and the spirit of the Council Fathers." He continues:

> I am convinced that the damage that we have incurred in these twenty years is due, not to the "true" Council, but to the unleashing *within* the Church of latent polemical and centrifugal forces; and *outside* the Church it is due to the confrontation with a cultural revolution in the West: the success of the upper middle class, the new "tertiary bourgeoisie," with its liberal-radical ideology of individualistic, rationalistic and hedonistic stamp.[65]

Ratzinger admits that "Vatican II was right in its desire for a revision of the relations between the Church and the world," however, he adds a word of caution, "but whoever thinks that these two realities can meet each other without conflict or even be identical would betray that he understands neither the Church nor the world."[66] Ratzinger's take on the hermeneutic of rupture or discontinuity, then, begins to become clear. The discontinuity exists precisely with regard to the tradition of the Church and it is caused by an indiscriminate attempt at continuity with the world on the part of the Church. Consequently, Ratzinger urges members of the Church to return to the authentic texts of Vatican II.[67] He argues against rupture, and for continuity. Defending the tradition, he argues, means defending the Council and not viewing it as a "'break' and abandonment of the tradition."[68] He adds in opposition to those who wish to ride the radical wave of the "spirit of the Council" right into Vatican III, that "the reading of the *letter* of the documents will enable us to discover their true *spirit*."[69]

Just over a decade later, on the brink of the new millennium, Ratzinger takes up the topic of the Council again. Here, in *Salt of the Earth*, Ratzinger clearly states "there are two interpretations of the Council." On the one hand, the texts of the Council stand "in continuity with the faith." On the other hand, people claim the texts are merely a starting point from which one can

---

"The Pre-political Moral Foundations," 207.
65. Ratzinger and Messori, *The Ratzinger Report*, 30.
66. Ratzinger and Messori, *The Ratzinger Report*, 36.
67. In fact, he repeats this call multiple times in *The Ratzinger Report*. See pp. 31, 34, 35, 40.
68. Ratzinger and Messori, *The Ratzinger Report*, 31.
69. Ratzinger and Messori, *The Ratzinger Report*, 40.

launch out and detach oneself.[70] With a nod toward Rahner, Ratzinger claims the progressives speak of a "winter of the Church," because expectations carried along by the "spirit of Vatican II" have not come to fruition.[71] Here, Ratzinger asserts that the results of the Council have been rather mixed for two tentative reasons. First, he believes they had expected too much, "that we wanted to see Christianity grow in breadth and did not recognize that the hour of the Church can also look quite different."[72] Second, he notes again the manner in which the media conveyed the Council to the public, wherein reform was reduced to "any kind of dilution of the faith."[73]

Finally, on the eve of his abdication of the Chair of Peter in 2013, Benedict XVI contrasts the Council of the Fathers—"the real Council"—with the Council of the media. The Council of the media picked up on the differing hermeneutics—reform and discontinuity. It promoted the latter. The Council of the media "was almost a Council apart," Benedict XVI says, "and the world perceived the Council . . . through the media. Thus, the Council that reached the people with immediate effect was that of the media, not that of the Fathers."[74] He continues:

> While the Council of the Fathers was conducted within the faith—it was a Council of faith seeking *intellectus*, seeking to understand itself and seeking to understand the signs of God at that time, seeking to respond to the challenge of God at that time and to find in the word of God a word for today and tomorrow . . . the Council of the journalists . . . was . . . conducted . . . within the categories of today's media, namely apart from faith, with a different hermeneutic. . . . For the media, the Council was a political struggle, a power struggle between different trends in the Church.[75]

The media ran with rupture and made that message accessible to people around the world. Thus, the Council of the media became most dominant force immediately after the Council. However, Benedict XVI concludes, "we see that this virtual Council is broken, is lost, and there now appears the true Council with all its spiritual force."[76]

---

70. Ratzinger, *Salt of the Earth*, 75.
71. Ratzinger, *Salt of the Earth*, 74.
72. Ratzinger, *Salt of the Earth*, 74.
73. Ratzinger, *Salt of the Earth*, 75.
74. Benedict XVI, "Parish Priests 2013."
75. Benedict XVI, "Parish Priests 2013."
76. Benedict XVI, "Parish Priests 2013."

Therefore, one can see that, decade-by-decade, Ratzinger's consistent reflection on the Council becomes more incisive, to the point of naming the two conciliar hermeneutics that "came face to face and quarreled with each other."[77] Ratzinger clearly believes the Council was an opportunity to solidify renewal efforts in the life of the Church for the sake of her mission. He approached Vatican II theologically—theological renewal for the sake of pastoral renewal was his chief concern—but this course would prove to be too shortsighted. The political ramifications within the Church, coupled with numerous centripetal forces at work without, allowed a hermeneutic of rupture to take hold and largely drown out the hermeneutic of renewal. The next chapter will explore Ratzinger's critique of the hermeneutic of rupture in the area of catechetics, which essentially amounts to his analysis of the positions outlined in Part I of this book.

77. Benedict XVI, "Christmas Greetings 2005."

CHAPTER SIX

Ratzinger Report: An Analysis of Catechetical Renewal Today

"The path from dogma to preaching has become very difficult," Ratzinger says. "There are no longer any patterns of thought and assumptions that carry the content of dogma into everyday life."[1] In the technological age "whose language and thought feed almost exclusively . . . upon experiences of the self-made world of man," where the traditional supports for catechesis—the family and the parish—are crumbling, "the experience of faith lived out in the living Church . . . seems to be condemned to remain mute."[2] The Second Vatican Council had aimed to address this problem as a reform council that ratified and catalyzed catechetical renewal. However, the Council itself provided relatively little instruction or guidance as to how to carry it out.[3] Despite catechetical creativity and some real advancement in carrying the faith into everyday life, Ratzinger concluded that modern catechetics twenty years after the conclusion of the Council was an "all too obvious . . . catastrophic failure."[4]

---

1. Ratzinger, *Dogma*, 7.

2. Ratzinger, *Handing on the Faith*, 14–15. See also Ratzinger, *New Song*, 44.

3. The Council did not formally call for the drafting of a universal catechism in its documents. Nevertheless, Council fathers did discuss the possibility thereof. Ratzinger notes that during the final session of the Council, Cardinal Jäger "proposed the commissioning of such a book in order to give concrete form to the work of aggiornamento in the area of doctrine" (Ratzinger and Schönborn, *Introduction to the Catechism*, 11). In 1971, however, the Congregation for the Clergy did produce the *General Catechetical Directory* to guide the process of aggiornamento.

4. Ratzinger, *Yes of Jesus*, 34–35. To be sure, not everyone felt this way, nor did all theologians at the time have the same type of self-critical attitude displayed by Hofinger. Many, in fact, denounced the whole project of developing a new catechism. Dulles, "The Challenge of the Catechism," offers a succinct overview of the project and commentary from its detractors.

Elsewhere, he said "that catechesis is having a difficult time is a platitude that does not need to be demonstrated at great length."[5]

Ratzinger does not blame Vatican II for the catechetical catastrophe. Instead, hinting at the hermeneutic of discontinuity, he says, "the damage that we have incurred . . . is due, not to the 'true' Council, but the unleashing *within* the Church of latent polemical and centrifugal forces; and *outside* the Church it is due to the confrontation with a cultural revolution in the West."[6] A hasty *aggiornamento* shot through catechetical renewal efforts like a bolt of lightning. Theology, Ratzinger says, "had to subordinate itself to a radical anthropocentrism," in order to be heard again.[7] Nobody listened to the theologian just as the townspeople ignored the circus clown from Kierkegaard's famous story. Ratzinger uses Kierkegaard's tale as an allegory to open *Introduction to Christianity* and as a way to highlight what was happening in theology immediately after the Council. In the narrative, a traveling circus in Denmark catches fire outside a nearby town. The circus manager sends the clown to the village to beg for help and to warn the townsfolk of the impending danger. Already made up for the evening's show, the citizens take the whole thing as a marketing scheme and merely laugh him away. Eventually, the fire spreads, destroying both circus and village. Prior to Ratzinger's use of the story, Harvey Cox, in his *The Secular City*, took up this allegory as analogous to the theologian today "who cannot make people really listen to his message" because they see him as "just giving a performance that has little or nothing to do with reality."[8] What can be done? In a manner of critique, Ratzinger asks, "Need we only call on the *aggiornamento*, take off our makeup, and don the mufti of a secular vocabulary or a demythologized Christianity in order to make everything all right? Is a change of intellectual costume sufficient to make people run cheerfully up and help to put out the fire that according to theology exists and is a danger to all of us?" At this point, Ratzinger levels such correlation attempts with a harsh critique, saying "the plain and unadorned theology in modern dress appearing in many places today makes this hope [of regaining credibility] look rather naïve."[9] Caught up in the spirit of the Council, such theologians and catechetical theorists, "without having produced anything genuinely new . . . could pretend to be interesting at a cheap price. They sold goods from the old liberal flea market as if they were new

---

5. Ratzinger, *Handing on the Faith*, 13.
6. Ratzinger and Messori, *The Ratzinger Report*, 30.
7. Ratzinger, *Handing on the Faith*, 16.
8. Ratzinger, *Introduction*, 40. See Cox, *The Secular City*, 256.
9. Ratzinger, *Introduction*, 41.

Catholic theology."[10] This resulted, however, in diminishing returns. Ratzinger captures this gradual relinquishing of the faith for those who employ the hermeneutic of discontinuity in the already referenced parable of "clever Hans." Here, Hans sees his lump of gold as too heavy and burdensome, so he trades it away and then makes additional exchanges in order to be more comfortable. He eventually ends up with a whetstone, which he throws into the water and finally has "the precious gift of complete freedom."[11]

To be sure, the Council Fathers certainly encouraged a sort of opening of the Church's relationship to the world. This was possible, that is, a dialogue with the world was possible, because the Council Fathers perceived that the Church had a sense of herself, a clear identity, and, consequently, she had something to say. Accordingly, the Church could open herself "with confidence to what is positive in the modern world," though always clarifying and correcting it in light of faith. However, in the years following the Council, there had been an "unrestrained and unfiltered opening to the world . . . to the dominant mentality."[12] Things shifted. Anthropology won out. Correlation now swung in reverse. The world did not have to conform to the Church, finding the ultimate answers to its questions in Christianity. The opposite was the case. Now the Church had to find herself in the world and stand corrected by it. Her own "given" had shifted.

The changing currents in theology, particularly in fundamental theology, catapulted catechetical renewal along a decidedly anthropocentric and tragically turbulent project plan. Now, *within* the Church, theologians and catechists clung to the revolutionary *zeitgeist* of the West with all their might, taking its flux as the new "given" and subtly (or not so subtly) rethinking theology according to its maxims. They attempted to illustrate how theology could measure up to modern principles, while developing catechetical principles and methods accordingly. However, modern history lacks stability, and catechetical renewal after the Council did too. Commenting on those who hectically and zealously produced new catechisms immediately after Vatican II, Ratzinger says "their hasty *aggiornamento*, had . . . already begun to look dated," for "it is inevitable that whoever binds himself too rashly to today already looks old-fashioned tomorrow." Eventually, the idea of an enduring catechism had to be abandoned altogether, because "catechesis had to be constantly written anew."[13]

---

10. Ratzinger, "*Communio*," 119.

11. Ratzinger, *Introduction*, 31. See also his brief commentary on this story in *Salt of the Earth*, 78.

12. Ratzinger and Messori, *The Ratzinger Report*, 35–36.

13. Ratzinger and Schönborn, *Introduction to the Catechism*, 12–13.

Ratzinger does not shy away from critically assessing the philosophical and theological positions behind the hermeneutic of rupture and its futile attempts at reform. Given Rahner's theological and pastoral prominence in the immediate decades after the Council, this chapter will consider Ratzinger's appraisal of Rahner's fundamental theology and its application to questions of salvation and mission in the form of anonymous Christianity. Ratzinger perceives a crisis of faith in such a position and in its practical outworking. This becomes increasingly apparent in the anthropological shift of the "vulgarized Rahnerians" who follow his blueprint for renewal and who develop a catechetical program that merely revolves around itself. In a real sense, this crisis of faith, which is a crisis of faith *in the faith of the Church*, provides the hermeneutic of rupture with its force in catechetics. Finally, I will explore Ratzinger's criticism of what we might call a "Postmodern Rahnerianism" that basically redefines faith and mission according to the demands of postmodern critical consciousness. Throughout this chapter, then, I will explore how the hermeneutic of rupture comes to bear on evangelization and catechesis in both its modern and postmodern forms through the lens of Ratzinger/Benedict XVI.

Ratzinger on Rahner's Fundamental Theology

As previously noted, a causal relationship exists between fundamental theology and a theology of evangelization. Therefore, Ratzinger's criticism of the anthropological shift in catechesis begins right at its Rahnerian core, in Rahner's serious dealings with the Heideggerian problematic. Ratzinger notes that Rahner's Christian conception of being, or creatureliness, rightly views temporality in a positive light. The two are intertwined in a sort of dynamic tension. "Creatureliness," he says, "means having one's origin, not in a passive idea, but in a creative freedom."[14] Whereas existentialism banishes the voice of Being, and Suárezian thinking silences history, Ratzinger sees Rahner as one who attempts to maintain this dynamic tension between Being and time. Rahner was dealing with the dichotomy between "the particularity of Christian history and its claim to the whole being *man*," and the question, "can a particular history justly claim to be

---

14. Ratzinger, *Principles*, 162. See also Ratzinger, *The Spirit of the Liturgy*, 24–34. Here Ratzinger affirms man's freedom. Ratzinger, however, does not affirm the far-reaching liberal notion of freedom-as-license, but grounds man's freedom in relation to God.

salvation not just for a particular history period but for man precisely *qua* man?"[15] Ratzinger notes two stages of development in Rahner's answer.

In the first stage, Rahner describes man as a hearer of the word, who from his very nature "waits for something that comes to him from without, for the word spoken in history, for revelation."[16] This sense of a *dasein*-like "standing open," could be viewed as another way to describe what Luigi Giussani calls "the religious sense,"[17] or the *Catechism*'s delineation of man as a "religious being."[18] Man needs that which comes from without in order to become himself. Ratzinger claims that man can only "find the 'universal' in himself only in tension with the 'particular,' with a history that comes from without, so that man can be described and postulated, as it were, *a priori*, as the receiver of a revelation history, as a 'hearer of the word.'"[19] In this sense, Christian history is not a purely particular or extrinsic thing, because it corresponds to an intrinsic and universal *a priori* need in man. As Ratzinger puts it, "Christian history thus loses its extrinsic character; it is, rather, a necessarily free answer to the free necessity and the necessary freedom of the being *man*."[20] Ratzinger finds no real fault in this first stage of Rahner's thought. It is the second stage, however, the stage which dominates Rahner's later work, which becomes problematic.

Rahner's second stage in dealing with the Heideggerian problematic basically concludes, as Ratzinger puts it, that "if revelation history is not to be understood as categorically extrinsic but refers, rather, to the human race as a whole . . . then it must also be present in the human race as a whole."[21] Ratzinger examines this conclusion. He argues that for Rahner, "man's being itself is historical in character," which refers "only to this historical character in general."[22] If man is historical in character, then history must be necessary in a universal sense—every moment in every age is necessary for man. However, Christianity claims that a particular history is universal. This is the fork in the road and Rahner begins to take his leave. Rather than reclaiming Christian particularity as having a universal import, Rahner attempts to legitimize other particular experiences in history by naturalizing the supernatural. He argues that "History is 'salvation history' because it is

15. Ratzinger, *Principles*, 163.
16. Ratzinger, *Principles*, 163.
17. See Giussani, *The Religious Sense*, 45.
18. CCC, §28.
19. Ratzinger, *Principles*, 163.
20. Ratzinger, *Principles*, 163.
21. Ratzinger, *Principles*, 163.
22. Ratzinger, *Principles*, 163–64.

everywhere and because it has always the role of forming man to his true nature." Ratzinger points out that Rahner most certainly comes to this conclusion by quoting Rahner directly as saying, "'salvation history is coexistent with the totality of human history,'" and "'by world history, then, we mean salvation history,'" and finally that "'revelation history' is 'coextensive with the totality of world and salvation history.'"[23] Following along the lines of Heidegger, Rahner's position takes history seriously, and absolutizes it. The historical character of Christianity is "subsumed in the universal";[24] it is incorporated into human history as a whole.

In order to avoid reducing theology to a philosophy of history, Rahner develops two thoughts that essentially build one on the other. "The first," notes Ratzinger, "consists in designating Christianity as a particularly successful apprehension of what is always more or less consciously acknowledged."[25] We have already seen this in full detail in Part I. Man, the transcendental being, in the very transcendental experience taking place "in" the supernatural existential, experiences or receives revelation. Man's revelational history reaches a high point in Christ, "not on the level of the event, but of consciousness: the particularity of Christianity with respect to the rest of history is now located in the realm of reflection; in Christianity is reflected that which, in itself, is always and everywhere."[26] Here, revelation and transcendental experience coincide, with revelation now situated, so to speak, in nebulous consciousness of transcendence rather than a concrete, interpersonal event.

Rahner's second attempt at maintaining Christianity's particularity involves a deeper consideration of Christ as Savior. Ratzinger explains:

> For Rahner, man is, in fact, self-transcendent being; hence the God-man can be deduced as the true Savior of mankind in terms of man's own being: the Incarnation of God is the highest instance of the ontological fulfillment of human reality, the successful, perfect transcendence. As the successful form of human self-transcendence, or, in other words, as the utterance of God in a finite subject, Christ, the Redeemer, is the expression and realization of the human universal.... [Ratzinger then quotes Rahner directly, as saying,] "The relationship to Jesus Christ, in which an individual ... makes Jesus, present within him, the mediator of his direct relationship to God" is such "that man

---

23. Ratzinger, *Principles*, 164. All direct quotations from Rahner's work can be found in his *Foundations*.
24. Ratzinger, *Principles*, 164.
25. Ratzinger, *Principles*, 164.
26. Ratzinger, *Principles*, 164.

> in his existence ... is always already within this ... relationship whether he is explicitly aware of it or not". From this, Rahner develops his basic formula of Christian existence, in which he seeks to express its simplicity and greatness, its full universality as present in its apparent particularity: "He who ... accepts his existence ... says ... Yes to Christ." ... To be a Christian is to accept one's existence in its unconditionality.... In the last analysis, this means "that the Christian is not so much an exception among men as simply man as he is."[27]

Christ is that evolutionary climax, the heights of transcendental being, who consciously and perfectly apprehends Being in time. In this way, in transcendental experience, Rahner maintains Christian particularity and superiority, thus rendering Christian the supernatural existential, that which is "in itself ... always and everywhere." With a christologized supernatural existential, every transcendental experience is now always already categorically Christian. The Christian proclamation simply makes known that which was already there in experience.

According to Ratzinger, Rahner's attempt at reconciling the particular and universal, history and being, "has something dazzling, something stupendous about it."[28] "The uniqueness of Christianity and the universality of man's being coincide."[29] The relationship with Christ is always already present in the unthematic embrace of reality. Embracing reality and accepting unconditionally one's existence is a Christian experience—whether or not one has ever heard of Jesus Christ, made an explicit act of faith, or participated in the life of the Church (i.e., anonymous Christianity).

Despite the dazzling and stupendous nature of Rahner's thesis, Ratzinger raises serious questions. These are worth listing here, as they clearly express his critique of Rahner and precisely what is at stake in all of this. Questioning Rahner, he says:

> Is it true that Christianity adds nothing to the universal but merely makes it known? Is the Christian really just man as he is? Is that what he is supposed to be? ... Is it not the main point of the faith of both Testaments that man is what he ought to be only by conversion, that is, when he ceases to be what he is? Does not Christianity become meaningless when it is reinstated in the universal, whereas what we really want is the new, the

---

27. Ratzinger, *Principles*, 165–66. See also O'Shea, "Vulgarised Rahnerianism," 346–50.

28. Ratzinger, *Principles*, 166.

29. Ratzinger, *Principles*, 166.

other, the saving trans-formation [*Ver-änderung*]? Does not such a concept, which turns being into history but also history into being, result in a vast stagnation despite the talk of self-transcendence as the content of man's being? A Christianity that is no more than a reflected universality may be innocuous, but is it not also superfluous?[30]

Ratzinger admits that Rahner could refute this entire critique by stating that he does take as a point of departure the Christian Event. However, Ratzinger leaves open whether or not this response does justice, practically speaking, to the particularity of Christ in salvation history.[31]

Thus, when Ratzinger applies spiritual considerations as the litmus test for Rahner's conceptual theory, he ultimately finds Rahner's theory lacking. On the spiritual level, Ratzinger finds that Rahner's theory amounts to nothing more than a pseudo-liberation. In Rahner's thought, the "intermingling of universal and particular, of history and being, of being a Christian and being a man 'as he is,' amounts to man's self-affirmation. To be a Christian is to accept oneself."[32] As Rahner himself puts it, "A Christian is simply man as he is. . . . [A Christian is] a person who accepts without reservations the whole of concrete human life with all of its adventures, its absurdities, and its incomprehensibilities."[33] Ratzinger summarizes Rahner's position in Rahner's own words, "He who . . . accepts his existence . . . says . . . Yes to Christ."[34] As such, one no longer needs to be burdened by Christian particularity or ecclesial bonds. One must simply accept him or herself and he or she is free, saved, and so forth. Ratzinger explains that "redemption is replaced by liberation in the modern sense, which can be understood in a more psychological-individual or political-collective way and which people like to connect with the myth of progress." Where there is progress, there is redemption, freedom. In this case, "Jesus *has* not redeemed us, but he can be a role model for the way redemption or liberation comes about."[35] This modernized approach is deistic at its core, seeing God's retreat from the world in his being limited "to the transcendental sphere" and offering "no 'categorical' instructions." God becomes "a general frame of reference without content," opening a vacuum wherein "the meaning of moral conduct must then be determined solely within the

---

30. Ratzinger, *Principles*, 166.
31. Balthasar, *The Moment of Christian Witness*, 107–9, argues that it does not.
32. Ratzinger, *Principles*, 166.
33. Rahner, *Foundations*, 402.
34. Ratzinger, *Principles*, 167, quoted from Rahner, *Foundations*, 228.
35. Ratzinger, *New Song*, 38.

world."³⁶ In the end, this amounts to "a spirituality of self-affirmation and the identification of 'humanness' as such with the notion of what it means to be Christian."³⁷ Elsewhere, with regard to this overemphasis on the self, Ratzinger observes that "in Kant's transcendental philosophy, the 'you' is no longer found."³⁸ If the Christian is simply man-as-he-is, one must simply accept himself in order to be saved, if one must simply be human, if it is merely "the canonizing of what already exists,"³⁹ then Ratzinger concludes that one's "liberation is not very far-reaching." Instead:

> One who escapes into the pure rationality of the human will have either to reestablish the particularity of the Christian claim or to acknowledge the emptiness of the universal rationalism that leaves man without a way yet challenges him again and again to seek for a concrete—for a particular—option.... Just to accept one's humanity as it is... that is not redemption; it is damnation.⁴⁰

Additionally, Ratzinger finds fault with Rahner's liberal concept of freedom and its ties to an idealistic philosophy which defines freedom as the "ability 'to be oneself.'" This consists of an "almost godlike ability for self-action," wed as it is to the Enlightenment ideal of the universal necessity of freedom and its understanding of history as the necessary human awakening of freedom. Hence, the synthesis that collapses being into time in light of freedom simply becomes another philosophy of necessity according to an all-embracing logic. Ratzinger concludes:

> A synthesis that combines being and history in a single, compelling logic of the understanding becomes, by the universality of its claim, a philosophy of necessity, even though this necessity is then explained as a process of freedom. By its very nature, insistence on freedom involves the rejection of a closed system. The logic of the whole is not something we can deduce. A synthesis adequate to the spiritual tension of Christianity must, therefore, be an open synthesis that rejects a definitive and all-embracing logic.⁴¹

---

36. Ratzinger, *New Song*, 41.
37. Ratzinger, *Principles*, 168.
38. Ratzinger, "Notion of Person," 118.
39. Ratzinger, *TT*, 54.
40. Ratzinger, *Principles*, 167.
41. Ratzinger, *Principles*, 170. Ratzinger also observes that Rahner's theology, functioning as a rational ideology, becomes susceptible to political exploitation by Marxist strains of thought. Marxism claims to know and order all things, but this

It appears Ratzinger accuses Rahner's attempt at reacting with Heidegger against "alienating forgetfulness of 'being' in onto-theology," of ironically falling into the same sin again but from the opposite perspective—anthropology. Then again, maybe this is simply another authentic manifestation of *Dasein*, whose essence, as Andrew Beards puts it, "is precisely that of the one who can fall away from his own nature. Icarus-like human beings must fall into the error and tragedy of history which are inevitable, given the human orientation to over-reach *Dasein*'s nature."[42] In Christian terms, this overreach goes by the name of sin.

Ultimately, Ratzinger concludes that Rahner's speculative exploits attempt too much. They devolve into yet another modern metanarrative—an ideological attempt to Christianly explain the whole of transcendental experience. While Rahner begins by noting that from revelation, one "can begin to reflect on the divine mysteries and come to understand with God's own understanding," he goes too far. For, as Ratzinger says, "revelation has given us no world formula . . . at best, [man] can have but an intimation of it in the fragmentary, the positive, the particular."[43] In Ratzinger's view, Rahner set out to overcome a certain ossification of the faith and within theology largely caused by Suárezian scholasticism. His attempt at naturalizing the supernatural, however, betrays his own neo-scholastic tendencies.[44] He fails to break from the nature-supernature paradigm. Here, Ratzinger notes that "Despite [Rahner's] early reading of the fathers, his theology was totally conditioned by the tradition of Suarezian scholasticism and its new reception in the light of German idealism and Heidegger."[45] Rahner, fails to escape *duplex ordo* thinking, but merely reworks it in terms of the human transcendental experience of the supernatural existential. To overcome the

---

knowledge comes at a great price—the exercise of a state police who ensure the freedom of the people (Ratzinger, *Principles*, 170). Marxism is eminently practical, a philosophy that "is essentially a 'praxis,' which does not presuppose a 'truth' but rather creates one," and wherein "the redemption of mankind . . . occurs through politics and economics, in which the form of the future is determined." Ratzinger concludes "this primacy of praxis and politics meant, above all, that God could not be categorized as something 'practical,'" so ultimately Marx's atheistic and antireligious philosophy required an idealized and reconfigured Jesus who embodied the proletariat's revolutionary charge (see Ratzinger, *Introduction*, 14–15; see also Ratzinger's treatment on the turn toward both historical and technical thinking in *Introduction*, 58–66). What is being described is Soviet Marxism. St. John Paul II takes a more nuanced view in his encyclical *On Human Labor*, alongside the harsh critique of Western capitalism. See John Paul II, *Laborem exercens*, §11.

42. Beards, "Addressing Philosophical Currents," 153.
43. Ratzinger, *Principles*, 169.
44. See Chapp, "The Wrath of the Lamb."
45. Ratzinger, *Milestones*, 128.

dichotomy, Rahner makes a Kantian-Heideggerian version of man and his transcendental experience the bridge between the natural and the supernatural. This sets the scene for the plummet of those who follow him in the areas of theology and catechetics.

Anonymous Christianity and the Crisis of Mission

Ratzinger is just as critical Rahner's influence in the Church's missionary efforts as he is of Rahner's fundamental theology. This criticism, however, must be contextualized. As noted above, prior to the Council, the exclusivist position vis-à-vis the Church and non-Christians had deteriorated. Even before the Council, the Church, it seems, had begun to adopt the pervasive "humanitarian" or "humanistic" attitudes of the West that emphasized the fundamental goodness of human beings. Benedict XVI claims that following Vatican II the "missionary commitment" tied to the exclusivist position that was fading prior to the Council, the conviction that "those who are not baptized are forever lost," is "finally abandoned." In this regard, he argues that in the hermeneutical quarrel following Vatican II the Church's understanding of evangelization undergoes a "profound evolution of dogma." A shift like this radically impacts the entire missionary enterprise of the Church *and* the vitality of faith itself.[46] The foundation of the Church's mission was crumbling. A new theological cornerstone had to be hewn to deal with the question of the universal necessity of Christ and the rise of humanism.[47] Such theological innovations appear in the theories of inclusivism and pluralism, and Ratzinger critiques both of them.

The first theory appears in Rahner's anonymous Christianity—a form of inclusivism that Ratzinger disagrees with from the outset.[48] As described in Chapter One, Rahner's anonymous Christianity theory begins from a presumption that the healthy element in man is "a fruit of the grace of Christ," and he calls "anonymously Christian" this person who "has not become consciously aware of himself" as a Christian (i.e., insofar as Christ has already healed him and made him holy).[49] Ratzinger describes Rahner's position further:

---

46. See Benedict XVI and Servais, "Full Text." See also John Paul II, *Redemptoris missio*, §2.
47. See Ratzinger, *TT*, 17.
48. See Ratzinger, *TT*, 16–17.
49. As quoted in Ratzinger, *TT*, 16–17.

> [Rahner] sustains that the basic, essential act at the basis of Christian existence, decisive for salvation, in the transcendental structure of our consciousness, consists in the opening to the entirely Other, toward unity with God. The Christian faith would in this view cause to rise to consciousness what is structural in man as such. So when a man accepts himself in his essential being, he fulfills the essence of being a Christian without knowing what it is in a conceptual way. The Christian, therefore, coincides with the human and, in this sense, every man who accepts himself is a Christian even if he does not know it.[50]

Here, "the uniqueness of Christianity and the universality of man's being coincide. If one accepts the uniqueness, one has the universality as well; if one has the universality, one possesses also the uniqueness."[51] By naturalizing the supernatural, Rahner blurs Christian particularity into universal human experiences, such that any transcendental experience is Christian.

The anonymous Christianity thesis validates the evolution of dogma with regard to mission, while attempting to maintain the uniqueness of Christ. However, in the end, it causes "a deep double crisis" for the Church and her faithful, because it ultimately calls into question the value and necessity of mission, which calls into question the value and necessity of explicit faith. If one can be saved outside of the Church, then is not that person better off than the one who bears the burden of the faith? And, if salvation can be attained apart from Christianity, what is the point of propagating the faith in the first place? In a 2016 interview, Benedict XVI describes the double-crisis, saying:

> On the one hand this seems to remove any motivation for a future missionary commitment. Why should one try to convince the people to accept the Christian faith when they can be saved even without it? But also for Christians an issue emerged: the obligatory nature of the faith and its way of life began to seem uncertain and problematic. If there are those who can save themselves in other ways, it is not clear, in the final analysis, why the Christian himself is bound by the requirements of the Christian faith and its morals. If faith and salvation are no longer interdependent, faith itself becomes unmotivated.[52]

Much earlier in his theological career, in his "The New Pagans and the Church," Ratzinger made a similar observation, that today:

50. Benedict XVI and Servais, "Full Text." See also Boeve, *God Interrupts*, 167–68.
51. Ratzinger, *Principles*, 166.
52. Benedict XVI and Servais, "Full Text."

> We cannot believe that the man next to us, who is an upright, charitable, and good man, will end up going to hell because he is not a practicing Catholic. So being somewhat confused by this, the believer asks himself: Why can those outside the Church have it so easy, when it is made so difficult for us? He begins to think and to feel that the faith is a burden, and not a grace. In any event, he still has the impression that, ultimately, there are two ways to be saved: through the merely subjectively measured morality for those outside the Church, and for Church members. And he cannot have the feeling that he has inherited the better part; in any event, his faithfulness is grievously burdened by the establishment of a way to salvation alongside that of the Church. It is obvious that the missionary zeal of the Church has suffered grievously under this internal uncertainty.[53]

If one can be "okay" without explicit faith in Christ, then what is the point of explicitly proclaiming Him? Why remain in the Church?

A Crisis of Faith: From Anonymous Christianity to the Catechetical Crisis

While centripetal forces certainly shaped the Church after Vatican II, Ratzinger argues that for catechetics, the "unleashing *within* the Church of latent polemical and centrifugal forces" were also at play. Ratzinger boils the forces down to one fundamental crisis. He says catechists have lost confidence in the organic whole of the faith due to a "crisis of faith, or, more precisely, to a crisis of the faith shared *with* the Church of all ages."[54] This mirrors his point at the of *Introduction to Christianity*, where he comments on the insufficiency of calling on the *aggiornamento*, removing the makeup, and donning the mufti of the secular culture in order to preach effectively today. Instead, he calls for an honest self-assessment, which will reveal "that it is not only a question of form, of the kind of dress in which theology enters upon the scene" that is the issue, but "the insecurity of his own faith, the oppressive power of unbelief in the midst of his own will to believe."[55] That Ratzinger hints at a Rahnerian foundation is clear enough at this point. For Ratzinger, the catechetical crisis is a crisis of faith *in the faith of the Church*, of the faith shared *with* the Church of all ages.

---

53. Ratzinger, "New Pagans."
54. Ratzinger, *Handing on the Faith*, 17.
55. Ratzinger, *Introduction*, 41.

The crisis of faith, that singular centrifugal force, appears in several forms. The first variation appears after the Council, as theorists declare the literary genre of "catechism" is outmoded. As a book, a catechism did not take hold until after the Reformation. However, what the books stands for, meaning "a basic structure for transmitting the faith, developed from the logic of the faith" is "as old as the catechumenate, which is to say that it is as old as the Church herself."[56] Renouncing a systematic, foundational schema that draws upon the whole tradition for the sake of transmitting the faith, means handing on arbitrary fragments detached from the whole, "haphazard and incoherent."[57] Ratzinger goes on to conclude that the evacuation of the idea of a catechism results in a hypertrophy of method.

The phenomenon of a hypertrophy of method over content, can be described a few different ways: praxis over theory, orthopraxy over orthodoxy, transcendental experience over tradition, or *ethos* over *logos*. Rowland explains that "*Logos* tends to be shorthand for the ideas or conceptual logic behind something, while *ethos* refers to the embodiment of ideas in institutional or social practices." Rowland goes on to note that Guardini was concerned about the general trend that granted "epistemic primacy to *ethos* or *praxis* over *logos*."[58] Ratzinger, for his part, maintains Guardini's position, that *logos* must stand before *ethos*; "before Doing," he says, "stands Being." Then Ratzinger adds, "In the beginning was not the 'deed' but, rather, the Word; it is mightier than the deed. Doing does not create meaning; rather, meaning creates doing."[59] Yet, in the movement from Vico's *verum quia factum* ("all that we can truly know is what we have made ourselves") to Marx's *verum quia faciendum* ("the truth with which we are now concerned is feasibility"),[60] the exaltation of history and the eventual forward-thinking thrust of *techne* over *logos*, human *ethos* dismantles divine *logos* and renders the future for itself. Rahner's fundamental theology,

---

56. Ratzinger, *Handing on the Faith*, 15. See also Ratzinger and Messori, *The Ratzinger Report*, 73; Kevane, "Introduction," xiii–lxxv.

57. Ratzinger, *Handing on the Faith*, 15.

58. Rowland, *Catholic Theology*, 34. See also Ratzinger, *TT*, 123–24; Millare, "Hermeneutic," 521–23. Robert Imbelli addresses the danger, here, of separating the pastoral from the doctrinal (or of placing the pastoral before the doctrinal), saying: "Some go so far as to contend that a new 'pastoral paradigm,' purportedly inspired by the magisterium of Pope Francis, is to replace the 'doctrinal paradigm' that may have served the Church in the past, but, in the present historical and cultural context, no longer authentically reflects the movement of the Spirit. . . . To separate them is dissect a living whole" ("No Decapitated Body," 769).

59. Ratzinger, *Dogma*, 94.

60. Ratzinger interprets the Latin phrases as such in *Introduction*, 59 and 63, respectively.

with its turn toward history and its "given" in transcendental anthropology, betrays a position wherein *ethos* oversteps *logos*.

In catechetics, Ratzinger ties the ascendency of *ethos* to a general movement in theology after the Council. This trend corresponds with that of modern educational theory outside the Church, which had become largely, or almost exclusively child-centered.[61] Such shifts establish method as the measure of content, and not the vehicle of it, whether in a secular or religious environment. "Supply is determined by demand," as the *Dutch Catechism* describes the new state of affairs.[62] Within catechesis, the catechist only supplies what is demanded, only brings in elements of the faith secondarily and when absolutely necessary, so as to not encumber the transcendental experience. Roland Millare, describing what happens in the areas of liturgy and eschatology when *ethos* overpowers *logos*, might as well be describing catechetics, when he says, "When we assert the primacy of *ethos*, then the liturgy and eschatology become subject (if such were possible) to the creation of the community, and they cease to be the

---

61. See Caldecott, *Beauty in the Word*, 20–25.

62. Ratzinger, *Handing on the Faith*, 16. In 1968, Ratzinger noted that the Dutch Catechism had attempted to take into account the findings of historical-critical scholarship, along with "the fundamental change in the presuppositions of our thinking by the mathematical-scientific-technological world" that has eclipsed that "old, static, geocentric world view, which took ontological thinking for granted." In short, the Dutch Catechism aimed at answering the questions of a "post-metaphysical" age dominated by positivism, and it did so in two fundamental ways: (1) by calling itself "new" in its "living voice; and (2) in assuming the perspective of a "post-metaphysical" age. The Dutch Catechism aims at a "new living voice" that cuts between Luther's claim that Scripture is self-interpreting without need of the Magisterium, and the Catholic position that Scripture needs the living voice of the Magisterium. Ratzinger notes that the problem with the *Dutch Catechism* lies in the fact that path between *sola scriptura* and Magisterium remains unclear. In its attempt at being "post-metaphysical," the *Dutch Catechism* proceeds according to phenomenology and "descriptive-narrative thinking" that attempts to discover the "question of meaning [*Sinnfrage*] and things that give meaning [*Sinngebung*] in the course of human life, in the events of history, and to situate the faith on the level of meaningful answer [*Sinngebung*] that can be detected in the course of events themselves." Ratzinger also points out that the work also operates in a decidedly anthropocentric fashion. He cites the chief editor, Fr. Guus van Hemert, as saying "Human existence is never left behind. The whole catechism moves within human existence," and J. Dreißen, as saying "Catechizing does not mean presenting to the child truths that it did not yet know. . . . The supply depends on the demand. . . . Life is believed, and the faith is lived." Already, then, in the late 1960s, Ratzinger questions the anthropocentric vision so closely related to the Rahnerian position. This anthropocentric vision poses a number of problems for theology and for evangelization: "Does Christian preaching really present nothing to us that we do not already know ourselves? . . . Can we fit catechesis into the scheme of supply and demand? . . . Should it only affirm and reinforce what already is . . . ?" (See Ratzinger, *Dogma*, 62–65).

*opus Dei.*⁶³ The potential of the faith to be an agent of change, to generate conversion, cripples, and instead, the faith itself must be changed. Ratzinger describes the shift:

> Catechetics now understood itself, no longer as a continuation and concretization of dogmatic theology or of systematic theology, but rather as a self-sufficient standard. This in turn corresponded to the new tendency to rank praxis over truth. . . . All of this overlapped with a far-reaching reductionism in anthropology: the priority of method over content means the priority of anthropology over theology, which had to subordinate itself to a radical anthropocentrism.⁶⁴

This shift appears in the catechetical work of Moran and Groome, where the Rahnerian blueprint styled according to transcendental anthropology and anonymous Christianity is clear enough. The center of the catechetical universe moves away from God and to the individual and his or her experience. Ratzinger explains that this shift calls for a "primacy of experience," which becomes "the measure for one's understanding of the faith heritage."⁶⁵ Following his 1983 lecture on catechesis, Ratzinger recalls receiving a letter from a French catechist who related how at the end of a catechetical course, the children seem to retain little despite her enthusiastic efforts. In asking herself what the problem might be, she did not simply blame the wickedness of the times (i.e., centripetal forces), but sees internal, centrifugal ones as the cause. In her analysis, she found that her catechetical program was pedagogically refined and up to date, however it "had almost no content at all but simply revolved around itself." She saw that "catechesis remained entirely a matter of accommodations designed to facilitate communication, never moving beyond them to deal with the subject itself."⁶⁶ Now, demand determines supply, and method determines content. The relegation of the traditional "organs of transmission" is simply the manifestation of a more profound movement in fundamental theology that grounds revelation in transcendental experience and makes the individual the ultimate arbiter for how he or she understands the tradition and whether he or she finds that tradition particularly helpful in unpacking personal experience. While this position does not deny dogma outright, it does diminish its importance and reconfigures it as "a sort of

---

63. Millare, "Hermeneutic," 523.
64. Ratzinger, *Handing on the Faith*, 16.
65. Ratzinger, *Handing on the Faith*, 16.
66. Ratzinger and Schönborn, *Introduction to the Catechism*, 13–14.

external frame of reference that no longer [has] much significance for the structure of catechesis or for its contents."[67]

Coupled with the relegation of doctrine for the sake of pure, unencumbered experience, Ratzinger also notes a similar subordination of dogmatic theology in relation to biblical theology—the third manifestation of the centrifugal force. To be sure, dogma is, in a real sense, the interpretation of scripture, however, "the explanation that had developed within the centuries-old faith no longer seemed quite compatible with the understanding of the texts that had been introduced in the meantime by the historical method."[68] Catechetical reformers followed along, no longer bothering with the "detour" of dogma, but operating directly from the sources of Scripture. As catechists vacated dogma, they attempted to construct the faith right out of the Bible (an act of pseudo-*sola scriptura*). Practically speaking, this shift ravages faith in Jesus Christ. Historical-criticism had attempted to unearth the "historical Jesus" who lays behind the Jesus of the Gospel by imposing the "normal causal framework," as determined by Enlightenment rationality, which aims to extricate the real Jesus from anything mythological. This ends up excluding even the divine in Jesus, as the "historical Jesus can only be a non-Christ, a non-Son."[69] Ratzinger points to Albert Schweitzer's conclusion on this point, that "there is nothing more negative than the result of the [historical-critical] research into the life of Jesus. The Jesus . . . who appeared upon the scene as the Messiah, proclaimed the morality of the kingdom of God, founded the kingdom of heaven upon earth, and died to consecrate his work never existed. He is a figure sketched by rationalism, brought to life by liberalism, and clothed by modern theology with historical scholarship."[70] Ratzinger sees the "evacuation of the figure of Jesus," along with a "deistic conception of God," as a chief reason why churches are empty and faith dwindling. He says, "the more or less romantic ersatz Jesus currently being offered is not enough. He lacks reality; he is too far away."[71] The "sanitized" Jesus is not a real person, as Ratzinger says elsewhere, but "the product of a historian."[72] By separating Scripture from dogma, by separating Scripture from the living community and Tradition from which Scripture came to be and is believed

---

67. Ratzinger, *Handing on the Faith*, 21–22.
68. Ratzinger, *Handing on the Faith*, 17.
69. Ratzinger, *New Song*, 37.
70. Quoted in Ratzinger, *Introduction*, 197n.
71. Ratzinger, *GCC*, 69.
72. Ratzinger, "Guardini on Christ in Our Century," para. 1.

to be Scripture, exegesis ends up suffocating the living word.[73] No longer a living part of the Church, exegesis simply becomes, as Ratzinger puts it, an act of "necrophilia: the dead burying their dead."[74] Without the Tradition holding Scripture as an organic unity, the Bible disintegrates leaving a question as to how it ought to be interpreted and who ought to do so, or, for catechetics, what should be emphasized as a foundation for catechesis. "In the end," Ratzinger concludes, "such questions are decided as matters of taste, and what is left of the Bible then is just good enough to provide applause for what we ourselves want."[75] This is similar to what happens with catechesis as a whole, when the catechist does not present the integrated and organic whole, but simply cherry-picked parts that seem to be helpful for thematizing the unthematic transcendental experience.

The rise of anthropocentrism, the turn towards the "sources" in a pursuit of the historical Jesus, and the syncing-up of Christianity with secular and political action all have the same root: "a certain embarrassment with regard to dogma."[76] Jettisoning the faith of the Church as the starting point results in a seismic shift from the traditional "sources" of catechesis, or "organs of transmission" (i.e., Scripture and tradition) to the human-agent-in-time. These are the marks of the anthropological shift. It is easy to see certain characteristics of Moran and Groome under fire, here. What begins as a reaction against an apparent metaphysical or onto-theological straitjacket in neo-scholastic catechesis accused of preventing access to the living "source," ends up perpetuating that which it was trying to overcome. In the Rahnerian trajectory for catechesis, the real "source" cannot be accessed; only subjective experience, shaped as it is, by those "experts" or "leaders" or "facilitators" who simply place a new interpretive grid (i.e., a modern worldview) over revelation. Thus, Ratzinger concludes that "the reduction of faith to experience robs it of its core," a core which exists to

---

73. See Ratzinger, *Handing on the Faith*, 18. Ratzinger quotes a famous passage from Albert Schweitzer, one he refers to often, where Schweitzer says: "What became of the research into the historical Jesus is remarkable. It set out to find the Jesus of history, thinking that it could then situate him in our own time just as he is, as Teacher and Savior. It loosed the bonds with which he had been chained for centuries to the rocks of Church doctrine, and then it rejoiced when the figure again showed life and movement and it saw the historical Jesus coming toward it. He did not stop walking, however; instead he went right past our time and returned to his own" (19).

74. Ratzinger, *Handing on the Faith*, 19.

75. Ratzinger, *Handing on the Faith*, 20; see also 22. See Ratzinger and Messori, *The Ratzinger Report*, 72.

76. Ratzinger, *Handing on the Faith*, 22.

"lead us into the land of the not-yet-experienced and thus bring us . . . to that broad place where true life begins to expand."[77]

In sum, we can see how this catechesis based on transcendental anthropology, along with an inclusive approach to mission, finds an inner impulse or primary structural support in Rahner's fundamental theology. Although Benedict XVI admittedly finds Rahner's theory fascinating,[78] even "dazzling" and "stupendous" in its apparent reconciliation of the particular and the universal, of history and being, he ultimately denounces it.[79] Ratzinger says, "it reduces Christianity itself to a pure conscious presentation of what a human being is in himself and therefore overlooks the drama of change and renewal that is central to Christianity."[80] When it comes to the hermeneutic of discontinuity at work in catechetical renewal efforts and the attempt to deal with the "evolution of dogma" in mission after the Council, it seems Rahner drafted the blueprint, and theorists like Moran and Groome set to work in building according to it.[81] Interestingly enough, John Henry Newman foresaw the crisis that the Church would live through following the Council. In an address at the opening of St. Bernard's Seminary, Newman identified the "spirit of liberalism in religion" as the sign of the impending crisis, for according to this spirit, "revealed religion is not a truth, but a sentiment and a taste; not an objective faith."[82] And so it happened.

The Pluralist Theory

The second theological response to the "evolution of dogma," that movement away from an exclusivist position regarding the Church's understanding of salvation and mission, appears in pluralistic approaches. With the onset of the postmodern condition, inclusivism had to be rejected as "a kind of Christian imperialism, as presumptive in relation to other religions: it is said to be not our business to see other religions as directed toward

---

77. Ratzinger, *Handing on the Faith*, 23.
78. Benedict XVI, "Full Text."
79. Ratzinger, *Principles*, 166.
80. Benedict XVI, "Full Text."
81. Ratzinger points out that all of the misrepresentations of Christianity that spin out of the hermeneutic of rupture "cannot be imputed to Rahner," for "it would be unfair to hold an author responsible for the conclusions others draw from his works unilaterally and against the whole tenor of his thought." However, the "factual misinterpretation" of those who follow Rahner, can "help him to isolate the weak spots and critical points of his synthesis . . . to give a new orientation to his theological reflection" (Ratzinger, *Principles*, 168).
82. Newman, "Sermon 9."

an end in Christ, and, thus, to take them over in a Christian sense."[83] As Boeve notes, modern theology must be recontextualized in order to survive. This interplay between cultural relativism (or, as some would argue, the postmodern condition) and the movement towards "spiritual but not religious," provide the key ingredients for the latest way of sensitively addressing the "evolution of dogma." Ratzinger calls this a "pluralist theology of religion."[84] This pluralist theology proceeds down two distinct paths. The first path could be described as relativistic pluralism and it is most often linked to the thought of Hick and Knitter.[85] The second path can be called "different inclusivism" and it appears in Boeve's thought.

Ratzinger describes the basic contours of the first approach (e.g., Hick and Knitter) in a 1999 address given at the Sorbonne. Here, Ratzinger engages the topic of Christianity in the "marketplace" of world religions, and he describes this plural reality in terms of a popular Buddhist tale. In the story, the different faith traditions are likened to the different ways in which blind men would perceive the same elephant from their various vantage points—one touching a leg, another an ear, a tusk, and so on. Rowland notes:

---

83. Ratzinger, *TT*, 80. Ratzinger sees a need to deal with the problem of the Christian theologian who, like a stick-in-the-mud, cannot get over his "know-it-all attitude" insofar as it appears in the "swaggering manner of apologists" (i.e., exclusivism) or "the friendly manner of contemporary theologians, who acknowledge . . . the other person to what extent he is already a Christian without being aware of it" (i.e., inclusivism) (Ratzinger, *TT*, 25). Marxism had claimed scientific certainty and made knowledge into *praxis*, and its collapse disillusioned many such that "the failure of the one system incorporating a scientifically based solution to human problems could only favor nihilism or at any rate absolute relativism" (Ratzinger, *TT*, 117). The revolutions of 1989 also revived religion—or, perhaps more accurately, revived spirituality. Ratzinger notes that for many, and Boeve makes this same point, "an institution is inconvenient, and dogma is bothersome." Instead, "they are looking for experience, an encounter with the entirely Other (Ratzinger, *Introduction*, 19. Cf. Boeve, *God Interrupts*, 16–21 and some references to this phenomenon in his article "Religious Bungee Jumping"). This movement towards spirituality-without-religion results in the relativization of individual religions. Differences and even contradictions are not ultimately relevant. Instead, what really matters is "contact with the ineffable, with the hidden mystery." This great mystery is not manifest in any one form of revelation, in any one religion, but is grasped only randomly and in a fragmentary way. Thus, "we cannot know God himself," as Ratzinger says, "everything that can be stated and described can only be a symbol" (Ratzinger, *Introduction*, 20).

84. Ratzinger, *Pilgrim Fellowship*, 209.

85. See Ratzinger, *TT*, 119–26. Relativism is the dominant philosophy of our time and one that does not adopt a merely negative position in front of truth—a "resignation in the face of the unfathomable nature of truth"—but a positive one "on the basis of the concepts of tolerance, dialectic epistemology, and freedom" (Ratzinger, *TT*, 117).

> The fable is often quoted by people who believe there is no possibility of one true religion. There is simply a kind of basic human question for contact with something divine, some force that is supra-human. Different faith traditions merely represent different human experiments fostered by this basic psychological need. Human beings have no capacity to understand the supra-human, no faculty for contact with the divine. They are like blind men grasping the parts of an elephant.[86]

Here, "all religions, each in their own way, would be ways of salvation and in this sense, in their effects must be considered equivalent."[87] For his part, Boeve also notes the allegory of the elephant, along with other images: distinct paths up the same mountain, varying perspectives in looking at a dew drop at dawn, colors of the rainbow, and so forth.[88] Ultimately, Boeve sees this pluralist strategy as weakening the constitutive character of Christianity and the confession in Jesus Christ. He points to how pluralist theologians "radically relativize the Christian truth claim," because they relativize all truth claims. Eventually, it becomes "difficult to take truth claims and identity seriously, let alone uphold them. If everything has the same truth value then nothing is ultimately true."[89] Jesus now exists, not above other religious leaders (e.g., Buddha, Mohammed, etc.), but on the same plane, opening a particular pathway to God and thus providing another way to fulfill humanity's religious desire.[90] Jesus is not the one who *is* God, but one who has experienced God in a special way, one who has been enlightened. Ratzinger calls this a "relativizing" of religion that attempts to bring peace, as each sees the other as a different way of reflecting upon the Eternal Being. However, Christian particularity fades. Jesus' person does not matter. Instead, the path he points to matters, and that path is just a different way to the top, a path no better or worse than the next.[91]

Ratzinger also speaks about a more radical, a more postmodernly sensitive form of the pluralist position, wherein one understands different religions as "unrelated blocks standing side by side or in opposition to each other." It is a position that "ultimately denies the unity of mankind and denies the dynamic of history, which is a process of various unions."[92] Here, he

---

86. Rowland, *Benedict XVI*, 114.
87. Benedict XVI, "Full Text."
88. Boeve, *God Interrupts*, 148.
89. Boeve, *God Interrupts*, 168–69.
90. Boeve, *God Interrupts*, 168.
91. Ratzinger, *Introduction*, 20. See also Ratzinger, *Pilgrim Fellowship*, 210–11.
92. Ratzinger, *TT*, 81.

seems to be alluding to a theological position like Boeve's, and his version of "different inclusivism," where the principle of inclusion is not Christ, but difference. Ratzinger explains that this position "relativizes" all religions, "and, at the same time, lets them stand in its relativity; the absolute value with which it surrounds them lies beyond anything that can be named; it is strictly 'non-categoric.' It can thus equally well be called 'being' as 'nonbeing,' 'word' as 'nonword;' it is obvious that this solution finds many supporters today." He then concludes this position "maintains that relativism which in certain respects has become the real religion of modern men."[93] Here, no human being can even claim the various religions are different paths up the same mountain. There is no "bird's eye view" that grants such an insight. All we know is the plural playing field that includes the possibility of encounters with difference-thinking that bursts open the bounds of one's own religious narrative constantly susceptible to closing upon itself as a new metanarrative. Different inclusivism, then, understands salvation, not in Christian terms, but in postmodern ones, recasting salvation in the light of postmodern critical consciousness, and rendering postmodern philosophy as the new savior of the world. With regard to God, then, Ratzinger argues this position maintains a certain "humility in the presence of the infinite,"[94] or the inability to know or to say anything for certain about God. Elsewhere Ratzinger calls this a "false humility and a false presumption: a false humility that does not recognize in the human person the capacity for truth, and a false presumption by which one places oneself above things, above truth itself, while making the extension of one's power, one's domination over things, the objective of one's thought."[95]

Speaking in a 2000 press conference regarding the presentation of *Dominus Iesus*, Ratzinger clearly ties together the dominant cultural force of relativism in the West, and the development of a "pluralist theology of religion" that has been gaining momentum since the middle of the twentieth century. Pluralist theologies of religion rest on a number of philosophical and theological presuppositions, and Ratzinger enumerates the following:[96] (1) the belief that divine truth cannot be apprehended and is ultimately ineffable; (2) a relativist attitude regarding truth, wherein what is true for some people is not true for others; (3) a radical opposition between the West's logical mode of thinking and the symbolic mode due to the East; (4) a subjectivism which takes human understanding as the only

---

93. Ratzinger, *TT*, 84.
94. Ratzinger, *Introduction*, 20.
95. Ratzinger, "Culture and Truth," 368; Benedict XVI, *Western Culture*, 162.
96. Ratzinger, *Pilgrim Fellowship*, 210.

source of knowledge; (5) the metaphysical (or ontological) emptying of the Incarnation; (6) a certain uncritical theological or religious syncretism; and (7) attempts to interpret the action of the Holy Spirit without reference to Tradition or the Magisterium.[97] These presuppositions impact theology in numerous ways, namely:

> The refusal to identify the unique historical figure of Jesus of Nazareth with the reality of God ... since it is held that absolute being, or the absolute being, can never be completely or finally revealed in history. In history ... there are only models, ideal figures, who point us toward the Wholly Other.... Some more moderate theologians ... recognize Jesus Christ as true God and true man but are of the opinion that on account of the limitations of the human nature of Jesus the revelation of God in him cannot be seen as final and complete but always has to be seen in relation to other possible revelations of God, like the great religious figures of mankind.... That means that the Church, dogma, and sacraments can have no absolute and necessary value.[98]

Rendering any of these elements "absolute" would risk universalizing the particular and overstepping one's human status by trying to hold the Wholly Other in one's hands, the Wholly Other who is "never at our disposal."[99] This relativizing means there is no universal, binding, and valid truth in history, no Truth that took flesh and is handed on by the Church.

When it comes to the renunciation of truth in religion, Ratzinger notes Wittgenstein's influence. Ratzinger quotes Wittgenstein's student, G. E. M. Anscombe, who summarizes Wittgenstein's position in two points:

> 1. There is no such thing as being true for a religion. This is perhaps suggested when someone says: "This religious statement is not the same as a statement of natural science." 2. Religious faith may be compared rather to a person's being in love than to his being persuaded that something is true or false.[100]

---

97. Cf. Ratzinger, *Pilgrim Fellowship*, 211.

98. Ratzinger, *Pilgrim Fellowship*, 210–11. The relativizing of Christian faith impacts the faith in two significant ways. First, Jesus is no longer seen as the man who is God, but as one who has experienced God in a special way and who points to a certain enlightened path that is, in the end, just one of many enlightened paths from which one may choose as he or she climbs the religious mountain. Second, God is no longer conceived of personally or impersonally, but only negatively (Ratzinger, *Introduction*, 21–22).

99. Ratzinger, *Pilgrim Fellowship*, 211.

100. Ratzinger, *TT*, 215. In light of the constant, "titanic" attempts by human beings "to take possession of the whole world," the "outbreaks of some cult of ecstasy, of self-transcendence and self-destruction," indicate, according to Ratzinger, that man is not

Accordingly, Wittgenstein concludes by his own logic that "it would make no difference to the Christian religion whether or not Christ had actually done some of the things recounted concerning him or whether indeed he had existed at all."[101] What God actually did or did not do, what is true and what is false, does not *really* matter. Instead, Christians *merely* need to understand themselves as being God's creatures and live a meaningful life in "the plane of play, of make-believe."[102] Religion is a game according to what Ratzinger calls "Wittgenstein's fiction . . . the theory concerning 'games,' which relativizes all religions," and Christianity is merely a player in it.[103]

With the pluralist theory of religion, the mutation within the evolution of dogma seems to reach its logical conclusion. What began with the Church's highly motivated concept of mission marked by exclusivist thinking, becomes more relaxed mission approached from within anonymous Christianity's inclusivism, before being completely renounced in the pluralist theory. The pluralistic conception, driven as it is by postmodern critical consciousness, calls the whole idea of "salvation" into question. It calls "conversion" and "mission" into question too, lest one assumes a "bird's eye view" over the religious landscape and subsumes all religions, each with its own particularities, under one narrative. For, to speak of "conversion" with regard to an individual's changing of religions to Christianity, "would assign a higher status to the Christian faith and thus contradict the idea of equality." Similarly, "mission" refers to "a kind of religious imperialism, which must be resisted."[104] In short, the universal truth claim of Christianity, or any religion for that matter, and its implications must be renounced. According to this theory, the call to evangelize must be either abandoned altogether or, at least reconfigured as interreligious dialogue, thus replacing an "urgent call to conversion."[105] Ratzinger claims this is not the kind of dialogue Vatican II promoted. Instead, it is a form of dialogue "no longer understood as a way to discover the truth," but one which aims "at relativizing 'dogma'" by

---

content with the verdict demanded by such false humility. He likens it to the man who is born blind who knows he was not born to be blind but to see, and as such, he seeks to overcome his blindness. He naturally works to see somehow. Ratzinger concludes, the "farewell to truth about God and about the essential nature of our selves, the seeming content at no longer having to bother about this, is deceptive" (*TT*, 164–65).

101. Ratzinger, *TT*, 215.

102. Ratzinger, *TT*, 215–16.

103. Ratzinger, *TT*, 216.

104. Ratzinger, *TT*, 105.

105. Ratzinger, *Pilgrim Fellowship*, 211. Benedict XVI sees tremendous value in interreligious dialogue, but not at the expense of mission. For example, see Benedict XVI, "Christmas Greetings 2012."

"setting one's own position, or one's own faith, and what the other person believes on the same level, so that everything is reduced to an exchange of opinions that are fundamentally relative and of equal value, with the aim of achieving a maximum of cooperation and integration between the different conceptions of religion." Therefore, Ratzinger concludes, "this is the opposite of 'conversion' and 'mission.'"[106]

While it sounds innocuous—each choosing for him or herself what is true, what he or she is, that "everything is relative," etc.—Ratzinger is not fooled by the supposed innocence of postmodern philosophy and its self-proclaimed hero status in defense of the *differend*. While proponents of the postmodern condition can see the Christian claim as a certain kind of fundamentalist metanarrative that opposes its critical consciousness, Ratzinger argues that postmodern thinking is not without its own hegemonic dangers. How, after all, can postmodern philosophy know that all positions are merely on a playing field and that one does not stand over and above the others unless it assumes the position of the "bird's eye view?" Is not the claim that there is no "bird's eye view," and that all positions are simply side-by-side and equal on the playing field, a metanarrative in its own right?

Critiquing postmodern philosophy's attempt to identify itself as a "condition" so as to avoid the obvious self-contradiction, Rowland notes that "progress" was the metanarrative of modernity, while "the celebration of 'difference'" is a "kind of master narrative of the culture of postmodernity. Although the postmoderns regard all master narratives as oppressive, the celebration of difference is regarded as an exception to this principle because it does not really affirm or privilege anything."[107] Sweeney adds to this, saying, that while most postmodernisms embrace flux as a way of preventing totalitarianism, "particularity becomes universality,"[108] and "there remains an enduring 'metaphysical' tendency to place absolute conditions on what can and cannot be said ... there is the tendency to continue thinking in terms of a closed system—what could be called metaphysical in the pejorative sense."[109] Sweeney claims that postmodernism, in an apparent posture of "humility," rejects the very possibility of an event "that would shatter both the self-sufficiency *and* the 'humility' of *Dasein*," and consequently risks limiting the mode of God's appearance—the same critique leveled against metaphysics.[110] Similarly, Ratzinger claims:

106. Ratzinger, *Pilgrim Fellowship*, 212.
107. Rowland, *Catholic Theology*, 161.
108. Sweeney, *Sacramental Presence*, 125.
109. Sweeney, *Sacramental Presence*, 186.
110. Sweeney, *Sacramental Presence*, 186.

Relativism, that is, letting oneself be "tossed here and there, carried about by every wind of doctrine", seems the only attitude that can cope with modern times. We are building a dictatorship of relativism that does not recognize anything as definitive and whose ultimate goal consists solely of one's own ego and desires.[111]

Accordingly, because man is not capable of truth (of discovering it, attaining it, or holding it in his hand), man is not capable of ethical values or standards. Now, one must arrange things reasonably for himself, while abiding by the opinion of the majority that has become the only criterion. Without truth, tolerance or "negative tolerance" become the "well-established standards of thinking that are supposed to be imposed on everyone." This, in effect, becomes a new form of intolerance, as "for the sake of negative tolerance [i.e., 'not offending anyone'] there must be no crucifix in public buildings." With this, however, "we are basically experiencing the abolition of tolerance, for it means . . . that the Christian faith is no longer allowed to express itself visibly,"[112] for tolerance always stands in relation to some position or value, as opposed to a completely valueless position. In this way, the "positive tolerance" (i.e., every position is equally and always as valid and acceptable as the next) and "negative tolerance" become the highest forms of reason, knowing all and defining the frame of reference that is now applied universally according to the *differend*. In short, relativity or particularity quickly become relativism or particularism, as "so-called Western reason—claims that it has now really recognized what is right and thus makes a claim to totality that is inimical to freedom."[113] While Bene-

---

111. Ratzinger, "Homily of His Eminence." To be sure, Lyotard would reject any accusation of relativism, as if he were "narrating the master narrative of the end of master narratives." Lyotard defends himself against this claim by describing his position as a contemporary version of Kant's tribunal of reason—a critical philosophy—that proceeds not from the Idea of freedom, but from "the framework of a philosophy of phrases," where philosophy is, "first and foremost analyses of phrase regimens and genres of discourse; it points to rules of formation and linking prescriptions, investigates phrases and validates them from the perspective of these rules." However, and this is where Lyotard attempts to extricate philosophy from the danger of hegemony, "philosophy . . . must especially keep open the heterogeneity of the diverse phrases and genres to which the linking bears witness," so that every *differend* is not turned into a litigation. In other words, philosophy is, as Boeve puts it, "the (non-hegemonic!) *discourse of the Idea of heterogeneity*" and the philosopher's task is to "foster this consciousness of heterogeneity" while critiquing "those who immediately try to fit the event into a hegemonic discourse." In this way, philosophy bears witness to heterogeneity as "a discourse genre that has as its rule *the constant search for its own rule*" (Boeve, *Lyotard*, 27; see also 72).

112. Benedict XVI, *Light of the World*, 52.

113. Benedict XVI, *Light of the World*, 53. To this he adds, "certain forms of behavior

dict XVI admits that truth claims have been abused, that "intolerance and cruelty have occurred in the name of truth." Nevertheless, while one must be careful to claim the truth—which we never have, "at best it has us"—"to simply dismiss it as unattainable is really as destructive."[114]

On Futile Reform

Undoubtedly impacted by various cultural forces outside the Church, and latent, polemical, centrifugal forces within, Ratzinger describes the post-Vatican II catechetical renewal efforts expressive of the hermeneutic of rupture as futile. He characterizes "futile reform" with the image of "the maker." The maker is one who "values his own activity above all,"[115] and holds that "the Church must no longer be fitted over us from above like a ready-made garment," for, instead, "we 'make' the Church ourselves, and do so in constantly new ways. It thus finally becomes 'our' Church, for which we are actively responsible. . . . The Church arises out of discussion, compromise and resolution."[116] Futile reform perceives that the Church as failed to live up to an ideal, so "a desperate attempt is undertaken to bring her into conformity with our wishes."[117] By taking matters into his own hands, the maker "restricts his horizon to the realm of things that he can grasp and that can become the object of his making. . . . He squeezes the world into the empirical realm, . . . [building] himself his own prison, against which he then noisily protests.[118]

---

and thinking are being presented as the only reasonable ones and, therefore, as the only appropriately human ones. Christianity finds itself exposed now to an intolerant pressure that at first ridicules it—as belonging to a perverse, false way of thinking—and then tries to deprive it of breathing space in the name of an ostensible rationality." Ratzinger admits that "there exist *pathologies in religion* that are extremely dangerous and that make it necessary to see the divine light of reason as a 'controlling organ.'" Religion must be purified by reason. At the same time, there are also "*pathologies of reason*, although mankind in general is not as conscious of this fact today" (Ratzinger and Habermas, *The Dialectics of Secularization*, 77–78; see also Benedict XVI, DCE, §28; Benedict XVI, "Faith, Reason, and the University").

114. Benedict XVI, *Light of the World*, 50.

115. Ratzinger, CC, 143. See also Bursa, "Provoking Renewal," 163–64.

116. Ratzinger, CC, 137. See also Ratzinger, CC, 158–60; Ratzinger and Messori, *The Ratzinger Report*, 45–49; Ratzinger, "Why I Am Still in the Church," 136, 140–41; Ratzinger, *Salt of the Earth*, 80; Benedict XVI, "Meditation"; Benedict XVI, *Western Culture*, 165, 169.

117. Ratzinger, CC, 136.

118. Ratzinger, CC, 143; see also 140.

Ratzinger goes on to identify several common markers of the maker's efforts. First, the maker perceives the Church as a fundamentally democratic organization. One must recall, here, as Ratzinger points out, that relativism is "the philosophical basis of democracy, which is said to be founded on no one's being able to claim to know the right way forward; and it draws life from all the ways acknowledging each other as fragmentary attempts at improvement and trying to agree in common through dialogue."[119] By democratizing the Church, the maker moves "from the paternalistic Church to the community Church," where all are active agents of Christian existence. This system comes equipped with representation, term limits, and majority vote.[120] This already anticipates Ratzinger's second characteristic of futile reform. Futile reform reduces faith to opinion. When the truth—the truths of the faith—are subject to majority vote, the whole of it is subjectively reduced to mere opinion, because, "everything that men make can also be undone again by others." In this case, "opinion replaces faith. And in fact, in the self-made formulas of faith with which I am acquainted, the meaning of the words 'I believe' never signifies anything beyond 'we opine.'"[121] Finally, futile reform conceives of its successes in empirical terms. In the pursuit of utopian idealism, everything becomes a matter of effectiveness and

---

119. Ratzinger, *TT*, 117. To this he adds, "A free society is said to be a relativistic society; only on this condition can it remain free and open-ended." In a certain sense, this is true. "One single correct political option does not exist," as Ratzinger notes. That is the error of Marxism and other totalitarian political ideologies. Yet, democracy cannot function as a form of absolute relativism—some things are wrong that will always be wrong, and right that can never become wrong. So, while relativism cannot be denied in democracy a certain right, it becomes problematic when "it sees itself as being unlimited," when there is nothing greater toward which it is being directed and for which it is working (see Ratzinger, *TT*, 117–18).

120. Ratzinger, *CC*, 137. For a relevant example of this attempted "democratization" of the Church, see the *Fundamental Text* of the German Synodal Way, which calls for "the conversion and renewal of the Church with regard to her order of power" based on a "successful inculturation into a democratic society" (3). In order to carry out ministry in today's world, the *Fundamental Text* states the Church "has the opportunity, but also the task, of developing the structures in which it organizes power in order to ... guarantee the shared responsibility and participation of all the faithful in both deliberative and decision-making processes" (19). The Synodal Way lays out the criteria by which the democratization should take place via voting rights, the election of officials, the ability of a "qualified majority" to overrule a bishop or pastor's veto, and government offices to handle complaints (see 28–31). This inculturation of Church power structures in light of democracy aims to achieve a truer sacramentality of the Church, hence rendering the Church credible again as a sign and instrument of what the Church is to be for society—which is apparently an idealistic and inclusive democratic society (see 16–19). See also Ratzinger, *CC*, 158; Ratzinger and Messori, *The Ratzinger Report*, 48–49; Benedict XVI, *Western Culture*, 167–67.

121. Ratzinger, *CC*, 139–40. See also Ratzinger, *CC*, 159; Ratzinger, *TT*, 129–30.

efficiency, of activity and performance. However, Ratzinger argues, "Statistics is not one of God's measurements.... I think we have to disregard quantitative measures of success.... We're not a business operation that can look at the numbers to measure whether our policy has been successful and whether we're selling more and more."[122]

Conclusion

By the mid-1980s, the impact of the hermeneutic of rupture within catechetics, marked as it was by a certain anthropological shift, had already become clear to Hofinger. He described the rather incomplete state of catechetical renewal as a house without a roof. Though the roof had been constructed, it lay on the ground and there was no clear plan as to how to place it on the actual edifice. Even before Hofinger's report, Ratzinger had already provided a drearier assessment, perhaps. He stated that "a real reform of the Church presupposes an unequivocal turning away from the erroneous paths whose catastrophic consequences are already incontestable," and he notes that Cardinal Julius Döpfner once remarked, with a similar analogy as Hofinger's, that "the Church of the post-conciliar period is a huge construction site. But a critical spirit later added that it was a construction site where the blueprint had been lost and everyone continues to build according to his taste."[123] Döpfner concludes, "The result is evident."[124] Ratzinger concludes in similar fashion, saying, "that catechesis is having a difficult time is a platitude that does not need to be demonstrated at great length."[125] Perhaps they had the wrong blueprint to begin with. Not long after Vatican II, a missionary "conviction was finally abandoned," which betrays a deeper issue, for "if faith and

---

122. Ratzinger, *Salt of the Earth*, 15–16. This kind of thinking can even creep into various endeavors within the New Evangelization. Here, individuals and organizations engaging the laws of supply and demand and search for a niche in the free market created by the concept of "new evangelization." When reduced to marketing and the empirical management market trends, however, fruitfulness is confined to statistical measurements. On this point, Rowland observes that approaches toward evangelization that mimic marketing schemes "complete with strategic plans, motivational posters and key performance indicators . . . [are] likely to fail because . . . grace cannot be subjected to the laws of supply and demand and other market forces. God is not a commodity. There needs to be a personal encounter with Christ which is something that cannot be artificially manufactured or conjured" (Rowland, "Christ, Culture, and the New Evangelization," 57).

123. Ratzinger and Messori, *The Ratzinger Report*, 30. See also Ratzinger, *Dogma*, 386.

124. Ratzinger and Messori, *The Ratzinger Report*, 30.

125. Ratzinger, *Handing on the Faith*, 13.

salvation are no longer interdependent, faith itself becomes unmotivated."[126] Faith in the faith of the Church had been lost—which is paramount to saying faith in Christ himself. Robert Imbelli asserts such. He says, "The critical issue, then [immediately after the Council], was and remains Christological," for "in truth, without Jesus Christ and his Paschal Mystery at its center the Church goes tragically astray. It lapses into apostasy."[127] The basic movement of the Rahnerian trajectory, then, as it appears in the progression of thought from Moran to Boeve, is one of a transition from displacing the tradition that carries forth the Word to silencing it.

---

126. Benedict XVI and Servais, "Full Text." Similarly, John Paul II describes the chief cause of the waning of mission in *Redemptoris missio*, saying, "In the Church's history, missionary drive has always been a sign of vitality, just as its lessening is a sign of a crisis of faith" (§2).

127. Imbelli, "No Decapitated Body," 759, 771.

CHAPTER SEVEN

The Revelation of the *Logos*

In contradistinction to the hermeneutic of rupture, Benedict XVI promotes a "hermeneutic of reform." Grounded in a theology and piety based upon Scripture, the Church Fathers, and tradition, Ratzinger describes this hermeneutic ten years after the Council as containing "the forces that made Vatican II possible and shaped it," though it was initially mistaken as an exercise in modernism.[1] Following the Council, however, it was steamrollered by the actual modernism operative in the hermeneutic of discontinuity.

It is worth noting that Benedict XVI does not call for some sort of facile "hermeneutic of continuity" that merely perpetuates the past. Instead, he calls for a "'hermeneutic of reform,' of renewal in the continuity," a "true reform," which contains a "combination of continuity and discontinuity at different levels," of "renewal in the continuity of the one subject-Church," because "she is a subject which increases in time and develops, yet always remaining the same, the one subject of the journeying People of God."[2] Pedraza explains:

> In Benedict's view, tradition is not static but, to quote *Dei Verbum*, it "makes progress." It blends continuity and discontinuity,

---

1. Ratzinger, *Dogma*, 382. Generally speaking, the theological journals *Concilium* and *Communio*, both of which emerge after Vatican II, concretize the two divergent interpretations of the Council and engage in a "theological star wars" over the heads of the faithful (Rowland, *Catholic Theology*, 4, 91, 93. For a brief overview of each journal, see Rahner and Schillebeeckx, "General Introduction," 1–2; Communio, "About Communio." See also Balthasar, *The Moment of Christian Witness*, 121; Ratzinger, "Communio," 127; Brotherton, "Development(s) in the Theology of Revelation," 661–76; Rowland, "Catholic Theology in the Twentieth Century," 42–43.

2. Benedict XVI, "Christmas Greetings 2005." Boeve and Benedict XVI use the same words (i.e., continuity and discontinuity), but with regard to differing referents. Boeve utilizes the terms relative to *the Church's relationship with context or the world*, and Benedict XVI with regard to the Church's relationship with her own tradition and ecclesiastical structures *in light of the call to faithfully announce the Gospel within the current context*.

fidelity and dynamism, retaining foundational "principles that express the permanent aspect" while innovating in "the practical forms that depend on the historical situation and are therefore subject to change." Such a position rightfully acknowledges that the Church develops in time, while nevertheless holding firm to the metaphysical truth that a being only remains the same being if there is substantial continuity in its essential nature, even as history continues on its way. . . . Benedict argues that true reform manifests continuity in foundational principles and possible discontinuity in contingent matters; false reform emphasizes discontinuity on both levels.[3]

Rather than finding the source of renewal in the context, Benedict XVI understands the need for a permanent "given," lest renewal efforts devolve into something other than the Catholic faith. He situates renewal from within the standpoint of the Church's faith. Provoked by context, Benedict XVI examines the Church in her current manifestation and human structures, in light of the tradition (i.e., continuity), for the sake of more profoundly seeing Christ (i.e., discontinuing that which now prohibits that view). For Benedict XVI, renewal exists as a constant reality so the Church might communicate the Gospel as clearly as possible today. Benedict XVI explains further:

> In this process of innovation in continuity we must learn to understand more practically than before that the Church's decisions on contingent matters . . . should necessarily be contingent themselves, precisely because they refer to a specific reality that is changeable in itself. It was necessary to learn to recognize that in these decisions it is only the principles that express the permanent aspect, since they remain as an undercurrent, motivating decisions from within. On the other hand, not so permanent are the practical forms that depend on the historical situation and are therefore subject to change. Basic decisions, therefore, continue to be well-grounded, whereas the way they are applied to new contexts can change.[4]

Church decisions on contingent matters are subject to change because they deal with a reality that is changeable in itself, while principles are permanent. If one discontinues permanent principles, one risks making the Church into

---

3. Pedraza, "Reform and Renewal in Catechesis," 4. For additional commentary on Ratzinger's theological position regarding ecclesial renewal, see Ramage, "*Extra Ecclesiam Nulla Salus*," 295–330; Mushi, "Benedict XVI's Hermeneutics of Reform," 279–94. For an overview of the Vatican II documents most relevant to the topic of renewal, see De Mey, "Church Renewal," 369–400.

4. Benedict XVI, "Christmas Greetings 2005."

a new subject, a different subject, rather than the same subject who grows in time and whose understanding develops. Pedraza goes on to describe Benedict XVI's approach to the Council as a "hermeneutic of tradition." He notes that Benedict XVI's view of tradition is not a static reality, but a dynamic one that "blends continuity and discontinuity, fidelity and dynamism," retaining foundational elements and innovatively renewing forms that are subject to change.[5] Conversely, false reform emphasizes discontinuity on both fundamental and contingent matters precisely because it takes context as its "given," whereas true reform maintains the tension between the continuity of foundational principles, and the discontinuity of contingent ones.

Ratzinger borrows an image Michelangelo to illustrate the interplay between continuity and discontinuity in authentic reform. For Michelangelo, the sculptor sees within the stone an image lying in wait, a pure image to be uncovered, so sculptor's task is one of *ablatio* (removal). The final sculpture is made of the same rock that was originally there (continuity!), but the form only appears through a process of chiseling away or removing that which obstructs the form (discontinuity!). For this reason, and in contradistinction to futile reform's "maker," Ratzinger personifies true reform in the image of "the wonderer." Applying *ablatio* to ecclesial renewal, Ratzinger says:

> This image [*ablatio*] contains the prototypical model of Church reform. The Church will constantly have need of human constructions to help her speak and act in the era in which she finds herself.... But they become obsolete; they risk setting themselves up at the essence of the Church and thus prevent us from seeing through to what is truly essential.... Reform is ever-renewed *ablatio*—removal, whose purpose is to allow the *nobilis forma*, the countenance of the bride, and with it the Bridegroom himself, the living Lord, to appear.[6]

Ratzinger sees this type of activity as constitutive of his own thought. He claims that his "basic impulse, precisely during the Council [and beyond], was always to free up the authentic kernel of the faith from encrustations and to give this kernel strength and dynamism."[7] Those human constructs, necessary and effective as they might have been, often become complex, cumbersome, obsolete, and an internal obstacle to mission.

---

5. Pedraza, "Reform and Renewal in Catechesis," 4.

6. Ratzinger, *CC*, 142–43. For more on this topic, see Bursa, "Provoking Renewal," 164–67.

7. Ratzinger, *Salt of the Earth*, 79.

Nevertheless, precisely how can this *ablatio* come about? In other words, just because the image flips from making to removing, how can one be sure God is acting and not simply man and his futile preferences? Whether "making" or "removing," is not the same temptation—carrying out the act according to one's own tastes and idealistic pursuits—at play? In terms of ecclesial renewal, the wonderer grounds his very wonder in an understanding that the Church is not something made by men, but is "given to us all."[8] The wonderer is not pre-occupied with an overemphasis on the Church or idealistic visions of what the Church could be, but rather, he is one who consistently looks to God, unites himself to God, and desires that God be known today.[9] The wonderer rejects empirical confinement, and instead "prepares . . . for the act of faith, which opens him to the horizon of the eternal and infinite."[10] The wonderer's faith reveals "a continual opening of oneself," to "God's action of breaking into the human world and in response to this man's breaking out toward God, which at the same time leads men toward one another."[11] In other words, the very act of faith, one which responds not to one's own ideals but to the revelation of God in the concrete, to the *prior datum* of Jesus Christ, this surrendering of oneself to Christ, brings about the necessary *ablatio*. Said yet another way: Jesus reforms the Church (cf. Eph 5:25–27). The more the members of the Church open themselves up to the encounter with Christ—which is possible precisely through the ministry of the Church—and live from it in a state of constant conversion and discipleship, the more the Church is renewed.

Benedict XVI argues that a hermeneutic of reform is in concert with his papal predecessors who oversaw the Council: John XXIII and Paul VI. He references both in his 2005 Christmas greetings. John XXIII introduces the proper hermeneutic, the hermeneutic of reform, when he says the Council aims:

> To transmit the doctrine, pure and integral, without any attenuation or distortion. . . . Our duty is not only to guard this precious treasure, as if we were concerned only with antiquity, but to dedicate ourselves with an earnest will and without fear to that work which our era demands of us. . . . [It is necessary that]

---

8. Ratzinger, *CC*, 140. Benedict XVI provides witness to this reality in his inaugural homily, "Homily of His Holiness." See also Ratzinger, *Salt of the Earth*, 74; Benedict XVI, "Meditation"; Benedict XVI, "Christmas Greetings 2005."

9. See Benedict XVI, "Address to Representatives from the World of Culture." Benedict XVI emphasizes the way in which cultural renewal was a byproduct of a more fundamental endeavor for the early monastic communities, namely the search for God.

10. Ratzinger, *CC*, 143.

11. Ratzinger, *TT*, 199–200.

adherence to all the teaching of the Church in its entirety and preciseness . . . [be presented in] faithful and perfect conformity to the authentic doctrine, which, however, should be studied and expounded through the methods of research and through the literary forms of modern thought. The substance of the ancient doctrine of the deposit of faith is one thing, and the way in which it is presented is another."[12]

For his part, Paul VI says, that while not intending to issue dogmatic proclamations, the Council thoroughly made "known its authoritative teaching on a number of questions," but it did so "with the accommodating friendly voice of pastoral charity . . . in simple, up-to-date, conversational style, derived from actual experience and a cordial approach which make it more vital, attractive and persuasive; it has spoken to modern man as he is."[13] Thus, Benedict XVI concludes, "It is clear that this commitment to expressing a specific truth in a new way demands new thinking on this truth and a new and vital relationship with it [which only comes] from an informed understanding of the truth expressed, and on the other hand, that a reflection on faith also requires that this faith be lived." He adds that John XXIII's program, then, "was extremely demanding, indeed, just as the synthesis of fidelity [i.e., continuity to the faith's essential nature] and dynamic [sic.] [i.e., discontinuity regarding contingent matters in order to allow for development] is demanding."[14]

This chapter, and those that follow, will attempt to survey Ratzinger's approach toward evangelization and catechesis as an example of "renewal in continuity" with the tradition. To pursue such a task, I will employ the same basic method as I have in previous chapters, moving from fundamental theology into its outworking in a theology of evangelization. Therefore, I intend to address the following: *How does the revelation of the Logos in Jesus Christ shape Ratzinger's vision for evangelization?* How does the theological trajectory of Ratzinger's answer to questions regarding fundamental theology establish a foundation and hint at appropriate methods for preaching and teaching?

From Fundamental Theology to Practical Theology (Again)

Early in his theological career, in the previously referenced Kierkegaardian tale of the clown found in *Introduction to Christianity*, Ratzinger says, "It is

12. Benedict XVI, "Christmas Greetings 2005."
13. Paul VI, "Address."
14. Benedict XVI, "Christmas Greetings 2005."

certainly true that anyone who tries to preach the faith amid people involved in modern life and thought can really feel like a clown, or rather, perhaps like someone who, rising from an ancient sarcophagus, walks into the midst of the world of today dressed and thinking in the ancient fashion and can neither understand nor be understood by this world of ours."[15] A central question for Ratzinger thus surfaces: How can one announce the Gospel today? In *Introduction to Christianity*, he acknowledges the difficulty of the task for the one "who seeks to preach the faith," and notes the tendency at the time to simply "modernize," and, thus, to correlate the faith in order to make the faith intelligible again. Ratzinger challenges this "modernizing" attitude and leans into the analogy even further, calling for the theologian and evangelist of that time to engage in a self-criticism that will reveal the question at hand is not fundamentally one about form (i.e., method—how to announce the Gospel), but of the insecurity of his own faith.[16] In other words, Ratzinger presses deeper, beyond methodological questions, to get to the heart of the matter—whether or not Christians of that time are terribly different from their non-believing fellow men. Is it not the case that Christians hold faith in their hands almost like water, which slips out of their grasp at any moment? Confronted with the problem of faith, he spends the rest of the book addressing this second, more pressing question: Can one actually, reasonably believe today? In a sense, he addresses Dostoyevsky's famous question: "Can one believe while being civilized, i.e., a European, believe without reservation in the divine nature of Jesus Christ, the Son of God?"[17] He addresses a question of fundamental theology, for without a solid answer to such a question, methods vaporize.

Over forty years later, on November 28, 2012, after the close of the Synod on the New Evangelization and weeks before announcing his resignation from the papacy, Benedict XVI asked the following: "How can we talk about God in our time? How can we communicate the Gospel so as to open roads to his saving truth in our contemporaries' hearts—that are all too often closed—and minds—that are at times distracted by the many dazzling lights of society?"[18] Again, note the progression of the line of questions. Benedict XVI moves from a question pertaining to fundamental theology into a question pertaining to practical theology. Therefore, Benedict XVI's inquiry remains consistent—from fundamental theology to a theology of

15. Ratzinger, *Introduction*, 41.
16. Ratzinger, *Introduction*, 41.
17. Dostoevsky, *Notebooks for "The Possessed,"* 237, quoted in Carrón, *Disarming Beauty*, 53.
18. Benedict XVI, *Transforming Power*, 42.

evangelization. But now, in 2012, the context in which the inquiry takes place has shifted away from modernity and into postmodernity. Modernity had claimed too much on the part of man—turning everything, including God, into a rational system—while the postmodern reaction claims to little—the inability to know anything definitively. Under the sway of the postmodern condition, we cannot know Being, and thus, we cannot speak about Being. In such a context, Benedict XVI's question "how can we talk about God?" carries a significant weight. The ability to speak about God, about Being, is no longer simply taken for granted as a "given."

Benedict XVI's answer addresses the postmodern critique head-on. He says:

> We can talk about God because he has talked to us; so the first condition for speaking of God is listening to all that God himself has said. God has spoken to us! God is therefore not a distant hypothesis concerning the world's origin; he is not a mathematical intelligence far from us. God takes an interest in us, he loves us, he has entered personally into the reality of our history, he has communicated himself, even to the point of taking flesh. Thus God is a reality of our life, he is so great that he has time for us too, he takes an interest in us. In Jesus of Nazareth we encounter the face of God, who came down from his heaven to immerse himself in the human world, in our world, and to teach "the art of living", the road to happiness; to set us free from sin and make us children of God (cf. Eph 1:5; Rom 8:14). Jesus came to save us and to show us the good life of the Gospel.[19]

Human beings can speak about God because God has spoken. It is true that on its own, created humanity cannot know or speak about uncreated Being, cannot claim some sort of perfect and full knowledge of Being. However, it is equally as prideful to claim that humanity can know nothing of Being. Instead, humanity can know precisely what Being chooses to reveal of itself. Ratzinger emphatically makes this point in *Dogma and Preaching*, saying, "God is made known through himself. He gives himself, on his own initiative, to be known in the man Jesus, who belongs divinely to God and is the active self-manifestation of God. God is not confined to our attempts, to our success or failure; he is (we repeat) made known by himself."[20] This is Ratzinger's foundational insight, his "given": the "object" of faith, so to speak, is not Being itself, but what Being chooses to reveal

---

19. Benedict XVI, *Transforming Power*, 42.
20. Ratzinger, *Dogma*, 87.

of itself. This revelation can be known by human beings; it is knowable because Being reveals it as such.

God, or Being, reveals himself through *Logos* ("reason," "mind," and also "person"). *Logos* becomes the starting point; *Logos* is clearly Ratzinger's "given." *Logos* is the "object" of faith. The revelation of the *Logos*, most fully manifest in Christ, becomes the critical reference point that offers unique access to Being itself, for without the word made flesh dwelling within us and among us, we cannot know God to this extent. Therefore, properly and most fully stated, Jesus Christ, the Son incarnate, becomes the starting point—and the end point for that matter. For Ratzinger, any understanding of reality that is embedded in (i.e., beginning in or ending with) anything other than Jesus Christ is a dead end. No one knows ultimate reality unless they come to know such through Him (cf. Matt 11:27; Luke 10:22).[21] And, nobody knows the ultimate reality about him or herself unless one discovers it "in the mystery of the incarnate Word," that is, in "Christ, the final Adam, by the revelation of the mystery of the Father and His love," who "fully reveals man to man himself and makes his supreme calling clear."[22]

When human beings limit God according to their understanding of Him, things fall apart. However, God and reality are not determined by our understanding. This was the tragic flaw of Rahner and those who immediately followed him. Looking upon man and his experience in history, they attempted to create a blueprint or map of meaning that could explain the whole, and then they tried to situate God in it. Similarly, the postmodern rendition of Rahnerianism claims there is no definitive map of meaning, nor does God reveal himself definitively. Modernity claims too much, and postmodernity too little—yet, ironically in doing so, it also claims too much. Conversely, Ratzinger argues that Being is not determined through transcendental anthropology, nor does it vanish into the apophatic ether. Instead, God speaks the first word. God creates. God reveals. God initiates. One can only speak about God because God has spoken in his Word, and human beings have heard and believed. Referring to Augustine's experience, Benedict XVI notes, "It is not we who possess the Truth after having sought it, but the Truth that seeks us out and possesses us."[23] Therefore, "the first condition for speaking of God," Benedict XVI says, "is listening to all that God himself has said. God is therefore not a distant hypothesis concerning the world's origin.... God ... has entered personally into the reality

---

21. Cf. Lane, *Reflections*, 16. Here, he says, "Revelation, then, *the Logos* as person, becomes 'the Given' in the journey toward Truth about God, the Cosmos and humanity."

22. Second Vatican Council, *Gaudium et spes*, §22.

23. Benedict XVI, *Transforming Power*, 30.

of our history, he has communicated himself, even to the point of taking flesh."[24] Renewal comes about, then, not through "making," but through praying and the opening of the Church to God. Rather than "making," the apostles "prayed and in prayer they waited, because they knew that only God himself can create his Church, that God is the first agent: if God does not act, our things are only ours and are insufficient; only God can testify that it is he who speaks and has spoken."[25] For Ratzinger, then, authentic renewal in fundamental and, consequently, in practical theology, springs from an objective and personal encounter with the revelation of God in the *Logos*—the subject objectively encounters the Subject. The revelation of the *Logos* in Christ, God's Word incarnate, and faith in this revelation, stands at the heart of Ratzinger's fundamental theology as the "given." Any adequate theology and methodology of evangelization begins here.

Ratzinger's Theology of Revelation[26]

In developing his theology of revelation, Ratzinger admits his debt to St. Bonaventure. In *Milestones*, Ratzinger summarizes Bonaventure's position as he had developed it in his *Habilitationschrift*:

> In Bonaventure (as well as in theologians of the thirteenth century) there was nothing corresponding to our conception of "revelation," by which we are normally in the habit of referring to all the revealed contents of the faith. . . . Such an identification would have been unthinkable in the language of the High Middle Ages. Here, "revelation" is always a concept denoting an act. The word refers to the act in which God shows himself, not to the objectified result of this act. And because this is so, the receiving subject is always also a part of the concept of "revelation." Where there is no one to perceive "revelation," no rev*el*-ation has occurred, because no *veil* has been removed. By definition, revelation requires someone who apprehends it.[27]

---

24. Benedict XVI, *Transforming Power*, 42. Cf. Benedict XVI, "Meditation."
25. Benedict XVI, "Meditation."
26. This section aims at providing a basic overview of Ratzinger's theology of revelation. For more thorough treatments of this topic, see Rowland, *Benedict XVI*, 48–70; Rowland, *Ratzinger's Faith*, 48–65; Nichols, *The Thought of Pope Benedict XVI*, 34–44; Lam, *Joseph Ratzinger's Theological Retractations*, 30–88; Gaál, *The Theology of Pope Benedict XVI*, 73–106; Collins, *The Word Made Love*, 21–54.
27. Ratzinger, *Milestones*, 108. See also Ratzinger, *On the Way*, 81–82.

Revelation is "the unveiling of the hidden."[28] Bonaventure, however, is not concerned to treat the nature of revelation in the same way current fundamental theology does. He does not deal with "revelation," as a singular, static reality, but of "revelations"—"the many individual revelations which have taken place in the course of history . . . never . . . one revelation which has taken place in these many revelations."[29] With this said, Ratzinger exercises due caution against an anachronistic reading of Bonaventure in light of current fundamental theology.

For Bonaventure, the general meaning of revelation—"unveiling"— leads in three directions. First, it has to do with an unveiling of the future. Second, and more often, Bonaventure uses the word to describe the "hidden 'mystical' meaning of Scripture that is referred to as the hidden mystery of *revelatio*. *Revelatio*, therefore, effects a pneumatic understanding of Scripture." Finally, the word refers to "that imageless unveiling of the divine reality which takes place in the mystical ascent."[30] With regard to the second, and most frequent use of *revelatio*, Ratzinger says for Bonaventure, "the content of faith is found not in the letter of Scripture but in the spiritual meaning lying behind the letter," and that "Scripture simply as a written document does not constitute revelation whereas the understanding of Scripture which arises in theology can be called revelation at least indirectly." Here, "'revelation' is understood to consist precisely in the understanding of the spiritual sense."[31] If this is the case, then it is precisely through Scripture (and with it, the other "organs of transmission"—tradition and the magisterial teaching) that one experiences revelation, or, more specifically, enters into the fullness of revelation in Christian revelation. Rather than discarding such organs of transmission for the sake of some sort of "pure" or unhindered transcendental experience, Scripture, tradition, and the magisterium aid in one's encountering God. They mediate an encounter with God; they mediate a consistent revelation.

Ratzinger's *Habilitationschrift* on Bonaventure lays a foundation that eventually impacts Vatican II in a significant way. Jared Wicks deserves credit for publishing a lecture found in the archives that Ratzinger gave regarding the schemata *De fontibus revelationis* (On the Sources of Revelation), at Cardinal Frings' request to the German-speaking bishops one day before the solemn opening of the Council.[32] In this lecture, Ratzinger

28. Ratzinger, *Theology of History*, 58.
29. Ratzinger, *Theology of History*, 57.
30. Ratzinger, *Theology of History*, 58–59.
31. Ratzinger, *Theology of History*, 66.
32. For Wicks' commentary on this lecture, see Wicks, "Six Texts," 241–43. The text

criticized the schemata's title as diverging from both Trent and Vatican I.[33] He says:

> Actually, Scripture and tradition are not the sources of revelation, but instead revelation, God's speaking and his manifesting of himself, is the *unus fons* [one source], from which then the two streams of Scripture and tradition flow out. This is the true way of speaking of tradition, which Trent took for granted . . . [Calling Scripture and tradition "sources" of revelation] is flawed in failing to distinguish the order of reality from the order of our knowing . . . Scripture and tradition are *for us* sources from which we know revelation, but they are not *in themselves* its sources, for revelation is itself the source of Scripture and tradition.[34]

While Scripture and tradition can rightly be called sources for theology, calling them sources of revelation "does not depict the order of reality . . . God's speaking and acting . . . comes before all historical formulations of this speaking, being the one source that feeds Scripture and tradition."[35] In fact, Ratzinger notes that calling Scripture and tradition "sources of revelation" leads to two major errors. First, it would mean beginning a treatment of revelation by starting with historicism and not with faith. Before speaking of Scripture and tradition, "one has to say something about God's action from which the documents come; otherwise, while they may well be tools of historians, they will not be wellsprings of faith and of life. . . . One has to speak here first of revelation in itself before saying anything about the witnesses to revelation."[36] If one does not proceed in this way, a second issue arises: revelation becomes identified with its "material principles." Here, one can assume a *sola scriptura* approach that claims Scripture and revelation are identical, a kind of positivism that "identifies revelation with its concrete attestations."[37]

---

itself appears beginning on p. 269. For further commentary on Ratzinger's assessment of *De fontibus revalationis*, see Lam, *Joseph Ratzinger's Theological Retractations*, 57–64.

33. See Wicks, "Six Texts," 270.
34. Wicks, "Six Texts," 270.
35. Wicks, "Six Texts," 270.
36. Wicks, "Six Texts," 271.
37. Wicks, "Six Texts," 271. Frequently, Ratzinger notes J. R. Geiselmann's contribution in this regard. See Ratzinger, *God's Word*, 47–48. Geiselmann, a dogmatician at Tübingen, argued prior to the start of Vatican II, that Trent's statement *"in libris scriptis et sine scripto traditionibus,"* traditionally been understood as meaning Scripture did not contain the whole truth and that there was no possibility of *sola scriptura*, should be interpreted in light of the first draft of the Tridentine text. The formulation in the first draft clearly divided revelation into two sources, saying that truth is contained *"partim*

A proper understanding avoids "scripturalism" or "historicism" because it grasps that revelation comes before "material attestations" and is always "more than its formulated witness in Scripture . . . [revelation] is the living reality that surrounds Scripture and expands it."[38]

Though he did not work on the text itself, Ratzinger's insights shaped the deliberations that eventually produced *Dei verbum*. *Dei verbum* presents revelation personally. Following the Council, in his commentary on *Dei verbum*, Ratzinger points out that, compared with Vatican I's *Dei Filius*, Vatican II's *Dei verbum*, with its emphasis on God himself "in his wisdom and goodness," gives "a far greater emphasis to the personal and theocentric starting point."[39] He adds, "It is God himself, the person of God, from whom revelation proceeds and to whom it returns, and thus revelation necessarily reaches—also with the person who receives it—into the personal centre of man, it touches him in the depth of his being, not only in his individual faculties, in his will and understanding."[40] Commenting on Ratzinger's comparison between Vatican I and II, Christopher Collins notes that in *Dei Filius*, "revelation is seen as a monologue from God to humanity rather than a dialogue between God and humanity," and one that follows the "material tradition" whereby God hands on that which is extrinsic to himself.[41] In other words, it operates from a neo-scholastic conception of revelation that results in a loss of the dynamism of dialogue that is central to a personalist conception of reality. Rowland describes this Suárezian theory of revelation as consisting of a "clutch purse of doctrines, a kind of pocketbook of theoretical propositions."[42] Suárez approached revelation as a matter of God giving to humanity truths *about* himself, as if the truths are extrinsic and outside of his person, instead of *giving* himself and inviting a personal response to that gift. Rowland identifies Ratzinger's work at Vatican II as laying the foundation for *Dei verbum*, which "set[s] aside the Suárezian approach," and

---

in libris scriptis partim in sine scripto traditionibus." In the final text, however, Trent dropped the "*partim*"—"*partim*," and Geiselmann sees this as not dividing truth into two sources, thus opening the door for a Catholic theologian to "argue the material sufficiency of Scripture," and "that Holy Scripture transmits revelation to us sufficiently" (Ratzinger, *God's Word*, 48). Geiselmann thus concludes that Trent intended to point in the direction of a thoroughly acceptable *sola scriptura*. Ratzinger critiques Geiselmann's thesis, though he appreciates the enthusiasm behind it for ecumenical progress. Nonetheless, he questions its historical and factual basis, along with the definition of "sufficiency of Scripture," etc.

38. Wicks, "Six Texts," 271–72.
39. Ratzinger, "Revelation Itself," 171.
40. Ratzinger, "Revelation Itself," 171.
41. Collins, *The Word Made Love*, 43.
42. Rowland, "What Did Dostoevsky Mean?"

presents revelation "as an historical event in which God the Son reveals God the Father to humanity through the aid of the Holy Spirit."[43] Hence, *Dei verbum* would proceed to develop "an understanding of revelation that is seen basically as dialogue."[44] With this, both the Council and Ratzinger move away from a neo-scholastic understanding of revelation, a propositional position in which "revelation chiefly meant a store of mysterious supernatural teachings, which automatically reduces faith very much to an acceptance of these supernatural insights."[45] Summarizing Ratzinger, here, Collins argues that at the heart of the narrative of salvation history one finds the *acts* of God, and "not simply the *content* of what is ultimately revealed. Revelation ... is not a static body of data or knowledge but rather always characterized by the dynamic of an *unfolding event*, in turn giving it a narrative texture rather than a propositional one ... what is *behind* Scripture is always more than the 'letter' of Scripture itself."[46] Rather than an intellectualist or extrinsicist approach that sees revelation and the handing over of certain divine truths, over and against human reality, which are to act as an interpretive grid for reality and received through faith, Ratzinger understands revelation to be a personal act of unveiling, revealing, disclosing the inner nature that is initiated by God and received by a human subject.

Similarities and Differences

From what has been determined thus far, the similarities between Ratzinger's position on revelation and that of Moran's are apparent. Like Moran, Ratzinger also believes the assertion that revelation "closed with the death of the last apostle must appear as far too simplistic."[47] Elsewhere he adds, "this cannot mean that a certain number of truths have now been impacted and God has decided to make no further communications," for the point of God's dialogue with man "was not, and is not, to say *something*, many kinds of things, but to utter himself in the Word."[48] On the contrary, to say revelation concludes with Christ

> Means that God's dialogue with man, God's entry into mankind in Jesus, the man who is God, has achieved its goal. . . . Thus

---

43. Rowland, "What Did Dostoevsky Mean?"
44. Ratzinger, "Revelation Itself," 171.
45. Ratzinger, "Revelation Itself," 172. See also Ratzinger, *On the Way*, 82; Ratzinger, *Principles*, 107–8.
46. Collins, *The Word Made Love*, 27.
47. Ratzinger, *God's Word*, 86.
48. Ratzinger, *Introduction*, 263.

his purpose is fulfilled, not when the greatest possible sum of knowledge has been communicated, but when through the Word love becomes visible, when in the Word "You" and "You" make contact. Its meaning does not lie in a third thing, in some kind of factual knowledge, but in the partners themselves. It is called "union." In the man Jesus, God has once and for all uttered himself: he *is* his Word and, as his Word, himself. Revelation ends here, not because God deliberately puts an end to it, but because it has reached its goal.[49]

Rahner, Moran, and Ratzinger all move down this path, decidedly away from a propositional understanding of revelation, opting instead for a dialogical position that reaches its high point in union with God in Christ. Because Christ lives, revelation continues to be accessible today.

At this point, however, Ratzinger and Moran's Rahnerian position diverge. Moran's "doctrine" of ongoing revelation ultimately relativizes Christian revelation and admits of a certain subjectivism (or a turn to the subject) which is radicalized in Boeve's position. By rendering revelation implicit, and by relegating the "organs of transmission," the possibility of moving away from Christ, the fullness of revelation, becomes quite real. Ratzinger anticipates such modern and postmodern problems within his study of Bonaventure, noting that Bonaventure's view does not "destroy the objectivity of revelation in favor of a subjective actualism." For Bonaventure, Ratzinger concludes, the deep meaning of Scripture in which one finds the *revelatio* and the content of faith "is not left up to the whim of each individual," instead "it has already been objectified in part in the teachings of the Fathers and in theology so that the basic lines are accessible simply by the acceptances of the Catholic faith . . . as it is summarized in the *Symbolum*."[50] Rather than relegating the faith of the Church and seeing it as prohibitive of the transcendent experience, Ratzinger, following Bonaventure, takes the faith of the Church as that which allows for revelations today. In and through the faith of the Church, one has the capacity of attaining a certain illumination, a process of inspiration, that makes it possible to understand the meaning of Scripture on this spiritual (or mystical) level.[51] In this light, with the Church's faith (and not without

---

49. Ratzinger, *Introduction*, 263.

50. Ratzinger, *Theology of History*, 66–67.

51. See Ratzinger, *Theology of History*, 65. Here, Ratzinger distinguishes three types of vision: (1) *visio corporalis*—external, bodily sight with the eyes; (2) *visio spiritualis*—imagination and dream; and (3) *visio intellectus*—understanding through divine illumination. For Bonaventure, revelation only takes place in light of this third understanding of vision, which is the "third heaven" into which St. Paul is taken up, but

it), Ratzinger can claim that Christian revelation remains accessible today. With a certain brilliance, Ratzinger captures all of this in his reflection on Christ, who is the same yesterday, today, and forever (cf. Heb 13:8):

> The first encounter with Jesus Christ occurs in the present; indeed, one can only encounter him because he is a today for many and therefore has a today. But to ensure that I get close to the whole Christ and not just to a piece of him perceived by chance, I must heed the Christ of yesterday as he reveals himself in the sources, especially in Scripture. If, in the process, I listen to him carefully and do not excise essential parts of his appearance because of a dogmatically asserted worldview, I see him open to the future and I see him coming from eternity, which embraces the past, the present, and the future all at once.[52]

Raymond de Souza offers a powerful commentary on this topic, examining the tendency of theology after the Council to jettison the "organs of transmission." He draws on the image of a river. Without the powerful current, a river is merely stagnant water, a ditch. However, without banks, the powerful river becomes a flood only to recede and leave behind shallow puddles of murky water. "Applied to theology," he says, "the influx of new ideas and new questions, and the retrieval of lost parts of the tradition, is what makes theology fresh and nourishing. Powerful currents even alter the shape of the banks over time. Yet the banks of authority, defined doctrine, and fidelity to settled tradition are needed to preserve the river." He concludes that theologians after the Council (characterized by Ratzinger and Hans Küng [1928–2021]) disagreed "on the necessity of the banks," with Ratzinger's renewal remaining within them "providing greater depth as the flow of neglected ideas, new and old, were explored."[53]

The Person of Christ Reveals the Personal "Content" of Revelation

The nature of revelation, as an event, an occurrence between the revealer and the receiving subject is one thing, but exactly *what* is revealed, or *who* is revealed, is another. For Ratzinger, *Logos* is the center of revelation. *Logos* is the

---

also that which is granted to all of the Apostles and the inspired authors of Scripture. Therefore, "it is identical with the process of inspiration." If one approaches Scripture with vision on the first or second levels, one will miss its meaning.

52. Ratzinger, *New Song*, 13.
53. De Souza, "The Rhine Breaches the Tiber."

key. *Logos* reveals Being. *Logos* is what Being freely reveals of itself, and *Logos* has taken flesh. Benedict XVI summarizes this entire thesis by saying:

> A God who is merely imagined and invented is not God at all. If he does not reveal himself, we cannot gain access to him. The novelty of Christian proclamation is that it can now say to all peoples: he has revealed himself. He personally. And now the way to him is open. The novelty of Christian proclamation does not consist in a thought, but in a deed: God has revealed himself. Yet this is no blind deed, but one which is itself *Logos*—the presence of eternal reason in our flesh. *Verbum caro factum est* (John 1:14): just so, amid what is made (*factum*) there is now *Logos*, *Logos* is among us. Creation (*factum*) is rational.[54]

To develop this central theme, David Bonagura's article, "*Logos* to Son in the Christology of Joseph Ratzinger/Benedict XVI,"[55] provides a guide for traversing Ratzinger's thought. Bonagura's treatment proceeds in the following progression: (1) God as *Logos*; (2) From *Logos* to Son; (3) the Word Incarnate. Here, I will follow Bonagura's basic outline, but I will expand in certain areas—particularly in the second movement where the sonship of the *Logos* opens into a full-scale treatment on a theology of personhood. This concept, and its corresponding theological anthropology, are central to Ratzinger's understanding of faith, as will become clear in the next chapter—a longer treatment on theological anthropology and its implications.

God as Logos

"In the beginning was the Word, and the Word was with God, and the Word was God" (John 1:1). John's recapitulation of Genesis 1 in a sentence "condenses creation theology into Logos theology."[56] "God is the Creator," a statement that "throws open the door to the proper field of human reason and to the province of world religions," Ratzinger says.[57] Though "distorted in many ways" and appearing "only in dubious refractions," God reveals himself in the world, for "there is a transparency of the world with respect to its Creator."[58] God's creative capacity reveals a certain might, and a Lordship. John's prologue, then, brings together this creative power

---

54. Benedict XVI, "Address to Representatives."
55. Bonagura, "*Logos* to Son," 475–88.
56. Ratzinger, *Dogma*, 93.
57. Ratzinger, *Dogma*, 91.
58. Ratzinger, *Dogma*, 91.

of God with the concept of *logos*. Here, John points out that "everything that exists comes from the 'Word,'" and that "'Word is mightier than the so-called facts . . . it is the fact of all facts.'"[59] All of this raises several questions: What is *logos*, exactly, and what does one mean by speaking of *the Logos*? What is the significance of the concept of Word? How does it differ from the concept of *logos*?

Logos signifies "reason, meaning."[60] In *Dogma and Preaching*, Ratzinger defines *logos* as "the same thing as 'mind.'"[61] Emphatically, Ratzinger claims that "The God who is *logos* guarantees the intelligibility of the world, the intelligibility of our existence . . . even though his understanding infinitely surpasses ours and to us may so often appear to be darkness."[62] Therefore:

> To say that the world comes from the Logos, accordingly, means: the world is intelligible; it is the creature of the Mind that expresses itself. Even before we *make sense* of anything, meaning is there. It embraces us. We stand upon it. The intelligibility does not depend on our creative effort but, rather, precedes and enables it. This means that the question about our Wherefore [our reason for being] is answered in our Whence [our origin]. The Whence itself is the Wherefore. . . . Thus, belief in the Creator ultimately has become a statement about what man is [as created] and what the world is [as created] by nature: the product of a creative Mind and thus empowered to bestow meaning that coexists with the meaning that is simply there.[63]

Similarly, in *Introduction to Christianity*, Ratzinger says:

> The world is objective mind; it meets us in an intellectual structure, that is, it offers itself to our mind as something that can be reflected upon and understood. From this follows the next step. To say "*Credo in Deum*—I believe in God" expresses the conviction that objective mind is the product of subjective mind and can only exist at all as the declension of it.[64]

The whole of the created universe, this being-thought, objectivized thought, "comes from thinking." "All being," Ratzinger concludes, "is ultimately

---

59. Ratzinger, *Dogma*, 93.

60. Ratzinger, *Introduction*, 26. See also Benedict XVI, "Faith, Reason, and the University."

61. Ratzinger, *Dogma*, 93. On p. 94, he also describes it as "meaning."

62. Ratzinger, *Introduction*, 26.

63. Ratzinger, *Dogma*, 93–94. See also Ratzinger, *In the Beginning*, 17–18, 22–25.

64. Ratzinger, *Introduction*, 155.

being-thought and can be traced back to mind as the original reality."[65] The world is intelligible, and all human thinking, human cognition, then, is not pure cognition, but *re*-cognition. It is re-thinking what has already been thought; it is the discovery of what already *is*. As Ratzinger puts it, "all our thinking is, indeed, only a rethinking of what in reality has already been thought out beforehand."[66] For this reason, Guardini speaks of the primacy of *logos* over *ethos*. "Before doing stands being," Ratzinger explains, adding, "doing does not create meaning; rather, meaning creates doing."[67]

Yet how did the Greek concept of *logos* come into contact with Christianity and shape the Church's understanding of God in the first place? Ratzinger argues that in answering this question, one must dig into the pre-Christian roots in Israel. Pablo Blanco Sarto comments on this, saying:

> In the history of Israel, God talks to his people in diverse ways and on numerous occasions.... In the tradition of the Jewish people, the Word [*dabar*]—as well as being an instrument for human communication—is above all the revealed mediation of God to his chosen people. The Logos is turned into *dia-logos*,

---

65. Ratzinger, *Introduction*, 156. The Church Fathers understood this fundamental intelligibility of all reality as the Book of Nature, as opposed to the Book of Revelation or of Scripture. See Tanzella-Nitti, "Two Books," 51–83. In numerous papal statements, Benedict XVI speaks of the book of creation. See, for example, his reference to the "Creator's handwriting" vs. historical revelation in Benedict XVI, "Christmas Greetings 2005"; Benedict XVI, "Address to the Participants of the General Assembly of the Italian Church"; Benedict XVI, *Caritas in veritate*, §51. Earlier in his theological career, we find in Ratzinger a consistent reference to the fundamental intelligibility "written" into nature, inscribed into the created order, as the basis of Ratzinger's teaching on the *logoi spermatikoi* or *semina verbi* found in other religions. These "seeds of the Word," from the one seed of the *Logos*, appear across and throughout human history. See Ratzinger, *Theology of History*, 7. See also the Congregation for the Doctrine of the Faith, *Dominus Iesus*, §21n85.

66. Ratzinger, *Introduction*, 153. In his article, "Einstein and God," Bishop Robert Barron describes what Ratzinger has developed in *Introduction* as a fundamental proof for the existence of God. He says Ratzinger's "simple but penetrating argument" is based on "the universal intelligibility of nature, which is the presupposition of all science, can only be explained through recourse to an infinite and creative mind which has thought the world into being. No scientist, Ratzinger said, could even begin to work unless and until he assumed that the aspect of nature he was investigating was knowable, intelligible, marked by form. But this fundamentally mystical assumption rests upon the conviction that whatever he comes to know through his scientific work is simply an act of re-thinking or re-cognizing what a far greater mind has already conceived. Ratzinger's elegant proof demonstrates that, at bottom, religion and science ought never to be enemies, since both involve an intuition of God's existence and intelligence."

67. Ratzinger, *Dogma*, 94.

because it is directed to humanity. . . . The *dabar* offered by God—the revelation in Christ—will be the origin in faith.[68]

For the Jewish people, God's word initiates a dialogue; God's word makes a dialogue with God possible while simultaneously making language sacred because God uses it as a means by which to speak to his people. Therefore, the root concept of "word" and "response," of *dabar* (or *logos*) and *dia-logos* exists at the heart of the old covenant. The union of thought crystallizes as the Septuagint interprets the Old Testament in light of Greek philosophy. This translation builds "the bridge from God over to Greek thought" by tying the self-revelation in Exod 3:14 ("I am who I am") to the Hellenistic concept of *logos*.[69] In the Septuagint, "I am who I am" becomes "I am he that is." The "he that is" refers to the eternal God, the *Logos*, the eternal reason, which, in being united to the Israelite "God of your fathers," means that God is not bound to a particular location like the pagan gods but brings about a convergence between the eternal and the personal, between the God of Israel's faith and the God of the philosophers. Ratzinger argues that the philosophical interpretation of the Hebrews weds belief to ontology, since the "biblical concept for God is here identified with the philosophical concept of God."[70] However, Ratzinger goes on to question precisely how the wedding of the two concepts of God could have taken place. He explains:

> Could one have ever given the Platonic "Being" a name and referred to it by this name as a kind of individual? Or is the fact that one can name this God not a sign of a fundamentally different conception? If one adds that it is an important detail of the text that one can name God only because he has named himself, then one only deepens still further the gulf between this conception and Platonic, absolute Being, the final stage of ontological thinking, which is not named and names itself still less.[71]

In other words, how do the personal God of faith and the eternal Being of Greek philosophy converge? Does not the convergence destroy the Greek concept *and* the Hebrew one?

Navigating the exegesis, here, Ratzinger ultimately concludes that "firm evidence of the name Yahweh before Moses or outside of Israel is lacking."[72] Israel's own nationhood, then, begins with "the final develop-

68. Sarto, "*Logos* and *Dia-Logos*," 501.
69. Ratzinger, *Introduction*, 119.
70. Ratzinger, *Introduction*, 119, quoted in Bonagura, "*Logos* to Son," 476.
71. Ratzinger, *Introduction*, 119.
72. Ratzinger, *Introduction*, 120.

ment of their own name for God," for "in the tangle of gods with whom people dealt, this word formation [of Yahweh] refers to the personal god, that is, the god who is concerned with man and is himself personal and person-centered. It is the God who, as the personal Being, deals with man as man."[73] Israel's understanding of God runs counter to the common conceptions of the time: God is not "the god of a place but the god of men: the God of Abraham, Isaac, and Jacob. . . . He is not anywhere in particular; he is to be found at any place where man is and where man lets himself be found by him."[74] God is not bound to this or that location, but "is seen on the plane of I and You," and thus "moves away into the transcendence of the illimitable and by this very fact shows himself to be he who is always . . . near, whose power is boundless."[75] In that mysterious phrase, in that name "I am," then, the God of Israel "confronts the gods and identifies himself as the one who *is*, in contrast to those who have been toppled over."[76] Israel's God is not a national god, but "the God of all people and of the whole universe," and Israel became convinced that "for this reason it alone worshipped the real God."[77] And, Bonagura concludes that the Old Testament's image of God becomes clear: God is both "personal and proximate," and "he is transcendent, absolute being, with power over space and time."[78] Therefore, the apparently unbridgeable gulf between the god of the philosophers and the biblical God is not as impassable as it initially appears. While the biblical God certainly differs from "the *esse subsistens*, the absolute Being, that is discovered in the lonely silence of philosophical speculation,"[79] the biblical God *is*, while the other gods *are not*; the biblical

---

73. Ratzinger, Introduction, 121. Ratzinger goes on to point out the significance of a name as opposed to a concept. A concept "tried to perceive the nature of the thing as it is in itself. The name, on the others hand . . . is concerned to make the thing nameable, that is, 'invocable,' to establish a relation to it" (134). Therefore, in naming himself for humanity, in revealing his name, "God has really become he who can be invoked," the God with whom man can have some sort of relationship (135). Then, in the Incarnation, the realism, here, reaches its climax, for "God has become one of us and so he has become the truly nameable, standing in coexistence with us" (135).

74. Ratzinger, Introduction, 123.

75. Ratzinger, Introduction, 123. Bonagura notes that this convergence of the eternal and the personal in God helps the Israelites to understand other dimensions: (1) God is the "most powerful God and force in the world"; (2) "he is the God of the Promise, of the future, rather than as a force of nature"; (3) "he transcends the bonds of singular and plural, thus preparing the way for the New Testament experience of God as Trinity" (Bonagura, "*Logos* to Son," 476).

76. Ratzinger, Introduction, 131.

77. Ratzinger, Introduction, 136.

78. Bonagura, "*Logos* to Son," 477.

79. Ratzinger, Introduction, 130.

God creates *ex nihilo*, and the biblical God transcends this or that locale, while remaining present in a radically personal manner.

John the Evangelist completes the bridge between the biblical God and the Greek concept of Being in his presentation on the *Logos*, the Word of God in Jesus Christ. The transition, here, from *Logos* to Word, means that the reality of *logos* does not remain in the abstract or distant. Ratzinger explains that for John, *logos* does not only mean "mind" or "meaning," "but also *verbum*—not only 'mind,' but also 'discourse.' . . . the Christian God is not just reason, objective meaning, the geometry of the universe, but he is speech, relation, Word, and Love."[80] Word describes "a meaning . . . that is relationship, that is creative."[81] This is a profound development in the concept of *logos*. "In the beginning was the *logos*, and the *logos* is God," Benedict XVI says, highlighting the "distillation" of a "rapproachment" between biblical faith and Greek thought.[82] Indeed, "God's word precedes human words, since he creates speaking beings by his word," Peter J. Leithart points out. "Yet God's word also follows human words. If God wants to make himself known to human beings, he must speak humanly. By speaking our language, the God who spoke first humbles himself, takes second place, and even allows his word to be mangled and distorted. But God's word couldn't reach its hearers at all without passing through this humiliation."[83] Ratzinger puts it similarly:

> The basic reason why man can speak with God arises from the fact that God himself is speech, word. His nature is to speak, to hear, to reply. . . . Only because there is already speech, "Logos," in God can there be speech, "Logos," to God. . . . Since there is relationship within God himself, there can also be a participation in this relationship. Thus we can relate to God in a way which does not contradict his nature. . . . And this is what the Incarnation of the Logos means: he who is speech, Word, Logos, in God and to God, participates in human speech. . . . Man is able to participate in the dialogue within God himself because God has first shared in human speech and has thus brought the two [i.e., divine speech and human speech] into communication with one another.[84]

80. Ratzinger, *Dogma*, 94.
81. Ratzinger, *Introduction*, 26.
82. Benedict XVI, "Faith, Reason, and the University."
83. Leithart, "A Birthday Card to Balthasar." See also Ratzinger, *The Feast of Faith*, 26.
84. Ratzinger, *The Feast of Faith*, 25–26.

The creative Word of God draws so close to man that *Logos*, Word, takes on flesh, *sarx* to reveal that which the Father wishes him to reveal and to draw humanity to participate in the divine dialogue. The implications are significant. Ratzinger says, "The Incarnation of the Logos brings eternity into time and time into eternity. It is not that God *is* time, but he *has* time."[85] God, as Creator, *made* time, and, more personally, in the *Logos* incarnate, God *enters* into time. God *makes time for us* and *has time for us*. Being does not stand entirely removed from time, nor does the Creator create and detach completely. Certainly, natural history and human history, grounded in and united as they are in the *logos*, manifest vestiges of the *logos*. Yet over and above this natural revelation, in Jesus Christ, Being has entered into time *in fullness* and in a profoundly different way—a way that allows for a deeply personal entry into the life of God—than what appears in the traces of the *logos* read in the book of nature.

Christianity, then, refers to revelation of *Logos*, Word, and its radical identification with the person, the man, Jesus Christ—this particular man, who lived at this particular time, in this particular place, with these particular people. John, therefore, takes the "central formula of his faith in God," the "I am" of the burning bush, and the "I am" of Deutero-Isaiah and the Wisdom literature,[86] and makes it "into the central formula of his Christology."[87] Now, God's name provided at the burning bush or in Isaiah, is "no longer merely a word, but a person: Jesus himself."[88] Now, "Being is accepted as a person, and the person accepted as Being itself."[89] Now, Ratzinger says, "in the Logos predicate, the belief in the Creator passes over into belief in Jesus Christ. In him we see the Father (John 14:9)."[90] Being becomes accessible to humanity inasmuch as Being reveals itself in and through the person of Jesus Christ, and humanity can now participate in God's inner life, his inner dialogue.

In making such points, Ratzinger holds that the early Christians, confronted by pagan cults with local deities, made another conscious decision in favor of *logos*, the "God of the philosophers" against those pagan, local gods—"the choice thus made meant opting for the *logos* against any kind of myth; it meant the definitive demythologization of the world and

---

85. Ratzinger, *The Feast of Faith*, 26.
86. See, for example, Isa 43; 44:6; 48:12.
87. Ratzinger, *Introduction*, 132.
88. Ratzinger, *Introduction*, 133.
89. Ratzinger, *Introduction*, 136.
90. Ratzinger, *Dogma*, 95.

of religion."⁹¹ This marks a radical coinciding of reason and God, for "the world comes from reason, and this reason is a Person, is Love—this is what our biblical faith tells us about God. Reason can speak about God; it must speak about God, or else it cuts itself short."⁹² As Bonagura puts it, "by seeing God as Being itself, they chose truth as the foundation of their faith rather than the customs and religious practices of pagans."⁹³ It was the culmination and coinciding in *logos* of a long chronology of Greek philosophy critiquing myths and prophets critiquing Israel's affairs with foreign gods.⁹⁴

While the Church Fathers chose the "god of the philosophers" over the local gods of the pagans, the Christian understanding of God-as-*Logos* does transcend the Greek concept of *logos* in several ways. In the first place, the philosophical God, the *logos*, for the Greeks, referred to the eternal rationality of being. This conceptualizes *logos* as isolated—pure being, or pure rationality. Ratzinger says, "*The philosophical God is essentially self-centered*, thought simply contemplating itself."⁹⁵ However, by wedding *logos* to the biblical image of God, *logos* is no longer thought-thinking-thought, because:

> The God of faith is basically defined by the category of relationship. He is creative fullness encompassing the whole. Thereby a completely new picture of the world, a completely new world order is established: the highest possibility of Being no longer seems to be the detachment of him who exists in himself and needs only himself. On the contrary, the highest mode of Being includes the element of relationship. . . . [T]he supreme Being no longer appears as absolute, enclosed autarchy but turns out to be at the same time involvement, creative power, which creates and bears and loves other things.⁹⁶

Judeo-Christianity recasts the *logos* of the philosophers in light of relationality, creativity, and love. Nothing that the creative *Logos* creates is too small or insignificant for relationship, for love.⁹⁷ Biblical faith transforms the philosophical understanding of *logos* as self-centered thought-thinking-thought, through

---

91. Ratzinger, *Introduction*, 137–38, quoted in Bonagura, "*Logos* to Son," 477. See also Ratzinger, *TT*, 21–22, 28.

92. Ratzinger, *Introduction*, 26.

93. Bonagura, "*Logos* to Son," 477.

94. See Ratzinger, *Introduction*, 139.

95. Ratzinger, *Introduction*, 147, quoted in Bonagura, "*Logos* to Son," 478.

96. Ratzinger, *Introduction*, 147–48, quoted in Bonagura, "*Logos* to Son," 478.

97. Ratzinger cites an aphorism from Hölderlin, "'Non coerceri maximo, contineri tamen a minimo, divinum est' (Not to be encompassed by the greatest, but to let oneself be encompassed by the smallest—that is divine)" (*Introduction*, 146).

the category of relationship, which is to say, the category of person. This fundamental insight into Being, made possible through the revelation of the *Logos* in Jesus Christ, provides the basis for a theology of personhood, which is foundational for Ratzinger's understanding of revelation.

Additionally, Christianity transcends a second prejudice, namely, "the exclusion of love from being."[98] The God of the philosophers is "based on the notion that thought and thought alone is divine," Ratzinger says. In Christianity, this notion is transcended by the "God of faith, [Who] as thought, is also love."[99] If the God of faith, the biblical God, is the same as the God of the philosophers (i.e., Being, truth), then this God of the philosophers "whose pure eternity and unchangeability had excluded any relation with the changeable and transitory," appears "to the eye of faith as the God of men [who are changeable and transitory], who is not only thought of all thoughts, the eternal mathematics of the universe, but also *agape*, the power of creative love."[100] He adds, "the God of faith, as thought, is also love. His image is based on the conviction that to love is divine."[101] In the *Logos*, love and truth coincide. Ratzinger argues, "the *logos* of the whole world, the creative original thought, is at the same time love; in fact this thought is creative because as thought, it is love, and, as love, it is thought."[102] Love is as great as truth. In fact, the truth is love. They are neither parallel, nor are they divergent realities. The ways in which the Christian God transcends the "god of the philosophers" will be subsequently unpacked in the next two sections of this chapter.

Logos *as Son: The God of the Philosophers Transcended by Relationality*

As noted above, Ratzinger argues that Christianity's understanding of the *Logos* first surpasses the "god of the philosophers" in the concept of

---

98. Bonagura, "*Logos* to Son," 478.

99. Ratzinger, *Introduction*, 148, quoted in Bonagura, "*Logos* to Son," 478.

100. Ratzinger, *Introduction*, 143. Ratzinger goes on to note Pascal's "Fire," his encounter-experience wherein he opposes a purely rational, purely mathematical God in favor of one who is creative, personal love. Ratzinger concludes, "In this sense there is the experience that the God of the philosophers is quite different from what the philosophers had thought him to be, though he does not cease to be what they had discovered; that one only comes to know him properly when one realizes that he, the real truth and ground of all Being, is at one and the same time the God of faith, the God of men" (144).

101. Ratzinger, *Introduction*, 148.

102. Ratzinger, *Introduction*, 148.

relationality. *Logos* is not merely thought-thinking-thought, but inherent relationality (a Trinity of persons) that grants freedom such that human beings in the created order can reach out in relation and discover themselves as part of a fundamental relationality. This fundamental relationality contradicts Greek thought, which, according to Ratzinger, "always regarded the many individual creatures... only as individuals, arising out of the splitting up of the idea in matter. The reproductions are thus always secondary; the real thing is the one and universal."[103] However, within the Christian understanding of God as *logos*, the concept of *logos* is not impersonal and individualistic, but personal and communal. Here:

> The last analysis is not mathematics but love, the minimum is a maximum; the smallest thing that can love is one of the biggest things; the particular is more than the universal; the person, the unique and unrepeatable, is at the same time the ultimate and highest thing.... The Christian sees in man, not an individual, but a person... this passage from individual to person contains the whole span of the transition from antiquity to Christianity, from Platonism to faith.... Then oneness is not the unique and final thing; plurality, too, has its own and definitive right.[104]

In his essay "Concerning the Notion of Person in Theology," Ratzinger attempts to uncover, or, better, to recover, the original understanding of the word "person," insofar as this original meaning grew out of Christian theology. Today, however, Ratzinger says thought regarding person "has distanced itself far from its origin and developed beyond it." Yet the original meaning "nevertheless lives, in a hidden way, from its origin." One must recover the origin to know what "person" truly means.[105] In other words, Ratzinger seeks to go beyond the mainstream definition that finds its source in Boethius' sixth-century definition of person as *naturae rationalis individua substantia* (the individual substance of a rational nature) in a return to the concept's origins.[106]

Ratzinger's philological pursuit traces the root of the word "person" to the Greek *prosopon* ("role"), the equivalent of the Latin word *persona* ("mask"). The poets of antiquity did not narrate as in a monologue but gave

---

103. Ratzinger, *Introduction*, 160.

104. Ratzinger, *Introduction*, 160–61. Also quoted in Bonagura, "Logos to Son," 480.

105. Ratzinger, "Notion of Person," 103–4.

106. Ratzinger, "Notion of Person," 112. See also Ratzinger, *Introduction*, 160–61, 181–84. Aquinas takes up this definition in the *Summa Theologica*, 1.29.1. See also the *Oxford English Dictionary Online*'s treatment of "person" and the emphasis on individuality at s.v. "person, n."

dramatic life to events through the appearance of certain *prosopa*. To illustrate the point, Ratzinger adds, "they placed words in the mouths of divine figures and the drama progresses through these words.... The poet creates the artistic device of roles through which the action can be depicted in dialogue."[107] *Prosopon* exists, at is origin, as an artistic device by which the ancient author gives life to a narrative through the drama of dialogue.

Early Christian theologians discovered within the texts of Scripture a similar dialogical character within the words attributed to God. In particular, they found curious the reality of God speaking "in the plural" or "with himself (e.g., 'Let *us* make man in our image and likeness,' or God's statement in Genesis 3, 'Adam has become like one of *us*,' or Psalm 110, 'The Lord said to my Lord,' which the Greek Fathers take to be a conversation between God and his Son)."[108] By applying the insights of prosopographic exegesis, an ancient interpretive technique that acknowledges the use of "roles" in the dramatic presentation of poems, the Fathers drew from such passages a new meaning. Within God, there are *prosopa*. However, here, *prosopon* no longer means "role." It is no longer a literary device, because "it takes on a completely new reality in terms of faith in the Word of God."[109] In God, *prosopon* describes a dialogical *reality*, not an artistic *device* for employing dialogical "roles." In the reality of God, the concept of "person—*persona*" is born. God, in and of himself, is a dialogical reality. Ratzinger notes, "The word *prosopon* = 'role' is thus at the transitional point where it gives birth to the idea of person."[110] Though God is one being, in his self-disclosure, Ratzinger says, "God seems to converse with himself . . . there are an 'I' and a 'You' in him."[111] In God's revelation, as indicated in the scriptural testimony, God conducts a dialogue, or rather, God *is* a dialogue. God is not a literary or dramatic device; He is real. God is, in himself, revealing event—the disclosure of one *persona* to another *persona*.

From here, Tertullian goes on to provide the first valid expression of a Trinitarian formula (c. 213), saying God is "one being in three persons."[112] The relatedness of God as Trinity does not destroy God's unity, but is the very essence of personal unity. As Ratzinger explains, "We have arrived at the trinitarian testimony, which is not a marginal feature of Christianity but rather represents its core. God exists as love, which means precisely that he

---

107. Ratzinger, "Notion of Person," 105. Cf. Hart, "Human Dignity."
108. Ratzinger, "Notion of Person," 105.
109. Ratzinger, "Notion of Person," 105.
110. Ratzinger, "Notion of Person," 105–6.
111. Ratzinger, *Introduction*, 182, quoted in Bonagura, "*Logos* to Son," 481.
112. Ratzinger, "Notion of Person," 104. See Tertullian, *Adv. Prax.* 2.

exists as Trinity. As love, he is from everlasting, in himself and by his nature, the fruitful encounter of I and Thou and precisely in this way the highest unity."[113] God's unity is not only found at the level of substance, but also, or precisely in the level of person. God is love, which is to say that God is *personal* love—the coming together, or, better said, *being* together of distinct persons existing in perfectly actualized relationship. Ratzinger concludes, "The idea of person expresses in its origin the idea of dialogue and the idea of God as the dialogical being... [who] lives in the word and consists of the word as 'I' and 'you' and 'we.'"[114] Ratzinger says that God "is not only *logos* but also *dia-logos*, not only idea and meaning but speech and word in the reciprocal exchanges of partners in conversation."[115]

By the turn of the fifth century, Trinitarian theology had developed such that a thesis could be clearly articulated: "God is a being in three persons."[116] Yet, by this point in time, person had come to be understood not only with regard to a dialogical reality, but as relation. It is, therefore, precisely through developments in Trinitarian theology that the concept of person matures. Ratzinger describes this maturation:

> According to Augustine and late patristic theology, the three persons that exist in God are in their nature relations. They are, therefore, not substances that stand next to each other, but they are real existing relations, and nothing besides.... In God, person means relation. Relation, being related, is not something superadded to the person, but it is the person itself. In its nature, the person exists only as relation.... Put more concretely, the first person does not generate in the sense that the act of generating a Son is added [accidental] to the already complete person, but the person is the deed of generating, of giving itself, of streaming itself forth. The person is identical with this act of self-donation. One could thus define the first person as self-donation in fruitful knowledge and love; it is not the one who gives himself, in whom the act of self-donation is found, but it is this self-donation, pure reality of act.[117]

Dauphinais and Levering provide further clarity, here, noting that person-as-relation is best understood in terms of a verb than a noun. They say, "There are not divine Persons who then relate; rather, the Persons are the

---

113. Ratzinger, *Dogma*, 89.
114. Ratzinger, "Notion of Person," 107.
115. Ratzinger, *Introduction*, 183, quoted in Bonagura, "*Logos* to Son," 481.
116. Ratzinger, "Notion of Person," 108.
117. Ratzinger, "Notion of Person," 108.

relating." They go on to describe the reality of fatherhood, where, prior to conception, the man was just a man, but after, he has been changed. "He exists now in a new relational way, as father of a child. . . . The same new relational existence is also in the child, who exists relationally as child of the father."[118] Relationality is what constitutes person as such.

God is one divine being in three persons. God's being is divine, and God's being is personal. God is self-donation and entrustment as perfectly actualized dialogical relationality. Dauphinais and Levering describe this reality by noting that the category of relation has two aspects: relation *to* and relation *in*. They say:

> The relation always exists in something, and the relation is always to another thing. Relation *to* gives us insight into how the relations in God are distinct: the Persons are distinct solely in relation (of origin) *to* each other. Relation *in* gives us insight into how the relations in God are each fully God, and how together they are fully God. Thus each Person is a distinct way of existing (subsisting) *in* "He who is," the simple divine Act. Since each divine Person is sheer subsisting relation, the Persons should be thought of not as static nouns, but as active verbs: the one divine Act is in act in three distinct relatings, or "Persons."[119]

"Relation *to*" allows for distinction, while "relation *in*" points to each divine Person as the divine being. As Dauphinais and Levering summarize, "God the Trinity is three Persons subsisting distinctly in relation *to* each other *in* the divine being."[120] Each divine Person is God, yet insofar as the Father gives/relates himself (eternally-begetting) to the Son, the Father is Father. The same holds true for the Son in his reciprocal relationship with the Father. Father could not *be* Father without the Son, nor could Son *be* Son without the Father.[121]

This understanding of "person" is a third fundamental category that demolishes the Greek division of reality between substance and accident. Ratzinger says, summarizing Augustine, "In God, person is the pure relativity of being turned toward the other; it does not lie on the level of substance—the substance is *one*—but on the level of dialogical reality, or relationality toward the other . . . in God there is nothing accidental, but only substance and relation."[122] Substance is not the only primordial form of

---

118. Dauphinais and Levering, *Knowing the Love of Christ*, 20–21.
119. Dauphinais and Levering, *Knowing the Love of Christ*, 22.
120. Dauphinais and Levering, *Knowing the Love of Christ*, 23.
121. Ratzinger makes this point in *The God of Jesus Christ*, 44. Cf. *CCC*, §255.
122. Ratzinger, "Notion of Person," 108.

being—person stands alongside. In *Introduction to Christianity*, Ratzinger describes consequence of this reality as follows:

> The experience of the God who conducts a dialogue, of the God who is not only logos but also dia-logos, not only idea and meaning but speech and word in the reciprocal exchanges of partners in conversation—this experience exploded the ancient division of reality into substance, the real thing, and accidents, the merely circumstantial. It now became clear that the dialogue, the *relatio*, stands beside the substance as an equally primordial form of being.[123]

Thus, via personal relationality, Ratzinger breaks free from the *duplex ordo*. The Old Testament makes this clear: God acts inter-relationally with His creation. He is outside of it, yet integral to it. Contra Rahner, relationality, not self-transcendence, bridges the gap between nature and supernature. Ratzinger, it seems, overcomes the dichotomy, not by thinking in substantial terms of natural/supernatural, but in relational ones: Creator/creation, Father/Son, Father/son, Being/being-thought, and so forth. While Rahner tried to solve the problem by starting with transcendental man, Ratzinger points out that *the* Man—*ecce Homo*—resolves the problem, the dichotomy between nature and supernature, once and for all. He does this by revealing the fullness, *in His person*, of interrelationality between God and humanity, that part of His creation God willed for itself, and by making it possible, *in His person*, for human persons to return to that fundamental relationality with the Father.[124]

The fundamental content of revelation, as made known in the very person of *Logos*-as-Son, is the primordial relationality of being in the Trinity of persons in the one God. Human beings, existing as that uniquely personal part of God's creation, in the "image and likeness" of the Trinitarian God, stand ever within and before the possibility of relationship with this eternal relationality. Person is being-in-relation. As Ratzinger concludes, "Person is the pure relation of being related, nothing else. Relationship is not something extra added to the person, as it is with us; it only exists at all as relatedness."[125] In traversing Ratzinger's thought on the nature of revelation, two striking features appear. The *Logos* is at once *the content revealed*

---

123. Ratzinger, *Introduction*, 183. In *Dogma*, Ratzinger says that the revelation of God existing in the relation Father-Son means that God is "comprehensible only as relation—whereby the essential and fundamental core of the doctrine of the Trinity is already stated and becomes clear in its true, central content" (86).

124. Second Vatican Council, *Gaudium et spes*, §22.

125. Ratzinger, *Introduction*, 183.

(i.e., the eternal rationality, the eternal logic, is relational, is *communio*), and *the one who reveals* (bringing humanity into that divine *communion*). These features coincide most fully in Jesus Christ. Said another way, "The form of revelation unveils its content."[126] In Jesus Christ, the *Logos* incarnate, God reveals himself personally as the personal God.

In God, person is the act of begetting, of self-gift, of being-in-relation. This means, following de Lubac, that God does not exemplify loneliness, but "ec-stasy" (the complete "going out" of himself), "the mystery of the Trinity has opened to us a totally new perspective: the ground of being is *communio*."[127] *Logos* reveals Being as perfect relationality. Being, as revealed by *Logos*, is, in itself, relational because it is personal. Commenting on the relationality that is the Trinity, Bonagura concludes, "Relation ... constitutes the essence of being, which is to say that in his essence God is relation."[128] The revelation of the *logos*, then, reveals God as *communio*—Being is *communio*—and creation exists as a profound expression of relationality and in *communio* with Being. "The 'objective' meaning of the world is a subject," Ratzinger says, "in relation to me."[129] Here, pure relativity (i.e., each person as he is relationally, or relative to the others),[130] or perfect relationality, coincides with the truth of Being, as revealed in the personal nature of God, meaning the truth takes on the form of perfect relationality. One finds *the* truth—it is possible to freely discover and to be embraced by *the* truth—in relation to the God who reaches out to His creation and who manifests Himself most fully in Christ, and one discovers through the truth of this relationship the inherent relationality of Being.

The initial development of person-as-relation within Trinitarian theology gives rise to a second stage, amid advances in Christology, where the concept of person fully matures. Ratzinger frequently conjectures that from the Gospels on, the Church set out to answer two inseparable questions: "Who is Jesus?" and "Where is he from?"[131] Ratzinger traces the Church's responses to these questions by considering the various titles that developed as a way of describing Jesus Christ. First, he considers the development of the title "Christ" (Messiah). He notes that this title made

---

126. Leithart, "A Birthday Card to Balthasar."
127. From Lubac, *La Foi chrétienne*, 14, quoted in Ratzinger, *Principles*, 22–23.
128. Bonagura, "*Logos* to Son," 481.
129. Ratzinger, *Dogma*, 94.
130. Cf. *CCC*, §255.
131. See Benedict XVI, *Jesus of Nazareth: The Infancy Narratives*, 1–4. See also Ratzinger, *Pierced One*, 15–22; Benedict XVI, *Jesus I*, 319–55, which is basically a later development of what appears in *Introduction*, 216–28.

little sense outside of Semitic culture,[132] and that it needed further explanation and clarification due to ambiguities in the understanding of the title within that very culture.[133] Consequently, "Christ" ceased to function as a title and melded with the name Jesus: Jesus Christ. Benedict XVI points out that "what began as an interpretation ended up as a name, and therein lies a deeper message: He is completely one with his office; his task and his person are totally inseparable from each other."[134] The next attempt at a suitable title also proved to be insufficient. The title, "Lord," when applied to Jesus, did claim a unity between him and God. However, the title is derived from the paraphrase for the divine name in the Old Testament, so something more distinctive of the Christian event would be necessary.[135] As was the case with the title "Lord," the title "Son of God" "connected him with the being of God himself," though the expression was intertwined with the political theology of the region and Jesus' exercise of power did not resemble the typical show of power.[136]

Thus, the clearest expression of Jesus' identity, its "further concentration," arrives in the word "Son," which, "comes in the end to be the only, comprehensive designation for Jesus. It both comprises and interprets everything else."[137] Therefore, Jesus' identity becomes most fully expressed in the title "the Son," or simply, "Son," which "is something quite distinct from the concept of 'son of God' . . . [and] has a different linguistic history and belongs to a different kind of language, namely, that of the coded parable."[138] This point is critical. Neither politics, nor mythology, nor philosophy drive the movement toward understanding *Logos*-as-Son. The real source of the phrase, Ratzinger points out, cannot be located so much in Jesus' public preaching, but in his "conversations with the inner circle of disciples. Its real source is probably to be found in Jesus' prayers; it forms the natural corollary to his new mode of addressing God, *Abba*."[139] Ratzinger adds:

132. Benedict XVI, *Jesus I*, 319. See also the *CCC*'s treatment of this title in §436–40.
133. Ratzinger, *Pierced One*, 16.
134. Benedict XVI, *Jesus I*, 319.
135. Benedict XVI, *Jesus I*, 320. For more on this title, see the *CCC*, §446–51.
136. Benedict XVI, *Jesus I*, 320. With regard to the title "Son of God," as it was understood in the Old Testament, see Ratzinger, *Introduction*, 216–23. Here he addresses the "king" theology of the Old Testament that is tied to the Davidic kingdom, as well as the title's application in the Emperor Augustus' political theology. As it is applied in Christianity, the title assumes the connotation of service. See also *Jesus I*, 335–39; Ratzinger, *God and the World*, 265–66; *CCC*, §441–45.
137. Ratzinger, *Pierced One*, 16. See also Benedict XVI, *Jesus I*, 339.
138. Ratzinger, *Introduction*, 223.
139. Ratzinger, *Introduction*, 223.

When Jesus' witnesses call him "the Son," this statement is not meant in a mythological or political sense—those being the two most obvious interpretations given the context of the time. Rather, it is meant to be understood quite literally: Yes, in God himself there is an eternal dialogue between Father and Son, who are both truly one and the same God in the Holy Spirit.[140]

The mysterious depth of Trinitarian relationality finally appears in those Gospel passages in which Jesus Christ reveals his prayer, his interior dialogue in which he identifies himself as "Son," and God as "Father"—the one can only be understood, can only exist, in light of the other. In Jesus, the Son, someone entirely original has arrived upon the scene, despite those who prefigure him in the Old Testament. "The term 'Son,' along with its correlate 'Father (Abba),' gives us a true glimpse into the inner being of Jesus—indeed, into the inner being of God himself," Benedict XVI says. "Jesus' prayer is the true origin of the term 'the Son.' It has no prehistory, just as the Son himself is 'new.'"[141]

When it comes to the title "the Son," Ratzinger holds that the decisive testimony in favor of this identification can be found in the Gospel of John and the *Jubelruf* (joyful shout) prayer recorded in the Gospels of Matthew and Luke (cf. Matt 11:25–27; Luke 10:21–22).[142] In Luke's gospel, Jesus exclaims, "no one knows the Father except the Son," which leads Benedict XVI to reflect on Plotinus' idea that Goethe captures as "If the eye were not sunlike, it could never see the sun."[143] Every process of knowing involves some similarity that allows for assimilation—a union between knower and that which is known. This is akin to the statement at the end of John's prologue: "No one has ever seen God; the only-begotten Son, who is in the bosom of the Father, he has made him known" (John 1:18). The *Jubelruf* is a filial dialogue that reveals that "the Son" means "perfect communion in knowledge, which is at the same time communion in being. Unity in knowing is possible only because it is unity in being."[144] The *Jubelruf* makes clear the divine unity of Father and Son.

---

140. Benedict XVI, *Jesus I*, 320.
141. Benedict XVI, *Jesus I*, 344.
142. Benedict XVI, *Jesus I*, 339.
143. Benedict XVI, *Jesus I*, 340.
144. Benedict XVI, *Jesus I*, 340. Ratzinger goes on to point out that the *Jubelruf* also highlights the unity of wills between Father and Son. The Son wills to whom the Father is revealed, but the Son's will is not arbitrary. It is always united with the will of the Father.

While John's Gospel also emphasizes the unity of Father and Son (cf. John 5:19, 30; 10:30), Ratzinger notes the evangelist carries the understanding of "the Son" further—into the realm of relation. Ratzinger says:

> By calling the Lord "Son," John gives him a name that always points away from him and beyond him; he thus employs a term that denotes essentially a relatedness. He thereby puts his whole Christology into the context of the idea of relation. . . . In that Jesus is called "Son" and thereby made "relative" to the Father, and in that Christology is ratified as a statement of relation, the automatic result is the total reference of Christ back to the Father. Precisely because he does not stand in *himself*, he stands in *him*, constantly one with him.[145]

He continues:

> The Son as Son, and insofar as he is Son, does not proceed in any way from himself and so is completely one with the Father; since he is nothing beside him, claims no special position of his own, confronts the Father with nothing belonging only to him, makes no reservations for what is specifically his own, therefore he is completely equal to the Father. The logic is compelling: If there is nothing in which he is just he, no kind of fenced-off private ground, then he coincides with the Father, is "one" with him. . . . To John, "Son" means being from another; thus, with this word he defines the being of this man as being from another and for others, as a being that is completely open on both sides, knows no reserved area of the mere "I" . . . this being is pure relation (not substantiality) and, as pure relation, pure unity.[146]

"Jesus is entirely 'Son' and is never enclosed in his own world," Ratzinger adds. "He is, with every fiber of his existence, relation to the Father."[147] In and of itself, the phrase "the Son" expresses relatedness to the Father, the referent without which it (i.e., the title "the Son") would not make sense.[148] "Son"

---

145. Ratzinger, *Introduction*, 185.
146. Ratzinger, *Introduction*, 186–87.
147. Ratzinger, *GCC*, 43.

148. It is important to note the ordering of the paragraphs in the *CCC* with regard to the Trinity. Following its treatment on belief in one God (§199–202), the *CCC* makes reference to the revelation of the Father by the Son (§238–42) and the revelation of the Father and the Son by the Spirit (§243–48), prior to explicating the dogma of the Trinity as one God in three persons (§249–56). This revelation leads the Church to develop its own terminology, indeed, she gave new meaning to words in order to signify "an ineffable master, 'infinitely beyond all that we can humanly understand'" (§251).

means nothing without "Father," and vice versa.[149] The *Catechism* echoes this point, saying "He is eternally Father in relation to his only Son, who is eternally Son only in relation to his Father."[150] With this title, John turns his Christology into one of relatedness. His emphasis remains on the person of the Son who is completely equal to the Father because he holds nothing for his own, just as the Father holds nothing as his own.

To further express the perfect relationality of "Son," Ratzinger describes the nature of sonship with the expression "being-from." Drawing from John's Gospel, Ratzinger notes, "The Son as Son, and insofar as he is Son, does not proceed in any way from himself and so is completely one with the Father; since he is nothing beside him, claims no special position of his own."[151] The Son's origin is "'from above—from God himself.... Only God is truly his 'father,'"[152] hence, any talk about "being-from" is talk of sonship, of filial relationship that ultimately has as its prototype the eternally begotten Son and the eternally begetting Father. Any filial relationship, humanly speaking, pales in comparison to that of the Son and the Father. All of this brings us back to the previous points about personhood and relationality. Regarding the threefold personhood of the Trinity, Ratzinger says, "The first Person does not beget the Son as if the act of begetting were subsequent to the finished Person; it *is* the act of begetting, of giving oneself, of streaming forth. It is identical with the act of self-giving."[153] The first Person of the Trinity does not beget the second Person subsequently, as if the first Person were "finished," and then proceeded to beget the second Person. The Father, as Giver, is the very *act* of giving, and the Son is the *act* of being given (receiving) and being given over/outpoured (the self-emptying of *kenosis*) in the Father's giving that extends to creation (cf. John 3:16). Eternally begotten is the Son—the pure act of the Father's self-giving is the Son. Again, this insight leads Augustine to say, "In God there are no accidents, only substance and relation."[154] Ratzinger says, "Person is precisely what the New Testament brings to light in the reality of the Father-Son relation: a consciousness that is essentially relation, creative, loving, knowing, relation."[155] This concept of person differs entirely from the concept of the

---

149. See Ratzinger, *Journey to Easter*, 137.

150. *CCC*, §240.

151. Ratzinger, *Introduction*, 186.

152. Benedict XVI, *Jesus of Nazareth: The Infancy Narratives*, 7–8. See also Ratzinger, *Introduction*, 271–72.

153. Ratzinger, *Introduction*, 184. See also Ratzinger, "Notion of Person," 108.

154. Ratzinger, *Introduction*, 184.

155. Ratzinger, *Dogma*, 86.

"individual" and reveals relation as that which ends thinking only in terms of substance.[156] As a final point here, Ratzinger adds that it is precisely in the perfect communion of persons in the Trinity, in the pure act of self-giving and self-receiving between persons in the Trinity—pure act that holds nothing as "individual" or "private"—that one finds, and can enter into, the unity which is the ground and sustenance of all reality.[157] The unity that exists between persons in the Trinity is found in that which is shared between Father and Son—the nothing and the all. In the Father-Son relationship, nothing is bracketed off for the self; all is shared.

Love Enfleshed and Given: The God of the Philosophers Transcended (Again)

Christianity's concept of *logos* first transcends that of the philosophers in its emphasis on personhood and inherent relationality. As "Son" becomes the primary descriptor for Jesus, this understanding of relationality in the Trinity reaches new heights. In addition to this initial transcendence of the philosophers, Christian understanding oversteps philosophy a second time in its reflection on the Incarnation, which claims "The historical man Jesus is the Son of God, and the Son of God is the man Jesus."[158] *Logos* does not "reside" in the realm of abstraction or in the universal idea, but in the very real, the very personal, and the very particular. In Jesus Christ, the Son of God, "the absolutely staggering alliance of *logos* and *sarx*," takes place.[159] *Logos*, then, encompasses two theological areas: (1) insofar as *logos* refers to word, creative reason, and love, it is decisive for understanding the Christian image of God; and (2) "the concept of *logos* simultaneously forms the core of Christology, of faith in Christ."[160] Now, "the Logos of all things can encounter me with a human face, the face of Jesus of Nazareth."[161] Bonagura argues, "The incarnation visibly manifests the *logos* as the choice of the personal, the particular, and the free over the impersonal, the universal, and the necessary; for in it the Logos, the eternal Word of God, freely assumed the particular, human flesh, so that the particular may share in the universal, life with God."[162] Ratzinger says, "If

---

156. Ratzinger, *Introduction*, 184.
157. Ratzinger, *Introduction*, 188.
158. Ratzinger, *Introduction*, 194.
159. Ratzinger, *Introduction*, 193.
160. Ratzinger, *Introduction*, 28, quoted in Bonagura, "*Logos* to Son," 475.
161. Ratzinger, *Dogma*, 94.
162. David Bonagura, "*Logos* to Son," 483.

it is true that the term *logos*—the Word in the beginning, creative reason, and love—is decisive for the Christian image of God, and if the concept of *logos* simultaneously forms the core of Christology, of faith in Christ, then the indivisibility of faith in God and faith in his incarnate Son, Jesus Christ, is only confirmed once more."[163] These two threads of *Logos* (i.e., the Christian image of God and faith in Jesus Christ) intersect, as Bonagura observes, most profoundly in John's Prologue.[164]

By applying the concept of *logos* to Jesus Christ in the Prologue of John's Gospel, the *Logos* now embraces particularity. Ratzinger holds that it would not be wrong to translate John 1:14 as "The meaning became flesh," given the Greek understanding of *logos*.[165] This "meaning" has turned towards men and women and addresses humanity, "given in a completely personal way to each of us ... God is not some distant sublime being that we can never approach. He is very near, within calling distance, easy to reach. He has time for us—so much time that he lay in the crib as man and remained eternally man."[166] With this deeply personal and profoundly particularized application, *logos* "no longer denotes simply the permeation of all being by meaning; it characterizes this man; he who is here is 'Word.' The concept of *logos*, which to the Greeks meant 'meaning' (*ratio*), changes here really into 'word' (*verbum*). He who is here is Word; he is consequently 'spoken' and, hence, the pure relation between the speaker and the spoken to."[167] Word is that which connects and makes relationship, makes communication possible between speaker and the one being spoken to, an "existence that is entirely way and openness."[168] The Word opens the way for communion—the Word is the Way of communion with the Father. Jesus Christ is the *Logos* of God, that meaningful Word who re-establishes the ground of man's existence as relationship with the Father. In the Word made flesh, the Son's relationship with the Father opens to incorporate all of mankind. Hence:

> The Logos stoops to assume as his own the will of man, and speaks to the Father with the "I" of this man, and thereby transforms the word of a man into the eternal Word, into his own blessed "Yes, Father." While giving to this man his own "I," his own identity, the Logos frees man, saves him, divinizes him. We

163. Ratzinger, *Introduction*, 28.
164. Bonagura, "*Logos* to Son," 475.
165. Ratzinger, *Seeking God's Face*, 84.
166. Ratzinger, *Seeking God's Face*, 84–85.
167. Ratzinger, *Introduction*, 189. For more on this transition from *logos* to Son, see Bonagura, "*Logos* to Son," 479–82. See also Ratzinger, *The God of Jesus Christ*, 77.
168. Ratzinger, *Introduction*, 189.

here touch almost palpably on the reality meant by the phrase "God became man."[169]

Humility appears as a hallmark of Being. For when the *Logos* takes flesh, he "who bears in himself the totality of Being reaches beyond the 'greatest,' so that to him it is small, and he reaches into the smallest, because to him nothing is too small. Precisely this overstepping of the greatest and reaching down into the smallest is the true nature of absolute spirit."[170]

While John's prologue highlights Jesus' identity as *Logos*, as Word, the transformation also includes the Cross.[171] Bonagura, quoting Ratzinger, points out that "in his surrender to the cross word, mission, and existence all converge, so that '[f]rom the cross faith understands in increasing measure that this Jesus did not just do and say *something*; that in him message and person are identical, that he is all along what he says."[172] In Jesus, word and work, mission and being coincide. Ratzinger says, "Jesus is 'word'; but a person who not only *has* words but *is* his word and his work, who is the *logos* ('the Word', meaning, mind) itself; that person has always existed and will always exist; he is the ground on which the world stands."[173] Because Jesus, "as a totality is Son, Word, and mission," Ratzinger says, "his activity reaches right down to the ground of being and is one with it."[174] Who He is and what He does are identical, for His person is pure act. The coinciding of being and mission appears most readily on the Cross. On the Cross, the *Logos* reveals itself as a radical love for man,[175] which is wholly "given over to obedience and love, loving to the end (cf. John 13:10), he himself becomes the true 'offering.'"[176]

The Cross, therefore, displays the radical convergence of *logos* and love not as "two parallel or even opposing realities but one, the one and only absolute."[177] In *Truth and Tolerance*, Ratzinger adds that "the primacy of the Logos and the primacy of love proved to be identical. The Logos was seen to be, not merely mathematical reason at the basis of things, but a creative love

---

169. Ratzinger, *Journey to Easter*, 102.

170. Ratzinger, *Introduction*, 146.

171. Bonagura makes this point in "*Logos* to Son," 484. See also Ratzinger, *Introduction*, 205–7, 225–28.

172. Bonagura, "*Logos* to Son," 484. See Ratzinger, *Introduction*, 206.

173. Ratzinger, *Introduction*, 206.

174. Ratzinger, *Introduction*, 226, quoted in Bonagura, "*Logos* to Son," 484.

175. Bonagura, "*Logos* to Son," 484. See also Benedict XVI, *DCE*, §12.

176. Benedict XVI, *Jesus I*, 334.

177. Ratzinger, *Introduction*, 148.

taken to the point of becoming sympathy, suffering with the creature."[178] For Christians, love is higher than thought, and thought is a kind of love. Love and *Logos* are identical. Here, Ratzinger says, "The *logos* of the whole world, the creative original thought, is at the same time love; in fact this thought is creative because, as thought, it is love, and as love, it is thought. It becomes apparent that truth and love are originally identical."[179] The convergence of *logos* and *sarx*—in the Incarnation of the Son and the manifestation of this love on the Cross—unites reason and faith. In the Word made flesh, the ground of the rational basis of faith is established,[180] because "the same Logos, the creative rationality from which the world has sprung, is personally present in this man Jesus. The same power that made the world is itself entering into the world and talking with us."[181]

Logos as love—incarnate and crucified—significantly transcends the "god of the philosophers." Liethart explains this, saying, "God gives himself to us in his Son, and this self-gift isn't a mere role God happens to play. His self-gift reveals the eternal life and being of God as Father, Son, and Spirit. In the light of this disclosure, we discern that self-gift is the basic reality of everything."[182] Leithart points out the consequences here, once again getting at the way the "god of the philosophers" must be transcended:

> From the viewpoint of Trinitarian ontology, Being itself has to be reimagined. Ancient ontology assumed that Being is what persists in a world of change. Trinitarian ontology insists instead on the primacy of love; love endures. Love is action, an out-going from the self to the Other. Within a Trinitarian ontology, the verb becomes the "new substantive." Things aren't most fully themselves when they're at rest, unchanging, alone. Being isn't isolated stasis. Beings exist and fulfill themselves not by holding back, but by giving. For created things as for God, "self-having [is] self-giving." Things are what they are, they possess themselves, in action, in motion, and in relation, in the movement of love.[183]

---

178. Ratzinger, *TT*, 182.

179. Ratzinger, *Introduction*, 148, quoted in Bonagura, "*Logos* to Son," 479. See also Benedict XVI, "Angelus Address, February 3, 2013."

180. Bonagura, "*Logos* to Son," 479.

181. Ratzinger, *God and the World*, 26, quoted in Bonagura, "*Logos* to Son," 475.

182. Leithart, "A Birthday Card to Balthasar."

183. Leithart, "A Birthday Card to Balthasar." Cf. Second Vatican Council, *Gaudium et spes*, §24.

Conclusion

The ability to speak about God at all, the whole problem of fundamental theology, stands at the fore of Ratzinger's inquiry regarding evangelization. In the area of fundamental theology, Ratzinger takes the *logos* as his "given." Even more specifically, he takes the revelation of the *Logos* in Jesus Christ, which is the consistent "given" throughout all the Christian tradition even if his visage is distorted or tarnished in various epochs. God is *logos*, and the incarnate *Logos* reveals God most fully. God, the *logos*, the fundamental intelligibility of the world, reveals himself as a deeply personal, relational reality that reaches us, encounters us, in the lowly humanity of Jesus Christ. In the radical realism present in Jesus Christ, the alliance of *logos* and *sarx*, the *Logos*, the Word identifies with *this man*, Jesus Christ, "in whom the mystery of the human being takes on light."[184] Without such a revelation, any talk of Being would be impossible, as postmoderns indicate. However, Being reveals itself in *logos*, and *logos* has taken flesh in Jesus Christ—the true object of Christian faith. We cannot know Being, but we can know that which Being reveals of itself. And Being reveals itself as *logos*, *logos* as Son, and Son as love.

---

184. Cf. Second Vatican Council, *Gaudium et spes*, §22.

CHAPTER EIGHT

A Theological Anthropology Revealed by the *Logos*

"The truth is that only in the mystery of the incarnate Word does the mystery of man take on light."[1] Thus claim the Council Fathers in *Gaudium et spes*, and with it, Ratzinger reads the whole Council in a Christocentric light.[2] He says:

> We are probably justified in saying that here for the first time in an official document of the magisterium, a new type of completely Christocentric theology appears. On the basis of Christ this dares to present theology as anthropology and only becomes radically theological by including man in discourse about God by way of Christ, thus manifesting the deepest unity of theology.[3]

In highlighting the revelation of God in the incarnate *Logos*, the generally "theologically reserved" text of *Gaudium et spes* reaches new heights and provides the basis for a theological anthropology in light of Christ. Taking cues from *Gaudium et spes*, Ratzinger develops a theological anthropology rooted in Christology. As beings made "in the image and likeness" of God's "image and likeness,"[4] the incarnate *Logos* reveals who man is and to what he is called. For Ratzinger, the revelation of the *Logos* in Jesus Christ "does not reveal something, nor does it reveal various kinds of things, but in the man Jesus, in the man who is God, we are able to understand the whole nature of man."[5] Ratzinger's anthropology has a clear "given": the *Logos* incarnate. In other words, Ratzinger's anthropology is decidedly Christocentric. It is an

1. Second Vatican Council, *Gaudium et spes*, §22.
2. Cf. Rowland, *Catholic Theology*, 94.
3. Ratzinger, "The Dignity of the Human Person," 159.
4. See Danielou, *From Shadows to Reality*, 46.
5. Ratzinger, "Dogmatic Constitution," 176.

applied Christology and the reverse of the Rahnerian trajectory. It moves from Christ to man and understands man in light of Christ, as opposed to mapping a vision for man and then showing how Christ always already fulfills the vision—understanding Christ according to an anthropological "given" drawn from contemporary thought.

The revelation of the mystery of man in Jesus Christ manifests at least two realities for human beings, and it does so simultaneously. On the one hand, Jesus Christ makes known the perfection of the human person, the standard, the bar, the heights to which humanity is called. Christ is "the fulfillment of the entire human being," he is "an indication for theology of how person is to be understood as such."[6] Insofar as *logos* has been revealed in Jesus Christ, indeed, *is* Jesus Christ, Jesus stands as the directional arrow for all humanity. In light of the revelation of the *Logos*, then, the mystery of man, the "image and likeness of God" takes on light in terms of a profound understanding of person-as-relation, and ultimately in terms of love—received and given within a communion of persons. On the other hand, and considering such a standard or directional arrow as Christ, man's radical shortfall caused by sin, which is made possible by the necessity of freedom (i.e., the ability to accept or reject fundamental relationality), appears in stupendous fashion. In other words, Jesus Christ lays bare both the heights and the depths of human personhood. Additionally, while "person is the relativity toward the eternal," and Christ reveals "what human being tends toward," the human being remains "on the way." As long as history is still on the way, the "goal is never fully reached."[7] This chapter will focus on Ratzinger's thought regarding the heights of the call, in order to set the stage for the next chapter, which will explore the impact of the depths caused by sin that reveal the deep-seated need the human being has for faith, which is, properly understood as a personal encounter that initiates ongoing conversion in time.

Christ, an Ontological Exception?

Before proceeding into the contents of the chapter, amid the post-Enlightened, liberal worldview, we must note two critical objections to a Christological basis for anthropology, namely that Jesus Christ appears to be some sort of ontological exception—at once too much and too little. Regarding the former, Anne Devlin notes that one may bristle before a distinctly theological starting point. This objection claims that a Christological starting

---

6. Ratzinger, "Notion of Person," 114.
7. Ratzinger, "Notion of Person," 116.

point is not "speaking about man as such."⁸ Ratzinger agrees that too often Christ is seen as "the simply unique ontological exception which must be treated as such."⁹ He responds by highlighting the methodological insight provided by Teilhard de Chardin who, reflecting on the discovery of radium in the natural sciences, asks if this discovery is an anomaly or if it opens the way for a new physics. According to de Chardin, if the discovery had been dismissed as an anomaly, modern physics would not have come to be. Making a Christological connection, Ratzinger observes:

> Something methodologically decisive for all human thinking becomes visible here. The seeming exception is in reality very often the symptom that shows us the insufficiency of our previous schema of order, which helps us to break open this schema and to conquer a new realm of reality. The exception shows us that we have built our closets too small, as it were, and that we must break them open and go on in order to see the whole. This is the meaning of Christology from its origin: what is disclosed in Christ, whom faith certainly presents as unique, is not only a speculative exception; what is disclosed in truth is what the riddle of the human person really intends.¹⁰

The uniqueness of Christ, his radical particularity, is not an anomaly that should be considered an exception to the rule and disregarded, but is, rather, he who breaks open the insufficiency of previous schemas and widens the horizon. It is Christ, who the New Testament presents as the "last Adam," the "second Adam," the "definitive Adam" who is the "image of God," who "alone appears [as] the complete answer to the question about what the human being is. In him alone appears the deepest meaning of what is for the present a rough draft. He is the definitive human being, and creation is, as it were, a preliminary sketch that points to him."¹¹ Christ is not the exception, but is, from his exceptional position, the rule.

Regarding the latter consideration, throughout history, various positions have seen Christ as somehow too little. The basic position sees the statement "Christ has only one person, namely, a divine person" as "a

---

8. Devlin, "The Theology of Human Personhood."

9. Ratzinger, "Notion of Person," 113.

10. Ratzinger, "Notion of Person," 114. Here, Ratzinger's argument sounds oddly similar to that of Boeve's theology of interruption, who borrows the concept from Lyotard. However, Ratzinger speaks of interruption in order to give credence to Christology in the realm of anthropology in general, as opposed to the manner in which Boeve's postmodern sympathies end up challenging the essential content of the faith itself. See chapter 3 of this study.

11. Ratzinger, *In the Beginning*, 48. See also Ratzinger, "Notion of Person," 114.

subtraction from the wholeness of Jesus' humanity."[12] This position holds that "person is the authentic and true apex of human existence," but Christ only has one person, a divine person. Recall that, according to the Christological doctrine, Jesus Christ "has two natures and one person, a divine and a human nature, but only a divine person."[13] "Therefore," Ratzinger says, this position holds "the entirety of human reality is not present in him," with this assumption serving as "the point of departure of various distortions and aberrations" in numerous heresies throughout Church history.[14] Such positions repeatedly attempt "to show where something is missing" in Jesus' personal existence.[15] Ratzinger points out that the problem running through such positions lies in conceiving of "person" in substantialist terms. Here, he implicates Boethius, and the prevalence of his concept of person in the West: *naturae rationalis individua substantia*. Ratzinger notes that in light of this idea coming from the Greek and Latin understanding of reality, "the concept of person stands entirely on the level of substance ... [which] cannot clarify anything about the Trinity or about Christology." Instead, "it is an affirmation that remains on the level of the Greek mind which thinks in substantialist terms."[16] Such a position almost inevitably results in seeing Christ's divine personhood as a subtraction from human personhood. It is somehow different; it is something other than a substantially human personhood.

In response, the Church rejects fundamental errors that somehow subtract from Jesus' humanity. The Council of Chalcedon holds the natures or essences, fully human and fully divine are to be acknowledged "without confusion or change, without division or separation" in "one and the same Christ, Lord, and only begotten Son." Chalcedon goes on to say, "The distinction between the natures was never abolished by their union but rather the character proper to each of the two natures was preserved as they came together in the one Person and one hypostasis."[17] Here, one must remember that the Christological formulation, understood in light the determinations of the first stage of development with regard to the notion of person, does not indicate substance, but relation. Or, as Ratzinger puts it, it is conceived not in substantialist but in existential terms.[18] In light of the theological

12. Ratzinger, "Notion of Person," 112.
13. Ratzinger, "Notion of Person," 111.
14. Ratzinger, "Notion of Person," 112.
15. Ratzinger, "Notion of Person," 112.
16. Ratzinger, "Notion of Person," 112.
17. Denzinger, *Compendium*, §302.
18. See Ratzinger, "Notion of Person," 112.

meaning of person, Christ's personhood does not refer to substance, but to a personal existence (a way of existing, of being, that is personal) that is, properly speaking, divine.[19] In the person of Jesus Christ, humanity and divinity comingle and coincide while remaining distinct, with humanity being lifted to the heights of existing in Christ's personhood such that relationship or relating to God occurs perfectly. In the Word made flesh, that staggering alliance of *logos* and *sarx*, human personhood now has the capacity of divine relationship—it is taken up into God's manner of relating. Far be it from Christ's divine personhood removing something from human personhood; theologically speaking, it makes the fullness of personhood possible.

Christological Advancements in Theological Anthropology

In the previous chapter on the revelation of God in the *Logos*, we noted Ratzinger's treatment of the first stage in the Church's understanding of the notion of personhood. This initial stage could be called the Trinitarian stage, as the Church Fathers worked out an understanding of personhood based upon the dialogical and relational nature of God—insofar as God reveals himself as Trinity. They utilize the word "person" to describe God's dialogical and relational nature: God is a perfectly relational being; God is one God in three persons. Christological developments mark a second stage in working out of the idea of person.

While the first six centuries of Christian theology focused on what the person of Christ is not,[20] a positive formulation of Christ's personhood remained elusive. Ratzinger notes that subsequent Christological developments have sought to overcome this deficiency in several ways. The first has to do with the nature of spirit. Ratzinger argues that "it is the nature of spirit to put itself in relation, the capacity to see itself and the other."[21] In other words, the spirit is relational. It is "not merely there; it goes back upon itself, as it were, it knows about itself; it constitutes a doubled existence

---

19. Ratzinger, "Notion of Person," 113. Ratzinger notes that at the beginning of the Middle Ages, Richard of St. Victor finds a way back to the original understanding of person, after it had been "substantialized" by Boethius. Richard defines the person existentially as "the incommunicably proper existence of spiritual nature." Scholastic philosophy and theology, including the likes of Aquinas, develop this category of existence. However, the whole thing is treated as a theological exception—limited to Christology and Trinitarian theology.

20. *CCC*, §464–69.

21. Ratzinger, "Notion of Person," 115.

which not only *is*, but knows about itself, *has* itself."[22] Conversely, matter is merely thrown upon itself. It simply is as it is. Spirit, however, throws itself forward, it transcends itself, and "in transcending itself it *has* itself; by being with the other it first becomes itself, comes to itself."[23] The essence of spirit, then, has to do with relatedness to the whole. The personal being, comes to itself through the spirit's relating to the other, and so, the personal being is a spiritual being. Taking this one step further, Ratzinger points out that spirit thinks not only about itself, but also about the wholly Other. This distinguishes the human spirit from any other form of consciousness—the capacity of the human spirit for relating to God. Ratzinger says:

> If the human person is all the more with itself, and is itself, the more it is able to reach beyond itself, the more it is with the other, then the person is all the more itself the more it is with the wholly other, with God.... Relativity toward the other constitutes the human person. The human person is the event or being of relativity. The more the person's relativity aims totally and directly at its final goal, at transcendence, the more the person is itself.[24]

This leads into Ratzinger's second attempt at developing a positive understanding of Christ's person. He argues that being with the other brings the person to himself. In Christ, that is, in the two natures in one person, "being with the other is realized radically." In Christ, one sees the perfect fulfillment of personal transcendence. Or, as Ratzinger puts it, "In Christ, in the man who is completely with God, human existence is not canceled, but comes to its highest possibility, which consists in transcending itself into the absolute and in the integration of its own relativity into the absoluteness of divine love."[25] A more positive formulation of Christ's personhood could run something like: Jesus Christ reveals the spiritual element of man as fundamentally relational and as that which is fully realized in relating to God, and of which he fulfills perfectly—Christ is the fullness of revelation.

---

22. Ratzinger, "Notion of Person," 115.

23. Ratzinger, "Notion of Person," 115.

24. Ratzinger, "Notion of Person," 115–16. Guerriero points out that Aquinas' definition of soul as "form of the body" seems to overemphasize the "essentialistic nature of the soul," while Ratzinger insists on the dialogical character of the soul (Guerriero, *Benedict XVI*, 241). When Ratzinger speaks of transcendence, then, it has to do with relationality and overcoming the tendency of isolating one's "I," as opposed to the awareness of and consequent acceptance of the soul as a being essentially capable of transcendence.

25. Ratzinger, "Notion of Person," 116.

A Theological Anthropology Grounded in Trinitarian Relationality as Revealed by the *Logos*

Ratzinger's theological anthropology could be called an expression of Trinitarian Christocentrism, in that Christ "brings human beings into relationship with the Blessed Trinity," and through Christ makes possible a self-understanding in light of the Trinity.[26] Grounded in the revelation of the *Logos* in Jesus Christ, Ratzinger's anthropology allows for that which has been revealed regarding the personal being of the Trinity to shape an understanding of what it means that the human person is made in God's "image and likeness." One can gain a foothold for Ratzinger's theological anthropology in a simple Trinitarian language construct: Being-from, Being-for, and Being-with.[27] He most clearly expresses the triadic principle in "Truth and Freedom," when he says, "The real God is by his very nature entirely being-for (Father), being-from (Son), and being-with (Holy Spirit). Man, for his part, is God's image precisely insofar as the 'from,' 'with,' and 'for' constitute the fundamental anthropological pattern."[28] With specific regard to the triadic formulation of the Trinity, in every case the "Being" is the same (*being*-from, *being*-for, *being*-with)—referring the to one Being, God. However, the distinction in relation (i.e., relation *to* not relation *in*) appears in the prepositions "for," "from," and "with," which clarify the nature of the relations: the Father is entirely "for" the Son, the Son is entirely "from" the Father, and the Spirit is entirely "with" the Father and Son. From here, from the Trinitarian relationality revealed by the *Logos*, Ratzinger establishes a full-blown theological anthropology. Brotherton notes the significance of this formulation within Ratzinger's corpus and for uniting anthropology with Trinitarian theology in Christ, saying:

> The triadic theme of being-for, being-from, and being-with appears in subtle ways throughout most of Ratzinger's writings,

---

26. O'Shea, "Human Embodiment," 456.

27. In *Introduction*, Ratzinger cites W. Eichrodt's *Theologie des Alten Testaments* as a source for developing the concept of Being-for. Here, he says that in the manifestation of God's name God reveals himself as a "God for Israel, as a God for man. 'I am' is as much to say 'I am here,' 'I am here for you;' God's presence for Israel is emphasized; his Being is expounded, not as Being in itself, but as a Being-for" (129).

28. Ratzinger, "Truth and Freedom," 160. On this point, Brotherton notes that "one can extrapolate from Ratzinger's reflections here and elsewhere that the notions of being-for, being-from, and being-with offer us a glimpse into the trinitarian life." At the same time, Ratzinger exercises due caution. Hence, Brotherton explains that "he does not push the parallelism so far that each corresponds directly with a divine person, although it is apparent that in the immanent Trinity these are most fittingly appropriated to Father, Son, and Spirit, respectively" (Brotherton, "Damnation and the Trinity," 140).

but the relative infrequency of these terms compared with other more common theological expressions does not undermine the almost programmatic function of this profound triad in his work. It plays the role of uniting his anthropology, which conceives the person as essentially relational and thus called to a *communio* of love, with his understanding of God's revealed being, where Christ is the bridge between the inner-divine exchange and the person as the center of the cosmos.[29]

Christ reveals God as a trinity of persons, which breaks open the "code" that lies underneath man's being created in God's "image and likeness." God is an essentially relational *Communio* of love. Man, made in God's image and likeness, stands as essentially relational and called to *communio* as well. Jesus Christ bridges the chasm between an understanding of God and an understanding of person. In Jesus Christ, new possibilities for theological anthropology arise, precisely because Christ manifests the trinitarian reality of Being. This threefold conception of God offers a roadmap for traversing Ratzinger's thought in anthropology. As such, the remaining parts of this chapter explore the principal divisions within Ratzinger's theological anthropology by moving from being-from (Son) to being-for (Father), and, finally, to being-with (Spirit).

The *Logos* Reveals Sonship: Being-from

To be Son means "being-from." Commenting on John's Gospel, Ratzinger notes, "The Son as Son, and insofar as he is Son, does not proceed in any way from himself and so is completely one with the Father; since he is nothing beside him, claims no special position of his own."[30] The Son's origin is "from above—from God himself. . . . Only God is truly his 'father,'"[31] hence, any talk about "being-from" is talk of sonship, of filial relationship that ultimately has as its prototype the eternally begotten Son and the eternally begetting Father. The first Person of the Trinity does not beget the second Person subsequently, as if the first Person were a complete person, and then proceeded to beget the second Person. Instead, eternally begotten *is* the Son—the pure *act* of the Father's self-giving is the Son.

The created human being, too, is a being-from. Genesis 2 describes this reality, as human beings are drawn from the clay of the "earth," and

---

29. Brotherton, "Damnation and the Trinity," 142–43.

30. Ratzinger, *Introduction*, 186.

31. Benedict XVI, *Jesus of Nazareth: The Infancy Narratives*, 7–8. See also Ratzinger, *Introduction*, 271–72.

carefully fashioned by the God who breathes into them the breath of life (cf. Gen 2:7–25). Elsewhere, scripture describes this relationship or relationality between divine personhood and human personhood by way of the words "image and likeness" (cf. Gen 1:26–27). These accounts make it clear that "the human being is directly related to God. . . . Each human being is known by God and loved by him. Each is willed by God, and each is God's image."[32] He goes on to point out that an image, by its very nature, points to that which is beyond itself and

> manifests something that it itself is not. Thus the image of God means, first of all, that human beings cannot be closed in on themselves. . . . To be the image of God implies relationality. . . . It means the capacity for relationship; it is the human capacity for God. . . . [They are] most profoundly human when they step out of themselves and become capable of addressing God on familiar terms. . . . The image of God also means that human persons are beings of word and of love, beings moving toward Another, oriented to giving themselves to the Other and only truly receiving themselves back in real self-giving."[33]

A person, according to the Scriptural understanding, is "not a substance that closes itself in itself, but the phenomenon of complete relativity, which is, of course, realized in its entirety only in the one who is God, but which indicates the direction of all personal being."[34] Created in God's "image and likeness," then, means to be made *in* the image of the one who *is* the image of God (cf. Col 1:15), sons and daughters (cf. Gen 1:26–27; 5:1–3) through the covenant established and re-established time and again.

Furthermore, Jesus Christ reveals the inherent relationality of the human person by revealing himself as Son and in calling his followers to follow him, to enter into relationship with him (cf. John 15:5; 17:11). Ratzinger observes:

> It is . . . part of the existence even of the disciples that man does not posit the reservation of what is merely and properly his own, does not strive to form the substance of the closed self, but enters into pure relativity toward the other and toward God. It is in this way that he truly comes to himself and into the fullness of his own, because he enters into unity with the one to whom he is related.[35]

---

32. Ratzinger, *In the Beginning*, 45.
33. Ratzinger, *In the Beginning*, 47–48.
34. Ratzinger, "Notion of Person," 109.
35. Ratzinger, "Notion of Person," 109.

Hence Ratzinger concludes, "To John, being a Christian means being like the Son, becoming a son; that is, not standing on one's own and in oneself, but living completely open in the 'from' and 'toward.'"[36] The person whose "I" has been encountered by the Son, the receiving subject of Christ's revelation, is in the state of becoming, in the Son, a being that does not belong to itself but is becoming itself by moving away from itself and into pure relatedness:

> What is so much yours as yourself, and what is so little yours as yourself? The most individual element in us—the only thing that belongs to us in the last analysis—our own "I," is at the same time the least individual element of all, for it is precisely our "I" that we have neither from ourselves nor for ourselves. The "I" is simultaneously what I have completely and what least of all belongs to me. Thus here again the concept of mere substance (=what stands in itself!) is shattered, and it is made apparent how being that truly understands itself grasps at the same time that *in* being itself does not belong to itself; that it only comes to itself by moving away from itself and finding its way back as relatedness to its true primordial state.[37]

The Son's Identification with the Father: Being-for

The *Logos* reveals Being; the Son reveals the Father (John 1:18). Later, John says, "Not that any one has seen the Father except him who is from God; he has seen the Father" (John 6:46). In Matthew's Gospel, we hear Jesus say, "All things have been delivered to me by my Father; and no one knows the Father except the Son and any one to whom the Son chooses to reveal him" (Matt 11:27; cf. Luke 10:22). Each of these passages point to the fact that God, the Father, Being itself, remains "unseen" or "unknown," save for that which has been revealed through the Son. Benedict XVI notes:

> True, no one has ever seen God as he is. And yet God is not totally invisible to us; he does not remain completely inaccessible. God loved us first . . . and this love of God has appeared in our midst. He has become visible in as much as he "has sent his only Son into the world, so that we might live through him"

---

36. Ratzinger, *Introduction*, 187. He goes on to say with stark honesty, "Insofar as the Christian is a 'Christian,' this is true of him. And certainly such utterances will make him realize to how small an extent he is a Christian."

37. Ratzinger, *Introduction*, 190. Cf. Second Vatican Council, *Gaudium et spes*, §24.

(1 John 4:9). God has made himself visible: in Jesus we are able to see the Father.[38]

God does not remain invisible. He can be known first, so to speak, in the vestiges of his revelation apparent in creation. However, in Jesus Christ, human beings can actually "see" the Father in his person. The incarnate Son reveals the Father—through the *Logos* incarnate, Being becomes visible and knowable. This, in fact, is the Gospel. God has spoken. As Benedict XVI emphatically puts it:

> God has broken his silence, God has spoken, God exists. This fact in itself is salvation: God knows us, God loves us, he has entered into history. Jesus is his Word, God with us, God showing us that he loves us, that he suffers with us until death and rises again. This is the Gospel. God has spoken, he is no longer the great unknown, but has shown himself and this is salvation.[39]

Jesus Christ, the *Logos*, the Word made flesh who is one with the Father, he has made the Father known. This is the Gospel—that God is for us and that God speaks to us most fully, most perfectly in Jesus Christ.

Ratzinger, therefore, describes the Son is the Father's ambassador. According to a late Jewish saying, the "ambassador of a man is like the man himself."[40] Jesus Christ, the new Moses,[41] who, from the Father's bosom, has seen the Father (cf. John 1:18), reveals the Father (cf. John 1:18; 10:30; 12:45; 14:9) and loses "his own identity in the role of ambassador; he is nothing but the ambassador who represents the other without interposing his own individuality."[42] This forms the basis of "mission" theology, insofar as it manifests the mission of the Trinity. Ratzinger notes that mission theology is a theology "of being in relation and of relation as a mode of unity."[43] To return to Ratzinger's triadic formula that highlights the fundamental relationality of the Trinity, the Father is being-for (i.e., pro-existence—existence given for another). The Son who is completely "from another," is the Father's ambassador for humanity and, therefore, completely "for." Joshua Brotherton points out that Ratzinger "says not only that 'Son' means being-from-another, but also that the Son defines himself on earth completely in terms of his Father; thus, he is being-for

---

38. Benedict XVI, *DCE*, §17.
39. Benedict XVI, "Meditation 2012."
40. Ratzinger, *Introduction*, 188. See also Ratzinger, "Notion of Person," 110.
41. See Benedict XVI, *Jesus I*, 4–6.
42. Ratzinger, *Introduction*, 188.
43. Ratzinger, *Introduction*, 188.

by mission because he is in himself being-from the Father."[44] The being-from (Son) is the being-for (Father). Jesus is nothing but the ambassador in John's Gospel, as he is completely one with the one who sent him, one whose being is interpreted as being "from" and being "for"—"being is conceived as absolute openness without reservation."[45]

In Jesus, personal identity and mission coincide, person and work exist as one. He becomes, or, better said, he *is* the mission of the Father. To be *from* means to exist as a person-in-relation wholly from another's act-of-giving and to receive that gift as one's own identity. In this case, the Father offers himself, is himself entirely *for* such that the Son (being-from) receives the "for-ness" as his own. Jesus' identity as Son does not proceed in any way from himself, thus his mission stands open "toward" the Father and, hence, "for" others. Jesus Christ, as the Son, is entirely from the Father, and as such, He is for the Father, and "for the many."[46] In other words, "the *being* of Christ ('Incarnation' theology!) is *actualitas*, stepping beyond oneself, the exodus of going out from self; it is, not a being that rests in itself, but the act of being sent, of being son, of serving. Conversely, this 'doing' is not just

---

44. Brotherton, "Damnation and the Trinity," 140.

45. Ratzinger, *Introduction*, 188.

46. Benedict XVI, *Jesus II*, 134–38. The concept of "for the many" introduces the "opposite angle" of pro-existence—the manner in which the Son assumes human flesh as the new Adam and offers himself on behalf of humanity to the Father. Viewed from this angle, pro-existence (a personal-ontological reality) appears in its correlative form known as vicarious representation (a personal-soteriological reality). Christopher Ruddy explains that "*Stellvertretung* [vicarious representation] literally means a representation standing for or in the place of something or someone else; but 'representation,' while it conveys the likeness of Jesus to us—i.e., in being fully human himself, he truly represents humanity—does not sufficiently convey the uniqueness of his identity and mission. And 'substitution,' while it conveys Jesus' uniqueness—i.e., he endures suffering and death in our place—fails to convey sufficiently that Jesus seeks also to involve us in his own paschal mystery. 'Vicarious representation' conveys more adequately both dimensions: uniqueness-substitution and participation-representation (Ruddy, "For the Many," 564n1). The fundamental law of salvation history "is one of vicarious representation, which manifests itself in several dimensions: divine election; the relationship between the 'few' and the 'many'; and the exchange between Christ and humanity, as well as between the Church and the world" (Ruddy, "For the Many," 567; see also Ratzinger, *Christian Brotherhood*, 75–79; Ratzinger, "Vicarious Representation," 210–16). Being chosen on behalf of others [election] is the fundamental pattern or law of salvation history, as the healing of the whole takes place according to the "dialectical antitheses of the few and the many" (Ratzinger, *Christian Brotherhood*, 75). Vicarious representation reaches its fulfillment in Jesus Christ, the one who allows himself to be completely rejected by man, and as such, is accepted by God in his very rejection as the vicarious representative of all those who have sinned and who have, therefore, rejected relationality (See Ratzinger, "Vicarious Representation," 212; Ratzinger, *Christian Brotherhood*, 78).

'doing' but 'being;' it reaches down into the depths of being and coincides with it. This being is exodus, transformation."[47]

The total relativity of the Son's existence as being-from and being-for is captured in the titles "the Word," "the one sent," and "I am." All indicate the "merging of the person in his work and in the total coincidence of the doing with the person himself, who keeps back nothing for himself but gives himself completely in his work. . . . The 'servant' aspect is no longer explained as a deed, behind which the person of Jesus remains aloof; it is made to embrace the whole existence of Jesus, so that his *being* itself is service. And precisely because this being, as a totality, is nothing but service, it is sonship."[48] The Son's perfect obedience is a consecration, a giving over of his human will to the divine will in such a way that it "expresses both total unity with the Father and total existence for the world. Jesus belongs entirely to God, and that is what makes him entirely 'for all.'"[49]

Jesus' mission as the ambassador of the Father reaches a high point in terms of realism in the Eucharist. When Jesus says, "this is my body" (see Matt 26:26; Mark 14:22; Luke 22:19; 1 Cor 11:22), he does not mean his body in contradistinction to his soul. Ratzinger points out that "Body, in the language of the Bible, denotes . . . the whole person, in whom body and spirit are indivisibly one."[50] To say, "this is my body," then, is to say, "this is me," or "this is my person" existing in bodily form. Now, as Ratzinger notes, the body carries within itself a certain contradiction. "On the one hand, the body is the boundary that separates us from others," he says.[51] Spatially, the body marks out a physical space for this person, such that where this person is, nobody else can be. However, the body also separates personally by establishing this individual as such. The body acts as something of a boundary that hides interiority, wherein corporeal existence prevents one from seeing the inner self of the other and even prevents us from looking into our own depths. Thus, "the body is a boundary that makes us opaque, impermeable for each other, which sets us beside each other and prevents our being able to see or to touch each other's intimate selves."[52] In this way, one could say the body divides; it is at the service of individuality. On the other hand, "the body is also a bridge. . . . [We] meet each other through the body; through it we communicate in the common material of creation; through it we can see

---

47. Ratzinger, *Introduction*, 230.
48. Ratzinger, *Introduction*, 226; see also pp. 188, 203; Benedict XVI, *Jesus I*, 319.
49. Benedict XVI, *Jesus II*, 86–87.
50. Ratzinger, "The Eucharist," 287.
51. Ratzinger, "The Eucharist," 288.
52. Ratzinger, "The Eucharist," 288.

ourselves, feel ourselves, come close to one another."[53] In this sense, the body expresses the person and makes personal existence possible, real. Therefore, Ratzinger concludes the body "is both boundary and means of communion in one."[54] To be sure, one can live bodily existence selfishly, such that he or she throws up boundaries, a walled off existence where the body is little more than a means of division and a mechanism for hiding one's inner self. Yet bodily existence can also be lived "as opening oneself up, as the developing freedom of a person who shares himself" by transcending bodily limits with a movement of the heart, even expressed bodily, that overcomes any boundaries thrown up by the body.[55] This is basically what resurrection means, "that the body ceases to be a limit and that its capacity for communion remains.... To have risen from the dead means to be communicable; it signifies being the one who is open, who gives himself."[56]

To return to the Eucharistic text, what is this "body?" Who is this "person" who says, "this is my body?" Ratzinger says, "What the nature of this person is, however, we learn from what is said next: 'which is given up for you.' That means: This person is: existing-for-others. It is in its most intimate being a sharing with others."[57] This person is the Son, the perfectly existing being-from the Father's "for," such that he identifies with the "for" as his own. The Son is, in his very person, existing-for-others. Such a statement reaches its full import on the Cross—the fulfillment of what Christ initiated at the Last Supper. On the Cross, the incarnate Son willingly offers himself manifesting the depths of the Father's "for." Jesus Christ reveals the Father's "for" and makes the profundity of this "for" accessible to men and women. As Benedict XVI puts it, "The Father's act of 'giving' is fully accomplished in the love of the Son 'to the end' (John 13:1), that is, to the Cross."[58] The Eucharist makes present, the Eucharist is the Son—crucified and risen—and receiving the Eucharist means becoming a son, becoming like the Son, and so entering into the Son's mission of being-for.

---

53. Ratzinger, "The Eucharist," 288.
54. Ratzinger, "The Eucharist," 288.
55. Ratzinger, "The Eucharist," 289.
56. Ratzinger, "The Eucharist," 289.
57. Ratzinger, "The Eucharist," 288.
58. Benedict XVI, *Jesus I*, 344.

The Holy Spirit as *Communio*: Being-with

Finally, Ratzinger's Trinitarian anthropology describes the Holy Spirit as being-with.[59] By way of introduction, Ratzinger notes that "pneumatology" and "spirituality" are connected in that the Holy Spirit (the "object" of pneumatology) is "recognizable in the way in which he forms human life [i.e., spirituality]. . . . Speaking about the Holy Spirit includes looking at him in man, to whom he has given himself."[60] Ratzinger continues by noting the difficulty of speaking about the Spirit who seems to be even more mysterious than Jesus Christ. Discussion about the Spirit often vacillates between speculation and fantasy. Therefore, in order to speak "meaningfully, reliably, and defensibly about the Holy Spirit," Ratzinger holds that three conditions must be upheld: (1) talk of the Holy Spirit cannot be pure theory but must be in reference to experienced reality that has been "interpreted and communicated in thought"; (2) experiences of the Spirit must be tested—discerned; (3) the experiences must be tested "in front of and standing in the context of the whole . . . one submits the experience of 'spirit' to the entirety of the Church."[61] In seeking a reliable theological foothold, Ratzinger settles upon Augustine's thought that has endured for 1500 years and from which he draws the foundation of his pneumatology and its anthropological implications. Augustine treats the Holy Spirit in a threefold manner: as *communio*, as love, and as gift.

Augustine begins his treatment on the Holy Spirit by exploring the name "Holy Spirit" itself. While "Father" and "Son" indicate characteristic uniqueness, the words "Holy" and "Spirit" seem to serve as descriptors for God in a generic fashion, as "God is spirit" (cf. John 4:24) and "being spirit and being holy is the essential description of God."[62] Augustine sees the answer to the question about the identity of the Holy Spirit in the tension created by this dilemma, for "when he is named by that which is the divinity of God, by what the Father and Son have in common, then his essence is just that, the *communio* of Father and Son. The particularity of the Holy Spirit is evidently that the Holy Spirit is what the Father and Son have in common.

---

59. It is worth noting that Ratzinger writes far less on the Holy Spirit than he does on Jesus Christ. Joseph Murphy makes this point and provides a helpful bibliography of Ratzinger's primary treatises on the Holy Spirit in *Christ Our Joy*, 139.

60. Ratzinger, "The Holy Spirit as *Communio*," 168. See also Ratzinger, *The God of Jesus Christ*, 120.

61. Ratzinger, "The Holy Spirit as *Communio*," 168–69.

62. Ratzinger, "The Holy Spirit as *Communio*," 170.

His particularity is being unity."[63] The Holy Spirit is that relation in whom and through whom Father and Son are eternally united. Ratzinger explains:

> The mediation of Father and Son comes to full unity not when it is seen in a universal ontic *consubstantialitas* but as *communio*. In other words, it is not derived from a universally metaphysical substance but from the person. According to the nature of God, it is intrinsically personal. The dyad returns to unity in the Trinity without breaking up the dialogue. Dialogue is actually confirmed in just this way. A mediation that backs into unity that was not another Person would break up the dialogue as dialogue. The Spirit is Person as unity, unity as Person.[64]

The *communio* of the Father and Son, their personal union, is the Holy Spirit. Ratzinger notes that the Holy Spirit "is that which is common, the unity of the Father and the Son, the unity in Person. The Father and the Son are one with each other by going out beyond themselves; it is in the third Person, in the fruitfulness of their act of giving, that they are One."[65] Brotherton summarizes this point, saying, "The Spirit is the unity of the being-for and being-from of God; He shares in the being-from of the Son and yet communes equally with the Father's being-for—he joins the being-from of the Son to the being-for of the Father in the being-with that is the love of God."[66]

With due caution given the limitation of analogy, one can see something of this mystery in the reality of family life. Here, in the sexual act between husband and wife, a mutually reciprocal exchange of giving and receiving personal love, the act itself has the capacity to generate a person (the mutual act of self-giving is not person, but has the potential to create new life). That person, the child, is, in a certain sense, an icon of relativity and of personal mediation. The child is the image of the act of personal love *in person*. The child is the living image of the "yes" of the union between husband and wife, and husband and wife are in union, and come back into union, in a personal, relational way (i.e., as father and mother) only in and through the reality of the child. The person of the child indicates reciprocity between his parents and is the relation through whom husband and wife relate to one another now as parents (as father and mother). Similarly, in returning to Ratzinger's treatment of Augustine's pneumatology, Ratzinger says, "Spirit is the unity that God gives himself. In this unity, he himself gives himself. In this unity, the Father and the Son give themselves back to

---

63. Ratzinger, "The Holy Spirit as *Communio*," 170.
64. Ratzinger, "The Holy Spirit as *Communio*," 170–71.
65. Ratzinger, *The God of Jesus Christ*, 119.
66. Brotherton, "Damnation and the Trinity," 142.

one another."⁶⁷ The Holy Spirit is the reciprocity of giving and receiving, that eternal exchange, between Father and Son. As *communio*, "The Holy Spirit does not represent a third reality somewhere next to or between the other two. He leads us to the unity of God."⁶⁸

In deepening his understanding of the Holy Spirit, Augustine argues that the Holy Spirit can also be called by the name "love" (*caritas*). While it is true that "God is love" (1 John 4:16), a statement first referring to the undivided Trinity, "love" also refers specifically to the Holy Spirit. Ratzinger traces Augustine's treatment of several verses from 1 John 4, namely:⁶⁹

- Verse 12: If we love one another, God abides in us . . .
- Verse 16b: God is love, and he who abides in love, God abides in him.
- Verse 13: We recognize that we abide in him and he in us because he has given us of his spirit.

Ratzinger explains:

> In the first instance, love gives abiding; in the second instance, love gives the Holy Spirit. In the above verses, *pneuma* takes the place of love and vice versa. Or literally: "The Holy Spirit, of whom he has given us, causes us to abide in God, and God in us. But love does this. He is, therefore, the God who is love." To clarify, Augustine adds that Rom 5:5 states that the love of God is poured out through the Holy Spirit who is given to us. It appears to me that these observations are correct in principle. The gift of God is the Holy Spirit. The gift of God is love. God communicates himself in the Holy Spirit as love.⁷⁰

Ratzinger comments on Augustine's treatment of 1 John 4:7, which states "Love is of God." Verse 16b, as noted above, says, "God is love." Juxtaposing the verses, then, Augustine notes that on one hand God is love, and on the other, love is from God. Putting these statements together, "love is 'God from God,'" which, for Ratzinger, "explains once again that this 'God from God'—God as the power to emerge and become near . . .—is the Holy Spirit and that we may receive what is said about *agape* as an equivalent elucidation of what the Holy Spirit is."⁷¹ If this is the case, then, the profound

---

67. Ratzinger, "The Holy Spirit as *Communio*," 171.
68. Ratzinger, *Images of Hope*, 65.
69. Scripture quotes are directly from Ratzinger, "The Holy Spirit as *Communio*," 172.
70. Ratzinger, "The Holy Spirit as *Communio*," 172–73.
71. Ratzinger, "The Holy Spirit as *Communio*," 174. On a practical note and as an

interrelationship between being-from, being-for, and being-with becomes apparent in the God who is Love in personal *communio*.

Ratzinger also notes that Augustine treats the Holy Spirit as "gift." Here, Augustine refers primarily to Jesus' interaction with the Samaritan woman (John 4:7–14), wherein Jesus repeatedly utilizes the words "gift," "give," and "given." Augustine compares this text with that in John 7:37, which reads "If anyone thirst, let him come to me and drink." As Scripture states, "out of his heart shall flow rivers of living water" (v. 38) and in v. 39, "This he said about the Spirit, which those who believed in him were to receive." To these verses, Augustine adds 1 Cor 12:13, which says, "all were made to drink of one Spirit." Ratzinger now points out the relationship between Christology and pneumatology, saying, "The crucified Lord is the generative source of life for the world. The well of the Spirit is the crucified Christ. From him each Christian becomes the well of the Spirit."[72] Christ is the well and the Spirit is the living water. This means the Christian, he who no longer lives in his own "I" but whose "I" has been and is becoming conformed to Christ's, is to be a well of the Spirit from whom men have access to the Holy Spirit who alone satisfies their infinite thirst.[73] This point must be developed further.

Ratzinger's treatment on the Ascension, which he calls "the gesture of blessing,"[74] provides the key insight. Christian iconography of the Ascension frequently portrays Jesus' raised hands in the gesture of blessing (cf. Luke 24:50). Ratzinger says, "He blesses; he has become blessing for us."[75] This explains the seemingly odd joy of the apostles, for they are ones blessed and not abandoned, ones who "knew that they were forever blessed and stood under blessing hands wherever they went."[76] This blessing can be a new experience of nearness, despite the Ascension (that "going away"), because Jesus *gives* the Counselor (cf. Luke 11:13; John 14:16). The blessing offered by Christ in the mystery of the Ascension is the Holy Spirit, who is the *gift* of Father and

---

aside, if love is the basic characteristic of the Holy Spirit, then love is the primary criterion by which one can proceed in discerning spirits. What is more, because love is abiding (i.e., constancy), love proves itself not in vacillation, disorder, or erratic behavior (i.e., not in any one moment alone), but over time. Ratzinger sees here a connection between love and the endurance of truth, saying, "Love in the full sense can exist only where constancy exists, where abiding exists. Because love has to do with abiding, it cannot take place anywhere except where there is eternity" (Ratzinger, "The Holy Spirit as *Communio*," 173).

72. Ratzinger, "The Holy Spirit as *Communio*," 175.
73. cf. Ratzinger, "The Holy Spirit as *Communio*," 175.
74. Ratzinger, *Images of Hope*, 56. See also Benedict XVI, *Jesus II*, 280–81.
75. Ratzinger, *Images of Hope*, 56.
76. Ratzinger, *Images of Hope*, 56.

Son.[77] In this way, the gift of the Holy Spirit, the blessing of God in giving the Holy Spirit, brings joy. Joy, as noted by Ratzinger, is the harmony one finds within himself when he accepts himself. However, no person can completely accept himself unless he has first been accepted by another—because another has said "yes" to him.[78] The joy of the apostles at the Ascension must stand as the fruit or "byproduct" of a "yes" given to them.[79] This "yes" that is the *gift* of blessing is nothing other than the *gift* of God himself—"what really matters is that God as gift is actually God; in other words, that the Holy Spirit is divine."[80] God's gift reigns where joy exists, and, conversely, "where joylessness rules and humor dies, we may be certain that the Holy Spirit, the Spirit of Jesus Christ, is not present."[81]

Elsewhere, Ratzinger points out that only the Spirit makes Jesus known by both bestowing remembrance and by listening. Ratzinger says, the Spirit allows for "a remembrance in which the particular is joined to the whole, which in turn endows the particular, which hitherto had not been understood, with its genuine meaning."[82] A person can only "be understood through himself," and it is the Holy Spirit, as the *communio* of Father and Son, who makes possible this kind of understanding of Jesus' identity.[83] This points to the second observation. Listening characterizes the Spirit, for the Spirit "does not speak in his own name, he listens and teaches how to listen." The Holy Spirit "does not add anything but rather acts as a guide into the heart of the Word, which becomes light in the act of listening."[84] Far be it from providing some sort of spirit-led ongoing revelation, the Holy Spirit simply leads one to listen to the Word. The Spirit's method is not violent amputation, but that which allows "what stands before me as an other [i.e., Jesus] to express itself and to enter into me."[85] Therefore, and now we return to the central concept of being-with, that "the Spirit effects a space of listening and remembering, a 'we,' which in the Johannine writings defines the Church as the locus of knowledge. Understanding can take place only within this 'we' constituted by participation."[86] The Church is that concrete partici-

77. Ratzinger, "The Holy Spirit as *Communio*," 181.
78. Ratzinger, *Principles*, 79–80.
79. Cf. Pieper, *An Anthology*, 32–39.
80. Ratzinger, "The Holy Spirit as *Communio*," 176.
81. Ratzinger, *The God of Jesus Christ*, 113. See also Ratzinger, *Principles*, 84.
82. Ratzinger, *Nature and Mission*, 55.
83. Ratzinger, *Nature and Mission*, 54–55.
84. Ratzinger, *Nature and Mission*, 55.
85. Ratzinger, *Nature and Mission*, 55.
86. Ratzinger, *Nature and Mission*, 55.

pation in being-with, that life in the Spirit, that living reality expressed in the unity of the statements of the Apostles' Creed "I believe in the Holy Spirit, the Holy Catholic Church, the communion of saints."[87] Here, faith in and through the "Spirit," and faith in and through the Church "interfere" with one another, Ratzinger says. Thus, "teaching about the Church must take its departure from teaching about the Holy Spirit and his gifts."[88] The Spirit is the *communio* of Father and Son, and within the concrete experience of *communio* on earth, the Church, one can listen to and remember the Word.

Conclusion

Who God is (as personal, as relational, as *Communio*) and how God loves (pro-existence) in Christ shines light on the gift and task of the human person, that "image and likeness" of God. For Ratzinger, the revelation of the *Logos* produces a theological anthropology grounded in the concepts of being-from, being-for, and being-with. Each is a particular manifestation of a different aspect of loving relationality. In sum, the whole of Ratzinger's theological anthropology, indeed, the whole of Christianity, can perhaps be expressed in the simple statement: love is enough.

In *What It Means to Be a Christian*, Ratzinger recalls a Jewish story popular in Jesus' time. Here, a pagan approached a rabbi with a challenge: explain the Jewish beliefs in the amount of time he could stand on one leg, and he would convert to Judaism. The rabbi dismissed him saying it was impossible. Unphased, he went down the road and found the next rabbi. This time, the rabbi took up the challenge summarizing the whole law by saying "Whatever is offensive to you yourself, do not do that to your neighbor." A similar story appears in the Gospel of Matthew, where a rabbi asks Jesus what he must do to achieve salvation, and to which Jesus responds with the greatest commandment (see Matt 22:35–40).[89] Parabolically, Jesus expresses the

---

87. In *Introduction*, Ratzinger notes that the original Greek text of this statement omitted the article. The sentence simply reads "I believe in Holy Spirit." Ratzinger notes that the original meaning, then, would have been understood in terms of salvation history and not in terms of the Trinity—though this does not exclude the Trinitarian interpretation. However, it does highlight that the Creed "refers in the first place, not to the Holy Spirit as the third person of the Godhead, but to the Holy Spirit as God's gift to history in the community of those who believe in Christ" (331).

88. Ratzinger, *Introduction*, 333. Here, Ratzinger does point out that an overemphasis on the Incarnation binds the Church's self-understanding as something "all too earthbound and finally explained entirely on the basis of power categories of worldly thinking," whereas a charismatic understanding preserves the Church from such devolvement.

89. Ratzinger, *What It Means*, 65–67.

same point "in full seriousness, without reservations" in the depiction of the Last Judgement in Matthew 25. Here, "the Judge does not ask what kind of theory a person has held about God and the world. He is not asking about a confession of dogma, solely about love. That is enough, and it saves a man. Whoever loves is a Christian."[90] Regarding this teaching, he adds:

> We may and should accept it in all its sublimity and simplicity, quite unconditionally—just as the Lord posited it. That does not mean, of course, that we should overlook the fact that these words represent a not inconsiderable proposition and make no small demand on someone. For love, as it is here portrayed as the content of being a Christian, demands that we try to live as God lives. He loves us, not because we are especially good, particularly virtuous, or of any great merit, not because we are useful or even necessary to him; he loves us not, because *we* are good, but because *he* is good. He loves us, although we have nothing to offer him; he loves us, even in the ragged raiment of the prodigal son, who is no longer wearing anything lovable. To love in the Christian sense means trying to follow in this path: not just loving someone we like, who pleases us, who suits us, and certainly not just someone who has something to offer us or from whom we are hoping to gain some advantage.[91]

To love in the Christian sense, that is, to love as an "image and likeness" of God in light of God's revelation in the *Logos* incarnate, means to be perfect as the Father is perfect (cf. Matt 5:48) in being-for others. Christology thus reveals man to himself and makes his supreme calling clear, which is little more than this: love perfectly.[92]

---

90. Ratzinger, *What It Means*, 68–69.
91. Ratzinger, *What It Means*, 69–70.
92. Cf. Second Vatican Council, *Gaudium et spes*, §22, 24.

CHAPTER NINE

Freedom—Sin—Death

The Christian is called to love as Christ loves (cf. John 15:12), to live according to the pattern of perfect relationality. But, what exactly does it mean to love? What is it? In *Deus caritas est*, Benedict XVI points out that "the term 'love' has become one of the most frequently used and misused of words, a word to which we attach quite different meanings." He notes the "vast semantic range of the word" and references common uses, like "love of country, love of one's profession, love between friends, love of work, love between parents and children, love of neighbor and love of God."[1] In *The Yes of Jesus Christ*, Ratzinger says the English word "love" "is today exposed to the danger of being downgraded to banality in a way that slowly seems to make its use impossible."[2] In light of such lexical elasticity, Benedict XVI asks, "are all these forms of love basically one, so that love, in its many and varied manifestations, is ultimately a single reality, or are we merely using the same word to designate totally different realities?"[3] Josef Pieper asks the same question in light of the same manifold problem, when he asks "What is the nature of love?"[4] Is there a common thread woven between all the various uses of the word "love"?

Pieper, to whom Ratzinger stands indebted, here, argues that the fact that one word exists amid such a multiplicity of uses seems to indicate that something common must stand underneath the "countless forms of love." There must be one reality, even if it has varying aspects. He goes on to conclude, however tentatively:

> In every conceivable case love signifies much the same as approval. This is first of all to be taken in the literal sense of the

---

1. Benedict XVI, *DCE*, §2.
2. Ratzinger, *Yes of Jesus*, 89.
3. Benedict XVI, *DCE*, §2.
4. Pieper, *About Love*, 18.

> word's root: loving someone or something means finding him or it *probus*, the Latin word for "good." It is a way of turning to him or it and saying, "It's good that you exist; it's good that you are in this world!" . . . I do not mean that the act of love necessarily involves any such bare statement, although that is quite possible. The approval I am speaking of is rather an expression of the *will*. . . . Loving is therefore a mode of willing.[5]

To love, in every case, has something to do with willing the approval of the goodness of someone or something. Ratzinger takes Pieper's conclusion as his own and summarizes it, saying "regardless of the multiplicity of its different aspects and levels we can say meanwhile that it denotes an act of fundamental assent to another; a 'yes' to the person towards whom the love is directed: 'it is good that you exist.' . . . The lover discovers the goodness of being in this person, is happy because of his or her existence, says 'yes' to his existence and confirms it."[6] In other words, this love-as-approval "precedes" the concepts of *eros*, *agape*, *philia*, *storge*, and so forth. On this point, Ratzinger observes:

> Even before any thought of self, before any desire or wish, there stands the simple business of being happy at the existence of the beloved, the "yes" to this "you." It is only in a second moment (not of time but of fact) that the lover discovers that in this way, because *your* existence is good, my own existence too has become better, more precious, happier. By saying "yes" to another, to "you," I receive myself made new and can now in a new way say "yes" to myself thanks to you.[7]

Love is, fundamentally, one reality, with different dimensions or manifestations. *Eros* and *agape*, for example, are not worlds apart. *Agape* did not destroy *eros* as Nietzsche so claimed.[8] *Eros* can only desire the good of the other for itself if the good exists and is recognized as such, and *agape* can only offer itself for the good of the other if that good exists and is recognized as such. *Eros* might will that the good of the other become my own good, and *agape* might will that my good might be sacrificed for the good of the other, only because the other is truly good in either case.[9] At the bot-

---

5. Pieper, *About Love*, 19.

6. Ratzinger, *Yes of Jesus*, 89. Ratzinger's explication of Pieper's conclusion parallels the thought of Conrad Baars who was writing in the field of psychology. See Baars, *Born Only Once*, 12–15. See also Ratzinger, *Principles*, 80.

7. Ratzinger, *Yes of Jesus*, 89–90.

8. Benedict XVI, DCE, §3.

9. On this point, Benedict XVI claims that "*eros* and *agape*—ascending love and

tom of it, love refers to the acknowledgement, approval, and affirmation of this fundamental goodness.

Therefore, despite the radical simplicity of that claim with which the last chapter ended: "whoever loves is a Christian," the imperative to love (perfectly) as God loves (perfectly) now seems to carry with it a seemingly impossible burden. Loving perfectly as *Logos* loves perfectly means perfectly affirming the existence of every "other," in every time and in every place. A Christological starting point for anthropology reveals the heights of the human call, but also the reality of the depths to which humanity can fall. For, as Ratzinger says:

> If we look at ourselves honestly and seriously, then there is not just something liberating in this marvelously simple message [that being a Christian means having love]. There is also something most disturbing. For who among us can say he has never passed by anyone who was hungry or thirsty or who needed us in any way? Who among us can say that he truly, in all simplicity, carries out the service of being kind to others? Who among us would not have to admit that even in the acts of kindness he practices toward others, there is still an element of selfishness, something of self-satisfaction and of looking back at ourselves?[10]

The call, then, throughout Judaism and into Christianity, remains abundantly clear: love God and love others as self. In other words, love persons perfectly. The breakdown happens its execution. This relational collapse, this falling-short-of-the-goal goes by the name of sin. Sin is nothing other than the rejection (in whole or in part) of relationality and the denial of the call—a rejection of the gift and the task. It manifests the stupendous capacity of human freedom, which carries with it the possibility of contradicting the *Logos*. In what follows, I will briefly explore Ratzinger's treatment of freedom, followed by his fundamental understanding of sin, before moving into the area of faith.

---

descending love—can never be completely separated. The more the two, in their different aspects, find a proper unity in the one reality of love, the more the true nature of love in general is realized" (*DCE*, §7). To this he adds, "Fundamentally, 'love' is a single reality, but with different dimensions; at different times, one or other dimension may emerge more clearly" (*DCE*, §8).

10. Ratzinger, *What It Means*, 73–74. See also Ratzinger, *Introduction*, 288.

Christianity as a Religion of Radical Freedom

Lyotard, as noted in chapter 3, accused Christianity of functioning as a metanarrative of love, wherein the *Logos*' "narrative" is a narrative of love, and his creation is the space in which the narrative plays out. However, if it is a narrative of love, then it is also a narrative of freedom. God's narrative of love in creation is a narrative of freedom, of dialogue—the story has been written *and* is being written. Word is the first word, which makes language possible, which makes a free response to Word possible. The narrative of reality is a dialogical one that fully allows room for human beings to "break the rule" initiated and proposed by Word, and to establish their own discourse genre. Man is free to respond to God, to be in dialogue, in relationship with God, and in so doing, man steps into himself, is himself. In this act of response, this act of giving himself, man is most fully "person."

Ratzinger describes this dynamic of freedom according to concepts employed in antiquity as a way of describing human life: *exitus* and *reditus*. Plotinus conceived of *exitus*, not as a going out, but a falling down—a falling away from divinity. This is clear in many ancient creation myths, where the human being is some sort of fallen being, a being lower than the gods. *Reditus*, on the other hand, marks the reversal, the journey back, a redemption from finitude—a climb that marks the burden of our lives. Christianity takes up this schema but understands them in a thoroughly positive manner:

> *Exitus* is not a fall from the infinite, the rupture of being and thus the cause of all the sorrow in the world. No, *exitus* is first and foremost something thoroughly positive. It is the Creator's free act of creation. It is his positive will that the created order should exist as something good in relation to himself, from which a response of freedom and love can be given back to him. ... The creature, existing in its own right, comes home to itself, and this act is an answer in freedom to God's love. It accepts creation from God as his offer of love, and thus ensues a dialogue of love, that wholly new kind of unity that love alone can create. ... This *reditus* is a "return", but it does not abolish creation; rather, it bestows its full and final perfection. This is how Christians understand God being "all in all."[11]

Christianity understands the reality of the person as thoroughly positive and free. It is marked by the free act of the creator—an act that gives freedom and respects freedom. Being is the author of reality and Being "speaks" reality through *Logos*/Word. God freely creates man and endows man with freedom

---

11. Ratzinger, *The Spirit of the Liturgy*, 32–33.

flowing from a fundamental relationship (*exitus*) and a freedom existing for *communio* (*reditus*). With this observation, one returns to the anthropological pattern explicated above (being-from, being-for, being-with). Man is being-in-relation insofar as man is made in the "image and likeness" of God. Because he is a being-in-relation to Love, he is a being-in-freedom. Man is free to choose if he will embrace the truth of his being-in-relation with God and his fundamental anthropological pattern, or not.

The Christian conception of reality and freedom has significant implications, for if creation is the completely serious "playground" of freedom,[12] then creation is marked by the very real possibility of choosing against God. In the dialogical reality necessary for a narrative of *love*, humanity is free to accept and to enter into relationship with Being, or to reject the offer and isolate. Man is free to denounce Word, to reject this original relationship (the positive *exitus*), and to renounce his *reditus*. He was designed by Relationship and made for relationship, by Love and for love, and the extent to which he freely accepts this reality, lives in it, and is transformed by it is the extent to which he is free.[13] Yet the converse also stands as an option, the human being can reject relationship under the guise of freedom and, as a self-proclaimed master of one's own universe, exercise a license to pursue whatever he wants, whenever he wants. The human being is, by his personal nature, therefore, confronted by an ethical decision from the outset, and is free to sin, i.e., free to cut off communion and to choose against his or her created nature. He is free to reject dialogue and mutter his own monologue. When it comes to man's freely choosing to sin, Ratzinger says:

> Everything is bound up with freedom, and the creature has the freedom to turn the positive *exitus* of its creation around, as it were, to rupture it in the Fall: this is the refusal to be dependent, saying No to the *reditus*. Love is seen as dependence and is rejected. In its place come autonomy and autarchy: existing from oneself and in oneself, being a god of one's own making. The arch from *exitus* to *reditus* is broken. The return is no longer desired, and ascent by one's powers proves to be impossible.[14]

In Adam's fall, the *exitus* that had existed at the origin as a positive and free act of creation-for-relationship is no longer seen as positive or desirable. Adam rejects the original relationship, refusing, as it were, his creaturely dependence on God, and cutting off the *reditus*. Ratzinger thus draws out

---

12. See Ratzinger, *Eschatology*, 216. See also See also Kaethler, "Freedom in Relationship," 397–411.

13. Cf. *CCC*, §1733.

14. Ratzinger, *The Spirit of the Liturgy*, 33.

sin as the antithesis of relationality, of communion, saying "Whenever there is an attempt to free ourselves from this pattern, we are not on our way to divinity [as, in our infinite pursuit of freedom might lead us to believe], but to dehumanization, to the destruction of being itself through the destruction of the truth."[15]

The present postmodern, post-Christian culture regards individual freedom to the utmost. Ratzinger notes the standard definition of freedom today would be "the right and the opportunity to do just what we wish and not to have to do anything which we do not wish to do . . . Freedom would mean that our own will is the sole norm of our action and that the will not only can desire anything but also has the chance to carry out its desire."[16] To this, Ratzinger adds, "The grand promises [metanarratives!] made at the inception of modernity have not been kept, yet their fascination is unabated . . . man's essence is undermined. It is an open question. I must decide myself what I understand by 'humanity,' what I want to do with it, and how I want to fashion it. Man has no nature, but is sheer freedom."[17] Rahner's fundamental theology tended toward this type of overreach of freedom, and those who follow him seem to bring this to a climax in postmodern theology that exalts the *testator*, the "self" as the ultimate arbiter of his existence and of tradition.[18] At the bottom of it, the radical cry to be like god—"a god who depends on nothing and no one, and whose own freedom is not restricted by that of another"[19]—requires an autarchic freedom. This is the new metanarrative. This radically individualistic approach toward freedom levels the original notion of personhood, attacking its core tenants, because it contradicts fundamental, created relationality.

15. Ratzinger, "Truth and Freedom," 159–60. See also Benedict XVI, *Verbum Domini*, §6.

16. Ratzinger, "Truth and Freedom," 148. Here, he also quotes Marx's description of this type of freedom: "to do one thing today and another tomorrow; to hunt in the morning, fish in the afternoon, breed cattle in the evening and criticize after dinner, just as I please."

17. Ratzinger, "Truth and Freedom," 156–57. See also Ratzinger, *Introduction*, 248.

18. The irony of the *testator* thesis lies, of course, in the fact that one's own capacity to "test" tradition and to choose what one accepts for himself depends on the tools given him by tradition itself. Thus, he ends up sawing off the branch upon which he sits. Ratzinger makes a similar comment, saying, "being a man means being a fellowman in every aspect, not just in the present moment, but in such a way that every man also contains the past and future of mankind. . . . One needs only to note that our mental life depends entirely on the medium of language and to add, then, that language was not invented today. It comes from a long way off; the whole of history has contributed to it and through it enters into us as the unavoidable premise of our present, indeed, as a constant part of it" (*Introduction*, 247).

19. Ratzinger, "Truth and Freedom," 159.

What is for the postmodern the ideal, is for the Church the beginnings of a contradiction of relationality that goes by the name of sin.

The Wages of Sin

Ratzinger treats the whole problem of sin in light of relationality and the free exercise of breaking down of or breaking free from relationship. He explains:

> Sin means the damaging or the destruction of relationality. Sin is a rejection of relationality because it wants to make the human being a god. Sin is loss of relationship, disturbance of relationship, and therefore it is not restricted to the individual. When I destroy a relationship, then this event—sin—touches the other person involved in the relationship. Consequently sin is always an offense that touches others, that alters the world and damages it.[20]

The human person is a relational event, a social being. The whole of human life is personal, interpersonal, and relational. Personal sin, therefore, exists as both an individual and social reality. This or that individual sins, but sin never only impacts merely this or that individual, but others as well. Sin operates on the level of the person and damages personhood as such (i.e., it damages the person-as-relation).

The very possibility of sin reveals the reality of human freedom. Personal sin is, therefore, an exercise in freedom of rejecting Love. It is the choice for autonomy—a counterfeit freedom that aims at a self-sufficient life without reference to God or any other. In this exercise of freedom, the person "refuses to recognize his own limitations and tries to be completely self-sufficient."[21] Elsewhere Ratzinger says, "at the very heart of sin lies human beings' denial of their creatureliness, inasmuch as they refuse to accept the standard and the limitations that are implicit in it. They do not want to be creatures, do not want to be subject to a standard, do not want be dependent . . . sin is, in its essence, a renunciation of the truth."[22] Sin is the expression of the autonomous "I" that is the antithesis of person-as-relation because it is the disruption of the fundamental relationship, a relationship without which "nothing else can be truly in order."[23] Sin is the rejection of

---

20. Ratzinger, *In the Beginning*, 72–73. See also *CCC*, §386.
21. Ratzinger, *Introduction*, 302.
22. Ratzinger, *In the Beginning*, 70–71.
23. Benedict XVI, *Jesus of Nazareth: The Infancy Narratives*, 43–44.

truth, the rejection of creatureliness and the fundamental, personal pattern of being-from, being-for, and being-with. It is an exercise in idolatry:

> To be totally free, without the competing freedom of others, without a "from" and a "for"—this desire presupposes not an image of God, but an idol. The primal error of such a radicalized will to freedom lies in the idea of a divinity conceived as a pure egoism. The god thought of in this way is not a God, but an idol. Indeed, it is the image of what the Christian tradition would call the devil—the anti-God—because it harbors exactly the radical antithesis to the real God. . . . Whenever there is an attempt to free ourselves from this pattern [i.e., being-from, being-for, being-with], we are not on our way to divinity, but to dehumanization, to the destruction of being itself through the destruction of the truth. The Jacobin variant of the idea of liberation . . . is a rebellion against man's very being, a rebellion against truth, which consequently leads man—as Sartre penetratingly saw—into a self-contradictory existence which we call hell.[24]

Sin is the shortfall in allowing oneself to be loved, and in loving others. Sin is the overexertion of freedom in a "will to power" against one's created nature that results not in humanization, but in an anti-personal, self-contradictory, dehumanized state known as hell.

Before exploring Ratzinger's thought on hell, one should note that the understanding of person-as-relation and revelation-as-dialogue lays a foundation for understanding original sin as well. Ratzinger says:

> Original sin is not an assertion about a natural deficiency in or concerning man, but a statement about a relationship that can be meaningfully formulated only in the context of the God-man relation. The essence of sin can only be understood in an anthropology of relation, not by looking at an isolated human being. . . . We could therefore describe original sin as a statement about God's evaluation of man; evaluation not as something external, but as revealing the very depths of his interior being. It is the collapse of what man is, both in his origin from God and in himself, the contradiction between the will of the Creator and man's empirical being.[25]

Original sin can only be rightly understood in light of the God-man relationship, that "collapse" of what man is and is meant to be as a person-in-relation. An anthropology of relationality reveals that the essence of

---

24. Ratzinger, "Truth and Freedom," 160.
25. Ratzinger, *Daughter Zion*, 69–70. See also Ratzinger, *Introduction*, 248–49.

original sin cannot to be found in the isolated human being (though the *Catechism* notes the effects of original sin for those in the "fallen state" are observable on this level in the intellect and will of the rational nature), but rather in the breakdown of relationality. Original sin describes the reality of damaged original dependence (*exitus*), and an impaired return to relationship (*reditus*), and a tendency toward autonomy and isolation instead. Ratzinger explains:

> When the network of human relationships is damaged from the very beginning, then every human being enters into a world that is marked by relational damage. At the very moment that a person begins human existence, which is a good, he or she is confronted by a sin-damaged world. Each of us enters into a situation in which relationality has been hurt. Consequently each person is, from the very start, damaged in relationships and does not engage in them as he or she ought. Sin pursues the human being, and he or she capitulates to it.[26]

Original sin exists on the level of relationship and signifies the original and fundamental broken relationship between Creator and creature, and the aftermath of the fundamental disunion—a network of broken relationships. The expression "original sin," then, not only refers to a moment in time, a primordial event (i.e., Adam and Eve's sin), but it describes a relational reality—a state of broken relationality on all levels. In other words, sin not only impacts one's personal relationship with God (i.e., the level of relation between the person and God), but between the person and others, and others and the person. Others become the victims of one's sin, and one becomes the victim of the sins committed by others. Original sin basically means the woundedness of others with whom I exist in a state of broken relationality, that relational woundedness enters into my life and wounds me. And, my own broken relationality does the same to them. Relationality, then, can be broken not only by actions for which one is responsible, but by those acts committed by others of which the person often bears no responsibility, and which cause one to become the unfortunate victim of a broken relationality. This all becomes clear in the various limitations or deficiencies of human love and affirmation manifest on a daily, hourly, or minute-by-minute basis.

In theological terms, and following Ratzinger's vision of the person and his understanding of the fallen person, mankind finds itself in a seemingly hopeless state when left its own devices. The radically individualistic misuse of freedom damages relationality, resulting in "a self-contradictory existence which we call hell." He notes that "the importance of the offense

---

26. Ratzinger, *In the Beginning*, 73.

varies according to the addressee. Since God is infinite, the offense to him implicit in humanity's sin is also infinitely important.... He [man] can offend infinitely—his capacity extends that far—but he cannot produce an infinite reparation; what he, as a finite being, gives will always be only finite."[27] The "rank" or "status," the "office" of the person sinned against, the addressee of the sin, determines the sin's gravity. In the case of an offense against God, who is infinite, the sin itself takes on an infinite proportion—man's freedom (and his finitude) is capable of this much. However, his finitude is not capable of bridging the infinite chasm that now exists in his fundamental relationship. "Human beings alone cannot save themselves," Ratzinger says. "We can only be saved—that is, be free and true—when we stop wanting to be God and when we renounce the madness of autonomy and self-sufficiency."[28] Here, again, the radical divergence between Ratzinger's position and the Rahnerian trajectory becomes clear. For Ratzinger, everything hangs on the *Logos* as author of life and source of salvation. The encounter with the *Logos* neither maintains or affirms life's trajectory as is, which is basically the case for Rahner, nor does it merely interrupt one's narrative with the shock of difference as proposed by Boeve, as a pause in a discourse ultimately to be resumed. Instead, the encounter alters the path significantly, entirely even, and it initiates a new story for one's life according to the *Logos* instead of the self. The "madness of autonomy and self-sufficiency" damages that fundamental relationship with God, and damage in this fundamental relationship means foundational damage for all interpersonal relationality. The converse is also true: damage in inter-personal relationships prohibits growth in the fundamental relationship with God (i.e., the source of all relationality). By freely adopting an attitude of self-sufficiency, man is given what he wants, he has delivered himself up to death.[29] As St. Paul puts it in his Letter to the Romans, "the wages of sin is death" (6:23).

When it comes to the topic of death, most immediately think of physical, biological death. This refers to "the physical process of disintegration which accompanies life . . . felt in sickness, and reach[ing] its terminal point in physical dying."[30] This reality stands as life's one, great, inescapable, non-negotiable metanarrative. Death stands as *the* metanarrative that even postmodernity cannot defeat. In fact, death itself ultimately does away with any and every *differend*, because death is a purely monological reality that consumes all its victims. It is the cessation of narratives, of word games, and

---

27. Ratzinger, *Introduction*, 232.
28. Ratzinger, *In the Beginning*, 73.
29. Ratzinger, *Introduction*, 302.
30. Ratzinger, *Eschatology*, 95.

the like. It is nothing. It silences human speech, disrupts communication, and blots out human existence. Death is simply fact, and its ominous nature lingers like a cloud over the whole of one's life, no matter how one attempts to hide it away or trivialize it. On biological death's doorstep, one stands staring at "a night into whose solitude no voice reaches."[31] This is the "door through which we can only walk alone—the door of death . . . all fear in the world is fear of this loneliness."[32] Yet, here, a second "dimension" of death becomes clear: loneliness appears as a type of death. Ratzinger explains:

> In the ultimate depths of every existence lies desperation, even hell. . . . One thing is sure: there will come a night when no word of comfort will penetrate the dark abandon, there will be a door which we must pass though in absolute solitude: the door of death. All this world's anguish is, in the final analysis, the anguish generated by this solitude. This is why in the Old Testament, the word indicating the kingdom of the dead was identical to the word for hell: *shêol*. Death, in fact, is absolute solitude. But this solitude which can no longer be illumined by love, which is so profound that love can no longer reach it, is hell.[33]

Death is not only physical disintegration, but "the nothingness of an empty existence" marked by the cessation of communication.[34] "It is simultaneously being and nonbeing, somehow still existence yet no longer life."[35] Death is not merely a biological event marked by the corruption of the body. It is not only an event that affects the substance of the individual, but one which fundamentally and existentially impacts one's personhood. Death is above all a relational disintegration of the person. Essentially, death, or hell, is that sphere of "dereliction, isolation, loneliness, and thus abandonment into nothingness."[36] In the biblical understanding of death, then, we have the coinciding of two terms, two realities—death and hell—both describing a state of being cut off from the land of the living or of being "banished into a noncommunication zone where life is destroyed precisely because relationship is impossible."[37]

---

31. Ratzinger, *Introduction*, 301.

32. Ratzinger, *Introduction*, 301.

33. Ratzinger, "The Anguish of an Absence," Meditation 2. See also Ratzinger, *Introduction*, 301.

34. Ratzinger, *Eschatology*, 95.

35. Ratzinger, *Eschatology*, 81.

36. Ratzinger, *Eschatology*, 81; see also 94–95.

37. Ratzinger, *Eschatology*, 81.

Man's own present existence, as a living being, is not safe from death and hell. For this reason, in the biblical thought of the Old Testament, sickness is described in the same manner as death. Sickness pushes one to the "realm of noncommunication, apparently destroying the relationships that make life what it is," and as the social sphere falls apart, death appears as that "sphere whose circumference reaches deep into human living."[38] Beyond physical ailment, living can be its own hell, marred as it is by the relational sickness of sin. The broken relationality caused by sin often renders human encounters superficial and incapable of curing the wound of loneliness. Sartre bases his anthropology upon this idea, as Ratzinger notes, "hell, despair, would dwell at the bottom of our existence, in the shape of that loneliness which is as inescapable as it is dreadful."[39] No idea, moral code, or philosophy can solve the riddle or ease the ubiquitous dysfunction that plagues human communities and drives people into isolation. In a certain sense, the existential philosophers of the twentieth century describe the harsh reality of the fallen man: he is alone, incapable of accessing real relationship, real communion, and, left as he is on his own, his life is a farce. With this more Scriptural and existential understanding, Ratzinger identifies the possibility of heaven and hell as current states of being, not as possibilities once one reaches the end of the line of his or her life. They are, according to McGregor, "two states [that] form the two poles of the total range of possible human existence. These two poles are existential rather than cosmic. It is possible for any human person to move to the hellish pole through the definite rejection of being-for the other."[40] Sin, both in its original and personal forms, is an anti-personal event that breaks relationality and results in loneliness, isolation, hell, and death—even in man's daily life, though not yet in a definitive or eternally fixed form.[41] The existential reality of death-as-hell, described as it is in relational terms as loneliness or isolation or abandonment, results from the reality of sin in all of its forms. Sin is the intentional, anti-personal, dehumanizing, and freely exercised breakdown of relationality. Death-as-hell is the existential state that results from sin, whether I am the one who commits the sin or the victim of the sin of another.

---

38. Ratzinger, *Eschatology*, 81.
39. Ratzinger, *Introduction*, 300.
40. McGregor, *Heart to Heart*, 268.
41. Ratzinger calls this eternally fixed form "second death"—the definitively fixed state of isolation following Christ's descent into hell. This is the ultimate and eternal rejection of God.

The Need for the Gospel

In a life marred by sin, a certain joylessness triumphs. A society, wounded by sin and because of sin, is a joyless state. According to Ratzinger, joy is a certain peace or harmony one has, or enjoys, when he acquiesces with his or her own being. Joy is that resting in the "yes" that one utters towards his or her own existence—a sign of affection toward oneself that says, "It is good that I exist." Ratzinger defines joy as, "the harmony [man] enjoys with himself. He lives in this affirmation. And only one who can accept himself can also accept the *thou*, can accept the world. The reason why an individual cannot accept the *thou*, cannot come to terms with him, is that he does not like his own *I* and, for that reason, cannot accept a *thou*."[42] The one who loves himself or herself in this way and who lives in this affirmation, this one can love others—love the neighbor *as self*. The command to love neighbor "as yourself," means, as Ratzinger puts it, "that self-love, the affirmation of one's own being, provides the form and measure for love of one's neighbor."[43] The terrible reality, however, is that one cannot accept him or herself due to an awareness of one's own fault in breaking down relationality with others through the failure to love. In other words, the reflective person sees him or herself as sinful, as one who does not love others as one ought, and, as such, as one who is unacceptable or unworthy of self-love. Incapable of self-love, one finds perfectly accepting others difficult or altogether impossible. As Sartre sees it, every human being is alien to the other; human beings objectify one another. Is there any way out? Is there an exit from this ubiquitously lonely and maddening situation?

The basis of joy is love. Joy is something of a byproduct of love, of being loved. Here, Pieper quotes Sartre, who notes that we must "feel that our

---

42. Ratzinger, *Principles*, 79.

43. Ratzinger, *Yes of Jesus*, 98. See also Ratzinger, *Principles*, 80. "Egoism and real self-love are not only not identical but exclude each other. Someone can be a great egoist and nevertheless be dissatisfied with himself. Indeed, egoism is often precisely a consequence of being torn apart oneself, of the attempt to create another ego for oneself, whereas the right relationship to the ego in freedom grows of itself. One could almost talk of an anthropological circle: to the extent that people are always seeking themselves, would like to bring about their own self-realization, and are intent on the success and fulfillment of their ego, this ego becomes objectionable, annoying, and unsatisfactory. . . . Only the 'yes' that is given me by someone else makes me capable for my part of addressing this "yes" to myself, in and with the other. The 'I' is realized by the 'you.' On the other hand it is true that only someone who has accepted himself can address a real "yes" to someone else. Accepting oneself, 'loving' oneself, once again presupposes truth and demands a continual pilgrimage towards the truth" (Ratzinger, *Yes of Jesus*, 99–100).

existence is justified" in order to be joyful and in order to love others. This is the way out: love—being loved. Pieper elaborates, saying:

> It does not suffice us simply to exist; we can do that "anyhow." What matters to us, beyond mere existence, is the explicit confirmation: It is *good* that you exist; how wonderful that you are! In other words, what we need over and above sheer existence is: to be loved by another person.... Being created by God actually does not suffice, it would seem; the fact of creation needs continuation and perfection by the creative power of human love.[44]

Ratzinger adds, "Of ourselves, we cannot come to terms with ourselves. Our *I* becomes acceptable to us only if it has first become acceptable to another *I*. We can love ourselves [and others] only if we have first been loved by someone else."[45] He adds, "Man is that strange creature that needs not just physical birth but also appreciation if he is to subsist."[46] Everyone needs to hear the loving affirmation: "It is good that you exist," not with words, but with an act of the other's being. Each person needs to be loved in order to be joyful, to accept him or herself, and to accept others. The reception of such a creative power as human love is the way out of the predicament caused by sin.

However, in a reality marred by the relational damage of sin, this "creative power of human love" given to me is also marred. It is imperfect, inconsistent, ignorant, and, above all, it is finite. No human being loves the other perfectly, consistently, and eternally—which is precisely what one longs for—a love in truth. In other words, a merely finite "yes" to one's existence from another human being is does not, in the end, satisfy the infinite longing of the human heart for a "yes" that can carry one across the void of death. Thus, without this kind of love, the human being does appear to be absurd, a hopeless passion. And, Ratzinger concludes:

---

44. Pieper, *About Love*, 27.

45. Ratzinger, *Principles*, 79–80.

46. Ratzinger, *Principles*, 80. The child's encounter with his or her mother instantiates this experience. A mother gives a child not only physical life, but also love, appreciation, and acceptance (See also Ratzinger, "On Hope," 30–31; Ratzinger, *Yes of Jesus*, 89–91; Pieper, *About Love*, 18–38; Bernanos, *The Diary of a Country Priest*, 14). Conor Sweeney adds: "To gaze at the mother's smile is to encounter the utter gratuitousness and gift-character of one's existence.... This experience is by 'nature' fundamental to every human being brought into this world. To gaze into the mother's eyes, to be bathed in the warmth of her smile, to be nourished by the sustenance of her breast: all of this is paradigmatic of the *gelassenheit* of human existence, of the call to entrust oneself to the other.... The child gazing at his mother has no need of 'proofs' for either his existence or hers. All that he 'knows' from this experience is that he is loved, and that love is really all there is and all that matters" (Sweeney, *Sacramental Presence*, 229–30).

Being is not good . . . if you have not experienced it as welcome, have not had "Yes" said to you, that is, if you have not been loved. This indicates that the fear which transcends all fears is the fear of losing love altogether, fear of an existence in which the little daily disturbances fill everything, without anything large and reassuring coming along to keep the balance. Then these little fears, if they constitute everything that can be expected of the future, will pass over into the great fear—fear of an unbearable life—because hope no longer dwells in it. In this case, death, which is the end of all hopes, becomes the only hope. . . . If the fear that transcends all fears is in the last resort fear of losing love, then the hope which transcends all hopes is the assurance of being showered with the gift of a great love.[47]

---

47. Ratzinger, "On Hope," 30.

CHAPTER TEN

Christian Faith as Encounter

Thus far, I have established that the sublimity of the Christian call consists in love. The one who loves perfectly as the Father loves perfectly, that one is Christian. *Love God; and love neighbor as yourself.* Karol Wojtyla sums up this greatest commandment, saying, "The commandment laid down in the New Testament demands from man love for others, for his neighbors—in the fullest sense . . . love for persons. For God, whom the commandment to love names first, is the most perfect personal Being."[1] This is the basic call: love persons perfectly. The problem, of course, lies in the human person's freely choosing non-love, freely choosing self, freely choosing to break from relationship and others. The criteria for such love, of course, is self-love, that loving acceptance that results in a certain state of joy. The problem, however, lies in the fact that one does not love himself as he ought. He must first (and always) be loved by another, by others, yet the "other" or the "others" fail to love him perfectly.

At this point, one bumps into a rather paralyzing catch-22. In order to love my neighbor perfectly, I must to love myself perfectly—which I do not. But, to love myself perfectly, I need to be loved by my neighbor perfectly—and he does not love me perfectly. Doomed, banished to the non-communication zone, one begins to enter the real depths of the human predicament, one grasps something of the real human need. "It is at this point that faith begins," Ratzinger says, "For what faith basically means is just that this shortfall that we all have in our love is made up by the surplus of Jesus Christ's love, acting on our behalf." He concludes by saying, "Ultimately, faith means nothing other than admitting that we have this kind of shortfall; it means opening our hand and accepting a gift. In its simplest and innermost form, faith is nothing but reaching that point in love at which we recognize that we, too, need to be given something."[2]

1. Wojtyla, *Love and Responsibility*, 40.
2. Ratzinger, *What It Means*, 74–75. See also Ratzinger, *Introduction*, 267.

Benedict XVI's famous line from *Deus caritas est* might best summarize his personalistic and dynamic understanding of the act of faith, and it does so in personalist terms (i.e., in terms of relationality). Here, he says, "Being Christian is not the result of an ethical choice or a lofty idea, but the encounter with an event, a person, which gives life a new horizon and a decisive direction."[3] Christianity is neither an ethical choice, an expression of mere moralism, nor is it a lofty idealism. It is not construed according to the ideals of rationalism, subjectivism, positivism, humanism, postmodernism, and so forth. It is not a binding narration, a monologue of reality. Instead, it is a personal encounter with the author of reality, the *Logos* who, in an act of pure freedom, reveals something of Being itself, and who provokes the full freedom of the person, for a response. Being Christian, then, is the result of an encounter with an objective reality, a fact, the Other who comes to humanity and who allows himself to be encountered as such. This wholly personal and human act (i.e., one which involves the intellect, will, and affectivity of the person), following the logic laid out in *Deus caritas est*, consists of at least three significant aspects: (1) faith as encounter; (2) faith as conversion (i.e., living according to a new horizon), and (3) faith as a journey of discipleship (i.e., life set upon a decisive direction, advancing on a "way"). For Ratzinger, the personal character of the act of faith weaves together these three aspects. The act of faith is an event, an encounter with Christ and the acceptance of perfect love that initiates a process of ongoing conversion and a path of personal healing. However, before developing this personalist account of faith—of what faith *means* for the person—one must grasp the basic dynamics of belief and faith.

Belief and Everyday Faith

What is faith in its plainest and simplest form? To pursue an answer, I first want to explore what Ratzinger calls "everyday faith," and what, more philosophically, Pieper labels "belief." With regard to the latter, one could say that belief means to regard something as true and real on the basis of another's testimony.[4] It is the acceptance and approval of the truth of something of which you are unfamiliar and which you have not seen for yourself, on the basis of another's account. As St. Paul puts it, "Faith comes from what is heard" (Rom 10:17). In essence, this means I believe "something"

---

3. Benedict XVI, *DCE*, §1. Pope Francis references this line in *Evangelii gaudium*, §7.

4. See Pieper, *Belief and Faith*, 18.

because I believe "someone."[5] Belief has trust as its prerequisite. Ratzinger describes this as a "mutual trust whereby another's knowledge becomes mine. . . . Through my trust I come to share in another's knowledge."[6] Belief, then, is a mediated way of coming to know something. One can boil down this concept into a little formula showing a twofold movement, or a parallel structure of belief: belief *in* and faith *that*. I believe (i.e., I place my complete trust) *in* someone, *that* what he has seen and told me is true. To believe, then, means "to participate in the knowledge of a knower," for "if . . . there is no one who sees and knows, then, properly speaking, there can be no one who believes."[7] My understanding about this or that comes from another, from my relationship with this or that other. In this sense, faith is a personal and quite natural way of coming to know something. Without this capacity to know something of which I have not seen for myself, my knowledge would be quite limited, indeed. Here, Ratzinger picks up with his concept of "everyday faith."

In a subtle, or not so subtle critique of those who advocate for a strict division between science and faith, Ratzinger observes that even a technological society organized by technocrats, a certain "everyday faith" remains and is necessary for human life. Ratzinger admits that faith seems to be temporary and that actually seeing the thing for what it is, actually knowing for oneself, propels the human being. Nevertheless, faith is unavoidable, because "nobody can actually know and master from his or her own knowledge and understanding all that in a technological civilization our life depends on."[8] One simply cannot start from the beginning and know, with scientific certainty, everything about each step of a technical process that stands behind the array of apparatuses that make living possible today. Doing so would be completely debilitating. Take, for example, the everyday occurrence of driving a car and consider how many acts of faith one makes, simultaneously, in the getting from here to there. Human beings simply must practice this kind of subconscious faith all the time, for without it, everyone would have to start from square one in each instant and never get anywhere. This kind of faith also relies upon a basic level of human trust, a fundamental reliance upon the experience, knowledge, and general goodwill of others. In other words, a certain "mutual trust" undergirds this kind of faith, "a common sharing in understanding and in mastering the world, and this aspect is essential

---

5. Pieper, *Belief and Faith*, 18.
6. Ratzinger, *Yes of Jesus*, 27.
7. Pieper, *Belief and Faith*, 34.
8. Ratzinger, *Yes of Jesus*, 6.

for the organization of human life."⁹ Ratzinger concludes his treatment on "everyday faith," by considering its existential structure in three points: (1) one directs this type of faith toward someone who knows and is an expert and trustworthy; (2) there is a certain trust of the majority, the many others who use things daily; and (3) the knowledge one obtains through "everyday faith" that allows one to live effectively today, this knowledge can be verified in everyday experience, even if it is not scientifically verified.[10] Again, driving a car suffices as an illustration.

Christian Faith

Thus far, the topic has revolved around a basic and reasonable human experience necessary for the survival of the human race, that goes by the name of "belief" or "everyday faith." How does Christian faith fit into this understanding? To be sure, there has always been a sort of natural knowledge of God.[11] The history of religions expresses this clearly enough—man is a religious creature. It is possible to read God's writing, so to speak, in the book of nature. It is possible to see those vestiges of the *logos* throughout all of creation, even if the possibility of obstruction remains significant. Ratzinger argues in favor of this basic experience of the *logos*, saying "that the rationality of the world cannot be sensibly and usefully explained on the basis of irrationality is evident. And thus the logos at the origin of all things remains as it always was the best hypothesis, and one that indeed demands of us that we should give up the gestures of domination and adopt those of humble receptivity."[12]

Indeed, there are two fundamental tendencies throughout human history. On the one hand, there is an "inner openness for God of the human soul," and, on the other hand, "the stronger force of immediate needs and experiences."[13] Those immediate needs and experiences drive a spirit of domination, a rewriting of reality, and, thus, they distract from one's ability to read the book of nature. Makability (Vico) and feasibility (Marx), as already noted, dominate modern ways of thinking. The modern man holds that "wherever he comes from, he can look his future in the eye with the determination to make himself into whatever he wishes; he does not need to regard it as impossible to make himself into the God who now stands at

---

9. Ratzinger, *Yes of Jesus*, 6–7.
10. See Ratzinger, *Yes of Jesus*, 7.
11. Cf. *CCC*, §36.
12. Ratzinger, *Yes of Jesus*, 26.
13. Ratzinger, *Yes of Jesus*, 26.

the end as *faciendum*, as something makable, not at the beginning, as *logos*, meaning."[14] In light of the modern mind, faith or even a natural knowledge of God, appears rather striking counter position.

Over and against the myth of modernity that reduces everything to what human beings can conceive of themselves, expressed as it is in the concept of the self-made man, biblical belief centers on the concepts of "stand—understand" with regard to an Other. Indeed, Christian faith, does not seek after observable facts, but is "a fundamental mode of behavior toward being, toward existence, toward one's own sector of reality, and toward reality as a whole."[15] Ratzinger asserts, "Belief operates on a completely different plane from that of making and 'makability.' Essentially, it is entrusting oneself to that which has not been made by oneself and never could be made and which precisely in this way supports and makes possible all our making."[16] Meaning, however, cannot be created through purely human activity—"meaning that is self-made is in the last analysis no meaning. Meaning, that is, the ground on which our existence as a totality can stand and live, cannot be made but only received."[17]

Despite the ways in which the *logos* is accessible to human beings in the book of nature, the human being longs for more—he longs for a relationship with this *logos*. Yet, "with our own resources we cannot build the bridges that would lead to a definitive relationship with this God. . . . God must cross over to them and talk to them if real relations are to be established."[18] This crossing over happens most fully, most definitively, in the incarnation of the *logos* in Jesus Christ, the *Logos* made flesh (John 1:14). True, in Israel's history, there had been those who knew God personally, who had even seen God's back, yet there were none who had truly seen God, who had beheld his face (cf. Deut 18:15; 34:10). Jesus Christ, the Son of God, is that one who has immediate contact with the Father (cf. John 1:18) and through whom human beings can "see" the Father (cf. John 14:9). "Of its essence," Ratzinger says, "Christian faith is sharing in the vision of Jesus, mediated by his word, which is the authentic expression of his vision. Jesus' vision is the point of reference of our faith, the point where it is anchored in reality."[19] Elsewhere, Ratzinger says, "to believe is to be granted a share in Jesus' vision [cf. John

14. Ratzinger, *Introduction*, 66.

15. Ratzinger, *Introduction*, 50.

16. Ratzinger, *Introduction*, 70. Faith is a definitive rejection of the idolatry. See Ratzinger, *Introduction*, 110–15.

17. Ratzinger, *Introduction*, 73.

18. Ratzinger, *Yes of Jesus*, 26–27.

19. Ratzinger, *Yes of Jesus*, 29.

6:56]. . . . Because Jesus is the Son, he has an unceasing vision of the Father. Because he is man, we can share this vision. Because he is both God and man *at once*, he is neither a historical person nor simply removed from all time in eternity. . . . He is in the midst of time, always alive, always present."[20] Christian faith basically says: I believe *in* you, Jesus Christ, *that* you are the *Logos*, the Son of God, and *that* your testimony is true.

For Ratzinger, faith means receiving the person of the *Logos*—entering into a personal relationship with the *Logos*—as the ground of one's existence, as that which gives meaning to the whole of one's life—a meaning which one did not and does not create for himself, but in which he participates. Such a meaning allows him to stand amid all the trials of life, allows him to stay firm amid the shifting sands of time. Here, Ratzinger argues that faith is understanding. Belief means accepting the meaning which is the ground of one's existence, which he did not make for himself but receives and that which holds him in existence. He says:

> For to believe as a Christian means in fact entrusting oneself to the meaning that upholds me and the world; taking it as the firm ground on which I can stand fearlessly. Using rather more traditional language, we could say that to believe as a Christian means understanding our existence as a response to the word, the *logos*, that upholds and maintains all things. It means affirming that the meaning we do not make but can only receive is already granted to us, so that we have only to take it and to entrust ourselves to it . . . [for] the receiving precedes the making.[21]

Ratzinger says, "Understanding means seizing and grasping as *meaning* the meaning that man has received as *ground*," and that understanding is grasping the "ground on which we have taken our stand as meaning and truth."[22] One must stand—stand firm—in the *Logos* in order to understand. This is a radical reversal or conversion from the rational and makable theses of modern praxis-oriented thinking to the reception of meaning in the revelation of Being in the *Logos*. Yet, precisely in this way, faith *is* rational, perhaps opening to the most reasonable position, because *logos*, as meaning, must also be truth. Understanding results from accepting the truth of *logos* as meaning, reason, rather than relying purely upon human reason.[23] Here,

---

20. Ratzinger, GCC, 27. See also Ratzinger, *Yes of Jesus*, 29–30.
21. Ratzinger, *Introduction*, 73.
22. Ratzinger, *Introduction*, 77.
23. Sarto describes Ratzinger's position clearly, saying that because Ratzinger understands *Logos* as both the eternal Word of the Father and as God's "reflection and projection in creation—the *logos*, the truth, the meaning of things . . . [which, in

human reason bows to and is dependent upon a source over and above it—human reason is "suspended," so to speak, from *Logos*.

This meaning, *logos*, which is the ground of our existence, does not come to humanity in the form of an idea or a book. In Jesus Christ, *Logos* appears as a person. Belief in the *Logos*, then, means belief in a "you," a person, who comes to me from outside of me, and who corresponds to the innermost recesses of my being which were written by that same *Logos*. *Logos* is not "reason" or "mind" alone. Ratzinger explains the implications of this reality:

> In Jesus' life from the Father, in the immediacy and intensity of his converse with him in prayer and, indeed, face to face, he is God's witness, through whom the intangible has become tangible, the distant has drawn near.... He is the presence of the eternal itself in this world. In his life, in the unconditional devotion of himself to men, the meaning of the world is present before us. ... Thus faith is the finding of a "you" that upholds me and amid all the unfulfilled—and in the last resort unfulfillable—hope of human encounters gives me the promise of and indestructible love that not only longs for eternity but also guarantees it. Christian faith lives on the discovery that not only is there such a thing as objective meaning but that this meaning knows me and loves me, that I can entrust myself to it like the child who knows that everything he may be wondering about is safe in the "you" of his mother. Thus in the last analysis believing, trusting, and loving are one, and all the theses around which belief revolves are only concrete expressions of the all-embracing about-turn, of the assertion "I believe in you"—of the discovery of God in the countenance of the man Jesus of Nazareth.[24]

At all times, Ratzinger begins with, remains in, and ends with the *Logos* incarnate. The most "fundamental feature of Christian faith or belief," then,

---

the case of humanity, means] endowment with the *logos*, the capacity for word and thought, communication and knowledge, reason and relationship, love and truth," "the answer of faith does not obviate or excuse the free exercise of rationality, but—on the contrary—it requires and reinforces it ... both [faith and reason] ultimately lead back to the divine Logos" (Sarto, "*Logos* and *Dia-Logos*," 501-2).

24. Ratzinger, *Introduction*, 79-80. See also Benedict XVI, *Transforming Power*, 14-15; Benedict XVI, *Verbum Domini*, §25; Ratzinger, *Ministers of Your Joy*, 48-49; and Benedict XVI's "Christmas Greetings 2012," which reads, "Christ, who is the truth, has taken us by the hand, and we know that his hand is holding us securely on the path of our quest for knowledge. Being inwardly held by the hand of Christ makes us free and keeps us safe: free—because if we are held by him, we can enter openly and fearlessly into any dialogue; safe—because he does not let go of us, unless we cut ourselves off from him. At one with him, we stand in the light of truth."

is "its personal character." Ratzinger says that Christian faith is more than a decision for the *logos* as the rational ground, the meaning of the world and of reality. Instead, its central formula is not "I believe in something," but "I believe in someone . . . you." Faith is a personal encounter with the *Logos*, "it is the encounter with the man Jesus, and in this encounter, it experiences the meaning of the world as a person."[25] Christian faith says, then, "I believe the meaning of the world is you, Jesus."

Faith as Encounter: An Interpersonal Event

Christian faith refers to the person of Jesus Christ and his testimony—relationship and testimony. Faith is the response of the receiving subject to the revelation of the *logos* in Jesus Christ. It describes a personal act—an act that involves the whole person of the receiving subject, because it involves encountering the event of the Son, the person of the Son in Jesus Christ. Benedict XVI describes this "meeting point" of revelation and faith, of Son and human being, as an *encounter*. The word "encounter" literally means a "meeting of adversaries, confrontation," and even "fight" in Old French. Msgr. Luigi Giussani describes an encounter as the confrontation with a fact, i.e., reality.[26] For Giussani, the method of encounter is marked by "the chance meeting with a reality external to the self, an objective, eminently 'encounterable' presence that, while 'outside' of the self, moves the heart. (The word 'encounter' has an exterior connotation just as decisive as the interior one.)"[27] For Giussani, an encounter means "something distinctly objective educated man's subjectivity,"[28] something or someone (i.e., an "objective" other) erupts onto the scene and brings about a change in the subject—moves the heart. Encounter denotes a real conflict. It is not simply an advertisable buzzword operative in the "free market" created by the concept of New Evangelization. No. It denotes a real change, a real transformation, an altered trajectory. Ratzinger seems to understand the concept in the same way as Giussani, with its somewhat violent connotation that implies a radical transformation or conversion of one's life.

Encounter, in the light of Christian faith, refers to the in-breaking of God's personhood, the "we" of Trinitarian *communio* alive in the completely open "I" of Love's *Logos*, entering into the *sheôl*, the isolation of the "I" that results from human sin. God does not confront man as an adversary

---

25. Ratzinger, *Introduction*, 79.
26. Giussani, *At the Origin*, 40.
27. Giussani, *Why the Church?*, 20.
28. Giussani, *Why the Church?*, 20.

(cf. 2 Cor 1:20), but sinful man is adversarial towards God. God is always and everywhere "yes" towards man, yet, in his sin, man expresses a "no" towards God. God's communal nature as "I," "You," and "We" stands in stark contrast to the isolating nature of sin that locks man in himself, in his "I," and, therefore, this isolated "I" stands in opposition to the radical relationality of God. Every encounter between God and fallen man is, by its nature, a "confrontation"—the God of love meeting the adversarial quality of the isolated (or isolating) "I" (e.g., Gen 3:8–10). Encounter refers to this: the "yes" of God encountering the "no" of man, or, said differently, the "yes" of God in the person of the *Logos* meeting and offering itself for the isolated "I" who mutters his "no" in the face of God's wholly humble love. The "yes" of God, the love of God *in* Jesus Christ encounters man, it is expressed to man *personally*. Through relationship, the Son of God, breaks through what could be called the "death of relationality" (i.e., loneliness) that results from the anti-personal activity known as sin. Ratzinger offers two striking entry points into a meditation on the reality of encounter in: (1) Jesus Christ's offering of himself to the Father "for the many" on the Cross, and (2) in the striking image of the harrowing of hell.

Encounters between God and humanity appear throughout history. Christianity holds that in the fullness of time, God chose to reveal his love for humanity in Jesus Christ, his only begotten Son. This manifestation reaches its own height in Jesus' "hour," in his passing over in his passion, death, and resurrection. Here, the Cross expresses most radically God's love for broken humanity. The Cross, in one moment, displays the depths of God's love for humanity, and the depths of humanity's sinfulness—indeed, the greatest of all sins, the cutting off of the Son of God. In a certain sense, the Cross is the manifestation of humanity's crisis of faith in the very possibility of a personal God of love. Human beings, it seems, cannot stand a God who cares this much, who draws this close, who loves this far. So, it "assails truth" and cuts it off, because unjust man always needs, as Ratzinger says, "the injustice of the next man in order to feel excused and thus canst not tolerate the just man who seems to rob thee of this excuse."[29] The Cross is the manifestation of humanity's self-imposed God-forsakenness. It cancels out the just one. Ratzinger explains:

> The truth about man is that he is continually assailing truth; the just man crucified is thus a mirror held up to man in which he sees himself unadorned. But the Cross does not reveal only man; it also reveals God. God is such that he identifies himself with man right down into this abyss and that he judges him by

---

29. Ratzinger, *Introduction*, 293.

saving him. In the abyss of human failure is revealed the still more inexhaustible abyss of divine love. The Cross is thus truly the center of revelation, a revelation that does not reveal any previously unknown principles but reveals us to ourselves by revealing us before God and God in our midst.[30]

As Brotherton puts it, "the Cross does not function here as the perfect image of God's own life, but it reveals the love God has for a sinful mankind."[31] "The Cross is revelation," Ratzinger says, "it reveals who God is and in what way man is."[32] The cross does not perfectly reveal the immanent life of God, but it does reveal something of the immanence of who God is for mankind: a God who sees and goes to the depths of mankind's condition caused by the rejection of the Truth. Ratzinger explains this, saying Jesus Christ's

> being stretched out from being in God [reaches] right down to the hell of "My God, why have you forsaken me?" Anyone who has stretched his existence so wide that he is simultaneously immersed in God and in the depths of the God-forsaken creature is bound to be torn asunder, as it were; such a one is truly "crucified." But this process of being torn apart is identical with love; it is its realization to the extreme (cf. John 13:1) and the concrete expression of the breadth it creates.[33]

God's judgment and expression of man's worth, despite man's free choice to distort or to damage the "image and likeness," is mercy, and opens the way for salvation.

The Cross responds to the need for love to be based upon truth. If it is not based upon truth, it is mere deception and joy becomes impossible. In every purely human case of being loved, one could raise a question: "Is it true . . . when someone says to me: 'It is good that you exist?' Is it really good? Is it not possible that that person's love, which wills my existence, is just a tragic error?"[34] Human love, with all of its inconsistency, ignorance, and finitude, cannot, it seems, overcome the gap of the unknown, the possibility of deception, and it certainly cannot overcome the grave. Human love is strong as death, perhaps, but not stronger than it. "Love alone is of no avail," Ratzinger says. "It serves no purpose if truth is not on its side. Only

---

30. Ratzinger, *Introduction*, 293. This is also quoted in Brotherton, "Damnation and the Trinity," 126.

31. Brotherton, "Damnation and the Trinity," 126.

32. Ratzinger, *Introduction*, 292.

33. Ratzinger, *Introduction*, 290. This is also quoted in Brotherton, "Damnation and the Trinity," 125.

34. Ratzinger, *Principles*, 80.

when truth and love are in harmony can man know joy. For it is truth that makes man free."[35] The Cross, then, is the loving acceptance, offered by such a Person in such an act that it reveals a perfectly-true loving-acceptance. In other words, the personal love encountered at the Cross makes joy possible. Recall that before all else, love is this radical acceptance and approval of the goodness of the other. Thus, with Jesus Christ, the Son, the *Logos*, the Cross manifests a being-loved-in-truth (accepting me despite everything unacceptable I have done) that consequently makes joy possible and the ability to love possible (cf. 1 John 4:19). Ratzinger explains:

> God finds man so important that he himself has suffered for man. The Cross ... is in truth the center of the *evangelium*, the glad tidings: "It is good that you exist"—no, "It is necessary that you exist." The Cross is the approbation of our existence, not in words, but in an act so completely radical that it caused God to become flesh and pierced this flesh to the quick; that, to God, it was worth the death of his incarnate Son. One who is so loved that the other identifies his life with this love and no longer desires to live if he is deprived of it; one who is loved even unto death—such a one knows that he is truly loved. But if God so loves us, then we are loved in truth. Then love is truth, and truth is love. Then life is worth living.... Christianity is, by its very nature, joy—the ability to be joyful.[36]

God knows. The living, consistent, committed, all-knowing, infinite God is, is the *Logos*, the truth, and knows the whole truth about man. God, the Son of God, knows what He is truly affirming in the sinful human person (cf. Rom 5:6–8). Following God's first "yes" to each person in the creative act, the Gospel is God's second "yes," directed, personally, to each person. He says, "God's second 'yes' that was made manifest on the cross is our rebirth.... It is only this rebirth that finally and definitively makes us alive.... People who have been affirmed by God in this way ... are called to share in this 'yes' ... to continue his creation ... by giving being to the other ... in the affirmation of love."[37] This second "yes" in the encounter with Christ crucified moves the person beyond what Pieper refers to as merely "existing," which one can do "anyhow," and into a state of being wholly him or herself. God himself vindicates himself of Pieper's scandalous indictment quoted above, that being created by God

---

35. Ratzinger, *Principles*, 80.

36. Ratzinger, *Principles*, 81.

37. Ratzinger, *Yes of Jesus*, 91. See also Ratzinger, *Principles*, 81; Ratzinger, *Introduction*, 201–3; Sarto, "The Theology of Joseph Ratzinger," 160.

is somehow insufficient, for the person stands in need of human love in order to thrive. Jesus Christ is the "human love" of God, that finite vessel through which infinite love reaches mankind. This "Yes" of God, this smile of God, reaches the "roots of our existence and proves its strength not least in the fact that it sustains us when all else about us is darkness,"[38] providing, "a way of life, indeed, life itself."[39] For this reason, "Christianity is, by its very nature, joy—the ability to be joyful," and the ability to love. Now, "in the authenticity of his being he lives by the fact that he is loved and is himself given the faculty to love."[40] This is the heart of the glad tidings of the Gospel. God's love makes joy possible; it makes love possible.

God's love in Jesus Christ solves the tripartite problem identified above: man's inability to love others perfectly, because he does not love himself perfectly, and he cannot love himself perfectly because he is not truly and perfectly loved by another. For this reason, Ratzinger believes faith still has a chance in a post-Christian age. Why? Because Christianity "corresponds to the nature of man."[41] Man is that being, that personal being that longs for the infinite, that longs for an infinite experience of the reality of love. Ratzinger says, "The longing for the infinite is alive and unquenchable within man. None of the attempted answers will do; only the God who himself became finite in order to tear open our finitude and lead us out into the wide space of his infinity . . . corresponds to the question of our being."[42] Jesus is this perfect love granted to man by the Other. Jesus, the *Logos*, is the "yes, it is good that you exist!" of the Father. Jesus Christ *is* the Father's affirmation of humanity in a gesture that goes beyond words but is the complete giving over of the Word. Here, the wholly personal aspect of faith becomes quite clear. Sure, faith in Jesus Christ can be characterized in a simple formula: I believe *in* you, Jesus Christ, *that* you are the Son of God (i.e., God). However, through an understanding of faith as encounter, in light of the Cross, this statement could be modified to say: I believe *in* you, Jesus Christ, *that* you are the Son and *that*, as God, you love me in truth. Now, this man or that man, can love himself insofar as he believes in the gift of God's "yes" to him in Jesus Christ and takes this "yes" as his own identity. Now, he sees himself and loves himself in light of this "yes," and, as such, he becomes capable of loving others, all of whom God has also loved with

---

38. Ratzinger, *Principles*, 81.

39. Ratzinger, *On the Way*, 42. See also Benedict XVI, *Jesus, the Apostles, and the Early Church*, 116).

40. Ratzinger, "The Anguish of an Absence," Meditation 2.

41. Ratzinger, *TT*, 137.

42. Ratzinger, *TT*, 137.

that same "yes," thus offering them the same "yes" he has received and making their joy possible. Now, mere human love is transformed into charity. It is possible and appropriate, then, to define evangelization, as a profound expression of love, of charity. It is the participation in, and communication of God's "Yes" to humanity in Jesus Christ (cf. 2 Cor 1:19–20). The word shared in evangelization, then, is the incarnate Word itself (cf. John 1:14), who was crucified to reveal the extent of the love of God for man, who defeated death, and who holds persons in common with himself and one another despite their ignorance, inconsistency, and finitude.

The "yes" of God in Jesus Christ (i.e., the inexhaustible abyss of divine love"), who identifies himself with man by "putting on the disguise of the smallest worm," counters humanity's "no" (i.e., "the abyss of human failure") to God.[43] In other words, the Cross reveals the extent to which God's "yes" to humanity in Jesus Christ (which is to say, Jesus Christ *is* the "yes" of God to humanity) confronts humanity's "no" with an unfathomable love. In Jesus Christ, God confronts humanity's "no" with an even greater "yes," a revelation that makes salvation and joy possible if one changes course, so to speak, by accepting the previously unfathomable "yes" of God in Jesus Christ. Despite humanity's "no," God still says "yes" with a love strong enough to stand ever before that "no" as a constant proposal and offering to break its bonds. In allowing himself to be silenced by humanity's non-reception of the gift of the *Logos*, for the sake of humanity, the *Logos* speaks God's love in mankind's profoundest depths. And, with this, that is, the Cross as the expression of God's "yes" confronting humanity's "no" in its profoundest depths, we have already anticipated another profound aspect of encounter discoverable in the harrowing of hell.

The Cross stands as one part—an initiatory event, so to speak—of a whole movement into God's direct dealings with humanity's hellish situation. Christ's descent into the realm of the dead, the act of harrowing hell, is the second part. We find in Christ's death and descent into hell, another aspect of the mystery of encounter. Brotherton explains, "Love for [Ratzinger] is a relational category (and the person is constituted by his capacity to love), which creates a problem when one is faced with the reality of damnation. He wants to indicate that God descended upon earth in order to rescue it from the darkness of rejecting love, where man lives the self-contradiction of '*Sheol*-existence.'"[44] *Sheol*-existence is a self-contradicting, anti-personal, anti-relational existence. For Ratzinger, *sheol* and death refer to the same relational reality: absolute loneliness, the "non-communication

---

43. Ratzinger, *Introduction*, 292–93.
44. Brotherton, "Damnation and the Trinity," 134.

zone." Hell describes the loneliness into which love can no longer reach. In a meditation on Holy Saturday, Ratzinger describes the anguish of the absence of presence that hell is—even now. He says:

> If a child had to venture out alone through a wood on a dark night, he would be afraid even if he were to be shown a hundred times that there was nothing to fear. He is not afraid of anything specific, to which he could put a name, but in the dark he feels insecure, an orphan, he feels the sinister character of inner existence. Only a human voice could console him; only the hand of a person he loves could banish the anguish, like a bad dream. There is an anguish—the true kind nesting in the profundity of our solitudes—which cannot be overcome by reason but only by the presence of a person who loves us. This anguish, in fact, doesn't have an object to which we could put a name. It is the terrible expression of our ultimate solitude.[45]

Hell is not limited to the physical experience of a biological corruption or disintegration known as death. No. Hell's shadows reach into existential reality any time relationship breaks down and one finds himself alone. As Ratzinger says, "life means communion, whereas the heart of death is the absence of relationship."[46] The Cross marks the in-breaking of Christ into this self-contradictory *Sheol*-existence with a personal presence that overpowers sin, death, human rejection, and isolation.

This understanding sets the stage for the article of the Creed which announces that Christ descended into hell:

> This article thus asserts that Christ strode through the gate of our final loneliness, that in his Passion he went down into the abyss of our abandonment. Where no voice can reach us any longer, there is he. Hell is thereby overcome, or, to be more accurate, death, which was previously hell, is hell no longer. Neither is the same any longer because there is life in the midst of death, because love dwells in it. Now only deliberate self-enclosure is hell or, as the Bible calls it, the second death (Rev 20:14, for example). But death is no longer the path into icy solitude; the gates of *sheol* have been opened.[47]

The Cross is the means by which Christ enters into the "abyss of our abandonment." The Cross is the door. In entering into this abandonment, which

---

45. Ratzinger, "The Anguish of an Absence," Meditation 2.

46. Ratzinger, *Eschatology*, 82.

47. Ratzinger, *Introduction*, 301. See also Ratzinger, "The Anguish of an Absence," Meditation 2.

was previously thought to be "un-enterable" by another, Christ overcomes hell, because now there is presence and not absence, there is an Other and not pure isolation. More clearly, perhaps, as Brotherton notes, "Christ has done the impossible of separating death from hell."[48] That first dimension of death, biological death, is hell no longer; it is no longer absolute loneliness. At the same time, human experiences of abandonment are no longer hell, because here, too, one finds an Other. Ratzinger explains that "In the descent of Jesus, God himself descends into Sheol," and "at that moment, death ceases to be the God-forsaken land of darkness, a realm of unpitying distance from God." Instead, "in Christ, God himself entered that realm of death, transforming the space of noncommunication into the place of his own presence."[49] Now, only "deliberate self-enclosure" or "second death" is hell—a definitive blotting out of God, of love, a definitive rejection of relationality.

In a real sense, the Trinitarian relationality that undergirds the harrowing of hell is the "key" to understanding what Ratzinger means by "encounter" in the real, existential experiences of today. The hellish anguish of absence caused by sin can only be overcome by a presence—a presence encounters the person in his or her anguish:

> "Descended into hell" . . . means that Christ passed through the door of solitude, that he descended into the unreachable and insuperable depth of our condition of solitude. This means, however, that also in that extreme night which no word penetrates, when we will all be like children, banished, weeping, there will be a voice that calls to us, a hand that takes our hand and leads us on. Man's insuperable solitude was overcome from the moment *He* entered it. Hell was beaten from the moment love entered the region of death and the no man's land of solitude was inhabited by him. In his profundity, man does not live by bread. In the authenticity of his being he lives by the fact that he is loved and is himself given the faculty to love. From the moment there is the presence of love in death's sphere, then life penetrates death. . . . In the hopeful certainty that when the hour of extreme solitude comes we will not be alone, we can already, now, presage something of what will happen. And in the throes of our protest against the darkness of the death of God we begin to be grateful for the light that comes to us from this same darkness.[50]

---

48. Brotherton, "Damnation and the Trinity," 127.

49. Ratzinger, *Eschatology*, 93.

50. Ratzinger, "The Anguish of an Absence," Meditation 2. See also Ratzinger, *Eschatology*, 80–103; Benedict XVI, "2007 Easter Vigil Homily."

Jesus Christ, as the Son, and always as Son, abides in perfect relationality with the Father. He may have been cut off from the land of human living, human relationships, but the divine relationality existing in the Holy Spirit between Father and Son is not severed. Therefore, when the Son, continually existing in perfect Trinitarian relationality, enters into death's sphere, "life penetrates death" because "life means communion." Where there is communion, where there is relationship, there is life. This is true, as a hope, not only at the end of life, but even now in the midst of present experiences of solitude. In these, too, one can find light breaking through and the insuperable solitude overcome. For Ratzinger, the encounter with Christ, the Son, is the revelation of God's relationality and love *and* its reception in faith—bursting open the self-enclosed space of the isolated "I" and incorporating that "I" into the expansive "I" of Jesus Christ. This takes place as Christ manifests God's profound "yes" for humanity in the depths of humanity's rejection of this great love and the hell that results from it. In this way, the encounter with Christ means that God's "yes" goes before us and enters into our abandonment as a way of meeting us in the depths and accompanying us on a path of healing known as conversion. The encounter with Christ means the "yes" of God's love meets humanity's "no" to loving relationship/relationality and renders these modes of anti-personalism personal or relational again. If hell is possible in our lives today, and Christ has already descended into it, then these hellish places of life initiated by sin, become privileged places of encounter.

The "New Horizon" of Faith: The Boundless Nature of Christian Conversion

Ratzinger says this encounter with "an event, a person" opens a new horizon. Prior to this encounter, sin sets the horizon by limiting or binding one's existence and locking it in the isolated "I." Sin essentially establishes certain boundaries according to one's own will or one's own perception of things in an attempt at making oneself joyful. Sin partitions off or breaks up relationality for the sake of the "I." Sin isolates the "I," either by one's free choice to cut off or damage relationship, or by becoming the victim of another's sin, another's isolating of the "I" and the cutting off and damaging of relationship.

In cutting off or damaging relationality with God, man freely crafts his own bunker wherein man is the ultimate arbiter of his existence who decides how he lives and what he is willing to change about himself.[51] Dietrich von

---

51. For more on the image of the bunker, though explained in a different context,

Hildebrand (1889–1977) characterizes this position in the "ethical idealist," who is a proponent of personal change, but only in those parts of life determined by the ideals of the idealist, and only up to a certain point. The ethical idealist sets boundaries and "wants to change only in certain respects but without letting the whole of his nature become involved."[52] This attitude betrays a position that is all-too-willing to change, but often by way of a frenetic, self-assertion for the sake of amounting to something in the eyes of the world.[53] Attempts to change often become a mere interruption—a particular aspect of life, a habit, a way of being, is interrupted, but, in the end, the person remains unaffected. This is not the Christian position. Again, contra Rahner, Ratzinger distinguishes Christianity according to its call for ongoing *metanoia*, constant renewal, and a "readiness to change" that is boundless in "its utter radicality."[54] Hildebrand notes that the boundlessness of Christian conversion differs from the manner in which the world conceives of conversion—from the limited horizon of the ethical idealist. In contradistinction to the self-imposed boundaries of the idealist, Ratzinger says, "To be a Christian, one must change not just in some particular area but without reservation even to the innermost depths of one's being."[55]

For the sinful man, for the ethical idealist of our day, the Other, and others lie outside the limited and limiting horizon caused by sin and selfishness. Conversion alone overcomes this diminished and shrunken horizon, because conversion means latching onto the activity something bigger, someone "above," who can break open self-imposed bounds to the possibility of a light which lies outside of their own meager flame. Faith requires trusting in something other than what one can grasp or make "on his own," so to speak. Faith demands an about-turn involving one's whole person—"a

---

see Benedict XVI, "The Listening Heart." Here, he says, "In its self-proclaimed exclusivity, the positivist reason which recognizes nothing beyond mere functionality resembles a concrete bunker with no windows, in which we ourselves provide lighting and atmospheric conditions, being no longer willing to obtain either from God's wide world. And yet we cannot hide from ourselves the fact that even in this artificial world, we are still covertly drawing upon God's raw materials, which we refashion into our own products." Elsewhere, Ratzinger says that man "must turn around to recognize how blind he is if he trusts only what he sees with his eyes. . . . Belief *is* the conversion in which man discovered that he is following an illusion if he devotes himself only to the tangible," and "it remains a turn that is new every day," a "lifelong conversion" (Ratzinger, *Introduction*, 51).

52. Ratzinger, *Principles*, 61. Here, Ratzinger is quoting from Hildebrand's *Transformation in Christ*.

53. Ratzinger, *Principles*, 61–62.

54. Ratzinger, *Principles*, 61. See also John Paul II, *Veritatis splendor*, §88.

55. Ratzinger, *Principles*, 60.

perishing of the mere self and precisely thus a resurrection of the true self."[56] Christian conversion, therefore, bears within it a boundless quality—it breaks open of self-imposed boundaries on one's personhood on all sides by the One who knows no bounds.

Ratzinger finds in St. Paul's *apologia pro vita sua* a profound explication of conversion. For Paul, conversion is nothing short of an exchange of "I's" in Gal 2:20: "It is no longer I who live, but Christ who lives in me." Ratzinger comments:

> This one phrase, like a sudden bolt of lightning, reveals in its light the inner event which took place in those outer events and which lies at their very foundation [cf. Gal 1:11—2:19]. This inner event is at one and the same time wholly personal and wholly objective. It is an individual experience in the highest degree, yet it declares what the essence of Christianity is for everyone. To explain it as meaning that becoming and being a Christian rest upon conversion would still be much too weak a way of putting things.... The Pauline sense is something much more radical than, say, the revision of a few opinions and attitudes. It is a death-event. In other words, it is an exchange of the old subject for another.[57]

"Faith is a perishing of the mere self and precisely thus a resurrection of the true self," Ratzinger says elsewhere.[58] Christ is the "new 'I' which bursts open the limits of subjectivity and the boundaries dividing subject from object, thus enabling me to say: 'It is no longer I who live.'"[59] Here, one sees a movement from the opening of the closed and isolated "I" to the "closing on," or "putting on" the radically open "I" of Christ. This exchange is more than the simple revision of opinions and attitudes. One gives over his "I," lays it to rest, so to speak, for the sake of the new "I."[60]

---

56. Ratzinger, *GCC*, 26.
57. Ratzinger, *Nature and Mission*, 50–51.
58. Ratzinger, *GCC*, 26.
59. Ratzinger, *Nature and Mission*, 58–59.
60. Ratzinger, *Nature and Mission*, 51. See also Ratzinger, *GCC*, 26; Ratzinger, *Yes of Jesus*, 35–38, 103. In *Principles*, Ratzinger identifies points of similarity and contrast between the biblical understanding of conversion (*metanoia*) and Greek thought. For the Greeks, in order for man to be himself, he must constantly turn away from external matters and turn within. If one turns to his innermost depths and penetrates deeply enough, he will access the divine in himself, "that, to be truly himself, man, as a whole, has need of a comprehensive movement of conversion and self-communion" (Ratzinger, *Principles*, 59). Instead, biblical belief, according to Ratzinger, is more critical and radical in that it does not only criticize that which man engages with externally, but the impurity that lies in man's interior as well. The whole of man, the external and

All said, the encounter with Christ could be described as a "death-event." In reality, it is a triple-death event. First, the sinful human subject finds him or herself subject to the reality of death, before which he or she is ultimately powerless.[61] Second, Christ gives himself freely over to death. As described above, this initiates an encounter between the Son who exists in the pure relationality of God (being-from, being-for, being-with) and the hell of the already isolated "I," leading into the third dramatic movement. The third movement arrives in the person's acceptance of Christ amid his hell, thus putting death to death by death. Ratzinger says, "The Christian dies into the death of Christ himself ... [uniting] the constantly experienced dispossession of self with the fundamental attitude of being created for love, a being that knows itself to be safe precisely when it trusts in the unexacted gift of love."[62] For the sinful individual, faith means willingly relinquishing one's icy grip on him or herself, by receiving the love of God and entrusting himself to it. In effect, this is, as Ratzinger says, "an exchange of the old subject for another. The 'I' ceases to be an autonomous subject standing in itself. It is snatched away from itself and fitted into a new subject. The 'I' is not simply submerged, but it must really release its grip on itself in order to then receive itself anew in and together with a greater 'I.'"[63]

The encounter initiated by God confronts the radical opposition to God within man, an opposition that damages the very nature of person-as-relation, and reconstitutes the person as such in an act of faith whereby the person receives relation and thereby allows God to burst the confines of the isolated "I." The "death-event" that is Christian conversion, when yielded to, knows no bounds as the "I" opens on all sides—a new and boundless horizon. In the exchange of "I's," Christian existence means being "put with Christ into the category of relationship." It means becoming a son in the Son, but for John, "Son" means "being from another ... being from another and for others [i.e., because the Father is being-for], as a being that is completely open on both sides," who "knows no reserved area

---

the internal, stands in need of salvation. Therefore, biblical conversion demands one to turn away from himself and toward "the God who calls" (Ratzinger, *Principles*, 60). He continues, "Man is oriented, not to the innermost depths of his own being, but to the God who comes to him from without, to the Thou *who reveals himself to him and, in doing so, redeems him*" (Ratzinger, *Principles of Catholic Theology*, 60; emphasis added). Christian faith is "turning" the whole of oneself in response to the God who reveals himself in Jesus Christ. Only in the "turning," only in the act of faith, is there revelation, redemption. The personal character of Christian faith is its most distinctive feature.

61. Ratzinger, *Eschatology*, 95–96.
62. Ratzinger, *Eschatology*, 97.
63. Ratzinger, *Nature and Mission*, 51.

of the mere 'I.'"⁶⁴ Elsewhere Ratzinger says, "being a Christian means essentially changing over from being for oneself to being for one another ... leaving behind the seclusion and tranquility of his 'I' [and departing] from himself in order by this frustration [*Durchkreuzung*] of his 'I' to follow the crucified Christ and exist for others."⁶⁵

Faith is the "yes" to the "You" of God in Jesus Christ, which opens into the "We" of the Trinity and which makes accepting the "we" of humanity possible. This is possible not because of the individual's devices but as a gift of communion.⁶⁶ The bursting open of anti-relational boundaries and stepping into boundless relationality is the "explanation of Christian existence." Ratzinger says, "being a Christian means being like the Son, becoming a son; that is, not standing on one's own and in oneself, but living completely open in the 'from' and 'toward.' Insofar as the Christian is a 'Christian,' this is true of him. And certainly such utterances will make him realize to how small an extent he is a Christian."⁶⁷ Christianity means placing Christ at the center of life, "so that our identity is marked essentially by encounter, by communion with Christ and with his Word.... [Then,] every other value is recovered and purified from possible dross."⁶⁸ Elsewhere, Ratzinger adds, "Communion with God is true reality, and by comparison with it everything, no matter how massively it asserts itself, is a phantom, a nothing.... Communication with God *is* reality, ... more real, even, than death itself."⁶⁹ The encounter with Christ becomes the "substance," so to speak, of one's existence. This encounter changes everything. It recovers, transforms, and purifies every value, every desire in one's life—breaking open boundaries and changing life forever.

Conversion of the Christian sort requires a certain "fluidity of existence," which is, however, the opposite of the contemporary "cult of constant activity." The Christian life requires an ongoing readiness to be changed by

---

64. Ratzinger, *Introduction*, 186.

65. Ratzinger, *Introduction*, 252–53. See also Benedict XVI, *Jesus, the Apostles, and the Early Church*, 116.

66. One this point, Ratzinger notes that conversion can only "be bestowed upon one by the 'not-I' and can never be achieved solely in the interiority of one's personal decision." The point of the exchange is that the "not-I" breaks open the bonds established by the "I." If the "I" were the one who initiated and undertook the exchange on its own, it would be illogical and absurd, because it would "still be the 'work' of the individual subject, thus confirming his hopeless self-imprisonment." Here, we anticipate the role of the Church in objectively making faith in Jesus Christ possible. See Ratzinger, *Nature and Mission*, 52.

67. Ratzinger, *Introduction*, 187.

68. Benedict XVI, *Jesus, the Apostles, and the Early Church*, 111.

69. Ratzinger, *Eschatology*, 89.

Christ, as the "I" must be broken open again and again due to the gravitational pull of "interest, of egoism," which is "always the one most 'natural' to him, . . . the more plausible way of acting."[70] In this sense, "the malleability of his existence must not decrease but increase," and that "truth remains always a way, a goal—that it never becomes something wholly one's own."[71] *Deus semper maior*. How is this boundless conversion possible? Following Ratzinger, I believe one can identify two key "ingredients" for boundless *metanoia*: (1) *pistis*, faith; and (2) forgiveness.

Perhaps paradoxically, Ratzinger, following Hildebrand, concludes that Christian readiness-to-change, ongoing conversion, or *metanoia*, is "to all intents and purposes, identical with *pistis* (faith, constancy)."[72] *Pistis* makes *metanoia* possible, and *metanoia* opens the person to a more profoundly constant *pistis*. Closing upon the truth revealed and offered in the *Logos* opens the way to boundless transformation. "Faith," as Ratzinger says, "is an orientation of our existence as a whole."[73] Faith is the radical reorientation of existence according to a fundamental relationality. The act of faith, as a personal—or interpersonal—event or exchange is the most personal act of transcendence, "an act of the whole self" wherein "all the energies of our existence go into maintaining it."[74] This means that after one's initial conversion (i.e., "encounter"), one cannot simply jettison the willingness and readiness to change as a past fancy. The gravitational pull of self-interest remains ever-present and in need of being renounced in favor of letting oneself be transformed in Christ. What is needed, then, is neither the self-affirming transcendental experience, nor interruption and its corresponding "open narrative." Neither is personal. The ongoing encounter with Christ and the entrustment of oneself once again to the Other who comes to him in Christ overpowers the gravitational pull of self-interest. Here, in "standing-firm in Christ," a "standing-firm against all tendencies to change that would mold us from below and a sensitive receptivity to every change that would mold us from above," one recommits to *communio*.[75] Ratzinger emphasizes that "The ability to remain constant in the Yes once given requires an unremitting readiness to change—a readiness in which one grows to maturity."[76] Clos-

---

70. Ratzinger, *Principles*, 62–63.

71. Ratzinger, *Principles*, 63.

72. Ratzinger, *Principles*, 62.

73. Ratzinger, *GCC*, 25. Here, he adds, "Faith is not a merely intellectual, or merely volitional, or merely emotional activity—it is all of these things together."

74. Ratzinger, *GCC*, 25.

75. Ratzinger, *Principles*, 62.

76. Ratzinger, *Principles*, 64.

ing on the truth, then, actually makes metanoia possible because it marks the Copernican revolution—the self ceases its isolating orbit around itself, an orbit that can be interrupted by the "other," and instead orbits around the Other, the Son, the ground of its existence.[77] Contra Boeve, it is in the *closing* of the "I" of Christ, or of allowing one to be completely possessed by the "I" of Christ (cf. Gal 2:20), that one becomes completely open, because uniting with the completely open "I" of Christ breaks open the bounds of one's own "I," however painfully and slowly.

When it comes to conversion and ongoing conversion, Ratzinger discusses forgiveness in addition to *pistis*. The relational nature of sin, its ramifications both personally and communally, reveal the deep need for constant reform through forgiveness.[78] Ratzinger explains, "Forgiveness, together with its realization in me by way of penance and discipleship, is first of all the wholly personal center of all renewal. But because forgiveness touches the very core of the person, it gathers men together and is also the center of the renewal of the community."[79] The finite human being cannot overcome his or her sinful offense committed against the infinite God. Finitude cannot bridge the gap; the sinful human being cannot propitiate God. As we have seen, God initiates this healing process. God forgives. In this way, and, in fact, only in this way, can one overcome the seemingly infinite chasm caused by sin. In a simple, yet striking commentary on the healing of the paralytic, Benedict XVI drives this point home:

> Forgiveness for sins [is] the foundation of all true healing.... Man is a relational being. And if his first, fundamental relationship is disturbed—his relationship with God—then nothing else can be truly in order. This is where the priority lies in Jesus' message and ministry: before all else, he wants to point man toward the essence of his malady, and to show him—if you are not healed *there*, then however many good things you may find, you are not truly healed.[80]

---

77. See Ratzinger, *What It Means*, 70, 73.

78. This said, Ratzinger is quick to note the line in the liturgy spoken by the priest each Mass, "look not on our sins, but on the faith of your Church." The understanding behind this line is simple, "everybody in the Church, with no exception, had to confess himself a sinner, beseech forgiveness and then set out on the path of his real reform. But this in no way means that the Church as such was also a sinner. The Church ... is a reality that surpasses, mysteriously and infinitely, the sum of her members" (Ratzinger and Messori, *The Ratzinger Report*, 52).

79. Ratzinger, *CC*, 153. See also Gibson, *The Rule of Benedict*, 301.

80. Benedict XVI, *Jesus of Nazareth: The Infancy Narratives*, 43–44. See also Ratzinger, *The Spirit of the Liturgy*, 21.

One can move towards God again insofar as he or she repents and believes in God's forgiving love that reaches out to embrace the sinner. Thus, the experience of being forgiven, literally, of being given back to oneself as person, of being seen by God as person, as son or daughter again, opens to a way to life, opens a way of loving others. Ratzinger places a particular emphasis on one's awareness of his need for forgiveness, and that this grace of forgiveness, of being forgiven, results in a desire to follow on the way of constant conversion and penance. Conversion through forgiveness and *pistis* marks the way of discipleship.

Christian Discipleship as a "Decisive Direction" —A Path of Healing

The "decisive direction" Benedict XVI describes that, for the one who has encountered Christ, life advances in a decisive direction. The Christian life is a way of life, a way of discipleship. The encounter radically alters one's life through the conversion of one "I" for another, thus inserting the person into the new relational horizon of Christ's radically open "I." This encounter opens for the person a new way of living life; it establishes a new trajectory for being in time due to the about-turn. In his funeral homily for Msgr. Luigi Giussani, Ratzinger draws the connection between the initial encounter with Christ, and discipleship. He says, "Christianity is not an intellectual system, a collection of dogmas, or moralism. Christianity is instead an encounter, a love story; it is an event. . . . To encounter Christ means to follow him. This encounter is a road, a journey."[81] Conversion is a path. It is not a one-time event, but a path of forgiveness—of repentance and belief.[82] Being a Christian is the result of the encounter with Christ, the encounter between divine communion and human isolation, the encounter of the isolated "I" and the "We" of the Father, Son, and Holy Spirit. However, being Christian is an ongoing, ever-deepening encounter. This fact appears within the very history of Christianity, for, as Ratzinger highlights, "In its very earliest beginnings, before the word 'Christian' was coined, the Christian religion was simply called 'the Way.'" To this, he adds that "when Christianity was called 'the Way,' it meant first and foremost that it was a way of living. Faith was not a mere theory; above all it was a 'way,' a *praxis*. . . . Faith included morality, . . . it gave concrete directions for human living."[83] In a recent essay

---

81. Ratzinger, "Funeral Homily," 184–85.

82. See Ratzinger, *New Song*, 188–89; Ratzinger, *Yes of Jesus*, 91–97; Ratzinger, *Dogma*, 126.

83. Ratzinger, "Christian Faith," 199–200.

published in *Western Culture*, Benedict XVI explains that "Christianity has been described from the beginning with the word *hodós* [Greek for "road"]. Faith is a path and a way to live."[84] Christianity is a way of life, or it is nothing at all. It is no mere theory, and it is not a lofty idea. "The knowledge of God is a way," Ratzinger says, "it means discipleship. It is not revealed to an uncommitted, permanently neutral observer but, rather, is disclosed in the measure in which one sets out on the way."[85] The new and boundless horizon, the boundless conversion, the Copernican revolution, becomes possible as one embraces the decisive direction of Christian discipleship that shapes the whole of life.

The decisive direction of discipleship is the living-out of this new horizon; it is the "gradual unfolding of [the] encounter."[86] Ratzinger describes discipleship in *Seek That Which Is Above*:

> Discipleship means accepting the entire path, going forward into those things that are above, the hidden things that are the real ones: truth, love, our being children of God. Discipleship of this kind only happens, however, in the modality of the Cross, in the true losing of self that alone can open the treasury of God and of the earth, that alone releases, as it were, the living wellsprings of the depths and cause the power of real life to stream into this world. Discipleship is a stepping-forward into what is hidden in order to find, through this genuine loss of self, what it is to be a human being. It also means discovering that store of joy of which the world stands in such urgent need. Not only do we have a right, we also have a duty to rejoice, because the Lord has given us joy and the world is waiting for it.[87]

Following Christ does not mean imitating a life that is "past and gone," nor is it an "activism" that turns discipleship into "a program for action with all kinds of compromises and revaluations."[88] Discipleship is not a "beginning" that is eventually transcended, but "is the fulfillment and destination of his life. He always remains a disciple."[89] Hence, discipleship is the process, beginning with encounter and ending with *theosis*, that brings about the healing of the human person, that brings about the freedom of the human

---

84. Benedict XVI, *Western Culture*, 155.
85. Ratzinger, *Dogma*, 87.
86. Benedict XVI, *DCE*, §17.
87. Ratzinger, *Seek That Which Is Above*, 55.
88. Ratzinger, *Seek That Which Is Above*, 54.
89. As quoted in Ratzinger, *The Meaning of Christian Brotherhood*, 62. Here, Ratzinger is quoting directly from Schelkle, *Discipleship and Priesthood*, 24.

person in accord with the truth of the person as a being-from, for, and with. The decisive direction of one's life, one's "new horizon" is a relational reality patterned on the Trinity. Discipleship, then, means learning to live this pattern.

Ratzinger's starting point for understanding discipleship centers around two parallel texts: Mark 3:13–19 and Luke 6:12–16.[90] Here, Jesus calls his disciples, from whom he names the Apostles, and the whole of the call, task, and mission are reflective of the Trinitarian pattern: being-from, being-with, and being-for.

In terms of being-from, both accounts note that Jesus is on the mountain, and Luke explicitly acknowledges that Jesus went up the mountain to pray.[91] In any case, "the hills are the place of Jesus's prayer. They are the place where he is alone, where he turns to the Father."[92] Benedict XVI continues:

> The calling of the disciples is a prayer event; it is as if they were begotten in prayer, in intimacy with the Father. The calling of the Twelve, far from being purely functional, takes on a deeply theological meaning: Their calling emerges from the Son's dialogue with the Father and is anchored there. . . . You cannot make yourself a disciple—it is an event of election, a free decision of the Lord's will, which in its turn is anchored in his communion of will with the Father.[93]

Disciples come *from* Jesus Christ's communion with the Father. Disciples are borne from the union of wills in the singular person of Jesus Christ, the Son of God, who is perfectly united with the Father. One cannot make himself a disciple—it is an event of election, an encounter initiated by the Lord, an invitation extended by the Father through the Son. One can only become a disciple as the result of Jesus' prayer, and one can only come to know who Jesus is as the disciple who is invited to participate in his prayer.[94]

The text from Mark's Gospel proceeds with a double-assignment: the Twelve are tasked "to be with him, and to be sent out to preach."[95] This seems to be contradictory at first glance. Ratzinger points out the difficulty, saying, "Either, one could say, Jesus wants them to form his entourage and

---

90. See Benedict XVI, *Jesus I*, 170–82; Benedict XVI, *Jesus, the Apostles, and the Early Church*, 14; Ratzinger, *Behold the Pierced One*, 18; Ratzinger, *Ministers of Your Joy*, 82–90.

91. See Benedict XVI's note on this point in *Jesus I*, 170.

92. Ratzinger, *Ministers of Your Joy*, 83.

93. Benedict XVI, *Jesus I*, 170.

94. See Ratzinger, *Behold the Pierced One*, 25–27.

95. Benedict XVI, *Jesus I*, 172.

always to accompany him; or he wants people he can send out who then will of course only be with him from time to time. If we transpose this question into the terminology of a later age, then one would say that here the monastic, contemplative vocation and the apostolic vocation seem to be intertwined."[96] Being-with and being-for must hold together in the life of the disciple. On this rather paradoxical point, he says:

> Being with Jesus and being sent by him seem at first sight mutually exclusive, but they clearly belong together. The Apostles have to learn to be with him in a way that enables them, even when they go to the ends of the earth, to be with him still. Being with him includes the missionary dynamic by its very nature, since Jesus' whole being is mission.[97]

Being with Jesus provides the Apostles with a safe haven, such that when they are sent to the ends of the earth, they remain, they abide in the security of knowing and being known by Christ. Said another way, being with Christ enables the Apostles to remain faithful to Him throughout their mission. Remaining with Jesus conforms the life of the disciple to the obedience of the Son, who, as *Logos*, unites both wills (human and divine) "in one assent to the will of the Father, that the communion between human and divine being is consummated. . . . The act of participation in this filial obedience, as truly effecting a change in man, is at the same time the only effective action that truly has power to change and renew society."[98]

The first "assignment," then, has to do with learning how to be-with Christ at all times. Benedict XVI says:

> They must be with him in order to get to know him; in order to attain that intimate acquaintance with him that could not be given to the "people"—who saw him only from the outside and took him for a prophet, a great figure in the history of religions, but were unable to perceive his uniqueness (cf. Matt 16:13–20). The Twelve must be with him so as to be able to recognize his oneness with the Father and thus become witnesses to his mystery. . . . One might say that they have to pass from outward to inward communion with Jesus.[99]

Discipleship marks this movement from the "outside" to the "inside" that is initiated by the encounter with Jesus Christ as the event of election by

---

96. Ratzinger, "In the Beginning Is Listening," 86.
97. Benedict XVI, *Jesus I*, 172. Cf. Ratzinger, *Ministers of Your Joy*, 86.
98. Ratzinger, *Pilgrim Fellowship*, 81–82.
99. Benedict XVI, *Jesus I*, 172.

which one begins the process of discipleship. Discipleship is the process of becoming a witness. Ratzinger calls the Twelve "eye-witnesses," and "ear-witnesses."[100] Being with Christ means participating in his inner life, in his prayer. Ratzinger claims that "since the center of the person of Jesus is prayer, it is essential to participate in his prayer if we are to know and understand him."[101] If the central act of the person of Jesus is prayer, "of unbroken communication with the one he calls 'Father,'"[102] then it is "only possible really to understand this person by entering into this act of prayer, by participating in it."[103] Ratzinger explains, "Only by entering into Jesus' solitude, only by participating in what is most personal to him, his communication with the Father, can one see what this most personal reality is; only thus can one penetrate to his identity. This is the only way to understand him and to grasp what 'following Jesus' means."[104] Being *with* Jesus implies a process of conversion, whereby one's will, indeed, one's entire person, is conformed to the Son, in whose incarnation, the union of the human and divine wills brings about the reconciliation of mankind with God.[105] Abiding in Christ makes possible the genuine passing-over of oneself, which is the nature of what it means to be human.[106]

Entering into the prayer of Jesus Christ is what Ratzinger means by the call to "be with" Jesus. One must enter into Jesus' communication with the Father in order to truly "see" Jesus, to "know" Jesus, as the Son. In order to be a witness, one must "be with" Jesus Christ in his communication, as

100. Ratzinger, *Ministers of Your Joy*, 87.

101. Ratzinger, *Behold the Pierced One*, 25. See also Biliniewicz, *The Liturgical Vision*, 9–10; Ratzinger, *The Feast of Faith*, 18–22.

102. Ratzinger, *Behold the Pierced One*, 26.

103. Ratzinger, *Behold the Pierced One*, 26.

104. Ratzinger, *Behold the Pierced One*, 19; see also 26.

105. It is worth noting here that Ratzinger takes up Constantinople III in both dealing with spiritual Christology directly (see Ratzinger, *Behold the Pierced One*, 32–42) and in his application of spiritual Christology to the Eucharist (see Ratzinger, *Pilgrim Fellowship*, 80–81). The relationship should be clear. The spiritual Christology of Constantinople III attempts to reveal the center of Jesus' person as prayer, i.e., the union of his human will with his divine will in the one divine Person. If discipleship marks the entry of the person, spiritually, into the life of Christ (i.e., spiritual Christology), then the Eucharist marks the *concrete* entry of the person into the Person of Christ. In the giving and receiving of the Eucharist by Christ and the Church, respectively, the individual participates in the Paschal Mystery whereby his will is purified and conformed to that of Christ's. For more on spiritual Christology, see Bonagura, "Joseph Ratzinger/Benedict XVI's Christology of Jesus' Prayer," 287–306; Hahn, *Covenant and Communion*, 143–45); Butler, "Benedict XVI," 144–67; Riches, "After Chalcedon," 201–11; McGregor's *Heart to Heart*.

106. See Ratzinger, *Seek That Which Is Above*, 55.

Son, with the Father. This said, being-with is also Ratzinger's descriptor for the Holy Spirit. Being with Jesus is being with Him in and through the Holy Spirit, and being with Jesus in his prayer means entering, with Him, into that life of the Spirit that is His *communio* with the Father. Mission bears forth from being with Jesus in the Holy Spirit, and, here, one can begin to grasp the spiritual depth of what Paul VI means when he calls the Holy Spirit the "principal agent of evangelization."[107]

As a final point in this treatment of discipleship as a living expression of being-with: Jesus does not call an isolated disciple. Discipleship is not a privatized event. Instead, Jesus calls together the many disciples, and from there, creates an even more intimate family that "is in principle intended to be universal. . . . This 'we' of the new family is not amorphous. Jesus calls an inner core of people specially chosen by him, who are to carry on his mission and give this family order and shape."[108] Therefore, in being called by Christ's prayer to enter into Christ's prayer, a transformation occurs on two levels. Vertically, discipleship refers to relationship with God through Jesus Christ. However, in discipleship, being-with does not only extend between Jesus and the disciple, but between disciples themselves. Horizontally, then, discipleship refers to the fact that God calls many people by name, drawing them into relationship with one another in himself, in his body. Therefore, discipleship always contains a social dimension—that is, being-with the other disciples—by its very nature.

Finally, Christian discipleship marks the dynamic entry into Jesus' pro-existence. Benedict XVI develops the connection between Christian discipleship and pro-existence rather poignantly in *Jesus of Nazareth: Holy Week*, when he says:

> Recent theology has rightly underlined the use of the word "for" in all four accounts [of the Last Supper], a word that may be considered the key not only to the Last Supper accounts, but to the figure of Jesus overall. His entire being is expressed by the word "pro-existence"—he is there, not for himself, but for others. This is not merely a dimension of his existence, but its innermost essence and its entirety. His very being is a "being-for." If we are able to grasp this, then we have truly come close to the mystery of Jesus, *and we have understood what discipleship is*.[109]

As noted above, the Son, as Son (i.e., being-from), receives as His own the Father's "being-for." In His mission as the Father's ambassador, the Son

---

107. Paul VI, *Evangelii nuntiandi*, §75.
108. Benedict XVI, *Jesus I*, 169.
109. Benedict XVI, *Jesus II*, 134; emphasis added.

reveals the Father ("being-for") to humanity. This singular identification of Son with the Father highlights the union for which discipleship calls and the mission in which discipleship shares. The disciple is one who is not for oneself, but who exists, with Christ, for others.

To summarize, Discipleship is basically an exercise in living the resurrected life. Resurrected life means abiding in another's eternally loving affirmation, abiding in an eternal communion. This life is one of abiding communion in Christ's transformed body "where men enter into communion with God and with one another and are thus able to live definitively in the fullness of indestructible life." Benedict XVI continues, saying that while we cannot conceive of resurrected life perfectly, it does indicate that "an ontological leap occurred, one that touches being as such, opening up a new dimension that affects us all, creating for all of us a new space of life, a new space of being in union with God."[110] The life of discipleship is essentially a road, a way of anthropological healing in union with Christ, that alters one's pattern of being from being for oneself to being from, being with, and being for.

Conclusion

Christian faith marks the explicit reception of God's gift of revelation, his *Logos*—Son—Love, in an encounter that restores the person as such and makes joy, and, therefore, makes love possible. "Faith is a supremely personal act," Ratzinger says.[111] It is the entirely personal act, carried out by the receiving subject in response to the initiative of the *Logos* in Jesus Christ. Ratzinger calls it "an orientation of our existence as a whole," an orientation that requires "all the energies of our existence to go into maintaining it. Faith is not a merely intellectual, or merely volitional, or merely emotional activity—it is all of these things together. It is an act of the whole self, of the whole person in his concentrated unity."[112] Msgr. Frank Lane describes this reality as follows:

> Logos as Person is, therefore, essential for Ratzinger for "Word" is not a book but a whole person who is ontologically God and existentially Human. To know Christ, is to solve the theological problem of the intelligibility of being that is not a purely rational process nor a completely existential encounter or experience. The whole person encounters the inner structure of all reality as

110. Benedict XVI, *Jesus II*, 274.
111. Ratzinger, *GCC*, 25.
112. Ratzinger, *GCC*, 25.

a person and therefore relationally. The receiving subject therefore knows both directly and through reason the God who gives himself to us in the total revelation of his son.[113]

Faith is not an act of an "individual substance of a rational nature" grasping propositions rationally. Nor is it an implicit transcendental experience. Instead, Christian faith describes an event of relationship—a personal encounter—between the *Logos* and the receiving subject that reconstitutes the "I" according to the "not I" of Christ.

At the bottom of it, the encounter with Christ initiates the violent process of surrendering a self-made, self-created understanding of life and of man, and accepting, being suspended by, or standing firmly upon meaning offered by the *Logos*. Faith cancels out the closed reality of the isolated "I" precisely by closing in on the completely open "I" of Christ. The encounter marks the beginning of a process of *metanoia*, ongoing conversion, that is nothing other than the life of discipleship, a life of anthropological healing and rehabilitation according to the Trinitarian pattern of being-from, being-with, and being-for.

In light of a Ratzingerian "theology of encounter," one can see both points of convergence and divergence with Rahner's and Boeve's theologies. For Rahner, transcendental anthropology highlights the openness of the person toward Being, but the main thrust of the effort assumes implicit faith and drives a certain self-acceptance that reaches its culmination in anonymous Christianity. Here, the "self" need not change at all, but must merely accept its "self" as a transcendental "self." Conversely, for Ratzinger, faith is an act of personal transcendence, wherein transcendence has to do with personal encounter—encountering the other person, and in so doing, being drawn out of the self and into communion, thus coming to oneself. Ratzinger says that precisely because faith is a personal act, "it transcends the self," because "where man as a whole comes into play, he transcends himself; an act of the whole self is at the same time always an opening to others, hence, an act of being together with others."[114] Here, Ratzinger's concept of transcendence outpaces Rahner's, which emphasizes the self-transcending quality of human consciousness, but its ability to get outside of conscious awareness is questionable. Ratzinger goes on to point out that self-acceptance is only possible, truly, because an Other accepts the self and, in that acceptance, and only in that acceptance, can one accept himself. However, doing so, in believing in the love of an Other, means the pulverizing of all forms of egoism and the idealism of selfish attempts

---

113. Lane, *Reflections*, 28.
114. Ratzinger, *GCC*, 25.

at self-acceptance. Encounter, properly speaking, means conversion and it implies a path of healing which mere self-acceptance could never initiate. Boeve's theology of interruption rightly acknowledges the need of the "other." However, interruption is merely interruption. It implies that a narrative path has only been impeded temporarily by the other, before it continues, though it does so with a heightened awareness of its own fragility and hegemonic tendencies. With Ratzinger, we are not talking about the mere continuation of the same narrative, but the beginning of a new narrative, in a certain sense. The encounter with Christ initiates a new narrative according to a new Author. Now one does not grasp for meaning amongst deconstructed human words but can live open and free in the one Word spoken by God and encountered today with the same effect as that Word had on Peter, James, John, the Samaritan woman at the well, Mary Magdalene, and the criminal on the cross next to His. This Word did not merely interrupt their lives, He radically changed them and led them down a path of ongoing conversion and healing.

CHAPTER ELEVEN

Evangelization as a Participation in the "Yes" of God

Despite all that has been said about revelation, faith, and loving relationality, the Trinitarian personalism that drives Ratzinger's understanding of these realities, one significant question remains: How is the Christian event, which is an interpersonal exchange, possible today? What allows for the encounter with Christ, conversion in him, and the opening of the path of discipleship today? As Ratzinger puts the question, "How can the cross of the Lord come through to me from history so that I am able to experience the living reality that Pascal perceived in his meditation on the Lord on the Mount of Olives: 'I shed those drops of blood for you?'"[1] How is the encounter with Christ possible today, two thousand years after Jesus walked the face of the earth? How does history mediate God's self-revelation? How is Christian joy possible today? Giussani puts the question as follows, "By what method can I reasonably adhere to the Christian proposal?"[2] Is the encounter with Christ a totally private affair? Rahner and the Rahnerians proposed transcendental experience as the means by which the Resurrected consciousness of Christ meets us today, and Boeve recontextualizes the question of Christ according to a radical hermeneutics. But, what about Ratzinger?

In following this inquiry, the present study dives headlong into this book's practical dealings with the second significant question. Recall that the first question had to do with the catechetical landscape after Vatican II. The second deals with Ratzinger's assessment of this landscape *and* his response to it. Following a lengthy treatment on Ratzinger's assessment and some basic elements of his fundamental theology, we are now poised to develop a Ratzingerian structure of proclamation—principles for approaching evangelization—both in terms of its content and method.

1. Ratzinger, *Yes of Jesus*, 101–2.
2. Giussani, *Why the Church?*, 10.

The Encounter with Christ and the Sacramental Structure of the Church

How can the person of Christ be encountered today? Giussani, whose thought bears a certain resemblance to that of Ratzinger's, notes that three cultural attitudes give rise to three different answers to the question. First, a rational view, shaped by an historical-critical approach to Christian history and its Scriptures, collects sources and then classifies, evaluates, and analyzes the sources in an attempt to gain certainty about the historical facts—to come into contact with the "historical Jesus." Such an approach takes "that concept of reason which sees reason as the measure of all things," and determines that the "ultimate reason for things is one our reason gives them." Giussani argues that this position ends up "projecting dimensions . . . onto reality and whatever presumes to go beyond these measures *does not exist* by an a priori definition."[3] In other words, the rationalistic approach that takes human reason as the measure for all things devolves into a deterministic position that precludes certain possibilities, especially divine ones. Giussani concludes that the "rationalistic attitude *diminishes the content of the Christian message even before taking it into consideration*."[4] A second position emerges in an opposite cultural position that recognizes the limitations of human reason. Human reason cannot possibly "grasp" God, so God becomes a presence and allows himself to be experienced. Thus, "the spirit of God itself . . . enlightens the heart, and inspiring it, makes one 'feel' the truth of the person of Jesus," Giussani says. "It is recognition by means of an inner experience."[5] Giussani calls this the fulcrum of the Protestant attitude that encourages a sincere interior encounter, a direct relationship with the Spirit. In the arena of Catholic catechetics, this position emerges as a driving force within Moran's work, for example. Such an approach provokes a few questions. How can one possibly know if what one "feels" is the result of a prompting of the Spirit or simply the consequence of one's own thoughts? Why would the one Spirit's attempt to help man result in so much confusion, so many denominational positions? Ultimately, Giussani believes both the rational position and the Protestant position share the same common denominator in an "ultimate subjectivism."[6]

Giussani argues that a third approach to Christ can be found in the Orthodox-Catholic view. This position aligns with how the Christian event

---

3. Giussani, *Why the Church?*, 13.
4. Giussani, *Why the Church?*, 14.
5. Giussani, *Why the Church?*, 17.
6. Giussani, *Why the Church?*, 19.

presents itself in history, where "something distinctly objective educated man's subjectivity."[7] Giussani continues, "The existence of this entirely human presence implies the method of *encounter*, of the chance meeting with a reality external to the self, an objective, eminently 'encounterable' presence that, while 'outside' of the self, moves the heart. (The word 'encounter' has an exterior connotation just as decisive as the interior one.)"[8] Ratzinger describes the interplay in the encounter with Christ, the interplay between objective and subjective, exterior and interior, in a similar manner. He argues that the encounter with Christ involves exchanging subjects. Hence, it involves a passive aspect on the part of the receiving subject; the encounter with Christ does not result from the person's activity, or from one's initiative. Instead, it is an event marked by a certain passivity on the part of the receiving subject—his or her receptivity. Ratzinger says, "For his 'salvation' man is meant to rely on receiving."[9] Man's salvation (i.e., the restoration of his relationship with God) does not come about from his own resources, from one's own planning or speculation, but "demands the positivity of what confronts us, what comes to us as something positive, something to be received . . . the intrinsic necessity of the apparently historical contingency of Christianity can be shown, the 'must' of its—to us—objectionable positivity as an event that comes from outside."[10] No one can undertake the encounter himself. No one can make it happen for himself as a perfectly private effort. It cannot be manufactured by one's own devices. As Ratzinger says, "No one can undertake on his own the exchange of subjects spoken of by St. Paul. Such an attempt would be illogical and absurd. . . . The exchange would still be the 'work' of the individual subject, thus confirming his hopeless self-imprisonment."[11] The isolated "I" cannot, by his own isolated attempt, un-isolate himself. He cannot actively overcome his self-imprisonment by himself. He must be aided by another.

Today, this encounterable, objective presence, meets men and women in the Church.[12] Ratzinger corroborates, saying, "What takes place is a sacramental event, hence, an event involving the Church."[13] Here, the Church assumes the active role, while the individual remains passive. The Church,

7. Giussani, *Why the Church?*, 20.
8. Giussani, *Why the Church?*, 20.
9. Ratzinger, *Introduction*, 267.
10. Ratzinger, *Introduction*, 268–69.
11. Ratzinger, *Nature and Mission*, 52.
12. Giussani is careful to note that this third attitude does not devalue the other positions. Indeed, it finds within each of them aspects worthy of affirmation. See Giussani, *Why the Church?*, 23–26.
13. Ratzinger, *Nature and Mission*, 52.

at work in "the unity of believers as a single subject," manifests the great love of God concretely and historically as the "body of Christ."[14] Ratzinger "locates" in the Church and in her sacraments the continuing incarnational presence of Jesus within the world, the concrete and contemporary "other." In this way, God still initiates, God still takes the initiative and acts while the person who is coming to believe remains passive. Here, Ratzinger touches on two sacramental realities as part of one whole when it comes to the encounter with Christ and its contemporaneity: (1) the Sacrament of Baptism itself; and (2) the Church as "sacrament of salvation."[15] Delving too deeply into Ratzinger's ecclesiology or his sacramental theology would take us far afield. However, framing his understanding of evangelization and catechesis, our purpose here, requires a brief treatment of these areas.

Baptism as *the* Encounter with Christ

In a certain sense, the Sacrament of Baptism is, itself, the sacramental structure of encounter. In other words, the definitive, objective encounter with Christ takes place in baptism. Benedict XVI describes the baptismal nature of the encounter with Christ, as he describes St. Paul's encounter:

> With these words [in Gal 2:20], Paul is not describing some mystical experience which could perhaps have been granted him, and could be of interest to us from a historical point of view, if at all. No, this phrase is an expression of what happened at Baptism. My "I" is taken away from me and is incorporated into a new and greater subject. This means that my "I" is back again, but now transformed, broken up, opened through incorporation into the other, in whom it acquires its new breadth of existence. Paul explains the same thing to us once again from another angle . . . in Chapter Three of the Letter to the Galatians . . . You have become one in Christ (cf. Gal 3:28). Not just one thing, but one, one only, one single new subject. This liberation of our "I" from its isolation, this finding oneself in a new subject means finding oneself within the vastness of God and being drawn into a life which has now moved out of the context of "dying and becoming". The great explosion of the Resurrection has seized us in Baptism so as to draw us on. Thus we are associated with a new dimension of life into which, amid the tribulations of our day, we are already in some way introduced. To live one's own life as a continual entry into

14. Ratzinger, *Nature and Mission*, 52.
15. Second Vatican Council, *Lumen gentium*, §48.

this open space: this is the meaning of being baptized, of being Christian. . . . The Resurrection is not a thing of the past, the Resurrection has reached us and seized us. We grasp hold of it, we grasp hold of the risen Lord, and we know that he holds us firmly even when our hands grow weak. . . . I, but no longer I: this is the formula of Christian life rooted in Baptism, the formula of the Resurrection within time. I, but no longer I: if we live in this way, we transform the world.[16]

For Ratzinger, the encounter with Christ is a sacramental event with a sacramental structure. The exchange between the "I" and the "not-I" cannot be achieved in the subjective interiority of personal decision or awareness. This real encounter, this transformative, objective exchange is something like the opposite of the view explored earlier, which attempts to view everyone as essentially Christian via rendering every transcendental experience an act of implicit faith. Instead of this anonymous and implicit approach, as Ratzinger points out, the encounter "has a sacramental structure. The 'I no longer live' does not describe a private mystical experience but rather defines the essence of baptism."[17] Baptism is the encounter with Christ—the definitive, objective encounter with the Paschal Mystery—and our incorporation therein—whereby the "yes" of God in Jesus Christ encounters one, breaking open the bounds of his or her isolated "I" and offering in its place a new, open "I" in a boundless conversion experience that opens into a life known as Christian discipleship. The Sacrament of Baptism makes the Paschal Mystery present, while at the same time drawing the person into its Mystery—it immerses or inserts the person into the Paschal Mystery. Baptism marks the death of the isolated "I" and the reception of the "not-I," an entirely new and wide open "I." Life as a baptized Christian means living in this open space created by the encounter, by the conversion; it means living discipleship.[18] For Ratzinger, Baptism stands as the definitive, paradigmatic encounter with Jesus Christ—a mystery prevenient and generative. It is *the* definitive, objective encounter with Christ made possible through the ministry of the Church. All other encounters either move toward this encounter, or they are the discovery of the repercussions of the encounter throughout the whole of one's life.

---

16. Benedict XVI, "2006 Easter Vigil Homily."
17. Ratzinger, *Nature and Mission*, 52.
18. See Ratzinger, *Introduction*, 335.

The Church and the Encounter

That the encounter with Christ has a sacramental structure—it is a sacramental, objective reality—ties it directly to the Church, the sacrament of salvation. Again, the baptismal encounter with Christ is a decisively objective and personal event or reality, and yet it is one which involves the whole Church and the whole of her tradition. God is a concrete, objective subject one encounters. This, it seems, is the consistent Scriptural testimony, for "only the concrete God can be something other than a new projection of one's own self."[19] In God's revelation of the *Logos* in Jesus Christ, "the one who became flesh has remained flesh. He is concrete. . . . [And] the Church is that new and greater subject in which past and present, subject and object come into contact. The Church is our contemporaneity with Christ: there is no other."[20] Or, as Ratzinger says, "The Church is by her essence the mediation of the living presence of the word of God in the world, the 'tent of the word.'"[21]

To develop his argument about the role of the Church in the encounter with Christ, Ratzinger leans on St. Paul's Letter to the Romans. Here, Paul describes Baptism as the committing of oneself to the subject of the Church. In Rom 6:17, Paul says, "Thanks be to God, that you who were once slaves of sin have become obedient from the heart to the standard [*typos*] of teaching to which you were committed." Ratzinger, in a 1979 homily, notes that obedience from the heart is not a form of servile submission or fear, and that, for Paul, "the opposite of slavery or lack of freedom is not the complete absence of limitations or commitments."[22] It is obedience, a willful listening and responding to an authority—one who encourages growth. The Christian is to be obedient from the heart, but obedient to what authority? For Ratzinger, this is the key. He says:

---

19. Ratzinger, *Nature and Mission*, 59.
20. Ratzinger, *Nature and Mission*, 60.
21. Ratzinger, *Il nuovo populo*, 162, quoted in Guerriero, *Benedict XVI*, 140. Lorenzo Albacete captures this point in all its existential profundity, when he says: "To believe that one becomes a Christian through proper philosophy, theology, spirituality, morality, or a cultural project, is a presumption; it is to see our efforts as the cause of our belonging to Christ. Instead, we become Christians because the Incarnation happened in history, because the Paschal Mystery happened, because Pentecost happened and because those events continue to happen in the world today. They happen now because they happened then and because the Church exists in the world as the life of a communion of persons created by these events, and making them present today through the sacraments" (Albacete, "The Key to the Christian Life").
22. This homily is quoted in Schönborn, *Jesus' School of Life*, 115.

> Obedience has a very specific content: Paul relates it to the "*typos* of teaching to which you were committed." Here the apostle is referring . . . to the profession of faith [the Creed] or else to a catechetical formulation of the teaching that is the content of baptism. . . . Tradition is not committed to the newly baptized person, but rather the newly baptized person is committed to the tradition. It does not become his property, which he can shape arbitrarily, but rather he becomes its property. It is the larger form that shapes him, and not the other way around.[23]

Balthasar reflects similarly upon the same chapter from St. Paul. He says, "Christ's dying for us is presented as an *a priori* of the Christian attitude," and that "this objective *a priori* element in Christ's action has its effect on Christian baptism, which, independently of any subjective belief, objectively postulates a state of being dead and buried with Christ." For Paul, "the existential attitude of the Christian should be shaped and determined by this *a priori* element."[24] Though speaking on another topic, that is, *communio*, Ratzinger offers an insight regarding Acts 2:42 that further supports this idea of obedience to the tradition, to the teaching of the apostles. He says, the four concepts of Acts 2:42 appear in two sets, with communion linked with apostolic teaching, for "Church unity is unthinkable without 'remaining in the teaching of the apostles,' that is, in the apostolic structure of the Church."[25] More emphatically, though deeply connected to Balthasar's point, he adds, "In order to remain in unity with the crucified and risen Lord, the practical sign of juridical unity, 'remaining in the teaching of the apostles,' is indispensable."[26] The apostles, who have authority of interpretation, give the norm—their teaching—to the newly baptized, or, rather, the newly baptized is given over to it.

One would do well to note that distinct differences appear between the Balthasar-Ratzinger position, and those who embrace the Rahnerian blueprint. For one, Rahner's *a priori* lies in the nebulous concept of the supernatural existential that has been "christologized," so to speak. This allows the vulgarized Rahnerians to definitively develop theories and methods based upon implicit faith, in which there is no real need for the objective encounter with Christ or the tradition. Boeve's *testator* theory also collapses before the standards listed in Acts and in St. Paul's letter.

---

23. Again, quoted in Schönborn, *Jesus' School of Life*, 115–16. Ratzinger makes the same point in *Nature and Mission*, 53.
24. Balthasar, *The Moment of Christian Witness*, 23.
25. Ratzinger, *Pilgrim Fellowship*, 67; Ratzinger, *GCC*, 30.
26. Ratzinger, *Pilgrim Fellowship*, 69.

The Christian is not the *testator*, who receives tradition, tests it (in light of the context), and decides which of its contents to keep, discard, or modify. No. For Paul, the reverse is true. The person is committed to the tradition, and, in being obedient to it, the person, the Christian is tested and purified. Tradition tests the person, the receiving subject. Tradition determines which of the aspects of the person (i.e., his or her personality, to be sure, but also customs, cultural traditions, ways of thinking, etc.) can be kept, discarded, or modified. Here, the role of the Church, and her faith, appears rather strikingly. It is not the Church that is entrusted to those who are baptized, as if they are now free to shape her according to their will, but the converse. The Church always stands as that greater subject, that "we" into whom individuals become constitutive parts, but always a subject who is the Lord's. Perhaps this latter point becomes clear in Paul's ecclesiology in 1 Cor 12:12. Here, Paul says, "As a body is one though it has many parts, and all the parts of the body, though many, are one body, so also Christ." Paul does not say the Church is this body with many parts, rather, he says it is "Christ" himself. Here, Ratzinger points out that Paul does not see the Church as "a separate subject endowed with its own subsistence," instead, "the Church is nothing but the space of this new unitary subject, which is, therefore, much more than social interaction."[27] The Church, a unitary subject in communion with Christ, comprises those who are entrusted to her in Baptism and who are obedient to the Tradition.

We have already established that faith is profoundly personal, meaning it is "an act of communication" that always refers to another and implies a relationship of trust.[28] Faith means believing *in* Jesus Christ, that his testimony (i.e., that He is the Son of God) is true. However, when it comes to a relationship with God, faith does not exist in a pure experience of "I-Thou." Instead, on either side, faith contains a "we-dimension," in that God is a Trinity of persons, and that human beings exist always and everywhere in the we-dimension, because no one can live alone, nor can anyone believe alone.[29] In regard to the "we" of the Trinity, Ratzinger says:

> This trinitarian "we," the fact that even God exists only as a "we," prepares at the same time the space of the human "we." The Christian's relation to God is not simply, as Ferdinand Ebner claims somewhat one-sidedly, "I and Thou," but, as the liturgy prays for us every day . . . through Christ in the Holy

---

27. Ratzinger, *Nature and Mission*, 54. This is not to say tradition does not develop. See, for example, Ratzinger, *In the Beginning*, 14–15.

28. See Ratzinger, *Yes of Jesus*, 35–36.

29. See Ratzinger, *GCC*, 25–26. See also Ratzinger, "Notion of Person," 117.

> Spirit to the Father. Christ, the one, is here the "we" into which Love, namely the Holy Spirit, gathers us and which means simultaneously being bound to each other and being directed toward the common "you" of the one Father.[30]

One encounters the "we" of God (i.e., the three persons in one God), one believes in the "we" of God, in and through one's encounter with, and one's standing in the "we" of the Church. It is true, then, that faith means one believes in Jesus Christ, that He is the Son of God. However, this vision of Jesus, Jesus' vision of the Father, comes to human beings in a "secondhand" fashion. One believes in Jesus Christ because of and as a response to the Church's belief in Jesus Christ and her enduring testimony of such belief. By its very nature, "faith involves other people: it is a breaking out of the isolation of my ego that is its own illness."[31]

Ratzinger engages the story of the Samaritan woman to illustrate the crucial role of the Church in the transmission of the testimony. The Samaritan woman encounters and interfaces with Jesus "firsthand," so to speak, at the well, and then leaves and tells the whole town about this Jesus. The townspeople believe in Jesus because of her testimony; they believe, initially, "secondhand" (cf. John 4:39–42).[32] The Samaritan woman, here, is an icon of the "we" of the Church, that body of believers who have encountered the Lord and through whose testimony, and in whose testimony, others come to encounter Him. In other words, to the formula "I believe *in* Jesus Christ, *that* He is the Son of God" must be added "I believe *in* the Church, *that* her testimony about Jesus is true," because it is through the Church that the testimony reaches humanity today, making faith in Jesus possible. Both aspects of belief—which could be described as the "I" and the "we"—are essential. The "'I' of the 'I believe,'" Ratzinger says, "is not absorbed but allotted its place" in the "We believe" of the Church.[33] To this, Benedict XVI adds:

> Profession of faith is an act both personal and communitarian. It is the Church that is the primary subject of faith. In the faith of the Christian community, each individual receives baptism, an effective sign of entry into the people of believers in order to obtain salvation. As we read in the *Catechism of the Catholic Church*: "'I believe' is the faith of the Church professed personally by each believer, principally during baptism. 'We believe' is the faith of the Church confessed by the bishops assembled in

---

30. Ratzinger, "Notion of Person," 117.
31. Ratzinger, *Yes of Jesus*, 36.
32. See Ratzinger, *Yes of Jesus*, 32.
33. Ratzinger, *Introduction*, 90.

council or more generally by the liturgical assembly of believers. 'I believe' is also the Church, our mother, responding to God by faith as she teaches us to say both 'I believe' and 'we believe.'"[34]

The mediation of faith in the Father through Jesus, and its secondary mediation through the Church, means that no individual can build his or her own bridge to the divine, but receives it as God's own gift of himself, mediated through others, through tradition. Hence, faith's contingency on other people breaks me "out of the isolation of my ego ... breaking down the door of my subjectivity."[35] This is precisely what Paul refers to in Gal 2:20, wherein his ego is broken open and finds itself again "united not only with Jesus but with everybody who has followed the same path ... churchly faith ... lives and moves in the 'we' of the Church, one with the common 'I' of Jesus Christ.... I cannot build my personal faith in a private dialogue with Jesus. Faith lives in this 'we,' or else it is not alive."[36]

In a certain sense, this "we" dimension, or "communitarian" dimension of faith, manifests what it means when one says one believes "in the Holy Spirit," or, to live life in the Holy Spirit. Ratzinger points out the original Greek text lacks an article, here. The line is simply "I believe in Holy Spirit," and Ratzinger takes this to mean this section of the Creed refers not to the Holy Spirit as the third Person of the Trinity, but to the Spirit as God's gift.[37] This does not preclude a Trinitarian interpretation, but it does prevent a certain division from forming between the gift of the Holy Spirit and the institutional structure of the Church. When one believes "*in* Holy Spirit, the Holy Catholic Church," one finds within the Church the living expression of being *in* the Spirit. Believing is possible precisely *in* the concrete communion of believers animated by the Spirit. The remaining statements of the Creed (i.e., communion of saints and forgiveness of sins), Ratzinger points out, "are to be understood as concretizations of the words about the Holy Spirit, as descriptions of the way in which the Spirit works in history."[38] The Spirit is the "being-with" of the Trinity, the Holy Spirit is *communio*, and it is precisely in this communion, as part of the "we" that one can utter the *credo*, "I believe." In following Pauline theology, Ratzinger identifies the Church as the sacrament, the "concrete" other who is outside and who now comes "in" to meet the individual from the outside, and with and in whom the definite

---

34. Benedict XVI, *Porta fidei*, §10.

35. Ratzinger, *Yes of Jesus*, 36.

36. Ratzinger, *Yes of Jesus*, 36–37; Ratzinger, *Introduction*, 93. Ratzinger also considers the social aspect of the phenomenon of faith in *Yes of Jesus*, 27–30.

37. See Ratzinger, *Introduction*, 331.

38. Ratzinger, *Introduction*, 334.

encounter with Christ in Baptism takes place.[39] The Church, as the "sacrament of salvation," concretely mediates the Word today; she is that "place" of encounter, that tent of meeting. The Church mediates the one *Logos* in time, across time, from generation to generation.

If being a Christian is the result of the encounter with Christ, and Baptism is the ecclesial and sacramental event of encounter, then the whole of the Christian life bears the mark of Baptism. Indeed, it is imbued with Baptism. Baptism shapes the whole of the Christian life, insofar as the encounter with Christ shapes this life. Baptism, then, acts as something of a temporal epicenter in the life of the Christian. The shock of the encounter with Christ—the Christian event cutting across time and made present in Baptism—that breaks open the fault line between the "I" and the "not-I," that rips apart the self-imposed boundaries of the isolated "I," carries within its potency certain foreshocks that anticipate it, and aftershocks as well. Baptism is like a theological earthquake in the life of the Catholic Christian. Baptism is *the* objective, sacramental encounter with Christ anticipated by certain foreshocks (e.g., the catechumenate, the faith of one's parents, etc.) and aftershocks (e.g., the other Sacraments, post-baptismal catechesis, etc.). The theological ripples in time draw the person, through the Church, into the death and resurrection of Christ in Baptism. Abiding in Christ, or living the Christian life as a disciple, means living from the encounter with Christ in Baptism as the very substance of one's existence. In this way, the whole of the Christian life can be seen in a baptismal, or catechumenal light.

The word "catechumen" typically refers to one who is in the process of being initiated into the Catholic faith—the catechumen is one who has not yet been baptized—through a process called the "catechumenate." However, for Ratzinger, in a real sense, the entire Christian life is the life of the catechumenate, the life molded entirely by Baptism—both in terms of the anticipation of Baptism, the actual encounter that takes place in Baptism, and the lifelong repercussions of the encounter. The word catechumen comes from the Greek *katekhoumenos* "one being instructed," and is the passive present participle of the Greek word *katekhein* (catechesis) "to teach orally." The catechumen opens him or herself to instruction, which flows from the Word, anticipating and preparing one for the sacramental encounter. The catechumenate cultivates the receiving subject for the encounter, and, following the sacramental encounter, the catechumenate endures, deepening

---

39. To be clear, when Ratzinger refers to the Church, he refers to "a cosmic breadth," in that the Church "extends beyond the frontier of death" for the communion of saints, those "who through this [Eucharistic] table are united among themselves," are bound together as one in receiving "the one Spirit and his one, life-giving power" (*Introduction*, 334–35). See also Ratzinger, *CC*, 82, 99.

conversion. Ratzinger, therefore, does not limit the catechumenate to a brief period of time in one's life prior to being received into the Church, rather, he associates it with the life of discipleship generated by the encounter with Christ, and the exchange of "I's." The whole of the Christian life is a catechumenal life—a life of journeying in the Holy Spirit with Christ and through Christ to the Father. Furthermore, Ratzinger points out that the whole catechumenate, i.e., the Church's process of bringing someone into *communio* through the baptismal confession of faith, is ordered to Baptism and, therefore, "the catechumenate itself is a part of baptism."[40] The encounter with Christ in Baptism marks the whole of life, meaning the Church exists as "the journeying community of catechumens, a community of both learning and living, in which our eyes are opened as we walk."[41] The catechumenate, then—whether it is pre- or post-baptismal in nature—provides an orientation for whole of the Church's evangelizing mission; evangelization is the Church's response to the catechumenal nature of Christian life.

Evangelization in Light of the Encounter with Christ

A Ratzingerian structure of proclamation, aligned as it is with Ratzinger's fundamental theology, goes by way of relationality. Imbued by charity, evangelization is simply the Church's activity—largely in and through her individual members—of introducing one friend to Another. The relational aspect clearly identifies evangelization as something more than the mere transmission of information. Instead, this word describes an interpersonal event, a process of coming to know and love the Other. The bearing forth of the Church's testimony is a revelational event for the receiving subject— God, insofar as God has revealed himself to mankind, is made known to a new receiving subject who did not know—all flowing from the objectivity of Baptism and leading toward it. The remainder of this chapter will focus on what evangelization is and why it is essential for the Church, before considering how one can approach it in the final chapter.

What is evangelization, exactly? The word "evangelization" etymologically breaks down to "the making/sharing of good news" (*evangel* = "good news/glad tidings" and the root of the word "gospel"; *-ization* = "making or doing").[42] To "evangelize" the world, then, means to "gospel" the world, or to "gospel-ize" the world. The pre-Christian history of that root word Gospel (*evangelium* in Latin, and *euangelisasthai* in Greek) provides tremendous

40. Ratzinger, *Principles of Catholic Theology*, 35.
41. Benedict XVI, "Christmas Greetings 2012."
42. Cf. Kittel, "εὐαγγέλιον," in *TDNT* 2:707–37.

insight into the reality conveyed by the word "evangelization." Benedict XVI explains that Homer utilizes the word as an announcement of victory, "and therefore the announcement of good, joy and happiness."[43] The prophet Isaiah uses the word (see Isa 40:9) in reference to a voice that "announces joy from God, a voice that makes it clear that God has not forgotten his people, that God, who apparently had almost withdrawn from history, it is here, he is present."[44] Here, "gospel" refers to a message of "glad tidings" for the poor, to those who suffer for God's sake."[45] In the Roman Empire, Augustus would take up the word as a message that comes from the Emperor. As such, it is a message that brings good, renewal to the world, salvation, imperial strength, and power.[46] The pre-Christian history of "evangelization" reveals that this word bears significant weight, that it comes from an authority, that it announces that which is to be good for all, and, therefore, that which brings joy. It has a *gravitas* that is more substantial than sharing about a good burger joint or a new Netflix original, even if those are ordinary examples of sharing good news. Benedict XVI explains that these messages from the Roman emperors were saving messages, "not just a piece of news, but a change of the world for the better."[47] In other words, borrowing from linguistic theory, *evangelium* "is not just informative speech, but performative speech—not just the imparting of information, but action, efficacious power that enters into the world to save and transform."[48] The history of the word *evangelium* reveals that both the *source* of the message and its *content* matter—both the *source* and the *content* are significant. At this point one can begin to feel the weight of the Christian "glad tidings."

Jesus' "gospel" challenges the political theology of the Roman empire, for the emperor of Rome did not establish the idealistic utopia about which the imperial gospel speaks. Only God can establish *the* kingdom. In examining the transition from the pre-Christian understanding of "gospel" to its properly Christian status, Ratzinger argues that in the New Testament, the word "Gospel" develops in three stages or layers: (1) Jesus' Gospel; (2) the "gospel" in the Gospels; and (3) Paul's Gospel.

---

43. Benedict XVI, "Meditation 2012." See also Ratzinger, *GCC*, 38–39.
44. Benedict XVI, "Meditation 2012."
45. Ratzinger, *GCC*, 38–39.
46. Benedict XVI, "Meditation 2012." See also Ratzinger, *GCC*, 39; Benedict XVI, *Jesus I*, 46–47.
47. Benedict XVI, *Jesus I*, 47.
48. Benedict XVI, *Jesus I*, 47.

Beginning with Jesus' gospel, insofar as it is transmitted by the evangelists, Ratzinger points out that Jesus links "gospel" with "kingdom of God."[49] Benedict XVI describes the core content of the Gospel in this declarative statement: "The Kingdom of God is at hand." This announcement is a gift offered to mankind that demands a response: repentance and belief (cf. Mark 1:15).[50] Following a lengthy discussion of various interpretations of the expression "kingdom of God" in *Jesus of Nazareth*, Benedict XVI concludes that "kingdom" refers to "God's actual sovereignty over the world," or, more simply, "When Jesus speaks of the Kingdom of God, he is quite simply proclaiming God, and proclaiming him to be the living God, who is able to act concretely in the world and in history and is even now so acting. He is telling us: 'God exists' and 'God is really God.' . . . God is acting now."[51] Benedict XVI argues that the "kingdom of God is God himself." So, when Jesus claims that this kingdom is near, he essentially means to say: "God himself is near. You are near God, he is near you. . . . God is a God who acts. God is not exiled in the 'transcendental' sphere that supposedly separates him from the 'categorical' sphere in which we act and live."[52] This is a clear rebuke of the Rahnerian position. In a 2012 meditation, Benedict XVI adds:

> The New Testament accepts this situation [that of the word's usage in imperial Rome]. St Luke explicitly compares the Emperor Augustus with the Child born in Bethlehem: "Evangelium"—he says—yes, it is the Emperor's word, the true Emperor of the world. The true Emperor of the world has made himself heard, he speaks to us. And this fact, in itself, is redemption because the great suffering of man—then, as now—is this: behind the silence of the universe, behind the clouds of history, is or isn't there a God? And, if this God is there, does he know us, does he have anything to do with us? Is this God good, then does the reality of good have any power in the world or not? This question is as relevant today as it was then. Many people wonder: is God just a hypothesis or not? Is he a reality or not? Why do we not hear him? "Gospel" means: God has broken his silence, God has spoken, God exists. This fact in itself is salvation: God knows us, God loves us, he has entered into history. Jesus is his Word, God with us, God showing us that he loves us, that he suffers with us until death and rises again. This is the

---

49. Ratzinger, *GCC*, 40.
50. Benedict XVI, *Jesus I*, 47.
51. Benedict XVI, *Jesus I*, 55–56.
52. Ratzinger, *GCC*, 40.

Gospel. God has spoken, he is no longer the great unknown, but has shown himself and this is salvation.[53]

In other words, when it comes to Jesus' Gospel, the message is the messenger. The Kingdom appears in Christ. Ratzinger adds, "God is now present and near in a much more radical way. He is present in Jesus himself. The Son is the kingdom."[54] This means Jesus' proclamation did not stand as an expression of mere words. His proclamation was more than mere words, it was sacramental because Jesus words are "inseparable from his 'I'—from his 'flesh.'" Jesus' passion, death, and Resurrection are the culmination of the Gospel, and they are silent events, yet in these silent events, "God's kingdom comes, ever anew," healing, restoring, forgiving, etc.[55] The Christian claim, the Christian event, the Christian *glad tidings* only make sense when one grasps the gravity of the situation caused by sin and death (i.e., the full extent of the "bad news") as examined above. Here, Jesus' gospel message is profoundly simple, "it is a message about the God who is present and who lives within calling distance from us."[56]

In addition to his treatment on Jesus' Gospel, Ratzinger considers the "gospel" in the Gospels. The Gospels themselves are evangelizing, insofar as they introduce men and women into relationship with Christ. These Gospels are not merely books, but "the written record of a proclamation,"[57] and a preeminent one at that. They proclaim the content of Jesus' Gospel. Therefore, one could say "that to evangelize means to acquaint men with Jesus as we come to know him through the Gospels. To evangelize is to introduce men into a communion of life with him as well as into the fellowship of disciples, the community that journeys with him."[58] The Gospels provide something of the benchmark or standard for evangelization. They are the checks and balances for evangelization, part of that enduring "teaching of the apostles" and a key element of the "organs of transmission" that ensure fidelity, ensure *communio*. To evangelize, then, according to the Gospels, is to bring people into contact, today, with the same Jesus of the past, that their life might be moved to live as disciples into the future.

Finally, Ratzinger treats Paul's Gospel, by noting that Paul speaks of "'my gospel,' whereby he expresses the special insight given to him in his encounter with the risen Christ on the road to Damascus, namely, that man

---

53. Benedict XVI, "Meditation 2012."
54. Ratzinger, *GCC*, 48.
55. Ratzinger, *GCC*, 51.
56. Ratzinger, *GCC*, 40.
57. Ratzinger, *GCC*, 51.
58. Ratzinger, *GCC*, 53.

is not justified before God by the works of the law but by faith."[59] This marks a significant development. One need not become Jewish in order to become Christian, but "when I am in communion with Jesus, I live in the kingdom of God."[60] Evangelization makes known a new way of life, life not according to the Law etched in the confines of stone, but its fulfillment in the "Torah in person," in the openness of relationship with God in Jesus Christ.[61] The Gospel transcends culture. Paul's experience becomes something of a model for everyone: "I must have met God in Christ in such a living way that I can 'count as dust' (Phil 3:7) my own cultural provenance, indeed, everything that was important to me in my own history. No studies, however subtle, will produce new cultural forms of Christianity unless they proceed from the liberating power of encounter with Christ."[62]

To evangelize, then, means sharing God who has spoken His definitive "yes" to humanity in Jesus Christ—the revelation of the *Logos* as Son, as Love—in a manner that is in accord with the tradition of the Church, and which has the capacity to become "glad tidings" for this or that individual. To evangelize is to testify to the joy that comes in Jesus Christ, and to do so in such a way that the other might come to encounter this love and to live in this "yes" in such a way that he or she, too, might be joyful (cf. 1 John 1:1–4). Along this line, in his 2000 address to religion teachers and catechists, Ratzinger says:

> Human life cannot be realized by itself. Our life is an open question, an incomplete project.... Each man's fundamental question is this: How will this be realized—becoming man? How does one learn the art of living?... To evangelize means: to show this path—to teach the art of living. At the beginning of his public life Jesus says: I have come to evangelize the poor (Luke 4:18); this means: I have the response to your fundamental question; I will show you the path of life, the path toward happiness—rather: I am that path.[63]

Christianity is a way of living according to the "yes" of God in Jesus Christ, a "yes" that encounters the human being, and which has the capacity to transform the whole of life and to make joy possible. To evangelize, then, means to show someone a new path of life, a way of living in accord with the "yes" of God that encounters humanity in Jesus Christ.

59. Ratzinger, *GCC*, 53.
60. Ratzinger, *GCC*, 54.
61. Ratzinger, *GCC*, 54.
62. Ratzinger, *GCC*, 54.
63. Ratzinger, "The New Evangelization."

This "yes," which comes to man as a gift of God, in the person of Christ and through the Holy Spirit, impels mission. In a certain sense, a disciple of Jesus Christ cannot help but be on mission. Discipleship, as already noted, is missional, and mission, in order to be part of the Christian mission, demands discipleship. Being-with is being-sent, and so forth. For the Christian, the "yes" that has grabbed hold of his or her whole existence, that frighteningly personal "yes," is also the same terribly personal "yes" offered by God to others. If one "participates" in this "yes" in a personal way, meaning embracing it as his or her own, then one "participates," so to speak, in the offering of the "yes" to others. This is the result that great transformation of the "I" resulting from the exchange of "I's" that takes place in the encounter with Christ. Now, living in this new "I," the "other is no longer a stranger at all for me: he is part of me. Christ wishes to use my faculties and capabilities for him, even when a purely human natural attraction does not exist. Now I can give him Christ's 'yes' that fills my life as my own 'yes' and yet his."[64] This great "yes" of God in Jesus reveals to men and women that they were not made for hell—for the non-communication zone—but for *communio*. Evangelization means participating in the mission of the *Logos*' "yes" to humanity.

The life of St. Paul, who is something of a model evangelist for Benedict XVI, makes this basic movement clear. Paul claims that he is set apart in service of the Gospel (cf. Rom 1:1). He cannot help but be set apart for the sake of the Gospel. When it comes to evangelization, the "protagonist is not man, but God, the breath of the Holy Spirit, that impels the Apostle on the highways of the world to bring the Good News to everyone: the promises of the Prophets are fulfilled in Jesus, the Christ, the Son of God, who died for our sins and was raised for our justification. Saul is no longer, instead there is Paul, indeed there is Christ who lives in him (cf. Gal 2:20) and wants to reach out to all people."[65] Earlier in his theological career, Ratzinger speaks of the "dramatic personalization Paul accomplishes in these words" of Gal 2:20, that "the Son of God loved *me* and gave himself up for *me*." Humanity is not an indistinct and indistinguishable mass before God. No:

> In all truth, Christ walked his path for me. This certainty is a grace given to accompany me in all the stages of my life, in my successes and failures, in my hopes and my suffering. He did all that he did for me and for every man who crosses my path in life: Jesus loved him, too, and gave himself up for him, just as he loved and loves me still. When we have learned to believe this

---

64. Ratzinger, *Yes of Jesus*, 103.
65. Benedict XVI, "Homily for the Solemnity of Sts. Peter and Paul."

again, when we are able to announce it to others as the message of truth, evangelization takes place. Then we know that the kingdom of God is near. And this knowledge gives us the strength to live and act out of this nearness.[66]

Compelled by the Spirit, Paul participates in the "yes" that God offers to all. Indeed, "an essential part of the Christian faith is the fact that it is meant to be handed on. It consists of coming to know a message that concerns everyone, because it is the truth and because man cannot be saved without the truth."[67] For this reason, Ratzinger can point out:

> Becoming a Christian simply means giving our assent to this movement [of the "yes"] and putting ourselves at its service.... Becoming a Christian is not ... something given to us so that we ... can pocket it and keep our distance from those who are going off empty-handed. No: in a certain sense, one does not become a Christian for oneself at all; rather, one does so for the sake of the whole, for others, for everyone.[68]

Evangelization is an expression of this service. At the bottom of it, evangelization is an exercise of charity.

What Is the New Evangelization?

Within ecclesiastical circles, the words "new evangelization" are common parlance. In a certain sense, one might even call them buzzwords. Their precise meaning, however, often remains unclear—as does its origin, and so forth.[69] What is certain, however, is that the New Evangelization is a critical part of the Vatican II-era church, and its promotion was a central impulse of Benedict XVI during his papacy.[70] Benedict XVI describes the New Evangelization with a noteworthy clarity. He says:

> The term, "new evangelization" recalls the need for a renewed manner of proclamation, especially for those who live in a

---

66. Ratzinger, *GCC*, 71.
67. Ratzinger, *Handing on the Faith*, 13.
68. Ratzinger, *What It Means*, 54. See also Ratzinger, *Introduction*, 249.

69. Benedict XVI notes certain points of the development, with roots in Vatican II and the teachings of Paul VI, before being formalized in the thought of John Paul II. See Benedict XVI, *Ubiqumque et semper*; Benedict XVI, "Homily for the Solemnity of Sts. Peter and Paul."

70. For example, Benedict XVI established a Pontifical Council for the New Evangelization. See Benedict XVI, *Ubiqumque et semper*.

context, like the one today, in which the development of secularization has had a heavy impact, even in traditionally Christian countries. . . . Highlighting that at this moment in history, the Church is called to carry out a *new* evangelization, means intensifying her missionary action so that it fully corresponds to the Lord's mandate.[71]

Two critical points emerge, here. On the one hand, the New Evangelization refers to the new, post-Christian context appearing within cultures once imbued with Christianity, but which now bear only vestiges of it. Benedict XVI describes the context as a "current crisis" that:

Brings with it traces of the exclusion of God from people's lives, from a generalized indifference towards the Christian faith to an attempt to marginalize it from public life. . . . Today . . . we are witnessing a drama of fragmentation which no longer acknowledges a unifying reference point [i.e., Christianity]; moreover, it often occurs that people wish to belong to the Church, but they are strongly shaped by a vision of life which is in contrast with the faith.[72]

Elsewhere, Benedict XVI identifies the "dynamics [of] the secularization process" as the cause of "a serious crisis of the meaning of the Christian faith and of belonging to the Church."[73] In 2000, Ratzinger described this emerging context as caused by a "progressive process of de-Christianization and a loss of the essential human values."[74] In the midst of this context, Benedict XVI notes, the Church's mission "has been particularly challenged by an abandonment of the faith—a phenomenon progressively more manifest in societies and cultures which for centuries seemed to be permeated by the Gospel."[75] As a plain fact, the faith is no longer "a self-evident presupposition for life in society." Instead, this presupposition is often "openly denied." Benedict XVI continues, noting that "in the past it was possible to recognize a unitary cultural matrix, broadly accepted in its appeal to the content of the faith and the values inspired by it," however "today this no longer

---

71. Benedict XVI, "Address to Participants in the Plenary Assembly." See also Second Vatican Council, *Ad gentes*, §6. For more on the new evangelization, see Rymarz, "The New Evangelization," 24–27.
72. Benedict XVI, "Address to Participants in the Plenary Assembly."
73. Benedict XVI, "Homily for the Solemnity of Sts. Peter and Paul."
74. Ratzinger, "The New Evangelization," I.1.
75. Benedict XVI, *Ubiqumque et semper*.

seems to be the case in large swathes of society, because of a profound crisis of faith that has affected many people."[76]

On the other hand, the New Evangelization refers to a "renewed manner of proclamation" and "intensifying her missionary action." It is true that today, "a large part of today's humanity does not find the Gospel in the permanent evangelization of the Church," which is precisely why, as Ratzinger puts it, "we are searching for . . . a new evangelization, capable of being heard by that world that does not find access to 'classic' evangelization. Everyone needs the Gospel . . . and this is why we are obliged to look for new ways of bringing the Gospel to all."[77] "We cannot accept that salt should become tasteless or the light be kept hidden (cf. Matt 5:13–16)," Benedict XVI says.[78] Instead, the Church must "propose anew the perennial truth of Christ's Gospel."[79] In a certain sense, Benedict XVI identifies a similarity between the pre-Christian world of the early Church, and the contemporary post-Christian one. As a result, he calls for an apostolic impulse:

> There is a dynamic continuity between the proclamation of the first disciples and ours. Throughout the centuries, the Church has never ceased to proclaim the salvific mystery of the death and Resurrection of Jesus Christ, but today that same message needs renewed vigour to convince contemporary man, who is often distracted and insensitive. For this reason, the new evangelization must try to find ways of making the proclamation of salvation more effective; a proclamation without which personal existence remains contradictory and deprived of what is essential.[80]

This apostolic impulse, this new evangelization, does not imply "that a single formula should be developed that would hold the same for all circumstances."[81] The methods and approaches of the New Evangelization will vary based upon the concrete context in which the local church carries out the mission. What is common in the New Evangelization throughout the Church, however, is "a renewed missionary impulse, an expression of a new, generous openness to the gift of grace," for "we cannot forget that the first task will always be to make ourselves docile to the freely given

---

76. Benedict XVI, *Porta fidei*, §2. Boeve makes the same point in describing the "factual overlap" at play in present-day Europe.
77. Ratzinger, "The New Evangelization," I.1.
78. Benedict XVI, *Porta fidei*, §3.
79. Benedict XVI, "Homily for the Solemnity of Sts. Peter and Paul."
80. Benedict XVI, "Address to Participants in the Plenary Assembly."
81. Benedict XVI, *Ubiqumque et semper*.

action of the Spirit."[82] Similarly, in his 2000 address to catechists, Ratzinger claims that "we are in need of a new evangelization—if the art of living remains an unknown, nothing else works. But this art is not the object of a science—this art can only be communicated by [one] who has life—he who is the Gospel personified."[83] The profundity of such a statement, of such a call, that is, to personify the Gospel, must be unpacked further, and it will be in the next chapter on method. For now, however, we will turn our attention to Ratzinger's treatment of catechesis, that critical moment within a process of evangelization.

Catechesis as a "Moment" in a Process of Evangelization

Catechesis (from the Greek *katekhein*) means "to sound from above," "to recount something to someone," "to inform," "to teach," "to instruct someone." Paul uses the word exclusively in the sense of "to give instruction concerning the content of faith."[84] It is a form of the ministry of the word and an "essential moment" within the process of evangelization.[85] It is the activity which can simply be "understood as promoting communion with Jesus Christ."[86] Ratzinger captures the essence of catechesis, saying "the essential task of catechesis is to lead to the knowledge of God and of the One whom he has sent, or, as the *Roman Catechism* advisedly says: to remind people of this knowledge, for it is written in the deepest part of each and every one of us."[87]

While catechesis remains a distinct moment within evangelization, there should be no bifurcation between evangelization and catechesis, as if catechesis is that which dries up the vivacity of the *kerygma* (i.e., the basic Gospel message). Emphasizing the need for a unified understanding of catechesis and the proclamation of the Gospel, John Paul II adds:

---

82. Benedict XVI, *Ubiqumque et semper*.
83. Ratzinger, "The New Evangelization."
84. Kittel, "κατηχέω," in *TDNT* 3:638.
85. John Paul II calls catechesis an "essential moment" within evangelization, making reference to the Sacred Congregation for the Clergy, *General Catechetical Directory*, §17–18; Paul VI, *Evangelii nuntiandi*, §17–24, 45. John Paul II notes that "there is no separation or opposition between catechesis and evangelization. Nor can the two be simply identified with each other." See John Paul II, *Catechesi tradendae*, §18; Pontifical Council for the Promotion of the New Evangelization, *Directory for Catechesis*, §31–37.
86. *GDC*, §80.
87. Ratzinger, *Handing on the Faith*, 27.

> Through catechesis the Gospel kerygma ... is gradually deepened, developed in its implicit consequences, explained in language that includes an appeal to reason, and channeled towards Christian practice in the Church and the world. All this is no less evangelical than the kerygma, in spite of what is said by certain people who consider that catechesis necessarily rationalizes, dries up and eventually kills all that is living, spontaneous and vibrant in the kerygma.[88]

The primary proclamation of the Gospel is a ministry of the word that addresses itself to "nonbelievers and those living in religious indifference," and "its functions are to proclaim the Gospel and to call to conversion."[89] Catechesis builds upon this primary proclamation and "presupposes a global adherence to Christ's Gospel as presented by the Church."[90] It "promotes and matures initial conversion" and "educates the convert in the faith and incorporates him into the Christian community."[91] Situated within the process of evangelization:

> Catechesis is that particular form of the ministry of the word which matures initial conversion to make it into a living, explicit and fruitful confession of faith.... He who is converted to Jesus Christ and recognizes him as Lord through the primary proclamation of the Gospel begins a process which, aided by catechesis, necessarily leads to explicit confession of the Trinity.[92]

---

88. John Paul II, *Catechesi tradendae*, §25.

89. *GDC*, §61.

90. *General Catechetical Directory*, §18. While this is true by way of proper definition for catechesis, in reality it is quite often the case that many participants in catechetical programs within the Church have not yet given personal adherence to Jesus Christ. In light of this, the *General Catechetical Directory* notes that evangelization can both "precede or accompany the work of catechesis proper," and that "in any case ... one must keep in mind that the element of conversion is always present in the dynamism of the faith, and for that reason any form of catechesis must also perform the role of evangelization." Other magisterial documents attuned to the present cultural situation and the often "blurry" lines between the moments of primary proclamation and catechesis, call for a "new evangelization," characterized by "kerygmatic catechesis" or "pre-catechesis." The *GDC*, §62, notes, "Only by starting with conversion, and therefore by making allowance for the interior disposition of 'whoever believes,' can catechesis, strictly speaking, fulfill its proper task of education in the faith." The *National Directory for Catechesis*, §19.A, states, "In many situations ... catechesis must also be concerned with arousing initial faith and sustaining the gradual conversion to complete adherence to Jesus Christ." See also John Paul II, *Catechesi tradendae*, §19.

91. *GDC*, §61.

92. *GDC*, §82.

John Paul II describes catechesis as the "teaching and maturation stage," that "endeavors to know better this Jesus to whom he has entrusted himself."[93] With greater emphasis, John Paul II says, "the definitive aim of catechesis is to put people not only in touch but in communion, in intimacy, with Jesus Christ: only He can lead us to the love of the Father in the Spirit and make us share in the life of the Holy Trinity."[94] Catechesis promotes intimate communion through knowing and loving more profoundly this Jesus Christ, through whom one comes to the Father in the Holy Spirit. Catechesis leads people into intimate communion with Christ by "maturing the initial faith and of educating the true disciple of Christ by means of a deeper and more systematic knowledge of the person and the message of our Lord Jesus Christ."[95]

Ratzinger, too, views conversion as a process, a process of evangelization in which catechesis plays a key part. It is a catechumenal journey, so to speak, and Benedict XVI describes this process insofar as it appears in the calling of two of John the Baptist's disciples (John 1:35-39):

> First of all, we have the simple act of proclamation. John the Baptist points towards Jesus and says: "Behold the Lamb of God!" ... The first and fundamental element is the straightforward proclamation, the kerygma, which draws its strength from the inner conviction of the one proclaiming. In the account of the two disciples, the next stage is that of listening and following behind Jesus, which is not yet discipleship, but rather a holy curiosity, a movement of seeking. Both of them ... are seekers ... [and] stimulated by the proclamation, their seeking becomes concrete. ... The third act is set in motion when Jesus turns round, approaches them and asks: "What do you seek?" They respond with a further question, which demonstrates the openness of their expectation, their readiness to take new steps. They ask: "Rabbi, where are you staying?" Jesus' answer "Come and see!" is an invitation to walk with him and thereby to have their eyes opened with him. The word of proclamation is effective in situations where man is listening in readiness for God to draw near, where man is inwardly searching and thus on the way towards the Lord. His heart is touched when Jesus turns towards him, and then his encounter with the proclamation becomes a holy curiosity to come to know Jesus better. As he walks with

---

93. John Paul II, *Catechesi tradendae*, §20.
94. John Paul II, *Catechesi tradendae*, §5.
95. John Paul II, *Catechesi tradendae*, §19.

Jesus, he is led to the place where Jesus lives, to the community of the Church, which is his body.[96]

An unspoken initial stage exists, here. It is the disciples' time with John the Baptist that prepares their hearts, that cultivates the "inward searching." Second, comes the primary proclamation of the Gospel followed by the curiosity that seeks after the Lord. Finally, discipleship, a catechumenal life lived with Jesus in the community of the Church. For Ratzinger, then, evangelization is a reference both to the whole process of both initial conversion brought about through a primary proclamation of the *kerygma*, and of ongoing conversion and being brought more and more deeply into the *communio* of God through the *communio* of the Church. Catechesis is "secondary," not in a sense of being less essential, but in terms of the movement of deepening communion from initial conversion to ongoing conversion. In any case, both evangelization and catechesis are not reducible to the handing on of extrinsic truths which are ratified by faith, but of fostering an initial and ongoing encounter and relationship with the Truth, Jesus Christ, and entry into the Way of life that is marked by the Gospel.[97]

Ratzinger on Catechesis

For his part, Ratzinger, in typical *ressourcement* fashion, traces the biblical-historical evidence of the word "catechize" and notes that it does not appear at all in the Septuagint. Paul is the first to give the word permanent significance for the Church.[98] Catechesis results from his apostolic activity, with the most significant passage appearing in Gal 6:6 with reference of the catechumen and the catechist[99] Luke-Acts also uses the word to describe Apollos, a man who is "'catechized' in the way of the Lord" (Acts 18:25).[100] Luke also writes his Gospel to Theophilus, "in order that the latter might come to know the trustworthiness of the words and realities (*logōn*) in which he has been catechized."[101] Yet it is the case that the "term 'catechesis' takes second place to 'gospel,' which remains the basic word."[102] Echoing Paul VI and John Paul II, Ratzinger holds that catechesis becomes necessary within

---

96. Benedict XVI, "Christmas Greetings 2012."
97. For more on Christianity as "Way," see Ratzinger, "Christian Faith," 199–200.
98. Ratzinger, GCC, 38.
99. Ratzinger, GCC, 56.
100. Ratzinger, GCC, 56.
101. Ratzinger, GCC, 56.
102. Ratzinger, GCC, 55.

the process of evangelization, and that evangelization moves into catechesis, which "aims at coming to know Jesus concretely. It is theoretical and practical initiation into the will of God as revealed in Jesus and lived by the community of the Lord's disciples, the family of God."[103] Throughout Ratzinger's discussion of catechesis, five distinctive points become clear and are worth exploring at length: (1) the ties between catechesis and the baptismal catechumenate; (2) catechesis as instruction; (3) the experiential and existential nature of such instruction; (4) the essential role of community in catechesis; and (5) the need for a catechism.

Baptism as the Objective Core of Catechesis

First, and not surprisingly, catechesis is clearly tied to the catechumenate—that process whereby one comes to know Jesus concretely in the Sacrament of Baptism. As previously noted, a catechumen is one who is instructed, one who is being instructed with specific regard to the sacraments of Christian initiation. Ratzinger views the catechumenate, and, by extension, all of catechesis, as an integral part of the sacrament of Baptism itself.[104] Ratzinger considers this insight tremendously important:

> On the one hand, it reveals the catechumenate as something quite different from religious instruction as it is generally understood. . . . On the other hand, the sacrament is not just a liturgical act but a process, a long road that demands an individual's whole strength, mind, will and heart. Here, too, the separation [between catechumenate/catechesis and sacrament] has had disastrous consequences. It has led to a ritualization of the sacrament and a doctrinalization of the word.[105]

The catechumenate is motivated by and, in a certain sense, anticipates the encounter with Christ at Baptism. It is as if the grace of one's Baptism extends in time as one whole movement consisting of both the catechumenate and Baptism itself.

Additionally, the catechumenate can and does extend beyond Baptism itself in the other direction. Post-baptismal catechesis re-proposes the Person of Jesus Christ and the objective, personal encounter one had with him in the sacrament of baptism. Perhaps for this reason, the *General Directory for Catechesis* claims that "in order that the parish may succeed in activating

---

103. Ratzinger, *GCC*, 56.
104. Cf. *CCC*, §1229–32.
105. Ratzinger, *Principles*, 36.

effectively the mission of evangelization . . . adult catechesis must be given priority. This involves 'a post-baptismal catechesis, in the form of a catechumenate, . . . presenting again some elements from the *Rite of Christian Initiation of Adults* with the purpose of allowing a person to grasp and live the immense, extraordinary richness and responsibility received at Baptism.'"[106] "Post-baptismal" catechesis "derives from the sacraments of initiation which were received as infants, 'who have been already introduced into the Church and have been made sons of God by means of Baptism. The basis of their conversion is the Baptism which they have already received and whose power they must develop.'"[107] Post-baptismal catechesis should be enriched by the principal elements of the baptismal catechumenate, namely, "comprehensiveness and integrity of formation; its gradual character expressed in definite stages; its connection with meaningful rites, symbols, biblical and liturgical signs; its constant references to the Christian community."[108] Joseph Ratzinger notes the importance of such catechesis when he says, "even if we were baptized as children, we must enter into the reality of our baptism; throughout our lives—in various stages, of course—we must enter into this initiation to communion with Christ in the Church . . . this fundamental experience of the Church."[109] This objective reality, this experience of encounter with the Other who sacrificed himself for each of us, personally, means that each of us owes our whole being to him, or, as Balthasar puts it, "the only way to express my thanks is with my whole being."[110] Baptism is this event whereby Christ's whole sacrifice personally touches the whole being of the catechumen and invites that person's complete response—a response that must be made, a response that must be penetrated with greater depth of understanding and more profound willingness throughout the course of one's life. This painful process of giving one's entire self to Christ is one that, for many, spans the whole of life.

Catechumenal Instruction

The catechumenate is a time of instruction—flowing from the intellectual dimension of the Gospel, which appeals to man's reason. What content does such instruction engage? The catechumenate teaches the baptismal formula

---

106. *GDC*, §258. For more on post-baptismal catechesis at the service of ecclesial renewal, see Bursa, "Provoking Renewal," 159–77.

107. *GDC*, §90.

108. *GDC*, §91.

109. Ratzinger, *New Outpourings*, 67.

110. Balthasar, *The Moment of Christian Witness*, 24.

or creed, the profession of which, at baptism, presupposes a long learning process and a response in the triple *metanoia* of prayer, morality, and sacramental living.[111] However, the Gospel does not solely appeal to the intellect; it is a way of life. Therefore, "the actual living out of this doctrine [taught through instruction] is an essential component of [catechesis], and man's intellect sees properly only when the heart is integrated into the mind."[112] Faith is not a theory, and revelation is not a list of propositions—it is an interpersonal event that shapes life according to a relationship. Before Christianity acquired its name, it was simply called "the Way," which means it was, and is, fundamentally a *praxis*.[113] It is not a *praxis* devoid of content, however, but a *praxis* derived from the Paschal Mystery that has concrete implications, including moral ones for the way in which one lives life. For this reason, the text of the creed itself cannot merely be studied as if its cognitive apprehension is the only prerequisite for initiation into Christianity, but that the text itself must be put into practice as "the expression of a definite existential orientation."[114] In other words, a kind of dynamism between doctrine and life appears: the meaning of the text of the creed only becomes fully apparent to the extent that one follows the way in which it points, and the way is knowable through the text of the creed.

Therefore, for Benedict XVI, catechesis and the experience of the catechumenate (whether pre- or post-baptismal) cannot remain a purely intellectual, speculative, or propositional affair. Insofar as catechesis introduces a person to a "definite existential orientation," it could be said that catechetical activity introduces and apprentices a person down the experiential path that is Christianity—the Way.

The Experiential Character of Catechesis

The third distinctive point in Ratzinger's conception of catechesis appears in its experiential character. Benedict XVI adds, "In the Church's most ancient tradition, the process of Christian formation always had an experiential character. While not neglecting a systematic understanding of the content of the faith, it centered on a vital and convincing encounter with Christ, as proclaimed by authentic witnesses. It is first and foremost the witness who introduces others to the mysteries. Naturally, this initial

---

111. See Kevane, *Catechesis in Augustine*, 43; Kevane, "Introduction," xvi–xvii.
112. Ratzinger, *GCC*, 56–57.
113. See Ratzinger, "Christian Faith," 199–200.
114. Ratzinger, *Principles*, 35.

encounter gains depth through catechesis."[115] One could liken this to swimming. One cannot simply read about swimming and learn to swim, as if it were possible on one's own. Instead, one learns the art of swimming from another who already knows the way and can show that way to the novice. Likewise, catechesis is an "existential training in existence with God."[116] And, as any person striving to faithfully live the vows of his/her baptism, this "existential training" is not something mastered (or master-able, perhaps), in this life. In this sense, every Christian, whether baptized or about to be (for those in RCIA right now), is a catechumen.

This kind of existential training deepens following Baptism, in the immediate form of post-baptismal catechesis known as mystagogy. Mystagogy is that stage in the process of the Rite of Christian Initiation for Adults immediately following the reception of sacraments that marks one's formal entry into the Church. It refers to a process whereby one comes to a deeper understanding of the sacramental mystery one has experienced in order to become more personally conformed to the mystery being celebrated.[117] In other words, mystagogy is an experience of constant renewal. For his part, Benedict XVI holds that mystagogical catechesis should respect three elements:[118] (1) "*It interprets the rites in the light of the events of our salvation*, in accordance with the Church's living tradition.... From the beginning, the Christian community has interpreted the events of Jesus' life, and the Paschal Mystery in particular, in relation to the entire history of the Old Testament"; (2) "A mystagogical catechesis must also be concerned with presenting the meaning of the signs contained in the rites. This is particularly important in a highly technological age like our own, which risks losing the ability to appreciate signs and symbols. More than simply conveying information, a mystagogical catechesis should be capable of making the faithful more sensitive to the language of signs and gestures which, together with the word, make up the rite"; (3) "Finally, a mystagogical catechesis must be concerned with bringing out the significance of the rites for the Christian life in all its dimensions—work and responsibility, thoughts and emotions, activity and repose. Part of the mystagogical process is to demonstrate how the mysteries celebrated in the rite are linked to the missionary responsibility of the faithful." As a final point, here, Benedict XVI again notes how the "process of Christian formation always had an experiential character... centered on

---

115. Benedict XVI, *Sacramentum caritatis*, §64.
116. Ratzinger, *GCC*, 33.
117. Benedict XVI, *Sacramentum caritatis*, §64.
118. The quotations that follow can be found in Benedict XVI, *Sacramentum caritatis*, §64.

a vital and convincing encounter with Christ, as proclaimed by authentic witnesses. It is first and foremost the witness who introduces others to the mysteries."[119] This is not to deny the importance of a systematic expression of the contents of the faith, but it does provide insight into key elements that must also be in place for a pre- or post-baptismal catechesis: namely, the person of the witness and an experiential character.

In an attempt to further define experience and to get at the experiential character of catechesis, Ratzinger follows Aquinas' formulaic summation of the Aristotelean axiom, "There is nothing in the intellect that was not first in the senses." From Aquinas' *Anima forma corporis* ("The soul is the form of the body"), "it follows that the way of human cognition always requires the combination of corporal instrument and spiritual appropriation. . . . All human knowledge must have a sensory structure; it must have its beginning in experience, in the perception of the senses."[120] To this point, Ratzinger adds two "correctives." The first he takes from Ignatius of Loyola and the expression "God is always greater," and "Whatever is discovered to exist, God always transcends it."[121] God is always "more" than any one religious experience, and it is, in fact, the road that experience invites us to embark upon that invites the "constant revision of our experiences."[122] The second "corrective" comes in the Platonic statement: "There is nothing in the senses without the prior action of the intellect." He goes on to say, "The senses experience nothing if no question has been raised, if there is no preceding command from the intellect without which sensory experience cannot take place . . . it is only when the intellect shines light on sensory experience that this sensory experience has any value as knowledge and that experiences thus become possible."[123] Avoiding any bifurcation, Ratzinger roots his understanding of "experience" in the "dynamic link between intellect and senses from which there is constructed a path to deeper knowledge."[124]

Following Jean Mouroux, Ratzinger next identifies various stages of experience with an eye to their application to catechesis. Mouroux's first stage is "empirical experience," which is the most immediate and uncritical sense perception. "Empirical experience" is uncritical and often inexact, and one which calls for a second stage—"experimental experience." Modern natural sciences have their roots in this stage as the intellect seeks to

---

119. Benedict XVI, *Sacramentum caritatis*, §64.
120. Ratzinger, *Principles*, 344.
121. Ratzinger, *Principles*, 345.
122. Ratzinger, *Principles*, 346.
123. Ratzinger, *Principles*, 348.
124. Ratzinger, *Principles*, 348.

experiment with perceived reality. However, when it comes to faith, "this stage is not appropriate to what is truly divine or truly human because the condition of experience at this level is, as it were, a putting to death of the object."[125] Heidegger calls the fact that nature is controlled in a scientific experiment a technique named *Ge-stell*, a "set-up," and Brague speaks of how experimentation removes the object's freedom. Kołakowski calls the manner in which natural sciences deal with the object (i.e., nature) a form of necrophilia. Ratzinger comments, "The fact that a similar way of dealing with faith and with God must of necessity lead to a God-is-dead theology need hardly be elaborated here."[126] The third stage, called "experiential" by Mouroux or "existential" by Beinert, makes the case that "the decisive factor is not control but letting oneself be controlled."[127] Balthasar points out that this opens the way for Christian experience, which is the fruit of overcoming one's self-will.[128] And Ratzinger concludes:

> To say that God is trinitarian means, in fact, to confess that he is self-transcendence, "unselfishness," and, consequently, that he can be known only in what reflects his own nature. From this there follows an important catechetical conclusion: the being-led to a religious experience, which must start in the place where man finds himself, can yield no fruit if it is not, from the beginning, directed to the acquisition of a readiness for renunciation. ... From the perspective of Christian faith, we might say that religious experience in its most exalted Christian form bears the mark of the Cross.... The Cross redeems, it enables us to see.[129]

This last point is essential and ties into what has already been described as the goal of discipleship being pro-existence. The Church's catechetical efforts aim to journey with the person who has been encountered by Christ deeper into this encounter to the point of being ready to renounce his or her very self. This being-for, again, is the goal of discipleship, thus revealing the link between catechesis and discipleship.

To Mouroux's three stages of experience, Ratzinger adds a fourth—the distinctly Christian experience. This experience "relies ... on the extent and richness of the experiences already accumulated throughout history by the

---

125. Ratzinger, *Principles*, 349.
126. Ratzinger, *Principles*, 349.
127. Ratzinger, *Principles*, 349.
128. Ratzinger, *Principles*, 349–50.
129. Ratzinger, *Principles*, 350. See also Ratzinger, "The Anguish of an Absence," Meditation 1.

world of faith."¹³⁰ The accumulated experiences go by the name of tradition and the Church is the place of such accumulated experiences. In other words, the Church herself is the mother of the Christian experience, the "source of new personal experience," in three ways:¹³¹

1. The communal life created by faith, along with liturgy, provides the experiential support wherein one's intellectual assimilation is constantly renewed by experience, and whereby one may be led outside of himself.

2. The one who grows in faith becomes a light for others. Others come to the Light through the light of this or that person of faith. Through such lights, people come to encounter Jesus in a "secondhand" way.

3. The higher form of the previous experience appears in the persons of the saints, "the living personifications of a faith actually experienced and tested. . . . [They] are themselves . . . places into which one can enter, in which faith as experience has been . . . stored, anthropologically seasoned and brought near."

Through his brief treatment on Mouroux and Christian experience, Ratzinger concludes there are three kinds of Christian experience, and notes that catechesis only concerns itself with the first two:¹³²

130. Ratzinger, *Principles*, 351.

131. See Ratzinger, *Principles*, 351–52. Ratzinger's proposal for catechesis and experience dovetails with Giussani's treatment on education. Giussani argues that one must "*educat[e] the human heart as God made it*" (Giussani, *The Risk of Education*, xxvii; all other references, here, appear from xxviii–ix). Catechesis is a particular education of the heart. Giussani argues that three points are most significant here: (1) "Education requires an *adequate proposal of the past*," and adequate depiction of tradition. (2) The past must be proposed to young people "*within a present, lived experience* that underscores its correspondence with the ultimate needs of the heart. That is to say: within a present experience that offers reasons accounting for itself." The emphasis on a lived experience brings Giussani right into Ratzinger's domain, and this present lived reality shows, in and of itself, how the Christian experience corresponds to, or is in harmony with the needs of the heart. This living experience of the tradition implies a community and witnesses that have embraced the tradition as a way. (3) Giussani claims a "true education must be *education to criticism*." Eventually, the "contents" of the tradition must be sifted through or criticized by the child him or herself. However, in this way, education is a risk, because it leaves open the possibility of, or exalts the individual freedom which might reject the proposal, the tradition.

132. Ratzinger, *Principles*, 352. One must note that Ratzinger is speaking here specifically about experience and not about doctrine, which, for Ratzinger, does not impede the first type of experience listed here. Additionally, we can also cite Benedict XVI, *The Transforming Power of Faith*, 33–35. Following a similar trajectory, Benedict XVI identifies the following as pathways: (1) The beauty of creation, (2) The thirst for the infinite that rests within man—his insatiable desire for happiness, (3) The faith of

1. "The experience of creation and history, which offers itself to man not only in the range of possibilities that are open to him for transcending the superficial but also as a road leading him to a meeting with the ground of being." This corresponds to the types of experience Mouroux discusses.

2. "The experience of the Christian community and of Christian individuals, in which the ways of transcending creation and history are opened to man, that is, in which the first type of experience is made ready, intensified and cast in a Christian mold."[133] This is the explicitly Christian experience.

3. "From a combination of types one and two, there develops, then, a very personal experience with God in Christ and, finally, the genuinely supernatural experience."

Far from disregarding the transcendent religious experience Moran and Groome seek to foster in their religious education models, Ratzinger highlights its value as a transcendent experience of beauty within creation and history that lead beyond to the truth of being. For Ratzinger, however, the whole thing does not revolve around the experience itself, but an objective encounter with *logos*, "the ground of being." In the second kind of Christian experience—the experience of the community in life and in worship (i.e., the pilgrim fellowship that familiarizes one with the lifestyle that is Christianity[134]), which is the experience of mutual support as a force that

---

those who believe. It is also important to note that Ratzinger does not espouse a facile attempt at making God "fit" into "worldly language." For one, language is bound up within a "language community" such that "a language that is available to everyone just does not exist." Ratzinger is not oblivious to the contextualization points made by the postmodern thinkers. However, he does not engage this problem here. Instead, he notes that all discourse about God only slowly leads up to God from the outside and is never capable of reaching Him. Religious experience ultimately carries man further. This means "preaching must enlist the whole breadth of reality so as to make it transparent, a window through which to look at God." However, contra Rahner and those who follow him, this preaching "is guided by the discourse that has already been uttered about God. . . . Jesus himself did not start from zero when he constructed his proclamation but, rather, developed it in a continuation of the prophetic tradition." The same is true of the preacher today, "he does not stand before a two-thousand-year gulf between him and the Bible—the living interpretation in the experience of the saints is the inner connection that supports him, and without it intimate acquaintance with the Bible degenerates into mere historicism" (Ratzinger, *Dogma*, 99–101).

133. Note the interplay between types 1 and 2. In other words, types 1 and 2 do not exist in a progression, but are, rather, two distinct experiences with the capacity for fruitful interrelation.

134. Ratzinger, GCC, 57, 59.

sustains life[135]—the Church acts a secondhand source of faith, "a light for others."[136] Evangelization and catechesis function on the first and second levels. This secondhand faith carries the new believer to the third kind of experience, a "firsthand" experience of encountering Another outside of oneself who comes into oneself, an experience that, in this life, is a mere foretaste of what is to come.[137]

In order to illustrate the points taken from Mouroux, and to make a catechetical connection, let us turn again to the account of the woman at the well (John 4:4–42). In the woman's initial interaction with Jesus, Ratzinger sees an example of the "empirical" experience. What appears to be at stake here is a drink of water. The conversation eventually transcends "empirical" experience, leading her to become aware of her "elemental thirst," her desire for life. However, her understanding remains on the biological, or "experimental" level. She desires something of a fountain of youth, some physical water source that will allow her to live forever and to be satisfied on earth. However, in the next stage, the "experiential" stage, the woman "no longer asks for *something*, for water or for any other single thing, but for life, for herself,"[138] as she says, "Sir, give me this water, that I may not thirst, nor come here to draw" (John 4:15). To this, Jesus says, "Go, call your husband" (John 4:16). This, Ratzinger says, is both "intentional and necessary":

> For her life as a whole, with all its thirst, is the true subject here. As a result, there comes to light the real dilemma, the deep seated waywardness, of her existence: she is brought face to face with herself ... a new transition has occurred—to preserve our earlier terminology, a transition from empirical and experimental to "experiential" experience, to "existential experience." The woman now stands face to face with herself. It is no longer a question now of *something* but of the depths of the *I* itself and, consequently, of the radical poverty that is man's I-myself, the place where this *I* is ultimately revealed behind the superficiality of the *something*. From this perspective, we might regard the conversation between Jesus and the Samaritan woman as the prototype of catechesis. It must lead from the *something* to the *I*. Beyond every *something* it must ensure the involvement of man himself, of *this* particular man.

---

135. Ratzinger, *Principles*, 351.
136. Ratzinger, *Principles*, 351.
137. Ratzinger, *Principles*, 352.
138. Ratzinger, *Principles*, 353.

It must produce self-knowledge, and self-acknowledgement so that the indigence and need of man's being will be evident.[139]

Jesus leads the woman from the ordinary and somewhat superficial, deeper into the depths of her being, into the depths of her desire, to a place of truth—the objective encounter leads her there. She has to admit to the other her desire for satisfaction—her desire for love in truth. She is at stake; her very identity is at stake. The surrender of her longing to Jesus allows her, experientially (to use Mouroux's language), to be led by, to be "controlled" by Christ. He leads her to confront the truth about herself and her feeble attempts to slake her thirst in her various love-affairs. The woman becomes aware of her waywardness, and in this way, aware of her real need.

In her openness to being led by Christ, the woman finds herself in adoration. Ratzinger identifies this with her question in John 4:20, saying, "It is only apparently without motivation but in reality inevitable that the woman should ask now: How do things stand with regard to adoration, that is, with regard to God and my relationship to him."[140] A catechetical process that has Christ (not transcendental experience, postmodern critical consciousness, i.e., the "self") as its "given," leads the person to adoration, where one "sees" the truth of him or herself, the depths of one's own being—where God himself initiates and establishes for the person "a relationship and communion with God."[141] Ratzinger says, "Only at this point does the offering of Jesus' true gift become possible. For the 'gift of God' is God himself, God precisely as gift—that is, the Holy Spirit (cf. verses 10 and 24)."[142] Jesus leads the woman to the depths of her thirst wherein she becomes aware of the real thirst that drives her, and she learns to receive that which satisfies her thirst. Catechesis aims at "exposing the *I*, so that it lets the masks fall and moves out of the realm of something into that of being. Its goal is *conversio*, that conversion of man that results in his standing face to face with himself."[143]

At this point in the story of the woman, however, catechesis itself is transcended, insofar as it leads to worship, to adoration. Catechesis leads into what Ratzinger calls "the question of all questions: How can I worship God?"[144] The answer: in Spirit and in truth. Catechesis aims at revealing the truth of the person to the person himself in its testimony of Jesus Christ, such that the catechumen might open to the gift of God that is the

---

139. Ratzinger, *Principles*, 353–54.
140. Ratzinger, *Principles*, 354.
141. John Paul II, *Pastores dabo vobis*, §45.
142. Ratzinger, *Principles*, 354.
143. Ratzinger, *Principles*, 355; emphasis added.
144. Ratzinger, *Principles*, 355.

Holy Spirit, and in this way, enter into his identity as a son in the Son and into that which he was created for: worship.[145] This "very personal" and "supernatural experience" of worship is not necessarily highly abstract or mystical. Instead, catechesis reaches its definitive end in the objective concreteness of the Eucharist. In other words, the act of evangelizing, containing therein the systematic *and* experiential nature of catechesis, aims at Eucharistic worship. For this reason, Ratzinger says, "*Christian preaching is not the presentation of a doctrinal system but, rather, training in Christian reality, the crystallization point of which is the eucharistic celebration.*"[146] Evangelization and catechesis present the revelation of the *Logos*, which is not merely a system of thought, but a personal revelation, an experience of personal union that shapes the whole of life and which exists in an enduring way in the Eucharist. At this point, the present study has come face-to-face with the concept of *logikē latreia*.

St. Paul takes up this reality of *logikē latreia*, that is, "worship and sacrifice with spirit and mind,"[147] or worship in "accordance with *logos*,"[148] in Rom 12:1, and it becomes central to Ratzinger's understanding of entering into Jesus' prayer in the Eucharist. Ratzinger frequently quotes Augustine on this point, who stresses the nature of the food of the Eucharist as that which is stronger than man. Typically, when human beings eat, they take food into themselves and transform that food into themselves, so to speak. In the Eucharist, the opposite is true. When one feeds on the Eucharist, the Eucharist transforms the person into itself.[149] This leads Ratzinger to conclude that entering into Jesus' prayer, and becoming "contemporary with the Pasch of Christ in the liturgy of the Church is also, in fact, an anthropological reality. The celebration is not just a rite, not just a liturgical 'game.' It is meant to be indeed a *logikē latreia*, the 'logicizing' of my existence, my interior contemporaneity with the self-giving of Christ."[150] In *Sacramentum caritatis*, Benedict XVI echoes his point from *The Spirit*

---

145. For an additional perspective on worship, especially as it pertains to leisure and living a full human existence, see Pieper, *Leisure*, 65–74.

146. Ratzinger, *Dogma*, 51.

147. Ratzinger, *The Spirit of the Liturgy*, 45. For more on *logikē latreia*, see Benedict XVI, *Sacramentum caritatis*, §70; Ratzinger, *New Song*, 152; Ratzinger, *Pilgrim Fellowship*, 114–18.

148. Ratzinger, *The Spirit of the Liturgy*, 50.

149. For example, see Benedict XVI, *Sacramentum caritatis*, §70. For more on the Eucharist as a sacrament of "transformations," see Ratzinger, "Eucharist—Communio—Solidarity," 368–70. Cf. Benedict XVI, *DCE*, §13.

150. Ratzinger, *The Spirit of the Liturgy*, 58.

of the Liturgy, noting how the Eucharist "logicizes" and transfigures every part of a person's life, saying:

> Christians, in all their actions, are called to offer true worship to God.... There is nothing authentically human—our thoughts and affections, our words and deeds—that does not find in the sacrament of the Eucharist the form it needs to be lived to the full. Here we can see the full human import of the radical newness brought by Christ in the Eucharist: the worship of God in our lives cannot be relegated to something private and individual, but tends by its nature to permeate every aspect of our existence. Worship pleasing to God thus becomes a new way of living our whole life.[151]

Catechesis leads one into Eucharistic worship, into *logikē latreia*, that "supernatural experience" in the realism of discipleship that allows one to live ever more fully the "for" of the Father manifest in Jesus Christ—as a "for" God and *the many*.

The Need for Pilgrim Fellowship

The previous points about the catechumenate being a sort of existential and experiential training marked by the impact of witnesses, thus leads directly into the fourth of Ratzinger's distinctive marks of the catechumenate and catechesis—the essential need for community, pilgrim fellowship. Ratzinger says, "Catechetical instruction also includes a pilgrim fellowship, a gradual familiarization with the new life-style of Christianity."[152] Living life with and within the community Church is an essential part of the catechumenate. Being a catechumen does not mean participating in a class at the parish once each week, but an entry into a common way of life. The catechumenate must become something of a community of pilgrims on the Way together, and this must be so in order to live Christianity as a way of life amid the post-Christian culture in which nascent or mature Christians find themselves. Ratzinger emphasizes this point, saying:

> Evangelization is never merely intellectual communication; it is a process of experience, the purification and transformation of our lives, and for this to happen, company along the way is needed. That is why catechesis necessarily assumes the form of the catechumenate, in which the requisite recoveries can take

---

151. Benedict XVI, *Sacramentum caritatis*, §71.
152. Ratzinger, GCC, 56–57.

> place, in which especially the connection between thinking and living is established.... The company of believers, who set up an alternative way of living... demonstrate that [living as a Christian in our time] is possible.[153]

Again, Benedict XVI stresses the point, though extending it beyond catechumens to all members of the Church:

> In the old Church, the catechumenate was created as a living space set apart from an increasingly demoralized culture, a space in which that distinctive innovation of the Christian way of life was practiced and, at the same time, protected from the common mode of living. I think that even today something like catechumenal communities are needed, so that Christian life, with all its character, can hold its own ground.[154]

Benedict XVI clearly extends and calls for this community of catechumens beyond the catechumenate, properly speaking, and to the whole Church, when he says that the one who is coming to know Jesus will be led into his body, the Church, "the journeying community of catechumens, a community of both learning and living, in which our eyes are opened as we walk."[155]

The Necessity of the Catechism

Finally, a fifth essential point in Ratzinger's approach to catechesis appears in the necessity of a catechism. It is a well-known fact that Ratzinger served as the chair of the committee of twelve Cardinals and Bishops tasked by John Paul II with drafting the *Catechism* in response to the desire of 1985 Synod of Bishops.[156] Though Vatican II did not formally call for the drafting of a universal catechism in its documents, nevertheless, Council fathers did discuss the possibility. Ratzinger notes that during the final session of the Council, Cardinal Jäger "proposed the commissioning of such a book in order to give concrete form to the work of *aggiornamento* in the area of doctrine."[157] Even without a universal catechism in its immediate wake, Vatican II renewed the vigor surrounding catechetical ministry and called for the composition of a directory "concerning the catechetical instruction

---

153. Ratzinger, *On the Way*, 51.
154. Benedict XVI, *Western Culture*, 154–55.
155. Benedict XVI, "Christmas Greetings 2012."
156. See John Paul II, *Fidei depositum*.
157. Ratzinger and Schönborn, *Introduction to the Catechism*, 11.

of the Christian people,"[158] which came to life in 1971 in the Congregation for the Clergy's *General Catechetical Directory*. Popes Paul VI and John Paul II, also following the trajectory of the Council, produced *Evangelii nuntiandi* and *Catechesi tradendae* respectively. These gave further shape to evangelization and contextualized catechesis therein. In addition to the positive progression toward the *Catechism*, several magisterial documents of the era issue concerns regarding the state of catechesis and other renewal efforts following Vatican II.[159] Therefore, the *Catechism* can rightly be seen both as the fruit of Vatican II insofar as the council was and is a "catechetical council," and also, framed from a more negative perspective, as a concrete response to certain catechetical developments following the Council, many of which were highlighted in chapter 6.

But, what is a catechism anyhow? What is the *Catechism of the Catholic Church*? Ratzinger responds to such questions by stating the *Catechism* is basically a testimony, universal in nature, that relies on the voice of the catechist to bring the testimony to life.[160] Ratzinger argues that the *Catechism* literary form is that of a testimony. It is "not . . . a theology book, but a book of the faith, for the teaching of the faith." Ratzinger continues, saying, "its literary form is more than anything else the testimony, the proclamation that comes from the internal certainty of the faith."[161] The *Catechism* announces

---

158. Second Vatican Council, *Christus dominus*, §44.

159. For example, see John Paul II's *Catechesi tradendae*, §17; 1985 Extraordinary Synod of Bishops, "The Final Report," §3–4.

160. See Bursa, "The Catechism," 348–49, 359–66.

161. Ratzinger, "Current Doctrinal Relevance." Ratzinger also emphasizes that the *Catechism* is not an exercise in ecclesiocentrism (see *GCC*, 69). The whole of the Church's testimony, here, focuses on God and his action. Ratzinger says, "The Church is the place from which the *Catechism* thinks. . . . But this subject does not look at herself. She exists precisely to give us those new eyes of faith without which we see nothing but distorted reflections of Jesus, not Jesus himself. The Church exists to let us see Christ and hear the Gospel" (*GCC*, 69–70). Additionally, catechesis, including the catechesis provided by the *Catechism*, makes theology possible. For, theology is "the effort to recognize the gift of knowledge that precedes the reflection" (Ratzinger, "Current Doctrinal Relevance"). Ratzinger continues, "The relation between the given, which God offers to us in the faith of the Church, and our effort to appropriate this given in rational understanding, is a fundamental part of theology. The goal of the *Catechism* is precisely that of presenting this given that precedes us" (Ratzinger, "Current Doctrinal Relevance"). Elsewhere Ratzinger says that the faith must exist and be taken as "a prior datum [*Vorgabe*] of reality. . . . This means: your baptismal faith, the knowledge communicated . . . is contact with reality itself and hence has priority over theory. The baptismal faith does not have to prove its credentials to theory, but rather theory must prove itself in the presence of reality, to the 'knowledge' of the truth that is given in the baptismal profession of faith" (Ratzinger, *Handing on the Faith*, 24). In order for theology to exist as such, "the given," the "prior datum," must remain pure and

something, namely the person of Christ as He has revealed himself, as He encounters persons in the sacraments of the Church, and as He invites individuals to follow him in a way of life and into intimacy with the Father through the spiritual life (i.e., the life in the Spirit).[162] Next, the *Catechism* is a concrete reminder of the universality of the Church's communion in both its synchronic development, and in its diachronic content. It is no local catechism. In its construction, it was a collaborative effort of cardinals and bishops from around the world. Ratzinger says the "work represents a signal event of episcopal 'collegiality' and that in it the voice of the universal Church speaks to us in all its fullness."[163] In the text itself, this synchronic effort of today's bishops was then complemented by the diachronic reality of the Church, as voices from the East and West throughout time deepen the *Catechism*'s catechesis in each section. Consequently, the *Catechism* overflows with references to Scripture, Creeds, Councils, the Fathers of the Church, saints, and so forth.[164] The synchronic and diachronic elements allow for a truly universal catechism and avoid any privatization of the faith.[165] Finally, while it is the case that the *Catechism* appeals to what Augustine calls the "interior teacher,"[166] Ratzinger holds that the *Catechism* needs the exterior teacher, the catechist, and the life of a communion of disciples to bring the testimony to life—lest the book remain dumb.[167] Rather than imposing some sort of pedagogical straightjacket, the *Catechism* maintains and encourages the freedom of the catechist in expressing the universal testimony in a manner fitting to the needs of unique audiences.[168]

Conclusion

If God had not spoken, those following the trajectory of a postmodern theology would be right: one could say nothing definitive about God, about Being. However, God has spoken, making faith possible. The more

---

accessible, and for this reason, the *Catechism* exists.

162. For more on faith shaping morality—a way of living life—see Ratzinger, *Handing on the Faith*, 26–27. See also Ratzinger's *Introduction*, 69–81.

163. Ratzinger and Schönborn, *Introduction to the Catechism*, 25. See also Ratzinger, *GCC*, 58.

164. See Ratzinger, *GCC*, 61–62.

165. See Ratzinger, *Handing on the Faith*, 27–28; *CCC*, §166–69, 1253, 2030.

166. See *CCC*, §1695, 1697, 2681.

167. Ratzinger, *GCC*, 59. See Ratzinger and Schönborn, *Introduction to the Catechism*, 17–18. See also John Paul II's *Fidei depositum*.

168. See Ratzinger, *Handing on the Faith*, 38–39; *CCC*, §24.

one allows that truth to penetrate, possess, transform oneself, the more one can speak about that which Being has revealed—even when one does not speak. Because of the revelation of the *Logos*, the Church can recognize and repeat what God has revealed about himself and she does so in every age. In other words, the Church makes the encounter with Christ possible today, and she does so preeminently in the sacrament of Baptism. Baptism is the epicenter of one's encounter with Christ, from which God reaches forward into one's life drawing the person into the Christian event, and from which God leads the person, always with an appeal to freedom, down a definitive path of discipleship. Evangelization and catechesis, then, exist within this sacramental context—flowing out of and into Baptism (and "from there," to the other sacraments).

Given Ratzinger's fundamental theology, his understanding of evangelization and catechesis is far from an exercise in doctrinalization or a return flight to propositionalism. Instead, considering the revelation of the *Logos*, it is something deeply personal. For Ratzinger, the Church's evangelizing mission requires the recovery and full-throated announcement of the Christian narrative—her own personal testimony—offered by the Christian witness at the service of *Logos*, and within a lived experience of a Christian community seeking together the *Logos* (who has already anticipated their search and has come to meet them). Ratzinger eschews a position that camouflages the Christian narrative amid modernity, or one that minimizes the Christian claim as a small narrative functioning as a pawn at the hands of a tyrannical one operating under the guise of beneficence. Instead, the Christian narrative, offered personally and as an appeal to personal freedom, exists as a proposal for a way of life, with the effectiveness of this way evidenced in the proof of life itself.

CHAPTER TWELVE

Communicating the Gospel Today

"How can we talk about God in our time?," Benedict XVI asks. We can speak of him because he has revealed himself in the *Logos* and the human receiving subject has received the revelation through the act of faith. In other words, "we can talk about God because he has talked to us."[1] As noted above, this initial question deals directly with fundamental theology, and the previous chapters have attempted to provide something of a basic survey of Ratzinger's understanding of revelation, faith, and the role of the Church in encounter. His second question, however, pertains directly to method—namely, "How can we communicate the Gospel so as to open roads to his saving truth in our contemporaries' hearts—that are all too often closed—and minds—that are at times distracted by the many dazzling lights of society?"[2] This must be answered. This methodological question flows naturally from the previous, more fundamental one, and it has to do with effective communication, a communication that has to account for the current culture—however closed, dismissive, or distracted it may be.

How can the Church communicate the Gospel effectively today? Is the Gospel communicable at all? Does it even matter? How can the Church convey the "yes" of God in Jesus Christ in such a way that the exchange of the "I" for the "not-I," the encounter, takes place? A seriously penetrating methodological inquiry, along with the requisite case studies, would take the present study far afield. It also would not square with Ratzinger's contribution, which, notably, is not methodological in kind.[3] Instead, this book, along with Ratzinger's work, is more about casting a vision for evangelization and catechesis, it is more about building the theological foundation necessary for a solid approach to evangelization, than the real minutiae of a

---

1. Benedict XVI, *The Transforming Power of Faith*, 42. See also the same general question in Benedict XVI, "Meditation 2012."
2. Benedict XVI, *The Transforming Power of Faith*, 42.
3. See Ratzinger, *New Song*, 42.

concrete methodology. This chapter will first explore aspects of the problem of communication, with particular regard given to the relationship between the Gospel and culture. After analyzing Ratzinger's image of the dresser of sycamore trees, an allegory borrowed from St. Basil, the chapter will go on to argue that evangelizing according to the *Logos* means evangelizing personally, that is, according to the "from," "with," and "for" pattern. In other words, authentic evangelization, i.e., evangelization in accord with the *Logos*, is a deeply personal activity marked by the Trinitarian pattern being-from, being-for, and being-with. This pattern maintains the source and goal of evangelization, while serving as a series of guideposts and benchmarks for Ratzinger's personalist approach to evangelization.

Communication

Evangelization is a matter of communication; it is a type of communication that brings or causes joy. Ratzinger notes that "it is quite evident ... that the two concepts 'communication' and 'evangelization' go together."[4] He adds that *the* question behind evangelization is simply, "How can the gospel cross the threshold from me to someone else? How can a communion in the gospel come about, so that it not only forms a bond between me and the other, but also unites us both to the Word of God, thereby producing a genuinely profound unity?" Communication can be defined as the transmission or exchange of information, knowledge, or ideas by use of various means (e.g., speech, writing, etc.). Perhaps more deeply, it refers to that which is held in common with another, or to that which has been made common.[5] It has to do with overcoming the "gap" between two or more individuals—thus making relationship possible. It is that which brings two or more people together.

Typically, this "making-common" happens through language, however systematic or unsystematic, formal or informal.[6] Language implies meaning. "Take away the word, the meaning," Augustine says, "[and] there is only a meaningless sound. The voice without the word strikes the ear but does not build upon the heart." Building up the meaning in the heart is critical for Augustine. He says, "When I think about what I am going to say, the word or message is already in my heart." The word, its genesis, its meaning, is the manifestation of the pondering heart, and communication

---

4. Ratzinger, *On the Way*, 42.
5. *Oxford English Dictionary Online*, s.v. "communication, n."
6. *Oxford English Dictionary Online*, s.v. "language, n. (and int.)."

the searching "for a way to share with your heart what is already in mine." Augustine continues:

> In my search for a way to let this message reach you, so that the word already in my heart may find place also in yours, I use my voice to speak to you. The sound of my voice brings the meaning of the word to you and then passes away. The word which the sound has brought to you is now in your heart, and yet is still also in mine. . . . The sound of the voice has made itself heard in the service of the word, and has gone away, as though it were saying: *My joy is complete.* Let us hold on to the word; we must not lose the word conceived inwardly in our hearts.[7]

In a dialogue between two persons, for example, the meaning of a particular word (or particular words) already "grasped" or "held" in the heart, is transmitted by the voice of one to the other. The voice carries the word to the other, and, once grasped by the other, the voice passes away and the meaning holds the dialogue partners in common in a certain sense. In communication, duality exists in unity—communion—in the meaning that holds them in common. The word stands as a "third-party" who makes the coming together of the two possible. In sum, communication refers to affinity—the transmission of meaning that holds human beings in common.

Evangelization is the communication, not of just any words, or of many words, but the communication of *the* Word of God. The announcement of this Word, as Ratzinger says, "is more than a word—it is a way of life, indeed, life itself."[8] This Word, when communicated, does not simply reside idly in the heart of the receiver, but alters life—the way in which life is lived. The "yes" of the Word is not just any "yes," but the "yes" of God incarnate. God's *Logos* is the expression "yes, it is good that you exist" of God in the person of the Son. Receiving this Word, then, is not, at the bottom of it, a matter of abstraction, moralism, or intellection. It is a personal event. In receiving the love of God in Jesus Christ, in receiving this Word, when this Word resides in my heart, I become capable of receiving the other and accepting the other—we abide, together, in the Word which is "bigger" or "over" all of our passing words. The Word of God holds us in common, as that "third party" that makes communication—communion—possible, and eternally so. This makes life possible. Rather, this is life itself, because life, as a human person, is relational. Really living, then, as a person, means taking up the way of the Word, the life-altering way that makes relationality as a way of life possible again. To evangelize is to communicate this Word that

---

7. Augustine of Hippo, *Sermo* 293, 3, cited in Catholic Church, *Liturgy of the Hours.*
8. Ratzinger, *On the Way*, 42.

changes life by rendering it personal, or relational; it is to make accessible life in abundance (cf. John 10:10) and eternally so.

The Reality of Culture

Regardless of its type, communication does not take place in a vacuum, as if a pure transmission were possible. The heart of the other is not a *tabula rasa*. Communicating anything, much less God's "Yes" to humanity, confronts, almost immediately, innumerable challenges. Culture exists as the foremost of such challenges. Ratzinger argues that culture designates the medium or space through which the voice carrying the word from one to another must pass.[9]

In a 1992 essay published in *Truth and Tolerance* under the title "Faith, Religion, and Culture," Ratzinger defines culture as "the social form of expression, as it has grown up in history, of those experiences and evaluations that have left their mark on a community and have shaped it."[10] Ratzinger goes on to analyze the individual parts of this definition in three ways. First, he argues that "culture has to do with perceptions and values,"[11] with grappling with what it means to be human. In every epoch and milieu, one must attempt to understand how to be human, how to relate and respond to the world so as to be happy. But this is not a herculean attempt by an isolated individual. Rather, one understands how to be human with the help of other human beings. In 2002, Ratzinger would expand upon this explanation, describing culture as "the stamp of a community that provides . . . patterns of thinking, feeling, and acting. . . . [A] system of notions and thought patterns that preconditions the individual human being."[12] Culture provides understanding and direction from the most significant questions of life to the most practical. Given its widespread influence, a culture's starting point, its point of reference, is critical in determining its perceptivity. Ratzinger says, "the question of correct perception is thus also a question concerning the proper shaping of the community. . . . Culture is concerned with understanding, which is a perception that opens the way for practical action, that is, a perception of which the dimensions of values, of morality, is an indispensable part."[13] Over and above other serious questions that define a culture, Ratzinger identifies the most foundational question as that stance a

---

9. Ratzinger, *On the Way*, 43. See also the *GDC*, §20.
10. Ratzinger, *TT*, 60.
11. Ratzinger, *TT*, 60.
12. Ratzinger, *On the Way*, 43–44.
13. Ratzinger, *TT*, 60–61.

culture takes with regard to the divine. He says, "No one can understand the world at all, no one can live his life rightly, so long as the question about the Divinity remains unanswered."[14] For this reason, Tracey Rowland observes that Ratzinger "rejects the proposition that the realm of culture can ever be theologically neutral."[15] In some way, shape, or form, culture takes a position in front of the question of the divine.

Second, Ratzinger describes culture as a "social agent," one "which accepts into itself the experiences of the individuals and, on the other hand also molds them. This social agent preserves and develops perceptions that go beyond what any individual is capable of—insights we may describe as prerational and suprarational."[16] The individual both shapes and is shaped by the culture.[17]

Finally, Ratzinger acknowledges culture as a temporal reality. He notes that "society progresses through time," and that "culture develops along the way, through the encounter with new realities and the assimilation of new perceptions."[18] On this point, Ratzinger highlights the way culture does not close upon itself, but opens to progress, to transformation, to encounter. A culture expresses its own individuality, and at the same time, a culture exists within the movement of history, within time, and so it is not a walled off space, but one capable of encountering, and one which does encounter other cultural agencies and reacts in various ways to them. Here, he distinguishes between what he calls "cosmic" or "static" cultures that are more prescriptive in nature, whose understanding of the universe always remains the same, and those "historical" cultures (e.g., Judaism and Christianity) which are "molded by a conception of history as a fundamental category."[19] Culture develops over time as a common and concentrated set of values that distinguish one particular community from another, with the particularities of the system of life being manifest in common language, government, law, custom, moral concepts, art, forms of worship, etc.[20]

The outcome of an encounter between cultures depends upon the extent to which one culture is open or closed to another. Ratzinger holds that engaging a different culture can deepen and purify a culture's perceptions

14. Ratzinger, *TT*, 61.
15. Rowland, *Benedict XVI*, 28.
16. Ratzinger, *TT*, 61.
17. Cf. John Paul II, *Fides et ratio*, §71.
18. Ratzinger, *TT*, 62.
19. Ratzinger, *TT*, 62. Ratzinger tempers this distinction by noting that the cosmic cultures address death and rebirth, and human life as a path. In this regard, they are not purely "static" realities.
20. Ratzinger, *On the Way*, 45.

and values, reshaping the previous form without necessarily violating or alienating it.[21] Ratzinger explains:

> [The case of a positive cultural transformation] may be explained by the potentially universal nature of all cultures, which is concretized in the acceptance of what is other and the change of what is its own. A process of this kind can in fact lead to a breaking open of the silent alienation of man from the truth and from himself that exists within that culture. This can represent the healing Pasch for a culture, which through an apparent death comes to new life and becomes then for the first time truly itself.[22]

By "universal nature," here, Ratzinger means that, despite the many variations and expressions of social structure and custom, "man . . . is a single being, one and the same . . . touched and affected in the very depth of his existence by truth itself. . . . The fundamental openness of all men to others . . . can only be explained by the hidden way our souls have been touched by truth."[23] However, no individual person or culture can grasp the whole truth, but rather, an aspect or a perception that complements the others and only with the others can form the whole. This leads Ratzinger to conclude that "only in the interrelating of all great works of culture can man approach the unity and wholeness of his true nature."[24] This universality of cultures, however true it might be, remains rather idealistic. While individual cultures, due to the universal nature of human beings, contain within them a potentially unifying common dimension, equally powerful forces of division are also present and apparent. These forces act as a barrier, preventing the openness of one culture toward the other. This "negative factor of human existence" alienates men, and "hinders our perceiving things . . . [cutting] men off from the truth and thus also from each other."[25] A culture can contain within itself, then, both the possibility of opening toward a universality of cultures—which risks losing itself altogether while allowing something of itself to be potentially transformed—or, of closing itself into a state of pure autonomy and isolation for the sake of self-preservation.

Given the realities of communication and culture, Ratzinger admits that the challenge of relativism makes evangelization increasingly difficult today. He says, "Faith cannot of course find points of contact with philosophies that exclude questions concerning the truth, but it can do so with movements

21. See Ratzinger, *TT*, 63.
22. Ratzinger, *TT*, 63.
23. Ratzinger, *TT*, 64–65.
24. Ratzinger, *TT*, 65.
25. Ratzinger, *TT*, 65.

that are trying to break out of the relativist prison."[26] Ratzinger does not mince his words or play language games when it comes to his dealings with postmodern critical consciousness. It is not a theological plaything, but a dictatorial, tyrannical power that does not recognize "anything as definitive and whose ultimate goal consists solely of one's own ego and desires."[27] Postmodern critical consciousness absolutely denounces metanarratives while simultaneously absolving itself of being such a thing. Under the sway of the postmodern condition, "culture is set against truth," and the relativism that marks the "basic attitude of enlightened people." Such societies substitute practice (*praxis*) for truth. Now, "we do not know what is true, but we do know what we should do: raise up and introduce a better society."[28] Even a cursory historical sketch of culture and religion will reveal:

> Christianity has more in common with the ancient cultures of mankind than with the relativistic and rationalistic world that has cut loose from the fundamental insights of mankind and is thus leading man into a vacuum, devoid of meaning, which risks being fatal for him unless the answer to it comes to him in time. For the knowledge that man must turn toward God, and toward what is eternal, is found right across all the cultures. ... [Then,] it is not relativism that is confirmed; rather, it is the unity of the human condition and its common experience of contact with a truth that is greater than we are.[29]

When it comes to the proclamation of the Gospel, then, at least in the West, this proclamation must confront the radically "other" culture of relativism. The question then becomes, what is necessary to communicate the Gospel in this cultural environment? How can *logos* meet man *in time*? Or, perhaps more specifically, how can *logos* meet man in time *at this time*? Can *the* truth come to man at all? Amid the complexity of contemporary cultural dynamics, the immediate question presses the Church with urgency: How can one have the audacity to even begin to transmit the Gospel from one culture to another?

---

26. Ratzinger, *TT*, 198–200.
27. Ratzinger, "Homily."
28. Ratzinger, *TT*, 72.
29. Ratzinger, *TT*, 79.

A Communication That "Cuts"

Every form of communication, and, therefore, every attempt to communicate Christ, must confront the reality of culture—that value-laden "space" through which the voice that carries the Word (i.e., meaning) must pass. Evangelization, for its part, aims to communicate a particular message (i.e., the Gospel) and to make it understood within the perceptions and values that presently shape an individual person or a group of persons. In so doing, in reaching the hearts of individual hearers, the Gospel—which is carried on in history through cultural apparatuses, yet which itself is separate from and above human cultural expressions—not only has the capacity to transform the individual hearer, but, through the individual hearer, the Gospel can impact and renew the culture "from the inside," so to speak—whether the culture is already or not yet Christian. How, though? How does one evangelize?

Ratzinger's answer to such a question draws from Basil the Great's struggle to evangelize a pagan people of Asia-Minor who were steeped in a pagan, Greco-Roman culture. Basil finds motivation—a foothold in the trial—in the prophet Amos who identifies himself as "a herdsman, and a dresser of sycamore trees" (Amos 7:14). The Septuagint translates the line more vividly as "one who slits the fruit of the sycamore."[30] Basil explains the enigmatic image:

> The sycamore is a tree that bears very plentiful fruit. But it is tasteless unless one carefully slits it and allows its sap to run out, whereby it becomes flavorful. That is why ... the sycamore is a symbol for the pagan world: it offers a surplus, yet at the same time it is insipid. ... When one manages to slit them by means of the Logos, [the pagan world] is transformed.[31]

The pagan world contains within itself a certain wealth of meaning, a richness of culture, but also certain deficiencies. Christian Gnilka, says, "As it is, it is insipid, unusable." This culture "needs a complete transformation, whereby the change does not destroy its substance; rather, it gives to it the qualities that it lacks." Just as the sycamore fruit remains fruit as it is slit, becoming flavorful, so too, the culture remains culture, even as it is

---

30. Ratzinger, *On the Way*, 46. While being banished from Bethel by Amaziah, Amos declares that he is not a prophet, nor does he belong to a company of prophets. By this, Amos meant was neither from a prophetic school, nor was he a prophet by trade.

31. Basil, *In Is* 9,228, PG 30, 516D/517A, quoted in Ratzinger, *On the Way*, 46.

transformed—becoming more lively, more complete. This, as Gnilka puts it, is a "process of purification."[32]

Taking Basil's image as a starting point, Ratzinger draws several conclusions for evangelization, insofar as evangelization must, necessarily, engage with various cultures. He points out:[33]

1. *Cultural renewal requires an outside source.* Just as a fig cannot cut itself, neither can a culture slit itself. Transformation requires a "cut" applied from the outside. "An intervention from outside, is necessary."

2. *The Gospel (i.e., the Logos itself) slits the culture, and initiates a process of purification.* The Gospel is that which cuts the culture and pierces the heart of the hearer (cf. Acts 2:37–42). The cut from the Gospel results in a painful, but necessary process of purification known as ongoing conversion.[34]

3. *The Logos invites us to participate in the mission.* Ratzinger says that while "ultimately only the Logos himself can guide our cultures to their true purity and maturity, but the Logos makes us his servants, the 'dresser of sycamore trees.'"[35] Highlighting the incredulous nature of such involvement, Jean-Baptiste Chautard cites letter written by Pope Leo XIII, saying, "How admirable the plan, the universal law laid down by Providence, *that it is through men, that men* are to find out the way to salvation."[36]

4. *An effective proclamation of the Gospel necessitates patience and preparation.* The dresser must thoroughly understand the fig and exercise patience to make the cut the right way and at precisely the right time. The same holds for evangelization. Ratzinger says one must understand "the culture from within," and gain "an appreciation for its dangers and its hidden or evident potential."[37] Understanding a culture requires the evangelist to both identify the positive features of the culture, those "seeds of the Word" that are open to the Gospel, and the inherent dangers within a culture before which the Gospel stands as a sign of contradiction. In other words, while faith accepts what is

---

32. Gnilka, *Chrêsis: Die Méthode der Kirchenväter im Umgang mit der antiken Kultur*, 84, quoted in Ratzinger, *On the Way*, 47.

33. The following list is an attempt to collate Ratzinger's insights from *On the Way*, 46–48.

34. Cf. Ratzinger, *Principles*, 60–64.

35. Ratzinger, *On the Way*, 47.

36. Chautard, *Soul of the Apostolate*, 5–6.

37. Ratzinger, *On the Way*, 48.

good in a culture, those features open to the Gospel, it "is also a sign of opposition to whatever in the culture bars the doors against the gospel. It is a 'cut,' as we have heard. Therefore it has always been critical of culture also, and it must continue fearlessly and steadfastly to critique culture, especially today."[38] To this point, Ratzinger adds, "Evangelization is not simply adaptation to the culture, either, nor is it dressing up the gospel with elements of the culture, along the lines of a superficial notion of inculturation that supposes that, with modified figures of speech and a few new elements in the liturgy, the job is done."[39]

5. *The cut is not a momentary effort*, but an "ongoing and patient encounter between the Logos and the culture . . . mediated by the service of the faithful."[40] He says, "The gospel is a slit, a purification that becomes maturation and healing. It is a cut that demands patient involvement and understanding, so that it occurs at the right time, in the right place, and in the right way; a cut, then, that requires sympathy and understanding."[41] For this reason, Ratzinger claims the evangelist must patiently come to know "the culture from within," which includes "an appreciation for its dangers and its hidden or evident potential."

According to Ratzinger's schema, the *Logos* itself, the one who is "the Gospel personified" in Jesus Christ, initiates and invites men and women to participate in his mission. Benedict XVI expounds upon this point, saying:

> The first word, the true initiative, the true activity comes from God and only by inserting ourselves into the divine initiative, only by begging for this divine initiative, shall we too be able to become—with him and in him—evangelizers. God is always the beginning. . . . On the other hand, however, this God, who is always the beginning, also wants to involve our activity, so that the activities are theandric, so to speak, made by God, but with our involvement and implying our being, all our activity.[42]

The *Logos* makes those who are disciples, and, therefore, called to mission, evangelizers—his servants, co-dressers of sycamore trees. Thus, for Ratzinger, one must approach evangelization in the light of the *Logos*—who

---

38. Ratzinger, *On the Way*, 49–50.
39. Ratzinger, *On the Way*, 48. This point seems to summarize Ratzinger's critique of the Rahnerian trajectory—in its vulgarized and postmodern forms. In the end, the Christian gospel simply becomes the gospel of modernity or of postmodernity.
40. Ratzinger, *On the Way*, 48.
41. Ratzinger, *On the Way*, 48.
42. Benedict XVI, "Meditation 2012."

initiates evangelization, who is the Gospel personified, who is the "yes" of God incarnate. Evangelization, teaching the art of living, "is not the object of a science," but is the communication of a message "by [one] who has life—he who is the Gospel personified."[43] In light of the theandric activity of the *Logos*, who renders human beings his servants in dressing the sycamore trees, the personification of the Gospel, then, in some way, extends to those human evangelizers, to the Church and her members. Now they "personify," so to speak, the Gospel *in time*. To evangelize is to become one with Jesus Christ and share in the mission of initiated by the *Logos* and according to the pattern revealed by the *Logos*.

As has already been noted, in Jesus Christ, the *Logos* incarnate, person and mission coincide. Jesus is what he does, and what he does is who he is. The Son (being-from) is the ambassador of the Father (being-for). Who he is as Son (being-from) identifies with the Father (being-for) such that they are perfectly in union, they are one. In the Word's mission, the Son's "from" *is* the Father's "for." Person and mission are identical. Brotherton captures the essence of this identification, saying:

> The Incarnate Word ... inculcates being-for, being a transparent window into the Father and even an example for men of paternal virtue. But it is the Father who is the very act of self-giving in God. Again, "'Father' is purely a concept of relationship. Only in being for the other is he Father." Moreover, the "completely open being" of Christ's being-from or being-toward, which does not stand on its own, must be "pure relation (not substantiality) and, as pure relation, pure unity."[44]

Ratzinger says, "'Mission' theology is again theology of being as relation and of relation as mode of unity . . . through the concept of the mission, being is interpreted as being 'from' and as being 'for.'"[45] God's activity (*oikonomia*) reveals his being, the mystery of his inner life (*theologia*), and the interrelationship between fundamental theology and practical theology (or theological and methodological considerations of evangelization) again appears.[46] Brotherton claims, "Thus, the category (or rather, transcendental) of *relatio* is revealed to us in the economy of creation and salvation history as a window into the inner life of God as well as into man as his image."[47] Relating, being-in-relation, is the mission, is who God has revealed himself

43. Ratzinger, "The New Evangelization."
44. Brotherton, "Damnation and the Trinity," 140.
45. Ratzinger, *Introduction*, 188–89.
46. See *CCC*, §236.
47. Brotherton, "Damnation and the Trinity," 142.

to be. If evangelization is the Church's response to and participation in the *Logos*' missional initiative, and in the *Logos* person and mission coincide, then to evangelize, on the part of the Church, is to do so according to the *Logos* itself—according to who the *Logos* is and how he reveals himself, that is, personally, as pure relationality-in-love. Ratzinger, then, basically conceives an approach to evangelization along personalist lines, according to the anthropological pattern revealed by the *Logos*. As Leithart says, "the form of revelation unveils its content."[48] God reveals himself personally as personal. To "unveil" God, the Gospel, today demands evangelizing according to God's form, hence, it demands evangelizing personally. Evangelization takes place according to the *Logos*, that is, in the personal (i.e., relational) love-pattern revealed by the *Logos*: being-from, being-with, and being-for. Here, *who* is not only *what* (i.e., the coinciding of person and mission), but also *how*. Approaching evangelization in response to the initiative of the *Logos* means approaching evangelization *with* and *in* the *Logos*, who is mission as a relational event of love. As a fundamentally relational endeavor, evangelization, initiated by the *Logos*, restores and unites the relationality of God with the relationality of human being according to the relational pattern established by the Trinity and through a human relationship. Approaching evangelization according to the *Logos* means approaching evangelization relationally according to God's trinitarian pattern.

Ratzinger describes the Church's evangelizing effort as expropriation—a submission on the part of the Church, a complete giving-over of herself to God in his service. He says that the correct method, the correct way of approaching evangelization, flows from God's revelatory initiative, and demands the "expropriation of one's person, offering it to Christ for the salvation of men."[49] Just as the Son lives and gives voice to the Father (not to himself), the evangelizer is to listen and to give voice to the Father. He is not looking for ways to speak in his own name, to establish a name for himself, or to speak from his own authority. "The Lord and the Spirit build the Church, communicate through the Church," Ratzinger says.[50] Human beings, alone, do not.

This law of expropriation invites the evangelist to give him or herself entirely over to God essentially means living the threefold anthropological pattern. It means that the evangelist is a being-from, he or she is one who prays. Jesus prays to the Father in order to acquire the disciples, and the same is true for the evangelizer today. Only evangelization that comes

---

48. Leithart, "A Birthday Card to Balthasar."
49. Ratzinger, "The New Evangelization."
50. See Ratzinger, "The New Evangelization."

from prayer can lead to prayer, and "without prayer, preaching dries up by itself."[51] Expropriation also demands suffering and death with Christ, who not only prayed, but who also suffered and died. The grain of wheat falls to the earth and dies to become fruitful (cf. John 12:24). The evangelist must live as a being-for, offering himself, with Christ, for the many. Finally, the evangelist has a duty to communicate the Gospel in as effective a way as possible today—knowing that language is limited, but nevertheless finding in it a way of accompaniment, of being-with humanity.[52]

With and in the *Logos*, those who evangelize do so according to this relational pattern. The relational pattern even appears in Ratzinger's treatment of Amos/St. Basil. In order to cut through culture and reach the heart and to purify with the Gospel, God chooses some to be his servants (being-from). The *Logos* initiates and calls, and men and women respond to this call to be(come) evangelizers. The one who is called (being-from), is called to give him or herself over for the sake of making the cut, announcing the Gospel (being-for). And, an effective proclamation of the Gospel requires remaining with the *Logos* and an ongoing patience and preparation with the person (being-with), both leading up to the cut and in following through in the process of purification. In what follows, here, I will develop, based upon Ratzinger's thought, concrete points for approaching evangelization along this relational line.

The Church Evangelizes as a Being-from

Effective evangelization does not come about by radical attempts at donning the mufti of secular vocabulary, demythologizing Christianity, pursuing the latest contextual demands to prove her relevance. The Church neither has to convert to the world, nor does she have to engage in countless ecclesiocentric exercises. Ratzinger opposes such methods for reaching a post-Christian West. He says:

> In the long run, the Church cannot avoid the need to get rid of, part by part, the appearance of her identity with the world, and once again to become what she is: the community of the faithful. Actually, her missionary power can only increase through such external losses. Only when she ceases to be a cheap, foregone conclusion, only when she begins again to show herself as she really is, will she be able to reach the ear of the new pagans

---

51. Ratzinger, *Dogma*, 103.
52. See Ratzinger, "The New Evangelization."

with her good news, since until now they have been subject to the illusion that they were *not* real pagans.[53]

The Church simply needs to be(come) herself—as established by God as a being-from for bringing men and women to God. In this way, the Church can make present God's *Logos* in the world, and minister according to Being's *Logos* in time. For the Church to find her voice of proclamation again—indeed, for the Church to have a voice—she must embrace being-from. Ratzinger highlights at least three concrete ways in which to cultivate being-from at the heart of proclamation: (1) Listening to the tradition; (2) Adopting a humble disposition; and (3) Embracing the Eucharistic core.

Concretely, for the Church to evangelize as a being-from, she must listen, or wonder. She does not initiate; she is always the receiving subject of the divine initiative, the first Word. Benedict XVI asserts, "It is important always to know that the first word, the true initiative, the true activity comes from God and only by inserting ourselves into the divine initiative, only by begging for this divine initiative, shall we too be able to become—with him and in him—evangelizers."[54] One can announce the Gospel only by first hearing it, listening and allowing the Gospel to transform his or her life. For Benedict XVI, St. Paul stands as a model in this regard. He reflects on two facts regarding Paul's life:

> The first real fact, therefore, is that Paul speaks, not of a philosophy that he developed, not of ideas that he found elsewhere or invented, but of a reality of his life; he speaks of the God who entered his life; he speaks of a real God, who is alive, who spoke with him and will speak with us, he speaks of the Crucified and Risen Christ. The second real fact is that Paul does not seek himself, he does not want to make a fan club for himself ... rather, Saint Paul proclaims Christ and wants to gain people for the true and real God.... Therefore, talking about God means making room for the One who enables us to know him, who reveals his face of love to us; it means emptying ourselves of our own ego, offering it to Christ, in the awareness that it is not we who can win over others for God, but that we must expect God to send them, we must entreat God for them. Talking about God, therefore, stems from listening, from our knowledge of God, which is brought about through familiarity with him, through the life of prayer and in accordance with the Commandments.[55]

---

53. Ratzinger, "New Pagans."
54. Benedict XVI, "Meditation 2012."
55. Benedict XVI, *Transforming Power*, 44.

First, St. Paul did not come up with a great idea and launch out with slogans and marketing strategies for the sake of spreading it. He did not have an interesting idea about God or a novel piece of theological speculation. His knowledge of God is a living knowledge—the fruit of an objective event, an encounter with Jesus Christ. Second, Paul is not concerned with gaining popularity or becoming something in the eyes of the world. His concern is not self-centered or egotistical. "We are not listening for ourselves—we do not want to increase the power and the spreading of our institutions," Ratzinger says.[56] In order to talk about God, in order to announce the Gospel, therefore, one must listen for God's voice and make room for His Word. This inevitably leads to two questions: Where does one find God's voice and know it to be so? How can one make room for God's Word?

The former question, regarding finding God's voice, could be asked in a different way: How is it that the Church can be sure she is making the real, historical Jesus known today? What is the guarantee that the "image of Jesus is more than an image? Where can I find the real Jesus and not merely ideas about him?"[57] Commenting on Heb 13:8, "Jesus Christ is the same yesterday and today and forever," Ratzinger claims, "we can see Jesus Christ correctly today only if we understand him in union with the Christ of 'yesterday' and see in the Christ of yesterday and today the eternal Christ. The three dimensions of time as well as going beyond time into that which is simultaneously its origin and future are always a part of the encounter with Christ."[58] Encountering Christ, which leads to proclaiming Christ (cf. Rom 10:14), occurs in the present, but his person does not shift with the changing tides in the successive epochs of history. Instead, the encounter with Christ in the present is the encounter with the same Christ who walked the face of the earth, and who will come in glory. Therefore, to ensure that one is encountering (or proclaiming) the whole Christ, and not a piece of him as can result from historical criticism that claims the freedom of scientific objectivity but often resorts to its own various hermeneutical straightjackets, one must "heed the Christ of yesterday as he reveals himself in the sources, especially in Scripture. If, in the process, I listen to him carefully and do not excise essential parts of his appearance because of a dogmatically asserted worldview, I see him open to the future and I see him coming from eternity, which embraces the past, the present, and the future, all at once."[59] Elsewhere, he adds, "The proclamation of

---

56. Ratzinger, "The New Evangelization."
57. Ratzinger, *Nature and Mission*, 60.
58. Ratzinger, *New Song*, 11.
59. Ratzinger, *New Song*, 13.

Christ, the proclamation of the Kingdom of God presupposes listening to his voice in the voice of the Church."[60] Concretely, this means listening within the Church's tradition and to the Church's tradition, for the following is true: (1) "the entire mystery of Christ's presence is in the first instance the whole reality that is transmitted in tradition, the decisive and fundamental reality that is always antecedent all individual explications ... and which represents what in actual fact has to be transmitted";[61] (2) consequently, tradition's concrete form is present in faith, which is "the indwelling of Christ";[62] (3) tradition's "organ" lies in the authority of the Church; (4) tradition is articulated in the creed (*fides quae*), the rule of faith.[63] The revelation of God in his Word is *the* source of revelation—it is *the* revelation—which Scripture and Tradition mediate, but the whole of which they cannot and do not contain, yet through which one can come to knowledge of Christ with the surety that this is not the "more or less romantic ersatz Jesus ... but the Jesus of the Gospels."[64] Listening, then, means listening for the whole Christ, in and through the tradition of the Church, so as to proclaim the whole Christ with and in the Church.

Regarding the latter question from above (i.e., How can the Church make room for God's Word, then?), what disposition allows for the necessary receptivity to the Word? The answer is fairly simple in theory, though, perhaps, more difficult in practice: humility. Thus Church must exercise humility. "The form of revelation unveils its content," and its content reinforces the method of transmission. To be sure, a certain humility, or even hiddenness, shrouds the revelation of God's love in Jesus Christ, though God's glory is most fully manifest in Jesus Christ. Ratzinger notes that "when he really did appear upon the scene, so other, so invisible in regard to his divinity, so unrecognizable, it was not the kind of otherness and strangeness that we had foreseen and expected, and he thus remained in fact unrecognized."[65] God hides himself in his closeness to humanity in Jesus Christ. While it is true that God reveals himself as the great cosmic power, the *pantokrator*, he also takes up another sign that "shows more truly his intrinsic nature."[66] The sign, of course, as Ratzinger points out, is the "sign of the lowly, which, measured cosmically, quantitively, is completely insignificant, actually a

---

60. Ratzinger, "The New Evangelization."
61. Ratzinger, *God's Word*, 63–64.
62. Ratzinger, *God's Word*, 64.
63. Ratzinger, *God's Word*, 64.
64. Ratzinger, GCC, 69.
65. Ratzinger, *Introduction*, 255.
66. Ratzinger, *Introduction*, 255.

pure nothing."⁶⁷ It is the sign of hiddenness apparent in the movement from the creation of the earth *ex nihilo*, to the adoption of the humble nation of Israel, to the Annunciation hidden in Nazareth, the banality of the Cross, and the leaven that remains hidden in the world in the form of the Church.⁶⁸ The humility of God's self-revelation in the Incarnation manifests God's self-giving nature, and God's existence as perfectly personal self-giving (as pure act) is most fully manifest on the Cross where a man hangs "whose life had been a failure." Yet, here, one comes to the point "at which one can actually touch God," because the Cross is "the real sign of God wherein the entirely Other shows itself, which even in relation to our expectations is once again the completely unrecognizable. The cosmic Nothing is the true All, because 'for' is the really divine thing."⁶⁹ The weight of God's glory consists in his humbly lowering himself and allowing himself to be discovered in such a sad state, for in it, God reveals something of the unfathomable depths of His love, which is to say, He reveals himself as He is.

Humility, this acknowledgement of one's real status before Being and opening up to God as his or her source and destiny, is most concretely manifest in prayer. The Church and her mission lives from this prayer and her mission is fruitless without it (cf. John 15:5). Ratzinger makes this point several ways. He reflects on wise words from an Italian priest, Don Didimo, who says "Jesus preached by day, by night he prayed." In emphasizing this point, Didimo and Ratzinger wish to say "Jesus had to acquire the disciples from God. The same is always true. . . . We must acquire [disciples] by God for God." Therefore, "all methods [of evangelization] are empty without the foundation of prayer. The word of announcement must always be drenched in an intense life of prayer."⁷⁰ Or, put another way, the apostles "prayed and in prayer they waited, because they knew that only God himself can create his Church."⁷¹ Prayer is the Church's acknowledgement, and, therefore, the

---

67. Ratzinger, *Introduction*, 256.

68. See Ratzinger, *Introduction*, 256. The "law of disguise" or the "sign of hiddenness" is a common motif in Ratzinger's theology. See, for example, Ratzinger, *Introduction*, 149–50; Ratzinger, "The Undefeated Light"; Benedict XVI, *Jesus of Nazareth: The Infancy Narratives*, 66–67.

69. Ratzinger, *Introduction*, 256–57. Though speaking about an essay by Klaus Hemmerle, Leithart's words can be appropriately applied here, as he concludes that a "God who humbles and elevates himself in revelation is a God who glorifies himself in humility" ("A Birthday Card to Balthasar").

70. Ratzinger, "The New Evangelization." See also Ratzinger, *Dogma*, 103. Here, Ratzinger says, "Discourse about God loses its unifying power and becomes divisive, empty theory when it no longer proceeds from the experiential context of living conversation with God. Without prayer, preaching dries up by itself."

71. Benedict XVI, "Meditation 2012."

evangelist's acknowledgement that she is not her own source. The Church belongs to Another, as does the Word of the evangelist. Beginning with a humility exercised concretely in prayer, the Church can avoid a fundamental temptation that stands at the outset of every missionary venture (cf. Matt 4:1–11), namely that of impatience, of making something happen for herself, of "the temptation of immediately finding the great success, in finding large numbers."[72] However, this is not God's way, which is better described according to the parable of the mustard seed (see Mark 4:30–34). God's method is one of humility, one of hiddenness, manifest most profoundly in the Incarnation all the way through the Cross.[73] "Large things," Ratzinger says, "always begin from the small seed, and the mass movements are always ephemeral . . . large realities begin in humility." Those who evangelize must always remain satisfied with the mustard seed, daring "once again and with the humility of the small grain," leaving it "up to God the when and how it will grow."[74]

In the humility of prayer, then, the evangelist unites him or herself to the *Logos* as his servant, trusting that this act of personal faith will bring about the renewal necessary for effective evangelization today. For:

> God is made known through men who know him, place themselves at his disposal, and make room for him in the world [as servants of the *Logos*]. The path to God leads concretely again and again by way of the man who is already standing by God. It does not lead by way of pure reflection [Rahner!] but, rather, through encounter, which of course is deepened with reflection and becomes more independent and thus at the same time communicable again. . . . In this statement the importance of the preacher comes to the fore with its full gravity.[75]

Nevertheless, despite the undeniable importance of the preacher in evangelization, the preacher's abilities are limited. Ultimately, "God is made known through himself."[76] The evangelist speaks a Word that is not his own and which his words can never contain, in the same way that revelation goes beyond the testimony of contained in Scripture. Nevertheless, the evangelist has access to the Word precisely through the Church, her Scripture, her tradition, and the guidance of her teaching office.

---

72. Ratzinger, "The New Evangelization."
73. Benedict XVI, *Transforming Power*, 43.
74. Ratzinger, "The New Evangelization."
75. Ratzinger, *Dogma*, 87.
76. Ratzinger, *Dogma*, 87.

As a final, and closely related point regarding being-from in general, the *Catechism* points out, drawing from the thought of de Lubac, "the Eucharist makes the Church."[77] Therefore, a word must be said about this mystical food that transforms men and women into beings-from. Benedict XVI describes a certain being-from-the-Eucharist as the "Eucharistic form of the Christian life."[78] Ratzinger does not shy away from St. Augustine's declaration that Christians are to "eat the bread of the strong," for human beings do not change the Eucharist into themselves through the same transferal of nutrients as with other foodstuffs, rather, in the Eucharist "I [Christ] will transform you into me."[79] This Eucharistic bread is "greater and more substantial than we are. We do not assimilate it into ourselves, but rather it assimilates us into itself, so that we are conformed to Christ."[80] In the Eucharist, "We are taken out of ourselves," Ratzinger says, "we are assimilated into him, that we become one with him and, through him, with the fellowship of our brethren."[81] The Eucharist transforms recipients, making them into Christ and uniting them with the other members of his body who now identify with one another.[82]

Ratzinger points out that the Eucharist is a Sacrament of transformation in at least five ways.[83] First, in Christ's saying "This is my body, which is given up for you," he "transforms" his body into gift, so to speak. He is gift and nothing else. Second, because Jesus is his body, identifies himself with his body, and because this body is complete gift, Jesus transforms "an act of violence against him into an act of self-giving for these men" (John 10:18). Here, the act of killing is transformed into an act of love and violence is conquered by love. Now death itself is transformed into life and Jesus' mortal body is transformed into a resurrected body. This makes the remaining transformations possible, the third of which is that bread and wine are transformed or transubstantiated such that "in them the Lord who gives himself—his gift, he himself—becomes present, because he *is* self-giving." When Jesus identifies himself with the bread and wine, and he identifies the bread and wine as gift, for he is entirely self-giving gift. Fourth, "the goal of the Eucharist is the transformation of those who receive it into authentic communion

---

77. *CCC*, §1396.

78. See Benedict XVI, *Sacramentum caritatis*, Title of Part III, Sec. 1. In *CC*, Ratzinger goes so far as to say, "the Church is the Eucharist" (75).

79. Ratzinger, "Eucharist—Communio—Solidarity," 362. See also Ratzinger, "The Eucharist," 287; Benedict XVI, *Sacramentum caritatis*, §70.

80. Ratzinger, "Eucharist—Communio—Solidarity," 362.

81. See Ratzinger, "The Eucharist," 287.

82. See Ratzinger, "Eucharist—Communio—Solidarity," 362.

83. Each point appears in Ratzinger, "Eucharist—Communio—Solidarity," 368–70.

with his [Christ's] transformation. And so the goal is unity ... instead of being separated individuals who live alongside or in conflict with one another, might become, with Christ and in him, one organism of self-giving." Thus, in receiving Christ's being-for, his complete self-gift in the Eucharist, the members of the Church become beings-from and are reconfigured as beings-with Him and one another. This leads into the fifth and final transformation, that those who have received Him, become themselves beings-for, thus transforming all of creation. To live according to the Eucharist, to live a Eucharistic form of life, as a being-from the Eucharist, is to live according to this singular transformation (i.e., from the "I" to the "not I"—Gal 2:20) that is possible in the Eucharist. In this way, the Eucharist "appears in all its power as the source and summit of the Church's life," because it "expresses at once both the origin and the fulfilment of the new and definitive worship of God, the *logiké latreía*."[84] The Eucharist reconfigures the whole of one's life, it transforms the whole of human reality, it transfigures every aspect of daily life, such that all of it can be offered as spiritual worship—as gift.[85] This is only possible because the Eucharist makes the Church, because God initiates the gift-giving, thus making a return possible.

As noted above, one receives the Word, which comes to humanity in the humility of human speech and human flesh, through the mode of humility and in the act of prayer. One receives the Word in its "organs of transmission" by opening to the Word in prayer. Similarly, one becomes capable of receiving the humility of the Word in the enduring sacramental presence of the Eucharist and thus entering into communion, by first assuming the humble posture of adoration. "Communion is ... always simultaneously adoration," Ratzinger says. He adds, "even genuine human love cannot mean that we have the other person all to ourselves and possess him; it includes our reverential recognition of something sublime and unique ... whom we can never entirely possess."[86] This experience attains a new level when the "partner" is the Word, Jesus Christ, who carries the relationship above and beyond any human one. Hence, "no one can receive Communion without first adoring."[87] Humility (i.e., being-from), then, stands as something of the fundamental building block for evangelization, for without acknowledging, accepting, and participating in the initiative of the Word, one merely perpetuates his own ideals, which, in the end, come to nothing (cf. John 15:5).

---

84. Benedict XVI, *Sacramentum caritatis*, §70.
85. Cf. Benedict XVI, *Sacramentum caritatis*, §71.
86. Ratzinger, "The Eucharist," 290.
87. Ratzinger, "The Eucharist," 291.

The Church Evangelizes as a Being-for

An inner dynamism exists between being-from and being-for, as one leads into the other and back again. Christianity means entering into, indeed, participating in, Jesus Christ's pro-existence. Christianity means not only being saved from sin and death, but also the stepping into mission in Christ. Said another way, in becoming part of the being-from (Church as body of Christ) means taking on the Father's "being-for." The Church shares in and identifies with Jesus' pro-existence as her own. As is the case with Christ, this pro-existence bears the form of vicarious representation. Ratzinger says, "The Church, as such and as a whole, is the bearer of this vicarious election, the highest mission of which is to become vicarious rejection. The task of the Church and of the individual Christian is a dynamic one. . . . Election is always, at bottom, election for others. For the Church as for the individual, election is identical with missionary obligation. . . . However important it is for the Church to grow into the unity of a single brotherhood, she must always remember that she is only one of two sons, one brother beside another, and that her mission is not to condemn the wayward brother, but to save him."[88] The deepest meaning of the Church's existence is "grounded wholly in the vicarious existence of Jesus Christ."[89] Here, we see the transition from Christology to Ecclesiology in Ratzinger's understanding of pro-existence, and we see all of evangelization cast in light of charity. Evangelization is an exercise of charity.

Pro-existence, or, said another way, charity itself, is the "energy" or "force" behind evangelization and the issuing of the "slit" of the *Logos*. As for the cut itself, the Gospel, God himself, cuts; the Word is the "knife" or "blade" that cuts through the culture and reaches the heart. While in every case, the Gospel cuts, the manner in which one employs the "knife" may differ. How a person slices the culture depends upon circumstances, and the amount of force applied to the blade based upon the thickness and toughness of the cultural skin varies. In *The Meaning of Christian Brotherhood*, Ratzinger considers three manifestations of the "force" behind the cut of the Gospel: (1) preaching and missionary activity; (2) *Agape*; and (3) vicarious suffering.[90] The present study will briefly consider each of these aspects, which can be applied both to the Church as a whole and to each individual member.

---

88. Ratzinger, *Christian Brotherhood*, 79–80. See also Ratzinger, "Vicarious Representation," 215; Ruddy, "Smaller but Purer?," 713–41.

89. Ratzinger, *Christian Brotherhood*, 80.

90. Ratzinger, *Christian Brotherhood*, 81–84.

First, the Gospel must be proclaimed within the "church that is already founded and already alive." This is an "ordinary preaching" that takes place within a catechetical setting. However, the missionary activity of preaching, properly speaking, pushes out as "the act by which she goes beyond herself and is founded anew where she does not yet exist . . . [the] surpassing of the closed circle and a proclamation of the faith to a new world, in which it must make itself comprehensible once again."[91] The Church is a community of disciples called, first and foremost, to preach the Gospel and gather the scattered man-monads into the new family of God that is the Church. Preaching is never, as Benedict XVI notes, "just words, never just instruction. It is an event, just as Jesus himself is an event, God's Word in person. By announcing him, the Apostles lead their listeners to encounter him."[92] Evangelization is the Church's participation in a Word that establishes relationship. It is a relational reality, a relationship-establishing and relationship-building event. In evangelization, God's personal nature comes to bear, or encounters, the problem of human "impersonalism" or "anti-personalism" due to sin, marking the restoration of the human being's personal nature. To evangelize, then, is to introduce another to the art of living—which is being-in-love, in relationship with God, perfect relationality and the source of relationality—with the *Logos*, the Gospel personified, as "personifications," or "disciples." The Church announces the Gospel precisely because persons were not made for hell, for self-imposed, or other-imposed banishment to the non-communication zone.

The content of missionary preaching aims to present a fundamental outline of the faith.[93] Ratzinger says, "Missionary preaching, which can be accomplished in a course of fasting and missionary sermons . . . should not deal with mere attitudes and individual points, but much more fundamentally present an outline of the faith, or the essential parts of it, in a way that the modern man can understand it."[94] In making this point, Ratzinger frequently returns to the following "highlights:"[95]

- Conversion—John the Baptist unites the Old and New Testaments with his call to conversion. Ratzinger says, "To convert means not to live as all the others live, not do what all do, not feel justified in dubious,

---

91. Ratzinger, *Dogma*, 20.

92. Benedict XVI, *Jesus I*, 173.

93. Ordinary preaching also takes this fundamental outline as its starting point and builds on it.

94. Ratzinger, "New Pagans."

95. I am taking these four points from Ratzinger's 2000 address to catechists, "The New Evangelization," to which I have added similar points made elsewhere.

ambiguous, evil actions just because others do the same; begin to see one's life through the eyes of God. . . . To come out of self-sufficiency to discover and accept our indigence—the indigence of others and of the Other, his forgiveness, his friendship. . . . Conversion is humility in entrusting oneself to the love of the Other, a love that becomes the measure and the criteria of my own life."[96]

- The Kingdom of God—The Kingdom is not a utopian reference to a social or political reality. "The Kingdom of God is God," Ratzinger says, "God exists. God is alive. God is present and acts in our world, in our—in my life."[97] The question of God is central, because ultimately "everything depends on the issue of God. Faith is belief in God or it does not exist."[98] With regard to God, Ratzinger emphasizes the importance of God's creative power—that God is the Creator—and that creation is His, He has power over it—not us.[99] Along with this, God is to be preached as *Logos*,[100] and, therefore, as we have already seen, as a Trinity of persons.[101]

- Jesus Christ—The theme of God becomes concrete in Jesus Christ. Here, Ratzinger critiques attempts at reducing Jesus to the "merely historical Jesus, into a pure man" who is ultimately "an artifact."[102] Preaching on Jesus Christ is tied to happiness, a union with God that satisfies our "thirst for the infinite: for an infinite freedom, for happiness without limits."[103] In *Dogma and Preaching*, Ratzinger notes that the central phases in Jesus' story should mark preaching on his person. Jesus Christ is incarnate, God becoming man and willing to become man. In the Incarnation, the creature is very close to God, yet God still remains far from man who does not recognize Him. The Cross reveals that God's omnipotence unites love and truth. The Resurrection makes it known that God gives a future, that "he is our

---

96. Ratzinger, "The New Evangelization."
97. Ratzinger, "The New Evangelization."
98. Ratzinger, *New Song*, 42.
99. Ratzinger, *New Song*, 43; Ratzinger, *Dogma*, 91–93.
100. See Ratzinger, *Dogma*, 93–95.
101. See Ratzinger, *Dogma*, 88–91.
102. Ratzinger, "The New Evangelization." See also Ratzinger, *New Song*, 43–44; Ratzinger, *Dogma*, 95.
103. Ratzinger, "The New Evangelization." In *New Song*, Ratzinger points out that Augustine pursues the whole subject of Christianity from this question of happiness. At the bottom of it, this thirst is satisfied not by superficial things, but by God, in Jesus Christ (43).

future," and that His creative power is not deistic, but engages the world. Finally, to affirm Jesus means to affirm God's freedom, His freedom to act in the world, a freedom whose measure "is not necessity but, rather, truth and love."[104]

- Eternal Life—In the attempt to show God's relevance to daily life, one must not forget eternal life and ultimate justice. Man will be judged and must account for things. This must be grasped in all its seriousness, yet, at the same time, it leads to the "other aspect of this proclamation, that is redemption, the fact that Jesus, in the cross, takes on our sins."[105] Naturally, this means that preaching must have something to do with morality. This is not to say that preaching is to be reduced to morality, but that it cannot be erased altogether. As Ratzinger points out, "the hallmark ... God of Jesus Christ is precisely the fact that he is a moral entity ... the fullness of moral values in person."[106]

Missionary preaching also casts out demons. Jesus ties preaching and, in a certain sense, exorcism together, calling the Twelve "to preach and have authority to cast out demons" (Mark 3:14). Benedict XVI says, "Because the world is ruled by the powers of evil, this preaching is at the same time a struggle with those powers."[107] Benedict perceives the connection between exorcism of proclamation in two ways. First, he considers the manner in which faith makes the world more rational—casting out the "indeterminable powers of chance" that comprise "chaos theory" and the forces and demons that seem to confront the *homo religiosus*. He says, "To 'exorcise' the world—to establish it in the light of the *ratio* (reason) that comes from eternal creative reason [*Logos*!] and its saving goodness and refers back to it—that is a permanent, central task of the messengers of Jesus Christ."[108] In addition to exorcising the world of its irrationality, Christian proclamation also confronts demonic powers. The Christian cannot overcome these forces by his own resources, but instead, "in faith, in communion with the only true Lord of the world, he is given the 'armor of God.' It enables him—in the communion of the whole body of Christ [being-from and being-with!]—to oppose these powers, knowing that the Lord's gift of faith restores the pure breath of life."[109] Matthew's Gospel pairs

---

104. Ratzinger, *Dogma*, 95–96.
105. Ratzinger, "The New Evangelization."
106. Ratzinger, *Dogma*, 97–98.
107. Benedict XVI, *Jesus I*, 173.
108. Benedict XVI, *Jesus I*, 174.
109. Benedict XVI, *Jesus I*, 175.

the restoration of life brought about by the exorcistic function of preaching with the mission to heal (cf. Matt 10:1). Christianity is a religion of healing, a religion of redemption. Miracles of healing are always "signs" that point to God and move men toward God.[110] However, the ultimate goal of Christian preaching and the ministry of healing is not bodily healing, but the "becoming-one with God" that is "the true process of man's healing."[111] Viewed in this light, one could argue that the primary (or initial) proclamation of the Gospel[112] breaks the bonds of sin and death (the powers of darkness or irrationality), while catechesis deepens the understanding of the mysteries and serves the ongoing healing of the person.

Preaching remains at the forefront of the Church's ministry, regardless of the context—whether ordinary or missionary. On this point, we might recall again Balthasar's terse imperative to Ratzinger, "Do not presuppose the faith but propose it."[113] Balthasar's advice immediately challenges on two fronts. On the one hand, Ratzinger notes that "faith is not maintained automatically. It is not a 'finished business' that we can simply take for granted. The life of faith has to be constantly renewed."[114] Here, missionary preaching reaches right back into "ordinary preaching," and catechesis. The fundamental points of faith, the *kerygma* requires ongoing reflection and constant witness. The central points of faith, namely "God, Christ, the Holy Spirit, grace and sin, sacraments and Church, death and eternal life—are never outmoded. They are always the issues that affect us most profoundly."[115] On the other hand, the faith of the Church is to be "proposed," not imposed. The announcement of the Gospel in missionary preaching is a proposal, an invitation—it is a dialogical event that acknowledges the freedom of the receiving subject, and not a monologue that disregards freedom. Evangelization, then, is a dialogical event. This is not to say that evangelization is reducible to interreligious dialogue, the contemporary form of which does not aim at conversion but understanding and does

---

110. Cf. Benedict XVI, *Jesus I*, 176.

111. Benedict XVI, *Jesus I*, 176.

112. See the *GDC*, §51, 58, 60, 61.

113. Ratzinger, *GCC*, 23. The profundity of this statement has clearly remained with Ratzinger since the words reached him. In *Western Culture*, Benedict XVI recalls them again, "The triune God, Father, Son, and Holy Spirit—do not presuppose him, but present him!" He notes that God is often not presented or dealt with in the concrete, but remains in the background, removed from the real things that concern men and women. "Yet, everything changes if one presents God instead of presupposing him, if one does not leave him somewhat in the background, but instead recognizes him as the center of one's thoughts, words, and actions" (164).

114. Ratzinger, *GCC*, 23.

115. Ratzinger, *GCC*, 24.

not question the identity of either party involved.[116] Interreligious dialogue can play a role, can open the door for evangelization.

In addition to missionary preaching, Ratzinger highlights the place of *agape* in evangelization. *Agape* love is unselfish in nature. Vis-à-vis *eros* (i.e., self-seeking, self-interested love), Benedict XVI says *agape* "now becomes concern and care for the other. No longer is it self-seeking, a sinking in the intoxication of happiness; instead it seeks the good of the beloved: it becomes renunciation and it is ready, and even willing, for sacrifice."[117] In light of Christ, the "last Adam" who is the completely open existence between "from" and "for," "being a Christian means essentially changing over from being for oneself to being for one another . . . leaving behind the seclusion and tranquility of his 'I' [and] departs from himself in order by this frustration [*Durchkreuzung*] of his 'I' to follow the crucified Christ and exist for others."[118] Being a Christian means embracing *agape* as a way of life.

Ratzinger points out that Christian living inculcates *agape* in two ways. First, "the relations of Christians among one another ought to have an attractive and exemplary force, constituting an effective active mission."[119] The love shared within the Christian community should stand as a witness to all as a lamp stand (cf. Mark 4:21) and as a city visible on the hill (cf. Matt 5:14).[120] This point is straightforward enough—the Christian community is to be one of untiringly selfless love. Second, the expression of Christian

---

116. Benedict XVI, "Christmas Greetings 2012." Benedict XVI adds, "These rules are correct, but in the way they are formulated here I still find them too superficial. True, dialogue does not aim at conversion, but at better mutual understanding—that is correct. But all the same, the search for knowledge and understanding always has to involve drawing closer to the truth. Both sides in this piece-by-piece approach to truth are therefore on the path that leads forward and towards greater commonality, brought about by the oneness of the truth. As far as preserving identity is concerned, it would be too little for the Christian, so to speak, to assert his identity in a such a way that he effectively blocks the path to truth. Then his Christianity would appear as something arbitrary, merely propositional. He would seem not to reckon with the possibility that religion has to do with truth. On the contrary, I would say that the Christian can afford to be supremely confident, yes, fundamentally certain that he can venture freely into the open sea of the truth, without having to fear for his Christian identity. To be sure, we do not possess the truth, the truth possesses us: Christ, who is the truth, has taken us by the hand, and we know that his hand is holding us securely on the path of our quest for knowledge. Being inwardly held by the hand of Christ makes us free and keeps us safe: free—because if we are held by him, we can enter openly and fearlessly into any dialogue; safe—because he does not let go of us, unless we cut ourselves off from him. At one with him, we stand in the light of truth."

117. Benedict XVI, *DCE*, §6.

118. Ratzinger, *Introduction*, 252–53.

119. Ratzinger, *Christian Brotherhood*, 82.

120. Ratzinger, *Christian Brotherhood*, 82.

agape is not to be limited only to members of the Church, as if it were only an intra-ecclesial practice. Instead, *agape* must motivate all interactions with those on the other side of the boundary line established by faith. On this point, Ratzinger says, "Christians can never, and must never, be satisfied with saluting and loving their brothers, that is, their fellow believers; they must follow the Lord who performed his work of love for those who neither knew nor loved him (see Rom 5:6), directing their love to all those who need them, without asking for thanks or a response."[121]

Whether is expressed between members of the Church, or spills out beyond the borders created by faith, *agape* demands a "deep personal sharing in the needs and sufferings of others," which "becomes a sharing of my very self with them: if my gift is not to prove a source of humiliation, I must give to others not only something that is my own, but my very self; I must be personally present in my gift."[122] *Agape* becomes infused by and an expression of *caritas* when, in sharing oneself, one shares Christ. *Agape*, in the Christian sense of the word, means that not just any "yes," but God's "yes," God's *caritas* has entered one's life, and is now given to others. This is akin to the point above regarding Paul's calling the Gospel "my Gospel." Here, Ratzinger says:

> Like every love, "supernatural" love comes from a "yes" that has been given to me but in this case from a greater "you" than any human being. It is the irruption of God's "yes" into my life through Jesus Christ's "yes" to us who had distanced ourselves from God's "yes," a "yes" upheld in the incarnation, the cross, and the resurrection. *Agape* thus presupposes that the crucified love of the Lord has become perceptible to me, that it touches me through faith.[123]

Now, "the consciousness that, in Christ, God has given himself for us, even unto death, must inspire us to live no longer for ourselves but for him, and, with him, for others."[124] The Church makes this love perceptible to the person today, and reconstitutes the person to the point where the new "I" (cf. Gal 2:20) is no longer strange for the person but is his "home" due to the transforming power of faith.[125] Only at this point, wherein the Church (i.e., member of the Church) becomes so rooted in a radical reception of the

---

121. Ratzinger, *Christian Brotherhood*, 83.
122. Benedict XVI, *DCE*, §33–34.
123. Ratzinger, *Yes of Jesus*, 101.
124. Benedict XVI, *DCE*, §34.
125. Ratzinger, *Yes of Jesus*, 103.

truth of God's love,[126] can *agape* spill out and over to the "stranger" who is no longer a stranger due to the all-embracing love of God in Jesus Christ. Thus, Ratzinger says:

> Christ wishes to use my faculties and capabilities for him, even when a purely human natural attraction does not exist. Now I can give him Christ's "yes" that fills my life as my own "yes" and yet his, even when and precisely when natural sympathy is not there. In the place of individual, private sympathies and antipathies there has entered Christ's sympathy, his compassion, his suffering with and loving with people. From this compassion of Christ that has been communicated to me and that becomes my own in the life of faith I can hand on a compassion, a "yes," that is greater than my own and enables the other to feel that profoundest "yes" that alone gives meaning and support to every human "yes." ... It presupposes that in the life of faith I come to the inward exchange of my ego with Christ so that his "yes" really penetrates into my being and becomes mine.... It is only in this kind of risk-taking, at first still unaccustomed and perhaps a little frightening, that the power to do so grows and the Easter connection becomes ever more recognizable: this crucifixion of oneself—self-denial—leads to a great inner joy, to "resurrection." The more I dare lose myself, the more I discover that it is precisely in this way that I find myself. Thus through the encounter with Jesus a new realism accrues to me, and he again strengthens me anew in acting from membership with him.... The challenge of the cross ... demands that I give my ego into Jesus' hands, not so that he may destroy it but so that in him it may become free and expand. The "yes" of Jesus Christ that I hand on is only really his if it has also become completely mine.[127]

One can draw a number of conclusions here. The "yes" of Jesus Christ is the Gospel—*evangelium*—and it becomes Gospel when it first penetrates the being of the believer to the point that he or she identifies with the "yes" given to him or her by God in the *Logos*, and can, in turn, venture this "yes" to the other regardless of his or her feelings towards the other. *Agape* becomes *caritas*, and as such, becomes capable of evangelization, when God's "yes" in Jesus Christ transforms the person such that this "yes" can be given to the other. This "yes" demands much of the believer—the dissolution of his own "I" and his willingness to join in Jesus' compassionate

---

126. See Ratzinger, *Introduction*, 254.
127. Ratzinger, *Yes of Jesus*, 103–4.

suffering-with and suffering-for.¹²⁸ Thus, in light of the first responsibility of the Church toward the "other brother," one can say that the proclamation of the Gospel occurs when, in *agape*, the Christian issues forth the "yes" of Jesus Christ to the non-believer, who, in accepting the affirmation of his existence by the God who loved him when he did not know God or love God (cf. Rom 5:6), he is able to then accept himself and others. Hence, the truth of Love Incarnate, must become, as Benedict XVI says, "the flame of love, a flame that truly ignites my being . . . the great passion of my being and so ignites my neighbour . . . truth becomes charity in me and charity like fire ignites my neighbour."¹²⁹

One who has *agape* expressed as *caritas* is willing to offer him or herself, regardless of whether or not the gift is received, regardless of whether or not the "yes" is accepted. This fact leads into Ratzinger's final point regarding the Church's relation to nonbelievers, one which he calls the "last and highest mission" of the Christian—"to suffer for them and in their place as the Master did."¹³⁰ He says:

> The disciples of Christ will always be "few," as the Lord said, and as such stand before the mass, the "many," as Jesus, the one, stands for the man (that is, the whole of mankind). . . . The disciples of Jesus are few, but as Jesus himself was one "for the many," so it will always be their mission to not be against but "for the many." When all other ways fail, there will always remain the royal way of vicarious suffering by the side of the Lord. It is in her defeat that the Church constantly achieves her highest victory and stands nearest to Christ.¹³¹

Jesus Christ, who willingly accepted being rejected by men who cannot stand a God who dares to love them so personally, is the model here. The Christian who dares to issue forth the "yes" to the other and who is rejected by the other, in that moment of rejection, and suffering, stands closest to Christ who was rejected, suffered, and died in rejected isolation. Being from God and with God—that continued clinging to the "yes" of Jesus Christ—allows one to remain in the midst of the "no" of rejection such that the "yes" may be present even in the face of the "no," and be received, in and through the Son, by the Father in place of the "no." Vicarious suffering means standing with Christ as a "sign that is spoken against" (Luke 2:34). Pro-existence, then, reaches its high point in a vicarious representation

---

128. See Benedict XVI, *Spe salvi*, §39–40.
129. Benedict XVI, "Meditation 2012."
130. Ratzinger, *Christian Brotherhood*, 83.
131. Ratzinger, *Christian Brotherhood*, 83–84.

that is vicarious acceptance and rejection. Such vicarious representation is precisely the way in which the Church breaks through the gates of the netherworld today (cf. Matt 16:18) as a presence amid the hell of isolation. It is the enduring "yes" of God's extension of relationality in the face of the anti-personal "no" of relationally broken human beings.

The offering of the Christian "yes" in the face of the "no" of sin and death goes by the name of "confession." On this point, Benedict XVI highlights the martyrological aspect of Christian witness, as confession highlights:

> The element of witnessing to faith in front of the enemy, even in situations of passion and of the danger of death. Christian confession essentially involves a willingness to suffer. . . . Again, in the essence of the *"confessio"* of our Creed, an openness to passion, suffering, indeed, giving up life is implied. And this guarantees credibility: the *"confessio"* is not just something that can be abandoned; the *"confessio"* implies the willingness to give up my life, to accept the passion. This is also truly the verification of the *"confessio."* It can be seen that for us *"confessio"* is not a word, it is more than pain, it is more than death.[132]

Missionary activity (i.e., the proclamation of the Gospel), holds within itself the need for witness. Gospel cannot be proclaimed as some outside piece of information that is passed along in some banal fashion. The proclamation of the Gospel is a *confessio* shaped by the *confessio* of the Creed, and one which lays a personal demand upon the evangelist—to witness with a testimony that is a personal confession of faith (i.e., "my Gospel") in the face of possible persecution. *Agape*, in its Christian form, extends so far as to embrace this threat and to love despite it.

The Church Evangelizes as a Being-with

Just as the Church is, in the Son, a being-from in a twofold sense (i.e., called by, or from God, and called from the world) and a being-for in a twofold sense (i.e., for God and "for the many"), she is, in the Holy Spirit a being-with in a twofold sense—she is both with God and with humanity. She is, in light of the Holy Spirit as *communio*, the visible manifestation of *communio* on earth. In identifying the Holy Spirit as a being-with, as "*Communio*," Ratzinger notes that the Holy Spirit always points to the Trinity—three divine persons, in *Communio*, in one God. He also notes that the Holy Spirit points to humanity as well. He says, "the trinitarian God is the archetype

---

132. Benedict XVI, "Meditation 2012."

of the new united humanity, the archetype of the Church... Church does not mean another idea in addition to man, but rather man on the way to himself."[133] God's plan for man is "unity according to the image of God," a love that is "entirely one, single, and that he is, however, at the same time counterpart, exchange, community."[134] Men and women are made for community, communication, and communion—which is the fulfillment of their personal nature. Persons, by nature of being persons, aspire beyond their own temporal, special, and bodily boundaries for relationship. This aspiration has seemingly been muted in recent years. While the problems of individuality, the inability to dialogue, the "ultimate inaccessibility of the other, the impossibility of giving oneself to another and understanding one another for any length of time" have been, in Ratzinger's opinion, all too apparent in the twentieth century, the reality of the Holy Spirit reveals "that we men among ourselves can become one only when we find ourselves in a higher unity, as it were, in a third party. Only when we are one with God can we be united among ourselves. The way to the other leads over to God."[135] Relationship with another is possible in the presence of "the all-embracing third," who is "greater and higher than individuals," and which is God who "in truth is the first."[136]

The Holy Spirit is that "third party" that makes human communion possible "as God's gift to history in the community of those who believe in Christ."[137] And, the Holy Spirit is operative in the Church. The Church, as *communio*, as that body that is not only "from" and "for," but also "with" God and "with" humanity, stands as the concrete "all-embracing third" throughout both space and time.[138] The Church stands as a trans-temporal visible body, the "space" in which God comes to man and man to God, and the "space" in which men come to each other. The Church is the union of "yeses"—that of God and of man. Because she is with God she can be with man. In her deepest nature, the Church is "the overcoming of the boundary

---

133. Ratzinger, *Images of Hope*, 65. The word "parish," denoting the geographical or physical "place" in which one's Catholic Christianity is concretely lived, captures this notion of man "on the way to himself," in the *status viatoris* (Pieper, *On Hope*, 11–21). Etymologically, the word "parish" is derived from the Greek word for "sojourner," one who is present in a place only temporarily as part of a longer journey. Furthermore, the word parish is derived from *para* ("near") and *oikos* ("house"). The parish is a "near house," a place where sojourner-neighbors gather on the Way.

134. Ratzinger, *Images of Hope*, 66.

135. Ratzinger, *Images of Hope*, 66.

136. Ratzinger, "*Communio*," 126.

137. Ratzinger, *Introduction*, 331.

138. Cf. *CCC*, §759–69.

between I and Thou, the union of men among themselves through the radical transcendence of self into eternal love," made possible, because the "Church is mankind being brought into the way of life of the trinitarian God."[139] The Church, as the *communion* between God and men through Jesus Christ in the Holy Spirit, makes communion between men and women possible insofar as she is the image and gift of the Holy Spirit.

The Church, this objective "third" that is the "space" in which persons come together in time, in the present moment, makes the Christian fact encounter-able today. Giussani calls the Church "a reality comprised of those who believe in him," and "the encounterable form of his presence."[140] Citing Acts 9:4, and the mysterious line "Saul, Saul, why do you persecute me?" Giussani comments that the gift of the Spirit assimilates the person into the single body of Christ in an ontological sense.[141] Furthermore, Giussani says:

> It is by encountering the unity of believers that we quite literally meet up with Christ, by encountering the Church as it emerges in the way it has been fixed by the Spirit. To encounter the Church, I must meet men and women in given surroundings. It is impossible to encounter the universal Church in its entirety ... we meet the Church as it emerges locally, in each environment ... it is the mystery of God that is present.[142]

The Church exists as *communio*, and is, therefore, at the service of an encounter with the *Logos*. The Christian event happens today—it still happens today—in the "now" of the mystery of the Church. The Church is that objective reality, that fact, which confronts the subject as such, and provokes a response. Therefore, it is incumbent upon the one evangelizing to do so as a being-with the Church—a member of the *communio* that takes shape in the teaching of the apostles, the breaking of the bread, and in prayer (cf. Acts 2:42).

The Church, as a whole, and in her individual members, carries out the mission in the relationality of being-with as an enduring accompanying presence. In order to explain further, I will look at each of these

---

139. Ratzinger, *Images of Hope*, 68–69. For Ratzinger, this is precisely why there cannot be such a thing as a church purely "from below." Nothing that originates "from below" is capable of attaining to the heights of Trinitarian life. Similarly, the Church "cannot become a national Church or be identified with a race or a class. She must ... be catholic.... The Church does not begin, therefore, as a club; rather, she begins catholic. She speaks on her first day in all languages, in the languages of the planet. She was first universal before she brought forth local churches" (69).

140. Giussani, *Why the Church?*, 21.

141. Giussani, *Why the Church?*, 21.

142. Giussani, *Why the Church?*, 22.

words—*enduring* and *accompanying* and *presence*—separately and in reverse order. First, and fundamentally, the Church is to be a presence. This presence can take a number of forms. For Ratzinger, its most fundamental form appears in personal relations and a basic neighborly concern for others—particularly unbelievers. Ratzinger says:

> The Catholic should be able to be a happy man among men.... And I mean that in his relations with his unbelieving neighbors, he must, above all, be a human being; therefore, he should not irritate them with constant preaching and attempts to convert them. In a friendly way, he will be offering him a missionary service by giving him a religious article, when he is sick to suggest the possibility of calling a priest, or even to bring a priest to see him. He should not be just a preacher, but also in a friendly and simple way, a fellow human being who cares for others.[143]

The Church is, and is to be a presence: a real, personal, concrete presence in the world. One could argue that Ratzinger takes the patristic interpretation of the Body of Christ (*Corpus Christi*) as his point of departure, here, for, in his study of Augustine, Ratzinger finds that Christ's body is "neither 'mystical' nor confused," but "quite concrete and by no means considered only metaphorically."[144] On this point and commenting on Ratzinger's conclusion, Heim argues that the "Fathers of the Church understand the Church herself as the *true Body of Christ* . . . whereas they originally describe the Eucharist as *corpus mysticum*."[145] Understood in this light, "the Eucharist makes the Church" (*CCC*, §1396) means the Eucharist is that mystical food, that sacramental food that makes the Church into the true Body of Christ and which allows Him to be present throughout the world in the Church. Therefore, the Church is a being-with only because she is a being-from Christ's own enduring presence, the being-for of the Eucharist.

The second form of being-with follows from the initial point on presence: the Church is to be an *accompanying* presence. Ratzinger ties accompaniment to Christ's accompaniment of humanity in truth and compassion. He says, "in all human suffering we are joined by one who experiences and carries that suffering *with* us; hence *con-solatio* is present in all suffering,

---

143. Ratzinger, "New Pagans." For a practical exposition on the importance of being-with in mission, see Mother Teresa, *A Simple Path*, 88–89.

144. Ratzinger, *Volk und Haus Gottes*, 324, quoted in Heim, *Joseph Ratzinger*, 244.

145. Heim, *Joseph Ratzinger*, 245. For more on the thirteenth-century shift of language indicated here, between "true Body of Christ" and "Mystical Body," please see Lubac, *Corpus Mysticum*; McPartlan, *Sacrament of Salvation*, 56–60.

the consolation of God›s compassionate love."¹⁴⁶ In addition to consolation, accompaniment also accounts for *veritas*, that is the connection of truth and love as it is visible in the Cross. Hence, evangelization concerns itself with forgiveness. Ratzinger defines forgiveness as "the restoration of truth, the renewal of being, and the overcoming of the lie that lurks in every sin: of its nature sin is always a departure from the truth of one's own being and thus from the truth of the creator, God. . . . Forgiveness is participation in the pain of transition from the drug of sin to the truth of love."¹⁴⁷ Hence, not only compassion (i.e., suffering-with) but forgiveness becomes central in Ratzinger's understanding of accompaniment, which means:

> Preceding and accompanying someone on this path of death and rebirth. Only preceding and accompanying addicts in this way (for sin is always a "drug," the lie of false happiness) can enable them to let themselves be led through the dark journey of suffering. It is only by going ahead to enter into the suffering and into the death involved in the way of transformation that makes this journey bearable, because it is only in this way that the dark night of the narrow way the light of hope in new life becomes visible. The reverse is true: only love gives the power to forgive, that is, to accompany the other on the road of the suffering that transforms. It is only this that makes it possible to accept and to endure with and on behalf of the other the death of the lie. It is only this that enables one to remain a bearer of the light in the pitch-black and seemingly endless tunnel and to make noticeable the fresh air of promise that leads to rebirth.¹⁴⁸

To accompany means to go ahead with Christ (i.e., Truth and Love) and so to enter into the death-event of the "I," or, by way of a secondary mediation, actually helping to initiate that painful event of identity-suffering—the "I" becoming the "not I"—by being-with the "I" amid its hellish relational situation. None of this is possible—in other words, evangelization is impossible—without the love that gives the power to forgive, without the love (*caritas* expressed in *agape*) that gives the evangelist the power to *for-give*, to go before the other and, with and in Christ's "for" the other, to "give" the other him/herself (i.e., rebirth).¹⁴⁹

Finally, in her being an accompanying presence for others (i.e., accompanying others in the truth), which allows her to make the "cut" with

---

146. Benedict XVI, *Spe salvi*, §39.
147. Ratzinger, *Yes of Jesus*, 95.
148. Ratzinger, *Yes of Jesus*, 95–96.
149. See Ratzinger, *Yes of Jesus*, 103.

the Gospel, the Church must continue to accompany beyond this initial slit. It is an *enduring* accompaniment. Ratzinger says the encounter between the *Logos* and the culture (or the person immersed in the culture) must be "ongoing and patient" and "mediated by the service of the faithful."[150] In the Church, both "ordinary preaching," as Ratzinger calls it, and catechesis are concrete forms of this service offered by the faithful in their being-with or staying-with those who have heard the Gospel and who are responding to it. Ratzinger describes ordinary preaching as "the word proclaimed in the liturgy, [which] can and should be relatively short, because it should not really announce new things, because its purpose is to dig deeper into the mystery of the faith, which has already, fundamentally, been accepted and affirmed."[151] Catechesis, for its part, has already been discussed at length in chapter 11, and is that part of the Church's evangelizing mission that systematically and comprehensively leads one deeper and deeper into the mystery that has pierced the heart of the hearer.

In terms of concrete initiatives according a certain being-with or accompaniment, and apart from that which happens in the ordinary circumstances of a Christian's life within the world, it seems Ratzinger/Benedict XVI encourages three initiatives. First, he encourages ecumenical relations with other Christians and Christian denominations, which should neither "suppress truths in order to not upset others," nor should they "regard the others as opponents to defend ourselves against." Instead, Ratzinger views ecumenism through a lens of gift, wherein one recognizes the others "as fellow believers, with whom we talk and from whom we can learn."[152]

Next, he supports interreligious dialogue. Benedict XVI notes that interreligious dialogue is one of three areas of dialogue (with states, society, and other religions) in which the Church engages for the sake of man and his humanity. In each case, the "Church speaks on the basis of the light given her by faith. But at the same time she incorporates the memory of mankind. . . . By entering into the thinking and understanding of mankind, this knowledge broadens the horizon of reason and thus it speaks also to those who are unable to share the faith of the Church."[153] The Church engages and enters into in the memory of mankind, because the Church

---

150. Ratzinger, *On the Way*, 48.

151. Ratzinger, "New Pagans."

152. From an interview with *La Repubblica* as quoted in Seewald, *Benedict XVI*, 406. See also Ratzinger and Messori, *The Ratzinger Report*, 155–68; Ratzinger, *God and the World*, 450–53; Benedict XVI, *Light of the World*, 86–97; Rowland, *Benedict XVI*, 138–42.

153. Benedict XVI, "Christmas Greetings 2012."

and the world do not exist according to some sort of strict dualism.[154] The Church, drawn out of the world for the sake of the world, requires that, as Rowland puts it, "any assessment of the relationship between the church and the world requires something much more theologically complex than a merely juridical understanding of the church and a merely sociological understanding of the world."[155] This fundamental relationship between the Church and the world makes interreligious dialogue possible. According to Benedict XVI, interreligious dialogue consists of multiple dimensions. The first dimension involves simply being together, listening, openness to purification, and taking common steps toward truth.[156] Additionally, Benedict XVI notes two "rules" that seem to be regarded as fundamental for interreligious dialogue today: (1) dialogue aims at understanding, not at conversion (hence, it is not, properly speaking, evangelization); and (2) both parties remain within their respective identities—which are not to be called into question. Benedict XVI agrees with such rules but finds them to be too superficial. Thus, Benedict XVI concludes that the search for knowledge "has to involve drawing closer to the truth," and, therefore, it involves a certain risk to one's position and the unity of differing positions as they gaze together on the truth. He says, "Both sides in this piece-by-piece approach to truth are therefore on the path that leads forward and towards greater commonality, brought about by the oneness of the truth."[157]

Finally, when it comes to those who do not believe at all, or to those "nones" who have left religion behind, Benedict XVI calls the Church to create a new "court of the Gentiles," a space similar to that which the Israelites offered the Gentiles in the Temple. Benedict XVI introduced his thoughts about this court in his 2009 Christmas greetings to the Roman Curia:

> The so-called "Court of the Gentiles" . . . [was] a free space for the Gentiles who wished to pray there to the one God, even if they could not take part in the mystery for whose service the inner part of the Temple was reserved. . . . [It was a] place of prayer for all the peoples . . . who know God, so to speak, only from afar; who are dissatisfied with their own gods, rites and myths; who desire the Pure and the Great, even if God remains for them the "unknown God" (cf. Acts 17: 23). They had to pray to the unknown God, yet in this way they were somehow in touch with the true God, albeit amid all kinds of obscurity. I think that today

---

154. See Rowland, "The World," 118–19.
155. Rowland, "The World," 117.
156. Benedict XVI, "Christmas Greetings 2012."
157. Benedict XVI, "Christmas Greetings 2012."

too the Church should open a sort of "Court of the Gentiles" in which people might in some way latch on to God, without knowing him and before gaining access to his mystery, at whose service the inner life of the Church stands. Today, in addition to interreligious dialogue, there should be a dialogue with those to whom religion is something foreign, to whom God is unknown and who nevertheless do not want to be left merely Godless, but rather to draw near to him, albeit as the Unknown.[158]

This pastoral initiative has since been taken up as a forum by the Pontifical Council for Culture.[159] In terms of the concrete, organizations like Alpha and their basic Alpha course create this kind of "court of the Gentiles" on the ground at parishes, while various forums or social media networks create a similar type of space online. In each case, the Church's genuine and authentic being *with* the other in charity opens space for the possibility of evangelization.

The "Saint" as Servant of the *Logos*

The way for the Church to evangelize—as a whole Body and as individual members—goes by way of the *Logos*. I mean this in a twofold manner. On the one hand, one can evangelize, one can speak about God because God has first spoken to us, and continues to do so. On the other hand, one evangelizes according to the manner in which the *Logos* evangelizes. This is to say that one evangelizes personally and according to the personal pattern revealed and employed by the *Logos*: being-from, being-for, and being-with. Such an approach maintains God as the source of evangelization and a theandric, participatory role for human beings that ultimately finds its end by sharing in the "being-for" of the Father toward humanity.

Ratzinger locates the ideal evangelist, the one who evangelizes personally, in the person of the "saint." Evangelization depends upon this kind of personal structure of proclamation. He says:

---

158. Benedict XVI, "Address of His Holiness Benedict XVI to Members of the Roman Curia." For more on the ideas presented in this paragraph pertaining to the "courtyard of the Gentiles," see Franchi, "The Catholic School," 57–76. Here, Franchi argues that the idea of a "courtyard of the Gentiles" might engage the tension Catholic schools feel between pluralism and tradition. Daniel Blackman argues that the dialogue between Catholicism and Judaism encouraged by *Nostra Aetate* has become detached from evangelization, and sees principles derived from the Judaism and the Temple as helpful for reinvigorating this dialogue. See Blackman, "The Courtyard of the Gentiles," 579–98.

159. See the Pontifical Council for Culture, "Courtyard of the Gentiles."

> The only really effective apologia for Christianity comes down to two arguments, namely, the *saints* the Church has produced and the *art* which has grown in her womb. Better witness is borne to the Lord by the splendor of holiness and art which have arisen in the community of believers than by the clever excuses which apologetics has come up with to justify the dark sides which, sadly, are so frequent in the Church's human history.[160]

By "saint," Ratzinger refers to St. Paul's reference to the Christians of the early Church. Here, the word does not denote only those canonized, or even canonizable Christians. The word does not refer to "a headlong leap into heroism that makes someone a saint," or "adventurous achievements of virtue."[161] Instead, the word refers to Christ's own sanctifying initiative and action that sanctifies the Church and her members, those "saints" who "with Jesus receive a ray of his brightness" and who are "called to use their experience of the risen Lord to become a point of reference for others that could bring them into contact with Jesus' vision of the living God."[162] The saints are witnesses, they are reference points or windows that allow the light of Christ to shine through to others. Ratzinger emphasizes the connection between evangelization and witness, when he says, "It is the role of the Church to speak to the world the word of God given in Christ, to witness before the world to the public saving work of God so that everyone can hear it."[163] "Saint" is another name for witness, and the saint is precisely the one who has been reconfigured according to the anthropological pattern revealed by the *Logos* and who evangelizes accordingly.

Time and time again, Ratzinger speaks of the saint-as-witness or the saint-as-reference-point. It is clear that he drives at the early Church's understanding of the word: not as a seemingly unattainable goal for a "few," but as that to which the "many" who comprise the "few" of the Church are called. For example:[164]

---

160. Ratzinger and Messori, *The Ratzinger Report*, 129–30.

161. Ratzinger, *Yes of Jesus*, 104–5. See also Benedict XVI, "The Holiness."

162. Ratzinger, *Yes of Jesus*, 30–33.

163. Ratzinger, *Christian Brotherhood*, 82. Ratzinger includes a point in this section worth noting. He claims that the Church must perform her missionary activity with "holy discretion," recognizing "that there are places where the word would be wasted, thrown away, if it were spoken. . . . He best disseminates the word who does not squander it but proclaims it." The soil must be prepared, so to speak, for the seed of the Gospel to sink in, lest, like the parable of the sower, much of the seed fail to bear the intended fruit.

164. Rowland has a treatment on this topic in *Benedict XVI*, 90–91.

- "Whoever had and lived the faith in Christ Risen was called to become a point of reference for all others, setting them in this way in contact with the Person and the Message of Jesus, who reveals the face of the Living God. And this holds true also for us: a Christian who lets himself be guided and gradually shaped by the faith of the Church, in spite of his weaknesses, his limitations, and his difficulties, becomes like a window open to the light of the living God, receiving this light and transmitting it to the world."[165]

- "Is there anyone who does not know Dostoyevsky's often quoted sentence: 'The Beautiful will save us'? However, people usually forget that Dostoyevsky is referring here to the redeeming Beauty of Christ. We must learn to see Him. . . . Nothing can bring us into close contact with the beauty of Christ himself other than the world of beauty created by faith and light that shines out from the faces of the saints, through whom his own light becomes visible."[166]

---

165. Benedict XVI, *Transforming Power*, 23.

166. Ratzinger, "The Feeling of Things." Under Benedict XVI's pontificate, the Pontifical Council for Culture, engaged the topic of the present culture and the Gospel and called for a *via pulchritudinis* (way of beauty). The plenary assembly's concluding document, "The *Via Pulchritudinis*: Privileged Pathway for Evangelization and Dialogue," claims, "Too often in recent years, the *truth* has been instrumentalised by ideologies, and the *good* horizontalised into a merely social act as though charity towards neighbour alone sufficed without being rooted in love of God. Relativism . . . continues to spread, encouraging a climate of miscomprehension, and making real, serious and reasoned encounters rare. Beginning with the simple experience of the marvel-arousing meeting with beauty, the *via pulchritudinis* can open the pathway for the search for God, and disposes the heart and spirit to meet Christ, who is the Beauty of Holiness Incarnate, offered by God to men for their salvation" (§II.1). The document goes on to identify three "ways of beauty" that can lead the person to God: (1) the beauty of creation (§III.1); (2) the beauty of the arts (§III.2); and (3) the beauty of Christ (§III.3). Regarding the last point, the document speaks of encountering Christ in the liturgy, and in the person of the saint. The Pontifical Council for Cultures' document quotes Pope Benedict XVI, saying, "the saint is the one who is so fascinated by the beauty of God and by his perfect truth that he is progressively transformed by it. For this beauty and this truth, he is ready to renounce everything, even himself" (§III.1.B). Elsewhere he says, "Today, for faith to grow, we must lead ourselves and the persons we meet to encounter the saints and to enter into contact with the Beautiful. The witness is the saint, and the saint cannot help but bear witness" (Ratzinger, "The Feeling of Things"). On this point, Louis J. Rouleau draws the connection between Benedict XVI's interest in the action of God in history and the enduring manifestation of this action through the Holy Spirit operative in the lives of the saints as manifest in Benedict XVI's General Audiences on the great figures in the history of the Church (given from March 15, 2006–April 13, 2011). Rouleau points out that Benedict XVI "is animated by the conviction that holiness possesses an evidential power," for it is the beauty of the image of Christ apparent in the saints that "establishes the credibility of Christianity" (Rouleau, "Holiness," 166).

- "Paul was effective, not because of brilliant rhetoric and sophisticated strategies, but rather because he exerted himself and left himself vulnerable in the service of the Gospel."[167]
- At the origin of every new catechetical endeavor, one finds the person of the catechist for whom "the Church has ceased to be something external for him but has 'awakened in his soul,'" and who can "with his dynamic of faith, retransform the letter into a living voice. He will face contradiction, but above all, he will evoke the joy that comes from meeting Jesus."[168]
- "The renewal of the Church is also achieved through the witness offered by the lives of believers: by their very existence in the world, Christians are called to radiate the word of truth that the Lord Jesus has left us."[169]
- "It is important that every form of proclamation keep in mind, first of all, the intrinsic relationship between the communication of God's word and Christian witness. The very credibility of our proclamation depends on this. On the one hand, the word must communicate everything that the Lord himself has told us. On the other hand, it is indispensable, through witness, to make this word credible, lest it appear merely as a beautiful philosophy or utopia, rather than a reality that can be lived and itself give life."[170]
- "Actually I must say that also for my personal faith many saints, not all, are true stars in the firmament of history. And I would like to add that for me not only a few great saints whom I love and whom I know well are 'signposts,' but precisely also the simple saints, that is, the good people I see in my life who will never be canonized. They are ordinary people, so to speak, without visible heroism but in their everyday goodness I see the truth of faith. This goodness, which they have developed in the faith of the Church, is for me the most reliable apology of Christianity and the sign of where the truth lies."[171]

Evangelization demands something personal of the "saint." The saint's vision, the *who* and *what* he or she has witnessed, opens and is meant to

---

167. Ratzinger, *Images of Hope*, 26.
168. Ratzinger, *GCC*, 59.
169. Benedict XVI, *Porta fidei*, §6.
170. Benedict XVI, *Verbum Domini*, §97.
171. Benedict XVI, "The Holiness." Similarly, he says in *The Feast of Faith*, 124: "Next to the saints, the art which the Church has produced is the only real 'apologia' for her history."

be opened so as to awaken others. The transformation of the saint's life by the "yes" of Jesus Christ, and the saint's own *fiat*, marks a giving over to Christ, and the corresponding transformation that results in the saint's being a window through which the light of Christ can shine. Here, it is also worth noting the emphasis in Ratzinger's writing on sanctity and weakness. The "saint" is not necessarily the person who is perfectly whole and who always has been. Instead, the "saint" is the one who knows Jesus because Jesus has exposed his own wounds (cf. John 20:20), because Jesus has entered into the wounds of the "saint," and has and is redeeming them. The "saint," like Paul, knows that God "will act in [his/her] weakness,"[172] and that his/her weaknesses and wounds that are being redeemed, are something of a window through which the other catches a glimpse of the Divine Physician himself.[173] The saint's weakness allows the strength of God to shine through and to be given for the other. In this way, the saint both gets "in the way" of the other, and simultaneously "out of the way" for God in a manner similar to a stained-glass window—which strikes the eye of the beholder as the light (from a source outside of it) strikes each of its various parts allowing the whole to be seen, and, in allowing the whole to be seen, allowing the light outside to become recognizable, perceivable.

As mentioned above, the light and love of God allows the saint, the one who is in communion with Christ, to become capable, in some sense, of giving him/herself over with Christ in his entry into the other's own hell (i.e., His encounter with the other). To evangelize is to make possible the "in-breaking" of the "body of Christ" in the very reality of the other. The saint is capable of being a presence in the other's isolation and, through his or her own being-in-*communio* and vulnerability, of issuing forth a word that can reach the other and draw them into contact with the Word.

> For the saints, "Hell" is not so much a threat to be hurled at other people but a challenge to oneself. It is a challenge to suffer in the dark night of faith, to experience communion with Christ in solidarity with his descent into the Night. . . . One serves the salvation of the world by leaving one's own salvation behind for the sake of others. In such piety, nothing of the dreadful reality of Hell is denied. Hell is so real that it reaches right into the existence of the saints. Hope can take it on, only if one shares in the suffering of Hell's night by the side of the One who came to transform our night by his suffering.[174]

---

172. Benedict XVI, *Transforming Power*, 45.
173. See also Paul VI, *Evangelii nuntiandi*, §21–22, 41.
174. Ratzinger, *Eschatology*, 218. See also Ratzinger, *Yes of Jesus*, 33.

When the person-in-*communio* willingly enters the hell of the other with Christ, and issues forth the word of hope whose content is simply "I believe in God,"[175] as a presence in that hell and announces the Gospel at just the right time and in the right way, and is received by the other, evangelization occurs. *Caritas* initiates and ignites *confessio*, missionary proclamation marked by a willingness to suffer, a willingness to give up one's life, to give oneself over to the Truth, in the Truth, and for the Truth; and in the face of the other, even in the midst of the other's hell, it becomes clear that the confession is worth suffering unto death in order for that which is stronger than death can break through for the other.[176] The Church's "setting out with Christ" to hand on the love of God essentially means the "saints" mediate the "yes" of God in the hellish "places" of human isolation present on this earth and so remove from the shoulders of men the burden of sin.

In order for faith to be "handed on," then, it must become visible in life in such a way that it is verifiable in itself. This, perhaps, stands as the basis of all evangelization—without which all strategies and techniques are merely empty shells. Therefore, Ratzinger poignantly states:

> After the end of the apostolic age the early Church had as yet developed only relatively little in the way of a direct missionary activity as a Church, that it did not have any particular strategy for proclaiming the faith to the heathen, and that nevertheless this became the age of the greatest missionary success. The conversion of the ancient world to Christianity was not the result of any planned activity on the part of the Church but the fruit of the proof of the faith as it became visible in the life of Christians and of the community of the Church. . . . The new evangelization we need so urgently today is not to be attained with cleverly thought out ideas, however cunningly these are elaborated: the catastrophic failure of modern catechesis is all too obvious. It is only the interaction of a truth conclusive in itself with its proof in the life of this truth that can enable that particular evidence of the faith to be illuminated that the human heart awaits: it is only through this door that the Holy Spirit enters the world.[177]

The life of faith becomes visible in the life of the communion of saints. The proof of the truth of the Christian claim becomes conclusive and verifiable in the life this truth animates. The life of the Christian community lived within the world is the evidence of the truth of the faith and that which is

---

175. Ratzinger, *GCC*, 26.
176. See Benedict XVI, "Meditation 2012."
177. Ratzinger, *Yes of Jesus*, 34–35.

in harmony for what the human heart awaits. For it is precisely through this *communio* of the Church within the world, a *communio* inspired by the Holy Spirit, that the Holy Spirit enters the world making the *communio* among men and women, and, hence, making joy possible.

Conclusion

When it comes to evangelization, which is to say, the communication of the Gospel through the medium known as culture, and evangelizing methods, for Ratzinger there is no other method than that which comes from the *Logos*. The *Logos* reveals himself as Son and as the love of the Father—loving relationality perfectly actualized. The *Logos* is, therefore, the Gospel personified, and the *Logos* invites disciples to participate in the slitting of the culture with the Gospel, by participating in His own deeply personal and incarnate method, and by entering fully into the life of discipleship as beings from, for, and with. God "re-makes" the Christian in His "image and likeness" in the encounter with Christ in the rebirth known as Baptism, and the disciple is the one who lives in and into this way of living from, with, and for. Trinitarian theology, as revealed by the *Logos*, acts as a reference point for all branches of theology, including that of concern for this book—practical theology. Ratzinger says, "it is the nature of Christian existence to receive and to live life as relatedness and, thus, to enter into unity with is the ground of all reality and sustains it. This will . . . make it clear how the doctrine of the Trinity . . . can become the reference point of theology."[178] For this field, Trinitarian theology makes it known that God's loving relationality, manifest in the *Logos*, invites humanity into communion to be sure, but in doing so, the *Logos* invites human persons into mission as well. Evangelizing requires living life in relatedness to God and to others, and so allowing these two levels of relationality to encounter one another. Thus, understanding evangelization according to the *Logos* means understanding it as an expression of charity.

The movement of evangelization is simple: one is known and loved by Christ, and, in turn, knows and loves Christ, and this experience of knowing and loving within the most fundamental relationships informs and forms how one knows and loves other people. Ratzinger says, "the relationship to God, to the 'You,' and to the 'We' are intertwined. . . . God wishes to approach man only through man; he seeks out man in no other way but in

---

178. Ratzinger, *Introduction*, 188.

his fellow humanity."[179] For this reason, Ratzinger does not shy away from quoting the *Roman Catechism*'s stated goal of catechesis:

> The whole purpose of teaching and instruction must be directed toward the love that never ceases. For whatever is proposed by the pastor, whether it be the exercise of faith, of hope, or of some moral virtue, the love of the Lord should at the same time be so strongly insisted upon as to show clearly that all the works of perfect Christian virtue can have no other origin, no other end than divine love.[180]

In the end, evangelization is basically introducing one friend to Another, and in this way the faith still stands a chance—because it introduces one, through a relationship, into *the* relationship capable of responding to the deepest longings of the human heart.

Taking this one step deeper, then, it seems one could say that for Ratzinger *the* method for evangelization is nothing other than the life of the saint, the living fruit of charity as a way of beauty in this person who is being made wholly relational and existing as a reference point.[181] The saint is a witness for others, who makes friendship with God accessible for others through one's own friendship with God. In a certain sense, God's own humble and personal method becomes concrete in friendship—the establishment of relationship, the capacity to relate "as equals" due to the incarnation of the *Logos*—so to evangelize and catechize according to the *Logos* means taking friendship, or the establishment of relationship, as the method. The saint is little more than the one who is a friend of God's because of what God has done in making such a friendship possible, and in this exchange of "I's," in God becoming "all in all," the greatness of becoming a saint comes clear. In this case, then, the person, the saint, whose personhood has been restored at the foundational level in the image of God as a being-from, being-for, and being-with, and this person's gift of self in charity toward one's friend becomes *the* method. It is incarnational.

All of this can be expressed another way: Given Ratzinger's emphasis in fundamental theology on the "encounter"—that impact between the revelation of the *Logos* and the reception in faith on the part of the receiving subject—a personal, and dare we say "person-generating" event centering on *conversion* (the real exchange of the "I" for the "not-I"), some sort of personal method seems necessary in order to generate such a personal event.

179. Ratzinger, *Introduction*, 94.

180. Catechism of the Council of Trent, preface X, p. 7, quoted in Ratzinger, *Handing on the Faith*, 40

181. See *CCC*, §1829.

This event takes place in the other's reception of the person of the saint, the witness. For, in seeing the saint and in seeing "through" the saint, one can come to "see" Christ. In knowing the saint and in knowing "through" the saint, one can come to know Christ. In receiving the saint, for him or herself and as he or she is, one begins down that personal journey of faith: I believe *in* you, *that* your testimony is true. Thus, the Church, as a body consisting of many members, through her enduring *communio* with *Logos* and in her sacramental structure (including the sacramentality of the saint), mediates that same *Logos* today (cf. Heb 13:8) and she does so personally.

Conclusion

The pages of this book grappled with how structures of proclamation came to have such a difficult time after Vatican II—how the Church seemingly lost her voice in proclamation and in catechesis. In carrying out a theological excavation of the catechetical worksite, it becomes clear that shifts in fundamental theology directly impact structures of proclamation—for better or for worse.

In my estimation, Rahner stands as the chief architect behind the modern and postmodern catechetical project, with his fundamental theology acting as the blueprint for the former and his correlational methodology as the stimulus of the latter. Rahner, in response to Heidegger's critique, takes Kant's transcendental anthropology as a given, and, with a Thomistic foothold, establishes a theology of revelation based on anthropology: a transcendental experience of the supernatural existential. This established a supernaturally natural way to God, thus calling into question the real necessity of Jesus Christ and his Cross. Now, it seemed, one could achieve salvation, through an implicit faith, by simply accepting himself as a transcendent being.

Theorists like Moran and Groome inaugurate the anthropological phase in catechetical renewal by taking Rahner a step further with the continuing revelation thesis and the necessary relegation of the Church's tradition to an altogether secondary role. This relativizes the whole concept of Christian revelation amid the myriad of human transcendental experiences. Whether or not it is explicitly *Christian* revelation does not matter so much, and if it does matter, the subject himself or herself decides in what manner and to what extent. The Church's tradition, if it is necessary at all, comes into play after the bare-naked transcendental experience, as something of an interpretive tool—if the individual so decides such a tool is necessary. This form of "vulgarized Rahnerianism" radically alters the catechetical landscape by definitively relegating the Church's organs of transmission and establishing the "first things" of catechesis in the self and one's personal, transcendental experience. The Moran—Groome project seems to be an exercise in spirituality over and above religion, and no wonder such a catechesis could play a role in producing "nones."

The subjectivism apparent in catechetical renewal efforts immediately following the Council has become radicalized in the recontextualization project of Boeve and Pollefeyt. Their efforts could be categorized as a sort of postmodern Rahnerianism, given their aim in perpetuating Rahner's correlation theology in the current context. With a Lyotardian lens, they see that the collapse of the metanarrative *is* the postmodern condition. For Lyotard, philosophy takes responsibility for the defense of the *differend*—to defend against all metanarratives, to be intolerant of any sort of injustice toward the *differend*. This project, though it denies that it, of itself, is a new metanarrative, carries out its apparently altruistic motives according to the tenants of something like a postmodern creed with its own propositions of particularization, individualization, detraditionalization, and pluralization, and banishes to hell any position that does not comply.[1] In their postmodern recontextualization project, Boeve and Pollefeyt aim to vindicate Christianity of its indictment as a metanarrative and to illustrate how theology can also function as an exponent of postmodern critical consciousness. In Boeve's attempt to establish a postmodern theology that is theologically legitimate and contextually adequate, the mission of the Church becomes almost indistinguishable from that of postmodern philosophy. It, too, defends the *differend* and must remain open to interruption lest it take on metanarrative tendencies.

In Boeve and Pollefeyt's postmodern fundamental theology, one loses a real sense of *the* "given" outside of the self. According to a Lyotardian postmodern theology, there can be no "given," and certainly no tradition or idea taken as such. The detraditionalized and deinstitutionalized self approaches reality with a radical sensitivity to and awareness of plurality, contextuality, contingency, and so forth. Here, postmodernity acknowledges one's concrete need for the "other," insofar as the "other" prevents the self, or one's own self-narrative, from becoming hegemonic. The encounter with the "other," i.e., with alterity, is necessary, insofar as the other serves to make one aware of one's own fragility, given that the self has no definitive "given" outside of the self. For Boeve and Pollefeyt, the encounter with the "other" becomes theologically necessary, reminding the self of, and acting as a radical hermeneutic of the present absence of the "Other." Thus, in the postmodern work of Boeve and Pollefeyt, a radical subjectivizing takes

---

1. See Wiess, "Stop Being Shocked." See also Benedict XVI, *Light of the World*, 52.

place and all that seems to remain is the self—alone and drifting, aware of alterity and unable to enter into *communio*—which could serve as an apt definition of hell as Scripture conceives of the thing.

The movement from Rahner to Boeve originated as a response to the Heideggerian problematic and the challenge it presented to a Suárezian interpretation of the deposit of faith (indeed, of the faith itself), wherein revelation had become a list of propositions to be mastered. Theology, and, to a certain extent, faith had ossified by the mid-twentieth century, and theologians like Rahner sought to bring it back to life through the renewal of fundamental theology. However, instead of going back to the tradition—a growing and increasing consciousness of the church's collective understanding of the revelation of the Logos in Jesus Christ and occurring within the very dynamic relationality of the Church and the Trinity—as the way to the "given," the Rahnerian project loosens its grip on tradition, leaves Logos behind, and clings more and more tightly to the self. Said another way, this whole Rahnerian process of grappling with the Heideggerian problematic via correlation, the concept of the Christian "given" (i.e., the revelation of the Logos in Jesus Christ as accessed through the tradition—the enduring consciousness and testimony of the Church) becomes blurry for Rahner, is reordered in Moran's thought, and seemingly disappears in Boeve's. Being, once accessible through faith in the revealed Word, collapses into time and slowly becomes almost indistinguishable from man himself—first in his modern, then postmodern form. Here, fundamental theology becomes little more than an attempt to correlate the faith to modernity, and then to recontextualize it and make it productive according to the postmodern critical consciousness. In the process, structures of proclamation are caught up in relentless "updating" and risk losing touch with the Logos—their source—altogether. The path from Rahner to Boeve is a path of subduing, relegating, and eventually silencing of the tradition which carries forth the Word. In the area of fundamental theology, this movement throws out the baby (dogmatic theology) with the bathwater (Suárezian scholasticism), ultimately leaving the self with the subject's own experience as its "given"—whether modern or postmodern—and then reinterprets evangelization and catechesis accordingly. By making faith into an almost entirely implicit reality and relaxing the tension caused by personal sin, either by diminishing its possibility altogether or shifting the reality altogether to institutions or metanarratives, the Church's missional impulse either fades into the background or faces an accusation of hegemony.

As the builders of the anthropological phase continued to construct their structure of proclamation, Ratzinger did not withhold his criticism, declaring that modern catechesis exists in a state of "crisis" that has become a "catastrophic failure." For Ratzinger, things went awry in fundamental theology in such ways that directly impact a theology of evangelization, and he locates the catalyst of such waywardness in the "hermeneutic of discontinuity" vis-à-vis the conciliar texts. Thus, Ratzinger concludes that following Vatican II, "There are basically two concepts of reform. The first concept has more to do with renouncing external power and external factors, in order to live all the more by faith. The other consists in making history more comfortable, to caricature this approach somewhat. And then things go awry, of course."[2] This hermeneutical break from the tradition, and the conciliar intention, betrays a loss of faith in the faith of the Church (which leads down a path of losing faith in God, or of banishing God to the level of the abstract and impractical).[3] It exalts context (first modern, then, postmodern), allowing the context to determine theology's legitimacy. Theology no longer has power to transform context but must become a contextual chameleon, succumbing to the criteria or dictates of context (i.e., a postmodern "creed") even if that means becoming something other.

Such are the basic contours of the genesis of the anthropological phase of catechetical renewal, in its modern and postmodern iterations. But, what of a response to the situation? How might the Church rediscover her voice? "A flight into pure doctrine," wherein "doctrine that would exist like a nature preserve separated from the daily world of faith and its needs would be at the same time an abandonment of faith itself" cannot be the answer.[4] Yet, neither a praxis-oriented, anthropological plunge into pure transcendental experience devoid of content, nor a false humility that claims Being cannot and does not speak, and which views reason and faith with suspicion, is not the answer either. Ratzinger does not perceive Christianity according to the category of metanarrative, because it is not a human ideology that attempts to explain the whole. Instead, Benedict XVI acknowledges that "one must be careful and cautious in claiming the truth. But simply to dismiss it as unattainable is really destructive."[5] To claim to know everything about everything, including Being, manifests a certain pridefulness. Yet, to dismiss truth and the capacity of human reason altogether is pride disguised as humility—a false humility. Indeed, we cannot *have* the truth. "At best it [the Truth] has us," Benedict XVI says.[6] Elsewhere, he says more emphatically, "We do not possess the truth, the truth possesses

---

2. Ratzinger, *Salt of the Earth*, 75.
3. See Benedict XVI, *Western Culture*, 163.
4. CNA Staff, "Benedict XVI."
5. Benedict XVI, *Light of the World*, 50.
6. Benedict XVI, *Light of the World*, 50.

us: Christ, who is the truth, has taken us by the hand, and we know that his hand is holding us securely on the path of our quest for knowledge."[7] For, "believing in God means giving up our own prejudices and accepting the actual face in which he revealed himself: Jesus of Nazareth."[8] In response to Suárezian Neo-scholasticism, Ratzinger offers an alternate path to that of the modern and postmodern Rahnerians. He does so by taking as his "given" the person of the *Logos*, which offers an alternate path or trajectory for renewal in a theology of evangelization. For Ratzinger, the revelation of the *Logos* in Jesus Christ is the "given," as opposed to the "idea of man" or the "self." Ratzinger's whole theological foundation could be described as "*Logocentric*"—which is to say Christocentric—as opposed to the various anthropocentric manifestations of the Rahnerian project.

Christianity is neither an idealistic abstraction, nor a hegemonic metanarrative. God is not the product of a philosophical system, nor can He be contained within the bounds of rational (or anti-rational) systems. God is not an idea, a mere narrative, the fruit of human genius. God is not an ideology. One does not and cannot have a perfect, rational grasp of Being, but that is not the real object of Christian faith anyway. The *Logos* is. Christianity is not the product of human thought, but the result of an event. As Timothy O'Malley puts it, "Postmodernity was not the defeat of metanarratives, but the Incarnation was."[9] Why? Through incarnate realism, through a frighteningly proximate personalism, God breaks every tendency toward idealism. If Christianity really is the Idea of love, then Lyotard might be right. However, it is not an Idea or the response to one, but the response to a Person and revelation. The Christian claim runs thus: God, the universal, the cosmic "everything," in his providence, has taken on flesh in Jesus Christ, the cosmic "nothing,"—not a loft idea or metannarative—and thereby encounters each individual person in his or her particularity, inviting them on the Way that overpowers the master narrative of death. Through the Incarnation, God becomes small and capable of reaching the smallest. Christianity is no mere idea writ large, but the manifestation of the fundamental relationality of Being in the humble revelation of the incarnate Logos. In this way, Christianity is a "small" narrative shrouded in the humility of God, and that through which God extends an invitation to an interpersonal relationship that is illuminating. It allows one to see more, a certain fullness, but not all. True, one cannot perfectly comprehend Being. But, one can encounter, receive, believe, and understand that which Being reveals about itself—*Logos*—and allow it

---

7. Benedict XVI, "Christmas Greetings 2012."
8. Benedict XVI, "Angelus Address, February 3, 2013."
9. O'Malley, "Joseph Ratzinger Is Not a Platonist."

to change everything.[10] In short, for Ratzinger, Christianity cannot function as a pawn in the hands of contemporary philosophy and Christian revelation does not act as merely another interrupter, another "other" who saves the interrupted from becoming hegemonic. Instead, it is more radical than that. Christianity, the Christian event, marks something new, something "violent" even: an encounter with the Other who breaks apart the selfish death-grip of the isolated "I" and who opens for us the horizon of eternal communion.

The revelation of God, incarnate in the *Logos*, reaches humanity today through the Spirit operative in the Church the *Logos* established as the unique means by which He might continue to encounter each person in each particular place and at each particular time. Contra Rahner, Ratzinger does not collapse *logos* into time, but acknowledges, rather, that in the *Logos*, God has time, and He has time for each human being. The timely reception of God's revelation on the part of the receiving subject goes by the name of faith. And, the timeliness of God's revelation is the reason "why . . . faith still [has] any chance at all" in the postmodern, post-Christian world of today. Faith remains as a possibility today, even amid a post-Christian western culture, "because it corresponds to the nature of man" as a relational creature made for and aching for an infinite relationship.[11] Faith in Jesus Christ still corresponds to this ache; Jesus continues to satisfy the deep longing of the hearts of men and women. Faith reestablishes the person according to his or her fundamental nature as an "image and likeness" of the Trinity, as a being from, with, and for, as a son or daughter. The Church personally mediates the encounter between Word and person.

The Church's enduring testimony makes joy possible. This is precisely what the Church has always meant by evangelization, and her leading people more deeply into communion with Christ is known as catechesis. Evangelization, including the key "moment" in the process known as catechesis, takes place according to the *Logos*. The "object" here, the *Logos*, determines the method by which it is to be known, or made known. The "object" is inherently and eternally personal and is known and made known as such. Said another way, the personal form of revelation reveals the personal content of the revelation, and the appropriately personal means by which others are to be led to encounter such a personal revelation. Evangelization, by its nature, must proceed personally. In light of the revelation of the *Logos*, one has access to a theological anthropology that has the capacity to shape the whole of life and provide certain "checks and balances" for evangelization efforts. This is to say, evangelization finds in the *Logos* a way of advancing according

10. See Guerrierio, *Benedict XVI*, 241.
11. Ratzinger, *TT*, 137.

to a Trinitarian pattern. Because human beings participate personally in the evangelizing mission of the Son, who is the Father's ambassador—a unity of person and work—through the Holy Spirit, evangelization, too, has a Trinitarian structure of being-from, being-for, and being-with. Theological anthropology can act as a key for holding in dynamic tension the tradition and the person, content and experience, the truth and humility. This Trinitarian structure allows evangelization and catechesis, in its content and methods, to remain faithful to, and firmly rooted in the revelation of the *Logos*, while opening out to encounter the "other."

In the end, evangelization participates in the mission of the *Logos* that appears in the humility of the Incarnation, which has already overcome the metanarratives even before postmodernity because Christianity is not a mere idea, but an event. It is a concrete, personal reality wherein the "yes" of God in Jesus Christ, the person, comes to bear, through the "saint's" facilitation of a personal meeting between the other and this "yes" of God.[12] This fact leads Ratzinger to respond to the question *How many ways are there to God?* with this answer:

> As many as there are people. For even within the same faith each man's way is an entirely personal one. We have Christ's word: I am the way. In that respect, there is ultimately one way, and everyone who is on the way to God is therefore in some sense also on the way of Jesus Christ. But this does not mean that all ways are identical in terms of consciousness and will, but, on the contrary, the one way is so big that it becomes a personal way for each man.[13]

Through the one Incarnation, and its continued presence through the mission of Holy Spirit manifest in the Church, God meets each man and woman along his or her path, touching down in each life and offering a way to God.

The person simply looking for *the* method, *the* skill set, or *the* series of techniques for evangelization and catechesis in Ratzinger's thought will likely be disappointed if he or she has read this far. Such "practicals" will not be found here. Ratzinger does not offer anything like a transcendental,

---

12. Giussani describes this as the exercise of charism, which he defines as "a gift of the Spirit, given to a person in a specific historical context, so that this person can initiate an experience of faith that might in some way be useful to the life of the Church. I emphasize the existential nature of charism: it makes the Christian message handed down by the apostolic tradition more convincing, more persuasive, more 'approachable.' A charism is an ultimate terminal of the Incarnation, that is, it is a particular way in which the Fact of Jesus Christ Man and God reaches me, and through me can reach others" (Giussani, *Communion and Liberation Movement*, 19–20).

13. Ratzinger, *Salt of the Earth*, 32.

subjective experience-driven Shared Christian Praxis, nor does he encourage the sort of anti-evangelistic, or redefinition-of-evangelization-according-to-the-postmodern-creed approach apparent in Boeve and Pollefeyt's multicorrelative Hermeneutical-Communicative Model. The answers to questions regarding a theology and methodology of evangelization will neither be found by relegating tradition, relativizing revelation, and rendering faith implicit, nor will they be discoverable in the radical subjectivizing that centers on the difference of alterity and the awareness of fragility it fosters. Instead, Ratzinger's theological project grounds the whole of a theology evangelization in Jesus Christ, the revelation of the *Logos*, to which the Church and her enduring and her tradition testify, and a corresponding methodology in humility and friendship. The one who finds himself in friendship with God through Jesus Christ becomes capable of sharing that friendship with others—in relationship. In humility, one encounters the humility of the *Logos* that makes friendship with God possible, and by sharing in the humble mission of the *Logos*, one extends that possibility of friendship to others. To evangelize with and according to the *Logos* demands something personal, because the *Logos* reveals God personally and invites men and women to participate in evangelizing. The evangelist, then, must be personally involved and not only propositionally, so to speak, whether the proposition is doctrinal or anthropological. At the bottom of it, evangelization is an interpersonal exchange, a deeply personal event, the introducing one friend to Another, and catechesis is its deepening. For this reason, Ratzinger simply encourages living out of charity in the all too real and all too particular instances of friendship, which cannot help but reveal, and open opportunities to introduce the source and goal of charity in the Word that encounters humanity in Jesus Christ. If I have interpreted Ratzinger's theological trajectory correctly, it seems that his vision for the Church (or, better, his vision for evangelization) lies not in the prophetic mystic who facilitates the transcendental experience for others, but in the "saint," the reference point, who shows the way to Christ by living from and with the tradition of the Church and existing, with Christ, "for the many."

By grounding his theology in the person of the *Logos*, Ratzinger avoids the overreaches and underreaches in fundamental theology apparent in the approaches cataloged in Part I, thus preventing catechetics from becoming a purely anthropocentric exercise at the expense of the real content of what *Logos* reveals—of which Catholic tradition testifies—and that which makes faith possible. Ratzinger's position runs fundamentally contrary those of Rahner, Moran, and Boeve. For Ratzinger, faith is an explicit act made possible through the objective encounter with the Other as mediated by the Church. Ratzinger agrees that in and of itself, Being is inaccessible to humanity—a present absence perhaps. However, Being chooses not to remain inaccessible, but comes as a presence. He discloses or reveals itself through *logos* in the vestiges apparent in the created order and ultimately in the self-disclosure of the Word accessible through the enduring testimony of Scripture and tradition as proclaimed and safeguarded by the Church's magisterium. In other words, a Ratzingerian vision for evangelization and catechesis according to the *Logos* presents a possible solution for the dissonance that has resulted from the catechetical "crisis" since Vatican II.

When it comes to catechetical renewal, a chief aim of the Council, Ratzinger, it seems, may not be terribly concerned with lifting the anthropological roof onto Hofinger's allegorical house and completing the renewal project anyhow. Perhaps elements of catechetical renewal became too rapt in a self-referential and ideological pursuit. In its attempt at countering the ossified propositionalist position, renewal efforts themselves fixated upon experience and method. The pendulum swung away from orthodoxy to orthopraxy—a reduction in the opposite direction. Indeed, the near occasion of merely "making" is an ever-present temptation for renewal efforts. For his part, Ratzinger does not seem to be interested in any "temple" made by human hands, which establishes its own set of criteria and exalts in its own accomplishments. Instead, his vision of renewal consists in wonder, in the act of faith, which is precisely the opposite of making. Rather than an eventual construction project relying heavily on human devices, Ratzinger's Christocentric focus remains fixed upon the new Temple which began with Christ's resurrection, "the living body of Jesus Christ, which ... now stand[s] in the sight of God and [as] the place of all worship."[14] If evangelization and catechesis have as a goal the encounter and abiding communion with Jesus Christ, the entry into eternal worship, there is ultimately only one "structure" that matters despite the necessity for various catechetical apparatuses in every age. These latter mechanisms, however, are simply means to a far greater end, and not ends in themselves. A perfectly constructed catechetical house cannot be the point; Jesus Christ *is*.

As a final word, then, Benedict XVI clearly states we can only speak about God because He has first spoken to us. God speaks to us most clearly, most fully, and most completely in the revelation of the *Logos* in Jesus Christ. Insofar as Christ commissions the Church to evangelize, the Church does so according to the personal pattern revealed by the *Logos* as Son and as love. In other words, the Church, and her individual members are and are to evangelize as beings from, for, and with. This is possible through personal and ongoing renewal, that act of faith in the God who reveals and whose

---

14. Ratzinger, *The Spirit of the Liturgy*, 43.

revelation is accessible today through the Church's enduring testimony. Renewal is not an ideological pursuit, or an idealistic attempt to "create a culture nor . . . to preserve a culture from the past."[15] Instead, as the witness of the monks in Christian history reveals, it is the result of "*quaerere Deum*"—seeking God. "Amid the confusion of the times, in which nothing seemed permanent," Benedict XVI says, "they wanted to do the essential— to make an effort to find what was perennially valid and lasting, life itself. They were searching for God. They wanted to go from the inessential to the essential, to the only truly important and reliable thing there is."[16] The *Lineamenta* for the Synod on the New Evangelization basically expresses the same thing. When confronted with a post-Christian culture, "the Church does not give up or retreat into herself; instead, she undertakes a project to revitalize herself. She makes the Person of Jesus Christ and a personal encounter with him central to her thinking, knowing that he will give his Spirit and provide the force to announce and proclaim the Gospel in new ways which can speak to today's cultures."[17] This echoes Benedict XVI's own words, which encourage an evangelization that flows from personal renewal, from a personal experience of fundamental theology into its being lived out. He says, "The rediscovery of the value of one's baptism is the basis of the missionary commitment of every Christian, because we see in the Gospel that he who lets himself be fascinated by Christ cannot do without witnessing the joy of following in his footsteps . . . we understand even more that, in virtue of baptism, we have an inherent missionary vocation."[18]

The Church can speak about God today because God has spoken and continues to speak to humanity. The Church can say that which God has said about himself in and through the person of the *Logos*, to which she has access in the testimony of her Scripture and her living tradition. And, the Church speaks in the manner in which God has spoken—personally. She can evangelize today on the basis of faith in Jesus Christ, the *Logos* incarnate, and she does so according to that same method by which the *Logos* evangelizes, which is to say, in humility and in relationality. The Church can speak about God today because God has spoken and continues to speak through the presence of the Holy Spirit, the interpreter of the *Logos* and bearer of all wisdom.

---

15. Benedict XVI, "Address to Representatives from the World of Culture."
16. Benedict XVI, "Address to Representatives from the World of Culture."
17. XIII Ordinary General Assembly of the Synod of Bishops, *Lineamenta*, §5.
18. Pope Benedict XVI, "Angelus Address, October 29, 2006."

Bibliography

XIII Ordinary General Assembly of the Synod of Bishops. *Lineamenta: The New Evangelization for the Transmission of the Christian Faith.* Vatican City: Libreria Editrice Vaticana, 2011.

1985 Extraordinary Synod of Bishops. "The Final Report of the 1985 Extraordinary Synod." https://www.ewtn.com/catholicism/library/final-report-of-the-1985-extraordinary-synod-2561.

Albacete, Lorenzo. "The Key to the Christian Life." http://archivio.traces-cl.com/aprilo3/thekeyto.html.

Aquinas, Thomas. *Summa Theologica.* https://www.newadvent.org/summa/1029.htm#article1.

Baars, Conrad. *Born Only Once.* Eugene, OR: Wipf & Stock, 2016.

Balthasar, Hans Urs von. *The Moment of Christian Witness.* Translated by Richard Beckley. San Francisco: Ignatius, 1994.

———. *Razing the Bastions: On the Church in This Age.* Translated by Brian McNeil. San Francisco: Ignatius, 1993.

Barron, Robert. "Einstein and God." *Word on Fire*, July 18, 2008. https://www.wordonfire.org/resources/article/einstein-and-god/325/.

Baumert, Susan. "Instruments of Change: The Christian Brothers' Catechetical Texts, 1943–1969." *U.S. Catholic Historian* 32.4 (2014) 55–76.

Beards, Andrew. "Addressing Philosophical Currents Underlying Sacramental Theology." In *Speaking the Truth in Love*, edited by Petroc Willey and Scott Sollom, 139–77. Steubenville, OH: Emmaus Academic, 2019.

Beaudoin, Tom. "The Theological Anthropology of Thomas Groome." *Religious Education* 100.2 (2015) 127–38.

Benedict XVI, Pope. "2005 Address to the Roman Curia Offering Them His Christmas Greetings." Vatican City: Libreria Editrice Vaticano, 2005.

———. "2006 Easter Vigil Homily." Vatican City: Libreria Editrice Vaticana, 2006.

———. "2007 Easter Vigil Homily." Vatican City: Libreria Editrice Vaticana, 2007.

———. "2012 Address of His Holiness Benedict XVI on the Occasion of Christmas Greetings to the Roman Curia." Vatican City: Libreria Editrice Vaticana, 2012.

———. "Address of His Holiness Benedict XVI to Members of the Roman Curia and Papal Representatives for the Traditional Exchange of Christmas Greetings." Vatican City: Libreria Editrice Vaticana, 2009.

———. "Address of His Holiness Pope Benedict XVI on the Occasion of Meeting with the Parish Priests and the Clergy of Rome." Vatican City: Libreria Editrice Vaticana, 2013.

———. "Address to the Participants of the General Assembly of the Italian Church." Vatican City: Libreria Editrice Vaticana, 2006.

———. "Address to Participants in the Plenary Assembly of the Pontifical Council for Promoting the New Evangelization." Vatican City: Libreria Editrice Vaticana, 2011.

———. "Address to Representatives from the World of Culture." Vatican City: Libreria Editrice Vaticana, 2008.

———. "Angelus Address, February 3, 2013." Vatican City: Libreria Editrice Vaticana, 2013.

———. "Angelus Address, October 29, 2006." Vatican City: Libreria Editrice Vaticana, 2006.

———. *Caritas in veritate*. Vatican City: Libreria Editrice Vaticana, 2009.

———. *Deus caritas est*. Vatican City: Libreria Editrice Vaticana, 2005.

———. "Faith, Reason, and the University." Vatican City: Libreria Editrice Vaticana, 2006.

———. "The Holiness: General Audience, April 13, 2011." Vatican City: Libreria Editrice Vaticana, 2011.

———. "Homily of His Holiness Benedict XVI: Mass, Imposition of the Pallium, and Conferral of the Fisherman's Ring for the Beginning of the Petrine Ministry of the Bishop of Rome." Vatican City: Libreria Editrice Vaticana, 2005.

———. "Homily for the Solemnity of Sts. Peter and Paul." Vatican City: Libreria Editrice Vaticana, 2010.

———. *Jesus, the Apostles, and the Early Church: General Audiences (15 March 2006–14 February 2007)*. San Francisco: Ignatius, 2007.

———. *Jesus of Nazareth: From the Baptism in the Jordan to the Transfiguration*. Translated by Adrian J. Walker. New York: Doubleday, 2007.

———. *Jesus of Nazareth: Holy Week*. Translated by the Vatican Secretariat of State. San Francisco: Ignatius, 2011.

———. *Jesus of Nazareth: The Infancy Narratives*. Translated by Phillip J. Whitmore. New York: Image, 2012.

———. *Last Testament*. Translated by Jacob Williams. New York: Bloomsbury, 2016.

———. *Light of the World: The Pope, the Church, and the Signs of the Times*. Translated by Michael J. Miller and Adrian J. Walker. San Francisco: Ignatius, 2010.

———. "The Listening Heart: Reflections on the Foundations of Law: Address of Pope Benedict XVI, September 22, 2011." Vatican City: Libreria Editrice Vaticana, 2011.

———. "Meditation during the First General Congregation." Vatican City: Libreria Editrice Vaticana, 2012.

———. *Porta fidei*. Vatican City: Libreria Editrice Vaticana, 2011.

———. "Reflections Published for the First Time on the Occasion of the 50th Anniversary of the Opening of the Second Vatican Council." https://www.vatican.va/special/annus_fidei/documents/annus-fidei_bxvi_inedito-50-concilio_en.html.

———. *Sacramentum caritatis*. Vatican City: Libreria Editrice Vaticana, 2007.

———. "Social Networks: Portals of Truth and Faith: New Spaces for Evangelization." Vatican City: Libreria Editrice Vaticana, 2013.

———. *Spe salvi*. Vatican City: Libreria Editrice Vaticana, 2007.
———. *The Transforming Power of Faith*. Translated by L'Osservatore Romano. San Francisco: Ignatius, 2013.
———. *Ubiqumque et semper*. Vatican City: Libreria Editrice Vaticana, 2010.
———. *Verbum Domini*. Vatican City: Libreria Editrice Vaticana, 2010.
———. *Western Culture: Today and Tomorrow*. Translated by Michael J. Miller. San Francisco: Ignatius, 2019.
Benedict XVI, Pope, and Jacques Servais. "Full Text of Benedict XVI's Recent, Rare, and Lengthy Interview." *Catholic News Agency*, March 17, 2016. https://www.catholicnewsagency.com/news/33591/full-text-of-benedict-xvis-recent-rare-and-lengthy-interview.
Bernanos, Georges. *The Diary of a Country Priest*. Translated by Pamela Morris. New York: Image, 1954.
Biliniewicz, Mariusz. *The Liturgical Vision of Pope Benedict XVI: A Theological Inquiry*. New York: Lang, 2013.
Blackman, Daniel. "The Courtyard of the Gentiles." *Israel Affairs* 16.4 (2010) 579–98.
Boeve, Lieven. "Beyond Correlation Strategies: Teaching Religion in a Detraditionalised and Pluralised Context." In *Hermeneutics and Religious Education*, edited by H. Lombaerts and D. Pollefeyt, 233–54. Leuven: Leuven University Press, 2004.
———. "*Christus Postmodernus*: An Attempt at Apophatic Christology." In *The Myriad Christ: Plurality and the Quest for Unity in Contemporary Christology*, edited by Terrance Merrigan and Jacques Haers, 577–93. Leuven: Leuven University Press, 2000.
———. "Conversion and Cognitive Dissonance: Evaluating the Theological-Ecclesial Program of Joseph Ratzinger/Benedict XVI." *Horizons* 40.2 (2013) 242–54.
———. "Critical Consciousness in the Postmodern Condition: New Opportunities for Theology?" *Philosophy & Theology* 10.2 (1997) 449–67.
———. "Experience according to Edward Schillebeeckx: The Driving Force of Faith and Theology." In *Divinising Experience: Essays in the History of Religious Experience from Origen to Ricoeur*, edited by Lieven Boeve and L. Hemming, 199–225. Leuven: Peeters, 2004.
———. "Faculty of Theology and Religious Studies." https://theo.kuleuven.be/en/research/researchers/00000317.
———. *God Interrupts History: Theology in a Time of Upheaval*. New York: Continuum, 2007.
———. *Interrupting Tradition: An Essay on Christian Faith in a Postmodern Context*. Louvain: Peeters, 2003.
———. *Lyotard and Theology*. New York, Bloomsbury, 2014.
———. "Negative Theology and Theological Hermeneutics: The Particularity of Naming God." In *Gott Nennen: Gottes Namen und Gotts als Name*, edited by Ingolf U. Dalferth and Phillip Stoellger, 189–207. Tübingen: Mohr Siebeck, 2008.
———. "Postmodern Sacramento-Theology." *Ephemerides Theologicae Lovanienses* 74.4 (1998) 326–43.
———. "Religious Bungee Jumping: Youth and Experience in Transcendence in Postmodern Culture." *Interface* 2.2 (1999) 54–66.
———. "Religious Education in a Post-Secular and Post-Christian Context." *Journal of Beliefs and Values* 33.2 (2012) 143–56.

———. "Richard Kearney's Messianism: Between the Narrative Theology of Hermeneutics and the Negative Theology of Deconstructionism." In *Between Philosophy and Theology*, edited by Chrisophe Brabant and Lieven Boeve, 7–18. London: Routledge, 2016.

———. "The Shortest Definition of Religion: Interruption (Part I)." *The Pastoral Review* 5.3 (2009) 4–9.

———. "The Shortest Definition of Religion: Interruption (Part II)." *The Pastoral Review* 5.4 (2009) 4–9.

———. *Theology at the Crossroads of University, Church, and Society: Dialogue, Difference, and Catholic Identity*. New York: Bloomsbury, 2014.

Bonagura, David. "Joseph Ratzinger/Benedict XVI's Christology of Jesus' Prayer and Two Contemporary Theological Questions." *Nova et Vetera* 12.1 (2014) 287–306.

———. "*Logos* to Son in the Christology of Joseph Ratzinger/Benedict XVI." *New Blackfriars* 93.1046 (2011) 475–88.

Boys, Mary C. *Biblical Interpretation in Religious Education*. Birmingham, AL: Religious Education, 1980.

Brotherton, Joshua R. "Damnation and the Trinity in Ratzinger and Balthasar." *Logos* 18.3 (2015) 123–50.

———. "Development(s) in the Theology of Revelation: From Francisco Marin-Sola to Joseph Ratzinger." *New Blackfriars* 97.1072 (2016) 661–76.

Bursa, Brad. "The Catechism and the Benedict XVI Option for Ecclesial Renewal." In *Speaking the Truth in Love*, edited by Petroc Willey and Scott Sollom, 345–66. Steubenville, OH: Emmaus Academic, 2019.

———. "Provoking Renewal through Post-Baptismal Catechesis." *Josephinum Journal of Theology* 26.1–2 (2019) 159–77.

Butler, Sarah. "Benedict XVI: Apostle of the 'Pierced Heart of Jesus.'" In *The Pontificate of Benedict XVI: Its Premises and Promises*, edited by William G. Rusch, 144–67. Grand Rapids: Eerdmans, 2009.

Caldecott, Stratford. *Beauty in the Word: Rethinking the Foundations of Education*. Tacoma, WA: Angelico, 2012.

Carrón, Julián. *Disarming Beauty*. Notre Dame: University of Notre Dame Press, 2017.

Catholic Church. *Catechism of the Catholic Church*. 2nd ed. Vatican City: Libreria Editrice Vaticana, 1997.

———. *The Liturgy of the Hours*. Vol. 1, *Advent Season, Christmas Season*. New York: Catholic Book Publishing, 1975.

Chapp, Larry. "The Wrath of the Lamb: A Critique and Retrieval of *Gaudium et Spes*." *Gaudium et Spes* 22 (blog), October 4, 2021. https://gaudiumetspes22.com/2021/10/04/the-wrath-of-the-lamb-a-critique-and-retrieval-of-gaudium-et-spes/.

Chautard, Jean-Baptiste. *Soul of the Apostolate*. Translated by A Monk of Our Lady of Gethsemani. Charlotte, NC: TAN, 1974.

Clement, Neville. "Thomas Groome and the Intersection of Narrative and Action: Praxis, Dialectic, and Hermeneutics." *Australian eJournal of Theology* 10 (2007) 1–12.

CNA Staff. "Benedict XVI Laments Lack of Faith within Church Institutions in Germany." *Catholic News Agency*, July 26, 2021. https://www.catholicnewsagency.com/news/248494/benedict-xvi-laments-lack-of-faith-within-church-institutions-in-germany.

Coffey, David. "The Whole Rahner on the Supernatural Existential." *Theological Studies* 65 (2004) 95–118.
Collins, Christopher. *The Word Made Love*. Collegeville, MN: Liturgical, 2013.
Colombo, J. A. "Rahner and His Critics: Lindbeck and Metz." *The Thomist* 56.1 (1992) 71–96.
Communio. "About *Communio*." https://www.communio-icr.com/about.
Congregation for the Clergy. *General Directory for Catechesis*. Washington, DC: United States Catholic Conference, 1998.
Congregation for the Doctrine of the Faith. *Dominus Iesus*. Vatican City: Libreria Editrice Vaticana, 2000.
Conway, Eamonn. "A Constant Word in a Changing World." *New Blackfriars* 87.1008, (2006) 110–20.
Cooper, Adam. *Naturally Human, Supernaturally God*. Minneapolis: Fortress, 2014.
Cox, Harvey. "The Myth of the Twentieth Century: The Rise and Fall of 'Secularization.'" In *The Twentieth Century: A Theological Overview*, edited by G. Baum, 135–43. Maryknoll, NY: Orbis, 1999.
———. *The Secular City*. London: Pelican, 1968.
Craig, Jason. "Should Men Retire?" *New Polity* (blog). https://newpolity.com/blog/should-men-retire.
Crowley, Paul. "Mystagogy and Mission: The Challenge of Nonbelief and the Task of Theology." *Theological Studies* 76.1 (2015) 7–28.
Danielou, Jean. *From Shadows to Reality*. Westminster: Newman, 1960.
Dauphinais, Michael, and Matthew Levering. *Knowing the Love of Christ*. Notre Dame: University of Notre Dame Press, 2002.
De Mey, Peter. "Church Renewal and Reform in the Documents of Vatican II: History, Theology, Terminology." *The Jurist* 71 (2011) 369–400.
Denzinger, Heinrich. *Compendium of Creeds, Definitions, and Declarations on Matters of Faith and Morals*. Edited by Peter Hünermann et al. 43rd ed. San Francisco: Ignatius, 2012.
Descartes, Rene. *Discourse on Method*. New York: BN, 2007.
de Souza, Raymond J. "The Rhine Breaches the Tiber." *First Things*, April 14, 2021. https://www.firstthings.com/web-exclusives/2021/04/the-rhine-breaches-the-tiber.
Devlin, Anne. "The Theology of Human Personhood according to Joseph Ratzinger." PhD diss., Catholic University of America, 2011.
DiAngelo, Robin. *White Fragility*. Boston: Beacon, 2018.
Dooley, Catherine. "The Religious Education Curriculum in Catholic Schools." In *The Catholic Character of Catholic Schools*, edited by James Youniss et al., 156–73. Notre Dame: University of Notre Dame Press, 2000.
Dostoevsky, Fyodor. *Notebooks for "The Possessed."* Edited by Edward Wasiolek. Chicago: University of Chicago Press, 1968.
Doyle, Dennis. "The Concept of Inculturation in Roman Catholicism: A Theological Consideration." *U.S. Catholic Historian* 30.1 (2012) 1–13.
Dulles, Avery. "The Challenge of the Catechism." *First Things*, January 1995. https://www.firstthings.com/article/1995/01/the-challenge-of-the-catechism.
———. "The Rebirth of Apologetics." *First Things*, May 2004. https://www.firstthings.com/article/2004/05/the-rebirth-of-apologetics.
———. *Revelation Theology*. New York: Herder and Herder, 1969.

Egan, Harvey D. "Karl Rahner (1904–1984) and His Mystical Theology." In *A Companion to Jesuit Mysticism*, edited by Robert Aleksander Maryks, 310–34. Boston: Brill, 2017.

Erdozain, Luis. "The Evolution of Catechetics: A Survey of Six International Study Weeks on Catechetics." In *Source Book for Modern Catechetics*, edited by Michael Warren, 86–109. Winona, MN: St. Mary's, 1983.

Fischer, Mark. "Karl Rahner's Transcendental Christology." *Philosophy & Theology* 26.2 (2014) 383–95.

Franchi, Leonardo. "The Catholic School as a *Courtyard of the Gentiles*." *Journal of Catholic Education* 17.2 (2014) 57–76.

Francis, Pope. *Evangelii gaudium*. Vatican City: Libreria Editrice Vaticana, 2013.

———. *Lumen fidei*. Vatican City: Libreria Editrice Vaticana, 2013.

Frankl, Viktor E. *Man's Search for Meaning*. Translated by Ilse Lasch. Boston: Beacon, 2006.

Gaál, Emery de. *The Theology of Pope Benedict XVI: The Christocentric Shift*. New York: Palgrave Macmillan, 2010.

Galvin, John. "Jesus Christ." In vol. 1 of *Systematic Theology: Roman Catholic Perspectives*, edited by Francis Schüssler Fiorenza and John Galvin, 251–322. Minneapolis: Fortress, 1991.

Gerkin, Charles. *The Living Human Document*. Nashville: Abingdon, 1984.

Gerl-Falkovitz, Hanna-Barbara. "Recent Developments in International Feminist Philosophy: Tendencies and Interpretation of 'Gender' Studies." Presentation, Laghi Chair Lecture Series College Symposium, Pontifical College Josephinum, March 21, 2002.

German Synodal Way. *Fundamental Text*. www.online-sw.de.

Gibson, David. *The Rule of Benedict*. New York: HarperSanFrancisco, 2006.

Giussani, Luigi. *At the Origin of the Christian Claim*. Translated by Viviane Hewitt. London: McGill-Queen's University Press, 1998.

———. *Communion and Liberation Movement: A Movement in the Church*. Edited by Davide Rondoni. Translated by Patrick Stevenson and Susan Scott. Montreal: McGill-Queen's University Press, 2000.

———. *The Religious Sense*. Translated by John Zucchi. London: McGill-Queen's University Press, 1997.

———. *The Risk of Education*. Translated by Mariangela Sullivan. London: McGill-Queen's University Press, 2019.

———. *Why the Church?* Translated by Viviane Hewitt. London: McGill-Queen's University Press, 2001.

Gleason, Philip. *Contending with Modernity*. New York: Oxford University Press, 1995.

Groome, Thomas. *Christian Religious Education*. San Francisco: Jossey-Bass, 1980.

———. "From Life to Faith to Life: Some Traces." *Journal of Adult Theological Education* 8.1 (2011) 8–23.

———. "Handing on the Faith: The Need for Total Catechetical Education." In *Handing on the Faith: The Church's Mission and Challenge*, edited by Robert P. Imbelli, 172–92. New York: Crossroad, 2006.

———. "The Purposes of Christian Catechesis." In *Empowering Catechetical Leaders*, edited by Thomas Groome and Michael J. Corso, 3–27. Washington, DC: National Catholic Educational Association, 1999.

———. "Religious Education and Practical Theology." *YouTube*, September 22, 2010. https://youtu.be/ii_2gvncWF8.

———. *Sharing Faith*. San Francisco: HarperSanFrancisco, 1991.

Guerriero, Elio. *Benedict XVI: His Life and Thought*. Translated by William J. Melcher. San Francisco: Ignatius, 2018.

Hahn, Scott. *Covenant and Communion*. Grand Rapids: Brazos, 2009.

Haight, Roger. *Jesus Symbol of God*. Maryknoll, NY: Orbis, 1999.

Harrison, Peter. "Correlation and Theology: Barth and Tillich Re-examined." *Studies in Religion/Sciences Religieuses* 15.1 (1986) 65–76.

Hart, David Bentley. "Human Dignity Was a Rarity before Christianity." *Church Life Journal*, October 26, 2017. https://churchlifejournal.nd.edu/articles/human-dignity-was-a-rarity-before-christianity/.

Heidegger, Martin. *Being and Time*. Translated by John Macquarrie and Edward Robinson. New York: HarperPerrennial, 2008.

———. *Introduction to Metaphysics*. Translated by Gregory Fried and Richard Polt. New Haven: Yale University Press, 2000.

Heim, Maximilian Heinrich. *Joseph Ratzinger: Life in the Church and Living Theology*. Translated by Michael J. Miller. San Francisco: Ignatius, 2007.

Hofinger, Johannes. *The Art of Teaching Christian Doctrine: The Good News and Its Proclamation*. Notre Dame: University of Notre Dame Press, 1962.

———. "Looking Backward and Forward: Journey of Catechesis." *Living Light* 20.4 (1984) 348–57.

Horell, Harold Daly. "Thomas Groome." https://www.biola.edu/talbot/ce20/database/thomas-groome.

Hughes, Kathleen. *Becoming the Sign: Sacramental Living in a Post-Conciliar Church*. New York: Paulist, 2013.

Imbelli, Robert. "No Decapitated Body." *Nova et Vetera* 18.3 (2020) 757–75.

Jarrett, Bede. *The Life of Saint Dominic*. Providence, RI: Cluny, 2018.

John XXIII, Pop. "Opening Address to the Council." In *The Encyclicals and Other Messages of John XXIII*, edited by The Staff of the Pope Speaks Magazine, 423–35. Washington, DC: TPS, 1964.

John Paul II, Pope. *Catechesi tradendae*. Vatican City: Libreria Editrice Vaticana, 1979.

———. *Fidei depositum*. Vatican City: Libreria Editrice Vaticano, 1992.

———. *Fides et ratio*. Vatican City: Libreria Editrice Vaticana, 1998.

———. *Laborem exercens*. Vatican City: Libreria Editrice Vaticana, 1981.

———. *Pastores dabo vobis*. Vatican City: Libreria Editrice Vaticana, 1992.

———. *Redemptoris missio*. Vatican City: Libreria Editrice Vaticana, 1990.

———. *Veritatis splendor*. Vatican City: Libreria Editrice Vaticana, 1993.

Jungmann, Josef. "An Adult Christian." *Worship* 27 (1952) 5–11.

Kaethler, Andrew T. J. "Freedom in Relationship: Joseph Ratzinger and Alexander Schmemann in Dialogue." *New Blackfriars* 95.1058 (2014) 397–411.

Kant, Immanuel. *Critique of Pure Reason*. Translated by J. M. D. Meiklejohn. New York: Barnes and Noble, 2004.

Kendi, Ibram X. *How to Be an Antiracist*. New York: One World, 2019.

Kerr, Fergus. *Twentieth-Century Catholic Theologians*. Oxford: Blackwell, 2006.

Kevane, Eugene. *Catechesis in Augustine*. Villanova: Villanova University Press, 1989.

———. "Introduction." In *Teaching the Catholic Faith Today*, edited by Eugene Kevane, xiii–lxxv. Boston: Daughters of St. Paul, 1982.

———. "Toward Research in Fundamental Catechetics." *Angelicum* 62.3 (1985) 357–77.

Lam, Cong Quy Joseph. *Joseph Ratzinger's Theological Retractations*. New York: Lang, 2013.

Lamb, Matthew L., and Matthew Levering. *Vatican II: Renewal within Tradition*. Oxford: Oxford University Press, 2008.

Lane, Frank. *Reflections*. Indy Pub, 2019.

Leithart, Peter J. "A Birthday Card to Balthasar." *First Things*, April 23, 2021. https://www.firstthings.com/web-exclusives/2021/04/a-birthday-card-to-balthasar.

Lubac, Henri de. *At the Service of the Church: Henri de Lubac Reflects on the Circumstances That Occasioned His Writings*. San Francisco: Ignatius, 1992.

———. *Corpus Mysticum*. Translated by Gemma Simmonds. Notre Dame: University of Notre Dame Press, 2006.

Lyotard, Jean-François. *The Differend: Phrases in Dispute*. Translated by Georges Van Den Abbeele. Minneapolis: University of Minnesota Press, 1988.

———. *The Postmodern Condition: A Report on Knowledge*. Translated by Geoff Bennington and Brian Massumi. Minneapolis: University of Minnesota Press, 1984.

MacIntyre, Alasdair. *Three Rival Versions of Moral Enquiry*. London: Routledge, 1999.

Mansini, Guy. "Experiential Expressivism and Two Twentieth-Century Catholic Theologians." *Nova et Vetera* 8.1 (2010) 125–41.

Marthaler, Bernard. "Introduction." In *Source Book for Modern Catechetics*, edited by Michael Warren, 13–20. Winona, MN: St. Mary's, 1983.

———. "The Modern Catechetical Movement in Roman Catholicism: Issues and Personalities." In *Source Book for Modern Catechetics*, edited by Michael Warren, 275–89. Winona, MN: St. Mary's, 1983.

Martin, Ralph. *Will Many Be Saved?* Grand Rapids: Eerdmans, 2012.

McCarthy, Robert, and John Vitek. *Going, Going, Gone: The Dynamics of Disaffiliation in Young Catholics*. Winona, MN: St. Mary's, 2017.

McCool, Gerald A., ed. *A Rahner Reader*. New York: Seabury, 1981.

McDermott, F. J. Michael. "Vatican II." In *The Student's Companion to the Theologians*, edited by Ian S. Markham, 527–40. Chichester: Wiley-Blackwell, 2013.

McGregor, Peter John. *Heart to Heart: The Spiritual Christology of Joseph Ratzinger*. Eugene, OR: Pickwick, 2016.

McPartlan, Paul. *Sacrament of Salvation: An Introduction to Eucharistic Ecclesiology*. New York: T. & T. Clark, 1995.

McWhorter, John. "The Dehumanizing Condescension of *White Fragility*." *The Atlantic*, July 15, 2020. https://www.theatlantic.com/ideas/archive/2020/07/dehumanizing-condescension-white-fragility/614146/.

———. *Theology and Social Theory: Beyond Secular Reason*. Oxford: Oxford University Press, 2002.

Milbank, John. *Theology and Social Theory: Beyond Secular Reason*. Oxford: Blackwell, 2006.

Millare, Roland. "The Hermeneutic of Continuity and Discontinuity between Romano Guardini and Joseph Ratzinger: The Primacy of Logos." *Nova et Vetera* 18.2 (2020) 521–63.

Montag, John. "The False Legacy of Suárez." In *Radical Orthodoxy*, edited by John Milbank et al., 38–63. London: Rutledge, 1999.

Moran, Gabriel. *Believing in a Revealing God: The Basics of the Christian Life*. Collegeville, MN: Liturgical, 2009.

———. *Both Sides: The Story of Revelation*. New York: Paulist, 2002.

———. "Catechetics in Context . . . Later Reflections." In *Sourcebook for Modern Catechetics*, edited by Michael Warren, 290–99. Winona, MN: St. Mary's, 1983.

———. *Catechesis of Revelation*. New York: Herder and Herder, 1966.

———. *Design for Religion*. New York: Herder and Herder, 1970.

———. *Missed Opportunities: Rethinking Catholic Tradition*. Bloomington, IN: iUniverse, 2016. Kindle.

———. *The Present Revelation: The Search for Religious Foundations*. New York: Herder and Herder, 1972.

———. *Showing How: The Act of Teaching*. Valley Forge, PA: Trinity Press International, 1997.

———. *Theology of Revelation*. New York: Herder and Herder, 1966.

———. "A Verb, Not a Noun: The Perils of 'Revelation.'" *Commonweal*, October 7, 2016. https://www.commonwealmagazine.org/verb-not-noun.

———. "What Is Revelation?" *Theological Studies* 25.2 (1964) 217–31.

Mother Teresa. *A Simple Path*. Compiled by Lucinda Vardey. New York: Ballentine, 1995.

Murphy, Joseph. *Christ Our Joy: The Theological Vision of Pope Benedict XVI*. San Francisco: Ignatius, 2008.

Mushi, Edward. "Benedict XVI's Hermeneutics of Reform and Its Implications for the Renewal of the Church." *Pacifica* 26.3 (2013) 279–94.

Nebrada, Alfonso. "Some Reflections on Father Gleeson's Paper on History and Present Scene in Religious Education." *Teaching All Nations* 11.2 (1974) 85–98.

Neuhaus, Richard John. "What Really Happened at Vatican II." *First Things*, October 2008. https://www.firstthings.com/article/2008/10/what-really-happened-at-vatican-ii.

Newman, John Henry. "Sermon 9: The Infidelity of the Future." https://www.newmanreader.org/works/ninesermons/sermon9.html.

Nichols, Aidan. "Rahner and Balthasar: 'Anonymous Christianity' in Question." In vol. 1 of *Beyond the Blue Glass: Catholic Essays on Faith and Culture*, 107–28. London: St. Austin, 2002.

———. *The Shape of Catholic Theology*. Collegeville, MN: Liturgical, 1991.

———. *The Thought of Pope Benedict XVI*. New York: Burns & Oates, 2007.

O'Malley, John W. *What Happened at Vatican II*. London: Belknap, 2008.

O'Malley, Timothy. "Joseph Ratzinger Is Not a Platonist." *Church Life Journal*, October 16, 2018. https://churchlifejournal.nd.edu/articles/joseph-ratzinger-is-not-a-platonist/.

O'Shea, Gerard. "Human Embodiment and Trinitarian Anthropology—Six Implications for Religious Education." *Studia Ełkie* 15.4 (2013) 455–66.

———. "Nature or Grace and the Appearance of Insincerity: Silencing the Catholic Voice." *Solidarity* 2.1 (2012) 1–13. https://researchonline.nd.edu.au/solidarity/vol2/iss1/6.

———. *Review of Religious Education for The Catholic Education Office: Diocese of Parramatta*. Sydney: University of Notre Dame Australia, 2014.

———. "Vulgarised Rahnerianism and Post-critical Recontextualisation: Solvents of Catholic Identity in Contemporary Catechesis." *Studia Ełckie* 16.3 (2014) 341–73.

Ott, Ludwig. *Fundamentals of Catholic Dogma*. Translated by Patrick Lynch. Ft. Collins, CO: Roman Catholic Books, 1954.

Parmach, Robert J. "Gabriel Moran." https://www.biola.edu/talbot/ce20/database/gabriel-moran#authors.

Paruch, Johanna. "The Catechism Responding to Catechetical Currents after Vatican II." In *Speaking the Truth in Love*, edited by Petroc Willey and Scott Sollom, 179–95. Steubenville, OH: Emmaus Academic, 2019.

———. "A Study of the Direct Ramifications of Vatican Council II on Catechetics, Including the Impact of Conciliar and Post-Conciliar Catechetical Documents on the Content and Method of Catechesis." PhD diss., Maryvale Institute, 2007.

Paul, Darel E. "Against Racialism." *First Things*, October 2020. https://www.firstthings.com/article/2020/10/against-racialism.

Paul VI, Pope. "Address of Pope Paul VI during the Last General Meeting of the Second Vatican Council." Vatican City: Libreria Editrice Vaticana, 1965.

———. *Evangelii nuntiandi*. http://w2.vatican.va/content/paul-vi/en/apost_exhortations/documents/hf_p-vi_exh_19751208_evangelii-nuntiandi.html.

Pauley, James. *Liturgical Catechesis for the 21st Century*. Chicago: Liturgical Training, 2017.

Pedraza, Brian. *Catechesis for the New Evangelization: Vatican II, John Paul II, and the Unity of Revelation and Experience*. Washington, DC: Catholic University of America Press, 2020.

———. "Reform and Renewal in Catechesis: The Council, the Catechism, and the New Evangelization." *Josephinum Journal of Theology* 19.1 (2012) 1–31.

Pew Research Center. "America's Changing Religious Landscape." *Pew Research Center*, May 12, 2015. https://www.pewforum.org/2015/05/12/americas-changing-religious-landscape/.

———. "In U.S., Decline of Christianity Continues at Rapid Pace." *Pew Research Center*, October 17, 2019. https://www.pewforum.org/2019/10/17/in-u-s-decline-of-christianity-continues-at-rapid-pace/.

Pieper, Josef. *About Love*. Translated by Richard Winston and Clara Winston. Chicago: Franciscan Herald, 1974.

———. *An Anthology*. San Francisco: Ignatius, 1989.

———. *Belief and Faith: A Philosophical Tract*. Translated by Richard Winston and Clara Winston. Chicago: Regnery, 1963.

———. *Leisure: The Basis of Culture*. Translated by Alexander Dru. San Francisco: Ignatius, 2009.

———. *On Hope*. Translated by Mary Frances McCarthy. San Francisco: Ignatius, 1986.

Pius XII, Pope. *Humani generis*. https://www.vatican.va/content/pius-xii/en/encyclicals/documents/hf_p-xii_enc_12081950_humani-generis.html.

Pollefeyt, Didier. "Biography." http://www.didierpollefeyt.be/biography/.

———. "The Difference of Alterity." In *Responsibility, God, and Society: Theological Ethics in Dialogue*, edited by Johan de Tavernier et al., 305–30. Leuven: Uitgeverij, 2008.

———. "Hermeneutical Learning in Religious Education." *Journal of Religious Education* 68.1 (2020) 1–11.

———. "Interreligious Dialogue beyond Absolutism, Relativism, and Particularism." In *Encountering the Stranger: A Jewish-Christian-Muslim Trialogue*, edited by Leonard Grob and John K. Roth, 245–59. Seattle: University of Washington Press, 2012.

Pollefeyt, Didier, and Jan Bouwens. "Framing the Identity of Catholic Schools: Empirical Methodology for Quantitative Research on the Catholic identity of an Education Institute." *International Studies in Catholic Education* 2.2 (2010) 193–211.

Pollefeyt, Didier, and Michael Richards. "Catholic Dialogue Schools: Enhancing Catholic Identity in Contemporary Contexts of Religious Pluralisation and Social and Individual Secularisation." *Ephemerides Theologicae Lovenienses* 96.1 (2020) 77–113.

Pontifical Council for Culture. "Courtyard of the Gentiles." http://www.cultura.va/content/cultura/en/dipartimenti/ateismo-e-non-credenza.html.

———. *The Via Pulchritudinis: Privileged Pathway for Evangelization and Dialogue.* Vatican City: Libreria Editrice Vaticana, 2006.

Pontifical Council for the Promotion of the New Evangelization. *Directory for Catechesis.* Washington, DC: United States Conference of Catholic Bishops, 2020.

Posset, Franz. *American Catechetics: Personal and Secular.* Winona, MN: St. Mary's College Press, 1969.

Quezada, R. L. "Global Student Teacher Transformation Experiences: Living the Faith through the Shared Christian Praxis Learning Process." *Journal of Catholic Education* 14.4 (2011) 417–40.

Rahner, Karl. "Concerning the Relationship between Nature and Grace." In vol. 1 of *Theological Investigations,* translated by Cornelius Ernst, 297–317. Baltimore: Helicon, 1961.

———. *Faith in a Wintry Season.* Edited by Paul Imhof and Hubert Biallowons. Translated by Harvey D. Egan. New York: Crossroad, 1990.

———. *Foundations of Christian Faith: An Introduction to the Idea of Christianity.* Translated by William V. Dych. New York: Crossroad, 1978.

———. *Karl Rahner in Dialogue: Conversations and Interviews, 1965–1982.* Translated by Harvey Egan. New York: Crossroad, 1986.

———. "A Short Formula of Christian Faith." In *A Rahner Reader,* edited by Gerald A. McCool, 205–11. New York: Seabury, 1981.

———. *Spirit in the World.* London: Sheed and Ward, 1968.

———. *Theological Foundations.* Vol. 14. Translated by David Bourke. London: Darton, Longman & Todd, 1976.

Rahner, Karl, and Joseph Ratzinger. *Revelation and Tradition.* New York: Herder and Herder, 1966.

Rahner, Karl, and Edward Schillebeeckx. "General Introduction." *Concilium* 1 (1965) 1–4.

Ramage, Matthew. "*Extra Ecclesiam Nulla Salus* and the Substance of Catholic Doctrine: Towards a Realization of Benedict XVI's 'Hermeneutic of Reform.'" *Nova et vetera* 14.1 (2016) 295–330.

Ratzinger, Joseph. "The Anguish of an Absence." http://www.30giorni.it/articoli_id_10282_l3.htm.

———. *Behold the Pierced One.* Translated by Graham Harrison. San Francisco: Ignatius, 1986.

———. *Called to Communion: Understanding the Church Today.* Translated by Adrian Walker. San Francisco: Ignatius, 1996.

———. "Christian Faith as 'the Way': An Introduction to *Veritatis Splendor.*" *Communio* 21.2 (1994) 199–207.

———. "The Church's Teaching Authority–Faith–Morals." In *Principles of Christian Morality*, translated by Graham Harrison, 47–73. San Francisco: Ignatius, 1986.

———. "*Communio*: A Program." In vol. 1 of *Joseph Ratzinger in Communio: The Unity of the Church*, translated by Peter Casarella, 118–30. Grand Rapids: Eerdmans, 2010.

———. "Concerning the Notion of Person in Theology." In vol. 2 of *Joseph Ratzinger in Communio: Anthropology and Culture*, edited by David L. Schindler and Nicholas J. Healy, translated by Michael Waldstein, 103–18. Grand Rapids: Eerdmans, 2013.

———. "Culture and Truth: Some Reflections on the Encyclical Letter *Fides et Ratio*." In *The Essential Pope Benedict XVI: His Central Writings and Speeches*, edited by John F. Thornton and Susan B. Varenne, 367–76. New York: HarperSanFrancisco, 2007.

———. "Current Doctrinal Relevance of the Catechism of the Catholic Church." Vatican City: Libreria Editrice Vaticana, 2002.

———. *Daughter Zion*. Translated by John M. McDermott. San Francisco: Ignatius, 1983.

———. "The Dignity of the Human Person." In vol. 5 of *Commentary on the Documents of Vatican II*, edited by Herbert Vorgrimler, translated by W. J. O'Hara, 115–63. New York: Crossroad, 1989.

———. *Dogma and Preaching: Applying Christian Doctrine to Daily Life*. Translated by Michael J. Miller. San Francisco: Ignatius, 2011.

———. "Dogmatic Constitution on Divine Revelation, Origin and Background." In vol. 3 of *Commentary on the Documents of Vatican II*, edited by Herbert Vorgrimler, 155–272. New York: Herder and Herder, 1966.

———. *Eschatology: Death and Eternal Life*. Translated by Michael Waldstein. Washington, DC: The Catholic University of America Press, 1988.

———. "Eucharist—Communio—Solidarity." In vol. 11 of *Joseph Ratzinger Collected Works: Theology of the Liturgy*, edited and translated by Michael J. Miller, 355–70. San Francisco: Ignatius, 2014.

———. "The Eucharist: Heart of the Church." In vol. 11 of *Joseph Ratzinger Collected Works: Theology of the Liturgy*, edited and translated by Michael J. Miller, 249–98. San Francisco: Ignatius, 2014.

———. *The Feast of Faith*. Translated by Graham Harrison. San Francisco: Ignatius, 1986.

———. "The Feeling of Things, the Contemplation of Beauty." Vatican City: Libreria Editrice Vaticana, 2002.

———. "Funeral Homily for Msgr. Luigi Giussani." In vol. 2 of *Joseph Ratzinger in Communio: Anthropology and Culture*, edited by David L. Schindler and Nicholas J. Healy, 184–87. Grand Rapids: Eerdmans, 2013.

———. *The God of Jesus Christ*. Translated by Brian McNeil. San Francisco: Ignatius, 2008.

———. *God and the World*. Translated by Henry Taylor. San Francisco: Ignatius, 2002.

———. *God's Word: Scripture—Tradition—Office*. Edited by Peter Hünermann and Thomas Söding. Translated by Henry Taylor. San Francisco: Ignatius, 2008.

———. *Gospel, Catechesis, Catechism*. San Francisco: Ignatius, 1997.

———. "Guardini on Christ in Our Century." https://www.ewtn.com/catholicism/library/guardini-on-christ-in-our-century-10882.

———. *Handing on the Faith in an Age of Disbelief*. Translated by Michael Miller. San Francisco: Ignatius, 2006.

———. "The Holy Spirit as *Communio*: Concerning the Relationship of Pneumatology and Spirituality in Augustine." In vol. 2 of *Joseph Ratzinger in Communio: Anthropology and Culture*, edited by David L. Schindler and Nicholas J. Healy, translated by Peter Casarella, 168–83. Grand Rapids: Eerdmans, 2013.

———. "Homily of His Eminence Card. Joseph Ratzinger: Mass Pro Eligendo Romano Pontifice." http://www.vatican.va/gpII/documents/homily-pro-eligendo-pontifice_20050418_en.html.

———. *Images of Hope: Meditations on Major Feasts*. Translated by John Rock and Graham Harrison. San Francisco: Ignatius, 2006.

———. *Introduction to Christianity*. Translated by J. R. Foster. San Francisco: Ignatius, 2004.

———. *'In the Beginning . . .': A Catholic Understanding of the Story of Creation and Fall*. Translated by Boniface Ramsey. Grand Rapids: Eerdmans, 1990.

———. *Journey to Easter*. Translated by Dame Mary Groves. New York: Crossroad, 1987.

———. *The Meaning of Christian Brotherhood*. Translated by W. A. Glen-Doepel. San Francisco: Ignatius, 1993.

———. *Milestones: Memoirs, 1927–1977*. Translated by Erasmo Leiva-Marikakis. San Francisco: Ignatius, 1998.

———. *Ministers of Your Joy*. Translated by Robert Nowell. Ann Arbor, MI: Servant, 1989.

———. *The Nature and Mission of Theology: Approaches to Understanding Its Role in the Light of Present Controversy*. Translated by Adrian Walker. San Francisco: Ignatius, 1995.

———. "The New Evangelization: Building the Civilization of Love—Address to Catechists and Religion Teachers." https://www.ewtn.com/new_evangelization/ratzinger.htm.

———. *New Outpourings of the Spirit*. Translated by Michael J. Miller and Henry Taylor. San Francisco: Ignatius, 2007.

———. "The New Pagans and the Church." *Homiletic and Pastoral Review*, January 30, 2017. Translated by Kenneth Baker. https://www.hprweb.com/2017/01/the-new-pagans-and-the-church/.

———. *A New Song for the Lord*. Translated by Martha M. Matesich. New York: Crossroad, 1996.

———. "On Hope." In vol. 2 of *Joseph Ratzinger in Communio: Anthropology and Culture*, edited by David L. Schindler and Nicholas J. Healy, translated by Esther Tillman, 28–41. Grand Rapids: Eerdmans, 2013.

———. *On the Way to Jesus Christ*. Translated by Michael J. Miller. San Francisco: Ignatius, 2005.

———. *Pilgrim Fellowship of Faith*. Translated by Henry Taylor. San Francisco: Ignatius, 2005.

———. "The Pre-political Moral Foundations of a Free State." In *Fundamental Speeches from Five Decades*, edited by Florian Schuller, translated by Michael J. Miller, 201–15. San Francisco: Ignatius, 2012.

———. *Principles of Catholic Theology: Building Stones for a Fundamental Theology*. Translated by Mary Frances McCarthy. San Francisco: Ignatius, 1987.

———. "Relativism: The Central Problem for Faith Today." In *The Essential Pope Benedict XVI*, edited by John Fr. Thornton and Susan B. Varenne, 227–40. New York: HarperSanFrancisco, 2007.

———. "Revelation Itself." In vol. 3 of *Commentary on the Documents of Vatican II*, edited by Herbert Vorgrimler, translated by Lalit Adolphus et al., 170–80. New York: Crossroad, 1989.

———. *Salt of the Earth: The Church at the End of the Millennium*. Translated by Adrian Walker. San Francisco: Ignatius, 1997.

———. *Seek That Which Is Above*. Translated by Graham Harrison. San Francisco: Ignatius, 2007.

———. *Seeking God's Face*. Translated by David Smith and Robert Cunningham. Chicago: Franciscan Herald, 1982.

———. *The Spirit of the Liturgy*. Translated by John Saward. San Francisco: Ignatius, 2000.

———. *Theological Highlights of Vatican II*. Translated by Henry Traub. New York: Paulist, 1966.

———. *The Theology of History in Bonaventure*. Translated by Zachary Hayes. Chicago: Franciscan Herald, 1989.

———. "Truth and Freedom." In vol. 2 of *Joseph Ratzinger in Communio: Anthropology and Culture*, edited by David L. Schindler and Nicholas J. Healy, translated by Adrian J. Walker, 147–67. Grand Rapids: Eerdmans, 2013.

———. *Truth and Tolerance*. Translated by Henry Taylor. San Francisco: Ignatius, 2004.

———. "The Undefeated Light." Translated by Tracey Rowland. *Hochland* (1959/60) 97–100.

———. *Values in a Time of Upheaval*. Translated by Brian McNeil. New York: Crossroad, 2006.

———. "Vicarious Representation." *Letter and Spirit* 7 (2011) 209–20.

———. *What It Means to Be a Christian*. Translated by Henry Taylor. San Francisco: Ignatius, 2006.

———. "Why I Am Still in the Church." In *Fundamental Speeches*, edited by Florian Schuller, translated by Michael J. Miller, 133–53. San Francisco: Ignatius, 2012.

———. *The Yes of Jesus Christ*. Translated by Robert Nowell. New York: Crossroad, 1991.

Ratzinger, Joseph, and Jürgen Habermas. *The Dialectics of Secularization*. Translated by Brian McNeil. San Francisco: Ignatius, 2006.

Ratzinger, Joseph, and Vittorio Messori. *The Ratzinger Report*. Translated by Salvator Attanasio and Graham Harrison. San Francisco: Ignatius, 1985.

Ratzinger, Joseph, and Christoph Schönborn. *Introduction to the Catechism of the Catholic Church*. Translated by Adrian Walker. San Francisco: Ignatius, 1994.

Rausch, Thomas. *Systematic Theology: A Roman Catholic Approach*. Collegeville, MN: Liturgical, 2016.

Reiss, Jana. "Religion Declining in Importance for Many Americans, Especially for Millennials." *Religion News Service*, December 10, 2018. https://religionnews.com/2018/12/10/religion-declining-in-importance-for-many-americans-especially-for-millennials/.

Reno, R. R. "The Woke Script." *First Things*, October 2020. https://www.firstthings.com/article/2020/10/the-woke-script.

Riches, Aaron. "After Chalcedon: The Oneness of Christ and the Dyothelite Mediation of His Theandric Unity." *Modern Theology* 24.2 (2008) 199–224.

Rise, Svein. "Karl Rahner." In *Key Theological Thinkers: From Modern to Postmodern*, edited by Stalle Johannes Kristiansen and Svein Rise, 225–38. Burlington, VT: Ashgate, 2013.

Rosenstock-Huessy, Eugen. *Out of Revolution*. Oxford: Berg, 1969.

Rouleau, Louis J. "Holiness and the History of the Church in Benedict XVI's General Audiences." *Logos* 17.3 (2014) 158–73.

Rowland, Tracey. *Benedict XVI: A Guide for the Perplexed*. London: T. & T. Clark, 2010.

———. "The *Catechism of the Catholic Church* and the Culture of the Incarnation." In *Speaking the Truth in Love*, edited by Petroc Willey and Scott Sollom, 219–30. Steubenville, OH: Emmaus Academic, 2019.

———. *Catholic Theology*. London: Bloomsbury, 2017.

———. "Catholic Theology in the Twentieth Century." In *Key Theological Thinkers: From Modern to Postmodern*, edited by Stalle Johannes Kristiansen and Svein Rise, 37–52. Burlington, VT: Ashgate, 2013.

———. "Christ, Culture, and the New Evangelization." In *The New Evangelization: Faith, People, Context, and Practice*, edited by Paul Grogan and Kirsteen Kim, 45–62. London: Bloomsbury, 2015.

———. "Dogmatic and Pastoral Theology." In *Healing Fractures in Contemporary Theology*, edited by Peter John McGregor and Tracey Rowland, 189–205. Eugene, OR: Cascade, 2022.

———. "Joseph Ratzinger as Doctor of Incarnate Beauty." *Church, Communication, and Culture* 5.2 (2020) 235–47.

———. "Neo-Scholasticism of the Strict Observance." In *T&T Clark Companion to Henri de Lubac*, edited by Jordan Hillebert, 29–56. London: Bloomsbury T. & T. Clark, 2017.

———. *Ratzinger's Faith*. New York: Oxford University Press, 2008.

———. "What Did Dostoevsky Mean When He Said, 'Beauty Will Save the World'?" *Dawson Society*, October 4, 2013. http://dawsonsociety.com.au/articles/what-did-dostoyevsky-mean-when-he-said-beauty-will-save-the-world/.

———. "The World in the Theology of Joseph Ratzinger/Benedict XVI." *Journal of Moral Theology* 2.2 (2013) 109–32.

Ruddy, Christopher. "'For the Many': The Vicarious-Representative Heart of Joseph Ratzinger's Theology." *Theological Studies* 75.3 (2014) 564–84.

———. "'Smaller but Purer'? Joseph Ratzinger on the 'Little Flock' and Vicarious Representation." *Nova et Vetera* 13.3 (2015) 713–41.

Rymarz, R. M. "The New Evangelization: A Look at the Growing Range of Reference." *Compass* 44.2 (2010) 24–27.

Sacred Congregation for the Clergy. *General Catechetical Directory*. Vatican City: Editrice Libreria Vaticana, 1971.

Sarto, Pablo Blanco. "*Logos* and *Dia-Logos*: Faith, Reason, (and Love) according to Joseph Ratzinger." *Anglican Theological Review* 92.3 (2010) 499–509.

———. "The Theology of Joseph Ratzinger: *Nuclear Ideas*." *Theology Today* 68.2 (2011) 153–73.

Schelkle, K. H. *Discipleship and Priesthood*. London, Sheed & Ward, 1966.

Schönborn, Christoph. *Jesus' School of Life*. Translated by Michael J. Miller. San Francisco: Ignatius, 2013.

Schoonenberg, Piet. "Revelation and Experience." In *Sourcebook for Modern Catechetics*, edited by Michael Warren, 303–12. Winona, MN: St. Mary's, 1983.

Second Vatican Council. *Ad gentes*. Vatican City: Libreria Editrice Vaticana, 1965.
———. *Christus dominus*. Vatican City: Libreria Editrice Vaticana, 1965.
———. *Dei verbum*. Vatican City: Libreria Editrice Vaticana, 1965.
———. *Gaudium et spes*. Vatican City: Libreria Editrice Vaticana, 1965.
———. *Lumen gentium*. Vatican City: Libreria Editrice Vaticano, 1964.
———. *Sacrosanctum concilium*. Vatican City: Libreria Editrice Vaticano, 1963.
Seewald, Peter. *Benedict XVI: A Life*. Vol. 1. Translated by Dinah Livingstone. New York: Bloomsbury, 2020.
Sloyan, Gerard. *Speaking of Religious Education*. New York: Herder and Herder, 1968.
Smith, Christian. *Souls in Transition: The Religious and Spiritual Lives of Emerging Adults*. New York: Oxford University Press, 2009. Kindle.
Sweeney, Conor. *Sacramental Presence after Heidegger*. Eugene, OR: Cascade, 2015.
Tanzella-Nitti, Giuseppe. "Two Books Prior to the Scientific Revolution." *Annales Theologici* 18 (2004) 51–83.
Theological Dictionary of the New Testament. 10 vols. Edited by Gerhard Kittel and Gerhard Friedrich. Translated by Geoffrey W. Bromiley. Grand Rapids: Eerdmans, 1964–76.
Thorbjørnsen, Svein Olaf. "Paul Tillich." In *Key Theological Thinkers: From Modern to Postmodern*, edited by Stalle Johannes Kristiansen and Svein Rise, 101–11. Burlington, VT: Ashgate, 2013.
Tillich, Paul. *Systematic Theology*. Vol. 1. London: SCM, 1979.
Tilmann, Klemens. "Origin and Development of Modern Catechetical Methods." In *Teaching All Nations*, edited by Johannes Hofinger, translated by Clifford Howell, 81–94. New York: Herder and Herder, 1961.
Tobin, Greg. *Holy Father: Pope Benedict XVI*. New York: Sterling, 2005.
United States Conference of Catholic Bishops. *National Directory for Catechesis*. Washington, DC: United States Conference of Catholic Bishops, 2005.
Valente, Gianni, and Pierluca Azzardo. "Interview with Alfred Läpple." *30 Days* 1 (2006) 60.
Vandervelde, George. "The Grammar of Grace: Karl Rahner as a Watershed in Contemporary Theology." *Theological Studies* 49.3 (1988) 445–59.
Vanhoozer, Kevin. "Theology and the Condition of Postmodernity: A Report on Knowledge (of God)." In *The Cambridge Companion to Postmodern Theology*, edited by Kevin Vanhoozer, 3–25. Cambridge: Cambridge University Press, 2003.
Vincelette, Alan. *Recent Catholic Philosophy: The Twentieth Century*. Milwaukee: Marquette University Press, 2011.
Von Hildebrand, Dietrich. *Transformation in Christ*. New York: Longmans, 1948.
Wahlberg, Mats. *Revelation as Testimony: A Philosophical-Theological Study*. Grand Rapids: Eerdmans, 2014.
Wheeler, Michael. "Martin Heidegger." In *Stanford Encyclopedia of Philosophy*, edited by Edward N. Zalta. https://plato.stanford.edu/archives/fall2017/entries/heidegger/.
Whittle, Sean. "Some Theological Reservations Surrounding One Contemporary Christian Approach to Teaching and Learning." *Journal of Education and Christian Belief* 18.2 (2014) 191–205.
Wicks, Jared. "Six Texts by Prof. Joseph Ratzinger as *Peritus* before and during Vatican Council II." *Gregorianum* 89.2 (2008) 233–311.
Wiess, Cari. "Stop Being Shocked." *Tablet*, October 14, 2020. https://www.tabletmag.com/sections/news/articles/stop-being-shocked.

Willey, Petroc. "Catechetical Thinking in the Face of Critical Theory: Developing a Marian Understanding." *Ecce Mater Tua* 1 (2018) 133–47.

———. "The Catechism Enshrines the Pedagogy of God." Keynote presentation at the Speaking the Truth in Love Conference, Steubenville, OH, October 2017.

———. "The Pedagogue and the Teacher." In *The Pedagogy of God*, edited by Petroc Willey et al., 29–50. Steubenville, OH: Emmaus Road, 2011.

Wojtyla, Karol. *Love and Responsibility*. Translated by H. T. Willetts. San Francisco: Ignatius, 1993.

www.ingramcontent.com/pod-product-compliance
Lightning Source LLC
Chambersburg PA
CBHW071227290426
44108CB00013B/1319